WHEN CRITICS ASK

WHEN CRITICS ASK

■

A Popular Handbook
on Bible Difficulties

Norman Geisler
and
Thomas Howe

VICTOR BOOKS

A DIVISION OF SCRIPTURE PRESS PUBLICATIONS INC.
USA CANADA ENGLAND

Copyediting: Robert N. Hosack
Cover Design: Paul Higdon
Cover Photo: Mike Marshall

Library of Congress Cataloging-in-Publication Data

Geisler, Norman L.
   When critics ask : a popular handbook on Bible difficulties
   Norman L. Geisler and Thomas A. Howe.
      p.   cm.
   Includes bibliographical references and index.
   ISBN: 0-89693-698-8
   1. Bible—Miscellanea. 2. Bible—Evidences, authority, etc.
I. Howe, Thomas A. II. Title.
BS612.G45   1992
220.6—dc20   92-411
                                                                   CIP

---

5   6   7   8   9   10   Printing/Year   96   95

CONTENTS

ACKNOWLEDGMENTS

*We wish to thank Paul Krisak and Trent Dougherty
for help in preparing this manuscript.
Especially do we thank Barbara Geisler
for untold laborious hours in checking
all the thousands of Scripture references.
This effort was a labor of love.*

PREFACE

When Bible critics ask, "How can you believe the Bible when it is riddled with errors?" what do you say? Many Christians punt to faith. They simply cling tenaciously to their belief no matter what the evidence may be against it. This, however, is contrary to both Scripture and sound reason. The Bible declares, "Walk in wisdom . . . that you may know how you ought to answer each one" (Col. 4:5-6). Peter urged believers, "Sanctify the Lord God in your hearts, and always be ready to give a defense to everyone who asks you of the reason for the hope that is in you, with meekness and fear" (1 Peter 3:15). Indeed, Jesus commanded us to "love the Lord your God with all your heart . . . soul . . . and . . . mind" (Matt. 22:37). Part of this loving duty to Christ is to find answers for those who criticize God's Word. For, as Solomon said, "Answer a fool according to his folly, lest he be wise in his own eyes" (Prov. 26:5).

Truth is able to stand on its own two feet. Jesus said, "You shall know the truth, and the truth shall make you free" (John 8:32). We have nothing to fear from the truth. Jesus said to the Father, "Your Word is truth" (John 17:17). The Bible has withstood the criticisms of the greatest skeptics, agnostics, and atheists down through the centuries, and it is able to withstand the feeble efforts of unbelieving critics today. Unlike many other religions today that appeal to mystical feeling or blind faith, Christianity says, "Look before you leap."

This is a book for those who believe we should *think* about what we believe. God places no premium on ignorance, nor does He reward those who refuse to look at the evidence. On the contrary, He will condemn those who refuse the plain evidence He has revealed (Rom. 1:18-20).

This book grows out of over forty years of attempts to understand the Bible and answer those who would undermine faith in God's eternal Word. It is written as a companion to the Bible, so that one may find the answer to a difficulty in the text at the very place the problem occurs. For example, as for the age-old question "Where did Cain get his wife?" the answer will be found right in the text which says "Cain knew his wife, and she conceived and bore Enoch" (Gen. 4:17). As you read through the Bible and encounter a difficulty, just look up the verse and study the comment on it. For those who have difficulty remembering where a particular verse is that raised a question, just look in the topical and person indices in the back and find where the difficulty is treated.

In many ways, this book is five books in one. First, it is a book on Bible difficulties that gives answers to all the major questions ever raised about the Bible—over 800 in all. Second, this is a work in apologetics, since it helps defend the faith once for all delivered to the saints. Third, it functions like a critical commentary, since it treats most of the difficult passages in the Bible. Fourth, it is a book that will help strengthen your spiritual life as you receive answers to questions and your faith in God's Word is increased. Finally, this is a book on evangelism. For as you witness for Christ, people will ask you questions for which you may not have an answer. Rather than stop sharing Christ because you fear questions you can't answer, you can continue in confidence because you have a ready guide to help answer the questions of those who sincerely seek to know the truth.

It is our prayer that God will use this book to strengthen your faith and to help bring many others to the faith. Our own confidence in the Sacred Scriptures has increased over the years as we have delved deeper into the marvels of His truth. We are confident that yours will too.

INTRODUCTION:
HOW TO APPROACH
BIBLE DIFFICULTIES

THE BIBLE: ERRORS, NO!

Critics claim the Bible is filled with errors. Some even speak of thousands of mistakes. The truth is there is not even one demonstrated error in the original text of the Bible. This is not to say that there are not *difficulties* in our Bibles. There are, and that is what this book is all about. It is only to point out that there are not actual *errors* in the Scriptures. Why? Because the Bible is the Word of God, and God cannot err. Come let us reason. Let's put it in logical form and then examine the premises:

GOD CANNOT ERR.
THE BIBLE IS THE WORD OF GOD.
THEREFORE, THE BIBLE CANNOT ERR.

As any student of logic knows, this is a valid syllogism (form of reasoning). So, if the premises are true, the conclusion is also true. As we will show, the Bible clearly declares itself to be the Word of God.[1] It also informs us that God cannot err. The conclusion, then, is inevitable. The Bible cannot err. If the Bible erred in anything it affirms, then God would be mistaken. But God cannot make mistakes.

God Cannot Err
The Scriptures declare emphatically that "it is impossible for God to lie" (Heb. 6:18). Paul speaks of the "God who cannot lie" (Titus 1:2). He is a God who, even if we are faithless, "He remains faithful; He cannot deny Himself " (2 Tim. 2:13). God is truth (John 14:6) and so is His Word. Jesus said to the Father, "Your Word is truth" (John 17:17). The psalmist exclaimed, "The entirety of Your word is truth" (Ps. 119:160).

The Bible Is the Word of God
Jesus referred to the OT as the "Word of God" which "cannot be broken" (John 10:35). He said, "until heaven and earth disappear, not the

smallest letter, not the least stroke of a pen, will by any means disappear from the Law until everything is accomplished" (Matt. 5:18, NIV). Paul added, "All Scripture is God-breathed" (2 Tim. 3:16, NIV). It came "from the mouth of God" (Matt. 4:4). Although human authors recorded the messages, "prophecy never had its origin in the will of man, but men spoke from God as they were carried along by the Holy Spirit" (2 Peter 1:20, NIV).[2]

Jesus said to the religious leaders of His day, "You nullify the Word of God by your tradition" (Mark 7:13, NIV). Jesus turned their attention to the written Word of God by affirming over and over again, "It is written . . . It is written . . . It is written . . ." (Matt. 4:4, 7, 10). This phrase occurs over ninety times in the NT. It is a strong indication of the divine authority of the written Word of God. Stressing the unfailing nature of God's truth, the Apostle Paul referred to the Scriptures as "the Word of God" (Rom. 9:6). The writer of Hebrews declared that "the Word of God is living and active. Sharper than any double-edged sword, it penetrates even to dividing soul and spirit, joints and marrow; it judges the thoughts and attitudes of the heart" (Heb. 4:12, NIV).

The Logical Conclusion: The Bible Cannot Err
Yes God has spoken, and He has not stuttered. The God of truth has given us the Word of Truth, and it does not contain any untruth in it. The Bible is the unerring Word of God.[3]

Can the Bible be Trusted in Science and History?
Some have suggested that Scripture can always be trusted on moral matters, but it is not always correct on historical matters. They rely on it in the spiritual domain, but not in the sphere of science. If true, however, this would render the Bible ineffective as a divine authority, since the spiritual is often inextricably interwoven with the historical and scientific.

A close examination of Scripture reveals that the scientific (factual) and spiritual truths of Scripture are often inseparable. For example, one cannot separate the spiritual truth of Christ's resurrection from the fact that His body permanently vacated the tomb and later physically appeared (Matt. 28:6; 1 Cor. 15:13-19). Likewise, if Jesus was not born of a biological virgin, then He is no different from the rest of the human race on whom the stigma of Adam's sin rests (Rom. 5:12). Likewise, the death of Christ for our sins cannot be detached from His shedding literal blood on the cross, for "without shedding of blood there is no remission" (Heb. 9:22). And Adam's existence and fall cannot be a myth. If there were no literal Adam and no actual fall, then the spiritual teaching about inherited sin and eventual or physical death are wrong (Rom. 5:12). Historical reality and the theological doctrine stand or fall together.

Also, the doctrine of the Incarnation is inseparable from the historical truth about Jesus of Nazareth (John 1:1, 14). Further, Jesus' moral teaching about marriage was based on His teaching about God's joining a literal Adam and Eve together in marriage (Matt. 19:4-5). In each of these cases the moral or theological teaching is devoid of its meaning apart from the historical or factual event. If one denies that the literal space-time event occurred, then there is no basis for believing the scriptural doctrine built upon it.

Jesus often directly compared OT events with important spiritual truths, such as His death and resurrection which were related to Jonah and the great fish (Matt. 12:40). Or, His second coming as compared to the days of Noah (Matt. 24:37-39). Both the occasion and the manner of that comparison make it clear that Jesus was affirming the historicity of those OT events. Indeed, Jesus asserted to Nicodemus, "If I told you earthly things and you do not believe, how will you believe if I tell you heavenly things?" (John 3:12) In short, if the Bible does not speak truthfully about the physical world, then it cannot be trusted when it speaks about the spiritual world. The two are intimately related.

Inspiration includes not only all that the Bible explicitly *teaches*, but also everything the Bible *touches*. This is true whether the Bible is touching upon history, science, or mathematics. Whatever the Bible declares, is true—whether it is a major point or a minor point. The Bible is God's Word, and God does not deviate from the truth in any point. All the parts are as true as the whole that they comprise.

If It Is Inspired, Then It Is Inerrant

Inerrancy is a logical result of inspiration. For, inerrancy means wholly true and without error. And what God breathes out (inspires) must be wholly true (inerrant). However, it is helpful to specify more clearly what is meant by "truth" and what would constitute an "error."[4] By truth we signify that which corresponds to reality. An error, then, is what does not correspond to reality. Truth is telling it like it is. Error is not telling it like it is. Hence, nothing mistaken can be true, even if the author intended his mistake to be true. An error is a mistake, not simply something that is misleading. Otherwise, every sincere utterance ever made is true, even those that were grossly mistaken.[5] Likewise, something is not true simply because it accomplishes its intended purpose, since many lies succeed.

The Bible clearly views truth as that which corresponds to reality. Error is understood as a lack of correspondence to reality, not as intentionally misleading. This is evident from the fact that the word "error" is used of unintentional mistakes (Lev. 4:2). The Bible everywhere implies a correspondence view of truth. For example, when the Ten Commandments declare "You shall not bear false testimony" (Ex. 20:16), it implies that misrepresenting the facts is wrong. Likewise, a correspondence view of truth is used when the Jews said to the governor about Paul, "By examining him yourself you will be able to learn the truth about all these charges we are bringing against him." In so doing, he adds, "You can easily verify the facts" (cf. Acts 24:8).

"Has God Said?"

Of course, wherever God has made the truth clear, Satan's strategy is to cast doubt on it. Whenever God has spoken with authority, the devil desires to undermine it. "Did God really say that?" he sneers (cf. Gen. 3:1). This confusion often takes the following form. The Bible may be the inspired Word of God in some sense, but it is also human words. It had human authors, and "to err is human." Hence, we are to expect some errors in the Bible. So goes the argument. In short, the clear and simple truth of God has been confused by the lie of Satan, the master of lies (John 8:44).

Let's analyze what is wrong with this reasoning. A simple analogy will help. Consider some parallel but equally faulty reasoning:

1) Jesus was a human being.
2) Human beings sin.
3) Therefore, Jesus sinned.

Any Bible student can readily see that this conclusion is wrong. Jesus was "without sin" (Heb. 4:15). He "knew no sin" (2 Cor. 5:21). Jesus was "a lamb without blemish or defect" (1 Peter 1:19). As John said of Jesus, "He is pure" and "righteous" (1 John 2:1; 3:3). But, if Jesus never sinned, then what is wrong with the above argument that Jesus is human and humans sin, therefore, Jesus sinned? Where does the logic go astray?

The mistake is to assume that Jesus is like any other human. Sure, mere human beings sin. But, Jesus was not a *mere* human being. He was a perfect human being. Indeed, Jesus was not only human, but He was also God. Likewise, the Bible is not a mere human book. It is also the Word of God. Like Jesus, it is both divine and human. And just as Jesus was human but did not sin, even so the Bible is a human book but does not err. Both God's living Word (Christ) and His written Word (Scripture) are human but do not err. They are divine and cannot err. There can no more be an error in God's written Word than there was a sin in God's living Word. God cannot err, period.

THE BIBLE: DIFFICULTIES, YES!

While the Bible is the Word of God and, as such, cannot have any *errors*, nonetheless, this does not mean there are no *difficulties* in it. However, as St. Augustine wisely noted, "If we are perplexed by any apparent contradiction in Scripture, it is not allowable to say, the author of this book is mistaken; but either the manuscript is faulty, or the translation is wrong, or you have not understood."[6] The mistakes are not in the revelation of God, but are in the misinterpretations of man.

The Bible is without mistake, but the critics are not. All their allegations of error in the Bible are based on some error of their own. Their mistakes fall into the following main categories.

Mistake 1: Assuming that the Unexplained Is Not Explainable.
No informed person would claim to be able to fully explain all Bible difficulties. However, it is a mistake for the critic to assume, therefore, that what has not yet been explained never will be explained. When a scientist comes upon an anomaly in nature, he does not give up further scientific exploration. Rather, he uses the unexplained as a motivation to find an explanation. No real scientist throws up her hands in despair simply because she cannot explain a given phenomenon. She continues to do research with the confident expectation that an answer will be found. And, the history of science reveals that her faith has been rewarded over and over again.

Scientists, for example, once had no natural explanation of meteors, eclipses, tornadoes, hurricanes, and earthquakes. Until recently, scientists did not know how the bumblebee could fly. All of these mysteries have yielded their secrets to the relentless patience of science. Neither do scientists know how life can grow on thermo-vents in the depths of the sea. But, no scientist throws in the towel and cries "contradiction!"

Likewise, the Christian scholar approaches the Bible with the same presumption that what is thus far unexplained is not therefore unexplainable. He or she does not assume that discrepancies are contradictions. And, when he encounters something for which he has no explanation, he simply continues to do research, believing that one will eventually be found. In fact, if he assumed the opposite, he would stop studying. Why pursue an answer when one assumes there is none. Like his scientific counterpart, the Bible student has been rewarded for his faith and research. For, many difficulties for which scholars once had no answer have yielded to the relentless pursuit of truth through history, archaeology, linguistics, and other disciplines. For example, critics once proposed that Moses could not have written the first five books of the Bible because there was no writing in Moses' day. Now we know that writing was in existence a couple of thousand years or more before Moses. Likewise, critics once believed that the Bible was wrong in speaking of the Hittite people, since they were totally unknown to historians. Now, all historians know of their existence by way of their library that was found in Turkey. This gives us confidence to believe that the biblical difficulties that have not yet been explained have an explanation and that we need not assume there is a mistake in the Bible.

Mistake 2: Presuming the Bible Guilty Until Proven Innocent.
Many critics assume the Bible is wrong until something proves it right. However, like an American citizen charged with an offense, the Bible should be presumed "innocent" until it is proven guilty. This is not asking anything special for the Bible, it is the way we approach all human communications. If we did not, life would not be possible. For example, if we assumed road signs and traffic signals were not telling the truth, then we would probably be dead before we could prove they were telling the truth. Likewise, if we assume food labels are wrong until proven right, we would have to open up all cans and packages before buying. And what if we presumed all the numbers on our currency were wrong? And what if we assumed all restroom signs were wrong! Well, enough is enough.

The Bible, like any other book, should be presumed to be telling us what the authors said and heard. Negative critics of the Bible begin with just the opposite presumption. Little wonder, then, that they conclude the Bible is riddled with error.

Mistake 3: Confusing Our Fallible Interpretations with God's Infallible Revelation.
Jesus affirmed that the "Scripture cannot be broken" (John 10:35). As an infallible book, the Bible is also irrevocable. Jesus declared, "Truly I say to you, until heaven and earth pass away, not the smallest letter or stroke shall pass away from the Law, until all is accomplished" (Matt. 5:18, NIV; cf. Luke 16:17). The Scriptures also have final authority, being the last word on all it discusses. Jesus employed the Bible to resist the tempter (Matt. 4:4, 7, 10), to settle doctrinal disputes (Matt. 21:42),

and to vindicate His authority (Mark 11:17). Sometimes a biblical teaching rests on a small historical detail (Heb. 7:4-10), a word or phrase (Acts 15:13-17), or even the difference between the singular and the plural (Gal. 3:16). But, while the Bible is infallible, human interpretations are not. The Bible cannot be mistaken, but we can be mistaken about the Bible. The meaning of the Bible does not change, but our understanding of its meaning does.

Human beings are finite, and finite beings make mistakes. That is why there are erasers on pencils, correcting fluid for typing, and a "delete" key on computers. And even though God's Word is perfect (Ps. 19:7), as long as imperfect human beings exist, there will be misinterpretations of God's Word and false views about His world. In view of this, one should not be hasty in assuming that a currently dominant view in science is the final word on the topic. Prevailing views of science in the past are considered errors by scientists in the present. So, contradictions between popular opinions in science and widely accepted interpretations of the Bible can be expected. But this falls short of proving there is a real contradiction between God's world and God's Word, between God's general revelation and His special revelation. In this basic sense, science and Scripture are not contradictory. Only finite, fallible human opinions about each can be contradictory.

Mistake 4: Failing to Understand the Context of the Passage.
Perhaps the most common mistake of critics is to take a text out of its proper context. As the adage goes, "A text out of context is a pretext." One can prove anything from the Bible by this mistaken procedure. The Bible says "there is no God" (Ps. 14:1). Of course, the context is that "The fool has said in his heart, 'There is no God' " (Ps. 14:1). One may claim that Jesus admonished us "not to resist an evil" (Matt. 5:39), but the anti-retaliatory context in which He cast this statement must not be ignored. Likewise, many fail to understand the context of Jesus' statement to "Give to him who asks you," as though one had an obligation to give a gun to a small child who asked, or nuclear weapons to Saddam Hussein just because he asked. Failure to note that meaning is determined by context is perhaps the chief sin of those who find fault with the Bible, as comments on numerous passages in this book will illustrate.

Mistake 5: Neglecting to Interpret Difficult Passages in the Light of Clear Ones.
Some passages of Scripture are hard to understand. Sometimes the difficulty is due to their obscurity. At other times, the difficulty is because passages appear to be teaching something contrary to what some other

part of Scripture is clearly teaching. For example, James appears to be saying salvation is by works (James 2:14-26), whereas Paul taught clearly that it was by grace (Rom. 4:5; Titus 3:5-7; Eph. 2:8-9). In this case, James should *not* be construed so as to contradict Paul. Paul is speaking about justification *before God* (which is by faith alone), whereas James is referring to justification *before men* (who cannot see our faith, but only our works).

Another example is found in Philippians 2:12 where Paul says, "work out your own salvation with fear and trembling." On the surface this appears to be saying salvation is by works. However, this is flatly contradicted by a host of Scriptures which clearly affirm that we are "saved by grace through faith, and that not of ourselves; it is a gift of God, not of works, lest anyone should boast" (Eph. 2:8-9). And, "to him who does not work but believes on Him who justifies the ungodly, his faith is accounted for righteousness" (Rom. 4:5). Also, it "is not by works of righteousness which we have done, but according to His mercy [that] He saved us" (Titus 3:5-6). When this difficult statement about "working out our salvation" is understood in the light of these clear passages, we can see that, whatever it *does* mean, it *does not* mean that we are saved by works. In fact, what it means is found in the very next verse. We are to work salvation *out* because God's grace has worked it *in* our hearts. In Paul's words, "for it is God who works in you both to will and to do for His good pleasure" (Phil. 2:13).

Mistake 6: Basing a Teaching on an Obscure Passage.
Some passages in the Bible are difficult because their meanings are obscure. This is usually because a key word in the text is used only once (or rarely), and so it is difficult to know what the author is saying, unless it can be inferred from the context. For example, one of the best known passages in the Bible contains a word that appears nowhere else in all existing Greek literature up to the time the NT was written. This word appears in what is popularly known as the Lord's Prayer (Matt. 6:11). It is usually translated, "Give us this day our daily bread." The word in question is the one translated "daily"—*epiousion*. Experts in Greek still have not come to any agreement either on its origin, or on its precise meaning. Different commentators try to establish links with Greek words that are well-known, and many suggestions have been proposed as to the resulting meaning. Among these suggestions are:

Give us this day our *continuous* bread.

Give us this day our *supersubstantial* (indicating supernatural, from heaven) bread.

Give us this day bread *for our sustenance*.

Give us this day our *daily* (or, what we need for today) bread.

Each one of these proposals has its defenders, each one makes sense in the context, and each one is a possibility based on the limited information that is available. There does not seem to be any compelling reason to depart from what has become the generally accepted translation, but this example does serve to illustrate the point. Some passages of the Bible are difficult to understand because the meaning of some key word appears only once, or very rarely.

At other times, the words may be clear but the meaning is not evident because we are not sure to what they refer. This is true in 1 Corinthians 15:29 where Paul speaks of those who were "baptized for the dead." Is he referring to the baptizing of live representatives to ensure salvation for dead believers who were not baptized (as Mormons claim)? Or, is he referring to others being baptized into the church to fill the ranks of those who have passed on? Or, is he referring to a believer being baptized "for" (i.e., "with a view to") his own death and burial with Christ? Or, to something else?

When we are not sure, then several things should be kept in mind. First, we should not build a doctrine on an obscure passage. The rule of thumb in Bible interpretation is "the main things are the plain things, and the plain things are the main things." This is called the perspicuity (clearness) of Scripture. If something is important, it will be clearly taught in Scripture and probably in more than one place. Second, when a given passage is not clear, we should never conclude that it means something that is opposed to another plain teaching of Scripture. God does not make mistakes in His Word; we make mistakes in trying to understand it.

Mistake 7: Forgetting that the Bible Is a Human Book with Human Characteristics.

With the exception of small sections, like the Ten Commandments which were "written with the finger of God" (Ex. 31:18), the Bible was not verbally dictated.[7] The writers were not secretaries of the Holy Spirit. They were human composers employing their own literary styles and idiosyncrasies. These human authors sometimes used *human sources* for their material (Josh. 10:13; Acts 17:28; 1 Cor. 15:33; Titus 1:12). In fact, every book of the Bible is the composition of a *human writer* — about forty of them in all. The Bible also manifests different *human literary* styles, from the mournful meter of Lamentations to the exalted poetry of Isaiah; from the simple grammar of John to the complex Greek of the Book of Hebrews. Scripture also manifests *human perspectives*. David spoke in Psalm 23 from a shepherd's perspective. Kings is written from a prophetic vantage point, and Chronicles from a priestly point of view. Acts manifests an historical interest and 2 Timothy a pastor's heart. Writers speak from an observer's standpoint when they write of the sun rising or setting (Josh. 1:15). They also reveal *human thought patterns*, including memory lapses (1 Cor. 1:14-16), as well as *human emotions* (Gal. 4:14). The Bible discloses specific *human interests*. For example, Hosea possessed a rural interest, Luke a medical concern, and James a love of nature.[8] But like Christ, the Bible is completely human, yet without error. Forgetting the humanity of Scripture can lead to falsely impugning its integrity by expecting a level of expression higher than that which is customary to a human document. This will become more obvious as we discuss the next mistakes of the critics.

Mistake 8: Assuming that a Partial Report is a False Report.
Critics often jump to the conclusion that a partial report is false. However, this is not so. If it were, most of what has ever been said would be false, since seldom does time or space permit an absolutely complete report. Occasionally the Bible expresses the same thing in different ways, or at least from different viewpoints, at different times. Hence, inspiration does not exclude a diversity of expression. The four Gospels relate the same story in different ways to different groups of people, and sometimes even quote the same saying with different words. Compare, for example, Peter's famous confession in the Gospels:

Matthew: "You are the Christ, the Son of the living God" (16:16).
Mark: "You are the Christ" (8:29).
Luke: "The Christ of God" (9:20).

Even the Ten Commandments, which were "written with the finger of God" (Deut. 9:10), are stated with variations the second time God gave them (cf. Ex. 20:8-11 with Deut. 5:12-15). There are many differences between the books of Kings and Chronicles in their description of identical events, yet they harbor no contradiction in the events they narrate. If such important utterances can be stated in different ways, then there is no reason the rest of Scripture cannot speak truth without employing a wooden literalness of expression.

Mistake 9: Demanding that NT Citations of the OT Always Be Exact Quotations.
Critics often point to variations in the NT's use of the OT Scriptures as a proof of error. However, they forget that every *citation* need not be an

exact *quotation*. It was then (and still is today) a perfectly acceptable literary style to give the *essence* of a statement without using precisely the *same words*. The same *meaning* can be conveyed without using the same *verbal expressions*.

Variations in the NT citations of the OT fall into different categories. Sometimes they vary because there is a change of speaker. For example, Zechariah records the Lord as saying, "they will look on *Me* whom they have pierced" (12:10). When this is cited in the NT, John, not God, is speaking. So it is changed to "They shall look on *Him* whom they pierced" (John 19:37).

At other times, writers cite only part of the OT text. Jesus did this at His home synagogue in Nazareth (Luke 4:18-19, citing Isa. 61:1-2). In fact, He stopped in the middle of a sentence. Had He gone any farther, He could not have said as He did, "Today this Scripture is fulfilled in your hearing" (v. 21). For the very next phrase, "And the day of vengeance of our God," is a reference to His second coming.

Sometimes the NT paraphrases or summarizes the OT text (e.g., Matt. 2:6). Others blend two texts into one (Matt. 27:9-10). Occasionally a general truth is mentioned, without citing a specific text. For example, Matthew said Jesus moved to Nazareth "that it might be fulfilled which was spoken by the prophets, 'He shall be called a Nazarene' " (Matt. 2:23). Notice, Matthew quotes no given prophet, but rather "prophets" in general. So it would be futile to insist on a specific OT text where this could be found.

There are also instances where the NT applies a text in a different way than the OT did. For example, Hosea applies "Out of Egypt have I called My Son" to the Messianic nation, and Matthew applies it to the product of that nation, the Messiah (Matt. 2:15, from Hos. 11:1). In no case, however, does the NT misinterpret or misapply the OT, nor draw some implication from it that is not validly drawn from it. In short, the NT makes no mistakes in citing the OT, as the critics do in citing the NT.

Mistake 10: Assuming that Divergent Accounts Are False Ones.
Just because two or more accounts of the same event differ, it does not mean they are mutually exclusive. For example, Matthew (28:5) says there was one angel at the tomb after the resurrection, whereas John informs us there were two (20:12). But, these are not contradictory reports. In fact, there is an infallible mathematical rule that easily explains this problem: wherever there are two, there is always one — it never fails! Matthew did not say there was *only* one angel. One has to add the word

"only" to Matthew's account to make it contradict John's. But if the critic comes to the Bible in order to show it errs, then the error is not in the Bible, but in the critic.

Likewise, Matthew (27:5) informs us that Judas hanged himself. But Luke says that "he burst open in the middle and all his entrails gushed out" (Acts 1:18). Once more, these accounts differ, but they are not mutually exclusive. If Judas hanged himself on a tree over the edge of a cliff and his body fell on sharp rocks below, then his entrails would gush out just as Luke vividly describes.

Mistake 11: Presuming that the Bible Approves of All it Records.
It is a mistake to assume that everything contained in the Bible is commended by the Bible. The whole Bible is *true* (John 17:17), but it records some *lies*, for example, Satan's (Gen. 3:4; cf. John 8:44) and Rahab's (Josh. 2:4). Inspiration encompasses the Bible fully and completely in the sense that it records accurately and truthfully even the lies and errors of sinful beings. The truth of Scripture is found in what the Bible *reveals*, not in everything it *records*. Unless this distinction is held, it may be incorrectly concluded that the Bible teaches immorality because it narrates David's sin (2 Sam. 11:4), that it promotes polygamy because it records Solomon's (1 Kings 11:3), or that it affirms atheism because it quotes the fool as saying "there is no God" (Ps. 14:1).

Mistake 12: Forgetting that the Bible Uses Non-technical, Everyday Language.
To be true, something does not have to use scholarly, technical, or so-called "scientific" language. The Bible is written for the common person of every generation, and it therefore uses common, everyday language. The use of observational, nonscientific language is not *un*scientific, it is merely *pre*scientific. The Scriptures were written in *ancient* times by ancient standards, and it would be anachronistic to superimpose *modern* scientific standards upon them. However, it is no more unscientific to speak of the sun "standing still" (Joshua 10:12) than to refer to the sun "rising" (Joshua 1:16). Contemporary meteorologists still speak daily of the time of "sunrise" and "sunset."

Mistake 13: Assuming that Round Numbers Are False.
Another mistake sometimes made by Bible critics is claiming that round numbers are false. This is not so. Round numbers are just that—round numbers. Like most ordinary speech, the Bible uses round numbers (1 Chron. 19:18; 21:5). For example, it refers to the diameter as being about one third of the circumference of something. It may be imprecise from

the standpoint of a contemporary technological society to speak of 3.14159265 . . . as the number three, but it is not incorrect for an ancient, non-technological people. Three and fourteen hundredths can be rounded off to three. That is sufficient for a "Sea of cast metal" (2 Chron. 4:2, NIV) in an ancient Hebrew temple, even though it would not suffice for a computer in a modern rocket. But one should not expect scientific precision in a prescientific age. In fact, it would be as anachronistic as wearing a wrist watch in a Shakespearian play.

Mistake 14: Neglecting to Note that the Bible Uses Different Literary Devices.
An inspired book need not be composed in one, and only one, literary style. Human beings wrote every book in the Bible, and human language is not limited to one mode of expression. So, there is no reason to suppose that only one style or literary genre was used in a divinely inspired Book. The Bible reveals a number of literary devices. Several whole books are written in *poetic* style (e.g., Job, Psalms, Proverbs). The synoptic Gospels are filled with *parables*. In Galatians 4, Paul utilizes an *allegory*. The NT abounds with *metaphors* (e.g., 2 Cor. 3:2-3; James 3:6) and *similes* (cf. Matt. 20:1; James 1:6); *hyperboles* may also be found (e.g., Col. 1:23; John 21:25; 2 Cor. 3:2), and possibly even *poetic figures* (Job 41:1). Jesus employed *satire* (Matt. 19:24 with 23:24) and *figures of speech* are common throughout the Bible.

It is not a mistake for a biblical writer to use a figure of speech, but it is a mistake for a reader to take a figure of speech literally. Obviously when the Bible speaks of the believer resting under the shadow of God's "wings" (Ps. 36:7), it does not mean that God is a feathered bird. Likewise, when the Bible says God "awakes" (Ps. 44:23), as though He were sleeping, it is a figure of speech indicating God's inactivity before He is aroused to judgment by man's sin. We must be careful in our reading of figures of speech in Scripture.

Mistake 15: Forgetting that Only the Original Text, Not Every Copy of Scripture, Is without Error.
When critics do come upon a genuine mistake in a manuscript copy, they make another fatal error—they assume it was in the original inspired text of Scripture. They forget that God only uttered the original text of Scripture, not the copies. Therefore, only the original text is without error. Inspiration does not guarantee that every copy of the original is without error. Therefore, we are to expect that minor errors are to be found in manuscript copies. But, again, as St. Augustine wisely noted, when we run into a so-called "error" in the Bible, we must assume one of

two things—either the manuscript was not copied correctly, or we have not understood it rightly. What we may not assume is that God made an error in inspiring the original text.

While present copies of Scripture are very good, they are not without error. For example, 2 Kings 8:26 gives the age of king Ahaziah as twenty-two, whereas 2 Chronicles 22:2 says forty-two. The later number cannot be correct, or he would have been older than his father. This is obviously a copyist error, but it does not alter the inerrancy of the original (see Appendix 2 for further examples).

Several things should be observed about these copyist errors. First of all, they are errors in the copies, not the originals. No one has ever found an original manuscript with an error in it. Second, they are minor errors (often in names or numbers) which do not affect any doctrine of the Christian faith. Third, these copyist errors are relatively few in number, as will be illustrated throughout the rest of this book. Fourth, usually by the context, or by another Scripture, we know which one is in error. For example, Ahaziah (above) must have been twenty-two, not forty-two, since he could not be older than his father. Finally, even though there is a copyist error, the entire message can still come through. In such a case, the validity of the message is not changed. For example, if you received a letter like this, would you understand the whole message? And would you collect your money?

"#OU HAVE WON THE FIVE MILLION DOLLAR READER'S DIGEST SWEEPSTAKES."

Even though there is a mistake in the first word, the entire message comes through—you are five million dollars richer! And if you received another letter the next day that read like this, you would be even more sure:

"Y#U HAVE WON THE FIVE MILLION DOLLAR READER'S DIGEST SWEEPSTAKES."

Actually the more mistakes of this kind there are (each in a different place), the more sure you are of the original message. This is why scribal mistakes in the biblical manuscripts do not affect the basic message of the Bible. So, for all practical purposes, the Bible in our hand, imperfect though the manuscripts are, conveys the complete truth of the original Word of God.

Mistake 16: Confusing General Statements with Universal Ones.
Critics often jump to the conclusion that unqualified statements admit of
no exceptions. They seize upon verses that offer general truths and then
point with glee to obvious exceptions. In so doing, they forget that such
statements are only intended to be generalizations.

The Book of Proverbs is a good example of such an issue. Proverbial
sayings by their very nature offer only general guidance, not universal
assurance. They are rules for life, but rules that admit of exceptions.
Proverbs 16:7 is a case in point. It affirms that "when a man's ways
please the Lord, He makes even his enemies to be at peace with him."
This obviously was not intended to be a universal truth. Paul was pleasing to the Lord and his enemies stoned him (Acts 14:19). Jesus was
pleasing the Lord, and His enemies crucified Him! Nonetheless, it is a
general truth that one who acts in a way pleasing to God can minimize
his enemies' antagonism.

Another example of a general truth is Proverbs 22:6, "Train up a child
in the way he should go, and when he is old he will not depart from it."
However, other Scripture passages and experience show that this is not
always true. Indeed, some godly persons in the Bible (including Job, Eli,
and David) had some very wayward children. This proverb does not
contradict experience because it is a general principle that applies in a
general way, but allows for individual exceptions. Proverbs are not designed to be absolute guarantees. Rather, they express truths that provide
helpful advice and guidance by which an individual should conduct his
or her daily life.

It is simply a mistake to assume that proverbial wisdom is always
universally true. Proverbs are *wisdom* (general guides), not *law* (universally binding imperatives). When the Bible declares "You shall therefore be
holy, for I am holy" (Lev. 11:45), then there are no exceptions. Holiness, goodness, love, truth, and justice are rooted in the very nature of an
unchanging God and therefore admit of no exceptions. But wisdom
takes God's universal truths and applies them to specific and changing
circumstances which, by their very nature as changing, will not always
yield the same results. Nonetheless, they are still helpful guides for life,
even though they may admit of an occasional exception.

Mistake 17: Forgetting that Later Revelation Supersedes Previous Revelation.
Sometimes critics of Scripture forget the principle of progressive revelation. God does not reveal everything at once, nor does He always lay
down the same conditions for every period of time. Therefore, some of
His later revelation will supersede His former statements. Bible critics

sometimes confuse a *change* of revelation with a *mistake*. The mistake, however, is that of the critic. For example, the fact that a parent allows a very small child to eat with his fingers, only to tell them later to use a spoon, is not a contradiction. Nor is the parent contradicting himself to insist later that the child should use a fork, not a spoon, to eat his vegetables. This is progressive revelation, with each command suited to fit the particular circumstance in which a person is found.

There was a time when God tested the human race by forbidding them to eat of a specific tree in the Garden of Eden (Gen. 2:16-17). This command is no longer in effect, but the later revelation does not contradict this former revelation. Also, there was a period (under the Mosaic law) when God commanded that animals be sacrificed for people's sin. However, since Christ offered the perfect sacrifice for sin (Heb. 10:11-14), this OT command is no longer in effect. Here again, there is no contradiction between the latter and the former commands. Likewise, when God created the human race, He commanded that they eat only fruit and vegetables (Gen. 1:29). But later, when conditions changed after the flood, God commanded that they also eat meat (Gen. 9:3). This change from herbivorous to omnivorous status is progressive revelation, but it is not a contradiction. In fact, all these subsequent revelations were simply different commands for different people at different times in God's overall plan of redemption.

Of course, God cannot change commands that have to do with His unchangeable nature (cf. Mal. 3:6; Heb. 6:18). For example, since God is love (1 John 4:16), He cannot command that we hate Him. Nor can He command what is logically impossible, for example, to both offer and not offer a sacrifice for sin at the same time and in the same sense. But these moral and logical limits notwithstanding, God can and has given noncontradictory, progressive revelation which, if taken out of its proper context and juxtaposed with each other, can be made to look contradictory. This, however, is just as much a mistake as to assume the parent is contradicting herself when she allows a child to stay up later at night as he gets older.

After forty years of continual and careful study of the Bible, one can only conclude that those who think they have discovered a mistake in the Bible do not know too much about the Bible—they know too little about it! This does not mean, of course, that we understand all the difficulties in the Scriptures. But it does lead us to believe that Mark Twain was correct when he concluded that it was not the part of the Bible he did not understand that bothered him the most, but the parts he did understand!

NOTES

1. For a more complete discussion, see Norman L. Geisler and William E. Nix, *A General Introduction to the Bible: Revised and Expanded* (Chicago: Moody Press, 1986), chapters 3–6.

2. See ibid., chapters 1–11.

3. For a defense of the inerrancy of the Bible by a coalition of evangelical scholars, see Norman L. Geisler ed., *Inerrancy* (Grand Rapids: Zondervan Publishing House, 1979).

4. For further discussion of this, see Norman L. Geisler, "The Concept of Truth in the Inerrancy Debate" in *Bibliotheca Sacra* (Oct–Dec, 1980).

5. This is the mistake of G.C. Berkouwer, *Holy Scripture* (Grand Rapids: Eerdmans, 1975) and Jack Rogers, *Biblical Authority* (Waco, TX: Word, 1978). Defining error as what misleads, rather than what is mistaken, they make all sincere errors unfalsifiable.

6. St. Augustine, *Reply to Faustus the Manichaean* 11.5 in Philip Schaff, *A Select Library of the Nicene and Ante-Nicene Fathers of the Christian Church* (Grand Rapids: Eerdmans, 1956), vol. 4.

7. For a proponent of verbal dictation see John R. Rice, *Our God-Breathed Book – The Bible* (Murfeesboro, Tenn: Sword of the Lord, 1969).

8. The biblical authors include a lawgiver (Moses), a general (Joshua), prophets (Samuel, Isaiah, et. al.), kings (David and Solomon), a musician (Asaph), a herdsman (Amos), a prince and statesman (Daniel), a priest (Ezra), a tax collector (Matthew), a physician (Luke), a scholar (Paul), and fishermen (Peter and John). With such a variety of occupations represented by biblical writers, it is only natural that their personal interests and differences should be reflected in their writings.

GENESIS

GENESIS 1:1 — How can the universe have a "beginning" when modern science says energy is eternal?

PROBLEM: According to the First Law of Thermodynamics, "Energy can neither be created nor destroyed." If this is so, then the universe must be eternal, since it is made of indestructible energy. However, the Bible indicates that the universe had a "beginning" and did not exist before God "created" it (Gen. 1:1). Is this not a contradiction between the Bible and science?

SOLUTION: There is a conflict of opinion here, but no real factual contradiction. The factual evidence indicates that the universe is not eternal, but that it did have a beginning just as the Bible says. Several observations are relevant here.

First of all, the First Law of Thermodynamics is often misstated to the effect that energy "cannot be created." However, science is based on observation, and statements such as "can" or "cannot" are not based on observation, but are dogmatic pronouncements. The First Law should be stated like this: "[So far as we can observe] the amount of *actual* energy in the universe remains constant." That is, as far as we know, the actual amount of energy in the universe is not decreasing or increasing. Stated this way, the First Law makes no pronouncement whatsoever about where energy came from, or how long it has been here. Thus, it does not contradict the Genesis declaration that God created the universe.

Second, another well-established scientific law is the Second Law of Thermodynamics. It states that "the amount of *usable* energy in the universe is decreasing." According to this Law, the universe is running down. Its energy is being transformed into unusable heat. If this is so, then the universe is not eternal, since it would have run out of usable energy a long time ago. Or, to put it another way, if the universe is unwinding, then it was wound up. If it had an infinite amount of energy it would never run down. Therefore, the universe had a beginning, just as Genesis 1:1 says it did.

Genesis (6:9; 9:12; 10:1, 32; 11:10, 27; 17:7, 9), is used of Adam and Eve (Gen. 5:1). Fourth, later OT chronologies place Adam at the top of the list (1 Chron. 1:1). Fifth, the NT places Adam at the beginning of Jesus' literal ancestors (Luke 3:38). Sixth, Jesus referred to Adam and Eve as the first literal "male and female," making their physical union the basis of marriage (Matt. 19:4). Seventh, Romans declares that literal death was brought into the world by a literal "Adam" (Rom. 5:14). Eighth, the comparison of Adam (the "first Adam") with Christ (the "last Adam") in 1 Corinthians 15:45 manifests that Adam was understood as a literal, historical person. Ninth, Paul's declaration that "Adam was formed first, then Eve" (1 Tim. 2:13-14) reveals that he speaks of a real person. Tenth, logically there had to be a first real set of human beings, male and female, or else the race would have had no way to begin. The Bible calls this literal couple "Adam and Eve," and there is no reason to doubt their real existence.

GENESIS 2:1 – How could the world be created in six days?

PROBLEM: The Bible says that God created the world in six days (Ex. 20:11). But modern science declares that it took billions of years. Both cannot be true.

SOLUTION: There are basically two ways to reconcile this difficulty.

First, some scholars argue that modern science is wrong. They insist that the universe is only thousands of years old and that God created everything in six literal 24-hour days (= 144 hours). In favor of this view they offer the following:

1. The days of Genesis each have "evening and the morning," (cf. Gen. 1:5, 8, 13, 19, 23, 31), something unique to 24-hour days in the Bible.
2. The days were numbered (first, second, third, etc.), a feature found only with 24-hour days in the Bible.
3. Exodus 20:11 compares the six days of creation with the six days of a literal work week of 144 hours.
4. There is scientific evidence to support a young age (of thousands of years) for the earth.
5. There is no way life could survive millions of years from day three (1:11) to day four (1:14) without light.

Other Bible scholars claim that the universe could be billions of years old without sacrificing a literal understanding of Genesis 1 and 2. They argue that:

1. The days of Genesis 1 could have a time lapse before the days began

(before Gen. 1:3), or a time gap between the days. There are gaps elsewhere in the Bible (cf. Matt. 1:8, where three generations are omitted, with 1 Chron. 3:11-14).

2. The same Hebrew word "day" (*yom*) is used in Genesis 1–2 as a period of time longer than 24 hours. For example, Genesis 2:4 uses it of the whole six day period of creation.

3. Sometimes the Bible uses the word "day" for long periods of time: "One day is as a thousand years" (2 Peter 3:8; cf. Ps. 90:4).

4. There are some indications in Genesis 1–2 that days could be longer than 24 hours:

   a) On the third "day" trees grew from seeds to maturity and they bore like seeds (1:11-12). This process normally takes months or years.

   b) On the sixth "day" Adam was created, went to sleep, named all the (thousands of) animals, looked for a helpmeet, went to sleep, and Eve was created from his rib. This looks like more than 24 hours worth of activity.

   c) The Bible says God "rested" on the seventh day (2:2), and that He is still in His rest from creation (Heb. 4:4). Thus, the seventh day is thousands of years long already. If so, then other days could be thousands of years too.

5. Exodus 20:11 could be making a unit-for-unit comparison between the days of Genesis and a work week (of 144 hours), not a minute-by-minute comparison.

Conclusion: There is no demonstrated contradiction of fact between Genesis 1 and science. There is only a conflict of interpretation. Either, *most* modern scientists are wrong in insisting the world is billions of years old, or else *some* Bible interpreters are wrong in insisting on only 144 hours of creation some several thousand years before Christ with no gaps allowing millions of years. But, in either case it is not a question of *inspiration* of Scripture, but of the *interpretation* of Scripture (and of the scientific data).

GENESIS 2:4 — Why does this chapter use the term "Lord God" rather than "God" as in chapter one?

PROBLEM: Many critics insist that Genesis 2 must have been written by someone different from the one who wrote Genesis 1, since Genesis 2 uses a different name for God. However, conservative scholars have always insisted that Moses composed Genesis, as indeed both Jewish and Christian scholars have down through the centuries. Indeed, the first five books of the OT are called "the Books of Moses" (2 Chron. 25:4) or "Law of Moses" (Luke 24:44) by both OT and NT writers.

SOLUTION: Moses did write the first five books of the OT (see comments on Ex. 24:4). The use of a different term for God in the second chapter of Genesis does not prove there was a different author; it simply shows that the same author had a different purpose (see comments on Gen. 2:19). In chapter 1, God is the *Creator,* whereas in chapter 2 He is the *Communicator.* First, man is seen in his relation to the *Creator* (hence, the use of "God" or *elohim,* the mighty one). Next, God is seen as the *Covenant-maker,* thus, the use of "Lord God," the One who makes covenants with man. Different names are used of God since they designate a different aspect of His dealings with man (see Gen. 15:1; Ex. 6:3).

GENESIS 2:8 – Was the Garden of Eden a real place or just a myth?

PROBLEM: The Bible declares that God "planted a garden eastward in Eden" (Gen. 2:8), but there is no archaeological evidence that any such place existed. Is this just a myth?

SOLUTION: First of all, we would not expect any archaeological evidence, since there is no indication that Adam and Eve made pottery or built durable buildings. Second, there is geographical evidence of Eden, since two of the rivers mentioned still exist today – the Tigris (Hiddekel) and the Euphrates (Gen. 2:14). Further, the Bible even locates them in "Assyria" (v. 14), which is present day Iraq. Finally, whatever evidence there may have been for the Garden of Eden (Gen. 2–3) was probably destroyed by God at the time of the Flood (Gen. 6–9).

GENESIS 2:17 – Why didn't Adam die the day he ate the forbidden fruit, as God said he would?

PROBLEM: God said to Adam, "in the day that you eat of it you shall surely die" (Gen. 2:17). But Adam lived to be 930 years old after he sinned (Gen. 5:5).

SOLUTION: The word "day" (*yom*) does not always mean a 24-hour day. For "one day (*yom*) is as a thousand years" (Ps. 90:4; cf. 2 Peter 3:8). Adam did die within a "day" in this sense. Further, Adam began to die physically the very moment he sinned (Rom. 5:12), and he also died spiritually the exact instant he sinned (Eph. 2:1). So Adam died in several ways, any one of which would fulfill the pronouncement of God (in Gen. 2:17).

GENESIS 2:19 — How can we explain the difference in the order of creation events between Genesis 1 and 2?

PROBLEM: Genesis 1 declares that animals were created before humans, but Genesis 2:19 seems to reverse this, saying, "the Lord God formed every beast of the field . . . and brought them to Adam to see what he would call them," implying Adam was created before they were.

SOLUTION: Genesis 1 gives the *order* of events; Genesis 2 provides more *content* about them. Genesis 2 does not contradict chapter 1, since it does not affirm exactly *when* God created the animals. He simply says He brought the animals (which He had previously created) to Adam so that he might name them. The focus in chapter 2 is on the *naming* of the animals, not on *creating* them. Genesis 1 provides the *outline* of events, and chapter 2 gives *details*. Taken together, the two chapters provide a harmonious and more complete picture of the creation events. The differences, then, can be summarized as follows:

GENESIS 1	GENESIS 2
Chronological order	Topical order
Outline	Details
Creating animals	Naming animals

GENESIS 3:5 — Is man made like God or does he become like God?

PROBLEM: Genesis 1:27 says "God created man in His own image." But in Genesis 3:22 God said, "the man has become like one of Us, to know good and evil." The former seems to affirm that humans are *made* like God, and the latter appears to assert that he *becomes* like God.

SOLUTION: The two passages are speaking of two different things. Genesis 1 is speaking about a human virtue by *creation,* while Genesis 3 is referring to what he had by *acquisition*. The first passage refers to Adam and Eve *before* the Fall, and the last is referring to them *after* the Fall. The former refers to their *nature* and the latter to their *state*. By creation Adam did not know good and evil. Once he sinned, he knew good and evil. Once these differences are understood, there is no conflict.

GENESIS 3:8 – How could Adam and Eve go from God's presence if God is everywhere?

PROBLEM: The Bible says that God is everywhere present at the same time, that is, He is omnipresent (Ps. 139:7-10; Jer. 23:23). But, if God is everywhere, then how could Adam and Eve be sent out "from the presence of the Lord"?

SOLUTION: This verse is not speaking of God's omnipresence, but of a visible manifestation of God (cf. v. 24). God is everywhere in His omnipresence, but from time to time He manifested Himself in certain places through certain things, such as a burning bush (Ex. 3), the pillar of fire (Ex. 13:21), smoke in the temple (Isa. 6), and so forth. It is in this latter localized sense that one can go "from the presence of the Lord."

GENESIS 4:5 – Does God show respect to certain persons?

PROBLEM: God is represented in the Scriptures as someone who "is no respect[er] of persons" (Rom. 2:11, KJV), and one who "shows no partiality" (Deut. 10:17). Yet, this verse tells us that God "did not respect Cain and his offering," which seems contradictory to the other verses.

SOLUTION: First of all, in the fundamental sense of the word, God respects every person for who he or she is, a creature made in His image and likeness (Gen. 1:27). If He didn't, He would not be respecting Himself. But, when the Bible says God is no respecter of persons, it means that He does not show partiality in meeting out His justice. As Deuteronomy 10 puts it, He "shows no partiality nor takes a bribe" (v. 17). In other words, God is completely fair and even-handed in His dealings.

However, there is a sense in which it can be said that God does not respect some persons because of their evil deeds. God "did not respect Cain *and his offering*" (Gen. 4:5) because it was not offered in faith (Heb. 11:4). Thus, the Bible also speaks of God hating Esau (Mal. 1:3) and the Nicolaitans (Rev. 2:6), not because of their person, but because of their practice. As John told the believers at Ephesus, they should "hate the deeds of the Nicolaitans" (Rev. 2:6). God loves the sinner, but hates the sin.

GENESIS 4:12-13 – Why wasn't Cain given capital punishment for the murder he committed?

PROBLEM: In the OT, murderers were given capital punishment for their crime (Gen. 9:6; Ex. 21:12). Yet Cain was not only set free after murdering his brother, but he was protected from any avenger (Gen. 4:15).

SOLUTION: There are several reasons why Cain was not executed for his capital crime. First, God had not yet established capital punishment as an instrument of human government (cf. Rom. 13:1-4). Only after violence filled the earth in the days before the flood did God say, "Whoever sheds man's blood, By man his blood shall be shed; For in the image of God He made man" (Gen. 9:6).

Further, who would have killed Cain? Cain had just killed Abel. At this early stage only Adam and Eve were left. Surely, God would not have called upon the parents to kill their only remaining son. In view of this, God, who alone is sovereign over life and death (Deut. 32:39), personally commuted Cain's death penalty. However, in so doing, God implied the gravity of Cain's sin and implied he was worthy of death by declaring that "the voice of your brother's blood cries out to Me [for vengeance] from the ground" (v. 10). Nonetheless, even Cain seemed to recognize that he was worthy of death, and he asked God for protection (v. 14). Finally, God's promise to protect Cain from vengeance implies capital punishment would be taken on any who took Cain's life (cf. v. 15). So, Cain's case is the exception that proves the rule, and by no means does it argue against capital punishment as established by God (see comments on John 8:3-11).

GENESIS 4:17 — Where did Cain get his wife?

PROBLEM: There were no women for Cain to marry. There was only Adam, Eve (4:1), and his dead brother Abel (4:8). Yet the Bible says Cain married and had children.

SOLUTION: Cain married his sister (or possibly a niece). The Bible says Adam "begot sons and *daughters*" (Gen. 5:4). In fact, since Adam lived 930 years (Gen. 5:5), he had plenty of time for plenty of children! Cain could have married one of his many sisters, or even a niece, if he married after his brothers or sisters had grown daughters. In that case, of course, one of his brothers would have married a sister.

GENESIS 4:17 — How could Cain marry a relative without committing incest?

PROBLEM: If Cain married his sister, this is incest, which the Bible condemns (Lev. 18:6). Furthermore, incestuous marriages often produce genetically defective children.

SOLUTION: First, there were no genetic imperfections at the beginning of the human race. God created a genetically perfect Adam (Gen. 1:27). Genetic defects resulted from the Fall and only occurred gradually over long periods of time. Further, there was no command in Cain's day not to marry a close relative. This command (Lev. 18) came thousands of years later in Moses' day (c. 1500 B.C.). Finally, since the human race began with a single pair (Adam and Eve), Cain had no one else to marry except a close female relative (sister or niece).

GENESIS 4:19 – Does the Bible approve of polygamy?

(See comments on 1 Kings 11:1)

GENESIS 4:26 – Did worship of God begin here or earlier?

PROBLEM: According to this verse, people did not begin "to call on the name of the Lord" until the days of Enosh, the third son of Adam and Eve. Yet their first son, Abel, brought an acceptable sacrifice to the Lord before this time (Gen. 4:3-4).

SOLUTION: The meaning of "call upon the name of the Lord" (in Gen. 4:26) is not clear. And what is not clear cannot be taken to contradict what is clear, namely, that Abel worshiped God before Enosh did. It is possible that calling on the Lord implied a regular, more solemn, and/or public worship of the Lord, or prayer (cf. Rom. 10:13) that was not practiced earlier. At any rate, there is no contradiction here, since it does not say that Abel or anyone else "called on the Lord" before this time – whatever it may mean.

GENESIS 5:1ff – How can we reconcile this chronology (which adds up to c. 4,000 years B.C.) when anthropology has shown humankind is much older?

PROBLEM: If the ages are added in Genesis 5 and 10 with the rest of the OT dates, it comes out to 4,000 plus years B.C. But, archaeologists and anthropologists date modern man many thousands of years before that (at least 10,000 years ago).

SOLUTION: There is good evidence to support the belief that humankind is more than 6,000 years old. But there are also good reasons to believe there are some gaps in the Genesis genealogies. First, we know there is a gap in the genealogy in the Book of Matthew. Matthew's genealogy says "Joram begot Uzziah" (Matt. 1:8). But when compared to 1 Chronicles 3:11-14, we see that Matthew leaves out three generations—Ahaziah, Joash, and Amaziah as follows:

Matthew	1 Chronicles
Joram	Joram
–	Ahaziah
–	Joash
–	Amaziah
Uzziah	Uzziah (also called Azariah)

Second, there is at least one generation missing in the Genesis genealogy. Luke 3:36 lists "Cainan" between Arphaxad and Shelah, but the name Cainan does not appear in the Genesis record at this point (see Gen. 10:22-24). It is better to view Genesis 5 and 10 as adequate *genealogies,* not as complete *chronologies.*

Finally, since there are known gaps in the genealogies, we cannot accurately determine the age of the human race by simply adding the numbers in Genesis 5 and 10.

GENESIS 5:5 — How could people live over 900 years?

PROBLEM: Adam "lived nine hundred and thirty years" (Gen. 5:5), Methuselah lived "nine hundred and sixty-nine years" (Gen. 5:27), and the average age of those who lived out their normal life span was over 900 years of age. Yet even the Bible recognizes that most people live only 70 or 80 years before natural death occurs (Ps. 90:10).

SOLUTION: First of all, the reference in Psalm 90 is to Moses' time (1400s B.C.) and later, when longevity had decreased to 70 or 80 years for most, though Moses himself lived 120 years (Deut. 34:7).

Some have suggested that these "years" are really only months, which would reduce 900 years to the normal life span of 80 years. However, this is implausible for two reasons. First, there is no precedent in the Hebrew OT for taking the word "year" to mean "month." Second, since Mahalalel had children when he was only 65 (Gen. 5:15), and Cainan had children when he was 70 (Gen. 5:12), this would mean they were less than six years old—which is not biologically possible.

Others suggest that these names represent family lines or clans that went on for generations before they died out. However, this does not make sense for a number of reasons. First, some of these names (e.g., Adam, Seth, Enoch, Noah) are definitely individuals whose lives are narrated in the text (Gen. 1–9). Second, family lines do not "beget" family lines by different names. Third, neither do family lines "die," as each of these individuals did (cf. 5:5, 8, 11, etc.). Fourth, the reference to having "sons and daughters" (5:4) does not fit the clan theory.

Consequently, it seems best to take these as years (though they were lunar years of 12x30 = 360 days) for several reasons: (1) First of all, life was later shortened to 120 years as a punishment from God (Gen. 6:3). (2) Life span decreased gradually after the flood from the 900s (Gen. 5) to the 600s (Shem 11:10-11), to the 400s (Salah 11:14-15), to the 200s (Rue 11:20-21). (3) Biologically, there is no reason humans could not live hundreds of years. Scientists are more baffled by aging and death than by longevity. (4) The Bible is not alone in speaking of hundreds of years life spans among ancients. There are also records from ancient Greek and Egyptian times that speak of humans living hundreds of years.

GENESIS 6:2 – Were the "Sons of God" angels who married women?

PROBLEM: The phrase "sons of God" is used exclusively in the OT to refer to angels (Job 1:6; 2:1; 38:7). However, the NT informs us that angels "neither marry nor are given in marriage" (Matt. 22:30). Furthermore, if angels married, their children would be half human and half angel. But, angels cannot be redeemed (Heb. 2:14-16; 2 Peter 2:4; Jude 6).

SOLUTION: There are several possible interpretations other than insisting that angels cohabited with humans.

Some Bible scholars believe "sons of God" refers to the godly line of Seth (from whom the redeemer was to come – Gen. 4:26), who intermingled with the godless line of Cain. They point out that (a) this fits the immediate context, (b) it avoids the problems with the angels view, and (c) it accords with the fact that humans are also referred to in the OT as God's "sons" (Isa. 43:6).

Other scholars believe that "sons of God" refers to great men of old, men of renown. They point to the fact that the text refers to "giants" and "mighty men" (v. 4). This also avoids the problems of angels (spirits) cohabiting with humans.

Still others combine these views and speculate that the "sons of God" were angels who "did not keep their proper domain" (Jude 6) and possessed real human beings, moving them to interbreed with "the daughters of men," thus producing a superior breed whose offspring were the "giants" and "men of renown." This view seems to explain all the data without the insuperable problems of angels, who are bodiless (Heb. 1:14) and sexless spirits (Matt. 22:30), cohabiting with humans.

GENESIS 6:3 – Does this contradict what Moses said in Psalm 90 about human longevity?

PROBLEM: This text seems to indicate that human longevity after the flood will not exceed "one hundred and twenty years." Yet in Psalm 90 Moses took it to be as 70 or 80 years at best (v. 10).

SOLUTION: First of all, it is not certain that Genesis 6:3 is referring to human longevity. It may be speaking about how many years remained before the flood would come.

Second, even if it does envision how long humans would live, it does not contradict the later reference to 70 or 80 years for two reasons: for one, it refers to an earlier period when people still lived longer (Moses himself lived to 120, Deut. 34:7); further, the 70 or 80 was probably not intended as an absolute upper limit, but merely as an average for people who died of old age.

GENESIS 6:6 – Why was God unsatisfied with what He made?

PROBLEM: In Genesis 1:31, God was satisfied with what He made, declaring it "very good." But here in Genesis 6:6, God declares that He is "sorry that He had made man on the earth." How can both be true?

SOLUTION: These verses speak of humankind at different times and under different conditions. The first deals with humans in the *original state of creation*. The second refers to the race *after the Fall* and just before the flood. God is pleased with what He made, but is not happy with what sin has done to His perfect creation.

GENESIS 6:14ff – How could Noah's ark hold hundreds of thousands of species?

PROBLEM: The Bible says Noah's ark was only 45 feet high, 75 feet wide, and 450 feet long (Gen. 6:15, NIV). Noah was told to take two of every kind of unclean animal and seven of every kind of clean animal

(6:19; 7:2). But scientists inform us that there are between one half a billion to over a billion species of animals.

SOLUTION: First, the modern concept of "species" is not the same as a "kind" in the Bible. There are probably only several hundred different "kinds" of land animals that would have to be taken into the ark. The sea animals stayed in the sea, and many species could have survived in egg form. Second, the ark was not small; it was a huge structure—the size of a modern ocean liner. Furthermore, it had three stories (6:16) which tripled its space to a total of over 1.5 million cubic feet!

Third, Noah could have taken younger or smaller varieties of some larger animals. Given all these factors, there was plenty of room for all the animals, food for the trip, and the eight humans aboard.

GENESIS 6:14ff — How could a wooden ark survive such a violent flood?

PROBLEM: The ark was only made of wood and carried a heavy load of cargo. But, a world-wide flood produces violent waters that would have broken it in pieces (cf. Gen. 7:4, 11).

SOLUTION: First, the ark was made of a strong and flexible material (gopherwood) that "gives" without breaking. Second, the heavy load was an advantage that gave the ark stability. Third, naval architects inform us that a long box-shaped, floating box-car, such as the ark was, is a very stable craft in turbulent waters. Indeed, modern ocean liners follow the same basic dimensions or proportions of Noah's ark.

GENESIS 7:24 — Did the flood rains last forty days or one hundred fifty days?

PROBLEM: Genesis 7:24 (and 8:3) speak of the flood waters lasting for 150 days. But, other verses say it was only 40 days (Gen. 7:4, 12, 17). Which is correct?

SOLUTION: These numbers refer to different things. Forty days refers to how long "the *rain fell*" (7:12, NIV), and 150 days speaks of how long the flood *"waters prevailed"* (cf. 7:24).

At the end of the 150 days "the waters decreased" (8:3). After this it was not until the fifth month after the rain began that the ark rested on Mt. Ararat (8:4). Then about eleven months after the rain began, the waters dried up (7:11; 8:13). And exactly one year and ten days after the flood began, Noah and his family emerged on dry ground (7:11; 8:14).

GENESIS 8:1 – Did God temporarily forget Noah?

PROBLEM: The fact that the text says that "God remembered Noah" seems to imply that He temporarily forgot him. Yet the Bible declares that God knows all things (Ps. 139:2-4; Jer. 17:10; Heb. 4:13) and that He never forgets His saints (Isa. 49:15). How then could He temporarily forget Noah?

SOLUTION: In His omniscience, God was always aware of Noah being in the ark. However, after Noah was left in the ark for over a year, *as if* he were forgotten, God gave a token of His remembrance and brought Noah and his family out of it. But, God had never forgotten Noah, since it was He that warned Noah in the very beginning in order to save him and the human race (cf. Gen. 6:8-13). We often use a similar expression when we "remember" someone on their birthday, even though we had never forgotten they existed.

GENESIS 8:21 – Did God change His mind about never destroying the world again?

PROBLEM: According to this verse, after the flood, God promised, "Nor will I again destroy every living thing." Yet Peter foretells the day in which "the heavens will pass away with a great noise, and the elements will melt with fervent heat; both the earth and the works that are in it will be burned up" (2 Peter 3:10).

SOLUTION: After the flood, God only promised never again to destroy the world in the *same way* "as I have done" (Gen. 8:21), namely by water. The rainbow is a perpetual symbol of this promise. The second time God destroys the world it will be by fire, not by water. It will "be burned up" (2 Peter 3:10). Even so, God will not then destroy all living things. Humans will be saved in their resurrected and imperishable physical bodies (1 Cor. 15:42).

GENESIS 8:22 – If seedtime and harvest were never to be interrupted, then why were there famines?

PROBLEM: God promised Noah: "While the earth remains, seedtime and harvest . . . shall not cease." However, there are many famines recorded, even in Bible times, when there has been no harvest (cf. Gen. 26:1; 41:54).

SOLUTION: "Cease" *(shabath)* means to come to an end, to be eliminated, to desist completely. This passage only promises that the *seasons* will not cease, not the *crops*. It refers to "seedtime" and harvesttime, not necessarily to the actual planting and harvesting of a crop. And the seasons have never stopped completely since this promise was made to Noah. Further, this general promise was not intended as a guarantee that there would be no *temporary* interruptions. It was only a statement about the *permanent* cycles of the year until the end of time.

GENESIS 9:3 – Did God ordain the eating of meat or only plants?

PROBLEM: When God created Adam, He commanded him to eat only "every herb that yields seed which is on the face of all the earth . . . to you it shall be for food" (Gen. 1:29). But meat was not given by God to eat. However, when Noah came out of the Ark, he was told, "Every moving thing that lives shall be food for you. I have given you all things, even as the green herbs" (Gen. 9:3). But this seems to contradict God's earlier command not to eat meat.

SOLUTION: This is a good example of progressive revelation where earlier commands are superseded by later ones. In matters that do not involve the change of any intrinsic moral standard (based on the nature of God), God is free to change the commands to His creatures to serve His overall purposes in the progress of redemption. For example, parents at one time will allow small children to eat with their fingers, only to instruct them a little later to eat their potatoes with a spoon. Then, a few years later, the same parent reprimands her older child, "Don't eat your potatoes with your spoon; use your fork!" There is no contradiction here at all. It is a simple matter of progressive revelation adapted to the circumstances and all geared to the ultimate goal. God works in a similar way.

GENESIS 10:5 (cf. 20, 31) – Why does this verse indicate that humankind had many languages when Genesis 11:1 says there was only one?

PROBLEM: Genesis 10:5, 20, 31 seem to suggest many dialects, which is an apparent conflict with Genesis 11:1 that clearly states, "the whole earth had one language and one speech."

SOLUTION: These texts speak of two different times. Earlier, while maintaining their tribal distinctions, the descendants of Ham, Shem, and Japheth all spoke the same language. Later, at the tower of Babel (Gen. 11), God punished their rebellious attempt by confusing their speech.

As a result, tribes could no longer understand one another, though possibly the subtribes and clans were allowed a mutually understandable language so they could still understand one another.

GENESIS 11:5 — How can God "come down" from heaven when He is already here (and everywhere)?

PROBLEM: God is omnipresent, that is, everywhere at the same time (Ps. 139:7-10). But this text declares that God "came down" to see the city that men had built. But if He is already here, then how can He "come down" here?

SOLUTION: God "came down" as a theophany, which is a special localized manifestation of the presence of God. These theophanies often appeared in the OT. Once God appeared to Abraham as a man (Gen. 18:2). God also came down to speak to Moses (Ex. 3), Joshua (Josh. 5:13-15), and Gideon (Jud. 6) in a similar manner.

GENESIS 11:28 — How could Abraham's family be from Ur of the Chaldees when elsewhere it says his ancestors came from Haran?

PROBLEM: There is an apparent conflict as to where Abraham is really from. Genesis 11:28 says Abraham came from Ur of the Chaldees (in southern Iraq), but Genesis 29:4 claims he is from Haran (in northern Iraq).

SOLUTION: This conflict is easily resolved. Abraham's family originated in Ur, but later migrated to Haran when God called him (Gen. 11:31–12:1). It is not unusual that Abraham would look back to Haran, where he had lived until he was 75 years old, as his homeland. Also, he quite naturally refers to the children of his two older brothers as part of his family.

GENESIS 11:32 — Was Abraham 75 years old when he left Haran, or was he 135 years old?

PROBLEM: Genesis 11:26 states, "Now Terah lived seventy years, and begot Abram, Nahor, and Haran." In Acts 7:4 Stephen states that Abraham did not leave Haran until after Terah, his father, died. Genesis 11:32 says that Terah died at 205 years of age. If Abraham was born when Terah was 70, and did not leave for Canaan until Terah died at

205, that would make Abraham 135 years old when he left Haran to travel to Canaan. However, Genesis 12:4 states, "And Abram was seventy-five years old when he departed from Haran." How old was Abraham when he left Haran? Was he 75 or was he 135?

SOLUTION: Abraham was 75 years old when he left Haran. Although it was customary to list the names of sons from the oldest to the youngest, this practice was not always followed. Genesis 11:26 does not say that Terah was 70 years old when Abraham was born. Rather it states that Terah lived for 70 years before he had any sons, then he had three sons, Abraham, Nahor, and Haran. Haran was probably the oldest son of Terah, indicated by the fact that he was the first to die (Gen. 11:28). Nahor was probably the middle son, and Abraham was the youngest. Abraham was listed first because he was the most prominent of Terah's sons. Since Abraham was 75 when he left Haran, this would mean that he was born when Terah was 130 years old.

GENESIS 12:10-20; 20:1-18 — Why did God let Abraham prosper by lying?

PROBLEM: We are told in the Bible not to lie (Ex. 20:16), but, when Abraham lied about Sarah, his wealth was increased.

SOLUTION: First, Abraham's increase in wealth should not be viewed as a divine reward for his lie. Pharaoh's gifts to him were understandable. Pharaoh may have felt obligated to pay amends for the wicked constraint that his corrupt society put on strangers who visited his land.

Furthermore, Pharaoh may have felt he had to make amends to Abraham for unwittingly taking his wife into his palace. Adultery was strictly forbidden by the Egyptian religion.

What is more, Abraham paid for his sin. The years of trouble that followed may have been a direct result of his lack of faith in God's protecting power.

Finally, although some people are portrayed as men of God, they are still fallible and responsible for their own sin (e.g., David and Bathsheba, 2 Sam. 12). God blessed them *in spite of,* not *because of,* their sins.

GENESIS 14 — Is the account of Abraham's defeat of the Mesopotamian kings historically reliable?

PROBLEM: Genesis presents this battle as factually true. But, according to the Documentary Hypothesis of biblical criticism, this story is a later addition and totally fictitious.

SOLUTION: We possess very little information about this period apart from Genesis itself. As a result, while we do not have direct archaeological confirmation, there is no good reason to doubt the event. Such doubt usually stems from an anti-biblical bias.

Furthermore, there is indirect support for the validity of this account. Noted archaeologist W.F. Albright has observed that, "In spite of our failure hitherto to fix the historical horizon of chapter 14, we may be certain that its contents are very ancient. There are several words and expressions found nowhere else in the Bible and are now known to belong to the second millennium [B.C.]. The names of the towns in Transjordania are also known to be very ancient" (Alleman and Flack, *Old Testament Commentary,* Philadelphia: Fortress Press, 1954, 14). In light of this, there is no good reason to doubt the authenticity of the biblical account of Abraham's battle with these Mesopotamian kings.

GENESIS 14:18-20 — Who was Melchizedek?

PROBLEM: There is some debate over the nature of Melchizedek. Was he a historical person, a super-normal being, or just a mythical figure?

SOLUTION: Based on Hebrews 7, some have interpreted Melchizedek as being an angel or even an appearance of Christ. This is not likely since the author of Hebrews was using Melchizedek to be a type of Christ. In Genesis, Melchizedek is presented in an ordinary, historical manner. He meets and speaks with Abraham in an ordinary manner. There is no reason, archaeological or otherwise, to question the historical character of Melchizedek.

GENESIS 15:16 — Did the Exodus occur in the fourth generation or in the sixth?

PROBLEM: Here the Bible speaks of the Exodus as being in the "fourth generation" from the time of Jacob's descent to Egypt. However, according to the genealogical tables in 1 Chronicles 2:1-9 (and Matt. 1:3-4) it was really the sixth generation (2:1-11), namely, Judah, Perez, Hezron, Ram, Amminadab, and Nashon.

SOLUTION: The word "generation" in Genesis 15:16 is defined in that very passage as 100 years, since "the fourth generation" (v. 16) is used to refer to "four hundred years" (v. 13). So Genesis 15 is referring to the *amount of time* and 1 Chronicles is speaking of the *number of people* involved in the same period of time.

GENESIS 15:17; cf. 19:23 — Why does the Bible use unscientific terms such as "the sun going down"?

PROBLEM: Evangelical Christians claim that the Bible is the inspired and inerrant word of God. However, if the Bible is inerrant in all that it affirms, including historical and scientific facts, why do we find such unscientific terms as "the sun going down" or "the rising of the sun"?

SOLUTION: The Bible is not claiming that the sun actually sets or rises. Rather, it is simply employing the same kind of observational language that we employ even today. It is a regular part of any weather forecast to announce the time of "sunrise" and "sunset." To claim that the Bible is "unscientific," or that there are scientific errors because of the use of such phrases, is a feeble argument. Such a charge would have to be equally leveled against virtually everyone today, including modern scientists who employ this type of language in normal conversation (see comments on Josh. 10:12-14).

GENESIS 19:8 — Was the sin of Sodom homosexuality or inhospitality?

PROBLEM: Some have argued that the sin of Sodom and Gomorrah was inhospitality, not homosexuality. They base this claim on the Canaanite custom that guarantees protection for those coming under one's roof. Lot is alleged to have referred to it when he said, "don't do anything to these men, for they have come under the protection of my roof " (Gen. 19:8, NIV). So Lot offered his daughters to satisfy the angry crowd in order to protect the lives of the visitors who had come under his roof. Some also claim that the request of the men of the city to "know" (Gen. 19:5) simply means "to get acquainted," since the Hebrew word "know" (*yada*) generally has no sexual connotations whatsoever (cf. Ps. 139:1).

SOLUTION: While it is true that the Hebrew word "know" (*yada*) does not necessarily mean "to have sex with," nonetheless, in the context of the passage on Sodom and Gomorrah, it clearly has this meaning. This is evident for several reasons. First of all, 10 of the 12 times this word is used in Genesis it refers to sexual intercourse (cf. Gen. 4:1, 25).

Second, it means to know sexually in this very chapter. For Lot refers to his two virgin daughters as not having "known" a man (19:8), which is an obvious sexual use of the word.

Third, the meaning of a word is discovered by the context in which it is used. And the context here is definitely sexual, as is indicated by the reference to the wickedness of the city (18:20), and the virgins offered to appease their passions (19:8). Fourth, "know" cannot mean simply "get acquainted with," because it is equated with a "wicked thing" (19:7). Fifth, why offer the virgin daughters to appease them if their intent was not sexual. If the men had asked to "know" the virgin daughters, no one would have mistaken their sexual intentions.

Sixth, God had already determined to destroy Sodom and Gomorrah, as Genesis 18:16-33 indicates, even before the incident in 19:8. Consequently, it is much more reasonable to hold that God had pronounced judgment upon these cities for the sins they had already committed, namely homosexuality, than for a sin they had not yet committed, that is inhospitality.

GENESIS 19:30-38 – Does the Bible condone incest?

PROBLEM: Incest is denounced in emphatic terms in many biblical passages (cf. Lev. 18:6; 20:17). In fact, the Lord declared, "Cursed is the one who lies with his sister, the daughter of his father or the daughter of his mother" (Deut. 27:22). Yet Lot committed incest with his two daughters here, from which came the nations of Moab and Ammon.

SOLUTION: There is no question that Lot sinned here in several ways, to say nothing of the violation of incest laws that Moses later gave as commands to Israel. Lot was drunk, and he committed adultery with his daughters. Lot's righteous soul was vexed with many sins due to his long association with the people of Sodom. But none of these sins are approved of in this passage. Indeed, the whole colorless tone of the narrative, without any positive comment by the narrator, indicates that there was no attempt to conceal the horror of his sins. Here is a good example of the principle that not everything recorded by the Bible is approved by the Bible (see Introduction).

GENESIS 20:12 – If incest is condemned, why did Abraham marry his sister?

PROBLEM: Abraham admitted here that Sarah his wife was really his "sister" (cf. Gen. 17:15–16). Yet incest is denounced in no uncertain terms in many passages (cf. Lev. 18:6; 20:17). Indeed, the Lord declared, "Cursed is the one who lies with his sister, the daughter of his father or the daughter of his mother" (Deut. 27:22).

SOLUTION: Abraham was not beyond sin, as his lie about Sarah to king Abimelech reveals (Gen. 20:4-5). And Abraham did admit that Sarah was "the daughter of my father, but not the daughter of my mother; and she became my wife" (Gen. 20:12). However, even granting this, there is no real proof Abraham violated any law for two reasons. First, the incest laws were not given by Moses until some 500 years after Abraham. So he surely could not be held responsible for laws that had not yet been promulgated. Second, the terms "sister" and "brother" are used with great latitude in the Bible, just as the terms "father" and "son." Jesus, for example, was the "son" (i.e., descendant) of David (Matt. 21:15). "Sister" means a near relative, but it does not as such indicate the degree of nearness we understand by the word "sister." Lot, Abraham's nephew, is called a "brother" (Gen. 14:12, 16). Likewise, "daughter" can mean granddaughter or great granddaughter.

Considering the age to which Abraham lived (175, Gen. 25:7), it is possible that he married only a granddaughter on his father's side, or even a niece or grand niece. In any event, there is no proof that Abraham's marriage to Sarah violated any existing incest law. But if it did, the Bible simply gives us a true record of Abraham's error. When God called Sarah Abraham's "wife" (Gen. 17:15), He was not legitimizing any alleged incest, but merely stating a fact.

GENESIS 21:32, 34 — Did the Bible mistakenly place the Philistines in Palestine at the time of Abraham?

PROBLEM: The earliest allusion to Philistines by Palestinian or Egyptian sources is the twelfth century B.C., yet these verses place them in the area some 800 years earlier.

SOLUTION: This is not the first time critics have come to false conclusions based on the general lack of historical knowledge concerning this period. Sodom and Gomorrah are examples of cities the Bible mentioned that were supposedly not historical. When the Ebla tablets were discovered, the charge of myth was refuted. These tablets contained references to both cities. It may just be a matter of time before similar evidence turns up to confirm the biblical testimony here regarding the Philistines. Until then, we can rest assured that the biblical record is accurate in this case, having confidence in the Scriptures based on its past record of trustworthiness. Furthermore, the critics' argument is the traditional fallacious argument from ignorance. Simply because we lack evidence from extrabiblical sources of the earlier date for the Philistines does not mean they didn't exist then. It simply means we *lack the information.*

GENESIS 22:2 – Why did God tell Abraham to sacrifice his son when God condemned human sacrifice in Leviticus 18 and 20?

PROBLEM: In both Leviticus 18:21 and 20:2, God specifically denounced human sacrifice when He commanded Israel, "Do not give any of your children to be sacrificed to Molech" (Lev. 18:21, NIV), and "Any Israelite or any alien living in Israel, who gives any of his children to Molech, must be put to death; the people of the community are to stone him" (Lev. 20:2, NIV). Yet, in Genesis 22:2, God commanded Abraham to "Take now your son, your only son Isaac, whom you love, and go to the land of Moriah, and offer him there as a burnt offering on one of the mountains of which I shall tell you." This appears to contradict His command not to offer human sacrifices.

SOLUTION: First, God was not interested, nor did He plan, that Abraham should actually kill his son. The fact that the angel of the Lord prevented Abraham from killing Isaac (22:12) demonstrates this. God's purpose was to test Abraham's faith by asking him to completely surrender his only son to God. The angel of the Lord declared that it was Abraham's *willingness* to surrender his son, not the actual killing of him, that satisfied God's expectations for Abraham. God said explicitly, "Do not stretch out your hand against the lad . . . for now I know that you fear God, since you have not withheld your son, your only son, from Me" (Gen. 22:12, NASB).

Second, the prohibitions in both Leviticus 18:21 and 20:2 were specifically against the offering of one's offspring to the pagan god Molech. So it is not strictly a contradiction for God to prohibit offering one's offspring to Molech and yet asking Abraham to offer Isaac to Him, the only true God. After all, offering Isaac to the Lord is not offering one's offspring to Molech, since the Lord is not Molech. God alone is sovereign over life (Deut. 32:39; Job 1:21), and therefore He alone has the right to demand when it should be taken. Indeed, He has appointed the day of everyone's death (Ps. 90:10; Heb. 9:27).

Third, Abraham so trusted in God's love and power that he willingly obeyed because he believed God would raise Isaac from the dead (Heb. 11:17-19). This is implied in the fact that, though Abraham intended to kill Isaac, he told his servants, "I and the lad will go yonder; and *we* will worship and *we* will return to you" (Gen. 22:5, NASB).

Finally, it is not morally wrong for God to order the sacrifice of our sons. He offered His own Son on Calvary (John 3:16). Indeed, even our governments sometimes call upon us to sacrifice our sons for our country. Certainly God has an even greater right to do so.

GENESIS 22:2 – How could Isaac be Abraham's "only son" when he already had Ishmael?

PROBLEM: Abraham was told here, "Take now your son, your only son Isaac." However, Abraham had Ishmael many years before (Gen. 16) and he also had other "sons" (Gen. 25:6).

SOLUTION: The other sons of Genesis 25 were probably born later, being mentioned three chapters after Isaac is called his "only son." Furthermore, they were sons by "the concubines which Abraham had" (Gen. 25:6) and were not counted as heirs of God's promise. Likewise, Ishmael was conceived in unbelief by a concubine and not counted as heir to the promised inheritance. In addition, the phrase "only son" may be equivalent to "beloved son" (cf. John 1:18; 3:16), that is, a special son. God said clearly to Abraham, "in Isaac your seed shall be called" (Gen. 21:12).

GENESIS 22:12 – Was God ignorant of how Abraham would respond?

PROBLEM: This verse implies that God did not know how Abraham would respond to His command, since it was only after Abraham obeyed that God said, "now I know that you fear God." However, the Bible declares elsewhere that God in "His understanding is infinite" (Ps. 147:5), that He knows "the end from the beginning" (Isa. 46:10), and has foreknown and predestinated us from the foundation of the world (Rom. 8:29-30).

SOLUTION: In His omniscience God knew exactly what Abraham would do, since He knows all things (cf. Ps. 139:2-4; Jer. 17:10; Acts 1:24; Heb. 4:13). However, what God knows by *cognition,* and what is known by *demonstration* are different. After Abraham had obeyed God's command, he demonstrated what God always knew, namely, that he feared God.

Here again the Bible, addressed as it is to human beings, speaks from the human perspective. In like manner, a math teacher might say, "Let's see if we can find the square root of 49," and then, after demonstrating it, declare, "Now we know that it is 7," even though she knew from the beginning what the answer was.

GENESIS 23 – How could the sons of Heth have been in Hebron in 2050 B.C. when their kingdom was in what is now modern Turkey?

PROBLEM: Heth was the progenitor of the Hittites, whose kingdom was located in what is now modern Turkey. But, according to some archaeological evidence, the Hittites did not become a prominent force in the Middle East until the reign of Mursilis I, which began about 1620 B.C., and who captured the city of Babylon in 1600 B.C.

However, several times in Genesis 23 reference is made to Abraham's encounter with the sons of Heth, who controlled Hebron about 2050 B.C. How could the Bible claim the presence of Hittites in control of Hebron so many years before they became a significant force in the area?

SOLUTION: More recent archaeological evidence from cuneiform tablets describes conflicts in Anatolia (modern Turkey), among the various Hittite principalities from about 1950 to 1850 B.C. Even before this conflict, however, there was a race of non-Indo-Europeans called Hattians. These people were subdued by invaders about 2300 to 2000 B.C. These Indo-European invaders adopted the name Hatti. In Semitic languages, like Hebrew, Hatti and Hitti would be written with the same letters, because only the consonants were written, not the vowels.

In the days of Ramses II of Egypt, the military strength of the Hittites was sufficient to precipitate a non-aggression pact between Egypt and the Hittite empire which set a boundary between them. At this time, the Hittite empire reached as far south as Kadesh on the Orontes river (modern Asi). However, additional evidence indicates that the Hittites actually penetrated further south into Syria and Palestine. Although the Hittite kingdom did not reach its zenith until the second half of the 14th century, there is sufficient evidence to substantiate a Hittite presence in Hebron at the time of Abraham, which was significant enough to control the area.

GENESIS 25:1 — Why does Genesis 25:1 call Keturah Abraham's wife, while 1 Chronicles 1:32 calls her his concubine?

PROBLEM: Genesis 25:1 says, "Abraham again took a wife, and her name was Keturah." However, 1 Chronicles 1:32 states, "Now the sons of Keturah, Abraham's concubine." Was Keturah Abraham's wife, or was she merely one of his concubines?

SOLUTION: The contradiction is only apparent, and the problem can be easily solved by closer consideration. First, although in Genesis 25:1 the normal Hebrew word for wife (*ishshah*) is used, it is also the normal word for woman. It is not necessary to take the word in this case to mean wife, especially in light of verse 6 and the statement in 1 Chronicles 1:32 that Keturah was his concubine. Genesis 25:1 can be read simply as, "And Abraham took another woman" as his concubine.

Second, although 1 Chronicles employs the Hebrew word for concubine (*pilegesh*) in reference to Keturah, Genesis 25:6 uses the same word when referring to the mothers of all his other sons apart from Isaac. This would obviously include Keturah as one of his concubines. Additionally, Genesis 25:1 begins with a Hebrew word (*vayoseph*) which can be translated, "And adding" or "And in addition to." Since Genesis 24:67 clearly states that Sarah, Abraham's wife, had died, verse 1 of chapter 25 could not mean that Abraham was adding to his number of wives. It is more reasonable to take this word as indicating that Abraham was adding to his number of concubines by taking another woman (*ishshah*).

GENESIS 25:1-2 — How could Abraham have children naturally here when years before he needed a miracle to have Isaac?

PROBLEM: As early as Genesis 17, Abraham "laughed" when God told him he would have a son (Isaac) by Sarah, since he was "a hundred years old" (v.17). But here in Genesis 25, many years later, he has children by Keturah, the wife he took after Sarah died (vv. 1-2).

SOLUTION: There are two possibilities here, either one of which would explain this difficulty. First, the Genesis 17 text does not say Abraham laughed because he knew he was too old to have children, but because Sarah was past childbearing age (cf. 17:17; 18:12). There was no sure way for a man in ancient times to know he was no longer fertile, as there was for a woman when her periods ceased. Since Abraham was only 100 here, and he lived to be 175, it is reasonable to assume that he was still fertile. By comparison, men who live till 80 today are still fertile in their 60s.

Second, even if it took a miracle on Abraham (as well as on Sarah) to restore fertility, there is no reason that his fertile state could not have lasted for many years into the future. Once animated, his virile powers could have lasted for decades. After all, he lived 75 more years. In any event, the imagined contradiction here is simply not established.

GENESIS 25:8 — Did the Hebrews have a concept of life after death at such an early point in their history?

PROBLEM: Critical scholars assert that the early Hebrews had a very rudimentary religion that over the centuries would undergo great evolutionary development before ultimately arriving at a concept of life after death. However, this phrase implies that the Hebrews had a concept of immortality at a very early stage in the development of the nation.

SOLUTION: First of all, this criticism is based on the highly problematic premise that there is an evolutionary development of religion, with highly developed monotheism being very late. Recent archaeological findings at Ebla, however, contradict such speculation showing that monotheism was a very early belief (even before 2000 B.C.). Furthermore, the expression "gathered to his people" certainly seems to indicate more than merely being buried close to his kinsmen. In fact, since Abraham had left his homeland in Ur of the Chaldees to go to the land which God promised him, it would be contrary to Abraham's life to have his body returned to the land of his father's house for burial. The idea that the soul continued to live after the death of the body was a belief held by many peoples in the time of Abraham, including the Sumerians, the Babylonians, the Egyptians, and others.

In addition, this is not the only early reference to the concept of life after death. The Book of Job is probably the oldest book of the OT, with the events of the book dating back to the time of Abraham and the patriarchs of Israel. Yet, as early as Job, we find not only the concept of life after death, but also the concept of a bodily resurrection. In Job 19:25-26 we find Job expressing his confidence that, though he may not see his personal vindication in this life, he knew that God would ultimately make things right. This confidence moved him to express his conviction that he would indeed stand before God even after his physical demise; "For I know that my Redeemer lives, and He shall stand at last on the earth; And after my skin is destroyed, this I know, that in my flesh I shall see God." This verse shows that the concept of life after death was a very early conviction, and that the people of God also believed in the resurrection of the body.

GENESIS 25:31-33 — Did Jacob purchase the birthright or get it by deception?

PROBLEM: This text says Esau was asked by Jacob to "sell" him the birthright. But Genesis 29:1ff tells how he got it by deception.

SOLUTION: Jacob purchased the "birthright," but he got the "blessing" by deception. These are distinct things. So there is no real discrepancy.

GENESIS 26:33 — Was Beersheba named by Abraham or later by Isaac?

PROBLEM: In Genesis 21:31 Abraham named this city Beersheba ("Well of the Oath"). But later (in Gen. 26:33), Isaac gave it the same name.

But it is highly unlikely that two different people at two different times would call the same place by the same name.

SOLUTION: This is not unlikely at all for two reasons. First, the second person was the son of the first person and may have been familiar with his father's experience there. Second, Isaac's similar experience may have occasioned the memory of the name his father gave to this same place. So it is not at all uncommon that Isaac would have later renewed the name his father had earlier given to this important place in their lives.

GENESIS 26:34—How many wives did Esau have?

PROBLEM: Genesis 26:34 states that Esau married Judith the daughter of Beeri the Hittite, and Basemath the daughter of Elon the Hittite. However, Genesis 36:2-3 states that Esau's wives were Adah the daughter of Elon the Hittite, Aholibamah the daughter of Anah, and Basemath, Ishmael's daughter. Did Esau marry Elon's daughter Basemath or his daughter Adah? Did Esau have two, three, or four wives?

SOLUTION: The wives of Esau were four—Judith, the daughter of Beeri; Basemath, who was also named Adah, the daughter of Elon; Aholibamah the daughter of Anah; and Basemath the daughter of Ishmael. The reason Judith is not mentioned in Genesis 36:2-3 is because she bore him no children, and Genesis 36 is a statement of "the records of the generations of Esau" (Gen. 36:1, NASB). Also, it was a common practice for men and women to be known by more than one name. Apparently, Basemath, the daughter of Elon, was also named Adah and is so identified in Genesis 36:2 in order to distinguish her from Basemath the daughter of Ishmael. So Esau had four wives.

GENESIS 27:42-44—Did Jacob return to Haran to flee Esau or to get a wife?

PROBLEM: Here Rebekah told Jacob, "Flee to my brother Laban in Haran. And stay with him a few days, until your brother's fury turns away." But, in Genesis 28:2 the reason given is to "take yourself a wife from there of the daughters of Laban your mother's brother." Which was it?

SOLUTION: Jacob returned for both reasons. Two or more reasons for the same thing are not uncommon in the Bible. Compare the following:

(1) Moses' exclusion from the Promised Land was for unbelief (Num. 20:12), for rebellion (Num. 27:14), for trespass (Deut. 32:51), and for rash words (Ps. 106:33).

(2) Moses' condemnation for numbering the people was for taxation (Ex. 38:26) and for a military enrollment (Num. 1:2-3; 2:32).

(3) Saul was rejected by God for an unlawful sacrifice (1 Sam. 13:12-13), for disobedience (1 Sam. 28:18), and for consulting the witch of Endor (1 Chron. 10:13).

GENESIS 29:21-30 — When was Rachel given to be Jacob's wife?

PROBLEM: In Genesis 29:27 Laban tells Jacob to complete the bridal week of feasting with Leah, and then Rachel would be given to him. However, the verse also says that the contract between Laban and Jacob stipulated that in return for another seven years of service Rachel would be given to Jacob. When was Rachel given to Jacob, at the end of Leah's bridal week, or at the end of the seven years service?

SOLUTION: The passage indicates that Rachel was given to Jacob after the seven days which comprised the bridal week of Leah. The marriage feast generally lasted seven days (cf. Jud. 14:12). Laban contracted with Jacob that Rachel would become his wife at the end of this seven day bridal feast, and, in return, Jacob would serve Laban for an additional seven years. Ironically, Jacob, who had taken Esau's birthright by deception, had himself been deceived by Laban.

GENESIS 31:20 — How could God bless Jacob after he deceived Laban?

PROBLEM: In Genesis 31:20, Jacob is said to have deceived Laban by not telling him that he was fleeing. However, God blessed Jacob by appearing to Laban and warning him not to speak either good or evil to Jacob (Gen. 31:24). How could God bless Jacob after he had deceived Laban?

SOLUTION: First, it is not necessary to translate the Hebrew word in Genesis 31:20 as "deceived." The passage literally states, "And Jacob stole Laban's heart." This is a Hebrew idiom which can be used in a given context to mean "to deceive" or "to outwit." Jacob did not tell Laban that he was going to leave, nor did he tell Laban that he was going to stay. He may have left in secret because he feared Laban (cf. Gen. 31:2). Neither was Jacob obligated to remain with Laban, since he had fulfilled all the requirements of the contracts between them. In spite of the accusations by Laban, Jacob was justified in his fear and his action to leave without telling Laban.

Second, even on the assumption that Jacob was involved in deception,

God would not bless him *because* of it, but *in spite of* his shortcomings. This kind of situation is an example of the principle that "Not everything recorded by the Bible is approved by the Bible" (see Introduction). God had chosen Jacob to become the father of the 12 tribes of Israel, not because of any righteousness in Jacob, but on the basis of God's grace. God could bless Jacob according to His grace even though he was a sinner. Through Jacob's experiences with Laban, and later his confrontation with Esau, and his wrestling with the angel of the Lord in the night, Jacob's character was changed so that he became a fit vessel for God to use.

GENESIS 31:32 — How could God bless Rachel when she stole Laban's idols and then lied to him about it?

PROBLEM: Genesis 31:32 makes the statement that Jacob did not know that "Rachel had stolen" Laban's idols. However, it seems that God blessed Rachel because she lied to Laban.

SOLUTION: God did not bless Rachel either for stealing the idols or for lying about her deed. Simply because Laban did not discover that Rachel was the thief does not mean that God blessed her. On the contrary, it is more reasonable to assume that God did not expose Rachel's theft in order to protect Jacob. Also, Genesis 35:16-19 reports that Rachel died in delivering her second son, Benjamin. In the intervening chapters between 31:32 and 35:19 very little is said about Rachel. The biblical record reveals that in fact God did not bless Rachel for what she did, but allowed her to fall into the background of importance until her painful death.

GENESIS 32:30 — Can God's face be seen?

PROBLEM: God declared to Moses, "No man shall see Me, and live" (Ex. 33:20, see comments on John 1:18). Moses was allowed only to see God's "back" (Ex. 33:23). Yet the Bible informs us that Moses spoke with God "face to face" (Deut. 5:4). How could he speak to God face to face without seeing His face?

SOLUTION: It is possible for a blind person to speak face to face with someone without seeing their face. The phrase "face to face" means personally, directly, or intimately. Moses had this kind of unmediated relationship with God. But he, like all other mortals, never saw the "face" (essence) of God directly.

GENESIS 46:4 — Did God bring Jacob out of Egypt or did he die there?

PROBLEM: In this verse, God promised Jacob, "I will go down with you to Egypt, and I will also surely bring you up again." However, Jacob died in Egypt (Gen. 49:33) and never returned to the Land of Promise.

SOLUTION: This promise was fulfilled to Jacob in several ways, any one of which would explain the difficulty. First, it was a promise to Jacob's posterity who were brought back out of Egypt. This is indicated by the statement, "I will make of you a great nation" (v. 3). Second, Jacob was probably brought back from Egypt along with Joseph, though not alive (Gen. 50:25; Ex. 13:19). Finally, after the resurrection Jacob will return to the Land alive (cf. Matt. 8:11).

GENESIS 46:8-27 — Why does the Bible speak about the twelve tribes of Israel when actually there were fourteen?

PROBLEM: The Bible often states that there were twelve tribes of Israel. Yet, in three different passages, the lists are different. In fact, there are 14 different tribes listed as one of the 12 tribes.

Genesis 46	Numbers 26	Revelation 7
1. Reuben	Reuben	Reuben
2. Simeon	Simeon	Simeon
3. Levi	—	Levi
4. Judah	Judah	Judah
5. Issachar	Issachar	Issachar
6. Zebulun	Zebulun	Zebulun
7. Joseph	—	Joseph
8. —	Manasseh	Manasseh
9. —	Ephraim	—
10. Benjamin	Benjamin	Benjamin
11. Dan	Dan	—
12. Gad	Gad	Gad
13. Asher	Asher	Asher
14. Napthali	Napthali	Napthali

Were there twelve tribes of Israel or fourteen?

SOLUTION: In response, it must be noted that Jacob had only twelve sons. Their descendants comprised the original twelve tribes. However, for various reasons these same descendants are rearranged at different times into somewhat different groups of twelve. For example, in Genesis

48:22, Jacob grants to Joseph a double portion of the inheritance. In the list in Numbers, Manasseh and Ephraim, the sons of Joseph, are substituted for the tribe of Joseph. Also, Levi was not given a portion of the land as an inheritance because the Levites functioned as priests. Scattered among all the tribes in 48 Levitical cities, they taught the tribes the statutes of the Lord (Deut. 33:10). Consequently, Joseph's double portion is divided between Manasseh and Ephraim, his two sons in order to fill the space left by Levi.

In the Revelation passage, Joseph and Manasseh are counted separately, possibly indicating that Joseph and Ephraim (Joseph's son) are counted as one tribe. Dan is omitted from that list, possibly because the Danites took their own allotment by force in an area north of Asher, effectively separating themselves from their original inheritance in the south. Further, the Danites were the first tribe to go into idolatry. Levi is listed here as a separate tribe, possibly because, after the cross, the Levites no longer function in the priestly office for all the tribes and, thus, could be given a specific land inheritance of their own. In each case, the biblical author is careful to preserve the original number 12, with its spiritual significance indicating heavenly perfection (cf. the gates and foundations of the heavenly City, Rev. 21).

GENESIS 49:5-7 — How can Jacob pronounce a curse upon Levi here and yet Moses blessed Levi in Deuteronomy 33:8-11?

PROBLEM: In Genesis 49:5-7, Jacob pronounces a curse upon Levi: "Cursed be their [Simeon's and Levi's] anger, for it is fierce; And their wrath, for it is cruel! I will divide them in Jacob and scatter them in Israel" (v. 7). However, in Deuteronomy 33:8-11, Moses blessed Levi: "They [the Levites] shall teach Jacob Your judgments, and Israel Your Law. . . . Bless his substance, Lord, and accept the work of his hands" (Deut. 33:10-11).

SOLUTION: Jacob pronounces this curse upon Levi and Simeon because of the cruel manner in which they took revenge upon the inhabitants of Shechem (Gen. 34:1-31). As a punishment for their crime, they would be scattered among the other tribes of Israel so that they would not obtain a land possession of their own. However, the curse upon Levi was turned into a blessing for all the tribes of Israel. For it was God's plan to scatter the descendants of Levi throughout Israel so that "They shall teach Jacob Your judgments, and Israel Your law" (Deut. 33:10).

There is no contradiction between these two proclamations. Levi's descendants were scattered, as Jacob prophesied, but they were used by God to function as the priestly tribe throughout all Israel, as Moses had proclaimed. Levi was not given an inheritance of land among the other tribes because, in Numbers 18:20, God had said, "You shall have no inheritance in their land, nor shall you have any portion among them; I am your portion and your inheritance among the children of Israel."

GENESIS 49:10 – Who or what is "Shiloh" in this verse?

PROBLEM: The word "Shiloh" is often understood to be a reference to Jesus Christ as the coming Messiah. The word appears in a phrase which is part of the prophetic pronouncements of Jacob upon his son Judah. It is through the tribe of Judah that the Messiah will come (cf. 2 Sam. 7; Mic. 5:2), so it seems appropriate to understand this verse as a reference to the Messiah, Jesus Christ. However, the NT does not make any reference to this prophecy as being fulfilled in Christ, nor to the name Shiloh.

SOLUTION: The solution to this problem involves the vowel pointing of the Masoretic Text (MT) of the OT (see Appendix 1). The New King James Version translates this portion of verse 10 as follows: "Until Shiloh comes." This version follows the vowel pointing of the MT and translates the Hebrew word *shylh* as the proper name "Shiloh." Shiloh was the name of a town situated approximately ten miles northeast of Bethel. Although some interpreters take the statement in Genesis 49:10 as a reference to this town, others have taken it to be a proper name for Messiah.

However, the majority of scholars propose a different vowel pointing and understand the word to mean "to whom it belongs." This proposal has the support of ancient translations, such as the Greek and Syriac versions of the OT, and others. These ancient versions, being much older than the MT, also render the phrase, "he to whom they belong." This reading is also supported by Ezekiel 21:27 which states, "Until He comes whose right it is." When this part of verse 10 is taken this way, the passage reads, "The scepter shall not depart from Judah, Nor a lawgiver's staff from between his feet, *Until He comes to whom it belongs,* And to Him shall be the obedience of the people." In light of this, the Messianic significance of the verse is much clearer. For it is fulfilled in the NT Messiah (Christ), as indicated by such passages as Matthew 2:6, Luke 1:30-33, Revelation 5:5, and 19:11-16.

GENESIS 49:10b – If Judah was to reign until the Messiah, why was Israel's first king from the tribe of Benjamin?

PROBLEM: Genesis 49:10 indicates that "the scepter shall not depart from Judah, Nor a lawgiver from between his feet, Until Shiloh comes." But history records that the first king of Israel (Saul) was from "the tribe of Benjamin" (Acts 13:21; cf. 1 Sam. 9:1-2).

SOLUTION: This problem is predicated on the assumption that "Shiloh" is a reference to the Messiah. Some scholars take it to refer to the city in Ephraim where the Tabernacle of Moses was erected. On this interpretation, Judah was to be the leader of the 12 tribes all during the wilderness, until they came into the Promised Land.

Even if "Shiloh" is a reference to the Messiah, there is no real problem here, since the Messiah came from the tribe of Judah (cf. Matt. 1:1-3, 16; Rev. 5:5). In God's eyes David (from the tribe of Judah), not Saul, was His choice for the first king of Israel (cf. 1 Sam. 15–16). So, the tribe of Judah was always the ruling line from which the Messiah was to come.

GENESIS 49:14-15 – Why did Jacob predict slavery for Issachar here, but in Deuteronomy 33:18-19 Moses predicted blessing?

PROBLEM: In Genesis 49:14-15 Jacob prophesies that Issachar would become "a band of slaves" (Gen. 49:15). However, in Deuteronomy 33:19 Moses predicts that Issachar will "partake of the abundance of the seas and of treasures hidden in the sand."

SOLUTION: The history of the tribe of Issachar indicates that Jacob was looking forward to a time when, for the sake of their earthly possessions, Issachar would bow to foreign invaders under Tiglath-pileser rather than fight for their liberty. Moses, however, was looking forward to a time before this invasion when the tribe would prosper in the fertile plain which lay between the mountains of Gilboa and Tabor. The prosperity which they gained led to a relative life of ease, a characteristic alluded to in the figure of a lazy donkey unwilling to move its burden (Gen. 49:14). This prosperity in a land which was often threatened by foreign invaders, and their unwillingness to forfeit their possessions for liberty, created the eventual servitude predicted by Jacob.

EXODUS

EXODUS 1:15 – How could two midwives take care of so many Hebrew women?

PROBLEM: According to Exodus 12:37 and Numbers chapters 1–4, the size of the nation of Israel as they departed from Egypt must have been about 2 million persons. This would mean that there must have been several hundred thousand women. However, Exodus 1:15 states that Pharaoh spoke only to the Hebrew midwives who were Shiphrah and Puah. How could two midwives care for such a large number of women?

SOLUTION: Pharaoh spoke only to them because they were the leaders of the midwives of the Hebrews. History records that the Egyptian society was highly organized. There were individuals who functioned as overseers for almost every profession and craft in Egyptian society. Much of the commerce was regulated by the government, and craftsmen were required to take orders from the government official in charge of their district. It would be in keeping with this type of structure for the Israelites to have appointed these two individuals to function as superintendents of a large group of Hebrew midwives (cf. Ex. 18:24-25). This type of organizational structure would have facilitated interaction with the Egyptian officials. When Pharaoh, or some other Egyptian official, needed to communicate some new mandate to the group, he would do so through these two superintendents.

EXODUS 1:15-21 – How could God bless the Hebrew midwives for disobeying the God-ordained governmental authority (Pharaoh) and lying to him?

PROBLEM: The Bible declares that "the authorities that exist are appointed by God" (Rom. 13:1). The Scripture also says, "Lying lips are an abomination to the Lord" (Prov. 12:22). But the Pharaoh (king) of Egypt had given a direct order to the Hebrew midwives to murder the newborn Hebrew boys. "But the midwives feared God, and did not do as the king of Egypt commanded them, but saved the male children alive" (Ex. 1:17). Not only did the midwives disobey Pharaoh, but when he questioned them about their actions, they lied saying, "Because the Hebrew women are not like the Egyptian women; for they are lively and give birth before the midwives come to them" (Ex. 1:19). In spite of this, Exodus 1:20 states that God "dealt well with the midwives . . . He provided households for them" (v. 21). How could God bless the midwives for disobedience and lying?

SOLUTION: There is little question that the midwives both disobeyed Pharaoh by not murdering the newborn male children, and that they lied to Pharaoh when they said they arrived too late to carry out his orders. Nonetheless, there is moral justification for what they did. First, the moral dilemma in which the midwives found themselves was unavoidable. Either they obeyed God's higher law, or they obeyed the lesser obligation of submitting to Pharaoh. Rather than commit deliberate infanticide against the children of their own people, the midwives chose to disobey Pharaoh's orders. God commands us to obey the governmental powers, but He also commands us not to murder (Ex. 20:13). The saving of innocent lives is a higher obligation than obedience to government. When the government commands us to murder innocent victims, we should not obey. God did not hold the midwives responsible, nor does He hold us responsible, for not following a lower obligation in order to obey a higher law (cf. Acts 4; Rev. 13). In the case of the midwives, the higher law was the preservation of the lives of the newborn male children.

Second, the text clearly states that God blessed them "because the midwives feared God" (Ex. 1:21). And it was their fear of God that led them to do what was necessary to save these innocent lives. Thus, their false statement to Pharaoh was an essential part of their effort to save lives.

Third, their lying is comparable to their having disobeyed Pharaoh in order to save the lives of the innocent newborns. This is a case where the midwives had to choose between lying and being compelled to murder innocent babies. Here again the midwives chose to obey the higher moral law. Obedience to parents is part of the moral law (cf. Eph. 6:1). But if a parent commanded his or her child to kill a neighbor or worship an idol, the child should refuse. Jesus emphasized the need to follow the higher moral law when He said, "He who loves father or mother more than Me is not worthy of Me" (Matt. 10:37).

EXODUS 3:22 – How could an all-loving God command the Hebrews to plunder the Egyptians of their riches?

PROBLEM: Exodus 3:22 states, "So you shall plunder the Egyptians." The Bible presents God as all-loving. However, it does not seem to be a loving thing for God to command the Hebrews to plunder the Egyptians.

SOLUTION: First, it is a misunderstanding of the text to claim that God commanded the Hebrews to plunder the Egyptians. Actually, God commanded the Hebrews to "ask" the Egyptians for various costly items, and God would give them favor in the eyes of the Egyptians. By asking the Egyptians for these items they would not plunder them. Plundering, or spoiling, in this instance would be the taking of the possessions of another people by means of force. But by their asking, and the willful giving by the Egyptians, the effect would be the same *as if* they had plundered them.

Second, the term used in this passage is not the normal word for plunder, but is used to indicate a delivering of something or someone. It is used here in a figurative sense. It is God who had defeated the Egyptians, and now His people would also spoil the defeated foe. However, this defeated foe would willingly deliver up the spoils of victory to the liberated Hebrew people.

Third, even if taken literally, the gifts given to the Israelites could hardly be considered unjust, considering they had been Egyptian slaves for centuries. They were small compensations for centuries of slave labor to Egypt.

EXODUS 4:21 – If God hardened Pharaoh's heart, how can Pharaoh be held responsible?

PROBLEM: The Bible quotes God as saying, "I will harden his [Pharaoh's] heart, so that he will not let the people go." But if God hardened Pharaoh's heart, then Pharaoh cannot be held morally responsible for his actions, since he did not do it of his own free will, but out of constraint (cf. 2 Cor. 9:7; 1 Peter 5:2).

SOLUTION: God did not harden Pharaoh's heart contrary to Pharaoh's own free choice. The Scripture makes it very clear that Pharaoh hardened his own heart. It declares that Pharaoh's heart "grew hard" (Ex. 7:13), that Pharaoh "hardened his heart" (Ex. 8:15), and that "Pharaoh's heart grew hard" the more God worked on it (Ex. 8:19). Again, when God sent the plague of the flies, "Pharaoh hardened his heart at this time also" (Ex. 8:32). This same or like phrase is repeated over and over (cf. Ex. 9:7, 34–35). In fact, with the exception of God's prediction of what would happen (Ex. 4:21), the fact is that Pharaoh hardened his own heart first (Ex. 7:13; 8:15, 8:32, etc.), and then God hardened it later (cf. Ex. 9:12; 10:1, 20, 27).

Furthermore, the sense in which God hardened his heart is similar to the way the sun hardens clay and also melts wax. If Pharaoh had been receptive to God's warnings, his heart would not have been hardened by God. But when God gave Pharaoh a reprieve from the plagues, he took advantage of the situation. "But when Pharaoh saw that there was relief, he hardened his heart and did not heed them [Moses and Aaron], as the Lord had said" (Ex. 8:15).

The question can be summarized as follows: does God harden hearts?

GOD DOES NOT HARDEN HEARTS	GOD DOES HARDEN HEARTS
Initially	Subsequently
Directly	Indirectly
Against free choice	Through free choice
As to their cause	As to their effect

(See also discussion under Rom. 9:17.)

EXODUS 4:24 — Whom did the Lord meet at the encampment, and why did He seek to kill him?

PROBLEM: Exodus 4:24 states, "And it came to pass on the way, at the encampment, that the Lord met him and sought to kill him." The verse does not explicitly say whom the Lord met in the encampment, but the context indicates that it was Moses. If so, why did God seek to kill him, since He had called him to lead Israel out of Egypt?

SOLUTION: First, it is clear that Moses had been selected by the Lord to be His instrument to deliver the people of Israel from Egyptian bondage and from the power of Pharaoh. But, as one of God's covenant people, Moses was obligated to circumcise his sons on the eighth day. For one reason or another, Moses had not performed the rite of circumcision on his son as one of the covenant people of the Lord. It was not possible for the Lord to permit His chosen deliverer to represent Him to the people of Israel when he had not complied with the dictates of the covenant relationship himself. Apparently, God took this drastic measure to prompt Moses to obey Him, knowing that Moses would not willingly go against the wishes of his wife Zipporah. Zipporah performed the circumcision, perhaps because Moses was incapacitated from an affliction which the Lord had brought upon him. As soon as the circumcision was performed, the Lord ceased from seeking to kill Moses.

Second, it is obvious that the Lord could have killed Moses suddenly if that were the intent of this incident. God certainly possessed the power to do this without delay. The incident clearly indicates that God's purpose was to cause Moses to comply with His requirements. God obviously did not want to kill Moses. What He wanted was Moses' obedience and complete commitment to His law, if he was going to be the great lawgiver to his people.

EXODUS 5:2 – Who was the Pharaoh of the Exodus?

PROBLEM: The predominant view of modern scholars is that the Pharaoh of the Exodus was Ramsees II. If this is right, that would mean that the Exodus took place about 1270 to 1260 B.C. However, from several references in the Bible (Jud. 11:26; 1 Kings 6:1; Acts 13:19-20), the Exodus is dated from ca. 1447 B.C. If this is true, then given the commonly accepted dating system, the Pharaoh of the Exodus was Amenhotep II. Who was the Pharaoh of the Exodus, and when did the Exodus take place?

SOLUTION: Although much of modern scholarship has proposed a late date for the Exodus, about 1270-1260 B.C., there is sufficient evidence to say that it is not necessary to accept this date, and alternative explanations provide a better accounting of all the historical data, and place the Exodus at about 1447 B.C.

First, the biblical dates for the Exodus place it in the 1400's B.C., since 1 Kings 6:1 declares that it was 480 years before the fourth year of Solomon's reign (which was about 967 B.C.). This would place the Exodus around 1447 B.C. This fits also with Judges 11:26 which affirms that Israel spent 300 years in the land up to the time of Jepthah (which was about 1000 B.C.). Likewise, Acts 13:20 speaks of there being 450 years of judges from Moses to Samuel who lived around 1000 B.C. The same is true of the 430 years mentioned in Galatians 3:17 (see comments) spanning from around 1800 to 1450 B.C. (from Jacob to Moses). The same figure is used in Exodus 12:40. All of these passages provide a 1400 B.C. date, not 1200 B.C. as the critics claim.

Second, John Bimson and David Livingston have proposed a revision of the traditional dating of the end of the Middle Bronze Age and the beginning of the Late Bronze Age from 1550 to shortly before 1400 B.C.

The Middle Bronze Age was characterized by large fortified cities, a description which fits well with the account which the spies brought back to Moses (Deut. 1:28). This would mean that the conquest of Canaan took place about 1400 B.C. Since the Scriptures state that Israel wandered in the wilderness for 40 years, that would put the Exodus at about 1440 B.C., in complete accord with biblical chronology. If we accept the traditional account of the reigns of the Pharaohs, this would mean that the Pharaoh of the Exodus was Amenhotep II who reigned from about 1450 to 1425 B.C.

Third, another possible solution, known as the Velikovsky-Courville revision, proposes a redating of the traditional chronology of the reigns of the Pharaohs. Velikovsky and Courville assert that there are an extra 600 years in the chronology of the kings of Egypt. Archaeological evidence can be mustered to substantiate this proposal which again places the date of the Exodus in the 1440s B.C. According to this view, the Pharaoh at this time was King Thom. This fits the statement in Exodus 1:11 that the Israelites were enslaved to build the city called Pithom, ("the abode of Thom"). When the biblical chronology is taken as the pattern, all of the historical and archaeological evidence fits together in a unified picture. (See Geisler and Brooks, *When Skeptics Ask,* Victor Books, 1990, chap. 9.)

EXODUS 6:3 – Was God known by His name "Lord" (Jehovah or Yahweh) before Moses' time?

PROBLEM: According to this text God told Moses, "I appeared to Abraham, to Isaac, and to Jacob, as God Almighty, but by My name, LORD [Jehovah, Yahweh], I was not known to them." However, the word "LORD" [Jehovah, Yahweh] occurs in Genesis in many places, both in combination with the term "God," as "LORD God" (Gen. 2:4, 5, 7, 8, 9, 15, etc.) and alone as LORD (Gen. 4:1, 3, 4, 6, 9, etc.).

SOLUTION: This difficulty can be explained in several ways. Some believe it was introduced into Genesis by way of anticipation. Others hold that *the full meaning* of the name was not known previously, even though it was in use. Or, perhaps some special character of the covenant-keeping God as was indicated by the sacred name "LORD" (Jehovah, Yahweh) was not revealed until Moses' time. Still others think Moses (or a later editor) placed the name in the text of Genesis retrospectively, after it had come into use. This would be like a biographer of the famous boxer referring to the childhood of Muhammad Ali, even though his name was really Cassius Clay at the time. In favor of this is the fact that the common suffix "-ah" (which stands for "Jehovah") attached to names (such as, Mic-ah, Jon-ah, Jeremi-ah) is not generally found in names before Moses' time.

EXODUS 6:9 – Did the children of Israel listen to Moses or disregard his words?

PROBLEM: Here the text claims that "they would not heed Moses." But earlier (in Ex. 4:31) it says "the people believed [Moses]," and even "bowed their heads and worshiped [God]."

SOLUTION: Apparently they readily received Moses at first, but when they did not experience immediate deliverance, they became discouraged and impatient and would no longer listen to him.

EXODUS 6:10-13 – Was Moses called by God in Egypt or in Midian?

PROBLEM: In Exodus 3:10, God revealed Himself to Moses and commissioned him to lead Israel out of Egypt (cf. 4:19). However, Exodus 6:10-11 declares that Moses was in the Desert of Midian when God told him to go to Pharaoh and ask for Israel's release.

SOLUTION: Moses was commissioned in Exodus 3–4, but because of Pharaoh's rejection (in chap. 5), combined with Moses' initial reluctance to God (cf. 4:1, 10), it was necessary for God to encourage Moses and reconfirm his call in Exodus 6.

EXODUS 6:16-20 – How could the people of Israel have been in Egypt for 430 years when there were only three generations between Levi and Moses?

PROBLEM: Exodus 6:16-20 indicates that there were only three generations between Levi, the son of Jacob, and Moses. However, Galatians 3:17 indicates that Israel was in Egypt for 430 years. How could there be only three generations between Levi, who went down into Egypt at the beginning of the 430-year period, and Moses, who delivered Israel from Egypt at the end of the 430-year period?

SOLUTION: First, it was a common practice in the Ancient Near East to record genealogies according to tribe, or family clan. In this type of genealogical record, several generations would be omitted from the record due to the fact that some persons were perhaps of lesser significance in the family tree. The Hebrew language did not have a word corresponding to our terms "grandfather" or "great grandfather," or "grandson" or "great grandson." Consequently, when Abraham is referred to as "our father," the only Hebrew term capable of indicating such ancestry was the normal Hebrew term for "father." The same goes for the term "son." For example, Exodus 6:16 states, "The sons of Levi . . . Gershon, Kohath, and Merari." Traditionally these are held to be the original sons of Levi. However, when Exodus 6:18 states, "And the sons of Kohath were Amram, Izhar, Hebron, and Uzziel," Kohath is given as the head of that branch of the tribe of Levi known as the Kohathites. Amram, Izhar, Hebron, and Uzziel were probably not the immediate sons of Kohath, but were descendants of Kohath. The Hebrew language used the term "son" to signify a descendant.

Second, according to Numbers 3:28, the census of the family of the Kohathites numbered 8,600 persons from one month old and above. If there were only three generations between Levi and Moses, this would mean that the "sons of Kohath," Amram, Izhar, Hebron, and Uzziel, would have had over 2,000 children each. Obviously, either the Amram listed in verse 18 as a son of Kohath was not the immediate father of Moses, and not the same Amram listed in verse 20, or there were in fact additional descendants of Kohath which are simply not listed in these verses because that information is not essential to the context. Either way, it is clear that there were more than three generations between Levi and Moses.

EXODUS 6:26-27 — Didn't someone besides Moses write these verses?

PROBLEM: The references to Moses and Aaron in verses 26 and 27 are written in the third person: "These are the same Aaron and Moses" and "These are the ones." How could Moses be the author of this passage and not speak of himself in the first person?

SOLUTION: This passage, which begins in verse 14 of chapter 6, is an objective, historical account of the genealogies of the ancestors of Moses and Aaron. In this type of writing, it is customary for an author, if he makes reference to himself, to do so in the third person. Many ancient writings follow this manner of reporting historical facts, such as the *Gallic Wars* and the *Civil Wars* written by Julius Caesar. In fact, it would have been quite awkward if, in the midst of this objective historical report, Moses had written, "It was Aaron and I to whom the Lord said . . ." or "Aaron and I were the ones who spoke to Pharaoh." For future generations of Hebrew readers, Moses wanted his genealogical record to be quite clearly reported, so that no mistake be made as to the identity and the pedigree of the one whom God had chosen to bring Israel out of the bondage of Egypt.

EXODUS 7:11 – How could the wise men and sorcerers of Pharaoh perform the same feats of power that God told Moses to perform?

PROBLEM: Several passages in Exodus (7:11, 22; 8:7) state that the wise men, sorcerers, and magicians of Pharaoh did the same works with their enchantments which God commanded Moses and Aaron to perform. However, Moses and Aaron claimed to have been sent from the Lord God. How could these men perform the same feats of power as Moses and Aaron did by the power of God?

SOLUTION: The Bible indicates that one of Satan's tactics in his effort to deceive humankind is to employ counterfeit miracles (see Rev. 16:14). Exodus 7:11 states, "But Pharaoh also called the wise men and the sorcerers; so the magicians of Egypt, they also did in like manner with their enchantments." Each of the other verses makes a similar claim. The passage states that the feats of Pharaoh's magicians were performed "by their [magical] enchantments."

Some commentators assert that the feats of the magicians were merely tricks. Perhaps the magicians had enchanted snakes so that they became stiff and appeared to be rods. When cast down upon the floor, they came out of their trance and began to move as snakes. Some say these were acts of Satan, who actually turned the rods of the magicians into snakes. This, however, is not plausible in view of the fact that only God can create life, as even the magicians later recognized (Ex. 8:18-19). Whatever explanation one might take regarding these feats, one common point holds for every account and is found in the text itself. It is clear that by whatever power they performed these feats, they were not accomplished by the power of God. Rather, they were performed "by their enchantments." The purpose of these acts was to convince Pharaoh that his magicians possessed as much power as Moses and Aaron, and it was not necessary for Pharaoh to yield to their request to let Israel go. It worked, at least for the first three encounters (Aaron's rod, the plague of blood, and the plague of frogs). However, when Moses and Aaron, by the power of God, brought forth lice from the sand, the magicians were not able to counterfeit this miracle. They could only exclaim, "This is the finger of God" (Ex. 8:19).

There are several points by which one can discern the difference between a satanic sign and a divine miracle.

DIVINE MIRACLE	SATANIC SIGN
Supernatural	Supernormal
Connected with truth	Connected with error
Associated with good	Associated with evil
Never associated with the Occult	Often associated with the Occult
Always successful	Not always successful

These differences can be seen in these passages in Exodus. Although the magicians appeared to turn their rods into snakes, their rods were swallowed up by Aaron's rod, indicating superiority. Although the magicians could turn water to blood, they could not reverse the process. Although the magicians could bring forth frogs, they could not get rid of them. Their acts were supernormal, but not supernatural.

Although the magicians could copy some of the miracles of Moses and Aaron, their message was connected with error. Basically they copied the miracles of God's chosen men in order to convince Pharaoh that the God of the Hebrews was no more powerful than the gods of Egypt. Although Pharaoh's magicians were able to copy the first three miracles performed by God through Moses and Aaron, there came a point at which their enchantments were no longer able to counterfeit the power of God.

EXODUS 7:19 — How could Israel escape this judgment if it came upon all the land of Egypt?

PROBLEM: Several times in the account of the plagues the Scripture states that the judgments would be upon "all the land of Egypt" (7:19; 8:16, 24; ["throughout," 9:22]). However, other passages assert that God protected Israel from the effects of the different plagues (8:22). Isn't it a contradiction for some passages to say that the plagues would affect all the land of Egypt while others indicate that Israel was not affected by these plagues?

SOLUTION: In the Hebrew language the normal word for *all* is not necessarily absolute. The context must dictate whether the term is to be taken as absolute or not. God told Moses to make sure that Pharaoh knew that Israel was not being affected by the plagues which were being brought upon Egypt. "Then say to him . . . 'And in that day I will set apart the land of Goshen, in which My people dwell, that no swarms of flies shall be there, in order that you may know that I am the Lord in the midst of the land' " (Ex. 8:20, 22).

Verse 24 states, "Thick swarms of flies came into the house of Pharaoh, into his servants' houses, and into *all the land of Egypt*." However, according to the message of God given to Pharaoh, this did not affect the land of Goshen and the Israelites. We find this again in 9:6 which states, "So the Lord did this thing on the next day, and all the livestock of Egypt died; but of the livestock of the children of Israel, not one died." In the context of the judgments of God upon Egypt, there is a clear distinction placed between the people of Pharaoh and the people of the Lord. There is no contradiction between these references, for the judgments of God fell upon all the land of the Egyptians and all the people of Pharaoh, but God set apart and protected His people from these terrible events.

EXODUS 7:20 – How could Moses have turned all the water to blood if the magicians had some left to do the same thing?

PROBLEM: Exodus 7:20 asserts that "all the waters that were in the river were turned to blood" by Moses. But only two verses later it says the magicians of Egypt performed the same feat (v. 22), which would have been impossible if Moses had really turned *all* the water to blood.

SOLUTION: First, it should be noted that "all" need not be taken in an absolute sense, but in the popular sense of "the vast majority." Further, it does not say that Moses turned all water to blood, but only all the water "in the river" (Ex. 7:20). There was still water from wells that were unaffected. Then too, some of the water may have been filtered out through the sand on the river bank. This may explain why it says the Egyptians "dug all around the river for water to drink" (v. 24), since it would act as a natural filter for the river water.

EXODUS 9:19-21 – If all the cattle died, then how did some survive?

PROBLEM: Exodus 9:6 asserts that "all the livestock of Egypt died" in the fifth plague. Yet only a few verses later it instructs them to "gather your livestock and all that you have in the field" into their houses (v. 19). But if all livestock died, then how could there be any left?

SOLUTION: First of all, the term "all" is often used in a general sense to mean "the vast majority." Further, the plague was apparently limited to the cattle "in the field" (v. 3). The animals in stalls would not have been affected. Finally, the word "cattle" does not generally denote horses, donkeys, and camels which could have been part of the "livestock" that were spared.

In view of these factors, there is no contradiction between the passages. Nor would any reasonable person assume one by the same author within the same chapter who gave such a vivid, firsthand account of the events.

EXODUS 11:3 — How could Moses have written these words of self-praise?

(See comments on Num. 12:3.)

EXODUS 12:29 — How could an all-loving God slay the firstborn of all the Egyptians?

PROBLEM: Exodus 12:29-30 describes that terrible night when God struck in the land of Egypt, "from the first born of Pharaoh who sat on his throne to the firstborn of the captive who was in the dungeon, and all the firstborn of livestock." This miraculous judgment was brought upon Egypt because Pharaoh had refused to let Israel go. However, the people of Egypt did not have control over Pharaoh's actions. How could an all-loving God strike the firstborn of those Egyptians who were not responsible for the decisions of Pharaoh?

SOLUTION: First, it is wrong to assume that because the Egyptian people may not have had control over Pharaoh's decisions that they were completely innocent. Every individual Egyptian certainly had the opportunity, throughout the long ordeal of God's judgment upon Egypt, to flee to Moses and the Hebrews for protection from those judgments. In fact, Exodus 12:38 states that "A mixed multitude went up with them [the children of Israel] also." No doubt there were many Egyptians who joined the Hebrews as a result of the judgments of God. The fact that most were not willing to turn to the living God even in the face of the nine previous plagues indicates that they were not innocent bystanders.

Second, is it also wrong to assume that simply because the Egyptian people *did not* change Pharaoh's mind that they *could not* have changed his mind. Although the power of the people is severely limited under a dictatorship as that of Egypt, it is conceivable that the people could have revolted so as to either force Pharaoh to change his mind, or to overthrow him. In fact, Exodus 12:33 states, "And the Egyptians urged the people, that they might send them out of the land in haste." Up until this point the Egyptian people had apparently not made any effort to urge the Hebrews to leave the land. The Egyptians were obviously content to leave such matters in the hands of their king. By doing so, they were not innocent of the decisions which were made by their king. The judgment of God was not directed only at Pharaoh or the heads of state of the land, but on Egypt as a whole, since they were equally responsible for the oppression and bondage of the people of God.

EXODUS 14:21-29 – How could 2 million people cross the Red Sea in such a short time?

PROBLEM: According to the account of the crossing of the Red Sea, the massive group of fleeing Israelites must have had no more than 24 hours to cross through the portion of the Red Sea which God had prepared. However, according to the numbers given, there were some 2 million of them (see Num. 1:45-46). But, for a multitude of this size, a 24-hour period is just not enough time to make such a crossing.

SOLUTION: First, although the passage may give the idea that the time that the nation of Israel had to make the crossing was short, this is not a necessary conclusion. The text states that God brought forth an East wind which drove back the waters "all that night" (Ex. 14:21). Verse 22 seems to indicate that it was the very next morning when the multitude of Israelites began their journey across the sea bed. Verse 24 then states, "Now it came to pass, in the morning watch, that the Lord looked down upon the army of the Egyptians." Finally, according to verse 26, God told Moses to "stretch out your hand over the sea, that the waters may come back upon the Egyptians." There is no time reference to this command, however, and it is not necessary to conclude that Israel had completed their crossing that very morning.

Second, even if we assume that the crossing took place in 24 hours, this is not as impossible as it may seem. The passage never states that the people crossed in single file, or that they crossed over on a section of ground the width of a modern superhighway. In fact, it is much more likely that God had prepared a section several miles wide. This would certainly fit the situation, since the camp of Israel on the bank of the Red Sea probably stretched out for three or four miles along the shoreline. When the time came for the people to cross on dry ground, they probably moved as one magnificent throng, moving as a great army advancing upon the enemy lines.

In Exodus 13:18, the sea is called the Red Sea. The Hebrew is *yam suph,* which should be translated, "Sea of Reeds." This was probably a reference to a body of water farther north than what is identified today as the Gulf of Suez. This seems to be the case for several reasons. First, the Gulf of Suez was not known for having reeds. Second, the Gulf of Suez is much farther south than Pi-hahiroth and Migdol where Israel camped by the sea according to 14:2. Third, for Israel to reach the northern most tip of the Gulf of Suez, they would have had to cross a large expanse of desert, and this type of trip is not indicated in the text.

The Sea of Reeds was not simply a shallow marshy stretch of land. This is evident for at least two reasons. First, 14:22 states that when the sea was parted, "the waters were like a wall to them on their right hand and on their left" (NASB). Such would obviously not be the case if the sea were only a marsh. Second, after the Egyptians had entered the sea in pursuit of Israel, God instructed Moses to stretch out his hand over the sea, and the sea "returned to its normal state . . . and covered the chariots and the horsemen, even Pharaoh's entire army that had gone into the sea after them" (14:27-28, NASB). This would not have been an accurate description if the "Sea of Reeds" had been merely a shallow marshy stretch. It is possible that the sea was what is known as Lake Ballah. This lake, though it has disappeared as a result of the construction of the Suez Canal, was probably no more than 10 to 15 miles wide. Obviously there would be very little problem of even such a great multitude to cross this distance in one day.

Even if we suppose that Israel did cross at the widest point of the Gulf of Suez, this does not present a problem either. If we assume that the current size of the Gulf is comparable to its size in ancient times, the average width of the Gulf was probably no more than 40 miles. The average person would have had to walk at a speed of less than two miles per hour to make a 40-mile crossing in 24 hours.

EXODUS 20:4 — Why did God command His people not to make carved images when He directed them to carve two cherubs for the Ark of the Covenant?

(See comments on Ex. 25:18.)

EXODUS 20:5a — Does God get jealous?

PROBLEM: The Bible not only says here that God is a "jealous God," but it also declares His very "name is Jealous" (Ex. 34:14). On the other hand, jealousy is a sin. But, if God is absolutely holy, then how can He be jealous?

SOLUTION: God is jealous in the good sense of the word, namely, He is jealous for the love and devotion of His people (cf. Ex. 20:5). Paul spoke of a "godly jealousy" (2 Cor. 11:2). The verses on God's jealousy are all in the context of idolatry. Like any true lover, God is jealous when anyone or anything else steals the devotion of His beloved.

Human jealousy is often coveting what does not belong to us. However, God's jealousy is protecting what does belong to Him, namely His own supremacy. It is not a sin for God to claim allegiance of His creatures because He is the Creator. And He knows that it is best for them not to make an ultimate commitment to what is less than ultimate (idols). Only an ultimate commitment to what is really Ultimate will ultimately satisfy the human heart. God is jealous to protect this.

EXODUS 20:5b — Does God ever punish one person for another's sins?

(See comments on Ezek. 18:20.)

EXODUS 20:8-11 — Why do Christians worship on Sunday when the commandment sets apart Saturday as the day of worship?

PROBLEM: This commandment states that the seventh day of the week, Saturday, is the day which the Lord selected as the day of rest and worship. However, in the NT the Christian church began to worship and rest on the first day of the week, Sunday. Aren't Christians violating the Sabbath commandment by worshiping on the first day of the week rather than the seventh day?

SOLUTION: First, the basis for the command to observe the Sabbath, as stated in Exodus 20:11, is that God rested on the seventh day after six days of work, and that God blessed the seventh day and sanctified it. The Sabbath day was instituted as a day of rest and worship. The people of God were to follow God's example in His pattern of work and rest. However, as Jesus said in correcting the distorted view of the Pharisees, "The Sabbath was made for man, and not man for the Sabbath" (Mark 2:27). The point which Jesus made is that the Sabbath was not instituted to enslave people, but to benefit them. The spirit of Sabbath observance is continued in the NT observance of rest and worship on the first day of the week.

Second, it must be remembered that, according to Colossians 2:17, the Sabbath was "a shadow of things to come, but the substance is of

Christ." The Sabbath observance was associated with redemption in Deuteronomy 5:15 where Moses stated, "Remember that you were a slave in the land of Egypt, and that the Lord your God brought you out from there by a mighty hand and by an outstretched arm; therefore the Lord your God commanded you to keep the Sabbath day." The Sabbath was a shadow of the redemption which would be provided in Christ. It symbolized the rest from our works and an entrance into the rest of God provided by His finished work.

Finally, although the moral principles expressed in the commandments are reaffirmed in the NT, the command to set Saturday apart as a day of rest and worship is the only commandment not repeated. There are very good reasons for this. New Testament believers are not under the OT Law (Rom. 6:14; Gal. 3:24-25). By His resurrection on the first day of the week (Matt. 28:1), His continued appearances on succeeding Sundays (John 20:26), and the descent of the Holy Spirit on Sunday (Acts 2:1), the early church was given the pattern of Sunday worship. This they did regularly (Acts 20:7; 1 Cor. 16:2). Sunday worship was further hallowed by our Lord who appeared to John in that last great vision on "the Lord's Day" (Rev. 1:10). It is for these reasons that Christians worship on Sunday, rather than on the Jewish Sabbath.

EXODUS 20:13 – How could God command people not to kill, and then, in Exodus 21:12, command that murderers be put to death?

PROBLEM: In the Ten Commandments, God prohibits killing when He says, "Thou shalt not kill" (KJV). However, in Exodus 21:12 God commands that the man who strikes another man so that he dies should be put to death. Isn't it a contradiction for God to command that we not kill and then command that we do kill?

SOLUTION: A great amount of confusion has arisen because of the misleading translation of the sixth commandment. The Hebrew word used in the prohibition of this commandment is not the normal word for killing (*harag*). Rather it is the specific term for murder (*ratsach*). A more proper translation of the command is provided by the NKJV and NIV: "You shall not murder." Exodus 21:12 is not a command to murder, but a command to carry out capital punishment for capital crime. There is no contradiction between the command for men not to commit murder, and the command that the proper authorities should execute capital punishment for capital crimes.

EXODUS 20:24 – Was the altar made of earth or of wood?

PROBLEM: Here the altar is constructed of earth, but in Exodus 27:1 it was constructed of "acacia wood."

SOLUTION: The altar itself was only a hollow case made of acacia wood and covered with bronze (Ex. 27:2). But when it was used it was filled with earth or stones so as to form a bed for the coals.

EXODUS 21:22-23 – Does this passage show that unborn children are of less value than adults?

PROBLEM: According to some translations of the Bible, this text teaches that when fighting men cause a woman to have a "miscarriage" they "shall be fined" (v. 22, RSV). But, if the fighting men caused the death of the woman, the penalty was capital punishment (v. 23). Doesn't this prove that the unborn was not considered a human being, as the mother was?

SOLUTION: First of all, this is a mistranslation of the verse. The great Hebrew scholar, Umberto Cassuto, translated the verse correctly as follows:

> When men strive together and they hurt unintentionally a woman with child, and her children come forth but no mischief happens – that is, the woman and the children do not die – the one who hurts her shall surely be punished by a fine. But if any mischief happens, that is, if the woman dies or the children, then you shall give life for life. (*Commentary on the Book of Exodus,* Magnes Press, 1967)

This makes the meaning very clear. It is a strong passage against abortion, affirming that the unborn are of equal value to adult human beings.

Second, the Hebrew word (*yatsa*), mistranslated "miscarriage," actually means to "come forth" or to "give birth" (as NKJV, NIV). It is the Hebrew word regularly used for live birth in the OT. In fact, it is never used for a miscarriage, though it is used of a still birth. But, in this passage, as in virtually all OT texts, it refers to a live, though premature, birth.

Third, there is another Hebrew word for miscarriage (*shakol*), and it is not used here. Since this word for miscarriage was available and was not used, but the word for live birth was used, there is no reason to suppose it means anything else than a live birth of a fully human being.

Fourth, the word used for the mother's offspring here is *yeled* which means "child." It is the same word used of babies and young children in the Bible (Gen. 21:8; Ex. 2:3). Hence, the unborn is considered just as much a human as a young child is.

Fifth, if any harm happened to either the mother or the child, the same punishment was given, "life for life" (v. 23). This demonstrates that the unborn was considered of equal value with the mother.

Sixth, other OT passages teach the full humanity of an unborn child (see comments on Ps. 51:5 and 139:13ff). The NT affirms the same view (cf. Matt. 1:20; Luke 1:41, 44).

EXODUS 21:29-30 — Why was capital punishment commuted in the case of some murders?

PROBLEM: Numbers 35:31 commands that "you shall take no ransom for the life of a murderer who is guilty of death, but he shall surely be put to death." However, Exodus 21 says if the guilty one has "imposed on him a sum of money, then he shall pay to redeem his life, whatever is imposed on him" (v. 30). But these are contrary instructions about punishing murderers.

SOLUTION: The reason for the difference is clearly stated in the text — one was *willful* murder, and the other was just *negligent* homicide. In the first case there was *malice,* but in the second case there was *no evil intent.* In fact, in the latter instance the guilty had not actually taken the other person's life. Rather, he had simply been negligent about confining an ox that was known to gore people (Ex. 21:28-29). In such a case a fine could be levied rather than capital punishment.

EXODUS 23:19 — Why is boiling a kid in its mother's milk prohibited?

PROBLEM: This verse commands: "You shall not boil a young goat in its mother's milk." What does this mean and why were the Israelites commanded not to do this?

SOLUTION: There are two distinct questions here, and they should be separated. First of all, *what* does this passage mean? Second, *why* was God opposed to their doing this? The answer to the first question is easy. Every word in the sentence is clear. The Israelites knew exactly what to do. They were not supposed to cook a baby goat in its mother's milk. So there was absolutely no problem in their knowing *what* God did not want them to do.

The real problem is *why* did God forbid this? There are many possible reasons given by commentators:

1. Because it was an idolatrous practice.

2. Because it was a magical (occult) practice to try to make the land more productive.

3. Because it was cruel to destroy a baby goat in the very milk which sustained it.

4. Because milk and meat are difficult to digest.

5. Because it shows contempt for the parent-child relationship.

6. Because it would symbolically profane the Feast of Ingathering.

7. Because God wanted them to cook with olive oil, not butter.

8. Because it was too luxurious or Epicurean.

The truth is that we do not know for sure *why* God commanded this. But it does not really matter, since the Israelites knew exactly *what* they were not to do, even if they did not fully understand *why*. So while there is a problem in understanding the *purpose* of this passage, there is no problem in understanding its *meaning*. It means exactly what it says.

EXODUS 24:4 – How could Moses have written this when modern scholars say several different authors (JEPD) are responsible for it?

PROBLEM: Modern critical scholars following Julius Wellhausen (19th century) claim that the first five books of the OT were written by various persons known as J (Jehovist), E (Elohimist), P (priestly), and D (deuteronomist), depending on which sections reflect the literary characteristics of these supposed authors. However, this verse declares that "Moses wrote all the words of the Lord." Indeed, many other verses in the Bible attribute this book to Moses (see points 6–9 below).

SOLUTION: Here is another example where negative criticism of the Bible is wrong. There is very strong evidence that Moses wrote Exodus. First of all, no other person from that period had the time, interest, and ability to compose such a record.

Second, Moses was an eyewitness of the events and as such was qualified to be its author. Indeed, the record is a vivid eyewitness account of spectacular events, such as the crossing of the Red Sea and receiving the Ten Commandments.

Third, the earliest Jewish teaching ascribes this book to Moses. This is true of the Jewish Talmud, as well as Jewish writers like Philo and Josephus.

Fourth, the author reflects a detailed knowledge of the geography of the wilderness (cf. Ex. 14). This is highly unlikely for anyone, unlike Moses, who did not have many years of experience living in this area. The same is true of the author's knowledge of the customs and practices of the people described in Exodus.

Fifth, the book explicitly claims that "Moses wrote all the words" (Ex. 24:4). If he did not, then it is a forgery which cannot be trusted, nor could it be the Word of God.

Sixth, Moses' successor Joshua claimed that Moses wrote the Law. In fact, when Joshua assumed leadership after Moses, he exhorted the people of Israel that "This Book of the Law" should not depart out of their mouths (Josh. 1:8) and that they should "observe to do according to all the law which Moses . . . commanded" (Josh. 1:7).

Seventh, a long chain of OT figures after Moses attributed this book to him, including Joshua (1:7-8), Josiah (2 Chron. 34:14), Ezra (6:18), Daniel (9:11), and Malachi (4:4).

Eighth, Jesus quoted from Exodus 20:12, using the introduction "for Moses said" (Mark 7:10; cf. Luke 20:37). So either Christ is right or the critics are. Since there is strong evidence that He is the Son of God, the choice is clear (see Geisler and Brooks, *When Skeptics Ask,* Victor Books, 1990, chap. 6).

Ninth, the Apostle Paul declared "Moses writes about the righteousness which is of the law" (Rom. 10:5, citing Ezek. 20:11). So we have it on apostolic authority, as well as on the authority of Christ, that Moses wrote Exodus.

EXODUS 24:9-11 — How could these people see God when God said in Exodus 33:20, "no man shall see me and live"?

PROBLEM: Exodus 24:9-11 records that Moses, Aaron, Nadab, Abihu, and seventy of the elders of Israel ascended the mountain of God and "saw the God of Israel." However, Exodus 19:12-13 says that the people could not even touch the base of the mountain without being put to death. And in Exodus 33:20 God says that no one can see Him and live. How could these people go up the mountain and see God and yet live?

SOLUTION: First, it should be noted that God invited them to see Him. In Exodus 19:12-13 God told Moses to set the boundaries around the mountain so that no one should even touch its base without the punishment of death. However, God specifically invited these people to ascend the mountain in order to consecrate them for the service to which they had been appointed, and to seal the covenant which had been established between God and the nation of Israel.

Second, it is clear from the description and from other passages of Scripture (Ex. 33:19-20; Num. 12:8; John 1:18), that what these people saw was not the *essence* of God, but rather a visual *representation* of the glory of God. Even when Moses asked to see God's glory (Ex. 33:18-23), it was only a likeness of God which Moses saw (cf. Num. 12:8 where the Hebrew word *temunah* — "form," "likeness" — is used), and not the very essence of God.

EXODUS 24:10 — Can God be seen?

PROBLEM: According to this verse, Moses and the elders "saw the God of Israel." Yet God told Moses that he could not see God's face (Ex. 33:20), and John states flatly that "No one has seen God at any time" (John 1:18).

SOLUTION: God cannot be known directly in this life, nor can He be known completely. For "now we see in a mirror, dimly, but then face to face. Now I know in part, but then I shall know just as I also am known" (1 Cor. 13:12). God can be known "by the things that are made" (Rom. 1:20), but He cannot be known in Himself. The following contrast summarizes the ways God can and cannot be known:

HOW GOD CANNOT BE KNOWN	HOW GOD CAN BE KNOWN
Completely	Partially
Directly	Indirectly
In Himself	In His creation
(His essence)	(His effects)
As Spirit	As incarnate in Christ

While "no one has seen God [in His essence]" (John 1:18), nonetheless, His only begotten Son has revealed Him. Thus, Jesus could say, "He who has seen Me has seen the Father" (John 14:9).

EXODUS 25:18ff — If it is wrong to make graven images, why did God command Moses to make one?

PROBLEM: God clearly commanded in Exodus 20:4: "You shall not make for yourself any carved image, or any likeness of anything that is in heaven above, or that is in the earth beneath." Yet here Moses is instructed by God to "make two cherubim of gold; of hammered work" (v. 18). If making images of any heavenly object is wrong, then why did God command Moses to make some on the ark of the covenant?

SOLUTION: The prohibition against making graven images was distinctly set in the context of worshiping idols. There are, then, several reasons why making the cherubim does not conflict with this command not to bow down to graven images. First, there was no chance that the people of Israel would fall down before the cherubim in the most holy place, since they were *forbidden* to go in the holy place at any time. Even the high priest went only once a year on the Day of Atonement (Lev. 16).

Further, the prohibition is not against making any carved image for decorative purposes, but of those used in *religious worship*. In other words, they were not to worship any other God or any image of any god. These cherubim were not given to Israel as images of God; they were angels. Nor were they given to be worshiped. Hence, there is no way in which the command to make them violated the commandment in Exodus 20.

Finally, the prohibition in Exodus 20 is not against religious art as such, which includes things in heaven (angels) and on earth (humans or animals). Rather, it was *against* using any image as an idol. That idolatry envisioned is evident from the fact they were instructed not to "bow down to them nor serve them" (Ex. 20:5). The distinction between non-religious use of images and a religious use is important:

THE USE OF IMAGES OR REPRESENTATIONS OF GOD

FORBIDDEN	PERMITTED
• Object of worship	• Not an object of worship
• Appointed by man	• Appointed by God
• Religious purposes	• Educational purposes
• To represent essence of God	• To affirm truth about truth
• Used without qualifications	• Used with qualifications

Even language about God in the Bible contains images. God is both a shepherd and a father. But each of these is appropriately qualified. God is not just any father. He is our *Heavenly* Father. Likewise, Jesus is not just any shepherd, but the *Good* Shepherd who gave His life for His sheep (John 10:11). No finite image can be appropriately applied to the infinite God without qualification. To do so is idolatry. And idols are idols whether they are mental or metal.

EXODUS 31:17 — Can God get tired?

(See comments on Gen. 2:1.)

EXODUS 31:18 — Does God have fingers?

PROBLEM: This verse says that the Ten Commandments were "written with the finger of God." But, elsewhere the Bible insists that "God is spirit" (John 4:24) and that spirits do not have "flesh and bones" (Luke 24:39). How, then, can God have fingers?

SOLUTION: God does not literally have fingers. The phrase "finger of God" is a figure of speech indicating God's direct involvement in producing the Ten Commandments. It is called an anthropomorphism (speaking of God in human terms).

The Bible uses many figures of speech when referring to God, including "arm" (Deut. 7:19), "wings" (Ps. 91:4), and "eyes" (Heb. 4:13). None of these should be taken literally, though all of them depict something that is literally true of God. For example, although God does not have literal arms, nonetheless, it is literally true that God can and does extend His strength to do great things that, were humans to do, it would require strong arms.

EXODUS 32:14 — Does God change His mind?

PROBLEM: While Moses was upon the mountain receiving the Law from God, the people were at the foot of the mountain worshiping the golden calf which they had constructed (32:4-6). When God instructed Moses to go down to them, He told Moses that He would "consume them" and make a great nation from Moses (32:10). When Moses heard this, he pleaded with God to turn from His anger. Verse 14 states, "So the Lord relented from the harm which He said He would do to His people." This implies that God changed His mind. However, in 1 Samuel 15:29 God says that "He is not a man, that He should relent," and in Malachi 3:6 God says, "For I am the Lord, I do not change." Also, in Hebrews, God demonstrated the "immutability of His counsel" (Heb. 6:17) by swearing an oath. Does God change His mind or doesn't He?

SOLUTION: It must be emphatically maintained that God does not change (cf. Mal. 3:6; James 1:17). He neither changes His mind, His will, nor His nature. There are several arguments that demonstrate the immutability of God. We will consider three.

First, anything that changes does so in some chronological order. There must be a point before the change and a point after the change. Anything that experiences a before and an after exists in time, because the essence of time is seen in the chronological progress from before to after. However, God is eternal and outside time (John 17:5; 2 Tim. 1:9). Therefore, there cannot be in God a series of before's and after's. But, if God cannot be in a series of before's and after's, then God cannot change, because change necessarily involves before and after.

Second, anything that changes must change for better or for worse, for a change that makes no difference is not a change. Either something that is needed is gained that was previously absent, which is a change for the better, or something that is needed is lost that was previously possessed, which is a change for the worse. But, if God is perfect He does not need anything, therefore He cannot change for the better, and if God were to lose something He would not be perfect, therefore He cannot change for the worse. Therefore, God cannot change.

Third, if anyone were to change his mind, it must be because new information has come to light that was not previously known, or the circumstances have changed that require a different kind of attitude or action. Now, if God changed His mind, it cannot be because He has learned some bit of information that He did not previously know, for God is omniscient — He knows all (Ps. 147:5). Therefore, it must be because the circumstances have changed that require a different attitude or action. But, if the circumstances have changed, it is not necessarily the case that God has changed His mind. It may simply be the case that, since the circumstances have changed, God's relationship to the new circumstances are different because *they* have changed, not God.

When Israel was at the foot of the mountain engaged in idol worship, God told Moses that His anger was burning against them and He was prepared to destroy them in judgment. However, when Moses interceded for them, the circumstances were changed. God's attitude toward sin is always anger, and His attitude toward those who call to Him is always an attitude of mercy. Before Moses prayed for Israel, they were under God's judgment. By Moses' intercession for the people of Israel, he brought them under God's mercy. God did not change. Rather, the circumstances changed. The language used in this passage is called anthropomorphic, or man-centered, language. It is similar to someone moving from one place to another and saying, "Now the house is on my right," "Now the house is on my left." Neither of these statements is meant to imply that the house has moved. Rather, it is language from a human perspective to describe that I have changed my position in relation to the house. When Moses said that God relented, it was a figurative way of describing that Moses' intercession successfully changed the relationship of the people to God. He brought the nation under the mercy of God's grace, and out from under the judgment of God. God does not change, neither His mind, His will, nor His nature.

EXODUS 33:3 – Did God change His mind about going with the Israelites into the Land of Promise?

PROBLEM: Here God declares "I will not go up in your midst." Yet later God did go with them in a mighty and victorious way, leading them to victory under Joshua (see Josh. 1–11).

SOLUTION: These passages speak of different times. The first addresses the first generation of rebellious Israelites, and the second speaks about the second generation who believed God and followed Joshua into the land. Not all of God's threats (or promises) are unconditional. This one was conditional. God would go with them if and when they trusted Him (which the second generation did), but He would not go with them if and when they did not (which the first generation did). God's irreversible purpose to bring them into the land allowed for some temporarily reversible conditions in attaining this end.

EXODUS 34:20 – Were unclean animals to be redeemed with money or killed?

PROBLEM: Numbers 18:15-16 instructs that unclean beasts should be redeemed with money. But Exodus had commanded that they be killed. How can this discrepancy be reconciled?

SOLUTION: God apparently instructed Moses to modify the earlier law in favor of revenues for the sanctuary. Money would be more useable than so many animals. Thus, the essence of the first law was being implemented in another way, due to the circumstances. Actually, their obedience to the first law may have occasioned the need for the second. There may have simply been too many animals given to the service of the tabernacle, when other things that money could buy were in greater demand.

LEVITICUS

LEVITICUS 3:2 – Was the blood poured on the altar or sprinkled on it?

PROBLEM: In Leviticus 3:2, the priest was commanded to "sprinkle the blood all around on the altar." But, in Deuteronomy 12:27, the blood was to be "poured" on the altar.

SOLUTION: The great Jewish scholar Maimonides said that part of the blood was sprinkled on the altar and the rest was poured at the bottom of it. Others believe that the word "pour" could mean sprinkle. Just as today when rain is coming down strongly in sprinkles, we say it is pouring. In any event, there is no contradiction between the two passages.

LEVITICUS 5:18 – Was the sacrifice to be brought to the priest or to the Lord?

PROBLEM: Leviticus 5:15 instructs that one "bring to the Lord an offering." But a few verses later it says to "bring it to the priest" (v. 18).

SOLUTION: It was brought to the priest to be offered to the Lord. In Israel, the priests were the representatives of the people to God, as prophets were God's representatives to the people.

LEVITICUS 11:5-6 – How can the Bible say that the hyrax and the rabbit chew the cud when science now knows that they do not?

PROBLEM: In Leviticus 11:5-6, two animals, the rock hyrax and the rabbit, were designated as unclean by Leviticus because, although they chew the cud, they do not divide the hoof. But, science has discovered that these two animals do not chew the cud. Isn't it an error when the Bible says they chew the cud when in fact they do not?

SOLUTION: Although they did not chew the cud in the modern technical sense, they did engage in a chewing action that looked the same to an observer. Thus, they are listed with other animals that chew the cud so that the common person could make the distinction from his or her everyday observations.

Animals which chew the cud are identified as ruminants; they regurgitate food into their mouths to be chewed again. Ruminants normally have four stomachs. Neither the rock hyrax (translated "rock badger" in the NASB) nor the rabbit are ruminants and technically do not chew the cud. However, both animals move their jaws in such a manner as to appear to be chewing the cud. This action was so convincing that the great Swedish scientist Linnaeus originally classified them as ruminants.

It is now known that rabbits practice what is called "reflection," in which indigestible vegetable matter absorbs certain bacteria and is passed as droppings and then eaten again. This process enables the rabbit to better digest it. This process is very similar to rumination, and it gives the impression of chewing the cud. So, the Hebrew phrase "chewing the cud" should not be taken in the modern technical sense, but in the ancient sense of a chewing motion that includes both rumination and reflection in the modern sense.

The list of clean and unclean animals was intended as a practical guide for the Israelite in selecting food. The average Israelite would not have been aware of the technical aspects of cud chewing, and may have otherwise considered the hyrax and rabbit as clean animals because of the appearance of cud chewing. Consequently, it was necessary to point out that, although it may appear that these were clean animals because of their chewing movement, they were not clean because they did not divide the hoof. We often follow a similar practice when talking to those who are not familiar with more technical aspects of some point. For example, we use observational language to talk about the sun rising and setting when we talk to little children. To a small child the daily cycle of the sun has the appearance of rising and setting (see comments on Josh. 10:12-14). The description is not technically correct, but it is functionally useful for the level of understanding of the child. This is analogous to the use here in Leviticus. Technically, although the hyrax and the rabbit do not chew the cud, this description was functional at the time in order to make the point that these animals were considered unclean.

LEVITICUS 12:5, 7 — If motherhood was so blessed by God, why did mothers have to bring a sacrifice to God to expiate for having children?

PROBLEM: The Bible exalts the position of motherhood saying, "Your wife shall be like a fruitful vine . . . your children like olive plants" (Ps.

128:3). Nevertheless, mothers were commanded to bring a sacrifice to the altar for "purification" and "atonement" after the birth of a child (Lev. 12:5-7).

SOLUTION: Some take this sacrifice as merely symbolic, but even then it must symbolize something that is literally true. It seems best to make a distinction between the office of motherhood as such and motherhood in a fallen world. God did create a wife for Adam and command them to have children (Gen. 1:27-28). In this original and pristine sense, motherhood is pure and unstained.

Unfortunately, since the Fall of Eve (with Adam) motherhood is not without the taint of sin. David confessed, "in sin my mother conceived me" (Ps. 51:5). Since motherhood, like everything else in this fallen world, is subject to sin, it too needed purification. After all, "the plowing of the wicked are sin" (Prov. 21:4) in a fallen world. As a result of the Fall, every woman bears children in pain (Gen. 3:16). It is appropriate, then, that mothers be reminded of God's gracious provision for them and through them by the offering of a sacrifice on the birth of a child.

LEVITICUS 13:47-59 — How can the Bible say that leprosy infected clothing?

PROBLEM: Leviticus 13 gives the laws concerning leprosy. In verses 47-59 there are laws concerning leprosy in garments. However, leprosy is an infectious disease caused by a bacterium and does not affect inanimate objects like garments. Was not the Bible wrong to talk about leprous garments?

SOLUTION: It is simply a matter of the confusing of names. The disease which has been identified in modern times as leprosy, commonly known as Hansen's Disease, is not the same type of infection that is described in the OT and is translated by the English word "leprosy." The disease which is identified today as leprosy is caused by a bacterium and does not produce the kinds of symptoms which are described in various OT passages. The Hebrew term *tsaraath,* translated "leprosy," is a more general term for any serious skin disease or sign of infection or defilement on the surface of inanimate objects. The defilement on garments, or walls as in Leviticus 14:33-57, was probably some type of fungus or mold which attacks these types of material. Garments found to be infected were burned (Lev. 13:52). Infected houses were cleansed. If the infection could not be eradicated, the houses were demolished and the ruins were taken outside the city (Lev. 14:45).

LEVITICUS 16:6-22 – Why did God set up the procedure of the scapegoat, and what does it represent?

PROBLEM: Leviticus 16 sets up the procedure for the Day of Atonement of killing one goat as a sin offering to make atonement for the Holy Place, and then confessing the sins of Israel upon the head of another goat and sending it away into the wilderness. However, this does not present a unified picture, for there is only one sacrifice for our sins, not two (Heb. 10:14).

SOLUTION: The procedure relating to the scapegoat does not present a confused or disunited picture of redemption. Each animal referred to in the description of the procedures to be taken on the Day of Atonement represents some aspect of the work of Christ in making a once for all atonement for our sins. The first goat was killed and his blood was shed (Lev. 16:15), representing the substitutionary death of Christ and the shedding of His blood for our sins. The High Priest was then to take the scapegoat, to confess the sins of Israel upon the head of the goat, and to send it out into the wilderness. This represented the carrying away of Israel's sins and symbolizes the work of Christ in bearing away our sins. As Isaiah 53:6 prophesied, "And the Lord has laid on Him the iniquity of us all." The various aspects of the work of Christ in redemption are symbolized by the different parts which the different animals played on the Day of Atonement.

LEVITICUS 18:22 – Have the laws against homosexuality been abolished along with laws against eating pork?

PROBLEM: The law against homosexuality is found in the levitical law (Lev. 18:22) along with laws against eating pork and shrimp (Lev. 11:2-3, 10). But these ceremonial laws have been done away with (Acts 10:15). This being the case, some insist that the laws prohibiting homosexual activity are no longer binding either.

SOLUTION: The laws against homosexual practices are not merely ceremonial. Simply because the Mosaic prohibition against homosexuality is mentioned in Leviticus does not mean that it was part of the ceremonial law that has passed away.

First of all, if laws against homosexuality were merely ceremonial (and therefore abolished), then rape, incest, and beastiality would not be morally wrong either, since they are condemned in the same chapter with homosexual sins (Lev. 18:6-14, 22-23).

Second, homosexual sins among Gentiles were also condemned by

God (Rom. 1:26), and they did not have the ceremonial law (Rom. 2:12-15). It was for this very reason that God brought judgment on the Canaanites (Gen. 18:1-3, 25).

Third, even in the Jewish levitical law there was a difference in punishment for violating the ceremonial law of eating pork or shrimp (which was a few days isolation) and that for homosexuality which was capital punishment (Lev. 18:29).

Fourth, Jesus changed the dietary laws of the OT (Mark 7:18; Acts 10:15), but the moral prohibitions against homosexuality are still enjoined on believers in the NT (Rom. 1:26-27; 1 Cor. 6:9; 1 Tim. 1:10; Jude 7).

LEVITICUS 18:22-24 — Is the curse of barrenness the reason God condemned homosexuality?

PROBLEM: According to Jewish belief, barrenness was a curse (Gen. 16:1; 1 Sam. 1:3-7). Children were considered a blessing from the Lord (Ps. 127:3). The blessing of God in the land was dependent on having children (Gen. 15:5). In view of the stress laid on having children, some have argued that it is not surprising that the OT Law would frown on homosexual activity from which no children come. Thus, they conclude that the Bible is not condemning homosexual activity as such, but only the refusal to have children.

SOLUTION: There is no indication in Scripture that homosexuality was considered sinful because no children resulted from it. First of all, at no place in the Bible is any such connection stated.

Second, if homosexuals were punished because they were barren, then why were they put to death? The dead can't have any more children! Since it is against the desires of homosexuals, heterosexual marriage would have been a more appropriate punishment!

Third, the prohibition against homosexuality was not only for Jews, but for Gentiles (Lev. 18:24). But Gentile blessings were not dependent on having heirs to inherit the land of Israel.

Finally, if barrenness was a divine curse, then singleness would be sinful. But both our Lord (Matt. 19:11-12) and the Apostle Paul (1 Cor. 7:8) sanctioned singlehood by both precept and practice.

LEVITICUS 23:32 — Was the feast observed on the ninth day or on the tenth day?

PROBLEM: According to this verse the fast associated with the Day of Atonement was to begin on the "ninth day of the month." But earlier in Leviticus 16:29 they were to begin fasting on the "tenth day of the month."

SOLUTION: This fast began on the ninth day and extended over to the tenth day (cf. Lev. 23:27). Hence, it was appropriate to speak of it as being either day. There are several other problems of a similar nature. For example, in like manner the feast was both seven days (Ex. 12:15) or six days (Deut. 16:8). God ended His work of creation on the seventh day (Gen. 2:2) and yet did it in six days (Ex. 20:11). Also, "after eight days" means the next Sunday (John 20:26; cf. 20:19).

LEVITICUS 23:42-43 — Did Israel dwell in booths or in tents?

PROBLEM: Here the people of Israel are told to "dwell in booths." But earlier in Exodus 16:16, it speaks of everyone being "in his tent."

SOLUTION: Since the people moved throughout the wilderness for 40 years, their homes were tents. However, the Leviticus passage does not speak of their homes in the wilderness, but about later instructions for celebrating the Feast of Tabernacles (Booths) in Jerusalem. Since it was only for a week, they were instructed to make temporary booths in which to live while at the feasts. There was, after all, no Holiday Inn in Jerusalem at the time.

LEVITICUS 26:30 — Did God abhor Israel?

PROBLEM: Time and time again God reminded Israel that they were the "apple of His eye" (Zech. 2:8), the object of His special blessing (Gen. 12:1-3). Yet here God says, "My soul shall abhor you."

SOLUTION: Only a few verses later (v. 44), God says, "I will not cast them away, nor shall I abhor them." The difference is due to the fact that He is speaking of two different times in which Israel is in two different conditions. When they are faithful to Him, God will not abhor them. But, when they worship other gods, He promises to "cast your carcasses on the lifeless forms of your idols" (v. 30). God hates the practice of idolatry, whether by His people or by pagans.

NUMBERS

NUMBERS 1:1 — How could Moses have written Numbers when critics claim it was written centuries after his death?

PROBLEM: Many modern critics claim that Moses did not write the first five books of the Bible traditionally attributed to him (see comments on Ex. 24:4). But the Bible declares here that "the Lord spoke to Moses" (1:1) and that "Moses wrote down" the events of this book (33:2).

SOLUTION: The critics have no real evidence for their claim, either historical or literary. The fact that Moses used different names for God (Elohim, Jehovah [Yahweh]) is no proof. Each name of God informs us of another characteristic of God that fits the narrative in which it is used (see comments on Gen. 2:4).

Furthermore, there is strong evidence that Moses wrote the Book of Numbers. First, there is all the evidence mentioned earlier (in comments on Ex. 24:4) that the book reflects a detailed, first-hand knowledge of the time, places, and customs of the period it describes — all of which Moses possessed.

Second, the book claims to have been written by Moses (1:1; 33:2). This would make the book an outright fraud, unless Moses is really its rightful author.

Third, there are a number of NT citations from the Book of Numbers which are associated with Moses (Acts 7; 13; 1 Cor. 10:2-8; Heb. 3:7-16). If Moses did not write Numbers, then these inspired NT books would be in error too.

Fourth, our Lord quoted from Numbers and verified that it was indeed Moses who lifted up the serpent in the wilderness (John 3:14; cf. Num. 21:9). This places the stamp of Christ's authority on the authenticity of the question.

NUMBERS 1:1-4:49 — How accurate is this census of the tribes of Israel?

PROBLEM: According to the census taken in chapters 1–4 of Numbers, the newly formed nation of Israel must have numbered about 2 million people. According to Numbers 1:1, this census was taken while the people were in the wilderness of Sinai at the beginning of their 40 years of wandering. However, the dry and desolate conditions of the Sinai desert would have made it impossible for such a large group to survive. So, is the census inaccurate?

SOLUTION: The naturalistic presupposition of this criticism is contrary to the historic facts. Although there has been some controversy over the meaning of the Hebrew word which is translated "thousand," the evidence is clear that this is the proper understanding of this word in this context. For example, Numbers 1:21 does not say, as some have claimed, that the children of Reuben numbered 46 *families* and 500. The verse clearly states that the number of individual men from twenty years old and up was 46 *thousand* and 500. According to the census in these chapters, the total number of male Israelites from 20 years old and up was 603,550. This number is confirmed by the passage in Exodus 12:37 which states that 600,000 males, along with women and children, departed from Egypt.

The fact that the arid and barren desert would not be able to sustain such a large group of people is a valid observation. However, the problem which modern scholarship has with the size of the multitude and the possibility of their survival in the wilderness rests upon an unwillingness to consider the supernatural element. Modern scholarship is decidedly anti-supernatural. Since the Book of Exodus records the divine judgments upon Egypt, and the miraculous deliverance of Israel from bondage, the daily provision for the people by the mighty hand of God is sufficient to explain the survival of the people of God in that destitute land. Indeed, many passages record the miraculous provisions which God made for His people, from the daily supply of manna (Ex. 16), which was provided for the whole nation until the new generation ate the food of the Promised Land (Josh. 5:12), to the miraculous provision of water from that supernatural rock which followed them (1 Cor. 10:4; Ex. 17:6), to the miraculous provision of meat in Numbers 11:31, to the fact that neither their clothes nor their sandals wore out in all their wanderings (Deut. 29:5). God was able to meet all their needs. Although the desert was not able to sustain, the Lord God of Israel certainly was (see also discussion on Deut. 32:13-14).

NUMBERS 1:46 – Was this census made here or earlier?

PROBLEM: According to Exodus 40:2, Moses took the census of the people of Israel the "first day of the first month." But in Numbers, the same census, yielding the same number of 603,550, was taken on "the first day of the second month" (Num. 1:1).

SOLUTION: These are apparently two different censuses for two different purposes. The first one (Ex. 38) was for *religious* purposes and the second for *military* purposes. The first one was connected with the "inventory of the tabernacle" (Ex. 38:21), that is, a collection of the offering used for the tabernacle. The later one had to do with how many men were "able to go to war in Israel" (Num. 1:3). Both yield the same result since they were taken so close together.

NUMBERS 3:12 – If God commanded that firstborn sons from all the tribes be given Him, why was the tribe of Levi given instead?

PROBLEM: God had commanded Moses that "all the firstborn of man among your sons you shall redeem" (Ex. 13:13; cf. 22:29). However, this was never done. Instead, one whole tribe was set apart to God for the work of the priesthood (Num. 3:12).

SOLUTION: The reason for the substitution is given in Numbers 3:12. The Lord declared: "I Myself have taken the Levites from among the children of Israel instead of every firstborn who opens the womb among the children of Israel." Since they belonged to Him, God had the right to make the substitution.

NUMBERS 4:3 – How can the age for Levitical service be 30, when Numbers 8:24 says 25, and Ezra 3:8 says 20?

PROBLEM: According to Numbers 4:3, at 30 years of age a Levite would "enter the service to do the work in the tabernacle of meeting." However, Numbers 8:24 states, "this is what pertains to the Levites: From twenty-five years old and above one may enter to perform service in the work of the tabernacle of meeting," and Ezra 3:8 says that Levites "from twenty years old and above" were appointed to oversee the work of rebuilding the house of the Lord. Is there a contradiction between these passages?

SOLUTION: First, there is a distinction made in the text between the type of service which is rendered in each case. In Numbers 4:3 the passage talks about anyone entering into the service to perform the business (*melakah,* business or occupation) of the tabernacle. Numbers 8:24 is referring to those who come "to perform service in the work (*baabodath,* meaning work or labor) of the tabernacle." The difference indicates that the younger men, referred to in Numbers 8:24, were probably apprentices who engaged in the manual labor while in training. Later they were admitted to the official service of the tabernacle business at age 30 according to Numbers 4:3.

Second, Ezra 3:8 specifically states that these Levites were appointed "to oversee the work of the house of the Lord." This was not the official service of the tabernacle. Rather, this was the work of overseeing the rebuilding of the temple. Also, due to the fact that the number of Levites who had returned from the captivity was, according to Ezra 2:40 and Nehemiah 7:43, only 74, it was necessary to employ them at a younger age to have a sufficient number to oversee the work. Also, David employed the Levites from age twenty, and he did so because, "They [the Levites] shall no longer carry the tabernacle, or any of the articles for its service" (1 Chron. 23:26). Apparently the work of transporting the tabernacle from place to place in the wilderness journeys required a more mature and stronger person. This practice, apparently begun by David, was followed down to Ezra's time.

NUMBERS 4:6 — Were the staves to remain in the Ark or to be removed?

PROBLEM: According to Exodus 25:15, "The poles shall be in the rings of the ark: they shall not be taken from it." But, in the Numbers passage it says that when the ark was moved by the Levites "they shall insert its poles." This seems to be conflicting instructions.

SOLUTION: The Hebrew word for "insert" (*sum* or *sim*) has a wide range of meanings, including, leave, put, place, set, and turn. Hence, it may mean no more than the priests were to fasten or adjust the poles when they moved the ark so that it did not slip when being moved. This would make sense in view of the command not to remove the poles from the ark.

NUMBERS 5:13-22 — Doesn't the Bible condone a superstition here?

PROBLEM: Paul condemns "old wives' fables" (1 Tim. 4:7). But, Moses here commands the practice of a superstition that has no basis in science. The accused wife was found guilty after drinking bitter water only if her stomach swelled. But, both the innocent and guilty wives drank the same bitter water, thus showing that there was no chemical or biological basis for one swelling and the other not.

SOLUTION: The text does not say that the difference in the guilty woman's condition had a *chemical* or *physical* cause. In fact, it indicates that the cause was *spiritual* and *psychological*. "Guilt" is not a physical cause. The reason the belly of a guilty woman might swell can be easily explained by what is known scientifically about psychosomatic (mind over matter) conditions. Many women have experienced "false pregnancies" where their stomachs and breasts enlarge without being pregnant. Some people have even experienced blindness from psychological causes. Experiments with placebo pills (sugar pills) indicate that many people with terminal illnesses get the same relief from them as from morphine. So, it is a scientific fact that the mind can have a great effect on bodily processes.

Now, given that the text says the woman was placed under an "oath" before God with the threat of a "curse" (v. 21) if she was actually "guilty," the bitter water would have worked like a psychosomatic lie detector. A woman who believed she would be cursed and knew she was guilty would be so affected. But those who knew they were innocent would not.

Furthermore, the text does not say anyone actually drank the water and experienced an enlarged stomach. It simply says "if " (cf. vv. 14, 28) she does, then this will result. No doubt just the *belief* that this would happen and that one would be found guilty would have convinced the woman who knew she was guilty not even to subject herself to the process.

NUMBERS 6:5 — Does the vow of the Nazarite contradict Paul's prohibition against long hair?

PROBLEM: Paul affirmed that it is against "nature" for men to have long hair (1 Cor. 11:14). But the vow of the Nazarite demanded that one not cut his hair.

SOLUTION: The general rule was for men not to dress like women (see comments on Deut. 22:5), nor to wear long hair like women (see comments on 1 Cor. 11:14). Any exception was born out of either perversity (e.g., homosexuality), necessity (health, safety), or special sanctity. The vow of the Nazarite falls into the latter category and is an exception that helps establish the rule. God wished to distinguish the sexes for purposes of social and moral propriety. However, a special vow of dedication to

God involving long hair but not wearing women's clothes would scarcely tend to violate the spirit of the divine design of keeping the sexes distinguishable. No one with evil intentions of confusing the sexes for perverse reasons would be making such a self-sacrificing spiritual vow.

NUMBERS 10:31 — If God lead Israel by a cloud then why was Hobab needed as a guide?

PROBLEM: Exodus 13:21-22 affirms that God supernaturally lead Israel through the wilderness by a cloud that was illuminated by night. However, Moses asked his father-in-law, Hobab, to come with them "inasmuch as you know how we are to camp in the wilderness, and you can be our eyes" (Num. 10:31). But why did they need a human guide when they had divine guidance?

SOLUTION: In response, several things should be observed. One is that Moses saw no contradiction between these and even mentions both the usefulness of Hobab (Num. 10:31) and the leadership of the pillar of cloud (Num. 10:34) only three verses later! Furthermore, there is an important difference between the *general route to take* (and how long to stay) provided by the cloud and *specific arrangements for the camp* supplied by human wisdom. An experienced person in the way of this wilderness could be invaluable for finding the most advantageous places for pasture, shelter, and other needed supplies. The critic shows a lack of understanding of the principle that God does not do for us what we can do for ourselves.

NUMBERS 10:33 — Was the Ark placed in the middle of the camp or in front of it?

PROBLEM: In this text, we read that "the ark of the covenant of the Lord went before them." Yet, earlier the tabernacle (with its ark) are said to be "in the middle of the camps" (Num. 2:17).

SOLUTIONS: Some scholars claim there were two arks, one made by Moses which was carried in front of the camp and which the Philistines later captured. The other was made by Bezaleel, containing the tables of the law, which stayed in the middle of the camp.

Other scholars believe that the ark was *generally* in the middle of the camp but that on certain occasions, as the three day journey (Num. 10:33), it was taken out in front of the camp.

Still others believe that the phrase "went before them" (Num. 10:33)

■

does not imply *locality* but *leadership*. Just as a general "went before" his army (that is, led them) and yet was surrounded by troops protecting them, even so the ark lead Israel, even though it was in the middle of them.

Finally, it is possible that the ark was only in the middle of the people while they were camped (Num. 2). But that as they broke camp, the ark then went out before them to lead them to their next destination. Any one of these suggestions would resolve the difficulty.

NUMBERS 11:8 — Did the manna taste like a honey wafer or like fresh oil?

PROBLEM: Here the manna's "taste was like the taste of pastry prepared with oil." But in Exodus 16:31 asserts that the "taste of it was like wafers made with honey."

SOLUTION: The latter description may have been what the manna tasted like in its *natural* state; the former, after it was *cooked*. Notice that in the same verse it speaks of the people who "ground it on millstones" and "cooked it in pans." But even granting the two passages are speaking about the manna in the same condition, they are not mutually exclusive.

NUMBERS 11:24 — Was the tabernacle outside the camp of Israel or inside it?

PROBLEM: Numbers 2 places the tabernacle inside the camp, but here in Numbers 11:24 (cf. 12:4) it is said to be outside the camp.

SOLUTION: It was both. The twelve tribes were camped around the tabernacle (Num. 2:3, 10, 18, 25), with a space between them and the tabernacle in the center (Num. 2:2). Hence, to get to the tabernacle they would have to go "outside" their camping area. And yet the tabernacle was literally "in the middle" of them.

NUMBERS 11:31-34 — How could God bring judgment on the people for eating the quail that He provided?

PROBLEM: God miraculously provided quail for the people to eat. However, the wrath of the Lord was aroused against them, and He struck them with a great plague so that many of them died (v. 33). How could the wrath of God be aroused against the people for eating the very meat

[101]

that He had miraculously provided?

SOLUTION: It is necessary to see the judgment of God in light of events which led up to it. In Numbers 11:1-3, we find that the people of God began to complain. In fact, the text indicates that they were acting like people who had suffered some misfortune. Numbers 11:1 says, "Now when the people complained, it displeased the Lord." This was a direct rejection of God's provisions for them. They had apparently forgotten the bondage from which they had been rescued. This attitude displeased God, and He brought judgment upon them as a disciplinary act.

In verse 4, the people began to complain again because they wanted meat to eat instead of the manna which God was providing for them. They had apparently not learned the lesson, and their attitude displeased God again. In fact, verse 10 says, "Moses also was displeased." God brought disciplinary judgment upon them again, this time by giving them exactly what they asked for. In response to their disobedient and ungrateful attitude, God told Moses to tell the people, "Therefore the Lord will give you meat, and you shall eat . . . until it comes out of your nostrils and becomes loathsome to you, because you have despised the Lord who is among you, and have wept before Him, saying, 'Why did we ever come up out of Egypt?' " (Num. 11:18-20)

Even after this warning they did not get the point. When God brought the quail, verse 32 says, "And the people stayed up all that day, all that night, and all the next day, and gathered the quail." The lust and unrepentant attitude of the people brought the judgment of God upon them. Verse 34 states, "So He called the name of that place Kibroth Hattaavah, because there they buried the people who had yielded to craving." So, God did not bring judgment on the people for eating the quail, but because of their lustful and ungrateful hearts.

NUMBERS 12:3 — How can this statement have been written by Moses?

PROBLEM: Numbers 12:3 says, "Now the man Moses was very humble, more than all men who were on the face of the earth." The conservative view of the Pentateuch is that Moses was the author of these five books. But, how could Moses make such a statement about himself if he were really humble?

SOLUTION: Of course, no one would claim that Jesus was being boastful or prideful by saying "I am meek and lowly in heart" (Matt. 11:29, KJV). Jesus was simply stating the facts. Likewise, Moses is not boasting or being prideful about his humility. Rather, he was simply stating a fact which was crucial for understanding the significance of the events he was reporting.

Earlier in chapter 11, after the Spirit of the Lord came upon Eldad and Medad so that they began to prophesy, Joshua approached Moses and said, "Moses my lord, forbid them!" (Num. 11:28) Moses' response is a perfect illustration of the humility that 12:3 describes: "Are you zealous for my sake? Oh, that all the Lord's people were prophets and that the Lord would put His Spirit upon them!" (Num. 11:29) Moses exhibited the character of a humble man who was not interested in his own glory, but only in the glory of the Lord.

When Moses is confronted by Miriam and Aaron in 12:1, Moses did not respond in his own defense. A humble person does not usually rise to his own defense. Why didn't Moses just tell them? Why didn't he set them straight? Why did God have to speak to Miriam and Aaron in Moses' behalf? The explanation is found in 12:3. Moses was not out for his own glorification. If Moses had responded in his own defense, he would have been justifying their complaints against him. But, Moses was not the leader of the people because of any ambition on his own part, or any self-confidence or self-assertive ladder climbing. He was appointed by God. So verse 12:3 is a vindication of Moses' character. It is not a statement of boastful pride. It is simply a statement of fact.

NUMBERS 13:16 — How can this passage say that Moses called Hoshea by the name Joshua since he was called Joshua in Exodus 17:9?

PROBLEM: Numbers 13:16 says that Moses called Hoshea the son of Nun, Joshua. But, as early as Exodus 17:9 Joshua is referred to by that name. How can this passage say that Moses was the one to give Hoshea the name Joshua?

SOLUTION: First, it must be remembered that Moses probably wrote this toward the end of the 40 years of wandering in the wilderness. Although Joshua may not have been given this name until the time referred to in Numbers 13:16, it would have been natural for Moses to refer to Hoshea as Joshua while composing the final drafts of the books of the Pentateuch. Also, the point at which Moses notes the fact that he referred to Hoshea as Joshua is quite appropriate. In recording the names of the spies whom he sent into the land, Moses endeavored to make it clear that Hoshea was the very same person to whom he had frequently made reference in other parts of the Pentateuch by the name Joshua.

Second, it is not necessarily the case that Hoshea was not called Joshua until this point in the process of the historical events. Perhaps it was simply the case that Hoshea was commonly known as Hoshea, but that Moses had called him Joshua from the beginning. The text does not say that Moses began to call Hoshea, Joshua at this point in time. The text simply states that Moses called Hoshea by the name Joshua. It may be significant to realize that the name Hoshea means "salvation," while the name Joshua means "Yahweh is salvation."

NUMBERS 13:32 — How could the ten spies report that the land devoured its inhabitants?

PROBLEM: In Numbers 13:32, ten of the spies who had been sent by Moses reported that the land was "a land that devours its inhabitants." However, in addition to the fact that Joshua and Caleb had reported that the land flowed with milk and honey (Num. 13:27), the spies had come back with evidence of the abundance of the land (Num. 13:26). How could the ten spies claim that the land was "a land that devours its inhabitants"?

SOLUTION: It would be a misunderstanding of the text to assume that this epithet indicated that the land was actually a desolate place. The testimony of all the spies agreed upon the richness of the land in its capacity to produce food and sustain life. Rather, it was precisely because the land was so rich that the ten spies could give their pessimistic report. The fertility of the land caused many different peoples to desire to dwell in the land, which caused much blood shed between inhabitants and invaders. There is no contradiction in this statement. The land was so rich, and desired by so many different peoples, it facilitated many conflicts resulting in the inhabitants being devoured in the midst of the conflicts to own the land.

NUMBERS 14:25 — Did the Amalekites live in the mountain or in the valley?

PROBLEM: This verse says the Amalekites and Canaanites "dwell in the valley." But verse 45 says the opposite, namely, they "dwelt in that mountain."

SOLUTION: There are two possibilities. One is that these two verses may be referring to different groups. Some of them may have lived in the mountain and some in the valley. Or, it may have reference to the same people who lived in a valley or plateau which was also a mountain relative to the lower area around it from which they "came down" to fight (v. 45).

NUMBERS 14:29 — If nearly all the men from twenty years up died in the wilderness, why have none of their graves been discovered?

PROBLEM: According to Numbers 14:29, the corpses of all the men older than 20 years would fall in the wilderness. The total was over 600,000. But, if so many died in the wilderness, why do their grave sites not litter the landscape?

SOLUTION: Because the people were condemned to wander in the wilderness, the conditions were such that they were not able to construct graves that could withstand the weather conditions or even the ravages of wild beasts. The graves were probably shallow burial places just beneath the sand or gravel. Consequently, neither the grave sites nor the skeletons of those who were buried could be preserved for any length of time.

NUMBERS 15:24 — Are there two kinds of sin offerings, or only one?

PROBLEM: Leviticus states that for unintentional sins of the whole congregation, when the sin is made known, "the assembly shall offer a young bull for the sin" (Lev. 4:14). However, here Numbers 15 speaks of offering two different sacrifices for the same sin — "one young bull as a burnt offering . . . and one kid of the goats as a sin offering" (v. 24).

SOLUTION: Some Bible scholars think the difference here may be due to the fact that the Leviticus passage refers to sins of *commission,* and the Numbers text to sins of *omission.* Others believe that in Numbers the sacrifices for the rulers and the people are listed *separately,* but in Leviticus, for brevity, the sacrifices for the rulers and for the congregation are listed *together.* In any event, the fact that one passage specifies two and the other specifies one, does not mean that the second passage *contradicts* the first passage, but that one merely *supplements* the other.

NUMBERS 16:31 — Was Korah swallowed by the earth or burned?

PROBLEM: In verses 31-32 it says the earth opened and swallowed Korah and his 250 rebellious associates. Yet verse 35 asserts that fire came from God and consumed Korah and his associates.

SOLUTION: Some scholars have suggested that Korah was burned along with the 250 other rebels. However, no verse actually affirms this and other verses seem to deny it (noted below).

It seems better to understand it as follows: Korah, Dathan, and Abiram (v. 27) were swallowed by the earth, while at the same time (cf. 26:10) a fire from God consumed the 250 other rebels who offered incense in the tabernacle (cf. Ps. 106:17-18).

NUMBERS 16:32 — Were all Korah's family killed with him or only some?

PROBLEM: This verse states that "the earth opened its mouth and swallowed them up, with their households and all the men with Korah." However, Numbers 26:11 speaks about Korah's descendants who did not perish in the judgment.

SOLUTION: Those who perished with Korah were all his *followers,* but not all his *family.* Numbers 26:11 states clearly: "Nevertheless the children of Korah did not die." Indeed, the prophet Samuel was a descendant of Korah (1 Chron. 6:22-28).

NUMBERS 20:1 — Was Kadesh in the wilderness of Zin or in Paran?

PROBLEM: In this text Kadesh is said to be in the "Wilderness of Zin." But in Numbers 13:26 it is said to be in the "Wilderness of Paran." Which was it?

SOLUTION: There are several possible explanations, any one of which resolves the problem. First, some believe there were two places named Kadesh, one in each wilderness. Second, the name Kadesh could have been applied to both a city and a region in which the city lay. Third, that the same city was positioned between two wildernesses so as to be appropriately associated with either.

NUMBERS 20:21 — How could this verse say that Israel went around Edom when Deuteronomy 2:4 says they passed through it?

PROBLEM: God would not allow Israel to do battle with the Edomites because He had given the land of Edom to Esau as an everlasting possession. Numbers 20:21 states that "Israel turned away from him." However, when Moses reviews these events in Deuteronomy 2:4, he states that the Lord said, "You are about to pass through the territory of your brethren, the descendants of Esau." Likewise, Deuteronomy 2:8 says Israel "passed beyond our brethren the descendants of Esau." Did they pass through Edom or did they go around it?

SOLUTION: In one sense it can be said that Israel passed through Edom when they entered it in order to make the request to continue their journey along the King's highway that ran through their land. However, the text never actually says that they did, or that they would pass through the land. Actually, the same Hebrew word (*abar*) is used in each case. It can be used to mean pass through or pass by. The historical record clearly describes their journey as passing along the eastern border of Edom (Deut. 2:8). God had warned Israel that as they would pass along the eastern border, they should not provoke the Edomites to war (Deut. 2:5).

NUMBERS 21:9 — Wasn't making this bronze serpent a form of idolatry?

PROBLEM: God commanded Moses not to make "any carved image" (Ex. 20:4), lest it be used as an idol. Yet here Moses was commanded to "make a bronze serpent, and put it on a pole." Later, the people worshiped this very image (2 Kings 18:4). Does not God command Moses to violate the very command He gave him against idolatry?

SOLUTION: First of all, the command against making "carved images" was a command against making idols. God did not command Moses to make an idol for the people to worship but a symbol to which they could look in faith and be healed. Later, the people made this symbol into an idol. But this does not make the symbol wrong. After all, people have worshiped the Bible. This does not mean that the Bible was intended by God as an idol.

Further, not all "images" are idols. Religious art contains images but is not thereby idolatrous. God also instructed Moses to make cherubim (angels) for the ark, but they were not idols. There is a difference between a God-appointed representation of symbol (e.g., the bread and wine in the Lord's Supper) and a man-made idol (see comments on Ex. 20:4).

NUMBERS 22:33 — Why did the angel of the Lord try to kill Balaam, since God had given him permission to go to the plains of Moab?

PROBLEM: In Numbers 22:20 God had told Balaam to go with the men to the plains of Moab. However, verse 22 says, "Then God's anger aroused because he went, and the Angel of the Lord took His stand in the way as an adversary against him." Also, in verse 33 the angel of the Lord says, "If she [the donkey] had not turned aside from Me, I would also have killed you by now, and let her live." Why did the angel of the Lord try to kill Balaam when God had already given him permission to go with the men from Moab?

SOLUTION: The account of Balaam's activities demonstrates that Balaam was torn between obeying the command of God, and the greed in his heart for the riches that Balak had promised. Although God had flatly told Balaam not to go with the men to Balak (Num. 22:12), Balak's offer of riches (v. 17) tempted Balaam, and he went to God a second time to seek permission to go to Balak. It was because of Balaam's evil heart of greed that the Lord sent His angel to stand in the way as Balaam's adversary. The intent was not to kill Balaam, evidenced by the fact that the angel of the Lord allowed Balaam's donkey to see him and, by turning aside, to prevent Balaam's death. Rather, the angel's purpose was to present a forceful reminder that Balaam was to speak only what the Lord would tell him.

Balaam's greed is clearly demonstrated in the fact that, although he would not curse Israel because the Lord would only allow him to bless His people, Balaam counseled Balak to corrupt Israel by allowing his women to marry the men of Israel and to lead them into idolatry (2 Peter 2:15; Rev. 2:14). Balaam's greed had devised a way to help Israel's enemies while not directly disobeying the Lord's command to speak only the words that He would give to him (Num. 31:16).

NUMBERS 24:7 — How could this oracle refer to Agag when he lived much later, in the time of Saul?

PROBLEM: The oracle of Balaam makes reference to the exaltation of Israel over Agag and his kingdom. However, Agag was an Amalekite king during the time of Saul who was king of Israel in the 11th century, almost 400 years later. How could this oracle refer to Agag when he lived later in the time of Saul?

SOLUTION: First, the name Agag was probably a royal title which the Amalekite kings took for themselves — comparable to the title Pharaoh.

The Amalekite king whom Saul would later defeat would have taken this title also.

Second, if Agag was a proper name, it is not necessary to conclude that the reference in Numbers is anachronistic. It was not uncommon for kings to have the same name as previous kings. Even in the history of Israel there were two kings with the name Jeroboam. This practice was common in Phoenicia, Syria, and Egypt. In Egypt there were four Pharaohs named Amenemhet in the 12th Dynasty alone.

Third, since the oracle of Balaam was given to him by the Spirit of God, it is possible that this is a prophetic announcement of the dominance which Israel would have over those people who were the first to attack them upon their departure from Egypt (Ex. 17:8ff). In any case, this reference is not anachronistic.

Other examples of so-called "premature mention" can be explained in similar ways. For example, the Amalekites may be mentioned by historic anticipation (in Gen. 14:7), even though they flourished much later (cf. Num. 13:29; 14:25; Jud. 6:3). Likewise, "the land of the Hebrews" (Gen. 40:15) could have been so named by anticipation of later fulfillment of God's promise (in Gen. 12:1-3; 15:4-7) or by the fact that Abraham and his descendants had already lived there for centuries. Hebron (Gen. 13:18) may have been its original name, later called Kirjath-Arba, and then replaced again by Hebron (Josh. 14:15). Or, a later editor of the OT manuscript may have simply updated the name, so that the people of his day would understand the place to which it referred. For example, one of the present authors was born in a city then called Baseline, Michigan but was no part of Warren, Michigan. When asked by people today about the city of his birth, he generally says "Warren," even though that was not its name at the time. Also, the Levite's land (Lev. 25:32-34; Num. 35:2-8) was probably mentioned by way of anticipation. And the "mountain" where the "sanctuary" of the Lord was (Ex. 15:13-17) was simply speaking about the way it would be when they got into the Land of Promise.

NUMBERS 25:9 — Why does this verse say that 24,000 died when 1 Corinthians 10:8 offers a different number?

PROBLEM: The incident at Baal-Peor resulted in God's judgment upon Israel, and, according to Numbers 25:9, 24,000 died in the plague of judgment. However, according to 1 Corinthians 10:8, only 23,000 died. Which is the correct number?

SOLUTION: There are two possible explanations here. First, some have suggested that the difference is due to the fact that 1 Corinthians 10:8 is speaking only about those who died "in one day" (23,000), whereas Numbers 25:9 is referring to the complete number (24,000) that died in the plague.

Others believe two different events are in view here. They note that 1 Corinthians 10:7 is a quote of Exodus 32:6 and indicates that the 1 Corinthians passage is actually referring to the judgment of God after the idolatrous worship of the golden calf (Ex. 32). The Exodus passage does not state the number of people that died as a result of the judgment of God, and the actual number is not revealed until 1 Corinthians 10:8. According to 1 Corinthians 10:8, 23,000 died as a result of the judgment of God for their worship of the golden calf. According to Numbers 25:9, 24,000 died as a result of the judgment of God for Israel's worship of Baal at Baal-Peor.

NUMBERS 31 — How can it be morally right for the Israelites to totally destroy the Midianites?

PROBLEM: According to the record of events in Numbers 31, Moses commanded the Israelites to utterly destroy the Midianites. Verse 7 states that they killed every Midianite male. Verse 9 records that they took all the women and children as captives, and verse 10 states that the Israelites burned all the cities and camps of the Midianites. Again, in verse 17, Moses commanded the people to kill every male child of the Midianites and every Midianite woman who had intercourse with a man, leaving only the female children and young virgins. How can such a total destruction be morally justified?

SOLUTION: First of all, it must be remembered that it was the Midianites who corrupted God's people by leading them into idolatry at Baal-Peor so that 24,000 Israelites died in the plague (Num. 25:9). It was necessary to totally eliminate this evil influence from Israel.

Further, it was not on the authority of Moses that Israel performed this destruction. Rather, it was at the direct command of God. Verse 2 records God's command to Moses to carry out the Lord's vengeance upon the Midianites. The abominable nature of the influence which the Midianites had upon Israel in leading them into idolatry merited the destructive judgment of God. God dealt severely and decisively with this cancer. The moral justification for this action is found in the fact that God has the right to give and take life. Since the wages of sin is death,

and the Midianites engaged in a terrible sin, they justly reaped the consequences of God's vengeance (see comments on Joshua 6:21).

NUMBERS 33:44-49 — Why is the list of places Israel stopped different here from the ones stated earlier (in Numbers 21)?

PROBLEM: Numbers 21 speaks of the Israelites stopping off at Oboth, Ije Abarim, Zered, Arnon, Beer, Mattanah, Nahaliel, Bamoth, and Mt. Pisgah in Moab. But the Numbers 33 list of stopoffs includes Oboth, Ije Abarim, Dibon Gad, Almon Diblathaim, mountains of Abarim near Mt. Nebo, and the Plains of Moab.

SOLUTION: Understanding several factors helps to reconcile the apparent discrepancy. First, both lists begin with the exact same names and end in the exact same place (east of Jordan near Jericho). Second, since both lists are in the same book the author saw no contradiction between them. Third, some places may have had more than one name. Ije Abarim, for example, is also called Ijim (Num. 33:44-45). Fourth, neither list may be complete, listing only the names that the author wished to stress at that time. Numbers 21 lists six places in between Ije Abarim and Moab, whereas Numbers 33 lists only three. The more complete list may be a *statistic* account and the smaller one a *historical* perspective. Fifth, the list in Numbers 33 may be the head quarters of Moses and the tabernacle. Sixth, since there were millions of people who covered a broad stretch of land, more than one city may have been occupied at the same time. Seventh, in their wandering Israel may have covered the same ground twice, first the more *circuitous* one and then a more *direct* route (cf. Num. 33:30-33).

NUMBERS 35:19 — Why did God permit avenging blood and yet forbid murder?

PROBLEM: God forbade murder (Ex. 20:13). Yet here He says, "The avenger of blood himself shall put the murderer to death; when he meets him, he shall put him to death."

SOLUTION: First of all, this was not an act of *murder,* but an act of *capital punishment* which God had ordained before the law (Gen. 9:6), and Moses had reaffirmed it under the Law (Ex. 21:12). Further, notice that it was only to be done to a "murderer," not simply to anyone. Also, the avenger had to be the nearest male relative of the one who was murdered, not just anyone who wished to take justice in his own hands.

In short, what is forbidden in Exodus 20 is the recognized crime of murder, and what is permitted in Numbers 35 is the recognized responsibility of capital punishment. These are not in conflict.

NUMBERS 35:30 — Does the need for two witnesses mean that it is wrong to condemn someone on other evidence?

PROBLEM: According to Numbers 35:30, a man accused of murder could be convicted and condemned on the testimony of two witnesses, but not on the testimony of only one witness. However, the great majority of crimes are not committed in the open for people to witness. Does this make it wrong to convict and condemn someone on the basis of other evidence when there have been no eyewitnesses?

SOLUTION: It would be wrong to assume that the Hebrew word translated "witness" (*ed*), is exactly equivalent to the English usage. Leviticus 5:1 gives a good example of the wider range of use of this Hebrew word: "If a person sins in hearing the utterance of an oath, and is a witness, whether he has seen or known of the matter — if he does not tell it, he bears guilt." In this verse, the same Hebrew word translated "witness" refers to someone who has either seen or known of a matter. According to the Mosaic Law, then, there were two types of witnesses who could offer testimony to the guilt of an individual. One was an eyewitness, the other was one who, though not an eyewitness, could provide testimony to the identity of the offender. This verse does not make it wrong to convict a person on evidence that is other than direct eyewitness evidence. Further, the OT writer did not have in view, nor intend to exclude, such modern things as fingerprints and audio and video tapes.

DEUTERONOMY

DEUTERONOMY 1:1 — How could Moses have written this when biblical criticism claims it was written many centuries later?

PROBLEM: According to this verse, "these are the words which Moses spoke." However, many biblical critics claim that Deuteronomy was written in the third century B.C., many centuries after Moses' time.

SOLUTION: There are many arguments that support the claim that Moses wrote the Book of Deuteronomy.

First, there is the repeated claim of the book that "these are the words of Moses (1:1; 4:44; 29:1). To deny this is to claim the book is a total fraud.

Second, Joshua, Moses' immediate successor, attributed the Book of Deuteronomy to Moses, exhorting the people of Israel to "observe to do . . . all the law which Moses . . . commanded" (Josh. 1:7).

Three, the remainder of the OT attributes Deuteronomy to Moses (cf. Jud. 3:4; 1 Kings 2:3; 2 Kings 14:6; Ezra 3:2; Neh. 1:7; Ps. 103:7; Dan. 9:11; Mal. 4:4).

Fourth, Deuteronomy is the book of the Law most quoted in the NT, often with words like "Moses truly said" (Acts 3:22), "Moses says" (Rom. 10:19), or "it is written in the law of Moses" (1 Cor. 9:9).

Fifth, our Lord quoted the Book of Deuteronomy (6:13, 16) as the authoritative Word of God when He resisted the devil (Matt. 4:7, 10), and He also directly attributed it to the hand of Moses, saying, "Moses said" (Mark 7:10) or "Moses wrote" (Luke 20:28).

Sixth, the geographical and historical details of the book display a firsthand acquaintance such as Moses would have had.

Seventh, scholarly studies of the form and content of Near Eastern covenants indicate that Deuteronomy is from the period of Moses (see Meredith Kline, *Treaty of the Great King,* Eerdmans, 1963).

In addition to all of this, the apparent references within the book to a later period are easily explained (see comments on Deut. 2:10-12). Of course, the last chapter of Deuteronomy, being about Moses' death (chap. 34) was probably written by his successor Joshua, in accordance with the custom of the day.

DEUTERONOMY 1:6ff — How could any from the former generation be present when they all died in the wilderness?

PROBLEM: According to Numbers 26:64-65, all the unbelieving generation of Israelites died in the wilderness, with "not a man of those who were numbered by Moses" remaining to go into the Promised Land. However, when Moses spoke to the people at the end of the wanderings he referred repeatedly to their being witnesses to what happened before the wanderings (cf. Deut. 1:6, 9, 14; 5:2, 5; 11:2, 7).

SOLUTION: First of all, in Deuteronomy, Moses is addressing the nation *as a nation* and, therefore, may not be making a distinction between individuals in the earlier period as opposed to those in the later period. Second, there were a large number of women present who had personally remembered the things to which Moses referred. Third, both the Levites and those who were under 20 years of age before the 40 years were exempt from the general pronouncement that none of the men would enter the Promised Land (Num. 26:64). So also were Joshua and Caleb, who had been faithful spies (Num. 32:12). So there were plenty of people present who could witness to what Moses was saying, even though a whole generation of men (above the age of 20) had perished in the wilderness, as God had said.

DEUTERONOMY 1:13 — Did Moses appoint the judges or did the people?

PROBLEM: Exodus 18:25 declares that "Moses chose able men out of all Israel, and made them heads over the people." However, here Moses told the people to choose their own judges (Deut. 1:13).

SOLUTION: Both are correct, as is indicated only two verses later, where it says Moses "took the heads of your tribes . . . and made them heads [judges] over you." The people had chosen their leaders and Moses appointed these as their judges. So it is proper to speak of either Moses or the people as choosing the judges.

DEUTERONOMY 2:7 — Were Israel's conditions in the wilderness comfortable or destitute?

PROBLEM: Many passages speak of Israel's privations in the wilderness (cf. Ex. 16:2, 3; Num. 11:4-6). Yet here Moses declared that they "lacked nothing."

SOLUTION: The passages are easily reconciled if it is kept in mind that their general state was relatively comfortable. They had ample food and clothes at all times. However, their murmuring and complaining brought acts of judgment from God which could be described as occasions of destitution. So, while the wandering Israelites "lacked nothing" in daily necessities, they certainly did not lack in plagues and punishment from the hand of God.

DEUTERONOMY 2:10-12 — How could this have been written by Moses when it refers to the land of promise which he never entered?

PROBLEM: Moses died before he could enter the Promised Land and was buried outside of it on the east side of the Jordan river (Deut. 34). But, this passage refers to the "land of their possession" as something that Israel possessed at the time it was written. Therefore, it would appear that Deuteronomy could not have been written by Moses, as it is traditionally claimed.

SOLUTION: Some scholars claim that these verses are parenthetical and may have been added by a later editor. This view is supported by noting the brevity of the verses, the fact that they are in parentheses, and that Moses was already buried before the children of Israel entered the Land (Deut. 34:4-6), a fact that was obvious to all readers. However, there is no need to conclude that Moses did not write these sections, since "the land of their possession" can easily refer to the Tribes who had already taken their possession on the east side of Jordan before Moses died (Deut. 3:12-17).

While most evangelical scholars recognize that there are small editorial and explanatory changes, like updating names, they oppose the critical belief that Moses did not write all of the first five books of the OT (except Deut. 34). These verses here seem to be more than minor explanatory insertions for later readers.

Evangelical scholars stress the difference between minor editorial changes in accordance with the original author's meaning and later redactional changes that are contrary to the meaning of the original text. The following chart illustrates the differences between the two.

EVANGELICAL VIEW	CRITICAL VIEW
Editing the text	Redacting the text
Grammatical changes	Theological changes
Changes in form	Changes in fact
Transmitting truth	Tampering with truth
Changing the medium	Changing the message
Updating names	Redacting events

There are serious problems with the claims of critics that later redactors changed the content of previous prophetic writings.

1. It is contrary to the repeated warning God gave not to "add to the word which I [God] command you" (Deut. 4:2; cf. Prov. 30:6; Rev. 22:18-19).

2. The redaction theory confuses canonicity and lower textual criticism. The question of scribal changes in transmitting a manuscript of an inspired book is one of textual criticism, not canonicity.

3. The "inspired redactor" theory is contrary to the biblical use of the word "inspired" (2 Tim. 3:16). The Bible does not speak of inspired writers, but only of inspired *writings*. Furthermore, inspired (*theopneustos*) does not mean to "breathe into" the writers, but to "breath out" the writings.

4. The redaction theory is contrary to the evangelical view that only the autographs (original writings) are inspired. If it is only the final redacted version that is inspired, then the original writings were not the ones breathed out by God.

5. Inspired redaction would also eliminate the means by which prophetic utterance could be tested by those to whom it was given.

6. The redaction model shifts the locus of divine authority from the original prophetic message (given by God through the prophet) to the community of believers generations later. It is contrary to the true principle of canonicity that God *determines* canonicity and the people of God merely *discover* what God determined and inspired.

7. A redaction model of canonicity entails acceptance of deception as a means of divine communication. It asserts that a message or book that claims to come from a prophet (such as Isaiah or Daniel) did not really come from him in its entirety, but rather from later redactors.

8. The redaction model of the canon confuses legitimate scribal activity, involving grammatical form, updating of names, and arrangement of prophetic material with the illegitimate redactional changes in actual content of a previous prophet's message.

9. The redaction theory assumes there were inspired redactions of the OT well beyond the period in which there were no prophets (namely, the 4th century B.C.). There can be no inspired works unless there are living prophets. (See Geisler and Nix, *A General Introduction to the Bible,* Moody Press, 1986, 250–55.)

DEUTERONOMY 2:19 – Was the land of Ammon given to Israel or not?

PROBLEM: Here God told Moses, "I will not give you any of the land of the people of Ammon." But elsewhere it asserts that Joshua gave Israel "half the land of the Ammonites" as a possession from God (Josh. 13:25).

SOLUTION: These passages speak of two different tracts of land. The land that the Ammonites possessed in Moses' time (Deut. 2) was not given to nor occupied by the Israelites. However, the Amorites had previously overpowered the Ammonites and taken a tract of land which Israel later occupied (Joshua 13).

DEUTERONOMY 4:10-15 – Was the law given at Horeb or at Mt. Sinai?

PROBLEM: Exodus 19:11 affirms that Moses received the Law at "Mt. Sinai" (cf. v. 18). But here in Deuteronomy 4:10 it claims that Moses got it "in Horeb." Which was it?

SOLUTION: There are several possible explanations of this discrepancy. Some scholars believe Sinai may be the older and Horeb the later name for the same place. Others hold that Horeb may be the general name of the mountain range and Sinai the particular peak. Still others believe Sinai is the name of the entire group of mountains, while Horeb refers to one specific mountain. Or, the two names could be interchangeable.

In any event, the biblical authors, many centuries closer to the original event than we are, saw no problem in using both names. Horeb is used 17 times and Mt. Sinai 21 times in the OT. Employing two different names is not uncommon. Mt. McKinley in Alaska, the official name of the highest peak in North America, is called Denali by native Americans and many others.

DEUTERONOMY 5:6-21 — How could Moses alter the wording of the Ten Commandments from that which God spoke to him?

PROBLEM: In Deuteronomy 5:6-21 Moses repeats the Ten Commandments to Israel. In reviewing the covenant which God made with Israel, Moses reviews the commandments which God gave to Israel at Sinai. However, Moses' wording of the commandments in this passage is not exactly the same as the wording of God in Exodus 20:2-17. How could Moses alter the wording of the Ten Commandments from wording which God gave to him?

SOLUTION: First, it must be remembered that Moses' purpose in reviewing the Law is not to provide an exact word-for-word recitation of the statements in Exodus. Moses is not only reviewing the Law, but he is expounding and explaining the Law and its implications and applications for entrance into and life in the Promised Land.

Second, Moses was also under the inspiration of the Holy Spirit as he spoke and wrote the words in these passages in Deuteronomy. Consequently, it is under the inspiration of the Holy Spirit that Moses altered, omitted, or added a word or phrase in his presentation of the Decalogue.

DEUTERONOMY 5:15 — Was the Sabbath instituted because of God's rest from creation or His redemption of Israel from Egypt?

PROBLEM: When Moses first gave the Law to Israel, the reason stated for the Sabbath observance was because "in six days the Lord made the heavens and the earth . . . and rested the seventh day. Therefore, the Lord blessed the Sabbath day and hallowed it" (Ex. 20:11). But, when Moses repeated the Law to the new generation entering the Promised Land, the reason given was that "God brought you out from there [Egypt] by a mighty hand and by an outstretched arm; therefore the Lord your God commanded you to keep the Sabbath" (Deut. 5:15). Why two different reasons?

SOLUTION: These are simply two reasons for the same observance. The first reason was patterned after God's rest from *creation* and the second after His act of *redemption*. Both are true and legitimate reasons. The former was the *initial* reason, and the latter was the *subsequent* reason. Since God had performed both mighty acts for them, He had a right to state both as grounds for observing His law.

DEUTERONOMY 8:2 – Didn't God know what Israel would do?

PROBLEM: This passage says that God led Israel into the wilderness in order "to know" what they would do. But if God knows everything already (Ps. 139:7-10; Jer. 17:10), then why did He need to do this to know whether they would obey Him?

SOLUTION: God in His omniscience was already *aware* of what they would do. He led them into the wilderness in order *to prove* them. The parallel expression in this very verse is to "test you, to know what was in your heart." (See also discussion under Gen. 22:12.)

DEUTERONOMY 9:3 – Were the Canaanites destroyed quickly or slowly?

PROBLEM: This verse claims the Canaanites were destroyed "quickly" (*maher*), but an earlier passages (Deut. 7:22) said it would *not* be quickly, but "little by little."

SOLUTION: There are two different ways to understand this. First, it may be an example where the same term is applied to the same thing in different senses. It was quick, relative to the *magnitude of the work,* but slow with regard to the *rate of their occupation.*

Or, it may be referring to two different things in the same basic sense. The *initial victories* were rapid, but *mop-up activity* took much longer. They *conquered* the land in a short time, but they *occupied* it much more slowly. The *major* battles did not take long, but all the subsequent *minor* skirmishes took some time.

DEUTERONOMY 10:1-3 – When was the Ark made?

PROBLEM: According to many other verses, the ark was made before the 40 years wandering (Ex. 25:10; 35:12; 37:1). But according to this passage Moses made the ark of the covenant after the 40 years wandering.

SOLUTION: Some believe the first ark may have been a temporary one and the later one more permanent (cf. Ex. 33:8). Some Jewish commentators believe there were two arks, one to go to war and the other to stay in the tabernacle. Other scholars believe Moses may have ordered the construction of the ark before he went up into Mt. Sinai by way of Bezaleel. Still others believe Moses may be combining here (in Deut. 10:1-3) things that were closely related in *concept* but separated in *time.* Thus, the phrase "make yourself an ark of [acacia] wood" would refer to the command given earlier (Ex. 25:10) and the command to hew two new tables of stone after Moses had seen the glory of God (Ex. 33).

DEUTERONOMY 10:6 — Did Aaron die at Moserah, or did he die at the top of Mount Hor?

PROBLEM: According to Deuteronomy 10:6, Aaron died in Moserah and was buried there. However, according to Numbers 20:27-28 and 33:38, Aaron died at the top of Mount Hor and was buried there. Where did Aaron die, in Moserah or on the top of Mount Hor?

SOLUTION: Both statements are true. Moserah was a location in which Israel camped during their journey from Egypt to the Promised Land. Moserah was probably an area near the border of Edom. It is reasonable to assume that Mount Hor was located within the boundaries of this area. Similarly, Horeb was the name of a group of mountains in which Mount Sinai was located. Consequently, it is not a contradiction to claim that Aaron died and was buried both in Moserah and on the top of Mount Hor. Moserah was the district, and Mount Hor the specific location.

DEUTERONOMY 10:8-9 — Are priests distinguished from Levites or not?

PROBLEM: In this passage priests and Levites are not distinguished from each other, but in other places they are (cf. Lev. 1:5, 8, 11; Num. 6:23).

SOLUTION: When several things are kept in mind, the problem disappears. First of all, the priests were also Levites, all being sons of Aaron. Second, in Deuteronomy, Moses is speaking in general terms to the whole nation and thus avoids the finer distinctions.

Third, some 38 years separate the two passages. It may be that the earlier distinction was no longer in general currency after the wilderness wandering.

DEUTERONOMY 11:25 — Isn't this a false prophecy?

PROBLEM: Moses told the children of Israel that "No man shall be able to stand against you; the Lord your God will put the dread of you and the fear of you upon all the land where you tread, just as He has said to you." But this seems clearly false both in the short view and in the long run. Even under Joshua, Israel lost some battles (Josh 7:4). And in the long run, they were overrun by the Assyrians (2 Kings 16:9) and the Babylonians (2 Kings 25:22).

SOLUTION: This was not a *false* prophecy—it was a *conditional* promise. Notice it is prefaced by the condition "if you diligently obey My commandments which I command you" (v. 13), and "if you carefully keep all these commandments" (v. 22). In short, these were not categorical predictions, but conditional projections. When the people of Israel obeyed God, they were invincible against the most formidable foe (cf. Josh. 6). But when they did not obey Him, they fled in the face of the tiniest adversary (cf. Josh. 7).

DEUTERONOMY 12:24—Was the blood poured out as water or covered with dust?

PROBLEM: According to this verse, the priest was to take the blood of the sacrifice and "pour it on the earth like water." But, earlier in Leviticus 17:13 they were instructed to "cover it with dust." How can these be reconciled?

SOLUTION: The fact that some critics raise this kind of problem shows how desperate they are to find something wrong with the Bible. The full passage in Leviticus provides the answer: "he shall pour out its blood and cover it with dust" (Lev. 17:13). So there is absolutely no problem whatsoever.

DEUTERONOMY 14:22ff—Doesn't this contradict Moses' other command not to redeem animals with money?

PROBLEM: In Numbers 18:17, the law commands, "The firstborn of a cow, the firstborn of a sheep, or the firstborn of a goat you shall not redeem; they are holy." However, in Deuteronomy 14:25 they were instructed to "exchange it for money" if they desired. This is in direct conflict with the other instructions.

SOLUTION: Contrary to what some infer, the Deuteronomy passage does not actually allow them to buy a firstborn sheep or goat for their consumption, rather than give it to the Lord. On the contrary, it simply allows them to "exchange it for money," which would be more convenient for traveling, so they could "go to the place which the Lord your God chooses" (Deut. 14:25). In short, it was simply a divinely appointed accommodation to make it easier for the offerer. The money they received for it had to be taken to the divinely prescribed place and spent for the prescribed purpose.

DEUTERONOMY 14:26 — How can this passage permit the use of strong drink when other passages condemn its consumption?

PROBLEM: According to Deuteronomy 14:26, God permitted the purchase of wine or strong drink for conducting a feast before the Lord. However, Leviticus 10:8-9 forbids the use of strong drink by the priests, and passages like Proverbs 20:1, 23:29-35, and 31:4-5 seem to forbid the use of strong drink by all. How can this passage permit the use of strong drink when these other passages clearly condemn its use?

SOLUTION: It is clear that the Scriptures condemn the use of strong drink. For example, Leviticus 10:8-9 forbids the priest from drinking wine or strong drink when he is supposed to minister in the tent of meeting. Also, Proverbs forbids the use of wine or strong drink by kings or rulers, lest they pervert justice. Further, many passages warn of the deceitfulness of strong drink (Prov. 20:1) and condemn the use of it in general.

The word translated "eat" in Deut. 14:26 is a general term for consuming and may include the idea of drinking as well as eating solid food. However, the passage does not grant permission to drink strong drink or to drink to excess. Such action is specifically condemned in the NT as well as the OT. It was a common practice to dilute the strong drink (i.e., normally fermented grape juice) with about three parts water to one part wine. In this weaker form, imbibed with meals in moderation, there was no fear of excess. It is only in this sense that "wine" was permitted in the Scriptures and then only in a culture that was not alcoholic. While moderate drinking of this diluted wine may be permissible, in a culture shot through with alcoholism (such as ours), it is not profitable. Paul warns us in 1 Corinthians 6:12 that "All things are lawful for me, but all things are not helpful." Paul declared that "It is better not to eat meat or drink wine or to do anything else that will cause your brother to fall" (Rom. 14:21, NIV). God desires that our lives be influenced by the Spirit, not by the spirits.

The Bible is opposed to both strong drink and drunkenness (1 Cor. 6:9-10; Eph. 5:18). It pronounces woes on those who drink either strong drink or who drink in excess (Isa. 5:11; Amos 6:1, 6; Micah 2:11). Christian leaders are urged to be temperate (1 Tim. 3:3, 8). All are warned that too much alcohol is abhored by God (Amos 6:1-8).

And although moderate amounts were recommended for medicinal purposes (1 Tim. 5:23), nowhere does the Bible commend strong drink as a beverage. The only reference to taking "strong drink" is as a pain killer in extreme circumstances: "Give strong drink to him who is perishing" (Prov. 31:6).

Deuteronomy 14:26 should not be taken as an excuse to imbibe strong drink for several reasons. First, the stated command was not to *drink* it, but simply to *buy* it. There were other legitimate uses for owning alcohol, namely for cooking, healing (cf. Luke 10:34), and pain-killing. Second, the very next verse speaks only of "eating" food, not of drinking strong drink. Third, even if drinking is implied along with eating (v. 26), the Jews always diluted it with about three parts water to one part wine before they drank it in moderation with their meals. Done in this light form in such moderate amounts with food guaranteed them against the excesses known in today's alcoholic cultures. Fourth, it is still always wrong to use an unclear passage (such as Deuteronomy 14:26) to contradict all the clear ones (cited above) against strong drink.

In view of all these factors, it is best to conclude with the Apostle Paul, "It is good neither to eat meat nor drink wine nor do anything by which your brother stumbles or is offended or is made weak" (Rom. 14:21).

DEUTERONOMY 15:4 — How can this passage say there would be no poor among them when 15:11 says the poor will always be in the land?

PROBLEM: According to Deuteronomy 15:4, God promises that there will not be any poor among the people. However, 15:11 clearly states, "For the poor will never cease from the land." How can one passage say there would be no poor among the people while another says that the poor will never cease from the land?

SOLUTION: Careful consideration of the context shows that there is no contradiction here. The promise of verse 4 is conditioned upon the people "carefully obey[ing] the voice of the Lord your God, to observe with care all these commandments which I command you today" (Deut. 15:5). One of the commandments was that if there was a poor man in Israel, the people were not to harden their hearts. Rather, they were to open their hands and lend him money and goods sufficient for his needs — "whatever he needs" (Deut. 15:8). Obviously, if this commandment were to be fulfilled by the people, then, for every poor person there would be one who was not poor. Conversely, if they did not obey God's command to supply for all the needs of every poor person in the land, then the poor would never cease to be in the land. There is no contradiction here. God promised that if the people would obey His command to supply for the poor, then there would be no poor among them. Each time the circumstances overcame someone, so that they lost everything and were left in poverty, the people of the land would come to their aid and supply their needs.

Verse 11 can be understood as a statement that there would always be individuals in need of assistance and that others would be required to supply their needs. If the people obeyed God in this, He would so prosper the land that there would always be an abundant supply to enable some to care for the needs of others. Verse 11 may also be viewed as a prophetic pronouncement of Israel's failure to obey God and the consequent continual presence of the poor in the land. In either case, there is no contradiction.

DEUTERONOMY 16:5 — Was the passover lamb to be slain at home or at the sanctuary?

PROBLEM: Exodus 12:7 instructs that the passover lamb be killed in one's place of residence, but Deuteronomy declares that it should not be slain "within any of your gates."

SOLUTION: This is an example of a change in revelation (see Introduction "Mistake 17") because of a change in conditions. When the Passover instruction was first given (Ex. 12), they had no common sanctuary. Later in Deuteronomy, they did and were instructed to kill the passover lamb there "in the place where the Lord chooses to put His name" (Deut. 16:2).

DEUTERONOMY 18:10-22 — How can false prophets be distinguished from true prophets?

PROBLEM: The Bible contains many prophecies which it calls upon us to believe because they come from God. However, the Bible also acknowledges the existence of false prophets (Matt. 7:15). Indeed, many religions and cults claim to have prophets. Hence, the Bible exhorts believers to "test" those who claim to be prophets (1 John 4:1-3). But what is the difference between a false prophet and a true prophet of God?

SOLUTION: There are many tests for a false prophet. Several of them are listed in these very passages. Put in question form, the tests are:

1. Do they ever give false prophecies? (Deut. 18:21-22)
2. Do they contact departed spirits? (Deut. 18:11)
3. Do they use means of divination? (Deut. 18:11)
4. Do they involve mediums or witches? (Deut. 18:10)
5. Do they follow false gods or idols? (Ex. 20:3-4; Deut. 13:3)
6. Do they deny the deity of Jesus Christ? (Col. 2:8-9)
7. Do they deny the humanity of Jesus Christ? (1 John 4:1-2)
8. Do their prophecies shift the focus off Jesus Christ? (Rev. 19:10)
9. Do they advocate abstaining from certain foods and meats for spiritual reasons? (1 Tim. 4:3-4)
10. Do they deprecate or deny the need for marriage? (1 Tim. 4:3)
11. Do they promote immorality? (Jude 7)
12. Do they encourage legalistic self-denial? (Col. 2:16-23)

(See Geisler and Nix, *A General Introduction to the Bible,* Moody Press, 1986, 241–42.)

A positive answer to any of this is an indication that the prophet is not speaking for God. God does not speak or encourage anything that is contrary to His character and commands. And most certainly the God of truth does not give false prophecies.

DEUTERONOMY 18:15-18 — Is this a prophecy about the prophet Mohammed?

PROBLEM: God promised Moses here, "I will raise up for them [Israel] a Prophet like you from among their brethren, and will put My words in His mouth, and He shall speak to them all that I command Him" (v. 18). Muslims believe this prophecy is fulfilled in Mohammed, as the Koran claims when it refers to "The unlettered Prophet [Mohammed], Whom they find mentioned in their own [scriptures], in the Law and the Gospels" (Surah 7:157).

SOLUTION: This prophecy could not be a reference to Mohammed for several reasons. First, the term "brethren" refers to Israel, not to their Arabian antagonists. Why would God raise up for Israel a prophet from their enemies.

Second, in this very context, the term "brethren" means fellow Israelites. For the Levites were told "they shall have no inheritance among their brethren" (v. 2). Third, elsewhere in this book the term "brethren" also means fellow Israelites, not a foreigner. God told them to choose a king "from among your brethren," not a "foreigner." Israel has never chosen a non-Jewish king.

Fourth, Mohammed came from Ishmael, as even Muslims admit, and heirs to the Jewish throne came from Isaac. When Abraham prayed, "Oh that Ishmael might live before You!" God answered emphatically: "My covenant I will establish with Isaac . . ." (Gen. 17:21). Later God repeated: "In Isaac your seed shall be called" (Gen. 21:12).

Fifth, the Koran itself states that the prophetic line came through Isaac, not Ishmael: "And We bestowed on him Isaac and Jacob, and We established the Prophethood and the Scripture among his seed" (Surah 29:27). The Muslim scholar Yusuf Ali adds the word "Abraham" and changes the meaning as follows, "We gave (Abraham) Isaac and Jacob, and ordained Among his progeny Prophethood and Revelation." By adding Abraham, the father of Ishmael, he can include Mohammed, a descendent of Ishmael, in the prophetic line! But Abraham's name is not found in the original Arabic text.

Sixth, Jesus perfectly fulfilled this verse, since 1) He was from among His Jewish brethren (cf. Gal. 4:4). 2) He fulfilled Deuteronomy 18:18 perfectly: "He shall speak to them all that I [God] command Him." Jesus said, "I do nothing of Myself; but as My Father taught Me, I speak these things" (John 8:28). And, "I have not spoken on My own authority; but the Father who sent Me gave Me a command, what I should say and what I should speak" (John 12:49). 3) He called Himself a "prophet" (Luke 13:33), and the people considered Him a prophet (Matt. 21:11; Luke 7:16; 24:19; John 4:19; 6:14; 7:40; 9:17). As the Son of God, Jesus was prophet (speaking to men for God), priest (Heb. 7–10, speaking to God for men), and king (reigning over men for God, Rev. 19-20).

Finally, there are other characteristics of the "Prophet" to come that fit only Jesus, not Mohammed, such as, He spoke with God "face to face" and He performed "signs and wonders" (see comments on Deut. 34:10).

DEUTERONOMY 20:16-18 — How can the command for wholesale slaughter of innocent lives be justified?

(See comments on Josh. 6:21.)

DEUTERONOMY 20:16-18 — Were the captives to be spared or killed?

PROBLEM: In Deuteronomy 20:11, 15, Moses commanded the Israelites to spare the lives of their captives and make them servants. But only a few verses later he instructs them to "let nothing that breathes remain alive" (v. 16).

SOLUTION: The *general rule* was to make captives of the people conquered. Only in the *specific case* of the "seven nations" of Canaan were they to exterminate them (see comments on Josh. 6:21). This was because of their "abominations" which were so obnoxious to God that the land "vomits out its inhabitants" (Lev. 18:25).

DEUTERONOMY 22:5 – Why did God call it an abomination for men to dress like women and vice versa?

PROBLEM: What is wrong with wearing the clothes of the opposite sex? Isn't this just a matter of cultural preference, with nothing intrinsically immoral about it?

SOLUTION: God's design here was apparently to make it possible to distinguish one sex from the other. Without distinctive clothes and length of hair (see comments on 1 Cor. 11:14), the sexes could be more easily confused and the bounds of social and moral impropriety would have been more easily transgressed. Of course, which clothes are masculine and which are feminine will be determined in large part by the culture. But whatever the case, transvestites were hereby excluded.

DEUTERONOMY 22:13-21 – Why is the method of testing chastity different here than in Numbers 5?

PROBLEM: The Numbers text instructed that chastity be tested by drinking bitter water and seeing if the woman's stomach would swell (see comments on Numbers 5:13-22). But, Deuteronomy 22 provides the blood stained sheet from the wedding night as evidence of virginity (cf. vv. 14-17).

SOLUTION: The two situations are different. The Numbers passage is a test for alleged unchastity *after* marriage. And the Deuteronomy text deals with alleged unfaithfulness *before* marriage.

DEUTERONOMY 23:17 – Was homosexuality condemned because it was connected with idolatry?

PROBLEM: Some argue that the biblical condemnations used against homosexuality were because of the temple cult-prostitutes who were associated with these idolatrous practices (Deut. 23:17). They insist that homosexuality as such is not thereby condemned, but only homosexual acts that are associated with idolatry, such as, the shrine prostitute (cf. 1 Kings 14:24).

SOLUTION: Homosexual practices are not condemned in the Bible simply because they were connected with idolatry. This is made evident by several things. First, the condemnations on homosexual practices are often given apart from any explicit idolatrous practice (Lev. 18:22; Rom. 1:26-27).

Second, when homosexuality is associated with idolatry (such as in temple cult-prostitution), it is not essentially connected. It is only a concomitant sin, but not an equivalent one.

Third, sexual unfaithfulness is often used as an illustration of idolatry (e.g., Hosea 3:1; 4:12), but it has no necessary connection with it. Idolatry is a spiritual form of immorality. But immorality is wrong not only if it is done in connection with idol worship.

Fourth, idolatry may lead to immorality (cf. Rom. 1:22-27), but they are different sins.

Fifth, even the Ten Commandments distinguishes between idolatry (First Table of the Law, Ex. 20:3-4) and sexual sins (Second Table, Ex. 20:14, 17).

DEUTERONOMY 23:19 — Why was usury (interest) forbidden only on some but not on all Jews?

PROBLEM: In Exodus 22:25, lending money with interest was only forbidden with the poor. But, here in Deuteronomy 23:19 it is forbidden with any other Jew. This raises two problems. First, why the change? Second, why the partiality?

SOLUTION: First, the change from Exodus to Deuteronomy was necessary because of the change in circumstances. Perhaps it was because it became difficult, in the process of time, to determine who was to be considered poor. Hence, it was deemed necessary to extend the prohibition to all Hebrews. Otherwise, no poor person would ever have gotten a loan, since loans would only have been made to those who could pay interest on it.

Of course, usury was not forbidden with strangers (non-Jews), but only with brothers (other Jews). If this seems partial, it is only because the laws forbidding usury on the poor (or one's brothers) were a divinely enjoined act of *benevolence,* not strictly a matter of business. When it comes to doing *business,* one is entitled to a reasonable profit on his investment. Since the risk of loss (from non-payment) must be covered, it is just to pay the investor an appropriate amount for his risk.

DEUTERONOMY 24:1-4 — Is Moses' teaching on divorce contrary to the teaching of Jesus and Paul?

PROBLEM: According to Deuteronomy 24:1-4, a man was allowed to divorce his wife if he had found her to be unfaithful. However, according to the teaching of Jesus in Mark 10:1-12, and the teaching of Paul in 1 Corinthians 7:10-16, it seems that a man is not permitted to divorce his wife and remarry. Is the teaching in Deuteronomy contrary to the teaching of Jesus and Paul?

SOLUTION: It would be a mistake to assume that the statements of Moses here gave divine sanction to divorce. The passage presents a hypothetical situation which was likely to happen among the people. It simply says that if a man divorces his wife because of some uncleanness in her, and if she remarries, and if her new husband dies or divorces her, it is unlawful for the first husband to take her back. This is not a sanction of divorce. Rather, it is an acknowledgement of the fact of divorce and the implementation of regulation concerning remarriage.

As Jesus said in Mark 10:5, Moses allowed divorce and gave the people this precept because of the hardness of their hearts, but this is not God's ideal. God's ideal for marriage was that there be a lifetime commitment between husband and wife. There is no contradiction here between Moses' teaching and the teaching of Jesus and Paul. Moses simply recognizes the fact of divorce, while Jesus and Paul present God's ideal for marriage, as it was from the beginning.

DEUTERONOMY 24:16 — How can this passage state that children will not be killed for the sins of their parents when there are examples of this in other passages?

PROBLEM: Deuteronomy 24:16 clearly states that the children shall not be put to death for the sins of their fathers. However, in 2 Samuel 12:15-18, the child of David and Bathsheba died as a result of David's sins. How can this passage say that the children will not be put to death for the sins of their fathers if this is what happened to David's child?

SOLUTION: First, the passage in Deuteronomy is a precept laid down by which the legal system of Israel would function once they were established in the land. It was not the right of the human courts to exact capital punishment from the children of guilty parents if the children were not personally guilty of the crime. However, that which restricts the power of human courts does not restrict the right or authority of God.

Second, the Scripture does not indicate that David's child was being punished for David's sin. Rather, the Bible indicates that the death of the child was David's punishment (2 Sam. 12:14). If it is thought that allowing the child to die was an unjust way to punish David, it must be remembered that David trusted in the righteousness of God when he said in faith, "I shall go to him, but he shall not return to me" (2 Sam. 12:23). David trusted that God had taken his child to heaven and that he would be with the child when he died. God always acts according to His righteousness, and the restrictions of such precepts as this are designed to prevent men from perverting justice.

DEUTERONOMY 30:6 — Does God circumcise the heart or was Israel to circumcise their own hearts?

PROBLEM: According to this verse, "the Lord your God will circumcise your heart." However, earlier in the same book Moses called on Israel to "circumcise the foreskin of your heart, and be stiff-necked no longer" (Deut. 10:16). But how can we have it both ways?

SOLUTION: The truth is that there is both an *active* and *passive* role for humans in salvation. We are active in *receiving* the gift, but we were not active in the *giving* of the gift. We actively *submit* our hearts to God, but we are not active in *saving* our own hearts. In short, while we are active in receiving or accepting salvation, we had absolutely nothing to do with providing or accomplishing salvation. Even though the one rescued is active in receiving the lifeline, nonetheless, he is passive in being rescued by the rescuer who pulls in the rope. Likewise, we actively submit to the life-saving operation, but we are passive in receiving the physician's skillful surgery that saves our life. The situation can be summarized as follows:

OUR ACTIVE ROLE IN SALVATION	OUR PASSIVE ROLE IN SALVATION
Reception of the gift	Giving of the gift
Submitting to salvation	Being saved
Believing	Being redeemed
Accepting salvation	Accomplishing salvation

DEUTERONOMY 32:13-14 – How could there be sufficient pasture for the herds of 2 million people in a desert?

PROBLEM: The Bible informs us that the children of Israel wandered in the "desert" for 40 years (cf. Ex. 19:2; 23:31). They numbered over 600,000 adult men (Ex. 12:37; Num. 1:1-4:49), which would be a total population of some 2 million. But, Deuteronomy 32:13-14 speaks of there being plenty of produce for them and their flocks, which seems highly improbable for this many people and flocks in a "desert."

SOLUTION: Several things should be kept in mind. First of all, the Hebrew word "desert" does not imply the total desolation that it may connote today. It can be translated "wilderness." There were rivers and pastures in this wilderness.

Second, there is good evidence, even from modern times, that this wilderness had far more water and vegetation than it presently does, as is demonstrated by archaeological exploration of the remains of previous civilizations in that area.

Finally, God Himself provided for all their needs in the wilderness in several ways:

1. God provided them ample food (manna) for the entire 40 years (Ex. 16:35).

2. He also gave water "abundantly" for them and their flocks (Num. 20:11).

3. Since they came with "a great deal of livestock" (Ex. 12:38), they would naturally have plenty of milk to drink.

4. Since the land was apparently more arid than today, there were undoubtedly natural rivers, springs, and pastures as well.

5. By commerce with the surrounding nations (Midianites, Edomites, and Ishmaelites), they could obtain other needed things with the large amount of silver and gold they took from Egypt (cf. Ex. 12:35-36).

DEUTERONOMY 33:2 – Is this a prediction of the Prophet Mohammed?

PROBLEM: Many Islamic scholars believe this verse predicts three separate visitations of God—one on "Sinai" to Moses, another to "Seir" through Jesus, and a third in "Paran" (Arabia) through Mohammed who came to Mecca with an army of "ten thousand."

SOLUTION: First of all, this contention can be easily answered by looking at a Bible map. Paran and Seir are near Egypt in the Sinai peninsula (cf. Gen. 14:6; Num. 10:12; 12:16-13:3; Deut. 1:1), not in Palestine where Jesus ministered. Nor was Paran near Mecca, but hundreds of miles away near southern Palestine in the north eastern Sinai.

Furthermore, this verse is speaking of the "LORD" (not Mohammed) coming. And He is coming with "ten thousands of saints," not ten thousand soldiers, as Mohammed did. There is absolutely no basis in this text for the Muslim contention.

Finally, this prophecy is said to be one "with which Moses the man of God blessed the children of Israel before his death" (v. 1). If it were a prediction about Islam, which has been a constant enemy of Israel, it could scarcely have been a blessing to Israel. In fact, the chapter goes on to pronounce a blessing on each of the tribes of Israel by God, who "will thrust out the enemy" (v. 27).

DEUTERONOMY 34:1ff — How could Moses have written this chapter which records his own death?

PROBLEM: Deuteronomy 34 is a record of the death of Moses in the valley of Moab. However, the Book of Deuteronomy has traditionally been held to be the work of Moses. How could Moses have written this chapter that records his own death and burial?

SOLUTION: First, it is not necessary to conclude that Moses could not have written his own obituary. It is entirely within the power of God to reveal the future in minute detail (cf. Daniel 2; 7; 9; 12). It is not unreasonable to believe that the Spirit of God, through Moses, penned this final chapter. Whether we take this chapter as from the pen of Moses or from the pen of Joshua or some other author, it does not at all imply that Moses was not the author of the text of Deuteronomy or the other four books of the Pentateuch.

Second, it is entirely reasonable to assume that someone, perhaps Joshua, added this final chapter to the books of Moses as a fitting conclusion to the life of this great man of God. It is not at all an uncommon practice for someone to add an obituary to the end of a work by a great man. This would be similar to the practice of one author writing a preface to the work of another author.

DEUTERONOMY 34:10 — Was Moses unparalleled among prophets or were others equal to him?

PROBLEM: This text claims that "since then there has not arisen in Israel a prophet like Moses." However, there were others, like Elijah and Elisha, who got revelations from God and performed miracles like Moses did (cf. 1 Kings 17:22; 2 Kings 1:10; 2:14; 4:34).

SOLUTION: First of all, this claim is qualified by the phrase "since then," which refers to the time these words were written, possibly by Joshua, his immediate successor (see comments on Deuteronomy 34:1ff). Further, even if one extends the time to a much later period, there is still another qualification that makes Moses unique. It adds "whom the Lord knew face to face" (v. 10). This has not been true of any mere human prophet since Moses' day. Moses was the great lawgiver, whom God spoke to directly and intimately, in a manner not repeated since Moses' day until the coming of Jesus, who was face to face with God (John 1:1).

DEUTERONOMY 34:10 — Does this verse support the Muslim claim that Jesus could not be the predicted prophet (of Deut. 18:18)?

PROBLEM: This verse claims that "there arose not a prophet since in Israel like unto Moses." (KJV) Muslims argue that this proves that the predicted prophet could not be an Israelite, but was Mohammed instead.

SOLUTION: In response, several things should be noted. First, the "since" means since Moses' death to the time this last chapter was written, probably by Joshua (see comments on Deut. 34:1ff). Even if Deuteronomy was written much later, as some critics believe, it still was composed many centuries before the time of Christ and, therefore, would not eliminate Him. Second, Jesus was the perfect fulfillment of this prediction of the prophet to come, not Mohammed (see comments on Deut. 18:15-18). Third, this could not refer to Mohammed, since the prophet to come was like Moses who did "all the signs and wonders which the Lord sent" (Deut. 34:11). Mohammed by his own confession did not perform signs and wonders like Moses and Jesus did (see Surah 17:90-93). Finally, the prophet to come was like Moses who spoke to God "face to face" (Deut. 34:10). Mohammed never even claimed to speak to God directly, but got his revelations through angels (cf. Surah 2:97). Jesus, on the other hand, like Moses, was a direct mediator (1 Tim. 2:5; Heb. 9:15) who communicated directly with God (cf. John 1:18; 12:49).

JOSHUA

JOSHUA 2:4-5 — How could God bless Rahab for lying?

PROBLEM: When the spies came to Jericho, they sought refuge in the house of Rahab. When the king of Jericho commanded Rahab to bring out the men, she lied saying that the men had already gone and that she did not know where they went. However, when Israel finally destroyed Jericho, Rahab and all her family were saved alive. How could God bless Rahab for lying?

SOLUTION: Some argue that it is not clear that God blessed Rahab for lying. God certainly saved Rahab and blessed her for protecting the spies and assisting in the overthrow of Jericho. However, nowhere does the Bible explicitly say that God blessed Rahab for lying. God could have blessed her in spite of her lie, not because of it. Actually, Rahab's act of protecting the spies was a demonstration of great faith in the God of Israel. She firmly believed that God would destroy Jericho, and she exhibited that belief by siding with Israel against the people of Jericho when she protected the spies from being discovered.

Others insist that Rahab was faced with a real moral conflict. It may have been impossible for her to both save the spies and tell the truth to the soldiers of the king. If so, God would not hold Rahab responsible for this unavoidable moral conflict. Certainly a person cannot be held responsible for not keeping a lesser law in order to keep a higher obligation. The Bible commands obedience to the government (Rom. 13:1; Titus 3:1; 1 Peter 2:13), but there are many examples of justified civil disobedience when the government attempts to compel unrighteousness (Ex. 5; Dan. 3, 6; Rev. 13). The case of the Hebrew midwives lying to save the lives of the male children is perhaps the clearest example (see comments on Ex. 1:15-21).

JOSHUA 3:17 — Did Israel cross the Jordan here or not?

PROBLEM: According to Joshua 3:17, the people crossed over the Jordan on dry ground. However, 4:5, 10-11 indicate that they had not yet crossed the river. How can these verses be reconciled?

SOLUTION: In 3:17, Joshua records that the priests who were carrying the ark of the covenant stood in the middle of the river while the people crossed over on dry ground. Chapter 4 begins with the statement, "And it came to pass, when all the people had completely crossed over the Jordan, that the Lord spoke to Joshua." The passage then goes on to describe how Joshua, according to the command of the Lord, directed twelve men, one from each tribe, to go back to the spot where the priests were still standing with the ark in order to dig up twelve stones from the midst of the river bed. Verses 10 and 11 describe how the priests, who were carrying the ark of the covenant, finally left their spot in the middle of the river bed after everything had been completed which the Lord had commanded Joshua.

JOSHUA 6:1ff — Hasn't archaeology shown that the account of the conquest of Jericho is inaccurate?

PROBLEM: Joshua 6 records the conquest and destruction of the city of Jericho. If this account is accurate, it would seem that modern archaeological excavations would have turned up evidence of this monumental event. However, haven't these investigations proven that the account in Joshua is inaccurate?

SOLUTION: For many years the prevailing view of critical scholars has been that there was no city of Jericho at the time Joshua was supposed to have entered Canaan. Although earlier investigations by the notable British archaeologist Kathleen Kenyon confirmed the existence of the ancient city of Jericho, and its sudden destruction, her findings led her to conclude that the city could have existed no later than ca. 1550 B.C. This date is much too early for Joshua and the children of Israel to have been party to its demise.

However, recent reexamination of these earlier findings, and a closer look at current evidence indicates that not only was there a city that fits the biblical chronology, but that its remains coincide with the biblical account of the destruction of this walled fortress. In a paper published in *Biblical Archaeology Review* (March/April, 1990), Bryant G. Wood, visiting professor to the department of Near Eastern Studies at the University of Toronto, has presented evidence that the biblical report is accurate. His detailed investigation has yielded the following conclusions:

1. That the city which once existed on this site was strongly fortified, corresponding to the biblical record in Joshua 2:5, 7, 15; 6:5, 20.

2. That the ruins give evidence that the city was attacked after harvesttime in the spring, corresponding to Joshua 2:6, 3:15, 5:10.

3. That the inhabitants did not have the opportunity to flee with their foodstuffs from the invading army, as reported in Joshua 6:1.

4. That the siege was short, not allowing the inhabitants to consume the food which was stored in the city, as Joshua 6:15 indicates.

5. That the walls were leveled in such a way to provide access into the city for the invaders, as Joshua 6:20 records.

6. That the city was not plundered by the invaders, according to God's instructions in Joshua 6:17-18.

7. That the city was burned after the walls had been destroyed, just as Joshua 6:24 says.

JOSHUA 6:21 – How can the total destruction of Jericho be morally justified?

PROBLEM: This passage states that the Israelites "utterly destroyed all that was in the city, both man and woman, young and old, ox and sheep and donkey, with the edge of the sword." But how can such a ruthless destruction of innocent life and property be justified?

SOLUTION: First, the Canaanites were far from "innocent." The description of their sins in Leviticus 18 is vivid: "The land is defiled; therefore I visit the punishment of its iniquity upon it, and the land vomits out its inhabitants" (v. 25). They were cancerously immoral, "defiled" with every kind of "abomination," including child sacrifice (vv. 21, 24, 26).

Second, it must be remembered that God had given the people of Palestine over 400 years to repent of their wickedness. The people of that land had every opportunity to turn from their wickedness. According to Genesis 15:16, God told Abraham that in 400 years the descendants of Abraham would return to inherit this land, but that the iniquity of the people was not yet full. This prophetic statement indicated that God would not destroy the people of the land, including those who dwelt in Jericho, until their sins were such that their guilt merited their complete destruction in judgment.

Third, as for the killing of the little children, several things should be noted. (1) Given the cancerous state of the society into which they were born, they had no chance to avoid its fatal pollution. (2) Children who die before the age of accountability go to heaven (see comments on 2 Sam. 12:23). This was an act of God's mercy to their souls to take them into His holy presence from such an unholy environment. (3) God is sovereign over life (Deut. 32:39; Job 1:21) and can order its end according to His will and in view of the creature's ultimate good.

Fourth, Joshua and the people of Israel were acting according to the direct command of God, not on their own initiative. The destruction of Jericho was carried out by the army of Israel, but the army of Israel was the instrument of judgment upon the sins of these people by the righteous Judge of all the earth. Consequently, anyone who would question the justification of this act is questioning God's justice.

Fifth, it was necessary to completely exterminate any trace of the city and its people. If anything had remained, except that which was taken into the treasure house of the Lord, there would have always been the threat of heathen influence to pull the people away from the pure worship of the Lord. Sometimes radical surgery is required to completely eliminate a deadly cancer from the body.

JOSHUA 7:15, 24 — Was God just in punishing Achan's family along with him?

PROBLEM: When Achan committed a capital crime against God, the Bible says the children were stoned along with their parents, and then "they burned them with fire after they had stoned them with stones" (v. 25). Yet the Scriptures insist that God does not punish the children for the sins of their parent (Ezek. 18:20), nor destroy the righteous with the wicked (Gen. 18:23).

SOLUTION: There are two responses to this problem.

Some have argued that Achan's children were not given capital punishment with him, but merely brought along so that the event could be an example to them. In favor of this, several things are offered. First, it is noted that nowhere does the text say anyone beside Achan committed the crime. God speaks of the guilty as "he who is taken with the accursed thing" (v. 15). Also, Achan confesses alone: "I have sinned" (v. 20) and "I coveted" (v. 21).

Second, the text declares that "Israel stoned him" (v. 25). The reference to "burning them" (v. 25) alludes to the silver, gold, and garment he had taken (see vv. 21 and 24).

Third, stoning Achan's family for his crime would be a clear violation of the OT law which says emphatically that "the son shall not bear the guilt of the father" (Ezek. 18:20).

The most serious problem with this position is that verse 25 says, "they burned *them* with fire after they had stoned *them* with stones." Stoning an inanimate object does not seem to make good sense. Rather, it seems to be a reference to Achan and his family.

Another view acknowledges that Achan's family was stoned with him, but argues that they were complicit with his crime, so they were being punished for their own sins, not his. This position notes the following:

First, it is argued that it is unlikely that Achan could have accomplished this deed and hidden the stolen material in the family tent without their knowing something about it.

Second, the guilt of the family is implied in their very punishment. Since it was forbidden to punish someone for another's sin, the family must have sinned with him or else they would not have been punished with him.

Third, God had the right to take life, since it is He who gave it (Deut. 32:39). Job rightly declared: "The Lord gave, and the Lord has taken away; Blessed be the name of the Lord" (Job 1:21).

Fourth, there is no reference to small children in the family, but even if there were, God has the sovereign right to take them and sometimes does in sickness without implying their guilt. Further, if the parents were killed, then there would be no parents to care for them. It would be more merciful for God to take them into His direct care. This is so because children who die before the age of accountability are saved (see comments on 2 Sam. 12:23); there is no problem about their eternal destiny.

JOSHUA 8:30 — How can Joshua's altar on Mount Ebal be justified when the Bible clearly condemns the building of "high places"?

PROBLEM: Joshua 8:30 records that Joshua built an altar to the Lord on Mt. Ebal and offered burnt offerings to the Lord and sacrificed peace offerings upon that altar. However, many passages indicate that the construction of high places was condemned by God (1 Kings 12:31; 15:14; etc.). How can Joshua's altar be justified in light of God's condemnation of high places?

SOLUTION: The high places which were later to be condemned by God were not altars built to the Lord or built according to the requirements laid down in Deuteronomy 27:5-6. Those high places were usually elevated sites that were employed in the worship of false gods. By contrast, Joshua 8 states that the altar was built "as Moses the servant of the Lord had commanded the children of Israel" (Josh. 8:31). In fact, Deut. 27:2-8 records that Moses commanded that the people of Israel build an altar at Mt. Ebal as a sign of their commitment to the covenant and to the commandments of the Lord. Joshua's construction of this altar was not only in keeping with the dictates of how an altar should be built, but was in fact done in obedience to the command of Moses.

JOSHUA 9:1ff — Why did Israel honor their contract with the Gibeonites once they discovered they had been deceived?

PROBLEM: Joshua 9 records how the Gibeonites deceived Israel into thinking that they were not actually people from the land which God had commanded Israel to destroy, but were from a far country. Thus, Joshua and all Israel entered into a contract not to destroy them. However, when they discovered that the Gibeonites had deceived them and were actually people whom God had commanded Israel to destroy, why did Israel not ignore this contract and exterminate the Gibeonites as God had originally commanded?

SOLUTION: Perhaps under different circumstances the contract which Joshua and Israel had made would have been nullified by the discovery of fraud. However, this contract had been entered into on the basis of a solemn oath sworn in the name of the Lord God of Israel (v. 18). This unfortunate situation befell Israel because "they did not ask counsel of the Lord" (v. 14). Because they had bound themselves by their oath in the name of the Lord, they could not break the covenant they had made with the Gibeonites. Although the Gibeonites did become the servants of the people of Israel, they were also a constant source of trouble throughout Israel's history.

JOSHUA 10:12-14 — How is it possible for the sun to stand still for a whole day?

PROBLEM: During the battle with the kings of the land, God gave Israel the power to overcome their enemies. As the armies of the people of the land fled from before Israel, Joshua sought the Lord to cause the sun to stand still so that they might have sufficient daylight to complete the destruction of their enemies. But how could the sun stand still in the midst of the heaven for a whole day?

SOLUTION: First, it is not necessary to conclude that the earth's rotation was totally halted. Verse 13 states that the sun "did not hasten to go down for about a whole day." This could indicate that the earth's rotation was not completely halted, but that it was retarded to such a degree that the sun did not set for about a whole day. Or, it is possible that God caused the light of the sun to refract through some cosmic "mirror" so that it could be seen a day longer.

Even if the earth's rotation was completely stopped, we must remember that God is not only capable of halting the rotation of the earth for a whole day, but He is also able to prevent any possible catastrophic effects that might result from the cessation of the earth's rotation. Although we do not necessarily know *how* God brought about this miraculous event, we know *that* He did it.

Finally, the Bible speaks in everyday observational language. So the sun did not *actually* stop; it only *appeared* to do so (see Introduction "Mistake 12").

JOSHUA 11:18 — Was Canaan conquered quickly or only gradually?

PROBLEM: This verse declares that "Joshua made war a long time with all those kings." But earlier (in Joshua 10:42) it affirms that "all these kings and their land Joshua took at one time."

SOLUTION: These two texts refer to different kings at different times. The first passage speaks of the southern campaigns which went rapidly. But the other verse has reference to the northern battles which took much longer.

JOSHUA 12:1-24 — Were these kings defeated here or not until later?

PROBLEM: The text declares that "these are the kings of the land whom the children of Israel defeated." However, many of these cities were not captured until later (cf. Josh. 15:63; 17:12; Jud. 1:22, 29).

SOLUTION: There is a difference between *defeating a king's army* on the field of battle and later *destroying his capital city*. Once defeated in battle, the king and his remaining troops would retreat to their stronghold where it was much more difficult to root them out. *Sudden victory* and *permanent vanquishing* are two different things. So understood, there is absolutely no contradiction between these texts.

JOSHUA 13:9-12 — What was the correct eastern boundary of the Promised Land?

PROBLEM: God promised Abraham, "To your descendants I have given this land, from the river of Egypt to the great . . . River Euphrates" (Gen. 15:18; cf. Deut. 11:24). However, when Joshua divided the land Israel inherited, the boundaries listed do not mention the Euphrates, but cities to the west of it (Josh. 13:9-12).

SOLUTION: Joshua is simply dividing up the land that was *taken* by the Israelites, not everything that was *given* to them. Even though Joshua's forces conquered the land *as a whole* (cf. Josh. 11:23), they obviously did not occupy all the land in *particular* (cf. Jud. 1:27-36). Much later in David's day they were still extending their border toward the Euphrates (2 Sam. 8:3). This reveals that they understood the repeated promise (cf. Gen. 15:18; Deut. 1:7; 11:24) to include land up to the Euphrates as their eastern border. Indeed, even Joshua mentions this same border when he repeats the promise to Israel (Josh. 1:4).

JOSHUA 18:28 — Was Jerusalem in the territory of Benjamin or in Judah?

PROBLEM: Joshua 15:8 lists Jerusalem in Judah, but Joshua 18:28 says it is in Benjamin.

SOLUTION: Both are true. Some scholars also point to a Jewish tradition that held the altars and sanctuary were in Benjamin, while the courts of the temple were in Judah. Be that as it may, the city was actually within the limits of Benjamin's territory, but it was also on the border of Judah's land. So it may properly be described as being part of both.

JOSHUA 19:2-7 — Were these cities in the territory of Judah or of Simeon?

PROBLEM: Here they are listed in the land of Simeon, but in Joshua 15:26-32 they are in Judah.

SOLUTION: The inheritance of Simeon fell within the boundaries of Judah (Josh. 19:1, 9). So it was proper to speak of them as in either place.

JOSHUA 23:16 — Was God's promise of the land to Israel conditional or unconditional?

PROBLEM: When God gave the Promised Land to Abraham (Gen. 12–15), Isaac (Gen. 26), and Jacob (Gen. 46), there were no conditions. It was an unconditional covenant ("I will bless you") with no conditions ("If you do such and such") in which God swore by His own unchangeable nature (cf. Heb. 6:13-18). However, later both Moses (Deut. 31:16-17) and Joshua (23:16) speak of God expelling Israel from the land if they sinned against God.

SOLUTION: There are two ways Bible scholars attempt to respond to this criticism: spiritually and literally.

Spiritual Fulfillment in the Church. Some claim this promise does not find any fulfillment in literal Israel, but in spiritual Israel, the church. They appeal to the verse which calls believers the "Israel of God" (Gal. 6:16) and the spiritual "seed" of Abraham (Gal. 3:29). They point to Romans 11 which says that Israel was "broken off" because of their rejection of their Messiah (v. 17). Thus, while literal Israel sinned, God nevertheless will keep the Abrahamic covenant with NT believers who were unconditionally elected in Christ (Eph. 1:4).

Literal Future Fulfillment in Israel. Other Bible scholars take the eternal land promises to Abraham's descendants literally, pointing to a future fulfillment of these when Christ returns to earth to reign (cf. Matt. 19:28; Rev. 19–20). In support of their position they note the following points.

First, the promises of possessing the land of Palestine "forever" (see Gen. 13:15) have never been fulfilled.

Second, unlike the Mosaic covenant (Ex. 19:1-8), this was an unconditional covenant based on God's unchangeable character (cf. Gal. 3:18; Heb. 6:17-18). Thus God must literally fulfill it to the very people to whom He promised it, or else God would have reneged on an unconditional promise — in which case, He is not God.

Third, the NT church does not fulfill the *literal land promises* to Israel, but only the promises to receive the spiritual blessings of salvation through the seed of Abraham, who is Christ (cf. Gal. 3:16, 29).

Fourth, the NT could not be the fulfillment of these unconditional promises to Abraham's descendants because they speak of them as yet future. Paul not only spoke of the nation Israel being cut off, but of their being "grafted in again" and being "saved" (Rom. 11:23, 26). Indeed, the Book of Revelation speaks of "one hundred and forty-four thousand of all the tribes of . . . Israel" being reinstated in the end times (Rev.

7:4). Those who advocate this position also note that the word "tribe" is never used in a spiritual sense in Scripture.

Finally, Scripture makes a clear distinction between covenants that are unconditional (e.g., the Abrahamic) and those that are conditional (e.g., the Mosaic law). Paul told the Galatians clearly that "if the inheritance is of the law, it is no longer of promise; but God gave it to Abraham by promise" (Gal. 3:18). In view of this literal interpretation, all threats of non-fulfillment of a covenant refer either to the conditional covenant made with Moses (Ex. 19) or else they are merely exhortations about relating to temporary delays in fulfillment of the Abrahamic covenant (Josh. 23:16).

JOSHUA 24:26 — Was the sanctuary originally at Shechem or at Shiloh?

PROBLEM: According to Joshua 24:25-26 (cf. v. 1), the sanctuary was at Shechem. But earlier (1 Sam. 3:21; 4:3), it was said to be in Shiloh.

SOLUTION: The term "sanctuary" (*miqdash*) here simply means "holy place" or "sacred spot." It need not refer to the "tabernacle" (*mishkan*) where the ark of the covenant rested, but simply to a sacred location, such as one consecrated by Abraham (cf. Gen. 12:6-7) and Jacob (Gen. 33:19-20; 35:2-3). The tabernacle was at Shiloh, as Joshua himself acknowledged earlier in this same book (Josh. 18:1).

JUDGES 1:20 – Did Caleb kill the sons of Anak or just expel them?

PROBLEM: In Judges 1:10, the three sons of Anak were "killed" by Judah. But, in verse 20 it says they were merely "expelled" from the land, which is what Joshua 15:14 says as well. Which was it?

SOLUTION: There are two basic views in response to this problem. One view assumes that these two passages refer to the same event, while the other view maintains that they refer to different events.

The Same Event. According to this position, the children of Judah were led by Caleb. Thus, one passage could refer to the men who did it and the other to their leader. Further, the Hebrew word for "expel" can mean to "drive out" or "destroy." In this sense they were expelled not only from the land of Judah, but also from the land of the living.

Different Events. According to this view, the first chapter of Judges does not follow in chronological order, being almost verbatim from Joshua 15:13-19. If so, the events would be as follows: when Joshua conquered the land, the sons of Anak were simply "expelled," only to return when Joshua turned elsewhere. Later, after the initial campaigns, Judah settled the land and Caleb and his men actually "killed" them. Either position would resolve the difficulty.

JUDGES 1:28ff – Were the Canaanites destroyed or merely subjugated?

PROBLEM: Joshua 10:40 declares that "Joshua conquered all the land . . . he left none remaining, but utterly destroyed all that breathed, as the Lord God of Israel had commanded." But only a short time later, when the people occupied the land they had conquered, Judges 1:28 says Israel "did not completely drive them out," but "put the Canaanites under tribute." But if they had been utterly destroyed, then how could they still be there a few years later?

SOLUTION: It seems evident that Joshua at first only conquered the land *as a whole,* but did not literally destroy *every part* of it. He first swept through and gained the *major* victories, leaving the *minor* battles for the later settlers to fight. So, "utterly destroying all that breathed" is either a figure of speech for his general victory or a hyperbole for his complete success. However, even if it is understood more literally, it is qualified by the phrase "left none remaining" (Josh. 10:40). This says nothing about those who fled only to return after Joshua's armies turned northward to fight other battles. No doubt, in this interim, many of the Canaanites returned to occupy their homes and to be a continual thorn in Israel's flesh.

JUDGES 3:20-21 — Does the Bible approve of assassinations?

PROBLEM: The Bible says "the Lord raised up a deliverer" (Jud. 3:15) for Israel over their oppressor, King Eglon of Moab. Then it records how Ehud "took the dagger from his right thigh, and thrust it into his [Eglon's] belly" (v. 21). How can the God who forbids murder (Ex. 20:13) condone a brutal assassination like this?

SOLUTION: This incident, and others like it (cf. Jud. 4:21), are a good example of the principle that "Not everything *recorded* in the Bible is *approved* by the Bible" (see Introduction). First of all, the text does not say that God approved of this evil act. It simply states that it occurred.

Second, the fact that God had "raised up" Ehud does not justify everything he did. God "raised up" Pharaoh too (cf. Rom. 9:17), but God nevertheless judged Pharaoh for his sins (cf. Ex. 12).

Third, there are many sins *contained* in the Bible which are not *condoned* by it. These include Abraham's lie (Gen. 20), David's sin with Bathsheba (2 Sam. 11), and Solomon's polygamy (1 Kings 11).

Fourth, while assassinations as such are wrong, God reserves the right to life (Deut. 32:39; Job.1:21). Should He desire to take a life He gives, He has the right to do so through any instrument He may desire, natural or artificial (see comments on Josh. 6:21).

JUDGES 4:21 — Does God condone assassinations?

(See comments on Jud. 3:20-21.)

JUDGES 4:21 – Was Sisera lying down when Jael killed him, or was he upright as Judges 5:27 seems to indicate?

PROBLEM: According to Judges 4:21, Sisera was lying down fast asleep when Jael approached him softly and drove the tent peg through his temple and into the ground. However, Judges 5:27 seems to indicate that Sisera fell down after Jael pierced his head with the tent peg. Was Sisera lying down or was he upright when Jael killed him?

SOLUTION: The poetic description of Judges 5:27 can be understood to describe possible convulsions which Sisera's body exhibited after the blow to the head. Also, the term "fell" is frequently used in a figurative sense to indicate someone's demise. This would be especially likely in the poetic structure of chapter 5. The poem is not describing a literal falling down to the ground, as if Sisera was upright. Rather, it is poetically picturing Sisera's demise. At the hand of this maiden, the mighty Sisera, captain of the army of the Canaanite king, has fallen. There is no contradiction here, merely the difference between historical narrative accurately reporting the events in a literal manner, and poetic expression accurately reporting the events in a poetic figure.

JUDGES 5:6ff – How can Jael be commended for such a cruel act of murder?

PROBLEM: The story of the death of Sisera at the hands of Jael depicts a violent and cruel murder (Jud. 4:21). However, the song of Deborah recorded in Judges 5 commends Jael for killing Sisera. How can Jael be praised for committing such a violent murder?

SOLUTION: First, it should be remembered that Sisera was a mighty warrior. When he came to Jael's tent, Jael was hardly in a position to refuse him entrance. Although it was Jael who went out to meet Sisera to encourage him to find refuge in her tent, it is clear from 4:17 that he was already planning to go to Jael's tent.

Second, Sisera was a cruel warrior who had viciously oppressed God's people. If Sisera had escaped from the battle, he would most certainly have lived to brutalize God's people again. If Jael had not acted, she would have been party to any future slaughter or oppression of God's people by this godless man.

Third, Jael's own commitment to the Lord God of Israel dictated the only course of action she could take. The enemies of the Lord and the Lord's people were Jael's enemies. She had to kill him. She could not hope to face such a warrior in combat. Her action had to be swift and certain. She could not take a chance on failing to kill him and perhaps merely wound him. She had to take decisive action that would result in the certain and sudden death of Sisera. Faced with the alternatives, Jael chose the greater good. To prevent the future slaughter and oppression of the people of God, Jael killed Sisera.

Fourth, although there is no place in the Bible where God honors or praises Jael for the manner in which she killed Sisera, the song of Deborah certainly praises her for her decisive action. Jael was an instrument in the hands of God to bring judgment upon this terrible enemy of God's people.

JUDGES 11:26 – How long did Israel dwell in Heshbon?

PROBLEM: This verse affirms that Israel was in the land from the time of Moses to the time of Samuel, a period of about "three hundred years." However, if one adds up all the reigns of the judges, it totals some 410 years.

SOLUTION: The obvious solution is that, like the later kings of Israel, there were overlapping reigns. In other words, while some of the land was under oppression by a foreign ruler, other parts may have been delivered by a judge of Israel. Furthermore, it was common for a ruler to claim the whole year when he reigned only a part of it. Thus, the same year would be counted by different judges.

Furthermore, the 300 years total between Joshua and Samuel (ca. 1400–1100 B.C.) fits well with other verses that place the whole time period from the Exodus to Solomon at 480 years (1 Kings 6:1), and Acts 13:20 which speaks of 450 years between Israel's conquering the Land and Solomon's death (ca. 1381–931 B.C.).

JUDGES 11:29-40 – How could God allow Jephthah to offer his daughter up as a burnt offering?

PROBLEM: Just before Jephthah went into battle against the people of Ammon, he made a vow to the Lord. The vow he made was that if God would grant him victory over his enemies, then "whatever comes out of the doors of my house to meet me, when I return in peace . . . I will offer it up as a burnt offering" (Judges 11:31). When Jephthah returned, the first one to come out to meet him was his daughter. Jephthah refused to go back on the vow he had made. But, the Bible clearly states that human sacrifice is an abomination to the Lord (Lev. 18:21; 20:2-5;

Deut. 12:31; 18:10). How could God allow Jephthah to offer up his daughter, and then list Jephthah among the champions of faith in Hebrews 11:32?

SOLUTION: Many have taken this to mean that Jepthah offered his daughter's life to the Lord, claiming the inviolable nature of an oath made to the Lord (cf. Ecc. 5:2-6). In addition, they note that a "burnt offering" involves a sacrifice of the life. They justify it on the grounds that a vow to God takes precedence over all else, even human life (cf. Gen. 22). God is sovereign over life and takes it if He wishes (Deut. 32:39), as He does eventually (Heb. 9:27).

However, for several reasons, it is not necessary to assume that Jephthah ever offered a human sacrifice. First, Jephthah was aware of the law against human sacrifice, and if he had intended to offer a human sacrifice, he would have known this would have been a blatant rejection of God's law.

Secondly, the text does not actually say he killed his daughter in a sacrificial offering. This is simply inferred by some from the fact that he promised that whatever came out of his house first "shall surely be the Lord's, and I will offer it up as a burnt offering" (11:31). As Paul indicated, human beings are to be offered to God "as a living sacrifice" (Rom. 12:1), not as dead ones. Jephthah could have offered his daughter to the Lord as a *living* sacrifice. For the remainder of her life, she would serve the Lord in the temple and remain a virgin.

Third, a living sacrifice of perpetual virginity was a tremendous sacrifice in the Jewish context of that day. As a perpetual virgin dedicated to the service of the Lord, she would not be able to bring up children to continue her father's lineage. Jephthah acted as a man of honor and great faith in the Lord by not going back on the vow that he had made to the Lord his God.

Fourth, this view is supported by the fact that when Jephthah's daughter went out to weep for two months, she did not go out to mourn her impending death. Rather, she went out "and bewailed her virginity" (v. 38).

Finally, if she was facing death at the end of the two month period, it would have been very simple for her to marry some young man and live with him for the two months prior to her death. There was no reason for Jephthah's daughter to mourn her virginity unless she was facing a life of perpetual virginity. Being the only child of Jephthah, his daughter was not mourning her virginity because of any illicit sexual desire.

JUDGES 14:4 – How could God use Samson's lust after the Philistine girl to accomplish the deliverance of Israel from oppression?

PROBLEM: When Samson went to Timnah, he saw a Philistine woman whom he wanted to marry. Although his parents warned him not to pursue such a relation with this godless pagan woman, Samson refused to listen to their counsel. However, Judges 14:4 indicates that Samson's desire for this woman was the work of God to use Samson to defeat the Philistines. How could God use the evil lusts of Samson to accomplish the deliverance of Israel from Philistine oppression?

SOLUTION: It must be realized that, although Samson had been dedicated by his parents from birth to serve the Lord as a Nazarite, he was not totally committed to the Lord. Samson became a willful and self-centered person. He was not of a mind to go to battle against the Philistines for spiritual reasons. Consequently, to arouse him to do battle with the Philistines, God used Samson's own self-interests to incite his anger against the Philistines and to bring about the deliverance of Israel from oppression. God sometimes uses evil men to accomplish His good purposes.

JUDGES 15:4 – How could Samson capture 300 foxes?

PROBLEM: According to Judges 15:4, Samson captured 300 foxes, tied torches between the tails of two foxes, lit the torches, and released the foxes into the fields of the Timnite farmers. But, how could Samson have captured this many foxes?

SOLUTION: It must be remembered that Samson was endowed with supernatural strength. Although the passage does not describe how Samson was able to capture so many foxes, it is not difficult to see that a man who could use the jawbone of an ass to kill "a thousand" warriors (Jud. 15:15) would have little problem capturing 300 foxes.

JUDGES 16:26-27 – If suicide is wrong, why did God bless Samson for doing it?

PROBLEM: Suicide is murder, and God said, "You shall not murder" (Ex. 20:13). There were many suicides in the Bible (see comments on 1 Sam. 31:4), and none of them received divine approval. Yet Samson committed suicide here with God's apparent blessing.

SOLUTION: Samson never *took* his life; he *sacrificed* it for his people.

There is a big difference. Jonah prayed, "Lord, please *take* my life from me, for it is better for me to die than to live!" (Jonah 4:3) But he never took his own life. Suicide is acting *"for one's self."* What Samson did was to lay his life on the line *for others* – his people. Samson's act was no more suicide than Christ's, when He said, "I lay down my life," for "the good shepherd gives His life for the sheep" (John 10:11, 17). In fact, "greater love has no one than this, than to lay down one's life for his friends" (John 15:13).

Of course, not every apparent death "for others" is really an act of love. Paul made this plain in his great love chapter: "though I give my body to be burned, but have not love, it profits me nothing" (1 Cor. 13:3). Even a martyr may not be dying out of love, but in an obstinate commitment to his own self-centered cause. Saul took self-death "lest these uncircumcised men come and thrust me through and abuse me" (1 Sam. 31:4). Abimelek sought death for himself "lest men say of me, 'A woman killed him' " (Jud. 9:54). Samson by contrast asked God for permission to die, praying, "Let me die with the Philistines" (Jud. 16:30). God granted his request, "so the dead that he killed at his death were more than he had killed in his life" (v. 30). Paul also was willing to be "accursed from Christ for my brethren" (Rom. 9:3). The soldier who falls on a hand grenade to save his buddies is not *taking* his life by suicide; he is *giving* his life for others. Likewise, Christ did not commit suicide when He came to "give His life a ransom for many" (Mark 10:45).

JUDGES 18:30 – How could this book have been written in the time or shortly after the time of the judges?

PROBLEM: The events of the Book of Judges cover a period from circa 1380 to 1050 B.C. Judges 18:30 makes reference to the fact that the sons of Jonathan were priests in Dan "until the . . . captivity of the land." However, the captivity of the land took place in 722 B.C. How could this book have been composed during the time or shortly after the time of the Judges?

SOLUTION: The phrase "until the day of the captivity of the land" does not necessarily refer to the captivity of the nation of Israel in 722 B.C. The context of the passage indicates that the term "land" in verse 30 is not a reference to the entire nation of Israel, but the land of Dan. Consequently, the captivity of the land would refer to an overwhelming defeat of the people of Dan by some foreign invader about 1000 B.C., not to the captivity of 722 B.C.

Second, the description of the sudden destruction of the people of Laish by the Danites (v. 27) indicates that this same type of destruction came upon the Danites because they "set up for themselves the carved image" (v. 30). The people had been warned on several occasions that if they turned back from following after the Lord, that He would bring upon them all the trouble that He had brought upon the inhabitants whom Israel had driven out of the land (Deut. 4:25ff, 31:1-29; Josh. 23–24). Although the Scripture does not specifically record this type of event in Dan, the context clearly indicates that this reference is to a devastating defeat and captivity of the people in the land of Dan.

RUTH

RUTH 3:7 — Doesn't this verse imply that Ruth had intercourse with Boaz after he was drunk in order to obligate him to redeem her?

PROBLEM: After Boaz had eaten and drunk, he went to lie down. After he lay down, Ruth came up softly, uncovered Boaz's feet, and lay with him. Doesn't this imply that Ruth had intercourse with Boaz to obligate him to redeem her?

SOLUTION: No! There is nothing in the text of Ruth that indicates any moral impropriety on the part of either Boaz or Ruth. First, Ruth did not come at night to hide an immoral relationship with Boaz. Rather, she came in the night so that Boaz would not feel the pressure of public scrutiny. Boaz would have the opportunity to decline the proposal to redeem Naomi and marry Ruth without facing any public embarrassment.

Second, the uncovering of the feet is not a euphemism indicating that Ruth had intercourse with Boaz. Rather, it is a literal description of a customary practice to demonstrate subjection and submission. Ruth merely pulled back the covering from over the feet of Boaz as a symbol of her submission to Boaz and willingness to become his wife.

Third, the passage states that after uncovering the feet of Boaz, Ruth lay down (v. 7). However, this is not the normal way to indicate sexual intercourse. Sexual intercourse is usually indicated by the phrase, "he lay with her." Without the accompanying indication of laying "with" someone, the word normally indicates merely that someone reclines.

Fourth, it was also a symbolic act for Boaz to spread the corner of his garment over Ruth. This refers to the practice of a man spreading a covering over his wife as well as himself. Ruth reminds Boaz of his responsibility according to the law of levirate marriage (Deut. 25:5-10). The word translated "wing" in the NKJV recalls the earlier blessing which Boaz pronounced upon Ruth at their first encounter (2:12). Ruth had sought refuge under the wings of the God of Israel, now she seeks refuge under the wing of Boaz.

RUTH 4:3-8 — Isn't the arrangement between Boaz and Ruth contrary to the law of the Levirate marriage?

PROBLEM: Deuteronomy 25:5-10 delineates what is known as the law of the levirate marriage. If a man dies and leaves his wife childless, the man's brother was morally obligated to take his brother's wife and raise up children in the name of his deceased brother. This practice insured that the brother's name would not die out. However, Boaz was not the brother of Ruth's dead husband. Wasn't this marriage arrangement contrary to the law of the levirate marriage?

SOLUTION: Although it was a more complicated incident, the arrangement between Boaz, Naomi, and Ruth was certainly not contrary to the law of the levirate marriage. The primary concern of the levirate marriage was to perpetuate the family line of the deceased. Certain factors indicate that by the time of Boaz and Ruth, some additional provisions had become customary. First, if there was no surviving brother in the immediate family, then the obligation of the levirate marriage became the responsibility of the nearest surviving male relative. In this case, there was one individual who was nearer to Naomi's family than Boaz. However, when he declined the invitation, Boaz became the nearest male relative and the next in line to legally fulfill this moral obligation.

Second, along with the responsibility to raise up children in the name of the deceased, there came the responsibility to redeem any property that belonged to the deceased and that had been sold or forfeited (Lev. 25:25). Because the nearest kinsman was not financially able to assume this responsibility (Ruth 4:6), he relinquished his right and responsibility to redeem Naomi and marry Ruth and passed that obligation on to Boaz. There is nothing in the account of the redemption of Naomi and the marriage of Boaz and Ruth that is contrary to the law of levirate marriage.

1 SAMUEL

1 SAMUEL 1:1 — Was Elkanah, the father of Samuel, an Ephraimite or was he a Levite as indicated in 1 Chronicles 6:16-30?

PROBLEM: In the short genealogical note in 1 Samuel 1:1, Elkanah is said to be from the mountains of Ephraim. However, in 1 Chronicles 6:16-23, the longer genealogical record indicates that Elkanah was a Levite. Which is correct?

SOLUTION: Both are correct. The fact that Eli took Samuel into the temple service as an apprentice, and that Samuel later carried out the functions of the priesthood, substantiate the genealogical report that Samuel, and his father Elkanah, were of the tribe of Levi. The statement in 1 Samuel 1:1 simply points out that Elkanah lived in the mountains of Ephraim. All the Levites were assigned to dwell in certain cities that were scattered throughout the tribes of Israel (Num. 35:6). It is quite probable that Ramathaim Zophim, the city where Elkanah lived, was one of these appointed cities. Elkanah was a Levite by tribal descent and an Ephraimite by geographical location.

1 SAMUEL 2:30-31 — Did God change His mind?

(See comments on Ex. 32:14.)

1 SAMUEL 3:13 — Did Eli correct his sons or not?

PROBLEM: This text informs us that Eli's sons "made themselves vile, and he did not restrain them." However, in the previous chapter, Eli rebuked his sons for their evil deeds (2:23-24).

SOLUTION: Eli may have reproved his sons too leniently or not soon enough. At any rate, they became so hardened that his attempt here was futile. Whatever efforts he made at discipline here were not effective.

1 SAMUEL 6:19 — How could Beth Shemesh have a population of over 50,000 men?

PROBLEM: After the people of the town of Beth Shemesh had received the ark of the covenant, some of the citizens ignored the sacredness of the ark and looked inside it. This passage states that the Lord "struck fifty thousand and seventy men of the people." However, a population of over 50,000 seems to be much too large for such a community.

SOLUTION: First, this is most probably a scribal or transcription error. The numerical designation in Hebrew usually follows a certain pattern in which the larger number is written first, then the smaller number. The normal manner to write such a number would be "fifty thousand men and seventy men." However, in this instance, the numbers appear backward. The text actually reads "seventy men fifty thousand men." In addition, numerical designations are almost always connected by the conjunction "and" so that the statement would read, "fifty thousand men and seventy men." Again this passage departs from the normal practice by omitting the "and." These factors have lead many to suspect that the text was inadvertently corrupted in transmission.

Second, it is also conceivable that some explanation for the size of the group has simply eluded investigation to the present. Some future archaeological excavation may uncover evidence to explain why there was in fact such a large group present, or at least involved in the judgment at Beth Shemesh. Although a population of over 50,000 may have been too great for a community like Beth Shemesh, such population sizes were not unheard of in major cities in the ancient world. This large number may yet be accounted for in some way.

1 SAMUEL 6:19 — Why did God strike the people of Beth Shemesh with such a severe judgment for looking into the Ark?

PROBLEM: When the Philistines returned the ark of the Lord to Israel, they placed it on an ox cart and sent it down the road without a driver. When the oxen had pulled the cart into the borders of Beth Shemesh, the people of Beth Shemesh took the ark off of the cart and placed it on a large stone. However, some of the men of Beth Shemesh looked into the ark, and the Lord "struck the people with a great slaughter" (v. 19). But why did God strike the people with such a severe judgment simply because they looked into the ark?

SOLUTION: The Lord struck the people with judgment because they committed a terrible sacrilege against God. The ark of the covenant was a symbol of the very presence of God among His people. Regulations concerning the ark and how it was to be treated were of the strictest nature because of the holiness of God and the sinfulness of man (Ex. 25:10-22; 26:32-34; 37:1-9). Such an impious act of disregard for God's holiness certainly merited the sudden and terrible judgment of God.

1 SAMUEL 7:13 — Were the Philistines expelled once and for all, or only temporarily?

PROBLEM: This verse says that "the Philistines were subdued, and they did not come anymore into the territory of Israel." However, only a few chapters later (9:16; cf. 10:5; 13:5, 17) they were repeatedly fighting the Philistines.

SOLUTION: There are two ways to explain this difficulty. One is that it may simply be a strong idiom, not to be taken as excluding all future incursions on their land by the Philistines. In other words, "they came no more" *for some time*. Or, it could simply mean that "they came no more" *at that time*. A third possibility is that "they came no more" to occupy and dwell in the territory of Israel, which would not exclude them coming back to fight again and again.

1 SAMUEL 7:15 — Did Samuel judge Israel all his days, or only until Saul was anointed king?

PROBLEM: In this verse, we are informed that "Samuel judged Israel all the days of his life." However, Samuel lived after Saul was anointed king (1 Sam. 8:5; 12:1; 25:1).

SOLUTION: Samuel only gave up his *civil* authority to Saul, not his *spiritual* authority. Under Israel's monarch there was a separation of power. Kings were forbidden to perform spiritual functions (cf. 2 Chron. 26:16-23), and the prophets no longer had political authority. Even so, the prophets, with their direct revelations from God, were a continual moral check on those in political power.

1 SAMUEL 8:7-9 — How could God condemn Israel's request for a king when the rules for selecting a king were given by God in Deuteronomy 17?

PROBLEM: The Scriptures testify to the fact that God had planned for Israel to have a king. Deuteronomy 17:14-20 specifically lays down the rules for selecting a king in Israel. However, when the people of Israel requested that Samuel appoint a king, the Lord told Samuel that the people "have not rejected you, but they have rejected Me, that I should not reign over them" (1 Sam. 8:7). How could God condemn Israel's request for a king when He had already given them the guidelines for selecting a king?

SOLUTION: The context of 1 Samuel 8 indicates that the people had the wrong motive and employed the wrong method in seeking a king for themselves. First of all, the people had the wrong *motive* for seeking a king. In the first verse of chapter 8 we read that Samuel was old when he appointed his sons to be judges in Israel. However, Samuel's sons did not do right in the eyes of God. When the people came to Samuel they requested that he appoint a king, not because they wanted to have God's man to rule over them. Rather, they wanted to have a man rule over them. The people had mistaken God's administration through Samuel for Samuel's acts. At Saul's inauguration, Samuel reminded the people that it was "your God, who Himself saved you out of all your adversities and your tribulations" (1 Sam. 10:19). They completely ignored the fact that it was God who protected them and led them, not Samuel or any human king whom Samuel would appoint. Consequently, it was not Samuel whom they were rejecting. Rather it was God whom they were rejecting.

Second, they *failed to seek the Lord* concerning a king to rule over them. They did not bother to ask for God's guidance. They simply requested that Samuel appoint a king. When the elders of Israel came to Samuel, they said, "Now make for us a king to judge us like all the nations" (8:5). However, in Deuteronomy 17:15 God specifically stated that the people would set a king over them "whom the Lord your God chooses." The request of the people in 1 Samuel betrays their lack of consideration for God's part in the process. They had truly rejected God from ruling over them. The Lord was displeased with the people because they did not seek God's man, and they did not employ God's method.

1 SAMUEL 10:1 – Does the Scripture give contradictory accounts of the anointing of Saul?

PROBLEM: According to 1 Samuel 10:1, Samuel anointed Saul at the outskirts of Ramah in the territory of Zuph (cf. 9:5). However, 1 Samuel 10:17-24 asserts that Saul was appointed king of Israel at Mizpah. Are these accounts contradictory?

SOLUTION: No. The only passage that describes the anointing of Saul is found in 1 Samuel 10:1. In 1 Samuel 10:17-24 we read of the public appointment of Saul in the presence of the whole nation. There is no statement of anointing him at this time. Also, in 1 Samuel 12 we find the confirmation ceremony of Saul's appointment as king of Israel and Samuel's farewell address to the nation. Nowhere in this section is there any reference to an anointing. According to the biblical record, Saul was anointed only once, and there is no contradiction among these accounts.

1 SAMUEL 10:20-21 — Was Saul chosen by God, by the people, or by casting a lot?

PROBLEM: The Bible says Saul was chosen by the people (1 Sam. 8:19), by the Lord (1 Sam. 9:17; 10:24), and by casting a lot (1 Sam. 10:20-21). Which was it?

SOLUTION: All three are true. Since the people demanded of God a king, He granted their request and guided their choice of Saul by means of casting a lot. Proverbs 16:33 declares that "the lot is cast into the lap, but its every decision is from the Lord" (cf. Acts 1:26).

1 SAMUEL 13:1 — What is the correct number in this verse?

PROBLEM: Among the several translations of the OT, 1 Samuel 13:1 is rendered as "one year" in the NKJV, by "forty" in the NASB, by "thirty" for the first number and "[forty-]two" for the second number in the NIV. Which of these is the right number or numbers for this verse?

SOLUTION: The problem arises from the fact that the number is missing in the manuscripts of the Masoretic text. The verse simply reads, "Saul was the son of . . . years when he became king, and he reigned two years over Israel." The verse does not include the word "reigned" in the first part. It literally says that "Saul was the son of . . . years." Consequently, the renderings of the various translations are simply the attempts of translators to fill in the missing information based on other data.

1 SAMUEL 13:5 — How could the Philistines have an army of 30,000 chariots?

PROBLEM: According to this passage, the Philistines gathered together 30,000 chariots and 6,000 horsemen. However, an army of 30,000 chariots has never been recorded in all of ancient history, even among the most powerful empires. How could the Philistines have amassed such a large group of chariots?

SOLUTION: It is probably an error that has crept into the manuscripts during transmission. It is very unlikely that there would be such a ratio of chariots to horsemen. It is much more likely that the original manuscripts recorded the number of chariots at 3,000. This would give a better ratio of chariots to horsemen. Because the Hebrew numbers are very similar, it is quite probable that some copyist simply miscopied the 3,000 as 30,000. The accurate recording of numerical designations is very difficult, leading to this kind of problem.

1 SAMUEL 13:12-13 — Was Saul rejected by God for offering an unlawful sacrifice (1 Sam. 13:12-13), for disobedience (1 Sam. 28:18), or for consulting the Witch of Endor (1 Chron. 10:13)?

All of the above. (See comments on Gen. 27:42-44.)

1 SAMUEL 13:13 — How could God have promised Saul a perpetual dynasty over Israel when that had already been prophesied of David?

PROBLEM: After Saul profaned the sacrifice, Samuel rebuked him and told him that, had he not sinned, God would have established him on the throne of Israel forever. However, in Genesis 49:10 we find the promise that the throne would be given to the tribe of Judah forever. How could God promise Saul an eternal kingdom when this was already promised to Judah?

SOLUTION: The statement of Samuel did not amount to a promise. Rather, Samuel is telling Saul what he had forfeited by his act of impiety. God knew from the beginning that Saul would show himself to be unworthy of sitting on the throne of Israel. However, as a free moral agent, Saul had to actually commit the acts of impiety which God had foreknown. The statement that God would have established Saul upon the throne was sincere and legitimate, although hypothetical. For God also knew that Saul would disqualify himself, so God prophesied that ultimately the throne would fall to the tribe of Judah, and David's line would be established in Israel forever.

1 SAMUEL 15:2-3 – Why did God destroy the Amalekites?

PROBLEM: God is depicted in the Bible as a God of mercy and compassion, freely forgiving those who turn to Him (Ps. 94:18-19; Lam. 3:22; James. 5:11; 2 Peter 3:9). By vivid contrast, this text informs us that God commanded the seemingly merciless slaughter of innocent Amalekites – men, women, and children. Why?

SOLUTION: The Amalekites were far from innocent. In fact, they were utterly depraved. What is more, they desired to destroy Israel (v. 2), God's chosen people, the channel of His redemptive plans for all humankind (Gen. 12:1-3). The act of their total destruction was necessitated by the gravity of their sin. Otherwise, some hard core remnant might rise to resume their hateful act toward God's people and plan.

As to the question about the innocent children, several observations are relevant. First, we are all born in sin (Ps. 51:5) and deserve death (Rom. 5:12). Everyone will eventually be taken by God in death – it is only a matter of when (Heb. 9:27). Second, God is sovereign over life and reserves the right to take it when He will (Deut. 32:39; Job 1:21). Third, all children who die before the age of accountability are saved (see comments on 2 Sam. 12:23). Hence, the act by which God took the children is far from merciless (see also comments on Josh. 6:21).

1 SAMUEL 15:11 – How can God say that He regretted setting up Saul to be king in Israel?

PROBLEM: After Saul had failed to carry out God's command to utterly destroy the Amalekites, God said to Samuel, "I greatly regret that I have set up Saul as king" (1 Sam. 15:11). However, in 1 Samuel 15:29, Samuel states that God is not a man that He should repent. How can God say that He regretted setting up Saul as king when other passages assert that God does not repent or change His mind?

SOLUTION: The statement which God made to Samuel does not mean that God relented or changed His mind, but that God was expressing deep emotional sorrow over Saul's failure and the trouble that it would bring upon Israel. God selected Saul to be king in Israel to accomplish certain tasks for which Saul was well suited. To regret some course of action which had to be taken is an experience we have all had. God does not actually change His mind (see comments under Ex. 32:14), but He does experience deep emotional sorrow over the things which people do.

1 SAMUEL 16:1ff — Did God encourage Samuel to lie?

PROBLEM: Abraham was judged by God for telling the half-truth that Sarah was his sister (she was his half sister) when she was really his wife (see comments under Gen. 12:10-20). However, in this passage God actually encourages Samuel to tell only half of the truth, namely, that he had come to offer a sacrifice, when he had also come to anoint David king as well. Two problems emerge from this. First, did not God encourage deception here? Second, why did God condemn Abraham for the same thing that He commanded Samuel to do?

SOLUTION: The first thing to note in response to this problem is that the two situations are not the same. In Abraham's case his so-called "half-truth" was a whole lie, for the question he was asked was, "Is Sarah your wife?" And his answer in effect was really "No. She is my sister." By this answer to this question Abraham intentionally misrepresented the facts of the situation, which is a lie.

Samuel's case was different. The question he was asked is "Why have you come to Bethlehem?" His answer was "I have come to sacrifice to the Lord" (1 Sam. 16:2). This was truthful in that it corresponded with the facts, namely, it is why he came and it is what he did. The fact that he also had another purpose for coming is not directly related to the question he was asked and the answer he gave, as it was in Abraham's case. Of course, had Samuel been asked "Do you have any other purpose for coming?" then he would have had to come clean. To say "No" would have been a deception.

Secondly, concealment and deception are not the same. Samuel certainly concealed one of the purposes of his mission so as to save his life (1 Sam. 16:2). It is not always necessary (even possible) to tell all the truth. The fact that God told Samuel to conceal one of the purposes of his visit to avoid possible death does not necessarily mean he was guilty of lying. Not telling part of the truth and telling a falsehood are not necessarily the same. Secrecy and concealment are not the same as duplicity and falsehood.

1 SAMUEL 16:9 — What is the correct spelling of the name of David's brother?

PROBLEM: According to 1 Samuel 16:9, the name of David's brother is "Shammah." However, in 1 Chronicles 2:13 his name is "Shimea." Which is the correct spelling?

SOLUTION: It is not uncommon for proper names to be spelled differently due to regional patterns of pronunciation. The name in 1 Samuel 16:9 has a double "m." This may indicate that the region of Judah tended not to pronounce the guttural letter "ayin" which appears in the spelling of the name in 1 Chronicles, and that this was compensated for by the doubling of the "m." Perhaps this points to the 1 Chronicles spelling as the correct spelling and the 1 Samuel spelling as a reproduction of the pronunciation pattern of the region. (See Appendix 2.)

1 SAMUEL 16:10 – Did Jesse have eight sons as indicated in this verse, or only seven as indicated in 1 Chronicles 2:13-15?

PROBLEM: Although 1 Samuel 16 only names the three oldest brothers of David, verse 10 states that Jesse made seven of his sons pass before Samuel before he brought David out. However, 1 Chronicles 2:13-15 indicates that David was the seventh son of Jesse. How many sons did Jesse have?

SOLUTION: The passage in 1 Chronicles records the names of seven sons of Jesse, perhaps because one of David's brothers died, and his name was not preserved as late as the composing of 1 Chronicles. It is not an uncommon practice for the surviving children to speak of their family in terms of the remaining number, so that any member of a family which would have been composed of eight sons, identifies himself as one of a group of seven brothers. This would very likely be the case in David's family if the brother had died before marriage, leaving no posterity, and had made no significant contribution during the rise and reign of David. There would have been no reason to retain his name among the genealogical records of the sons of Jesse.

1 SAMUEL 17:50 – Why does this verse say David killed Goliath when 2 Samuel 21:19 says Elhanan killed Goliath?

PROBLEM: In 1 Samuel 17:50-51, David is said to have cut off the head of Goliath after striking him with the stone from his sling. However, according to 2 Samuel 21:19, it was Elhanan the son of Jaare-Oregim that killed Goliath. Why does one passage claim that David killed Goliath when the other claims that Elhanan did?

SOLUTION: The passage in 2 Samuel 21:19 which reads, "Elhanan the son of Jaare-Oregim the Bethlehemite killed Goliath the Gittite, the shaft of whose spear was like a weaver's beam" (the italicized words *"the brother of"* are not in the Hebrew text), is obviously a copyist error. This is substantiated by the fact that there is a parallel passage in 1 Chronicles 20:5 that reads, "and Elhanan the son of Jair killed Lahmi the brother of Goliath the Gittite, the shaft of whose spear was like a weaver's beam." The corruption of the passage in 2 Samuel 21:19 is traceable to the confusion by a copyist of several letters and words which, when combined in a certain way, could yield the reading found in the 2 Samuel passage.

1 SAMUEL 17:54 — How could Goliath's head be carried to Jerusalem when it was held then by the Jebusites.

PROBLEM: When David killed Goliath and cut his head off, the city of Jerusalem was still in the hands of the Jebusites. David did not conquer the city until much later (2 Sam. 5:6-9).

SOLUTION: It does not say that Goliath's head was taken *immediately* to Jerusalem. But David took his trophy there *eventually* when he made Jerusalem the place of his throne.

1 SAMUEL 17:57-58 — Why did Saul not recognize his harp player David as the one who killed Goliath?

PROBLEM: In 1 Samuel 16, Saul hired David to play the harp for him, and yet, in chapter 17, after David killed Goliath the giant, Saul did not seem to recognize who he was.

SOLUTION: There are two possibilities here. First, it would not be unusual that a busy preoccupied king had not taken enough notice of this humble hired musician so as to recognize him as the same person who killed Goliath. However, once David performed the notable feat of killing the giant, the king could not help but take note of him and ask who he was.

On the other hand, it is possible that Saul knew who David was, but, after David had performed this feat, was only inquiring who David's father was. This fits the exact nature of Saul's question which was, "Whose son are you, young man?" (17:58). Had he not recognized David he should have asked "What is your name?" Saul was known for placing the most valiant men in his bodyguard (14:52). Saul may have wondered if David had any more brave brothers. Or he may have simply wished for more complete identification of this brave young man so that he could properly reward his extraordinary accomplishment. In either case there is no contradiction here.

1 SAMUEL

1 SAMUEL 18:1-4 — Were David and Jonathan homosexuals?

PROBLEM: This Scripture records the intense love David and Jonathan had for each other. Some see this as an indication that they were homosexual. They infer this from the fact that Jonathan "loved" David (18:3); that Jonathan stripped in David's presence (18:4); that they "kissed" each other with great emotion (1 Sam. 20:41). They point also to David's lack of successful relations with women as an indication of his homosexual tendencies. Is this a valid conclusion to draw from these texts?

SOLUTION: There is no indication in Scripture that David and Jonathan were homosexual. On the contrary, there is strong evidence that they were not. First of all, David's attraction to Bathsheba (2 Sam. 11) reveals that his sexual orientation was heterosexual, not homosexual. In fact, judging by the number of wives he had, David seemed to have too much heterosexuality.

Second, David's "love" for Jonathan was not sexual (*erotic*) but a friendship (*philic*) love. It is common in eastern cultures for heterosexual men to express love and affection toward one another.

Third, Jonathan did not strip himself of all his clothes in David's presence. He only stripped himself of his armor and royal robe (1 Sam. 18:4) as a symbol of his deep respect for David and commitment to him.

Fourth, the "kiss" was a common cultural greeting for men in that day. Furthermore, it did not occur until two and a half chapters after Jonathan gave David his clothes (1 Sam. 20:41).

Finally, the emotion they expressed was weeping, not orgasm. The text says, "they kissed each other and wept together — but David wept the most" (1 Sam. 20:41, NIV).

1 SAMUEL 18:10 — How could a good God send an evil spirit to Saul?

PROBLEM: According to this passage, the evil ("distressing," NKJV) spirit came upon Saul so that he prophesied in his house, and then tried to kill David with a spear. However, the verse clearly states that the evil spirit was from God. How could a good God send an evil spirit to bring distress to Saul?

SOLUTION: Because God is absolutely sovereign, the actions of any evil spirit would be subject to the authority of God. Therefore, it was according to God's permission that the spirit was allowed to come upon Saul to bring him distress. Saul had already rejected God, and God had rejected him from being king. God had a special reason for allowing this spirit to incite Saul to action against David. Saul's attempt to kill David only made Saul realize that God was with David. By sending David away and making him captain over a thousand, Saul inadvertently increased David's popularity with the people and hastened his own demise. The sending of the evil spirit upon Saul is similar to God's allowing Satan to afflict Job. God allows evil, but always uses it to accomplish His own good purposes (see comments on 1 Kings 22:22).

1 SAMUEL 19:23-24 — How could it be said that the Spirit of God was upon Saul when God had already rejected him?

PROBLEM: When Saul came to Naioth in Ramah to try to capture David, he sent soldiers up to bring David back in chains. When his soldiers came back empty-handed, Saul decided to go up himself. However, when he came near to Naioth, the Spirit of the Lord was upon him and he danced and prophesied before Samuel. How could it be said that the Spirit of God was upon Saul when God had already rejected him?

SOLUTION: The Spirit of the Lord was not upon Saul at this time in the same way that the Spirit of the Lord was upon him before his rejection. Originally, the Spirit came upon Saul to *minister through him*. On this occasion the Spirit came upon him to *resist his evil intentions*. In this incident, Saul's intent was to capture and ultimately kill David, but Saul was unwilling to chance a face-to-face encounter with the prophet Samuel. Twice Saul sent messengers to capture David and bring him back in chains, but each time the Spirit of the Lord overcame them so that they were unable to accomplish their task. Finally, Saul went up himself. However, when he came near to Naioth, the Spirit of the Lord overcame him so that he could not control himself. He danced and prophesied until he fell exhausted on the ground. The Spirit of the Lord overcame Saul and thwarted his efforts to capture David.

1 SAMUEL 19:24 — Why did Saul strip off his clothes as he danced and prophesied before Samuel?

PROBLEM: Samuel was conducting a service in which the group of prophets were prophesying. When Saul's men came to capture David, they were overcome by the Spirit of the Lord and they also prophesied. However, when Saul came, he prophesied, danced, and stripped off his clothes. Why does Saul do this when apparently none of the others did?

SOLUTION: Some commentators say that this was apparently an act of judgment upon Saul in that Saul was humiliated in the presence of Samuel and the prophets. Saul was a man who was characterized by drastic mood changes (cf. 1 Sam. 16:14-23; 18:10-11; 19:9). Saul was so carried away by his enthusiasm that he stripped off his clothes and danced until he fell to the ground totally exhausted and remained there over night.

Others claim that the Spirit of God overcame Saul to a greater degree than in the case of the others in an attempt to soften the hard heart of Saul. If Saul continued in his obstinate way after this powerful experience of divine grace, then Saul would be swiftly hardened and ultimately destroyed.

1 SAMUEL 21:9 – Was Goliath's armor kept in David's tent or in Nob?

PROBLEM: In this text the sword of Goliath was located in Nob (cf. v. 1). However, in 1 Samuel 17:54 it says David "put his [Goliath's] armor in his tent."

SOLUTION: At first it was placed in his tent, but later it was taken to Nob. The two verses speak of different times.

1 SAMUEL 28:7ff – How could God allow the Witch of Endor to raise Samuel from the dead when God condemned witchcraft?

PROBLEM: The Bible severely condemns witchcraft and communication with the dead (Ex. 22:18; Lev. 20:6, 27; Deut. 18:9-12; Isa. 8:19). In the OT those who practiced it were to receive capital punishment. King Saul knew this and even put all witches out of the land (1 Sam. 28:3). Nevertheless, in disobedience to God, he went to the witch of Endor for her to contact the dead prophet Samuel (1 Sam. 28:8ff). The problem here is that she appears to be successful in contacting Samuel, which lends validity to the powers of witchcraft which the Bible so severely condemns.

SOLUTION: Several possible solutions have been offered to this episode at Endor. Three will be summarized here.

First, some believe that the witch worked a miracle by demonic powers and actually brought Samuel back from the dead. In support of this they cite passages which indicate that demons have the power to perform miracles (Matt. 7:22; 2 Cor. 11:14; 2 Thes. 2:9-10; Rev. 16:14). The objections to this view include the fact that death is final (Heb. 9:27), the dead cannot return (2 Sam. 12:23) because there is a great gulf fixed by God (Luke 16:24-27), and demons cannot usurp God's authority over life and death (Job 1:10-12).

Second, others have suggested that the witch did not really bring up Samuel from the dead, but simply faked doing so. They support this by reference to demons who deceive people who try to contact the dead (Lev. 19:31; Deut. 18:11; 1 Chron. 10:13) and by the contention that demons sometimes utter what is true (cf. Acts 16:17). The objections to this view include the fact that the passage seems to say Samuel did return from the dead, that he provided a prophecy from Samuel that actually came to pass, and that it is unlikely that demons would have uttered truth of God, since the devil is the father of lies (John 8:44).

A third view is that the witch did not bring up Samuel from the dead, but God Himself intervened in the witch's tent to rebuke Saul for his sin. In support of this view is the following: (a) Samuel seemed to actually return from the dead (v. 14), but (b) neither humans nor demons have the power to bring people back from the dead (Luke 16:24-27; Heb. 9:27). (c) The witch herself seemed to be surprised by the appearance of Samuel from the dead (v. 12). (d) There is a direct condemnation of witchcraft in this passage (v. 9), and thus it is highly unlikely that it would give credence to witchcraft by claiming that witches can actually bring people back from the dead. (e) God sometimes speaks in unsuspecting places through unusual means (cf. Baalam's donkey, Num. 22). (f) The miracle was not performed through the witch, but *in spite of* her. (g) Samuel seems to really appear from the dead, rebukes Saul, and utters a true prophecy (v. 19). (h) God explicitly and repeatedly condemned contacting the dead (see above) and would not contradict this by giving credence to witchcraft. The major objections to this view are that the text does not explicitly say that God performed the miracle, and that a witch's tent is a strange place to perform this miracle.

1 SAMUEL 31 — The report of Saul's death in this passage contradicts that given in the next chapter (2 Sam. 1)

PROBLEM: First Samuel 31 says that King Saul committed suicide by falling on his sword, but 2 Samuel 1 records that he was killed by an Amalekite as he was about to lean on his sword.

SOLUTION: Some claim that both stories are true, taking the Amalekite's story as supplementary. They claim that Saul attempted suicide, but was not dead when the Amalekite arrived and finished the job. They point to the fact that the Amalekite had Saul's sword and bracelet as evidence that his account was true, as well as the fact that David punished him by death for killing the king. The objections to this view are that it contradicts the statements of 1 Samuel 31, that "Saul took a sword and fell on it" and that his armorbearer "saw that Saul was dead" (vv. 4-5), as well as the inspired record that says "so Saul . . . died" (v. 6).

Others see the 1 Samuel story as the correct version and the one in 2 Samuel 1 as a true record of the fabrication of the Amalekite who came upon Saul after he died and thought he could gain favor with David by taking credit for the feat. They point to the fact that the story contradicts the record in 1 Samuel 31, that the Amalekite did not seem to know that Saul died by a sword, not a spear, and that 1 Chronicles 10 repeats the story as recorded in 1 Samuel, but not the fabrication of the Amalekite. The main objections to this view are that 2 Samuel does not say his story is a lie, and that David killed him for his act. In response, he may have been killed on the basis of his self-confession (2 Sam. 1:16). And the fact that his story was in contradiction to that in 1 Samuel may have been taken as sufficient evidence that his story was a fabrication.

1 SAMUEL 31:4 — Was Saul's suicide justifiable?

PROBLEM: King Saul was mortally wounded, and he asked his armorbearer to assist him in committing suicide. Was this justified?

SOLUTION: Suicide is murder, and the Bible says, "You shall not murder" (Ex. 20:13). It makes no difference that the life taken is one's own. All life belongs to God, and He alone has the right to take it (Deut. 32:39; Job 1:21).

Even the most desperate believers in the Bible who desired death never considered suicide a morally viable alternative. Rather, recognizing the sovereign hand of God over human life, they prayed like Jonah: "Lord, please *take* my life from me, for it is better for me to die than to live" (Jonah 4:3). Though they wanted God to take it, they never considered it right to take it themselves.

Furthermore, with the exception of Samson (see comments on Jud. 16:26-27), there are at least five cases of suicide recorded in Scripture, and none of them is approved by God — Abimelech (Jud. 9:50-56); Saul (1 Sam. 31:1-6); Zimri (1 Kings 16:18-19); Ahithophel (2 Sam. 17:23); and Judas who betrayed Christ (Matt. 27:3-10). Each met a tragic death, and none met with divine approval. Suicide is an attack on the image of God in man (Gen. 1:27) and an attempt to usurp God's sovereignty over human life.

2 SAMUEL

2 SAMUEL 2:10 — How could Ishbosheth have reigned only two years
  when 2 Samuel 5:5 says David reigned for seven and one half years?

PROBLEM: After the death of Saul, his son Ishbosheth reigned over
Israel. According to 2 Samuel 2:10, Ishbosheth reigned for two years.
While Ishbosheth reigned in Israel, Judah followed after David (2 Sam.
2:10). After Ishbosheth was killed, the people of Israel came to David to
crown him king of all Israel. However, according to 2 Samuel 5:5, David
reigned in Hebron for seven and one-half years. How could David have
reigned over Judah for seven and one-half years when Ishbosheth reigned
over Israel for only two years?

SOLUTION: Although Ishbosheth was eventually crowned king of Israel,
this did not take place until five years after the death of Saul. The
Philistines had been a major obstacle in uniting the ten tribes of Israel
and establishing Israel under the reign of Ishbosheth. Once the armies of
Israel under Abner's direction had sufficiently driven back the Philistines,
Abner set up Ishbosheth as king over Israel. During the entire period of
Abner's conflicts with the Philistines, and during the two years of
Ishbosheth's reign, David reigned as king of Judah.

2 SAMUEL 8:4 — Did David capture 1,700 horsemen or 7,000 as
  1 Chronicles 18:4 says?

PROBLEM: After David had defeated Hadadezer, he took prisoners from
Hadadezer's army. According to 2 Samuel 8:4, David captured "one
thousand, seven hundred horsemen" (the word "chariots" added by some
translations is not in the Hebrew text). However, the passage in
1 Chronicles 18:4 states that David captured 7,000 horsemen. Which
number is correct?

SOLUTION: This is undoubtedly a copyist error. Probably an early copyist inadvertently omitted the word "chariot" that we find supplied in

some translations. This in turn created a problem for a later copyist who would have recognized that it was not proper Hebrew structure to write "one thousand seven thousand horsemen," so he would have reduced the second "thousand" to "hundred" resulting in the reading we now have in 2 Samuel 8:4. It is probably the 1 Chronicles passage that retains the correct number.

2 SAMUEL 8:18 — How could David's sons be priests when they were not Levites?

PROBLEM: According to this verse, "David's sons were chief ministers." Yet Numbers 3:10 forbids anyone except the sons of Aaron from being priests (cf. Num. 16:40).

SOLUTION: Some scholars believe that the priesthood was extended to include David's sons, granting them a kind of honorary priesthood. However, since there is no indication of this in the text, it does not seem likely.

Probably a broader understanding of the word for priest is employed here. The Hebrew word for "priest" (*kohen*) is also used for servant, minister, or counselor. David's sons did not offer sacrifices (only Aaron's sons did), but they were domestic priests or *spiritual advisors*.

2 SAMUEL 12:15-23 — How could a loving God take the life of David's child because of the sin of David?

PROBLEM: As a result of David's sin with Bathsheba, the life of the child that Bathsheba bore to David was taken. However, 2 Samuel 12:15 states that it was the Lord who struck the child with illness so that it died. How could a loving God commit such an act?

SOLUTION: The taking of the life of the child was not a judgment upon the child, but upon David. The Word of God assures us that death is not the end. This passage in particular indicates that David's child was taken to heaven upon its death (see comments on 2 Sam. 12:23). Consequently, the child was probably spared a life of sorrow and trouble as the illegitimate offspring of the illicit relationship of David and Bathsheba. David's faith in the all-loving God is clearly illustrated in verses 22-23. While the child was alive, David fasted and wept in hopes that God would graciously allow the child to live. However, when the child died, David trusted in the goodness of God to take the child to be with Him in heaven, and that one day David would be reunited with the child.

■

2 SAMUEL 12:21-23 — Should we pray for the dead?

PROBLEM: Based on a verse in 2 Maccabees 12:46 (Douay), Roman Catholics believe it is a holy and wholesome thought to pray for the dead that they may be loosed from their sins. However, David refused to pray for his dead son. Does the Bible teach that we should pray for the dead?

SOLUTION: There is nothing in inspired Scripture that supports the Roman Catholic doctrine of praying for the dead that they may be released from their sins. This conclusion is based on strong evidence from many passages. First, the only verse supporting prayers for the dead comes from the 2nd century B.C. apocryphal book of 2 Maccabees (see comments on 1 Cor. 3:13-15) which the Roman Catholic Church added to the Bible in A.D. 1546 in response to the Reformation that condemned such practices.

Second, the doctrine of prayers for the dead is connected with the unbiblical doctrine of purgatory. The prayers are for the purpose of releasing them from purgatory. But there is no basis for the belief in purgatory (see comments on 1 Cor. 3:13-15).

Third, nowhere in all of inspired Scripture is there a single example of any saint who prayed for the dead to be saved. Surely as passionately as many saints wished for their loved ones to be saved (cf. Rom. 9:1-3), there would be at least one example of a divinely approved prayer on behalf of the dead.

Fourth, the Bible makes it unmistakably clear that death is final and there is no hope beyond the grave. Hebrews declared, "it is appointed for men to die once, but after this the judgment" (Heb. 9:27). Jesus spoke of those who rejected Him as dying "in their sins" (John 8:21, 24), which implies that there is no hope for sins beyond the grave.

Fifth, Jesus set the example in John 11 by weeping for the dead and praying for the living. Upon coming to His friend Lazarus' grave, "Jesus wept" (v. 35). Then He prayed for "the people who are standing by . . . that they may believe" (v. 42).

Sixth, the dead pray for the living (cf. Rev. 6:10), but there are no instances in the inspired Word of God where the living pray for the dead. The martyred saints in glory were praying for vengeance on the wicked (Rev. 6:9). And since there is rejoicing in heaven over one soul saved on earth (Luke 15:10), there is no doubt that there is prayer in heaven for the lost. But the Bible does not hold out even the slightest hope for anyone who dies in their sins (see comments on 2 Thes. 1:9).

2 SAMUEL 12:23 — Do those who die in infancy go to heaven?

PROBLEM: The Scriptures teach that we are born in sin (Ps. 51:5) because we "all sinned [in Adam]" (Rom. 5:12). Yet David implies here that his baby, who died, will be in heaven, saying, "I shall go to him" (v. 23).

SOLUTION: There are three views regarding children who die before the age of accountability, that is, before they are old enough to be morally responsible for their own actions.

Only Elect Infants Go to Heaven. Some strong Calvinists believe that only those babies that are predestined go to heaven (Eph. 1:4; Rom. 8:29). Those who are not elect go to hell. They see no greater problem with infant predestination than with adult predestination, insisting that everyone is deserving of hell and that it is only by God's mercy that any are saved (Titus 3:5-6).

Only Infants Who Would Have Believed Go to Heaven. Others claim that God knows the end from the beginning (Isa. 46:10) and the potential as well as the actual. Thus, God knows those infants and little children who would have believed in Christ had they lived long enough. Otherwise, they contend, there would be people in heaven who would not have believed in Christ, which is contrary to Scripture (John 3:36). All infants whom God knows would not have believed, had they lived long enough, will go to hell.

All Infants Go to Heaven. Still others believe that all who die before the age of accountability will go to heaven. They base this on the following Scriptures. First, Isaiah 7:16 speaks of an age before a child is morally accountable, namely, "before the child shall know to refuse the evil and choose the good." Second, David believed in life after death and the resurrection (Ps. 16:10-11), so when he spoke of going to be with his son who died after birth (2 Sam. 12:23), he implied that those who die in infancy go to heaven. Third, Psalm 139 speaks of an unborn baby as a creation of God whose name is written down in God's "book" in heaven (vv. 14-16). Fourth, Jesus said, "Let the little children come to Me, and do not forbid them; for of such is the kingdom of God" (Mark 10:14), thus indicating that even little children will be in heaven. Fifth, some see support in Jesus' affirmation that even "little ones" (i.e., children) have a guardian angel "in heaven" who watches over them (Matt. 18:10). Sixth, the fact that Christ's death for all made little children savable, even before they believed (Rom. 5:18-19). Finally, Jesus' indication that those who did not know were not morally responsible (John 9:41) is used to support the belief that there is heaven for those who cannot yet believe, even though there is no heaven for those who are old enough and refuse to believe (John 3:36).

2 SAMUEL 12:31 – How can we justify David's cruelty to his enemies?

PROBLEM: This passage implies that David tortured his enemies, since he "put them under saws, and under axes or iron, and made them pass through the brick-kiln" (KJV). But torture is wrong, and Jesus said "love your enemies" (Luke 6:35).

SOLUTION: Several things should be observed in response to this criticism. First, the KJV translation is open to this misinterpretation here. More recent translations clear up the difficulty. The NKJV correctly renders it, David "put them to work with saws and iron picks and iron axes, and made them cross over to the brick works." Likewise, the NIV says, David "brought out the people who were there, consigning them to labor with saws and with iron picks and axes, and he made them work at brick-making."

Second, the writer is merely relating these events here—he is not necessarily placing his stamp of approval on them. As noted earlier (see Introduction), not everything *recorded* in the Bible is *condoned* by the Bible.

Third, the punishment of forced labor given to these vicious enemies of God's people is not extreme. Considering the cruelties they unleashed on the children of Israel (cf. 1 Sam. 11:2; Amos 1:13), by comparison, their treatment was humane.

2 SAMUEL 14:27 – Why does this passage say Absalom had three sons when 2 Samuel 18:18 says he had none?

PROBLEM: The passage in 2 Samuel 14:27 states that Absalom had three sons and one daughter. However, in 2 Samuel 18:18 Absalom set up a pillar for himself because, as he says, "I have no son to keep my name in remembrance." Which is correct?

SOLUTION: Both passages are correct. It is significant that 14:27 names Absalom's daughter (Tamar), but does not give the names of Absalom's three sons. Probably, these sons died in infancy, and their names were not recorded because they left no posterity. Consequently, Absalom set up a monument in a vain attempt to memorialize his name precisely because he had no male children who could carry on his family name.

2 SAMUEL 18:6 — Was the land of Ephraim west or east of Jordan?

PROBLEM: According to Joshua (17:15-18), the Ephraimites settled on the west side of Jordan. But in 2 Samuel 18:6 it speaks of the "woods of Ephraim" as being on the east side of Jordan.

SOLUTION: Some believe this battle (2 Sam. 18) took place on the west side of Jordan in the territory of Ephraim. However, this is unlikely for several reasons. Both armies were on the east side before the battle, and there is no mention of their crossing Jordan. The army returned back to the west side after the battle (19:3). David had to cross the Jordan to get back home in Jerusalem (v. 15) on the west side.

Other scholars believe that the "woods" of Ephraim were not within their territory, but on the east side of Jordan. They think the forest may have received its name from the earlier slaughter of Ephraimites in that area (cf. Jud. 12:1-6), even though it did not belong to the tribe of Ephraim. It is not unheard of for a section of one province to bear the name of another. After all, Michigan City is just across the border in the state of Indiana!

2 SAMUEL 18:17 — Was Absalom buried in the forest of Ephraim or in the Kidron Valley?

PROBLEM: After Absalom was killed by Joab's men, they took his body and threw it into a pit and covered him with a large stone. However, according to 2 Samuel 18:18, Absalom had erected his own tomb in the Kidron Valley. Where was Absalom buried?

SOLUTION: Absalom was buried in the pit as 2 Samuel 18:17 describes. The memorial Absalom built, which has come to be known as the Tomb of Absalom, was not necessarily erected to function as a burial place. Rather, it was a memorial of remembrance to Absalom's name, and there is no claim in Scripture that he was buried there.

2 SAMUEL 21:19 — This verse says "Elhanan . . . killed Goliath" but 1 Samuel 17 declares that David did.

PROBLEM: First Samuel 17 records the dramatic story of how David the son of Jesse killed the giant Goliath. However, 2 Samuel 21:19 says clearly: "Elhanan . . . killed Goliath the Gittite." But both texts cannot be right.

SOLUTION: The 2 Samuel text is probably a scribal error in copying the manuscript and should read "Elhanan . . . slew *Lahmi the brother of* Goliath the Gittite." This conclusion is supported by a parallel report of the story in 1 Chronicles 20:5 which has the missing highlighted phrase "Lahmi the brother of," thus showing it was the brother of Goliath that Elhanan killed and not Goliath, whom David slew just as 1 Samuel 17 reports.

2 SAMUEL 23:11 – Was this a field of barley or lentils?

PROBLEM: Here in 2 Samuel it is called a field of "lentils," but in 1 Chronicles 11:13 it is called "barley."

SOLUTION: There are two basic possibilities here. One, these could be different occasions when God gave Israel deliverance from the Philistines in the midst of a field. More likely, however, it may be a copyist mistake, since the Hebrew words for lentils and barley are similar enough to be mistaken, especially if there were some smudge or imperfection on the manuscript copy. Either possibility would take care of the difficulty.

2 SAMUEL 24:1 – How can this passage claim that God moved David to number Israel when 1 Chronicles 21:1 claims that it was Satan?

PROBLEM: This passage reports the sin of David in numbering the people of Israel and Judah. Verse one affirms that God moved David to number the people. However, according to 1 Chronicles 21:1, it was Satan who moved David to number the people. Who was responsible for prompting David to act?

SOLUTION: Both statements are true. Although it was Satan who immediately incited David, ultimately it was God who permitted Satan to carry out this provocation. Although it was Satan's design to destroy David and the people of God, it was God's purpose to humble David and the people and teach them a valuable spiritual lesson. This situation is quite similar to the first two chapters of Job in which both God and Satan are involved in the suffering of Job. Similarly, both God and Satan are involved in the crucifixion. Satan's purpose was to destroy the Son of God (John 13:2; 1 Cor 2:8). God's purpose was to redeem humankind by the death of His Son (Acts 2:14-39).

2 SAMUEL 24:9 – Why do the numbers of men recorded in 2 Samuel 24:9 and in 1 Chronicles 21:5-6 disagree?

PROBLEM: When David was moved to number the people of Israel and Judah, he sent Joab to carry out the task. According to the report in 2 Samuel 24:9, the number of the men of valor in Israel was 800,000, and the number of the men of valor in Judah was 500,000. However, according to 1 Chronicles 21:5-6, the number of the men who drew the sword in Israel was 1,100,000, and the number of the men who drew the sword in Judah was 470,000. Which of these calculations is correct?

SOLUTION: This discrepancy involves the difference in who was included in each report. In the report in 2 Samuel, the number of men of valor who drew the sword was 800,000, but did not include the standing army of 288,000 described in 1 Chronicles 27:1-15, or the 12,000 specifically attached to Jerusalem described in 2 Chronicles 1:14. Including these figures gives the grand total of 1,100,000 men of valor who composed the entire army of the men of Israel. The figure of 470,000 in 1 Chronicles 21 did not include the 30,000 men of the standing army of Judah mentioned in 2 Samuel 6:1. This is evident from the fact that the Chronicler points out that Joab did not complete the counting of the men of Judah (1 Chron. 21:6). Both calculations are correct according to the groups which were included and excluded from each report.

2 SAMUEL 24:13 – Why are the numbers of the years of the famine different from those in 1 Chronicles 21?

PROBLEM: God spoke to Gad and instructed him to offer David three alternative punishments for his sin. According to 2 Samuel 24:13, the famine was to be seven years. However, according to 1 Chronicles 21:12, the famine was to be three years. Which one of these is correct?

SOLUTION: There are two possible ways to reconcile these accounts. Some commentators propose that the prophet Gad actually confronted David on two occasions. This proposal is based on the difference in language used to present the alternatives to David. In the 2 Samuel passage, Gad presents the alternatives as a question, "Shall seven years of famine come to you in your land" (v. 13). In the 1 Chronicles passage the alternatives are presented more along the lines of a command, "Choose for yourself, either three years of famine, or three months to be defeated" (vv. 11-12). Those who offer this solution assume that perhaps the 2 Samuel passage records the first encounter of Gad and David in which the alternatives are presented for David's consideration, and that after some fasting and prayer, Gad returned for David's decision by which time God had reduced the duration of the famine from seven to three years in response to David's supplication.

Another group of commentators suggests that the record in 2 Samuel is a copyist error. They point out that there are more reliable manuscripts which preserve the number "three" for the duration of the famine and that the NIV has employed this manuscript reading in its translation.

2 SAMUEL 24:14 – Is it fearful to fall into the hands of God?

PROBLEM: David here implies that it is not fearful to fall into the hands of the living God. In fact, he chooses it over all other options. At the same time, the writer of Hebrews declares that "It is a fearful thing to fall into the hands of the living God" (Heb. 10:31).

SOLUTION: The two passages are speaking of two different conditions. In David's case, it was a matter of choosing his own punishment for his self-acknowledged sin. The Hebrews passage speaks of those who, far from being repentant, had sinned "willfully" after having "received the knowledge of the truth" (v. 26). In brief, whether it is fearful or not will depend on the condition of the person who falls into God's hands.

IT IS FEARFUL FOR:	IT IS NOT FEARFUL FOR:
The sinner	The righteous
The unrepentant	The repentant
The unfaithful	The faithful

2 SAMUEL 24:24 – Why does this passage say that David paid Araunah 50 shekels of silver when elsewhere it says he paid 600 shekels of gold?

PROBLEM: When David offered to buy the oxen and the threshing floor for a sacrifice and altar to the Lord, 2 Samuel states that he paid for them with 50 pieces of silver. However, according to 1 Chronicles 21:25, David gave Araunah 600 shekels of gold. Which is the correct record?

SOLUTION: Both accounts are correct. The passage in 2 Samuel 24 records David's purchase of the oxen and the threshing floor. The passage in 1 Chronicles 21 states that David paid 600 shekels of gold "for the place" (v. 25). The Hebrew phrase that is translated "the place" includes more than just the oxen and the threshing floor. Araunah must have possessed a large portion of land on Mount Moriah which would prove valuable to David in the future.

1 KINGS

1 KINGS 4:26 – How can this verse say Solomon had 40,000 stalls when 2 Chronicles 9:25 says he had only 4,000 stalls?

PROBLEM: In recording the prosperity of Solomon, this passage states that he had 40,000 stalls of horses for his chariots. However, 1 Chronicles 9:25 affirms that Solomon had only 4,000 stalls for horses. Which one is right?

SOLUTION: This is undoubtedly a copyist error. The ratio of 4,000 horses to 1,400 chariots, as found in the 2 Chronicles passage, is much more reasonable than a ratio of 40,000 to 1,400 found in the 1 Kings text. In the Hebrew language, the visual difference between the two numbers is very slight. The consonants for the number 40 are *rbym*,[1] while the consonants for the number 4 are *rbh* (the vowels were not written in the text). The manuscripts from which the scribe worked may have been smudged or damaged and have given the appearance of being forty thousand rather than four thousand.

1 KINGS 6:1 – How can this be an accurate calculation if Ramses the Great was the Pharaoh of the Exodus?

PROBLEM: The predominant view of modern scholarship is that the Pharaoh of the Exodus was Ramses II. If this is right, it would mean that the Exodus took place about 1270 to 1260 B.C. However, since the fourth year of Solomon's reign was 967 B.C., adding 480 years to that date would put the Exodus at about 1447 B.C. which is in the reign of Amenhotep II. How can this calculation be correct if Ramses the Great was the Pharaoh of the Exodus?

---

1. The "y" in the word *rbym* is normally represented by the long "i" vowel. However, since the consonant *yod* was written to represent long vowels before the vowel points were added, it is inserted here as a transliteration of the letter which would have appeared in the unpointed text.

SOLUTION: If the present chronology of the kings of Egypt is accepted, the Pharaoh of the Exodus was not Ramses the Great, but Amenhotep II. If Egyptian chronology is revised, then Ramses lived 200 years earlier and could be the Pharaoh of the Exodus. Although modern scholarship has proposed a late date for the Exodus, ca. 1270–1260 B.C., there is no longer any reason to accept this date, and alternative explanations provide a better account of all the historical data and place the Exodus at about 1447 B.C. (See comments under Ex. 5:2.)

1 KINGS 7:23 – Doesn't the calculation in this verse represent an inaccurate value of pi?

PROBLEM: According to 1 Kings 7:23, Hiram constructed a "Sea of cast bronze ten cubits from one brim to the other; it was completely round. Its height was five cubits, and a line of thirty cubits measured its circumference." From this report we learn that the ratio of the circumference to the diameter is three to one. However, this is an inaccurate value of pi which is actually 3.14159.

SOLUTION: This is not an error. The biblical record of the various measurements of the different parts of the temple are not necessarily designed to provide precise scientific or mathematical calculations. Rather, the Scripture simply provides a reasonable approximation. The rounding of numbers or the reporting of approximate values or measurements was a common practice in ancient times when exact scientific calculations were not used.

1 KINGS 9:22 – How can this verse claim that Solomon did not make forced laborers of the Israelites when 1 Kings 5:13 says he did?

PROBLEM: According to 1 Kings 9:22, Solomon did not make forced laborers of the children of Israel in his building campaigns. However, 1 Kings 5:13 says Solomon raised up a labor force out of all Israel. Which one of these reports is correct?

SOLUTION: Both reports are correct. The reconciliation of these statements is found in the fact that there are different Hebrew words used of two different types of laborers in the building projects of Solomon. According to 1 Kings 5:13 (5:27 in the Hebrew text), Solomon raised up a "labor force" (*mas* or *hammas*) from all Israel. In this context, labor force was a group conscripted from the population to participate in the building project. It was apparently composed of both Israelites and non-Israelites. However, in 1 Kings 9:21 the author delineates those people from whom Solomon drafted "slave labor." The word used here is *mas-obed* which indicates forced slave labor. Then, in 9:22 the author points out that Solomon did not employ any Israelites as "slaves" (*abed*). There is no contradiction here, because, although Solomon did draft young men of Israel to labor in the construction of the temple, a practice which brought him great trouble later in his reign, he did not force any Israelite to become a slave laborer.

1 KINGS 11:1 — How could God allow Solomon to have so many wives when he condemns polygamy?

PROBLEM: First Kings 11:3 says Solomon had 700 wives and 300 concubines. And yet the Scriptures repeatedly warn against having multiple wives (Deut. 17:17) and violating the principle of monogamy — one man for one wife (cf. 1 Cor. 7:2).

SOLUTION: Monogamy is God's standard for the human race. This is clear from the following facts: (1) From the very beginning God set the pattern by creating a monogamous marriage relationship with one man and one woman, Adam and Eve (Gen. 1:27; 2:21-25). (2) Following from this God-established example of one woman for one man, this was the general practice of the human race (Gen. 4:1) until interrupted by sin (Gen. 4:23). (3) The Law of Moses clearly commands, "You shall not multiply wives" (Deut. 17:17). (4) The warning against polygamy is repeated in the very passage where it numbers Solomon's many wives (1 Kings 11:2), warning "You shall not intermarry with them, nor they with you." (5) Our Lord reaffirmed God's original intention by citing this passage (Matt. 19:4) and noting that God created one "male and [one] female" and joined them in marriage. (6) The NT stresses that "Each man [should] have his own wife, and let each woman have her own husband" (1 Cor. 7:2). (7) Likewise, Paul insisted that a church leader should be "the husband of one wife" (1 Tim. 3:2, 12). (8) Indeed, monogamous marriage is a prefiguration of the relation between Christ and His bride, the church (Eph. 5:31-32).

Polygamy was never established by God for any people under any circumstances. In fact, the Bible reveals that God severely punished those who practiced it, as is evidenced by the following: (1) Polygamy is first mentioned in the context of a sinful society in rebellion against God where the murderer "Lamech took for himself two wives" (Gen. 4:19, 23). (2) God repeatedly warned polygamists of the consequences of their actions "lest his heart turn away" from God (Deut. 17:17; cf. 1 Kings 11:2). (3) God never *commanded* polygamy—like divorce, He only permitted it because of the hardness of their hearts (Deut. 24:1; Matt. 19:8). (4) Every polygamist in the Bible, including David and Solomon (1 Chron. 14:3), paid dearly for his sins. (5) God hates polygamy, as He hates divorce, since it destroys His ideal for the family (cf. Mal. 2:16).

In brief, monogamy is taught in the Bible in several ways: (1) by *precedent,* since God gave the first man only one wife; (2) by *proportion,* since the amount of males and females God brings into the world are about equal; (3) by *precept,* since both OT and NT command it (see verses above); (4) by *punishment,* since God punished those who violated His standard (1 Kings 11:2); and, (5) by *prefiguration,* since marriage is a typology of Christ and His bride, the church (Eph. 5:31-32). Simply because the Bible records Solomon's sin of polygamy does not mean that God approved of it.

1 KINGS 11:4 — In light of David's sin with Bathsheba, how could this passage say his heart was loyal to the Lord?

PROBLEM: When Solomon was old, his wives turned his heart away from the Lord (1 Kings 11:4). This verse contrasts Solomon and David by asserting that Solomon's heart was not loyal to the Lord his God as David's heart was. However, in light of David's sin of adultery with Bathsheba, and his killing of her husband Uriah, how can this text say that David's heart was loyal?

SOLUTION: It must always be remembered that a person's acceptance with God is not based on his or her own works, but upon God's grace. David was not a man after God's own heart because of any acts of righteousness which he had done. Rather, David's heart was loyal to the Lord his God because of his faith in God. The verse literally says, "and his [Solomon's] heart was not fully devoted to the Lord his God as the heart of David his father." The contrast between Solomon and David is found in the fact that, while Solomon was enticed by his wives to worship other gods, David worshiped only the God of Israel. Although David had committed some very grievous sins, he never worshiped or served other gods. His heart was completely loyal to the Lord, and his faith was reckoned unto him as righteousness.

1 KINGS 12:25 — Was Jeroboam's residence in Shechem or at Tirzah?

PROBLEM: In 1 Kings 12:25 Jeroboam's home is said to be in Shechem, but later it is listed as Tirzah (1 Kings 14:12-17).

SOLUTION: He may have moved later to a different location. Or, one place could have been a vacation or retreat home. It was not uncommon for kings to have more than one place of residence.

1 KINGS 15:5 — Is this the only sin David committed?

PROBLEM: According to this verse, David was without sin except on one occasion—the sin involving Bathsheba! It claims David "had not turned aside from anything that He [God] commanded him all the days of his life, except in the matter of Uriah the Hittite." But, this is both contrary to general statements about fallen human beings (cf. Gen. 6:5; Jer. 17:9; Rom. 3:10-23) and specific condemnations of David on other occasions. David himself said, after God convicted him for numbering Israel (1 Chron. 21:1), "I have sinned greatly" (v. 8).

SOLUTION: The statement in question is by no means a pronouncement of David's virtual sinlessness for several reasons. First of all, it is a general and true characterization of David's life. Just as Job was not sinless, but was called "blameless and upright" (Job 1:1), even so David's life was without major fault. Second, this commendation of David is not absolute, but relative to all the sins Abijam had committed (cf. 1 Kings 15:1, 3). David did, with one major exception, "that which was right in the eyes of the Lord" (v. 5). Third, even when he sinned, he did what was right, namely repented immediately when confronted by God (cf. 2 Sam. 12:1ff and 1 Chron. 21:8). Fourth, the exception clause ("except in the matter of Uriah the Hittite") is not found in many manuscripts of the OT, including the Vatican Ms. Without it, the point that this was only a general commendation of David has even stronger force. Fifth, the phrase "had not turned aside" indicates that God is speaking of the generally steadfast direction of David's life, not every specific sin in it. This would account for why David's other sins are not mentioned, since they did not turn him from the generally forward direction of his life in serving the Lord to this point.

1 KINGS 15:14 — Did Asa destroy the high places or leave them standing?

PROBLEM: Second Chronicles 14:3 asserts that "he [Asa] removed the altars of the foreign gods and the high places." But here, 1 Kings says that, during the reign of king Asa, "the high places were not removed."

SOLUTION: There are several possible explanations. One is that these passages may refer to different times in Asa's reign. In his early period, he may have been more active in putting idolatry down. Or, it may have been that Asa was unsuccessful in carrying through his reforms, so that the high places were not completely removed. Some have suggested that he may have only torn down the high places to other gods (as 2 Chronicles notes) but allowed the ones to the Lord to remain (which 1 Kings speaks about). Any one of these would take care of the difficulty.

1 KINGS 18:27 — Why was Elijah blessed for ridiculing the prophets of Baal when the Bible urges us to use kind words to our enemies?

PROBLEM: The Bible says here that "Elijah mocked them" and suggested that their god was "meditating, or he is busy, or he is on a journey, or perhaps he is sleeping and must be awakened." However, the Scriptures teach in other places to "love your enemies" (Matt. 5:44), "bless and do not curse" (Rom. 12:14), and "let your speech always be with grace" (Col. 4:6). Elijah's conduct hardly seems exemplar of these truths.

SOLUTION: First, it should be pointed out that the text does not specifically commend every word Elijah uttered. It simply says that God answered his prayer to vindicate him by sending fire to consume the sacrifice and the prophets of Baal (v. 38).

Further, it can be argued that Elijah did not violate any of these scriptural exhortations. Nowhere does the Bible say Elijah hated the prophets of Baal or cursed them. As for Elijah's alleged ridicule, it was no doubt cutting, but not outside the limits of a forceful but legitimate use of irony. The same passage that exhorts us to always speak with "grace" also notes that it can be "seasoned with salt." This was perhaps an example of a more salty remark. In any event, there is no indication that Elijah did it with malice. Ultimately, his act was benevolent in that it saved the lives of those who were witnesses of this marvelous intervention of God.

1 KINGS 18:32-35 – Where did Elijah get all the water if there had been a drought for three years?

PROBLEM: Even the brook had dried up because the drought was so severe (1 Kings 17:7; cf. 18:2). Yet before Elijah prayed for fire from heaven he doused the sacrifice with water three times until it filled the trenches around the altar.

SOLUTION: There was a severe drought, but there was still water to drink, both for man and beast, from the springs around the land (1 Kings 18:5), and from the brook Kishon (v. 40). The drought was not so bad that the people were literally dying from thirst. The amount of water Elijah used was not astronomical, being only twelve "waterpots" full (18:33-34). Although waterpots varied in size from those small enough to be carried by one person, some were big enough to hold 20 gallons. However, the author of Kings notes that the trench was big enough to hold about two seahs of seed, equivalent to about one-fourth of a bushel. The fact that Elijah commanded his servants to fill the waterpots indicates that they were small enough for one person to carry. The total amount of water probably amounted to about 13 quarts.

1 KINGS 18:40 – Wasn't killing too severe a punishment for the prophets of Baal?

PROBLEM: Isn't this a classic example of religious intolerance, a notorious example of overkill? Further, wasn't it contrary to Jewish law to kill the prophets of Baal because of their beliefs?

SOLUTION: According to the Law of Moses, even Jewish prophets were to be killed for giving false prophecies (Deut. 18:20). Furthermore, idolatry was punishable by death (Ex. 22:20), as was blasphemy (Lev. 24:15-16) and adultery (Lev. 20:10), all of which the prophets of Baal were guilty. Given that these false prophets were also engaged in treason against the Jewish theocracy, the punishment is not surprising and certainly justifiable by a God who is not only sovereign over all life (Deut. 32:39; Job 1:21), but also absolutely fair in executing justice (Gen. 18:25).

1 KINGS 21:19 – How could the prophecy of this verse claim to be fulfilled in the events recorded in 1 Kings 22:37-38?

PROBLEM: God told Elijah to prophesy to Ahab that his blood would be licked by the dogs in the same place where dogs had licked the blood of

Naboth. According to 1 Kings 22:37-38, when the chariot of King Ahab was washed in a pool in Samaria, the dogs licked the blood according to the word of the Lord. However, if Naboth was executed outside the city of Jezreel, and since Ahab's chariot was washed in a pool in Samaria which was over 20 miles away, how can the one be the fulfillment of the other?

SOLUTION: Nowhere in the Bible do we find a specific statement about where the dogs licked the blood of Naboth. First Kings 21:13 states that Naboth was taken outside the city of Jezreel and stoned to death. However, there is no statement about the dogs licking the blood of Naboth. Although it may seem likely that the licking of Naboth's blood took place in the same place where he was stoned, this is only an assumption. It is possible that those who killed Naboth transported his body to Samaria, perhaps for verification by Jezebel, in which case the washing of Naboth's chariot, and the licking of Ahab's blood would have taken place in the same spot.

1 KINGS 22:22 – How could God use "lying spirits" to do His will since He forbids lying?

PROBLEM: The Scriptures teach that God is truth (Deut. 32:4) and that it is impossible for Him to lie (Heb. 6:18). Furthermore, God commands us not to lie (Ex. 20:16), and He will severely punish those who do (Rev. 21:8). And yet, in spite of all this, God is portrayed in this passage as enlisting lying spirits to entice wicked king Ahab to seal his own doom. The text says, "Now therefore, look! The Lord has put a lying spirit in the mouth of all these prophets of yours" (v. 23).

SOLUTION: Several factors should be considered in understanding this situation. First, this is a vision. As such, it is a dramatic picture of God's sovereign authority spelled out in regal imagery. Second, this dramatic vision represents God in all His sweeping authority so that even evil spirits are represented as being subjected to His ultimate control. Third, the God of the Bible, in contrast to gods of pagan religions, is in sovereign control of everything, including the forces of evil which He uses to accomplish His good purposes (cf. Job 1–3). Fourth, the Bible sometimes speaks of God "hardening" people's hearts (see comments on Rom. 9:17) or even sending them strong delusions (2 Thes. 2:11). However, on closer examination of the text, we discover that God did this only on those who freely harden their own hearts (Ex. 8:15) and who "did not believe the truth" (2 Thes. 2:12). In short, God is not *commending* lying here. He is simply *utilizing* it to accomplish His purposes. God is not *promoting* lying, but *permitting* it to bring judgment on evil. That is, God, for His own purposes of justice, allowed Ahab to be deceived by evil spirits whom He knew in His omniscience would be used to accomplish His sovereign and good will.

1 KINGS 22:49 — How can this verse say that Jehoshaphat refused Ahaziah's request when 2 Chronicles says they worked together?

PROBLEM: According to 1 Kings 22:48, Jehoshaphat built several merchant ships. When Ahaziah requested that Jehoshaphat take some of his servants, Jehoshaphat refused. However, according to 2 Chronicles 20:35, Jehoshaphat allied himself with Ahaziah to build these merchant ships. How can one passage state that Jehoshaphat refused to let Ahaziah's servants sail on the ships when the other verse claims that they worked together on building these ships?

SOLUTION: Although Jehoshaphat did join together with Ahaziah to build the merchant ships, Jehoshaphat changed his mind once Eliezer prophesied that God was displeased with Jehoshaphat's alliance with Ahaziah. The passage in 1 Kings records the fact that Jehoshaphat refused an alliance with Ahaziah, while the passage in 2 Chronicles points out that although the alliance was the original arrangement, God used His prophet to change Jehoshaphat's mind.

2 KINGS

2 KINGS 1:17 — When did Jehoram son of Ahab begin his reign as king of Israel?

PROBLEM: According to 2 Kings 1:17, Jehoram son of Ahab became king of Israel in the second year of the reign of Jehoram son of Jehoshaphat, king of Judah. However, according to 2 Kings 3:1, Jehoram son of Ahab became king of Israel in the eighteenth year of the reign of Jehoshaphat, king of Judah. When did Jehoram son of Ahab become king in Israel?

SOLUTION: Both statements are correct. Before Jehoshaphat joined Ahab in the military campaign against Ramoth-Gilead, Jehoshaphat appointed his son Jehoram as co-regent in Judah. When Jehoram son of Ahab became king in Israel, it was both the second year of the reign of Jehoram son of Jehoshaphat, and the eighteenth year of the reign of his father Jehoshaphat.

2 KINGS 2:23-24 — How could a man of God curse these 42 young men so that they were mauled by she-bears?

PROBLEM: As Elisha was going up to Bethel, he was confronted by some young people who mocked him saying, "Go up, you baldhead!" When Elisha heard this, he turned and pronounced a curse on them, and two she-bears came out of the wood and mauled 42 of the young men. How could a man of God curse these young men for such a minor offense?

SOLUTION: First of all, this was no minor offense, for these young men held God's prophet in contempt. Since the prophet was God's mouthpiece to His people, God Himself was being most wickedly insulted in the person of His prophet.

Second, these were not small, innocent children. They were wicked young men, comparable to a modern street gang. Hence, the life of the prophet was endangered by their number, the nature of their sin, and their obvious disrespect for authority.

Third, Elisha's action was designed to strike fear in the hearts of any other such gang members. If these young gang members were not afraid to mock a venerable man of God such as Elisha, then they would have been a threat to the lives of all God's people.

Fourth, some commentators note that their statements were designed to challenge Elisha's claim to be a prophet. They were essentially saying, "If you are a man of God, why don't you go on up to heaven like Elijah did?" The term "baldhead" might be a reference to the fact that lepers shaved their heads. Such a comment would indicate that these young men looked upon Elisha as a detestable outcast.

Fifth, it was not Elisha who took their lives, but God who alone could have providentially directed the bears to attack them. It is evident that by mocking this man of God, these young men were revealing their true attitudes toward God Himself. Such contempt for the Lord was punishable by death. The Scriptures do not say that Elisha prayed for this kind of punishment. It was clearly an act of God in judgment upon this impious gang.

2 KINGS 3:18-19 — Didn't Israel violate the law of warfare by destroying fruit trees?

PROBLEM: Moses had commanded the armies of Israel about their enemy's land saying, "You shall not destroy its trees" (Deut. 20:19). However, here in 2 Kings they were instructed to "cut down every good tree."

SOLUTION: Some scholars believe that the Deuteronomy law applies only to using fruit trees for siege-works, since it says "do not cut them down to use in the siege" (Deut. 20:19). This fits with the fact that Deuteronomy explicitly states that the reason for not destroying fruit trees was that "the tree of the field is man's food" (Deut. 20:19).

It is also possible that the command not to destroy them applies only to the land of the Canaanites which they would immediately occupy, whereas 2 Kings refers to destroying Moab which they were not going to occupy.

2 KINGS 6:19 — Didn't Elisha lie to the Syrian troops who were coming to capture him?

PROBLEM: When Elisha went out to meet his enemies, he told them "this is not the way, nor is this the city. Follow me, and I will bring you to the man whom you seek" (2 Kings 6:19). How could a man of God lie to these Syrian troops?

SOLUTION: What Elisha told them was not actually a lie. The Syrian troops were sent to Dothan to capture Elisha. The Lord blinded them, and Elisha came out of the city to meet them. What Elisha told them was "this is not the way, nor is this the city." Once Elisha came out of the city he was no longer in Dothan. Consequently, entering Dothan was no longer the way to capture Elisha, neither was it the city. Elisha also instructed them, "follow me and I will bring you to the man whom you seek." This was also true. Elisha went before them into Samaria, and when they arrived, the Lord opened their eyes and they saw Elisha, and that they were in Samaria. (As to whether lying is ever justified, see comments on Ex. 1:15-21.)

2 KINGS 8:25 — Did Ahaziah become king in the twelfth year of Jehoram or in the eleventh year of Jehoram?

PROBLEM: According to 2 Kings 8:25, Ahaziah son of Jehoram became king of Judah in the twelfth year of the reign of Jehoram son of Ahab, king of Israel. However, 2 Kings 9:29 states that Ahaziah became king of Judah in the eleventh year of the reign of Jehoram over Israel. Which is right?

SOLUTION: Both are correct. The difference stems from the manner in which the reign of a king was calculated in Israel and in Judah. At the time of the reign of Ahaziah in Judah, the system used to calculate the years of the reign of a king was the accession-year system. According to this system, the first official year of the reign of a king did not begin until the beginning of the new year after that king had taken the throne. The calculation system employed in Israel, however, was the nonaccession-year system in which the year that a king came to the throne was counted as his first official year. Consequently, what was the eleventh year according to the accession-year system was the twelfth year according to the nonaccession-year system.

2 KINGS 8:26 — Was Ahaziah 22 years old when he began to reign in Judah, or was he 42 years old?

PROBLEM: According to the statement in 2 Kings 8:26, Ahaziah was 22 years old when he began to reign in Judah. However, in 2 Chronicles 22:2 (KJV) we find the claim that Ahaziah was age 42 when he took the throne in Judah. Which is correct?

SOLUTION: This is clearly a copyist error, and there is sufficient evidence to demonstrate that Ahaziah was 22 years old when he began to reign in Judah. In 2 Kings 8:17, we find that Joram, father of Ahaziah and son of Ahab, was 32 years old when he became king. Joram died at age 40, eight years after becoming king. Consequently, his son Ahaziah could not have been 42 when he took the throne after his father's death, otherwise he would have been older than his father.

2 KINGS 9:7 — How could God condemn Jehu for bloodshed when God had commanded him to exterminate the house of Ahab?

PROBLEM: In 2 Kings 9:6-10, we find the commissioning of Jehu by the Lord to strike down the house of Ahab. According to 2 Kings 10:30, God commended Jehu for having destroyed the house of Ahab. However, Hoshea prophesied that God would "avenge the bloodshed of Jezreel on the house of Jehu" (Hosea 1:4). How could God condemn Jehu for shedding blood when it was God who had commanded him to do so?

SOLUTION: God praised Jehu for obeying Him in destroying the house of Ahab, but condemned Jehu for his sinful motive in shedding their blood. Although 2 Kings 10:30 states that God told Jehu that he had done right in killing the relatives of Ahab, the previous verse observes that Jehu "did not turn away from the sins of Jeroboam . . . from the golden calves . . . " and verse 31 states that Jehu "took no heed to walk in the law of the Lord God of Israel with all his heart." Obviously, since Jehu worshiped other gods and did not walk in God's Law, he did not destroy Ahab's family out of any devotion to the Lord.

2 KINGS 10:13-14 — Were Ahaziah's brothers slain or were they his brother's sons?

(See comments on 2 Chron. 22:8.)

2 KINGS 14:3, 7 — Why is Amaziah commended for abhorring Edomites when God said not to do so?

PROBLEM: The record says that Amaziah did "what was right in the sight of the Lord" (v. 3) and that "he killed ten thousand Edomites in the Valley of Salt" (v. 7). This is in spite of the fact that the law commanded, "You shall not abhor an Edomite, for he is your brother" (Deut. 23:7).

SOLUTION: It should be observed in response to this objection, first of all, that although Amaziah's life was commended in general, the passage does not explicitly approve of this particular action. In fact, even his general commendation is not without stated reservation by God (cf. v. 3).

Second, the text does not state that he killed Edomites because he "abhorred" them. It may have been an act of just retaliation. His other act of vengeance was in accord with the Law of Moses, inasmuch as he did not kill the children for their father's sins (cf. v. 6).

2 KINGS 14:29 — Are the dead asleep or conscious?

PROBLEM: As in this passage, the Bible often speaks of death as the time when one "sleeps with his fathers" (e.g., 1 Kings 2:10; 11:21, 43; 14:20, KJV). Jesus said, "Lazarus sleeps" (John 11:11) when he was "dead" (John 11:14). Paul speaks of believers who have "fallen asleep" in the Lord (1 Thes. 4:13; cf. 1 Cor. 15:51). Yet, in other places, the Bible speaks of persons being conscious in the presence of God after they die (cf. 2 Cor. 5:8; Phil. 1:23; Rev. 6:9).

SOLUTION: The first set of verses refers to the *body,* and the second set to the *soul.* "Sleep" is an appropriate figure of speech for the death of the body since death is only temporary, awaiting the resurrection when the body will be awakened from its sleep. Further, both sleep and death have the same posture, lying down.

The Bible is very clear about the fact that the believer's soul (spirit) survives death (Luke 12:4), is consciously present with the Lord (2 Cor. 5:8) in a better place (Phil. 1:23) where other souls are talking (Matt. 17:3) and even praying (Rev. 6:9-10). Likewise, the unbeliever's soul is in a place of conscious torment (Matt. 25:41; Luke 16:22-26; Rev. 19:20–20:15).

2 KINGS 15:27 — How can this verse say Pekah ruled over Samaria for 20 years when he took Samaria 8 years before the end of his reign?

PROBLEM: According to 2 Kings 15:27, Pekah ruled over Israel in Samaria for 20 years. However, Hoshea the son of Elah killed Pekah only 8 years after Pekah had taken Samaria from Menahem. How could Pekah have reigned over Israel for 20 years when he only reigned from Samaria for 8 years?

SOLUTION: Although Pekah did not have control over the city of Samaria, he was considered to be the only lawful king of Israel, and therefore his reign over Israel, and its capital city Samaria, was calculated from the time he claimed the throne after the death of Zechariah in 752 B.C. Pekah actually took up official residence in Samaria in 740 B.C., approximately two years after Menahem died. However, only eight years later, in 739 B.C., Hoshea led a conspiracy against Pekah and killed him.

2 KINGS 17:4 — How can this verse mention a king of Egypt named "So" when there are no records of such a king?

PROBLEM: When Shalmaneser king of Assyria came to do battle with Hoshea king of Israel, Shalmaneser discovered a conspiracy which Hoshea had begun when he "sent messengers to So, king of Egypt" (2 Kings 17:4). However, besides this statement in the Bible, there are no records of a king of Egypt named So. Is this an error?

SOLUTION: The name translated "So" can also be translated "Sais" which was the name of the capital city of Tefnakht the king of Egypt at the time Hoshea ruled in Israel. Thus the passage should read, "He [Hoshea] sent to Sais, to the king of Egypt." The word "So" in the NKJV is not the name of the king of Egypt, but of the capital city of the kingdom of Egypt. There is no error here.

2 KINGS 17:41 — How could the nations fear the true God and serve false gods?

PROBLEM: This text says plainly that "these nations feared the Lord" (cf. v. 32). Yet this same passage claims that they "served their own gods" (v. 33). Isn't this a flat contradiction?

SOLUTION: Not all *verbal* contradictions are *actual* contradictions (see comments on Ps. 53:5). This is a good example of using the same word ("fear") in different senses (see also comments on 1 John 4:18). The contrasting senses in which they feared God is revealed in verse 41: "So these nations feared the Lord, yet served their carved images." In other words, they feared God in *general*, but not on this *particular* matter. They did not cease being *monotheists*, but they were *idolatrous* ones.

2 KINGS 18:13 — How can this verse say that Sennacherib invaded Judah in the fourteenth year of Hezekiah?

PROBLEM: 2 Kings 18:13 claims that "in the fourteenth year of King Hezekiah, Sennacherib king of Assyria came up against all the fortified cities of Judah and took them." Since archaeological evidence has established Sennacherib's invasion at 701 B.C., this would mean that Hezekiah became co-regent with his father Ahaz in 719 B.C., and sole ruler of Judah in 715 B.C. However, according to 2 Kings 18:1, Hezekiah became co-regent in 729 B.C., and he became sole ruler of Judah when his father died in 725 B.C. This is a discrepancy of ten years. Which account is correct?

SOLUTION: The claim that Sennacherib invaded Judah in the fourteenth year of Hezekiah is clearly a copyist error. Sennacherib actually invaded Judah in the twenty-fourth year of the reign of Hezekiah of Judah. The error is easy to explain since the difference between the two numbers is a single Hebrew letter. The Hebrew consonants for "fourteen" are *rb srh,* while the Hebrew consonants for "twenty-four" are *rb srm* (the ancient manuscripts did not write the vowels, see Appendix 2). The final letters are the only difference in the written text. In fact, the words are the same, only the word "twenty" is simply the plural form of the word "ten." We might express the way the Hebrew is written as "four ten," or "four twenty." It is simply a case where a copyist miscopied the form from "four twenty" to "four ten."

2 KINGS 20:11 — How could the shadow retreat by ten degrees on the stairway of Ahaz?

PROBLEM: In response to Hezekiah's prayer, God instructed Isaiah to prophesy to Hezekiah that God would add 15 years to Hezekiah's life. When he heard this, Hezekiah asked for a sign to confirm God's promise. The sign was that the shadow would retreat ten degrees. But, this would involve making the shadow go backward instead of forward as the sun set. How could the shadow retreat?

SOLUTION: Obviously, this was a miracle. Hezekiah realized that it would not be a miraculous confirmation of God's promise if the sign involved some phenomenon that could be easily explained (2 Kings 20:10). It was the miraculous nature of the event that qualified it as a sign from God. Any attempt at an explanation of how this was accomplished would be pure speculation. Although God can employ the forces of nature to accomplish His purposes, He can also accomplish His will in a way that defies natural explanation. God can perform miracles, and this was a miracle.

2 KINGS 20:12-15 — How can these verses speak of the visitors from Berodach-Baladan as coming after the invasion of Sennacherib?

PROBLEM: According to the sequence of events as they are presented in 2 Kings 20:12-15, the delegation sent from Berodach-Baladan (spelled Merodach-Baladan in Isa. 39:1) came to visit Hezekiah after the invasion of Sennacherib in 701 B.C. However, according to historical evidence, Berodach-Baladan had fled to Elan after having been expelled from Babylon by Sennacherib in 702 B.C. How can the chronology of these verses be reconciled?

SOLUTION: The fact that the description of the invasion of Sennacherib in both 2 Kings and Isaiah comes before the description of the visit of the delegation from Berodach-Baladan does not mean that this is the actual order. In 2 Kings 20:1 we find the introductory phrase "In those days." However, this does not necessarily indicate that the following events took place in the same time period as the previous section. This phrase is sometimes used to introduce a new section and is similar in function to the phrase "And it came to pass." We find this type of use in Judges 17:6, 18:1, 19:1, and Esther 1:2. It may also be pointed out that the Hebrew word *hem* that is translated here as "those" can also be rendered "these." It is the context that determines its function. The beginning phrase could be translated, "In these days."

The visit recorded in 2 Kings 20:12-15 actually took place before the invasion of Sennacherib recorded in 2 Kings 18–19. This is attested by the fact that Hezekiah died sometime between 698 and 696 B.C. Since God extended his life by 15 years, this would put the time of Hezekiah's illness at about 713 B.C. This time frame would coincide well with a visit by a delegation from Berodach-Baladan who was expelled by Sennacherib in 702 B.C.

2 KINGS 23:30 — Did Josiah die at Megiddo or at Jerusalem?

PROBLEM: This verse says Josiah died in the city of Megiddo, but elsewhere it affirms he died in Jerusalem (2 Chron. 35:24).

SOLUTION: The Chronicles passage merely states that he died; the Kings text tells us specifically where he died. It says clearly, "Pharaoh Necho killed him at Megiddo when he confronted him. Then his servants moved his body in a chariot from Megiddo, brought him to Jerusalem, and buried him in his own tomb" (2 Kings 23:29-30).

2 KINGS 24:6 — Did Jehoiakim die in Jerusalem, as this passage suggests, or did he die in Babylon, as 2 Chronicles 36:6 implies?

PROBLEM: The statement in 2 Kings 24:6 indicates that Jehoiakim died a peaceful death at home. However, 2 Chronicles 36:6 describes Jehoiakim's capture and deportation to Babylon by Nebuchadnezzar, which indicates that Jehoiakim died a terrible death in a foreign land. Which is correct?

SOLUTION: The fact is that neither passage actually identifies where Jehoiakim died. The deportation described in 2 Kings 24:10-16 is not the same event as that described in 2 Chronicles 36:5-8. There is a difference in the severity of the action of Nebuchadnezzar. Whereas 2 Chronicles 36:7 indicates that Nebuchadnezzar took only Jehoiakim and *some* of the articles of the temple, 2 Kings 24:13 points out that Nebuchadnezzar took *all* of the treasures of the house of the Lord, that he carried all of Jerusalem into captivity (v. 14), and that only the poorest were left in the land (v. 14). The two accounts clearly report two different events. Consequently, it is quite possible that after the first captivity—when Jehoiakim was taken to Babylon, according to the report in 2 Chronicles 36—Jehoiakim was allowed to return to Jerusalem at a later time and died there. However, it is also possible that Jehoiakim died in captivity. The Scriptures are simply silent on this point.

2 KINGS 24:8 — How old was Jehoiachin when he became king?

PROBLEM: The record in 2 Kings 24:8 states that Jehoiachin was 18 years old when he became king. However, in 2 Chronicles 36:9 we find the claim that Jehoiachin was age 8 when he became king. Which is correct?

SOLUTION: This is probably a copyist error. Most likely, Jehoiachin was 18 when he became king. The observation that he "did evil in the sight of the Lord, according to all that his father had done" (2 Kings 24:9), is a description of an older man rather than a young boy. Additionally, the fact that the Chaldeans condemned him to prison in 597 B.C., indicates that they considered him to be a responsible adult.

1 CHRONICLES

1 CHRONICLES 1:32 — Why does 1 Chronicles 1:32 call Keturah Abraham's concubine, while Genesis 25:1 calls her his wife?

(See comments under Gen. 25:1.)

1 CHRONICLES 2:18 — Was Caleb's father Hezron, Hur, or Jephunneh?

PROBLEM: According to this verse, Caleb's father was Hezron. But verse 50 says it was Hur, and Joshua 14:6 lists it as Jephunneh.

SOLUTION: Several solutions are possible. Some scholars believe there may have been two or three Calebs. Others note that the word "son" may mean grandson of even great-grandson. Hence, these men could refer to Caleb's father, grandfather, and great-grandfather. Also, some think that 1 Chronicles 2:50 may not affirm that Caleb is the son of Hur. By placing a period after Caleb (see NASB), the phrase "these are the descendants of Caleb" refers to the preceding verse. If so, Hur would not be the father of Caleb.

1 CHRONICLES 3:19 — What is the correct genealogical relationship of Pedaiah, Shealtiel, and Zerubbabel?

PROBLEM: According to the statement in 1 Chronicles 3:19, Zerubbabel was the son of Pedaiah. However, according to Ezra 3:2, Zerubbabel was the son of Shealtiel. What is the correct genealogical relationship?

SOLUTION: In 1 Chronicles 3:16-19 we find the following genealogy.

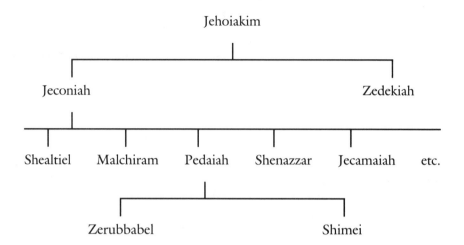

This record shows that Zerubbabel was the son of Pedaiah and the nephew of Shealtiel, Pedaiah's older brother. Although the Bible does not record the death of Pedaiah, it is reasonable to assume that he died shortly after Shimei was born, and Shealtiel, the oldest of the sons of Jeconiah, adopted Zerubbabel as his own son.

1 CHRONICLES 5:22 – How could the God of peace conduct war?

PROBLEM: In 1 Chronicles 5:18-22, the war of the sons of Reuben, the Gadites and the half tribe of Manasseh, against the Hagrites is described. Verse 20 states that the children of Israel cried out to the Lord in the midst of the battle, and God helped them in their fight against the Hagrites. In fact, verse 22 states, "for many fell dead, because the war was God's." However, if God is good (Ps. 100:5) and if God is the God of peace (Rom. 15:33), how can He make war?

SOLUTION: Waging war and being a God of goodness and peace are not necessarily incompatible. First, it is wrong to suppose that waging war is inconsistent with goodness. A surgeon takes drastic action against a cancer to bring about the ultimate good of the patient. Yet, spiritual evil is much more serious than physical evil. When God waged war in the OT, it was against the forces of spiritual evil. God took drastic action to rid the land of the evil influence of the inhabitants.

Second, it is wrong to suppose that waging war is inconsistent with peace. There would be no peace in the world if God did not oppose evil. Indeed, the peace of God is now available to all who believe, because

God waged war against the forces of evil—a warfare that culminated at the Cross where the blood of God's only Son was shed. Ultimately, the enemy will be cast into the lake of fire as a defeated foe. Sometimes war is necessary to bring about lasting peace.

Because God is good, He never wages war in an unrighteous manner. Because God is the God of peace, He only wages war against the enemies of peace. God is the God of war because He has defeated the forces of evil who would bring upon all people spiritual destruction forever.

1 CHRONICLES 6:16-23 — Was Elkanah, the father of Samuel, a Levite, or was he an Ephraimite as 1 Samuel 1:1 indicates?

(See comments under 1 Sam. 1:1.)

1 CHRONICLES 8:33 — Was Ner the father of Kish or the son of Abiel?

PROBLEM: 1 Samuel 14:51 refers to "Ner the father of Abner" who was Saul's cousin. For Saul's father, Kish, and Abner's father, Ner, were brothers, having the same father, Abiel (1 Sam. 14:51, NIV). But in 1 Chronicles 8:33 "Ner begot Kish, Kish begot Saul," which would make Ner Saul's grandfather. But if Ner was the father of Abner (as 1 Sam. 14:51 says), who was Saul's cousin, then Ner would have been Saul's uncle. Which was he?

SOLUTION: There were probably two men named Ner, one Saul's uncle and the other his great grandfather. The same names were not uncommon in family trees. The genealogy would look like this:

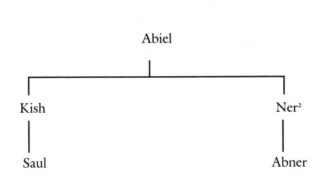

Thus, Saul had both an uncle and a great grandfather by the same name, Ner.

1 CHRONICLES 9:1 – What happened to the missing "Book of Kings"?

PROBLEM: The Books of Chronicles often refer to other missing books on which the inspired record in Chronicles is based in part (cf. 1 Chron. 9:1; 27:24; 29:29; 2 Chronicles 9:29; 13:22; 16:11; 25:26; 27:7; 28:26; 32:32; 33:19; 35:27; 36:8). Some of these books were written by prophets (1 Chron. 29:29). How could books that were written by prophets of God, or were the basis of prophetic books, perish? Why did not God preserve His Word?

SOLUTION: Prophets as a class were usually an educated group able to read and write. Samuel even led a "group of prophets" (1 Sam. 19:20, NIV). It was only natural that as moral educators in Israel they would keep a record of events in addition to whatever prophecies God may have given them. Thus, the records of Iddo the Seer may have been normal (uninspired) records which he kept (1 Chron. 29:29). It is noteworthy that they are not referred to as "visions" or "prophecies."

Further, it is not unusual for inspired books of the Bible to cite uninspired ones. The Apostle Paul even cited pagan poets (Acts 17:28; 1 Cor. 15:33; Titus 1:12). This does not mean that they were inspired, but simply that they uttered a truth on that occasion which a prophet or apostle incorporated into his inspired book.

1 CHRONICLES 10:6 – Did all of Saul's family die with him or not?

PROBLEM: Here we read, "Saul and his three sons died, and all his house died together." But, in 2 Samuel 2:8, Saul's son Ishbosheth was not killed and was even later made king.

SOLUTION: Ishbosheth was not encompassed by this statement, since he was not part of Saul's house who had attended him or followed him to war. So he was not part of the group referred to as "all Saul's men." First Samuel 31:6 states that "Saul, his three sons, his armorbearer, and all his men died together [in battle] that same day." Further, not all the grandchildren were killed, since Saul's son Jonathan had a handicapped son named Mephibosheth who also survived (2 Sam. 4:4). It is understandable that someone in his condition was not part of Saul's army and, therefore, did not die with Saul's other men in battle.

1 CHRONICLES 10:14 – Did Saul inquire of the Lord or not?

PROBLEM: First Samuel 28:6 says "when Saul inquired of the Lord, the Lord did not answer him." However, this verse says just the opposite, namely, "he [Saul] did not inquire of the Lord; therefore He killed him." But how can both be true?

SOLUTION: It should be noted first that two different words with different meanings are used here. Samuel uses the Hebrew word *shaal,* which usually means simply to ask, to consult, or to request. Chronicles, however, uses the word *darash* which often means to search for, or to seek after. In other words, Saul did not sincerely inquire of the Lord because He really wanted to know God's will, but because he was hoping God would agree with his will.

In brief, Saul inquired *casually* but not *sincerely.* He went through the *ritual,* but he was not seeking the *reality.*

1 CHRONICLES 21:1 – How can this passage claim that Satan moved David to number Israel when 2 Samuel 24:1 claims that God did?

(See discussion under 2 Sam. 24:1.)

1 CHRONICLES 22:14 – How could David have given 100,000 talents of gold when 1 Chronicles 29:4 says he gave only 3,000 talents?

PROBLEM: In preparation for the building of the temple, David states in 1 Chronicles 22:14 that he had donated 100,000 talents of gold. However, 1 Chronicles 29:4 affirms that David had given only 3,000. Which is correct?

SOLUTION: Both amounts are correct. Each of these passages records a different donation given by David. The 1 Chronicles 29 text clearly distinguishes the 3,000 talents of gold here recorded from the 100,000 talents given earlier. David points out in 29:3, that "because I have set my affection on the house of my God, I have given to the house of my God, *over and above all that I have prepared for the holy house, my own special treasure of gold and silver.*"

First Chronicles 22:14 records the amount given for the preparation of the building of the house of God. First Chronicles 29:4 states the amount given out of David's own private treasures, over and above what was raised by David for the preparation of the temple.

2 CHRONICLES

2 CHRONICLES 7:8-10 — Why did Solomon fail to keep the fast as the law commanded?

PROBLEM: Leviticus 16:30 commanded that a fast should be kept in connection with the Day of Atonement. However, Solomon did not observe a fast in connection with the Day of Atonement celebration that he held here in 2 Chronicles 7:8-10 (cf. also 1 Kings 8:65-66).

SOLUTION: First of all, it cannot be shown from the texts that Solomon failed to keep the fast as Leviticus had commanded. The text declares that Solomon celebrated for "fourteen days" (1 Kings 8:65). It is quite possible that on the actual Day of Atonement, which was the tenth day of the seventh month, that Solomon did keep the fast.

Furthermore, strictly speaking, the Leviticus passage does not use the word "fast." It simply says they were to "afflict their souls" (Lev. 16:29). This could mean to keep the celebration with appropriate solemnity, not necessitating that no food be eaten. It does forbid that no work be done (v. 29), but it does not really say that no food could be eaten, although this has been the general understanding of the phrase throughout Jewish history.

Finally, even if it could be shown that Solomon did not keep the Law correctly, all this would prove is that Solomon erred in not keeping the fast. It would not show that the Bible erred in recording what Solomon in truth did.

2 CHRONICLES 7:12ff — Does God dwell in a chosen temple?

PROBLEM: God told Solomon, "I have heard your prayer, and have chosen this place for Myself as a house of sacrifice" (v. 12), that "My name may be there forever" (v. 16). Yet, even Solomon in his dedicatory prayer acknowledged that God could not dwell in His temple, saying, "Behold, heaven and the heaven of heavens cannot contain You. How much less this temple which I have built!" (1 Kings 8:27). Other Scriptures likewise affirm that God does not "dwell in temples made with hands (Acts 17:24; cf. Isa. 66:1).

SOLUTION: It should be noted, first of all, that God did not actually promise Solomon that He would "dwell" in this temple. He only said He chose it as a "house of sacrifice" (2 Chron. 7:12), to which He would attach His "name" (v. 16).

Further, when the Bible speaks of God being "in" something, it does not mean that His infinite nature can be "contained" (1 Kings 8:27) by it, but simply that He is there in a special sense to bless it or manifest Himself to His people. Usually, this took the form of a theophany (Isa. 6:1), or shekinah cloud of glory (Ex. 40:34). But, there is no way that the transcendent God of Scripture can be encompassed by the walls of any human building (cf. Isa. 40:21-22).

2 CHRONICLES 9:21 — Did Solomon's ships get gold from Tarshish or from Ophir?

PROBLEM: Here the Chronicler affirms that Solomon's ships "went to Tarshish" and brought back gold. However, in 1 Kings 9:28 it claims they "went to Ophir" and acquired gold.

SOLUTION: Solomon had more than one fleet of ships and they went to more than one location. Every three years they went to Tarshish (Spain) and brought back "gold, silver, ivory, apes, and monkeys" (1 Kings 10:22; cf. 2 Chron. 9:21). This appears to be different from their mission to "Ophir" (Africa) which was for "gold" (1 Kings 9:28); Ophir was renown for gold in ancient times (cf. Job 28:16; Ps. 45:9; Isa. 13:12). That Ophir is a different trip seems evident from the fact that it brought back different things. For "the ships of Hiram, which brought gold from Ophir, brought great quantities of almug wood and precious stones from Ophir" (1 Kings 10:11), as opposed to "gold, silver, ivory, apes, and monkeys" mentioned in the trip to Tarshish (1 Kings 10:22).

2 CHRONICLES 9:25 — How can this verse say Solomon had 4,000 stalls when 1 Kings 4:26 says he had 40,000 stalls?

(See comments under 1 Kings 4:26.)

2 CHRONICLES 13:4-22 — Was Abijah a wicked or a righteous king?

PROBLEM: According to 1 Kings 15:3, Abijah was a wicked king who "walked in all the sins of his father." However, here in 2 Chronicles he is represented as giving a speech against idolatry and in defense of God's appointed priests and temple in Jerusalem.

SOLUTION: Abijah is not the first, nor will he be the last, politician on record who could give an occasional pious speech when it served his purposes. The fact is, his deeds did not match his words. That is, in general, whatever occasional exceptions there may have been, he was an evil king, just as 1 Kings 15:3 declares.

2 CHRONICLES 14:9 — How can this verse make reference to Zerah the Ethiopian, when there are no historical records of such a person?

PROBLEM: When Asa was king in Judah, he was confronted by Zerah the Ethiopian who marshalled an army of 1 million men. However, there are no historical records of such a person. Is this an error?

SOLUTION: This is not an error. It is true that until now no extra-biblical records of Zerah the Ethiopian have been found. However, simply because extra-biblical records of Zerah have not been discovered does not mean the biblical record is in error. To doubt the historical accuracy of the Bible on the basis of the silence of extra-biblical sources is to engage in faulty reasoning. Through the years, critics have doubted the existence of many historical figures of the Bible, only to be refuted by additional historical and archaeological discoveries (e.g., the existence of the Hittites and of Sodom and Gomorrah).

2 CHRONICLES 16:1 — How can this verse say Baasha king of Israel built Ramah in the thirty-sixth year of the reign of Asa?

PROBLEM: Asa began his reign in about 911 B.C. The thirty-sixth year of his reign would have been about 876 or 875 B.C. However, Baasha began his reign in 909 and reigned until 886 B.C. when Elah his son became king (1 Kings 16:8). How could 2 Chronicles 16:1 say Baasha built Ramah in the thirty-sixth year of Asa, 11 years after Baasha's death?

SOLUTION: The number "thirty-six" is undoubtedly a copyist error. The actual number was probably "sixteen." This error is explained by the fact that the numbers were probably written in numerical notation. In this type of notation, the difference between the letter representing the number 10 xx and the letter representing the number 30 xx was only two small strokes at the top of the letter. It is quite possible that a copyist misread the original and wrote the wrong letter for the number, possibly as the result of a smudged or damaged manuscript at his disposal.

2 CHRONICLES 21:12 — How could Elijah have sent a letter long after his departure into heaven?

PROBLEM: When Jehoram became king in Judah, "he made high places in the mountains of Judah, and caused the inhabitants of Jerusalem to commit harlotry, and led Judah astray" (2 Chron. 21:11). In 2 Chronicles 21:12, we find that, in response to Jehoram's sin, Elijah sent a letter to Jehoram. However, if Elijah was translated prior to the reign of Jehoram the son of Jehoshaphat, then how could he have sent a letter to Jehoram?

SOLUTION: Elijah was not translated until some time during the reign of Jehoram son of Ahab. Jehoram son of Ahab reigned in Israel from about 852 to 841 B.C. Jehoram son of Jehoshaphat reigned in Judah from 848 to 841 B.C. Therefore, since Elijah was not translated until some time in the reign of Jehoram of Israel, it is perfectly reasonable that he could have sent this letter to Jehoram of Judah.

2 CHRONICLES 22:1 — Were Jehoram's sons taken captive or were they killed?

PROBLEM: According to 2 Chronicles 21:16-17, Jehoram's sons were only taken captive by the Philistines and the Arabians. By contrast, this passage says they "killed all the older sons."

SOLUTION: There is no contradiction here for two reasons. First, it was only the "older" sons who were killed, not all of them. The others could have been taken captive. Second, they could have first taken them captive and then afterward killed them.

2 CHRONICLES 22:8 — Were Ahaziah's brothers slain or were they his brother's sons?

PROBLEM: Here we are told that it was king Ahaziah's brother's "sons" who were killed. But 2 Kings 10:13-14 says it was Ahaziah's "brothers" that were slain.

SOLUTION: The Hebrew term for "brother" can mean "near relative." For example, Abraham's nephew Lot was called his "brother" (Gen. 14:12, 16). Since Ahaziah, the youngest son, was born when his father was only 18, he could have had many nephews and cousins or "brethren." Since the 2 Chronicles passage refers to his brother's sons, the word "brother" can be taken in the strict sense here.

It is also quite possible that both statements are literally true. Since Jehu was commanded by God to exterminate the house of Ahab, and since Ahaziah "walked in the way of the house of Ahab," it is conceivable that Jehu took it upon himself to destroy the house of Ahaziah also, including his brothers and his brothers' sons. In fact, in the 2 Kings passage, the report of the killing of Ahaziah's brothers (2 Kings 10:13-14) takes place after Jehu had killed Ahaziah (2 Kings 9:27), while the 2 Chronicles passage reports the killing of the sons of Ahaziah's brothers before the killing of Ahaziah (2 Chron. 22:8-9).

2 CHRONICLES 28:24 — Did Ahaz encourage or oppose worship in the Jerusalem temple?

PROBLEM: In 2 Kings 16:15, Ahaz encouraged the worship of the Lord in the temple. But, in 2 Chronicles 28 he is said to have "shut up the doors of the house of the Lord, and made for himself altars in every corner of Jerusalem" (v. 24).

SOLUTION: First of all, even in 2 Kings, during his earlier reign, Ahaz was said to be an evil king who "did not do what was right in the sight of the Lord his God" (16:2). He even "took the silver and gold that was found in the house of the Lord . . . and sent it as a present to the king of Assyria" (v. 8). During this period, he encouraged only a corrupt form of worship in the pilfered Jerusalem temple (v. 15).

Furthermore, the 2 Chronicles passages refers to a later, even more corrupt, part of his reign. During this period of apostasy, he shut up the house of the Lord completely and set up his own centers of worship.

2 CHRONICLES 33:10-17 — Why is the repentance of Manasseh recorded here, but no mention is made of it in 2 Kings?

PROBLEM: According to this text, upon his return, Manasseh repented of his earlier sin and reinstituted the worship of the Lord in Judah. However, the record of the career of Manasseh as found in 2 Kings 21 does not mention this glorious repentance. Why?

SOLUTION: Apparently the author of 2 Kings did not record the repentance of Manasseh because of the lack of influence it had upon the steady decline of the nation. The Book of 2 Kings concentrates primarily upon the actions of the covenant people of God as a whole. The repentance and reforms of Manasseh did relatively little to turn the nation around from its path to judgment, while his sinful leadership early in his reign did much more damage to the nation. Even in the 2 Chronicles passage we find this statement: "Nevertheless the people still sacrificed on the high places, but only to the Lord their God" (2 Chron. 33:17). Even though the people dedicated their sacrifices to the Lord, they were still committing sin, because sacrifices were to be made at the temple, not upon high places which were originally altars to false gods. Despite the efforts of Manasseh, the people would not totally dedicate themselves to the Lord.

2 CHRONICLES 34:3-5 — If Josiah demolished idolatry, then why does it say Manasseh did it earlier?

PROBLEM: Here we are informed that Josiah destroyed the altars and idols, but earlier (in 2 Chron. 33:15) Manasseh had destroyed them.

SOLUTION: No human king can root out the depraved human desire for idolatry. Therefore, Josiah had to redo the same work that his predecessor had done. A good human king can destroy idols, but not the love of idols. And, as long as this love exists, idolatry will live to rear its ugly head again and again.

2 CHRONICLES 36:6 — Was Jehoiakim carried to Babylon or did he die in Jerusalem?

PROBLEM: The Chronicler declares that Nebuchadnezzar "came up against him [Jehoiakim], and bound him in bronze fetters to carry him off to Babylon." But elsewhere "Jehoiakim rested with his fathers" (2 Kings 24:6) and was "buried with the burial of a donkey, dragged and cast out beyond the gates of Jerusalem" (Jer. 22:19; cf. 36:30).

SOLUTION: Apparently, Jehoiakim was bound and fettered with the intention "to carry him off to Babylon" (2 Chron. 36:6), but he was slain instead, and his body ignominiously treated "and cast out beyond the gates of Jerusalem" (Jer. 22:19). The phrase "rested with his fathers" (2 Kings 24:6) refers to death, not necessarily to a burial in the same place. Of all the kings of Judah, Jehoiakim is the only one whose official burial is not mentioned.

EZRA

EZRA 1:8 – Who is Sheshbazzar?

PROBLEM: When Cyrus the king of Persia allowed the Israelites to return to Jerusalem, he gave back the articles of the house of the Lord which Nebuchadnezzar had taken. According to Ezra 1:8, Cyrus counted out into the hands of Sheshbazzar the prince of Judah the treasures that Nebuchadnezzar had taken. Who was this Sheshbazzar?

SOLUTION: There have been two proposals as to the identity of Sheshbazzar. First, some commentators claim that Sheshbazzar was the court name of Zerubbabel. The giving of court names was quite common during the captivity of Israel in Babylon. Daniel's court name was Belteshazzar (Dan. 1:7). One weakness of this view is that it is not clear whether or not Sheshbazzar is a Babylonian name, and usually, an Israelite who had received a court name, had also been given a Hebrew name by his parents. Neither Sheshbazzar nor Zerubbabel are Hebrew names, and neither can be conclusively identified as Babylonian.

Second, other commentators claim that Sheshbazzar is the court name of Shealtiel, Zerubbabel's adopted father. This involves an explanation as to why Sheshbazzar is identified as "the prince of Judah" in Ezra 1:8. It is proposed that Shealtiel/Sheshbazzar was assigned to this position by the Babylonian governor, and that this position passed on to Zerubbabel after Shealtiel/Sheshbazzar's death. Ezra 5:16 states that it was Sheshbazzar who "laid the foundation of the house of God." Since Ezra 3 does not specifically name Sheshbazzar as participating in the laying of this foundation, it can be assumed that Shealtiel/Sheshbazzar and Zerubbabel participated in the project together as a father/son team, and Sheshbazzar is just not mentioned. One weakness of this position is that there is no indication that there were two persons functioning as joint governors of Jerusalem. Also, there is the fact that the name Sheshbazzar is not mentioned in the long list recorded in Ezra 2 of those who came back with Zerubbabel.

The fact that Sheshbazzar's name is not mentioned again after Ezra 5:16 can be explained from the point of view of either proposal. If Sheshbazzar and Shealtiel are one person, then perhaps he died shortly after the laying of the foundation. If Sheshbazzar and Zerubbabel are one person, then the court name was simply dropped, and the given name Zerubbabel was retained. Either explanation, however, provides a reasonable solution, and there is no real reason to assume an error or contradiction here.

EZRA 2:1ff — Why are many of the numbers in Ezra's list of those who returned to Jerusalem different from those in Nehemiah 7?

PROBLEM: In the record of those who returned to Jerusalem under the leadership of Zerubbabel as recorded in Ezra, there are 32 family units identified and numbered. In 18 of these instances, the numbers in Ezra are exactly the same as those found in Nehemiah 7. However, in 14 instances, the numbers differ. The difference ranges from as little as one to as much as 1,100. Why are these numbers different?

SOLUTION: First, it is possible that each of these is a copyist error. One of the most problematic areas of transcription for the Jewish scribe was copying numbers. It is certainly conceivable that out of these rather large lists of names and numbers there would be a number of copyist errors (see Appendix 2).

Second, it is also possible that Ezra and Nehemiah compiled their lists at different times. Ezra may have compiled a list of those who left Babylon with Zerubbabel, while Nehemiah compiled his list of those who actually made it to Jerusalem. In some cases, people who left Babylon with the intention of going back to rebuild Jerusalem may have turned back or died along the way. In other cases, a family may have enlisted recruits to bolster their numbers. Perhaps family members in other lands got word of the migration and rendezvoused with their relatives along the way from Babylon to Jerusalem.

EZRA 3:10 — How could the rebuilding have begun during the reign of Cyrus when Ezra 4:24 says it was in the reign of Darius I?

PROBLEM: According to Ezra 3:8-13, the rebuilding of the temple began under the reign of Cyrus the Great (cf. Ezra 5:16), who reigned in Persia from about 559 to 530 B.C. However, Ezra 4:24 says the rebuilding of the temple took place during the reign of Darius, King of Persia, about 520 B.C. Also, Haggai 1:15 implies that the building of the temple did not begin until 520 B.C. How can these statements be reconciled?

SOLUTION: The statements in Ezra 3:10 and 5:16 are references to *laying the foundation,* while Ezra 4:24 and Haggai 1:15 concern the *resuming the rebuilding project* after a long period of delay. Ezra 4:4 points out that as soon as the people of the land heard about the rebuilding project, they discouraged the people and frustrated their efforts throughout the reign of Cyrus. The project was abandoned for 16 years. At this point, God directed Haggai to prophesy to the people of Jerusalem to motivate them to begin the project again. This is referred to in Ezra 4:24. The rebuilding of the temple was resumed about 520 B.C. during the time of Darius and was completed in 516 B.C.

EZRA 4:23 – How could foreign influence have caused the work to cease when Haggai 1:2 blames it on the indifference of the leaders?

PROBLEM: Ezra 4:7-23 records that after the great beginning made by the people in laying the foundation of the temple, foreign enemies came up to force the people to stop the rebuilding project. However, Haggai 1:2 implies that the people were indifferent toward the building project. What was the real reason for the delay in rebuilding the temple?

SOLUTION: Both statements are true. Although the military force of the enemy caused the rebuilding to *stop,* it was the indifference of the people that was responsible for the fact that the project was not *restarted.* During the reign of Cyrus the Great, the climate was hostile toward the people, and the building project faced stiff opposition. Once Darius I had taken power in Persia in about 522 B.C., the opportunity to restart the building project was much more favorable. However, the leaders of the people had become so involved in their own affairs that they were not interested in undertaking such an enormous project.

EZRA 10:10-44 – Why did God command Israelite men to put away their unbelieving wives, but Paul said not to do so?

PROBLEM: Ezra made all the returning Israelites put away their "pagan wives" because they were "adding to the guilt of Israel" (Ezra 10:10). However, when Paul was asked whether a believer should divorce an unbelieving spouse, he said, "If any brother has a wife who does not believe, and she is willing to live with him, let him not divorce her" (1 Cor. 7:12). Aren't these contradictory instructions?

SOLUTION: The different advice is given at different times, for different peoples, and for different reasons. First of all, Ezra's command was given in OT times to the Jews, and Paul's command was given in NT times to Christians. New Testament believers are not under OT laws to Israel (see comments on Matt. 5:17-18).

Furthermore, even assuming that the moral principle embodied in this OT command is still binding today, the situations are different for three reasons. First, the wives in the OT were not just "unbelievers" who were "willing" to be "sanctified" by the believing husband (1 Cor. 7:14). They were "pagans," that is, they were probably Babylonian *idol worshipers* (cf. Neh. 13:25-26), who were having a pagan influence on their husbands. God told Solomon that his pagan wives, "will turn away your hearts after their gods" (1 Kings 11:2). Second, these were not just any pagans, for they included descendants of Moab and Ammon (Ezra 10:30; cf. Neh. 13:23) and other surrounding nations of which God had told the Israelites explicitly that they should not marry them (cf. Ex. 34:16; Deut. 7:3). Third, they may even have been *extra* wives (cf. Ezra 10:44), and God forbid polygamy (see comments on 1 Kings 11:1). If so, they had violated the laws about polygamy (Deut. 17:17) and idolatry (Ex. 20:4-5). This is a different situation from Paul's instruction to keep a non-idolatrous monogamous wife (cf. 1 Cor. 7:2), if she wished to remain under the sanctifying influence of a believing husband.

NEHEMIAH

NEHEMIAH 2:19 – Why is Nehemiah's adversary named Geshem here and Gashmu in Nehemiah 6:6? (KJV)

PROBLEM: As soon as Nehemiah set about to rebuild the walls of Jerusalem, the surrounding enemy mounted an opposition. One of those who opposed the work was identified as Geshem the Arab. However, in Nehemiah 6:6 this same person is identified as Gashmu. Which is the correct spelling?

SOLUTION: Both spellings are correct. The difference lies in the way the Hebrew and Arab languages treat the spelling of proper names. The Arabic pronunciation is preserved in Nehemiah 6:6 with the customary "u" ending. The Hebrew pronunciation is preserved in Nehemiah 2:19 with the elimination of the "u" along with the appropriate short vowels to produce the name "Geshem."

NEHEMIAH 7:1ff – Why are many of the numbers in Nehemiah's list of those who returned to Jerusalem different from those in Ezra 2:1ff?

(See comments under Ezra 2:1ff.)

NEHEMIAH 7:32 – If Ai was destroyed earlier, why is it still inhabited here?

PROBLEM: After an earlier embarrassing defeat because of disobedience to God, Joshua's forces completely destroyed the city of Ai (Josh. 8:28). But it is still flourishing many years later (Neh. 7:32).

SOLUTION: This is many centuries later, and the city was rebuilt by survivors or others. Phrases like "utterly destroyed" (Josh. 8:26) refer to all who got caught. It does not say that some did not escape. Nor does it eliminate the possibility that others moved in later to occupy the site.

This same explanation applies to the Amalekites who were completely destroyed (1 Sam. 15:7-8), yet survived to be overthrown at a later date (1 Sam. 30:1, 17). Likewise, Bethel and Gezer were conquered by Joshua (Josh. 12:12, 16) and later under the judges (Jud. 1:22-29). However, Genesis 32:3 may refer to the settlement of Edom by anticipation (cf. Gen. 36:6, 8).

NEHEMIAH 8:17 — Was this feast not celebrated since Joshua's time or was it celebrated later by Zerubbabel?

PROBLEM: According to this passage, the Feast of Tabernacles had not been celebrated by Israel "since the days of Joshua the son of Nun." Yet, Ezra 3:4 declares that Zerubbabel and the Israelites "kept the Feast of Tabernacles" after they returned from the Babylonian captivity.

SOLUTION: The Nehemiah passage means there had been *nothing like this celebration* since Joshua's day. It does not mean no one had ever celebrated this feast since Joshua's day. Nehemiah's celebration was unique in many ways. First, it was commemorated by "the whole congregation" (Neh. 8:17). Second, it was celebrated with "great gladness" (v. 17). Third, it was celebrated with a Biblethon, that is, with continual Bible reading for one week. Fourth, they celebrated it exactly as Moses had commanded, with a restored priesthood and temple (8:18; cf. 12:1ff). Nothing like this had occurred since Joshua's day.

ESTHER

ESTHER — How could this book be part of the Holy Scriptures when God is not even mentioned?

PROBLEM: Although the rabbis at Jamnia, in about A.D. 90, debated whether the book should continue to be counted among the inspired Scriptures, the Book of Esther has enjoyed a long history of acceptance among the books of the Hebrew canon. However, the Book of Esther is the only book in the entire Bible in which the name of God is not mentioned. How can it be part of the Word of God?

SOLUTION: Even though there is an absence of the *name* of God, it is evident that there is no absence of the *hand* of God. The entire book overflows with the providence of God in human affairs. God so directed the lives of those involved that He had the right person at precisely the right place at precisely the right point in time. As Mordecai observed, "Yet who knows whether you have come to the kingdom for such a time as this" (Es. 4:14).

Further, the name of God is found in the Book of Esther in acrostic form. At four crucial points in the story (1:20; 5:4; 5:13; 7:7), twice forward and twice backward, God's name (YHWH) is present. The devout Jew would have recognized this, while the Persians would not. This may have been God's way of preserving His sacred name from pagan perversion. Even apart from any explicit use of God's name, the hand of God in directing the affairs of men is glaringly obvious throughout the narrative. Yet, the free moral agency of each participant is perfectly preserved. Although He can, God does not need to invade the normal process of daily affairs to accomplish His will. His providence delicately intertwines into the acts and decisions of people so that He accomplishes all His will with divine perfection and precision, without violating human free choice. The Book of Esther, like no other book, reveals the hidden, supernatural providence of God in directing all of His creation according to the good purpose of His will. Even in the explicit absence of God's name, Esther reminds us that He is always present and always in control.

ESTHER 2:1-18 — How could Esther participate in a pagan beauty contest?

PROBLEM: It is evident that Esther was selected by God as His instrument to deliver Israel from evil at the appointed time (Esther 4:14). However, as a devout Jew, how could Esther take part in a pagan pageant and then become part of the harem of King Xerxes?

SOLUTION: First, it is not clear that Esther had a choice as far as being part of the display of beautiful women before the king. According to Esther 2:8, Esther was "taken to the king's palace." This seems to imply that Esther had no choice in the matter, but was drafted into the service of the king.

Second, it is not clear that participants in the pageant had to do anything explicitly immoral to be in the contest. Knowing Esther's character, we can be sure she would have refused to do anything contrary to God's law.

Finally, once she had been chosen by the king, she was compelled to belong to his court. It was the providence of God that brought Esther to this place at precisely the appropriate moment. When the time was right, Esther was willing to place her life on the line for the people of her God.

ESTHER 4:16 — Didn't Esther disobey human government which God had ordained?

PROBLEM: Romans 13:1 informs us that even pagan governments are "appointed by God," and Peter adds, "submit yourselves to every ordinance of man for the Lord's sake" (1 Peter 2:13; cf. Titus 3:1). But it says that what she did was "against the law" (4:16). So, didn't Esther violate the God-ordained laws of Persia by going before the king?

SOLUTION: Sometimes it is necessary to disobey human government, namely, when it compels us to sin. For example, if the government says we cannot pray to God (Dan. 6) or we must worship idols (Dan. 3) or we must kill innocent babies (see comments on Ex. 1:15-21), then we must disobey. In Esther's case, however, there was no law compelling her to sin. But neither did she disobey the law of the land, since the law allowed for someone to come before the king unannounced at their own risk (Es. 4:11). Knowing of this provision of the law and accepting the risk of her life, Esther went before the king to save the lives of her people. In this case there was no need to disobey the law, since it was not compelling her to kill anyone or to commit any other act of sin.

JOB

JOB 1:1 — If all are sinners, then how can Job be perfect?

PROBLEM: God declared that Job was "blameless and upright, and one who feared God and shunned evil" (1:1). Yet the Bible insists that "there is none righteous, no, not one," for "all have sinned and fall short of the glory of God" (Rom. 3:10, 23).

SOLUTION: God's praise of Job was not absolute, as is clear from His later condemnation of him (in chap. 38) and from Job's own confession, "I abhor myself, And repent in dust and ashes" (Job 42:6). Further, God only pronounced Job "blameless" *before man,* whereas Romans is speaking about no one, apart from Christ's work, being blameless *before God* (cf. Rom. 3:19).

JOB 1:1 — Was Job a real historical person?

PROBLEM: The first verse of the Book of Job introduces the main character as a historical figure who actually existed in the land of Uz. However, modern scholars have questioned the historicity of the man Job. Was Job a real historical person?

SOLUTION: Job was a person in human history. First of all, verse one of the book plainly asserts that Job actually existed. There are no literary indications that this statement should be understood any other way than as a statement of historical fact. There is every reason to accept it with the same assurance one would accept the historicity of any such statement in the Bible.

Second, the historicity of Job is attested by references in other parts of the Scripture. In Ezekiel 14:14, 20, God names Job along with Daniel and Noah as examples of righteousness. To question the historicity of Job, one would have to question the historicity of Daniel and Noah. Additionally, this would call into question the veracity of God, for He makes reference to these men (through Ezekiel) as real historical figures.

Finally, in James 5:11 we find a reference to Job in which Job is held to be an example of patience in the midst of tribulation. James makes a matter-of-fact reference to Job that assumes the historicity of both the man and the events recorded in the book that bears his name. There would have been no real force to James' appeal if Job were merely a fictional character. For in that case, what actual comfort would his life be to real people?

JOB 1:5 — Why does Job offer a burnt offering for his sons if they had blessed God?

PROBLEM: According to Job 1:5, Job was such a pious man that he even offered burnt offerings for his sons just in case they had sinned and cursed God. However, the Hebrew word used here, and in 1:11 and 2:5, is not "cursed," but "blessed." Why do these passages use the word "blessed" instead of the word "cursed"?

SOLUTION: Two solutions have been proposed. First, the Hebrew people had a sublime reverence for God's name. In fact, they would not even pronounce God's name lest they possibly commit blasphemy in the act. When the name Yahweh appeared in the text of the Scripture, the pious Hebrew would not say God's name out loud, but would substitute the word "Adonai," which means "Lord." It has been proposed that perhaps the author of Job (or a later editor), recognizing this reverence, did not wish to write or speak the word "curse" with reference to God. Therefore, he substituted the word "bless" and allowed the context to supply the necessary idea.

Second, others have suggested that the verb used here, *barak,* means "to say good-bye to." Several passages are cited in support of this use, such as Genesis 24:60, 32:1 and 47:10. The function of this word in this context is viewed as a antiphrastic euphemism. This is the use of a word or phrase that usually has one meaning in common speech, but is used to mean the opposite. We do this at times even today. For example, someone might sarcastically say "yes" when the obvious meaning is "no." Job's statement in 1:5, then, can be translated, "It may be that my sons have sinned and dismissed God in their hearts." In each of these instances, the word gives the idea of dismissing or rejecting God.

JOB 1:6 — How can Satan come before God when he was dismissed from heaven?

PROBLEM: Job 1:6 states that the sons of God came to present themselves to God, and "Satan also came among them." However, this implies that Satan has access to the throne of God when elsewhere it is declared that he has been banished from God's presence (Rev. 12:7-12).

SOLUTION: Satan has been *officially* expelled from heaven, but he still *actually* has access there. Several places in Scripture present the idea that Satan has access to the presence of God in order to accuse the saints. In Zechariah 3:1 we find a vision of Joshua standing before the angel of the Lord with Satan on his right hand accusing him. Revelation 12:10 identifies Satan as the accuser of the brethren "who accused them before our God day and night." Apparently, as the prince of the power of the air (Eph. 2:2), Satan has had opportunity to appear before God for the purpose of accusing God's people of sin. This is what he is doing against Job in both Job 1:6 and 2:1.

JOB 1:6 — Who are the sons of God mentioned in this verse?

PROBLEM: The introduction of Satan into the story of Job takes place before the throne of God. Satan comes before God among a group identified as "the sons of God." But, who are these sons of God?

SOLUTION: These are angels. Several other passages in the Bible refer to angels as the sons of God, such as Job 2:1 and Job 38:7 (cf. Pss. 29:1 and 89:6 where the Hebrew uses the phrase "sons of God"). The angels are the "sons" of God in the sense that they are His creation. (Also see comments on Gen. 6:2ff.)

JOB 1:20-21 — Does this verse teach reincarnation?

PROBLEM: The Bible speaks against the belief in reincarnation (Heb. 9:27). But here Job speaks of a person returning again after he dies.

SOLUTION: Job is not speaking about the "return" of the soul to another body to live again, but of the return of the body to the grave. God told Adam he would "return to the ground" for "dust you are and to dust you shall return" (Gen. 3:19). And the Hebrew word for "womb" (*beten*) is used figuratively in Job's poetic expression of the "earth." The ideas of "earth" and "womb" are used in Psalm 139, saying, God formed us in our "mother's womb" in "the lowest parts of the earth" (vv. 13, 15). Like the ancient Hebrew book of wisdom (Ecclesiasticus 40:1), Job believed that men labor "from the day they come forth from their mother's womb, till the day they return to the Mother of all [i.e., the womb of the earth]." Likewise, Job used the poetic expression "return there [i.e., to my mother's womb]" to refer to the earth from which we all come and to which we all return (cf. Ecc. 12:7).

Furthermore, even if one insisted on a literal understanding of this figure of speech, it would not prove reincarnation. It would only show that the person returns to his mothers womb after he dies, which is absurd!

Finally, Job did not believe in reincarnation into another mortal body; he believed in resurrection in an immortal body. He declared: "I know that my redeemer lives, And He shall stand at last on the earth; And after my skin is destroyed this I know, that *in my flesh* I shall see God" (Job 19:25-26). He realized that this corruptible flesh would put on incorruptible flesh (cf. 1 Cor. 15:42-44). But reincarnation, by contrast, does not believe we will be raised once in an immortal physical body; it is the belief that the soul will be reincarnated many times into mortal bodies that will die again. So there is no basis for claiming Job believed in reincarnation.

JOB 5:13 — Why does Paul quote these words of Eliphaz if Eliphaz was rebuked by God in Job 42:7 for what he said?

PROBLEM: Eliphaz was one of the friends of Job who came to comfort him in his affliction. In Job 5:13, Eliphaz makes the following observation which Paul quotes in 1 Corinthians 3:19: "He [God] catches the wise in their own craftiness." However, in Job 42:7, God rebukes Eliphaz and his friends because "you have not spoken of Me what is right, as My servant Job has." How could Paul quote Eliphaz since God rebuked him for not saying the right things?

SOLUTION: Although God rebuked Eliphaz for his overall view of God, this does not mean that every statement Eliphaz made was incorrect. There were many *particular* things which Job said that were not right; however, Job's view of God was right in *general*. At times, even Job recognized that some things that Eliphaz and his friends said were true. Their problem was that they misdirected the truth they knew and improperly applied it to what God was doing in Job's life.

JOB
■

JOB 7:9 — Does this verse contradict the Bible's teaching about resurrection?

PROBLEM: The Scriptures teach that all people will be raised bodily from the tomb (cf. Dan. 12:2; 1 Cor. 15:22; Rev. 20:4-6). Indeed, Jesus said that one day "all who are in the graves will hear His voice and come forth" (John 5:28-29). However, Job seems to say just the opposite, when he wrote: "he who goes down to the grave does not come up" (cf. also Job 14:12; Isa. 26:14; Amos 8:14).

SOLUTION: As the first set of passages clearly reveals, there will be a resurrection of all the dead, both the just and the unjust (Acts 24:15; cf. John 5:28-29). Job himself expressed belief in the resurrection, declaring, "After my skin is destroyed, this I know, that in my flesh I shall see God" (Job 19:26). What he meant when he spoke of someone going down to the grave and not coming up (7:9) is explained in the very next verse. "He shall never return *to his house*" (v. 10). In other words, those who die do not return to their mortal lives again. Indeed, the resurrection is to an immortal life (1 Cor. 15:53), not to the same mortal life one had before.

Job 14:12 does not deny there will be any resurrection, but simply that there will be none until "the heavens are no more," that is until the end of the age. But, that is precisely when the resurrection will take place, namely "at the time of the end" (Dan. 11:40; cf. 12:1-2; John 11:24). In fact, the passage actually teaches resurrection. For Job simply spoke of being hidden in the grave by God until an appointed time when God would again remember him (14:13) in the resurrection.

Likewise, the Isaiah passage (Isa. 26:14) does not deny the resurrection. Here too the resurrection is affirmed in the succeeding verse which states clearly, "Your dead shall live; together with my dead body they shall arise" (v. 19). Obviously, then verse 14 means "they will not live" *until the resurrection.* The memory of the wicked will perish from the earthly scene. Not until the heavenly scene dawns will they be raised again.

Also, some texts which may appear to deny the resurrection (e.g., Amos 8:14) simply refer to the enemies of God falling, never to rise to oppose Him. They will never resume their former sway over God's people. In short, God overthrew them irretrievably.

JOB 11:7 – Can God be known by humans?

PROBLEM: Job seems to imply that God cannot be known by human reason. Paul also declared that God's judgments are "unsearchable . . . and His ways past finding out" (Rom. 11:33). On the other hand, the Bible declares that God has revealed Himself to all people (Rom. 1:20) so that they "are without excuse" (v. 20). Indeed, the Bible is said to be a special revelation of God by which we can know Him and serve Him (2 Tim. 3:16-17).

SOLUTION: God cannot be known *directly* in this life, nor can He be known *completely*. For "now we see in a mirror, dimly, but then face to face. Now I know in part, but then I shall know just as I also am known" (1 Cor. 13:12). God can be known "by the things that are made" (Rom. 1:19), but He cannot be known in Himself. The following contrast summarizes the ways God can and cannot be known:

HOW GOD CANNOT BE KNOWN	HOW GOD CAN BE KNOWN
In Himself (His essence)	In His creation (His effects)
Directly	Indirectly
Completely	Partially
As Spirit	As Incarnate in Christ

While "no one has seen God at any time [in His essence]" (John 1:18), nonetheless, His only begotten Son has revealed Him. Thus, Jesus could say, "He who has seen Me has seen the Father" (John 14:9).

JOB 14:12 – Does this contradict the Bible's teaching on the resurrection?

(See comments on Job 7:9.)

JOB 19:17 – How could Job have children here when they were all killed earlier?

PROBLEM: In Job 1:2, 18-19 (cf. 8:4) all of Job's children were killed in a great windstorm. Yet here he speaks of his breath being "repulsive to the children of my own body."

SOLUTION: The term "children" can mean "grandchildren" or even his "blood relatives." With seven sons and three daughters, including their own families (cf. 1:2, 18), Job undoubtedly had many grandchildren. Job lived 140 more years after his sickness (Job 42:16). So, in his long life, he had many years to have many grandchildren and great grandchildren.

JOB 19:26 – Does this verse indicate that the resurrection body will be a body of flesh?

PROBLEM: Satan had afflicted Job's body, and his flesh was rotting away. However, Job expressed his faith in God by saying, "in my flesh I shall see God" (Job 19:26). Does this mean that the resurrection body will be a body of flesh?

SOLUTION: Yes. Although the preposition "from" (*min*) may be translated "without," it is a characteristic of this preposition that when it is used with the verb "to see," it has the meaning "from the vantage point of." This idea is strengthened by the use of contrasting parallelism employed in this verse. Hebrew poetry often employs two parallel lines of poetic expression which sometimes express contrasting words or ideas (called antithetic parallelism). Here the loosing of Job's flesh is contrasted by his trust in God to restore the body that is decaying before his eyes, and that in his very flesh, he would see God. This is a most sublime expression of Job's faith in a literal, physical resurrection (see also Dan. 12:2; Luke 24:39; John 5:28-29; Acts 2:31-32).

JOB 37:18 – Does the Bible err in speaking of a solid dome above the earth?

PROBLEM: Job speaks of God who "spread out the skies" like "a cast metal mirror" (37:18). Indeed, the Hebrew word for the "firmament" (*raqia*) which God created (cf. Gen. 1:6) is defined in the Hebrew lexicon as a solid object. But this is in clear conflict with the modern scientific understanding of space as non-solid and largely empty.

SOLUTION: It is true that the origin of the Hebrew word *raqia* meant a solid object. However, meaning is not determined by *origin* (etymology), but by *usage*. Originally, the English word "board" referred to a wooden plank. But when we speak of a church board member, the word no longer has that meaning. When used of the atmosphere above the earth, "firmament" clearly does not mean something solid. This is evident for several reasons. First, the related word *raqa* (beat out, spread out) is correctly rendered "expanse" by many recent translations. Just as metal spreads out when beaten (cf. Ex. 39:3; Isa. 40:19), so the firmament is a thinned out area.

Second, the root meaning "spread out" can be used independently of "beat out," as it is in several passages (cf. Ps. 136:6; Isa. 42:5; 44:24). Isaiah wrote, "So says Jehovah God, He who created the heavens and *stretched them out,* spreading out the earth and its offspring (Isa. 42:5, MKJV). This same verb is used of extending curtains or tents in which to dwell, which would make no sense if there was no empty space there in which to live. Isaiah, for example, spoke of the Lord "who sits on the circle of the earth, and its people are like grasshoppers; who *stretches out the heavens like a curtain, and spreads them out like a tent to dwell in . . ."* (Isa. 40:22, MKJV).

Third, the Bible speaks of rain falling through the sky (Job 36:27-28). But this makes no sense if the sky is a metal dome. Nowhere does the Bible refer to little holes in a metal dome through which the drops fall. It does speak figuratively of the "windows of heaven" opening for the Flood (Gen. 7:11). But this should probably not be taken any more literally than our idiom, "It is raining cats and dogs."

Fourth, the Genesis creation account speaks of birds that "fly above the earth across the face of the firmament" (Gen. 1:20). But this would be impossible if the sky was solid. Thus, it is more appropriate to translate *raqia* by the word "expanse" (as the NASB and NIV do). And in this sense there is no conflict with the concept of space in modern science.

Fifth, even taken literally, Job's statement (37:18) does not affirm that the "skies" *are* a "metal mirror," but simply that they are *"as* [like]" a mirror. In other words, it is a comparison that need not be taken literally, any more than God is really a "strong tower" (cf. Prov. 18:10). Further, the point of comparison in Job is not the solidity of the "skies" and a mirror, but their durability (cf. word "strong" [*chazaq*]; v. 18). So when all is considered, there is no evidence that the Bible affirms that the firmament of the sky is a metallic dome. And thus there is no conflict with modern science.

JOB 41:1 — Does this passage make reference to the mythological figure Leviathan?

PROBLEM: Job 41:1 makes reference to the mythological figure Leviathan. But, how can the Bible talk about Leviathan as if it were a real sea monster?

SOLUTION: Although this is basically the same name used in the Ugaritic documents about a mythological sea monster, it is not at all clear that Job 41:1 is a reference to this monster. Some commentators have proposed that this is a reference to a large crocodile, and that the name "Leviathan" is used to heighten the emphasis on its uncontrolability.

Further, this type of expression is often used today, as when someone refers to an adversary as a "monster." This is not a claim that monsters actually exist. It is merely the application to the person or thing of the fearsome characteristics that are usually associated with a monster.

Finally, even if it is assumed that this is a reference to the same mythological creature of the Ugaritic tales, its use in this poetic text is not necessarily a claim that it really exists. It could be simply a poetic figure employing the image of an untamable sea monster to illustrate a point. Whereas Job is merely a man incapable of taming such a fearsome beast, God is all-powerful, and it is He who sets the bounds of both man and beast. As such, it would be like someone today saying "Jesus (whom they believe is historical) is stronger than Superman (whom they believe to be mythical)." Poetic expressions often employ symbolic figures in an effort to heighten the emotional impact of the literal message being conveyed. This does not, however, mean that the author accepts the pagan mythology that has given rise to this figure.

PSALMS

PSALM 1:2 – Should Christians meditate, or is this a Buddhist practice?

PROBLEM: David declared here that the righteous person "meditates day and night." However, meditation is associated with Eastern religions, such as Buddhism and Hinduism, which are contrary to Christianity. Should Christians engage in meditation?

SOLUTION: There is a significant difference between Christian meditation and mystical meditation found in many eastern religions, popularly known in western forms as "New Age" religions. The differences are brought out in this contrast:

	CHRISTIAN	EASTERN RELIGIONS
Object	Something (God)	Nothing (void)
Purpose	Worship of God	Merge with God
Means	Divine revelation	Human intuition
Sphere	Through reason	Beyond reason
Power	By God's grace	By human effort
Experience Immediate	Objective reality	Purely subjective
State	Concentration	Relaxation

(See Geisler and Amano, *The Infiltration of the New Age,* Tyndale, 1989, 135)

There is a big difference between emptying one's mind to meditate on nothing and filling one's mind with the Word of God to meditate on the Living God. David said he meditated on God's "law" – the Word, not on the void. His purpose was spiritual fellowship with Yahweh, not a mystical union with Brahman or the Tao of eastern religions. The two forms of meditation are entirely different.

PSALM 3:1 — How could David have written this Psalm when critics insist that most Psalms were not completed until much later?

PROBLEM: The inscription on this psalm, as on many others, says, "A Psalm of David." However, biblical critics argue that the form and style of the psalm reflects a much later period than David's time.

SOLUTION: Most scholars do not believe these inscriptions are part of the inspired text, but were added later. However, there is strong evidence that David did write this psalm, as well as some 70 others attributed to him. Consider the following.

First, these inscriptions are very old and reflect the most ancient documentary evidence about the authors of these psalms.

Second, David, being a true poet (cf. 2 Sam. 1:17-27) was certainly capable of writing these psalms.

Third, there is evidence that David possessed the rich imagination needed to write Hebrew poetry (cf. 2 Sam. 1:19-27).

Fourth, David was also a good musician (cf. 1 Sam. 16:18-23) which would greatly aid him in composing these psalms that comprised the ancient hymnal of Judaism.

Fifth, David probably composed the music used in Solomon's temple (1 Chron. 6:31-32) in which these psalms were later sung.

Sixth, the Bible declares that David was endued with the Spirit of God (1 Sam. 16:13), thus enabling him to write such inspired poems.

Seventh, David was deeply spiritual in both character and heart (cf. 2 Sam. 7), something obviously true of the author of the psalms attributed to him.

Eighth, Psalm 18, for example, is also recorded in 2 Samuel 22, where it is directly attributed to King David.

Ninth, David swore on his death bed that God spoke through his mouth as the "sweet psalmist" of Israel (2 Sam. 23:1).

Finally, both our Lord and NT writers verified by name that David wrote specific psalms attributed to him in these OT inscriptions. For example:

> Psalm 2 is cited in Acts 4:25-26 as by David
> Psalm 32 is cited in Romans 4:7-8 as by David
> Psalm 95 is cited in Hebrews 4:7 as by David
> Psalm 110 is cited in Matthew 22:44 as by David.

In brief, there is an ancient and unbroken teaching extending to modern times, which includes our Lord and His apostles, that King David is indeed the author of the psalms attributed to him. No one has provided any solid evidence to the contrary, but have offered instead mere speculations about literary form which generally either beg the question or are based on the fallacious argument from ignorance.

PSALM 5:5 – How can this verse say God hates the wicked when John 3:16 says that God loves the world?

PROBLEM: Psalm 5:5 states, "You [God] hate all workers of iniquity." However, John 3:16 says God loves the world. Don't these verses contradict each other?

SOLUTION: There is no contradiction in these statements. The difficulty arises when we wrongly assume that God hates in the same way men hate. Hatred in human beings is generally thought of in terms of strong emotional distaste or dislike for someone or something. However, in God, hate is a judicial act on the part of the righteous Judge who separates the sinner from Himself. This is not contradictory to God's love, for in His love for sinners, God has made it possible for sin to be forgiven so that all can be reconciled to God. Ultimately, the sinner will reap the harvest of God's hatred in eternal separation from God, or the harvest of God's love by being with Him for all eternity. But, God is "not willing that any should perish but that all should come to repentance" (2 Peter 3:9). God's justice demands that sin be punished. God's love carried that punishment for every man in the person of His Son (2 Cor. 5:21).

PSALM 10:1 – Is God approachable or unapproachable?

PROBLEM: Throughout the Bible God is depicted as eminently approachable, for "God is our refuge and strength, a very present help in trouble" (Ps. 46:1; cf. 73:28; James 4:8). On the other hand, in this psalm God is portrayed as inaccessible. For example, "Why do You stand afar off, O Lord? Why do You hide Yourself in times of trouble?" (Psa. 10:1; cf. Isa. 14:15; Ezek. 20:3).

SOLUTION: The psalmist is speaking figuratively here. Just as "drawing near" to God (James 4:8) is figurative, not literal, likewise, neither does God literally "hide" from us. It may seem to us as though He does simply because He does not respond as fast as we would like or in the way we would like. Nonetheless, the Scriptures assure us that God is both listening and acting in our best interest (cf. Heb. 4:14-16; 12:11). There is no text of Scripture that says God does not respond to the earnest and penitent prayers of believers (see comments on John 9:31).

PSALM 11:5 – How can this verse say God hates some people when John 3:16 says God loves everyone?

(See discussion under Ps. 5:5.)

PSALM 24:2 – Is the earth founded upon the seas or on nothing?

PROBLEM: The psalmist declares that the earth was "founded upon the seas." But Job said, "He hangs the earth on nothing" (Job 26:7).

SOLUTION: The first text speaks about the obvious fact that the earth is situated *above* the seas so that they cannot overflow and destroy it. The verse in Job may refer to the scientific fact that the earth is suspended in space, something that could have been inferred from observation of other heavenly bodies visible to the eye, and inferences made from eclipses. Indeed, Aristotle (4th century B.C.) concluded that the earth was round in a similar way.

PSALM 30 – Why does the subtitle to Psalm 30 make reference to the dedication of the house of David when the psalm says nothing about it?

PROBLEM: The subtitle to Psalm 30 is "A Song at the dedication of the house of David." However, the psalm itself makes no reference to the house of David, and the content is concerned with a personal experience of God's grace in time of trouble. Is this subtitle an error?

SOLUTION: The titles and subtitles that appear in our Bibles were not part of the original inspired psalms. These were added at a later time in much the same way that study Bibles today provide titles and subtitles over various sections of a given book. In many cases they provide valuable information about the psalms with which they are connected.

However, some scholars believe that some of these sentences that have been understood to be titles of one psalm have come to be seen as postscripts of the previous psalm. This may be the case with the subtitle over Psalm 30. Some think that Psalm 29 is much better suited as a psalm of dedication, and perhaps what has been taken to be the subtitle of Psalm 30 is actually the postscript of Psalm 29.

PSALM 34 — Why does the subtitle of this Psalm have the name Abimelech when the name should be Achish?

PROBLEM: The subtitle of Psalm 34 states, "A Psalm of David when he pretended madness before Abimelech, who drove him away, and he departed." However, David's act of madness, recorded in 1 Samuel 21:13, took place before Achish, not Abimelech. Is this an error?

SOLUTION: It must be remembered that the titles and subtitles of the various psalms were not part of the original, inspired psalms. Therefore, it is possible that those who added these titles made an error in this instance.

Others have proposed that perhaps Abimelech was another name for Achish. It was not an uncommon practice in ancient times to have two names. Gideon was also named Jerubbaal (Jud. 6:32; 7:1), and Solomon also went by the name Jedidiah (2 Sam. 12:25). It is possible that the name Abimelech was a recurring name in a certain dynasty of the Philistines.

PSALM 37:9, 34 — When the wicked are cut off, are they annihilated?

PROBLEM: The psalmist affirms that "evildoers shall be cut off." Elsewhere (Ps. 73:27; Prov. 21:28), it says they will perish (see comments on 2 Thes. 1:9). But, does being cut off forever mean they will be annihilated?

SOLUTION: Being "cut off" does not mean to be annihilated. If it did, then the Messiah would have been annihilated when He died, since the same word (*karath*) is used of the death of the Messiah (in Dan. 9:26). But, we know that Christ was not annihilated, but lives on forever after His death (cf. Rev. 1:18; also see comments on 2 Thes. 1:9).

PSALM 37:25 — Do the righteous ever beg bread?

PROBLEM: David declares here, "I have not seen the righteous forsaken, nor his descendants begging bread." But this is obviously not always true. Many of the starving thousands in the world today are Christians. Even the Bible spoke of "a certain beggar named Lazarus" who was in heaven (Luke 16:20). David's statement seems to be clearly false.

SOLUTION: Several things should be kept in mind about David's statement. First of all, strictly speaking it is not a universal claim — it is simply a statement about his own personal experience. He begins it by saying, "I have been young, and now am old; *yet I have not seen*" (v. 25).

Second, he is not claiming that no righteous person ever starves, but simply that he has not seen them "begging bread." There is a difference.

Third, the context of his statement was the OT Jewish economy wherein no one needed to starve because the Law provided that they could glean in the fields (cf. Lev. 19:10; Deut. 24:21). In this system, there was generally no need to "beg bread" — it could be gleaned freely from the fields.

Finally, like Proverbs, this statement need not be taken universally, but only as a general rule that in a society ordered according to God's law, those who live righteously will seldom find it necessary to beg for food.

PSALM 44:23 — Does God sleep?

PROBLEM: According to Psalm 121:4, God shall "neither slumber nor sleep." Yet, in this verse the psalmist calls on God, "Awake! Why do You sleep, O Lord?"

SOLUTION: The psalmist uses "sleep" as a figure of speech referring to the fact that God had deferred judgment, showing at that moment no signs of activity (cf. Ps. 44:9-10).

PSALM 45:3-5 — Is this a prediction of Mohammed?

PROBLEM: Since this verse speaks of one coming with the "sword" to subdue his enemies, Muslims sometimes cite it as a prediction of their prophet Mohammed, who was known as "the prophet of the sword." They insist it could not refer to Jesus, since He never came with a sword (Matt. 26:52).

SOLUTION: This contention, however, fails for several reasons. First, the very next verse (v. 6) identifies the person spoken of as "God" whom Jesus claimed to be (John 8:58; 10:30). But Mohammed denied he was God, saying he was only a human prophet. Second, the NT affirms that this passage refers to Christ (Heb. 1:8). Third, although Jesus did not come the first time with a sword, He will at His second coming (cf. Rev. 19:11-16).

PSALM 51:5 — Was man brought forth in iniquity or made upright?

PROBLEM: David said he was "brought forth in iniquity," but Solomon taught that "God made man upright" (Ecc. 7:29). Which is true?

SOLUTION: Both are correct, but each is speaking about something different. Solomon is referring to man's *original creation* before he "sought out many schemes" (Ecc. 7:29). David is alluding to how humans have been "brought forth" from *actual "conception"* in their mother's womb since the Fall.

PSALM 51:5 – Does this verse support the position that an unborn fetus is only a potential human being?

PROBLEM: David claimed that he was "conceived" in sin in his mother's womb. However, he could not have actually sinned at the moment of conception, since he had no moral consciousness or free will which are necessary for moral acts (see Isa. 7:15; John 9:41).

SOLUTION: This text does not support the view that a human embryo is merely a potential human being, as opposed to an actual human being. This is evident for several reasons. First, even if it were teaching that humans are potential *sinners* from conception, it does not follow that they are potential *humans*.

Second, in whatever sense the unborn are declared sinners from the point of conception, it reveals, nevertheless, that they are human, that is, they are part of the fallen human race. For it is only by virtue of being part of the Adamic human race that we are conceived in sin (see comments on Rom. 5:12).

PSALM 51:16 – Did David disavow the sacrificial system of Moses?

(See comments on Hosea 6:6.)

PSALM 53:5 – Doesn't this verse contradict itself?

PROBLEM: The psalmist said, "they are in great fear where no fear was." But how could they be in fear if there was no fear there?

SOLUTION: The Bible critic here manifests two serious flaws — utter presumption that the biblical writer was so stupid as to contradict himself in the same sentence, and complete ignorance of the fact that the same word is often used in different senses, even in the same sentence. For example, "You know *perfectly* well that you do not know anything *perfectly*." (See also comments on Prov. 26:4-5 and Phil. 3:15.) The meaning in this psalm is captured by the NIV: "There they were, overwhelmed with dread, where there was nothing to dread."

PSALM 58:3 — How can an innocent child be wicked from the womb?

PROBLEM: Over and over the Bible speaks of the innocence and guilt-lessness of little children (cf. Deut. 1:39) who do not "know to refuse evil and choose the good" (Isa. 7:15), and who are part of the kingdom of God (Matt. 18:3-4; cf. Rom. 9:11). Yet, in this verse David insists that "the wicked are estranged from the womb; they go astray as soon as they are born, speaking lies." But, if a baby is morally guiltless, then how can he or she speak lies?

SOLUTION: It is clear that this cannot refer to *actual* sins, but only *potential* ones, since the baby has not yet developed its moral conscious-ness and responsibility. The Scriptures clearly speak of "children not yet being born, nor having done any good or evil" (Rom. 9:11). The sense in which a person is "sinful at birth" (Ps. 51:5, NIV) is by way of *inclination,* not by way of moral *action.* All persons are "by nature chil-dren of wrath" (Eph. 2:3) because they are born with a *tendency* to sin, but they are not born in sin *in reality.* The condemnation over the head of everyone who comes into Adam's race is judicial guilt, not personal guilt. We stand condemned before God because "all sinned" in Adam our representative (Rom. 5:12). This situation can be summarized as follows.

WE ARE NOT BORN IN SIN	WE ARE BORN IN SIN
Actually	Potentially
By action	By inclination
In reality	In tendency
Personally	Judicially

PSALM 73:20 — How can this verse talk about God awakening when Psalm 121:3 states that God never sleeps?

(See comments on Ps. 44:23.)

PSALM 88:11 — Do the dead have remembrance of anything?

(See comments under Ecc. 9:5.)

PSALM 97:7 — Doesn't this verse imply there are many gods?

PROBLEM: The psalmist commands, "Worship Him, all you gods." Yet the Bible elsewhere insists there is only one God (Deut. 6:4).

SOLUTION: First of all, there is no other *God,* but there are many *gods.* There is only one *true* God, but there are many *false* gods. Indeed, Paul declares that there are demons behind false gods (1 Cor. 10:20). And one day even the demons will bow before the true and living God and confess that He is Lord (Phil. 2:10).

Furthermore, good angels are sometimes called "gods" (*elohim*) in the Bible (Ps. 8:5; cf. Heb. 2:7). This verse (Ps. 97:7) could be a command for the angels to worship God, as they are so commanded in Psalm 148:2: "Praise Him, all His angels."

PSALM 104:5 — Will the earth abide forever or will it be destroyed?

PROBLEM: This verse, and several others (cf. Ps. 78:69; Ecc. 1:4), speak of the earth being "established forever." By contrast, the Bible also teaches that the heavens and the earth "will perish" (Ps. 102:26) or "pass away" (Luke 21:33), being "burned up" (2 Peter 3:10).

SOLUTION: First, the Hebrew word for "forever" (*olam*) often simply means a long period or an indefinite time. Hence, one need not take the verses that speak of the earth lasting "forever" as literally meaning without any end. Further, even taken literally an important distinction must be made. While the earth will not abide forever *in its present form,* its *constituent elements* will remain, and it will be reformed into a "new heaven and a new earth" (Rev. 21:1) which will never pass away. In this sense, both are true — the basic elements of the universe God created will last forever, but not in their present shape which has been infected by sin and decay (Rom. 8:18ff). God will one day destroy the universe in its present form and reconstruct it into a perfect world, "a new heaven and a new earth" (Rev. 21:1) which contains no disease, death, or decay (cf. Rev. 21–22).

PSALM 109:1ff — How can the God of love in the NT be reconciled with the vengeful God of these cursing Psalms?

PROBLEM: This psalm, like many others in the OT (e.g., Pss. 35; 69), pronounces curses on one's enemies. Thus they are called imprecatory (cursing) psalms. David says, "Let his children be fatherless, and his wife a widow" (109:9). By contrast, Jesus said, "Love your enemies . . . and pray for those who . . . persecute you" (Matt. 5:44). How can the God of vengeance of the OT be the same as the God of love of the NT (1 John 4:16)?

SOLUTION: Several important factors must be kept in mind in understanding these imprecatory or so-called cursing psalms.

First, the judgment called for is based on *divine justice* and not on *human grudges.* David said clearly of his enemies in this psalm, "they have rewarded me evil for good, and hatred for my love" (v. 5). While David did pray this imprecation (curse) on his enemies, he nonetheless loved them and committed them to the justice of God for a due reward for their wicked deeds. David's action in sparing Saul's life is vivid proof that revenge was not a motivation behind this psalm. In spite of the fact that Saul stalked David's life, David forgave Saul and even spared his life (cf. 1 Sam. 24; 26). Further, they can't be a grudge, since there are self-imprecations (cf. Ps. 7:4-5).

Second, judgment in these psalms is expressed in terms of the culture of the day. Since being fatherless or a widow was considered a tragedy, the curse is expressed in these commonly understood categories.

Third, since the Hebrew culture made no sharp distinction between the sinner and his sin, the judgment is expressed in personal terms rather than abstractly. Furthermore, since the Hebrew family was a solidarity, the whole family was saved (cf. Noah, Gen. 7–8) or judged together (cf. Achan, Josh. 7:24).

Fourth, the phenomenon of imprecation is not unique to the OT. Jesus urged His disciples to curse cities that did not receive the Gospel (Matt. 10:14). Jesus Himself called down judgment on Bethsaida and Capernaum in Matthew 11:21-24. Paul declared anathema any who did not love the Lord Jesus (1 Cor. 16:22). Even the saints in heaven cried out to God for vengeance on those who martyred believers (Rev. 6:9-10).

Fifth, imprecations are not a primitive or purely OT phenomenon. Justice executed on evil is just as much a part of God, as is blessing on the righteous. Both are true of God in the OT as well as in the NT. In fact, God is mentioned as being loving more often in the OT than in the NT.

Sixth, because the OT emphasis was on earthly reward, connected with family, prosperity, and the land, the OT curses were expressed in these terms. With the NT revelation expressed more in terms of eternal destiny, there was less need to express imprecations in earthly terms.

Even in these OT imprecations one can see an anticipation of Christ.

God has committed all judgment to the Son (John 5:22). So those who long for justice are not only aspiring to His righteous kingdom, but can wait patiently for Him who comes quickly to execute it justly (Rev. 22:12).

PSALM 115:17 — Can the dead praise God or are they unconscious?

(See comments on Ecc. 9:5 and 2 Kings 14:29.)

PSALM 119:110 — Is it true that David never erred from God's precepts or did he go astray from them?

PROBLEM: David appears to contradict himself in the same psalm. First he says to God, "I have not strayed from Your precepts" (v. 110). But later he admitted, "I have gone astray like a lost sheep" (v. 176). However, it would seem that both cannot be true.

SOLUTION: David has two different things in mind. In the first case he is speaking in *general,* and in the latter he is speaking in *particular.* In verse 110 David states that the general trend of his life has been faithfulness to God. But, in verse 176, David affirms what we must all acknowledge, namely, the *universal* truth that "all we like sheep have gone astray" (Isa. 53:6). So understood, there is no real contradiction here. (See also comments on 1 Kings 11:4.)

PSALM 137:9 — How could the Psalmist rejoice at the thought of little ones being dashed against rocks?

PROBLEM: When the psalmist considers the ultimate judgment that will be brought against Babylon, he appears to rejoice that babies will be injured. How could a man of God rejoice over such a tragic and cruel event?

SOLUTION: The psalmist is not rejoicing over the dashing of babies. Rather, he is rejoicing over the retributive justice of God that would ultimately return the cruelty of the Babylonians upon them as a just punishment for their crimes. The Babylonians had treated the Hebrews and their children with just such acts of brutality. Ultimately, God would bring the Medes and Persians to inflict His judgment upon Babylon. In the hands of God, the armies of the Medes and Persians would balance the scales of justice, for the Babylonians would reap what they had sown (see comments on Ps. 109:1ff).

PSALM 139:13-16 — Can it be inferred from this verse that the Bible considers abortion to be murder?

PROBLEM: According to this passage, God looks upon the unborn as a human being. However, if the unborn is fully human, then abortion would be the willful killing of the innocent — murder. Does this passage indicate that God considers abortion to be murder?

SOLUTION: Yes. Several other passages reinforce this position. First, the unborn are known intimately and called out by God. In Jeremiah 1:5, God says, "Before I formed you in the womb I knew you; before you were born I sanctified you; and I ordained you a prophet to the nations."

Second, the unborn are said to possess personal characteristics — sin, as in Psalm 51:5; or joy, as in Luke 1:44.

Third, anyone who harms the unborn receives the same punishment for harm done to an adult. Elsewhere (see comments on Ex. 21:22-23), equal punishment is given for harm done to a woman or to the child she carries. God looks upon the unborn as fully human. And the willful taking of an innocent human life is murder.

PROVERBS

PROVERBS 1:1 — How could Solomon's writings be part of the Scripture since 1 Kings 11:6 said Solomon did evil in the sight of the Lord?

PROBLEM: Solomon began his reign as a man who loved the Lord (1 Kings 3:3). Later in his life he began to turn away from following the Lord and did that which was evil in God's sight. How can the writings of an evil man become Scripture?

SOLUTION: The reason any book is in the Bible is not based upon the life of the human author, but on the inspiration of the Holy Spirit (2 Tim. 3:16, cf. 2 Peter 1:20-21). Every human author was a sinful human being. It is by the grace of God that humans were used to communicate God's revelation. Solomon asked God for the capacity to judge Israel and to "discern between good and evil" (1 Kings 3:9). Solomon's writings are in the Bible because God supernaturally spoke to him (1 Kings 3:10-15) and gave him wisdom to share with others. In short, he was a prophet or mouthpiece through whom God spoke, imperfect though he was.

PROVERBS 8:22-31 — Who is referred to as "wisdom" in these verses?

PROBLEM: Many commentators have claimed that the person identified as wisdom in Proverbs 8:22-31 is Jesus, because 1 Corinthians 1:30 states that Jesus is the wisdom of God. However, though the NKJV translates 8:22 as "The Lord *possessed* me," the Hebrew uses the word *qanah* which is usually translated "to create." If this passage is a reference to Jesus, then why does 8:22 affirm that the Lord created wisdom? If "wisdom" in Proverbs is not a reference to Jesus, then who is it?

SOLUTION: This passage is not a direct reference to any person. Poetic expression often takes an abstract idea and talks about it as if it were a person. This is called personification. The wisdom referred to here is not a reference to Jesus. Rather, it is a personification of the virtue or character of wisdom for the purpose of emphasis and impact. However, since Jesus is the perfect wisdom of God, He is the only one who perfectly personified and exemplified the wisdom spoken of in Proverbs—for "in Whom are hidden all the treasures of wisdom and knowledge" (Col. 2:3).

PROVERBS 11:31 — Are the righteous rewarded in this life or in the next one?

PROBLEM: Here Solomon speaks as though the godly person receives his reward in this life, claiming, "the righteous will be recompensed on the earth." However, the Bible repeatedly speaks of the rewards of the believer as being yet future, after Christ returns (cf. 1 Cor. 3:12-15). Jesus said, "Behold, I am coming quickly, and My reward is with Me, to give to every one according to his work" (Rev. 22:12).

SOLUTION: Rewards only *begin* in this life—they are not *completed* until the next life. They are only *partially* passed out on earth—they will be *fully* given in heaven. The same is true of punishment for the wicked. The same retributive justice that governs this world will also rule the world to come. The wrath of God is already abiding on unbelievers (John 3:36), yet we are told to flee from the wrath to come (Matt. 3:7).

PROVERBS 12:21 — Does God always spare the godly from grave trouble?

PROBLEM: In some places the Bible promises, "No grave trouble will overtake the righteous" (Prov. 12:21; cf. 1 Peter 3:13). But, in other places, such as the fate of Job, it makes a point to show how the godly sometimes suffer great troubles.

SOLUTION: Two factors help to explain this apparent contradiction. First, the promise in Proverbs is only *general,* not universal. For example, the promise that the enemies of the godly will be at peace with him (Prov. 16:7) is surely not universal. Paul pleased God, and yet his enemies stoned him (Acts 14:19). Surely Jesus pleased God, and yet His enemies crucified Him!

Second, the believer is not promised that no tribulation would befall him. In fact, he is warned that "in the world you will have tribulation" (John 16:33). On the contrary, God deliberately allowed Job to undergo grave trouble (Job 1), another man to be born blind for His glory (John 9:3), and the Apostle Paul to have an affliction (2 Cor. 12:7-9). What the believer is promised is that no *permanent* or *ultimate* evil will befall him. No evil will beset us out of which God cannot bring some greater good (cf. Gen. 50:20; Rom. 8:28).

PROVERBS 13:22 — Are believers obligated to leave an inheritance to their children?

(See comments on 1 Tim. 5:8.)

PROVERBS 16:4 — Does God make people to be doomed?

PROBLEM: On the one hand, the Bible speaks of human beings as having free choice (Matt. 23:37; 2 Peter 3:9) and being responsible for their own destiny (cf. Ezek. 18:20; John 3:36). On the other hand, Solomon declares here that "the Lord made . . . even the wicked for the day of doom." Indeed, Paul speaks of some people being "vessels of wrath" (Rom. 9:22). How can we justify God making people in order to destroy them?

SOLUTION: God does not create people in order to destroy them. God loves "the world" (John 3:16), and Christ died "for the whole world" (1 John 2:2). Indeed, Christ's blood "bought" even those who deny Him (2 Peter 2:1). And God "is not willing that any should perish" (2 Peter 3:9). There is a hell, but it was not prepared for human beings. Jesus said it was "prepared for the devil and his angels" (Matt. 25:41).

How then can we explain the fact that God made the wicked for the day of doom? The word "made" (*asah*) has broad usage in Hebrew. It can mean "appoint" or "institute" or even "administer." God is in sovereign control of the entire universe. Even when humans intend something for evil, God can mean it for good (Gen. 50:20). In this sense, "Surely the wrath of man shall praise You" (Ps. 76:10). For "in all things God works for the good" (Rom. 8:28, NIV). So even the "day of doom" is "for" God in the sense that He is in control of it and it will ultimately redound to His glory. For God's love is magnified in heaven, and His justice is manifest in hell.

Of course, it is not God's directive will that anyone be judged, but in His sovereign will He has appointed ("made") that even judgment on sin will magnify Him. Nonetheless, God "desires all men come to be saved and to come to the knowledge of the truth" (1 Tim. 2:4). Even the "vessels of wrath" were only "prepared for destruction" (Rom. 9:22) because they refused to repent, since God patiently "endured [them] with much longsuffering," waiting for them to repent (cf. 2 Peter 3:9).

In brief, God's *prescriptive* will is that all be saved. His *permissive* will is that some be lost (those who refuse to repent). And God's *providential* will is that He will bring ultimate good, even out of evil. In this sense, all things are made for (i.e., appointed by) Him.

PROVERBS 22–24 — Wasn't this section of Proverbs copied from the Egyptian work titled "The Wisdom of Amenemope?"

PROBLEM: An Egyptian document containing a book titled "The Wisdom of Amenemope" was discovered in 1888. Many of the sayings are similar to those found in Proverbs chapters 22–24. However, if these chapters in Proverbs are simply a copy of this Egyptian book, then at least this section was not written by Solomon, as it claims to be (cf. 1:1; 25:1).

SOLUTION: First, there is no reason why God could not guide Solomon to use other human sources in writing God's Word. Other authors of Scripture did this (cf. Luke 1:1-4). However, it is not clear that Solomon used this Egyptian source. For, although there are sentences and contents that are quite similar, the fact is that the differences outweigh the similarities. The two books deal with the same general subject matter, and this fact alone can account for the similarities. Furthermore, closer examination by scholars has revealed that, if there was any borrowing, it was more likely that the Egyptian author borrowed from the Hebrew author. Ultimately, of course, God is the source of all truth, wherever it is found. Thus the proverbial wisdom found in these chapters of Proverbs is from the Holy Spirit whatever human source He employed.

PROVERBS 22:6 — How can this verse be true when experience teaches us that often children abandon the principles of their training?

PROBLEM: According to Proverbs 22:6, if a child is trained in the way to live, he or she will not depart from this training even when older. However, experience shows that this is not always true. Isn't this proverb contradicted by experience?

SOLUTION: This proverb does not contradict experience because it is only a general principle that allows for individual exceptions. Proverbs are not designed to be absolute guarantees. Rather, they express truths that provide helpful advice and guidance for wise living by which individuals should conduct their daily lives. It is generally true that the diligent training of godly parents will influence children to follow that training in later years. However, circumstances and individual personalities and problems might work against the training a child has received. The proverb encourages parents to diligently fulfill their responsibilities, and to trust the future to the grace and sovereignty of God.

PROVERBS 24:11 — Does this verse justify breaking the law to stop abortions?

PROBLEM: Solomon urged here that we "Deliver those who are drawn toward death, and hold back those stumbling to the slaughter." Does this justify illegal attempts to "rescue" babies by blocking pregnant women's path into legal abortion clinics?

SOLUTION: This passage does not justify breaking the laws of God-ordained human government (cf. Rom. 13:1; 1 Peter 2:13), even if we believe they are unjust laws. The only time believers are allowed to disobey the law is when it *compels* them to sin, not when it *permits* someone else to sin (see comments on Ex. 1:15-21). Otherwise, we would be obligated to block the doors to non-Christian churches or temples where they are sinning by worshiping false gods. We should disobey a law that *compels* us to worship idols (Dan. 3), but we should not disobey one that *permits* others to do so.

Furthermore, this text (Prov. 24) does not support illegal attempted "rescues" for several reasons. First, the chapter does not support civil disobedience; it commands civil obedience. It says, "fear the Lord and the king" (v. 21), and fear implies obedience to His commands (cf. Rom. 13:1, 3 and Titus 3:1). Second, those being led away to death (24:11) are victims of those breaking the law; they were not the lawbreakers. In other words, they were being carried away contrary to the law, whereas legal abortion is occurring in accordance with the law.

There is no indication in this passage (or any other) that believers have the right to illegally take away the legal rights of others simply because they personally believe the laws are unjust. By the same illogic used by so-called "rescuers" we should block the path of anyone — judge, jury, or police — taking a lawbreaker to the place of legal sentence if we believe the conviction is unjust. Further, if it is right to "rescue" lives by blocking clinic doors, then why not rescue them by bombing clinics, destroying their power supplies, or even assassinating the doctors and nurses doing it. Perish the thought! The truth is that two wrongs do not make a right, and the end does not justify the means, whether it is an active or a passive means of disobeying God-ordained human government that has issued non-compulsory laws that permit others to sin.

PROVERBS 25:1 — How can Solomon be the author of Proverbs when Hezekiah's men copied them?

PROBLEM: The Book of Proverbs claims to be written by Solomon (1:1; 10:1). Conservative Jewish and Christian scholars have long attributed this book to King Solomon. However, Proverbs 25:1 speaks of King Hezekiah's men "copying" these proverbs long after Solomon's death. Further, the last two chapters claim to be written by Agur (30:1) and King Lemuel (31:1) and not by Solomon.

SOLUTION: Since Solomon wrote some 3,000 proverbs (1 Kings 4:32) — many more than are in this book — it is possible that the Book of Proverbs was not put together from Solomon's many proverbs until after his death. If so, then God would have guided His servants who compiled it so that they selected the ones He wanted in His authoritative Word.

It is also possible that Solomon himself wrote the Book of Proverbs and that the reference to "copying" by Hezekiah's men simply refers to their later transcribing what Solomon wrote on another manuscript. The last two chapters could have been included by Solomon himself or added later since they too were inspired wisdom like that of Solomon's, even though they were written by other men of God named Agur (30:1) and Lemuel (31:1).

PROVERBS 26:4-5 — How can contradictory commands both be true?

PROBLEM: Verse 4 says "Do not answer a fool according to his folly;" and verse 5 tells us to "Answer a fool according to his folly." But this looks like a flat contradiction.

SOLUTION: This would be contradictory if it were not qualified by the accompanying phrases. We *should* answer a fool according to his folly if not doing so will leave him "wise in his own eyes" (v. 5). But, we *should not* answer him according to his folly if in so doing we will "also be like him." In other words, it depends on the circumstances. Sometimes we should and sometimes we should not answer a fool. The wise man will know the difference. And if one lacks wisdom, let him ask of God (James 1:5).

PROVERBS 27:22 — Is foolishness correctable?

PROBLEM: Proverbs 22:15 teaches that "Foolishness is bound up in the heart of a child, But the rod of correction will drive it far from him." But, according to this verse, foolishness is irremediable, because, "Though you grind a fool in a mortar with a pestle along with crushed grain, yet his foolishness will not depart from him."

SOLUTION: There are two significant differences in these passages. First, one is speaking of a *child,* who is still teachable. The other is referring to an *adult* who is beyond hope. Second, the correctable foolishness is only *waywardness,* whereas the incorrigible foolishness is *beyond hope.*

PROVERBS 28:13 — Is it right to cover sins or not?

PROBLEM: God warns here that "He who covers his sins will not prosper." However, elsewhere God commends those who have had their sins covered, saying, "Blessed is he . . . whose transgression is covered" (Ps. 32:1).

SOLUTION: In response, several crucial differences should be observed. First, anyone who attempts to cover *his own sin* is condemned, but the one who confesses his sins and has *God cover his sins for him* is blessed. Second, in the first case, it is an *unjustified concealment* of sin that God is condemning. In the other passage it is a God-appointed means of *remission* or *atonement.* Third, one passage is condemning anyone who attempts to *cover up* his sin. The other is commending those who have God *cover* their sins by blood atonement.

PROVERBS 30:30 — If the fear of man is on all beasts, why do lions not fear humans?

PROBLEM: God told Noah that "the fear of you and the dread of you shall be on every beast of the earth" (Gen. 9:2). However, this is not the case, for even Proverbs 30:30 admits that the lion "does not turn away from any."

SOLUTION: Several things help us to understand this problem. First, "the turn away" may refer to other beasts, not to humans. Second, unless they are desperately hungry or defending their young or turf, beasts do try to steer clear of human beings. Third, whatever exceptions there may be only serve to establish the rule that the presence of human beings tends to intimidate lower forms of life.

PROVERBS 31:6 — Does this verse encourage drinking strong alcoholic beverages?

PROBLEM: On the one hand the Bible speaks against strong drink, claiming it is a "mocker" and arouses "brawling" (Prov. 20:1). On the other hand, Solomon declares here that we should "give strong drink to him who is perishing, and wine to those who are bitter of heart." Doesn't this encourage drinking strong alcoholic beverages?

SOLUTION: The Bible strongly condemns the *social* abuse of strong drink (see comments on 1 Tim. 5:23), but not its *medicinal* use. This is clearly a medicinal use here, since it was to be given to those who are dying ("perishing") or in deep pain or shock ("bitter distress" or "misery," v. 7). Used in this way and for this purpose is not forbidden in Scripture. Indeed, alcohol properly administered has healing power both on the inside of the body (1 Tim. 5:23) and on the outside (Luke 10:34). But to abuse strong drink or engage in drunkenness is forbidden in Scripture (cf. 1 Cor. 5:11; 1 Tim. 3:8).

ECCLESIASTES

ECCLESIASTES 1:1 – If this book is inspired, why isn't it quoted in the NT?

PROBLEM: The NT writers quote the vast majority of the OT from Genesis to Malachi. There are literally hundreds of citations from every major section of the OT. Yet, the Book of Ecclesiastes is not quoted once. If it was inspired, then why isn't it cited at least one time?

SOLUTION: There are several OT books that are not directly quoted in the NT, including Ruth, 1 and 2 Chronicles, Esther, Song of Solomon, and Ecclesiastes. However, all these books were considered inspired by both Judaism and Christianity. Several points should be kept in mind.

First, being quoted in the NT was not a test for the inspiration of an OT book. Rather, the question was whether it was written by a spokesperson accredited by God and accepted by His people. Ecclesiastes meets this test.

Second, while no *text* of Ecclesiastes is cited as such in the NT, many of its *truths* are. For example:

What we sow we reap	Ecc. 11:1, cf. Gal 6:7
Avoid lust of youth	Ecc. 11:10, cf. 2 Tim. 2:22
Death is divinely appointed	Ecc. 3:2, cf. Heb. 9:2
Love of money is evil	Ecc. 5:10, cf. 1 Tim. 6:10
Don't be wordy in prayer	Ecc. 5:2, cf. Matt. 6:7

Third, the NT writers had no occasion to quote from every book in the OT. Few Christians have quoted recently from 1 Kings, yet the NT did (Rom. 11:4). Indeed, few believers ever cite 2 or 3 John, and yet they are part of the inspired Word of God. Whether, or even how often, a book is quoted does not determine whether it is inspired.

ECCLESIASTES 1:2 – How can this book be part of the Scriptures since it contains such skepticism?

PROBLEM: Several statements that Solomon makes throughout this book indicate a skepticism that seems contrary to the Bible as a whole. In Ecclesiastes 9:5 Solomon says, "For the living know that they will die; *but the dead know nothing.*" However, the Book of Ecclesiastes is included in the canon of Holy Scriptures as an inspired book. How can such a skeptical book be inspired Scripture?

SOLUTION: Although Ecclesiastes does contain statements that, when taken in isolation, appear to be contrary to the teaching of the Bible, the book is not a book of skepticism. Once these statements are understood in their contexts, their meaning is compatible with other Scriptures. Such statements as found in Ecclesiastes 1:2 are not designed to produce or to promote skepticism. Rather, Solomon is recording his search for happiness and meaning in life by pursuing everything that this world offers. Each of these seemingly skeptical observations is aimed at demonstrating that, apart from God, everything "under the sun" is only vanity, and that the only source of true happiness and lasting peace is the Lord our God. Solomon's investigations led eventually to the conclusion that the whole duty of man is to "fear God and keep His commandments" (Ecc. 12:13).

ECCLESIASTES 1:9-10 – Isn't it false to claim there is nothing new under the sun?

PROBLEM: Solomon declared here that "there is nothing new under the sun." But not only is this contrary to science and human history, but it is opposed by other verses of Scripture (cf. Isa. 43:19; Jer. 31:22) where God says He will do "a new thing."

SOLUTION: Of course there are new inventions, and God does new things. Solomon is not speaking about these, but as to how a human being can be satisfied "under the sun" (v. 8). All the regular means of wine, wealth, wisdom, and works (see Ecc. 2) have already been tried and found wanting.

ECCLESIASTES 1:18 – Is wisdom the source of happiness, or the means of sorrow?

PROBLEM: Solomon affirms here that "in much wisdom is much grief, and he who increases knowledge increases sorrow." However, Proverbs asserts that "Happy is the man who finds wisdom, and the man who gains understanding" (Prov. 3:13). Does wisdom bring sorrow or happiness?

SOLUTION: It all depends on the purpose for which wisdom or knowledge are sought. In Ecclesiastes, Solomon is seeking wisdom "under the sun" (cf. 1:3), that is, apart from God, as the source of happiness. This he rightly concludes is "vanity and grasping for the wind" (1:14). However, if wisdom is viewed as based in "the fear of the Lord" (Prov. 1:7), then it is the very means of obtaining true happiness. Indeed, Solomon came to this very conclusion in Ecclesiastes (see 8:12; 12:13). Also, the OT understanding of wisdom is not the accumulation of great amounts of knowledge. For Solomon, wisdom is first and foremost living a successful life of righteousness and peace in obedience to God. Knowledge alone does not bring wisdom. Indeed, the message of Ecclesiastes is that knowledge alone brings only sorrow. Wisdom is the accumulation of the right kind of knowledge coupled with a life that is in harmony with God's commands and at peace with Him.

ECCLESIASTES 2:2 — Is laughter good or bad?

PROBLEM: Sometimes the Bible speaks as though laughter is good and other times as though it is bad. Solomon concluded, "I said of laughter, 'It is madness'; and of mirth, 'What does it accomplish?' "(Ecc. 2:2). He added that "sorrow is better than laughter" (7:3). Jesus added, "Woe to you who laugh now" (Luke 6:25). On the other hand, the Bible encourages laughter, claiming that "a merry heart does good, like medicine" (Prov. 17:22). Solomon even "commended enjoyment, because a man has nothing better under the sun than to eat, drink, and be merry" (Ecc. 8:15).

SOLUTION: The answer lies in another verse. "To everything there is a season, a time for every purpose under heaven . . . a time to laugh; a time to mourn" (Ecc. 3:1, 4). What the Bible says about laughter can be summarized in the following contrast.

WHEN LAUGHING IS GOOD	WHEN LAUGHING IS BAD
The means of enjoying life	The end (goal) of life itself
Means of expressing happiness	Means of attaining happiness
In a cheerful spirit	In riotous derision
As reasonable merriment	As senseless hilarity

ECCLESIASTES 2:24 – Is Solomon commending hedonism here?

PROBLEM: Solomon concluded, "There is nothing better for a man than that he should eat and drink, and that his soul should enjoy good in his labor." But this is hedonism, which is condemned elsewhere in the Bible (Luke 12:19-20; 1 Cor. 10:7).

SOLUTION: Solomon is not recommending pleasure-seeking hedonism apart from God. There is a big difference between the hedonist's "Eat, drink, and be merry for tomorrow we die" and Solomon's exhortation to enjoy life because it comes "from the hand of God" (Ecc. 2:24). The kind of pleasures Solomon commended is that "which God gives him under the sun" (Ecc. 8:15), and that "is the gift of God" (Ecc. 3:13).

God is not a cosmic killjoy or a heavenly scrooge. He "gives us richly all things to enjoy" (1 Tim. 6:17) and at His "right hand are pleasures forevermore" (Ps. 16:11). However, Solomon warns, "Rejoice, O young man, in your youth, and let your heart cheer you in the days of your youth; walk in the ways of your heart, and in the sight of your eyes; but know that for all these God will bring you into judgment" (Ecc. 11:9). God wants us to enjoy this life, but to live it in the light of the next one.

ECCLESIASTES 3:19 – Is man's fate the same as that of animals?

PROBLEM: Solomon seems to claim here that there is no difference between the death of humans and animals. "One thing befalls them: as one dies, so dies the other." Yet Solomon asserts later that, unlike animals, when a human dies, "the spirit will return to God who gave it" (Ecc. 12:7). How can this conflict be explained?

SOLUTION: There are both similarities and differences between the death of animals and humans. In both cases, their bodies die and return to dust. Likewise, their death is certain, and both are powerless to prevent it. In these respects, the *physical* phenomena are the same for both humans and animals.

On the other hand, humans have immortal souls (spirits), and animals do not (Ecc. 12:7; cf. 3:21). Of no beasts does the Bible say, "to be absent from the body . . . [is] to be present with the Lord" (2 Cor. 5:8). Likewise, nowhere does the Bible speak of the resurrection of animals, as it does of all human beings (cf. John 5:28-29; Rev. 20:4-6). So there is a big difference in the *spiritual* realm between the death of humans and animals. Consider the following summary:

HUMAN AND ANIMAL DEATHS

SIMILARITIES	DIFFERENCES
Physically	Spiritually
In the body	In the soul
Life before death	Life after death
Mortality of the body	Immortality of the person
How the body decays	That the body is raised
No control over death	Experience of a resurrection

ECCLESIASTES 3:20 — If all return to dust, how can there be a resurrection?

PROBLEM: Some have argued against a physical resurrection on the grounds that the scattered fragments of decomposed corpses cannot be reassembled, since some become plants, or others are eaten by animals or even cannibals. Yet, the Bible declares that all bodies will "come forth" from the "graves" (John 5:28-29).

SOLUTION: Several things must be noted in this connection. First, as many scholars have pointed out, if necessary, it would be no problem for an omnipotent God to bring all of the exact particles of one's body together again at the resurrection. Certainly He who created every particle in the universe could reconstitute the relatively few particles (by comparison) in a human body. The God who created the world out of *nothing* is surely able to fashion a resurrection body out of *something*.

Second, it is not necessary to believe that the *same particles* will be restored in the resurrection body. Even common sense dictates that a body can be the *same physical body* without having the *same physical particles*. The observable fact that bodies eat food and give off waste products, as well as get fatter and skinnier, is sufficient evidence of this. Certainly, we do not say that one's body is no longer material or no longer her body simply because she gains or loses weight.

Third, in the light of modern science it is unnecessary to believe that God will reconstitute the exact particles one had in his pre-resurrection body. The physical body remains physical even though, according to science, the exact physical molecules in it change every seven years or so. So, the resurrection body can be just as material as our present bodies and still have new molecules in it.

ECCLESIASTES 3:20-21 — If there is life after death, why does Solomon declare that man has no advantage over the beasts?

PROBLEM: The Bible teaches that the soul survives death (Phil. 1:23; 2 Cor. 5:8; Rev. 6:9). But, Ecclesiastes insists that "all go to one place: all are from the dust, and all return to dust" (v. 20). Hence, "man has no advantage over beasts, for all is vanity" (3:19).

SOLUTION: The reference here is to the human body, not to the soul. Both men and beast die and their bodies return to dust. However, humans are different in that their soul "goes upward" (v. 21). In fact, Solomon speaks of "eternity" in the human heart (Ecc. 3:11) and of its immortality when he declares that at death "man goes to his eternal home" (12:5). He also emphasized that we should fear God because there is a day when "God will bring you into judgment" after this life (11:9). So Ecclesiastes is not denying life after death; it is warning about the futility of living only for this life "under the sun" (cf. 1:3, 13; 2:18). (See prior comments under 3:19.)

ECCLESIASTES 7:16 — How is it possible to be too righteous?

PROBLEM: Jesus commanded His followers to be "perfect just as your Father in heaven is perfect" (Matt. 5:48). God said, "You shall therefore be holy, for I am holy" (Lev. 11:45). But, Solomon instructs us not to be "overly righteous" (Ecc. 7:16). How can someone be too righteous? Surely one cannot be too just or too loving?

SOLUTION: A person cannot be *too* righteous, but he can be *overly* righteous. The Pharisees were a good case in point. They were so righteous that they were self-righteous. For, "being ignorant of God's righteousness, and seeking to establish their own righteousness, [they] have not submitted to the righteousness of God" (Rom. 10:3).

ECCLESIASTES 8:12 — Are the lives of the wicked prolonged or shortened?

PROBLEM: According to this verse, "the sinner does evil a hundred times, and his days are prolonged" (cf. Job 21:7). Yet elsewhere the Bible says, "the years of the wicked will be shortened" (Prov. 10:27; cf. Ecc. 8:13).

SOLUTION: The texts that speak of the wicked living short lives affirm the general principle that such living tends to shorten human life. Whatever exceptions there are prove the general rule. The texts that speak of the wicked living long lives speak only of some, not all. These become the occasion of the godly cry as to why? The answer, of course, is that not all justice is accomplished in this life.

ECCLESIASTES 9:5 — Do the dead remember anything?

PROBLEM: Taken at face value, Solomon seems to be claiming that the dead have no more knowledge of anything. He wrote here, "the dead know nothing." Likewise, the psalmist said, "in death there is no remembrance" (Ps. 6:5). But, this seems to contradict the many passages that speak of souls being conscious after death (e.g., 2 Sam. 12:23; 2 Cor. 5:8; Rev. 6:9).

SOLUTION: The Bible teaches that the soul survives death in a conscious state of knowledge (see comments on 2 Kings 14:29). The passages which say there is no knowledge or remembrance after death are speaking of no memory *in* this world, not of no memory *of* this world. Solomon clearly qualified his comment by saying it was "in the grave" (Ecc. 9:10) that there was "no remembrance." He affirmed also that the dead do not know what is going on "under the sun" (9:6). But while they do not know what is happening *on earth,* they certainly do know what is going on *in heaven* (cf. Rev. 6:9). In short, these texts refer simply to man in relation to *this present life* — they say nothing about the *life to come* immediately after this one.

ECCLESIASTES 11:9 — Should a young man follow his own way or God's way?

PROBLEM: In this text, Solomon encourages a young person to "walk in the ways of your heart, and in the sight of your eyes." But this flies in the face of other Scriptures that urge them to seek not after "your own heart and your own eyes" (Num. 15:39).

SOLUTION: There are several ways to understand this Ecclesiastes passage that do not conflict with other Scriptures. First, some have suggested that it is an example of *irony,* meaning, therefore, they were not to go their own way but God's. Since irony is a perfectly legitimate human literary form that the Holy Spirit may use (see Introduction), this is entirely possible.

Second, even taken *literally,* the advice is not without qualification, since Solomon adds quickly, "But know that for all these God will bring you into judgment. Therefore . . . put away evil from your flesh, for childhood and youth are vanity" (Ecc. 11:9-10). In this sense, Solomon's advice would be, enjoy yourself. Do what your heart desires, but at the same time bear in mind that you are accountable to God, "who gives us richly all things to enjoy" (1 Tim. 6:17).

SONG OF SOLOMON

SONG OF SOLOMON 1:1 — How did a sensual book like this get in the Bible?

PROBLEM 1: The Bible condemns the lust of the flesh and sensuality (Rom. 6:6; Gal. 5:16-21; 1 John 2:16). Yet this love song is filled with sensual expressions and sexual overtures (cf. 1:2; 2:5; 3:1; 4:5).

SOLUTION 1: The Bible does not condemn sex, but only perverted sex. God created sex (Gen. 1:27), and He ordained that it should be enjoyed within the bonds of a monogamous marriage and in a relationship of love. The Scriptures declare, "Rejoice with the wife of your youth. As a loving deer and a graceful doe, let her breasts satisfy you at all times; and always be enraptured with her love" (Prov. 5:18-19).

After warning against those who forbid marriage (1 Tim. 4:3), the apostle declares that "every creature of God is good" (v. 4), and he goes on to speak of the God "who gives us richly all things to enjoy" (6:17). Hebrews insists that "marriage is honorable among all, and the bed undefiled; but fornicators and adulterers God will judge" (Heb. 13:4).

God realizes that normal people will have sexual desires, but He adds, "Nevertheless, because of sexual immorality, let each man have his own wife, and let each woman have her own husband" (1 Cor. 7:2). So, sex itself is not sinful, nor are sexual desires. God created them and intends that they be enjoyed within the loving bonds of a monogamous marriage. The Song of Solomon is a divinely authoritative example of how sensual love should be expressed in marriage.

PROBLEM 2: Some question whether this book should be in the Bible, claiming that some rabbis rejected it. Was it always a part of the Jewish Scriptures?

SOLUTION 2: From the very earliest times, this book was part of the Jewish canon. Centuries after it was accepted into the canon of Scriptures, the school of Shammai (A.D. 1st century) expressed doubt about its inspiration, but the view of Rabbi Akiba ben Joseph (c. A.D. 50–132) prevailed when he declared, "God forbid!—No man in Israel ever disputed about the Song of Songs . . . for all the ages are not worthy the day on which the Song of Songs was given to Israel; for all the writings are holy, but the Song of Songs is the Holiest of Holies" (See Geisler and Nix, *A General Introduction to the Bible,* Moody Press, 1986, 259).

PROBLEM 3: Many modern scholars propose that this book of Solomon is simply a collection of love poems that have been put together on the basis of their similarity in theme. However, as a whole, this book is said to have been written by Solomon. How can it be a book written by Solomon if it is really only a loosely connected group of poems?

SOLUTION 3: Actually, the Song of Solomon is not a loosely connected group of love poems. The structure of the book demonstrates that it is a single poetic expression of the relationship between Solomon and his Shulamite bride. The structure of the Song of Solomon is revealed in the repetition of key phrases.

OPENING PHRASES	CLOSING PHRASES
2:8 "The voice of my beloved! Behold, he comes."	2:7 "I charge you O daughters of Jerusalem . . ."
3:6 "Who is this coming . . ."	3:5 "I charge you O daughters of Jerusalem . . ."
6:10 "Who is she . . ."	6:9 "The daughters saw her . . ."
8:5 "Who is this coming . . ."	8:4 "I charge you O daughters of Jerusalem . . ."

The structure of this book can be illustrated by the following outline.

I. The mutual compassion of the lovers	1:2–2:7	A
II. Pre-wedding events	2:8–3:5	B
III. Wedding details	3:6–6:9	C
IV. Post-wedding events	6:10–8:4	B
V. The mutual contentment of the lovers	8:5–8:14	A

The repetition of "A"s and "B"s is a pattern called chiasm that was frequently employed by the Hebrew poets as a means of structuring their material. This structure not only indicates the unity of the book, but it provides evidence of a single author who put the material together in this manner to tell a true story and communicate a message. This literal account of the love of Solomon for his wife teaches the sanctity of human love in the marriage relationship (cf. Heb. 13:4).

SONG OF SOLOMON 1:2 – Why do so many people who claim to interpret the Bible literally, spiritualize the Song of Solomon?

PROBLEM: Evangelical Christians defend the literal interpretation of the Bible. They insist that it should be taken in its normal, historical-grammatical sense, not in some hidden, mystical, or allegorical sense. To do so in the Gospels, for example, leads to liberalism, denying the historicity of the life, death, and resurrection of Christ. However, many evangelicals do not take the Song of Solomon literally, but give it an allegorical or spiritual meaning. Is this not inconsistent?

SOLUTION: There are three basic interpretations of the Song of Solomon – the literal, the allegorical, and the typical.

First, there is a *literal interpretation*. According to this view, it is a literal story about King Solomon and his love for his wife and her love for him, although scholars differ over just which of his 700 wives and 300 concubines (1 Kings 11:3) this might be. Some say it was "the daughter of Pharaoh" (1 Kings 11:1). Others suggest it was a lowly maiden known as the Shulamite. But all who take it literally insist that it is about the historical King Solomon and a love affair he had with a woman. They insist, then, that the book is intended to extol the beauty, purity, and sanctity of marriage.

Second, others take an *allegorical interpretation* of the book, shying away from the more sensuously descriptive parts of the story. They prefer to see a deeper meaning, such as Yahweh's love for His people Israel (cf. Hosea) or, more broadly, God's love for His people in general.

Third, many Christians opt for a *typical interpretation* of this canticle, seeing in it the prefiguration or type of Christ and His love for the church (cf. Eph. 5:28-32). This view also denies that the book should be taken in a literal sense, insisting rather on a deeper spiritual meaning.

Whatever *application* this love story may have to God's relation to His people, or Christ's love for His church, it seems better to insist on a literal *interpretation* of this book for the following two basic reasons. First, it is inconsistent to allegorize this story and insist on taking the

Gospels and other parts of Scripture literally. Second, taking it literally does not contradict any other teaching of Scripture. Rather, it complements it in many ways. God instituted marriage (Gen. 2:23-24). God created sex and gave it to humans to enjoy within the bonds of marriage (Gen. 1:27; Prov. 5:17-19). Paul declared that sex should be exercised within a monogamous marriage (1 Cor. 7:1-5). Timothy was informed that sex within marriage should not be forbidden (1 Tim. 4:1-4) and that God "gives us richly all things to enjoy" (1 Tim. 6:17). The Song of Solomon is a beautiful example of a real romance between two actual people that extols the biblical view of sex and marriage.

Since a literal marriage does, according to Paul, exemplify the love of Christ for His bride, the church, there is no reason we cannot take this literal love story as a *picture* of God's love. However, to claim the story is not literally true, or that it is a type or *prediction* of Christ's love for the church goes beyond the meaning of the text.

SONG OF SOLOMON 6:8 — Why are Solomon's wives and concubines listed as 140 when he had 1,000?

PROBLEM: Here Solomon is said to have had only 140 wives and concubines, but 1 Kings 11:3 gives the number of 1,000.

SOLUTION: These two passages may refer to two different times in his life, the lower number being the earlier one. Or, it may be that there were different ways of counting his wives. First Kings 11:3 does not really say he had seven hundred wives but "seven hundred wives, princesses." In other words, many of these were more political alliances rather than actual marriages. Further, in the Song of Solomon it speaks of "virgins without number" (Song 6:8) being part of Solomon's female entourage. This general statement could easily account for the total of 1,000 mentioned in 1 Kings 11.

ISAIAH

ISAIAH 1:1 — Hasn't it been shown that Isaiah is actually two or more books, and that it was not all written by one Isaiah in the 8th century B.C.?

PROBLEM: The traditional view of the Book of Isaiah is that it was written by Isaiah, son of Amoz, some time between 739 and 681 B.C. However, modern critics have argued that Isaiah is actually composed of at least two individual books. What has been designated as First Isaiah encompasses chapters 1 through 39, while Second Isaiah encompasses chapters 40 to 66. Is the Book of Isaiah actually several books put together, or is it one book written by the one prophet Isaiah who lived in the 8th century B.C.?

SOLUTION: The traditional view that the Book of Isaiah is a single work written by the prophet Isaiah is supported by several arguments. First, the critical view that separates Isaiah into two or more books is based on the assumption that there is no such thing as predictive prophecy. Modern scholars claim that the prophecies in chapters 40–55 concerning Cyrus must have been written after Cyrus ruled in Persia. This view is antisupernatural and tries to explain these sections of Isaiah as history rather than predictive prophecy. However, since God knows the end from the beginning (Isa. 46:10), it is not at all necessary to deny the supernatural element in Isaiah's prophecies.

Second, the differences between the two halves of the book can be explained in other ways than the two-author approach. Chapters 1 through 39 prepare the reader for the prophecies contained in chapters 40 through 66. Without these preparatory chapters, the last section of the book would make little sense. Chapters 1 through 35 warn of the Assyrian menace that threatens to destroy God's people. Chapters 36–39 form a transition from the previous section to chapters 40–66, by looking forward to the invasion of Sennacherib (chaps. 36–37), and looking back to the spiritual decline that has caused the downfall of Jerusalem (chaps. 38–39). These four intervening chapters (36–39) are not in chronological order because the author is using them to prepare the reader for what is to follow.

Third, the difference in words and style of writing between the two sections of the book has been used by critical scholars to substantiate their claim that there are at least two different books. However, these differences are not as great as has been claimed, and the differences that do exist can be explained as a difference in subject matter and emphasis. No author writes in exactly the same style using precisely the same vocabulary when writing about different subject matter. Nevertheless, there are a number of phrases that are found in both sections that attest to the unity of the book. For example, the title "the Holy one of Israel" is found 12 times in chapters 1–39 and 14 times in 40–66. The following list illustrates these kinds of similarities.

CHAPTERS 1–39	CHAPTERS 40–66
1:15 – "Your hands are full of blood."	59:3 – "For your hands are defiled with blood."
28:5 – "For a crown of glory and a diadem of beauty to the remnant of His people."	62:3 – "You shall also be a crown of glory in the hand of the Lord, and a royal diadem in the hand of your God."
35:6 – "For waters shall burst forth in the wilderness, and streams in the desert."	41:18 – "I will make the wilderness a pool of water, and the dry land springs of water."

Fourth, in Luke 4:17 we find that when our Lord rose to read in the synagogue, "He was handed the book of the prophet Isaiah." The people in the synagogue and Jesus Himself assumed that this book was from the prophet Isaiah. Other NT writers accepted Isaiah as the author of the entire book. John 12:38 states that Isaiah was the one who made the statement that is found in Isaiah 53:1. Other instances where the NT ascribes portions of chapters 40–66 to Isaiah include Matthew 3:3 (Isa. 40:3), Mark 1:2-3 (Isa. 40:3), John 1:23 (Isa. 40:3), Matthew 12:17-21 (Isa. 42:1-4), Acts 8:32-33 (Isa. 53:7-8), and Romans 10:16 (Isa. 53:1).

Fifth, the Dead Sea Scrolls include a complete copy of the Book of Isaiah, and there is no gap in the scroll between chapters 39 and 40. This indicates that the Qumran community accepted the prophecy of Isaiah as one book in the 2nd century B.C. The Greek version of the Hebrew Bible, which dates from the 2nd century B.C., treats the Book of Isaiah as a single book by the single author, Isaiah the prophet.

ISAIAH 1:11-13 — Did the prophet Isaiah disavow the sacrificial system of Moses?

(See comments on Hosea 6:6.)

ISAIAH 7:14 — Is this verse a prophecy about the virgin birth of Jesus Christ?

PROBLEM: The prophecy of Isaiah 7:14 concerns the conception of a virgin and the bringing forth of a son whose name would be Immanuel. However, verse 16 seems to place the birth of the child before the invasion of the Assyrian armies and the fall of Samaria in 722 B.C., and Isaiah 8:3 seems to be a fulfillment of this prophecy. How can this be a prophecy about the virgin birth of Jesus?

SOLUTION: The fulfillment of this prophecy may be two-fold. Because of the desperate situation which the people of Israel faced, God promised to give them a sign that would assure them that He would ultimately deliver His people out of bondage. Many scholars believe this sign came in two ways. First, it came as a sign of the physical deliverance of Israel from the bondage to which they were going under the invading Assyrians. Second, it came as a sign of the spiritual deliverance of all of God's people from the spiritual bondage to Satan. The first aspect of the sign was fulfilled in the birth of Maher-Shalal-Hash-Baz as recorded in Isaiah 8:3. The second aspect of the sign was fulfilled in the birth of Jesus Christ at Bethlehem as recorded in the Gospels.

The word translated "virgin" (*almah*) refers to a young maiden who has never had sexual relations with a man. The wife of Isaiah who bore the son in fulfillment of the first aspect of the prophecy was a virgin until she conceived by Isaiah. However, according to Matthew 1:23-25, Mary, the mother of Jesus, was a virgin even when she conceived and gave birth to Jesus. The physical conception and birth of the son of Isaiah was a sign to Israel that God would deliver them from physical bondage to the Assyrians. But, the supernatural conception and birth of the Son of God was a sign to all of God's people that He would deliver them from spiritual bondage to sin and death.

ISAIAH 9:6 – Why is Jesus called "the everlasting Father" if He is the Son of God?

PROBLEM: The orthodox Christian doctrine of the Trinity holds that God is one Essence in three Persons – Father, Son, and Holy Spirit. However, Isaiah 9:6 calls the Messiah "the everlasting Father." How can Jesus be both the Father and the Son?

SOLUTION: This verse is not a Trinitarian formula that calls Jesus Christ the Father. Actually, it is easier to grasp the idea when the phrase is rendered literally into English, "Father of eternity." The first part of verse six makes reference to the incarnation of Jesus. The part that lists the names by which He is called expresses His relationship to His people. He is to us the Wonderful Counselor, the Mighty God, the Father of Eternity, the Prince of Peace. Considered in this way, we see that Jesus is the One who gives us eternal life. By His death, burial, and resurrection, He has brought life and immortality to light. Truly, He is the Father of eternity for His people. The name "Father of eternity" indicates that, as a loving father provides for His children, so Jesus loves us and has provided for us by giving us everlasting life.

ISAIAH 14:12 – Who is Lucifer in this verse?

PROBLEM: Many commentators consider this passage to be a reference to Satan, because the name "Lucifer" is used. However, in Isaiah 14:4 this entire poetic section stretching from 14:4 through 14:27 is a proverb against the king of Babylon. How can this be a reference to Satan when it is against the king of Babylon?

SOLUTION: This passage is a literal reference to the king of Babylon, but its significance encompasses the ultimate defeat and fall of Satan. There have been many different views as to the identity of this king of Babylon. Some propose that this is a reference to Sennacherib, a fierce enemy of God's people. Others see the poetic figure of personification in which the kingdom of Babylon as a whole is referred to in personal terms. The Hebrew word translated in the NKJV as "Lucifer" literally means "shining one." Verse 12 could be translated "How you are fallen from heaven, O shining one, son of the morning." Because the king of Babylon desired to set himself up as God, his fall would be as from heaven.

The parallels between this passage and such NT passages as Luke 10:18 and Revelation 20:2 indicate that this passage may have a broader application. The prophecy was given for those who lived in Isaiah's day, and it had immediate significance for them. God was promising them that their enemy, the king of Babylon and the evil empire itself, would ultimately be torn down. Yet, the prophecy may have significance for us as a picture of the ultimate demise of the evil ruler of this world whom God will ultimately destroy (Rev. 20:10).

ISAIAH 21:7 – Does this passage predict the coming of Mohammed?

PROBLEM: Some Muslim commentators take the rider on the "donkeys" to be Jesus and the rider on "camels" to be Mohammed, whom they believed superseded Jesus.

SOLUTION: This is a totally unfounded speculation with no basis in the text or the context. Actually, the passage is speaking of the fall of Babylon (v. 9) and the news of its fall that spread by various means, namely, those riding on horses, donkeys, and camels. There is absolutely nothing here about the prophet Mohammed.

ISAIAH 26:14 – Does this contradict the Bible's teaching on the resurrection?

(See comments on Job 7:9.)

ISAIAH 30:26 – Will the light of the sun and moon be increased or decreased in the future kingdom?

PROBLEM: Isaiah has two apparently contradictory predictions. One is that the light to the heavenly bodies will be increased sevenfold (Isa. 30:26). The other is that it will be "ashamed" in the light of the Lord Himself (Isa. 24:23).

SOLUTION: Some scholars believe these are mutually compatible poetic predictions that even though the light of the sun and moon is increased manifold (perhaps, figuratively), nevertheless, the light of the Lord will outshine them.

Others take these as literal predictions about two different future times. They hold that the natural light of the heavenly bodies will be increased during the reign of Christ for "a thousand years" (Rev. 20:4-6). But after that, when the "new heaven and a new earth" (Rev. 21:1) are created, there will be "no need of the sun or of the moon to shine in it, for the glory of God illuminated it" (Rev. 21:23).

ISAIAH 40:5 – Will the wicked behold God's glory?

PROBLEM: Isaiah declares in this passage that "the glory of the Lord shall be revealed, and all flesh shall see it together." However, earlier Isaiah contended that the wicked "will not behold the majesty of the Lord" (Isa. 26:10). How can both be true?

SOLUTION: First, the answer lies in the fact that the wicked do not *voluntarily* recognize God's glory, as the godly do. Further, the wicked do not *presently* recognize God's majesty, but one day every knee will bow to Him – both the godly and the wicked (Isa. 45:23; cf. Phil. 2:10). Understood in this way there is no disharmony between the texts.

ISAIAH 40:25 – If nothing is like God, then how can humans be in the image of God?

PROBLEM: Isaiah wrote: " 'To whom will you liken Me, or to whom shall I be equal?' says the Holy One." Yet the Bible says "God created man in His own image" (Gen. 1:27).

SOLUTION: Isaiah is not denying all similarity between God and His creatures. In fact, the Bible affirms elsewhere, "He who planted the ear shall He not hear? He who formed the eye, shall He not see?" (Ps. 94:9) Indeed, God is reflected in the mirror of His creation (cf. Ps. 19:1; Rom. 1:19-20). Isaiah is simply affirming that the transcendent God is *more than* His creation, even though He is not totally *unlike* it.

ISAIAH 44:28 – How could Isaiah talk in such specific terms about a king that would not exist for some 200 years?

PROBLEM: In Isaiah 44:28 and 45:1, Isaiah specifically names Cyrus in connection with the future restoration of Israel and the laying of the foundations of the temple. However, Isaiah conducted his ministry some time between 739 and 681 B.C., while Cyrus would not even become king of Persia until 539 B.C. That is a period of at least 150 years. How could Isaiah specifically name Cyrus before he even lived?

SOLUTION: This is an instance of supernatural prophecy. Although it was not in the power of Isaiah to look into the future, it is certainly in the power of God who declares "the end from the beginning" (Isa. 46:10). Not only does God know who will come to power, but, "the Most High rules in the kingdom of men, and gives it to whomever He chooses" (Dan. 4:32). It is God who sets up kingdoms, and it is God who brings them down. It is no small wonder, then, that God is able to name a king almost 200 years before he takes the throne. (See comments on Daniel 1:1.)

ISAIAH 45:7 — Is God the author of evil?

PROBLEM: According to this verse, God "creates good and evil" (KJV, cf. Jer. 18:11 and Lam. 3:38; Amos 3:6). But many other Scriptures inform us that God is not evil (1 John 1:5), cannot even look approvingly on evil (Hab. 1:13), and cannot even be tempted by evil (James 1:13).

SOLUTION: The Bible is clear that God is morally perfect (cf. Deut. 32:4; Matt. 5:48), and it is impossible for Him to sin (Heb. 6:18). At the same time, His absolute justice demands that He punish sin. This judgment takes both temporal and eternal forms (Matt. 25:41; Rev. 20:11-15). In its temporal form, the execution of God's justice is sometimes called "evil" because it seems to be evil to those undergoing it (cf. Heb. 12:11). However, the Hebrew word for evil (*rā*) used here does not always mean moral evil. Indeed, the context indicates that it should be translated, as the NKJV and other modern translations do, as "calamity." Thus, God is properly said to be the author of "evil" in this sense, but not in the moral sense — at least not directly.

Further, there is an indirect sense in which God is the author of moral evil. God created moral beings with free choice, and free choice is the origin of moral evil in the universe. So, ultimately God is responsible for making moral creatures who are responsible for moral evil. God made evil *possible* by creating free creatures, but the free creatures made evil *actual*. Of course, the possibility of evil (i.e., free choice) is itself a good thing. So, God created only good things, one of which was the power of free choice, and moral creatures produced the evil. However, God is the author of a moral universe and in this indirect and ultimate sense is the author of the possibility of evil. Of course, God only *permitted* evil, but does not *promote* it, and He will ultimately *produce* a greater good through it (cf. Gen. 50:20; Rev. 21–22).

The relation of God and evil can be summarized this way:

GOD IS NOT THE AUTHOR OF EVIL	GOD IS THE AUTHOR OF EVIL
In the sense of sin	In the sense of calamity
Moral evil	Non-moral evil
Perversity	Plagues
Directly	Indirectly
Actuality of evil	Possibility of evil

ISAIAH 53:3 – Was Jesus despised by men or respected by them?

PROBLEM: According to Isaiah, Jesus was "despised and rejected by men." Yet in the Gospels, even Jesus' enemies seemed to respect Him, saying as Pilate did, "I find no fault in Him at all" (John 18:38). The Roman soldiers who crucified Jesus exclaimed, "Certainly this was a righteous Man" (Luke 23:47). Indeed, Luke says that Jesus "increased . . . in favor with God and men" (2:52). Which is true—was Jesus respected or despised?

SOLUTION: Both are true. In general, He was respected by His *friends* and rejected by His *enemies*. He was honored by His disciples, but crucified by His foes.

Further, Jesus was more accepted in general in His *early* ministry, but the antagonism became more intense in His *later* ministry. So, it depends on who is speaking and when, as to whether Jesus was despised or respected.

ISAIAH 56:3 – Did Isaiah predict there would be homosexuals in the kingdom?

PROBLEM: According to some pro-homosexual interpreters, Isaiah 56:3 prophesied homosexuals will be brought into the kingdom of God. The Lord said, "to them I will give within my temple and its walls a memorial and a name better than sons and daughters; I will give them an everlasting name that will not be cut off" (NIV). Should this be taken to mean that Isaiah predicted the day of acceptance for homosexuals into God's kingdom?

SOLUTION: The Bible makes no predictions about homosexuals being accepted into the kingdom of God. First of all, Isaiah's prophecy is about "eunuchs," not homosexuals. And enunuchs are asexual, not homosexual.

Second, the "eunuchs" spoken of are probably spiritual, not physical.

Jesus spoke of spiritual "eunuchs" who had given up the possibility of marriage for the sake of the kingdom of God (Matt. 19:11-12).

Third, this is a classic example of reading one's beliefs into the text (eisegesis), rather than reading the meaning out of the text (exegesis). This is the very thing homosexuals charge heterosexuals of doing with Scripture.

Finally, the Bible says emphatically that "neither fornicators . . . nor homosexuals . . . will inherit the kingdom of God" (1 Cor. 6:9). The Scriptures repeatedly and consistently condemn homosexual practices (see comments on Lev. 18:22; Rom. 1:26). God loves all persons, including homosexuals. But He hates homosexuality.

ISAIAH 57:15 — Does God dwell in eternity or with men?

PROBLEM: Isaiah speaks of God as "the High and Lofty One Who inhabits eternity." Yet John claims that "God is with men, and He will dwell with them" (Rev. 21:3). Is God in eternity or in time?

SOLUTION: God is in both. He is "out there" as well as "in here." In technical terms, He is both transcendent over the universe and yet immanent in it. All of God is everywhere, in heaven and on earth (Ps. 139:7-10). He is over all and in all. He created the universe and has manifested Himself in it, but He is not identical to the universe (Col. 1:15-16). God is in the world, but God is not the world. Like a painter and his painting, God put Himself in His creation but is still more than it.

JEREMIAH

JEREMIAH 1:5 — Does Jeremiah teach reincarnation in this verse?

PROBLEM: God told Jeremiah: "Before I formed you in the womb I knew you; before you were born I sanctified you; and ordained you a prophet to the nations." But if God knew Jeremiah before he was formed in the womb, then He must have preexisted as a soul before he was incarnated into a body, which is what reincarnation teaches.

SOLUTION: These verses do not speak of the soul preexisting before birth, but of God calling and setting apart people for the ministry long before they are born. "I knew you" does not refer to a *preexistent soul,* but to the *prenatal person.* They were known by God "in the womb" (Jer. 1:5; cf. Ps. 51:6; 139:13-16). The word "know" (*yada*) implies a special relationship of commitment (cf. Amos 3:2). It is supported by words like "sanctified" (set apart) and "ordained," which reveal that God had a special assignment for Jeremiah (and Paul, Gal. 1:15-16), even before birth. Therefore, these passages do not imply *preexistence* of a soul; rather, they affirm *preordination* of an individual to a special ministry.

JEREMIAH 2:22 — Were Israel's sins eradicable or not?

PROBLEM: Jeremiah seems to imply that nothing could wash away Israel's sins. " 'For though you wash them with lye, and use much soap, yet your iniquity is marked before Me,' says the Lord God." However, later Jeremiah changes his tune and calls upon them to "Wash your heart from wickedness that you may be saved" (4:14). Why the difference?

SOLUTION: The solution seems to lie in the fact that the first passage is speaking about mere *outward* washing that does not cleanse their hearts. That is, no *external* ritual can purify a sinful heart. As the prophet said elsewhere, they needed to "circumcise" their hearts, not just their flesh (Jer. 4:4; cf. Deut. 10:16). What was wrong with them could only be purified by true penitence, not by phony practices.

JEREMIAH 6:20 – Do the later prophets disavow the earlier sacrificial system of Moses?

(See comments on Hosea 6:6.)

JEREMIAH 12:1 – Do the wicked prosper or not?

PROBLEM: Jeremiah complained, "Why does the way of the wicked prosper?" The same complaint is heard elsewhere in Scripture (cf. Job 12:6; Ps. 73:7). However, other passages of Scripture contend that the wicked do not prosper. Rather, "evil pursues sinners" (Prov. 13:21) and "evil shall slay the wicked" (Ps. 34:21).

SOLUTION: Jeremiah is speaking of *temporary* prosperity, which the wicked often enjoy. The *transitory* nature of their prosperity, however, is due to the longsuffering of God, wherein He delays judgment in favor of mercy and in the hope of repentance (2 Peter 3:9). When the Bible speaks of God slaying the wicked, it does not always mean immediately, but *ultimately*. When understood in this way, there is no real conflict between these passages.

JEREMIAH 15:6 – Can God repent?

PROBLEM: The prophet speaks of God repenting so many times that He is "weary of relenting." Yet in other places the Bible affirms that "He is not a man that He should relent" (1 Sam 15:29; cf. Mal. 3:6).

SOLUTION: God does not actually change, but only appears to change as we change, just as the wind appears to change when we turn and go in another direction (see comments on Gen. 6:6 and Ex. 32:14). God cannot change His character nor His unconditional promises (Heb. 6:17-18), because they are based in His unchangeable nature (cf. 2 Tim. 2:13). In fact, it is because God is unchangeable in Himself that He appears to change in relation to humans who vary in their character and conduct. God's immutability demands that His feelings and actions toward different human beings be different. Since He always feels the same revulsion toward sin (Hab. 1:13), God cannot feel the same toward a person who has just fallen in sin as toward that same person when he confesses his sin and calls upon God's mercy for salvation. In this case, it is not God who changes, but the person who changes in relation to God.

JEREMIAH 20:7 — Did God deceive Jeremiah?

PROBLEM: The KJV of this verse reads, "O Lord, thou has deceived me, and I was deceived." But, God is a God of truth who cannot lie (Heb. 6:18), nor can He tempt others to sin (Jas. 1:13). How then could He deceive Jeremiah?

SOLUTION: The Hebrew word (*patah*) translated "deceived" by the KJV does not imply moral deception here. It can be translated "induced" or "persuaded" (NKJV and NIV note). It simply means that God persuaded or constrained Jeremiah into a ministry of which he was not fully aware of all the consequences. But this is a good description of marriage. And who but the most cynical would insist that all romance and courtship are moral deception simply because the couple could not foresee all they were getting into.

JEREMIAH 22:30 — Was Jehoiachin childless or did he have heirs?

PROBLEM: Jeremiah was told here to "write this man down as childless." However, Jechoiachin had a son, Shealtiel, who is listed in Matthew 1:12.

SOLUTION: First of all, the verse does not say he would actually be childless. Jeremiah was simply told to write him down "as *if* childless" (NIV). Further, this is explained by the last part of the verse, namely, "none of his descendants shall prosper, sitting on the throne of David, and ruling anymore in Judah." This is true of His immediate successors. And it is even true of his long-range successor, Christ, who was not an *actual* son of Jehoiachin but only a *legal* son through his legal father, Joseph (see comments on Matt. 1:17). Jesus, however, was the actual son of David through Mary, His actual mother (cf. 2 Sam. 7:12ff; Luke 3:23, 31).

JEREMIAH 27:1 — Is this passage about Jehoiakim or Zedekiah?

PROBLEM: In the NKJV, this passage reads, "In the beginning of the reign of Jehoiakim." However, verses 3 and 12 identify Zedekiah as king of Judah, and 28:1 indicates that the prophecy of chapter 27 was given during the time of the reign of Zedekiah, not Jehoiakim. Should it be Zedekiah or Jehoiakim here?

SOLUTION: It is most likely the case that a scribe miscopied the text by inadvertently placing the heading of chapter 26 over chapter 27. There is good textual evidence from the Syriac and the Greek versions of the OT that there is a scribal error here. While the Syriac version reads "Zedekiah," the Greek version omits this verse altogether. This could indicate that a problem had developed in the early stages of the transmission of this portion of Jeremiah's text, and the Greek translators were not able to decipher the verse at all and merely left it out. The context and the historical situation indicates that the original read "Zedekiah" instead of "Jehoiakim."

JEREMIAH 32:31 – Did God delight in Zion (Jerusalem) or did it provoke His anger?

PROBLEM: The psalmist declared that "the Lord loves the gates of Zion." (Ps. 87:2). In fact, "the Lord has chosen Zion . . . [as] My resting place forever" (Ps. 132:13-14). But, in this text, Jeremiah quotes God as saying, "This city has been to Me a provocation of My anger and My fury from the day that they built it, even to this day." Well, then, does God delight in Zion forever, or has He been provoked by it from the beginning?

SOLUTION: Actually both are true, whether taken in a spiritual sense or in a literal sense. Some scholars take this *spiritually,* as a reference to God's eternal blessing on His heavenly Zion, the church (cf. Heb. 12:22; Rev. 21–22).

Other Bible scholars understand this literally as yet to be fulfilled when Israel is restored to their land forever as God promised (see comments on Rom. 11:26). Accordingly, the city of Jerusalem which was chosen by God as the capital of His people Israel was a perpetual pain to God. But, when the Messiah returns to set up His throne and reign there (cf. Zech. 13–14; Matt. 19:28), it will be a source of endless delight to God.

JEREMIAH 34:3 – Did Zedekiah see the King of Babylon or not?

PROBLEM: Jeremiah declared here to King Zedekiah: "your eyes shall see the eyes of the king of Babylon . . . and you shall go to Babylon." However, 2 Kings 25:7 says the Babylonian invaders "put out the eyes of Zedekiah, bound him with bronze fetters, and took him to Babylon." How then could he see the king of Babylon, if he was blind?

SOLUTION: These passages are perfectly harmonious, once all the factors are known. First, the king of Babylon summoned that the captured King Zedekiah be brought to his headquarters in Riblah (cf. 2 Kings 25:6).

There, after seeing the king of Babylon "face to face" (Jer. 34:3), Zedekiah's eyes were put out. Then Zedekiah was bound and taken to Babylon. So Zedekiah saw the *king* of Babylon, but not the *city* of Babylon.

JEREMIAH 36:28 — How can this book be inspired if the original manuscript of Jeremiah perished?

PROBLEM: According to evangelical scholars, only the original manuscripts (autographs) were inspired and inerrant, not the copies, since there are minor errors in the copies. But according to this passage, the king destroyed the original manuscript in the fire.

SOLUTION: When evangelicals refer to the "original manuscripts" alone being inspired (autographs), they do not exclude the fact that a biblical author may have had a "second edition" in original manuscripts too. Nor do they exclude the fact that, if the original is destroyed, God can inspire another one just like it. Indeed, Jeremiah was told, "Take yet another scroll, and write on it all the former words that were in the first scroll" (v. 28). So both manuscripts were inspired, only the first one perished without a copy. So the second one is now the "original" one.

Technically, we should not claim that only the original *manuscripts* are inspired, but the original *text*. For example, a perfect copy (e.g., a photo copy) of an original manuscript is as inspired as is the original manuscript itself. Likewise, all existing manuscript copies of the original are inspired in so far as they have accurately reproduced the original manuscript. God in His wisdom has not deemed fit to preserve the original manuscripts of Scripture. Some believe this is so men would not make an idol of it (cf. 2 Kings 18:4). Others claim it was His way of keeping it from human distortion by diffusing so many copies that it would be impossible to distort all of them. Whatever the case, the copies we do have are earlier, more numerous, and more accurate than those of any other book from the ancient world. They bring us all the truth of the original text, and the minor differences do not affect any doctrine of the Christian faith.

JEREMIAH 36:30 — How can this verse say that Jehoiakim shall have no one to sit on the throne when his son reigned after him?

PROBLEM: Because Jehoiakim burned the book of the prophecy of Jeremiah, God told Jeremiah to prophesy again to Jehoiakim that he "shall have no one to sit on the throne of David" (Jer. 36:30). However, according to 2 Kings 24:6, Jehoiachin the son of Jehoiakim "reigned in his place." Is this contradictory?

SOLUTION: This is not a contradiction. Although Jehoiachin did take over after the death of his father, he was in Jerusalem only three months before the city fell to the invading armies of Nebuchadnezzar. After reigning in Jerusalem for only three months, Jehoiachin was taken into captivity, and Zedekiah was placed on the throne in his stead. The Hebrew idea expressed in the phrase "sit on the throne" indicates a more permanent enthronement. God was telling Jehoiakim that his family name would not continue in the place of leadership, and that no dynasty in his name would continue. The extremely short reign of Jehoiachin, and his almost immediate removal and captivity, were a fulfillment of this prophetic statement.

JEREMIAH 43:8-13 — How can these verses talk about the invasion of Nebuchadnezzar when there is no evidence that it ever happened?

PROBLEM: According to this prophecy of Jeremiah, Nebuchadnezzar would attack and devastate Egypt. However, the Greek historians made no mention of this event, and there does not seem to be sufficient historical evidence to substantiate the claim that there ever was such an invasion. Is this an error in the biblical record of history?

SOLUTION: No, there is no historical error. Until recently, the only testimony from ancient historians was the record of Josephus, the Jewish historian. Modern scholars rejected Josephus' testimony as a fabrication to support the Hebrew Scriptures. However, a small fragment of a Babylonian chronicle from about 567 B.C. confirms both the record of Josephus and the biblical record concerning Nebuchadnezzar's invasion of Egypt. There is also confirmation from an inscription on the statue of Nes-hor, governor of southern Egypt under Hophra. Nebuchadnezzar did indeed invade and devastate Egypt as Jeremiah had prophesied.

JEREMIAH 46:2 — Does this date of the defeat of the Egyptian armies by Nebuchadnezzar contradict the date given in Daniel 1:1?

(For a consideration of the historical accuracy of this statement, see comments under Dan. 1:1.)

LAMENTATIONS

LAMENTATIONS 3:22 – Is God compassionate or ferocious?

PROBLEM: This and many other verses in Scripture describe God as merciful and compassionate, slow to wrath and plentiful in kindness (cf. Ps. 94:9; James 5:11; 1 John 4:16). By contrast, there are numerous passages in the Bible which reveal God as wrathful and vengeful. God told Moses, "You shall destroy all the peoples whom the Lord your God delivers over to you; your eye shall have no pity on them" (Deut. 7:16; cf. 1 Sam. 6:19; 15:2-3; Jer. 13:14; Heb. 12:29).

SOLUTION: In each case, the object is different. God executes His wrath on the wicked, as His justice demands, and He bestows His kindness on the righteous, as His love constrains Him. These are consistent acts of God in accordance with His own unchangeable essence (Mal. 3:6; James 1:17). But since the objects are different it only appears that God is acting contradictorily when in fact they are eminently compatible in a holy, loving God.

EZEKIEL

EZEKIEL 1:5-28 — Is this a manifestation of UFOs and extraterrestrial intelligence?

PROBLEM: Ezekiel speaks here of "living creatures" whose faces were in "the likeness of a man" which moved "like a flash of lightning" (v. 14). They were "lifted up from the earth" (v. 19) and their "wheels were lifted up together with them" (v. 20). Some have taken this to be a reference to UFOs and extraterrestrials. Are there human-like UFO creatures in outer space?

SOLUTION: This is not a reference to UFOs, but is a vision of the glory of God. This is evident for several reasons. First, the text states clearly that "This was the appearance of the likeness of the glory of the Lord" (Ezek. 1:28).

Second, these are called "visions" in the very first verse. Visions are usually given in highly symbolic form (cf. Rev. 1:9-20). Hence, the "likeness" (v. 28) given of things should not be taken literally, but symbolically.

Third, the "living creatures" were angels, since they had "wings" (v. 6) and flew in the midst of heaven. They compare to the angels mentioned in Isaiah 6:2 and especially to the "living creatures" (angels) which were around God's throne (in Rev. 4:6).

Fourth, their message was from the "Lord God" of Israel to the Prophet Ezekiel (cf. 2:1-4), not from some alleged UFO beings. The context was a message from the God of Israel through the Jewish prophet Ezekiel to His "rebellious nation" (2:3-4; cf. 3:4).

Fifth, there is no real evidence that any UFO, human-like creatures exist anywhere in the universe. There are, of course, demonic spirits which the Bible calls a "lying spirit" (1 Kings 22:22) and "deceiving spirits" (1 Tim. 4:1). These demons or evil angels may deceive people into thinking they are extraterrestrials. But they can be known by their false teaching and the evil practices they encourage, such as idolatry, witchcraft, astrology, divination, fortune telling, and contacting departed spirits (cf. Deut. 13:1-9; 18:9-14; 1 Tim. 4:1-3).

EZEKIEL 14:9 — Did God deceive these false prophets?

PROBLEM: Ezekiel declares that God "induced" the false prophets to speak and then would "destroy" them for doing so. But this sounds deceptive.

SOLUTION: God's action was neither deceptive nor morally coercive. Giving false prophecies is exactly what false prophets like to do. So, there is no coercion by God in inducing them to ply their trade. The sovereign God so ordered the circumstances that these evil men would, by their own free will, utter false prophecies that would reveal their true character and lead to their eventual doom. It is because they did not love the truth that God gave them over to error and its eventual consequence, destruction (see 2 Thes. 2:10-11).

EZEKIEL 16:47 — Did Israel imitate the heathen or not?

PROBLEM: In Ezekiel 5:7, the Israelites were condemned because they had "multiplied disobedience more than the nations that are all around" them. Yet, here in Ezekiel 16:47 they were condemned by God who said, "You did not walk in their ways nor act according to their abominations."

SOLUTION: There are two possible explanations of this discrepancy. Some scholars hold that the Israelites had imitated the pagan nations in *some* regards, but not in *all*. They had not gone so far as to incur the same judgment of God as the heathen around them, even though their present course was not consistent with God's Law.

Others believe that both texts indicate they were not merely *imitating* the heathen, but that they had gone far beyond them in their moral corruption. When the last passage is taken in its entirety, this becomes more clear: "You did not walk in their ways nor act according to their abominations; but, as if that were too little, you became more corrupt than they in your ways." In other words, "They were not *like* them; they were *worse* than them!" They were not *following* the heathen; they were so bad that they were the *leaders* in evil.

EZEKIEL 16:49 — Was the sin of Sodom selfishness rather than homosexuality?

PROBLEM: Ezekiel described the sin of Sodom as selfishness: "Now this was the sin of your sister Sodom: She and her daughters were arrogant, overfed and unconcerned; they did not help the poor and needy" (NIV). No mention is made of homosexuality or related sexual sins. Contrary to the traditional view, they were apparently condemned simply because they were selfish, not because they were homosexuals.

SOLUTION: Sodom's sin was not *only* selfishness, but *also* homosexuality. This is evident from several facts. First of all, the context of Genesis 19 reveals that their perversion was sexual (see comments on Gen. 19:8).

Second, the sin of selfishness related by Ezekiel (16:49) does not exclude the sin of homosexuality. As a matter of fact, sexual sins are a form of selfishness, since they are the satisfaction of fleshly passions.

Third, by calling their sin an "abomination," the very next verse (v. 50, NKJV) indicates that it was sexual. This is the same word used to describe homosexual sins in Leviticus 18:22.

Fourth, the notorious nature of Sodom's sexual perversity is revealed in the very word "sodomy" which has come to mean homosexual activity.

Fifth, the sin of Sodom is referred to elsewhere in Scripture as a sexual perversion. Jude even calls their sin "sexual immorality" (v. 7).

EZEKIEL 18:20 — Does God ever punish one person for another's sin?

PROBLEM: Ezekiel says clearly God does not punish the sons for their fathers' sins, but that "the soul who sins shall die [for its own sins]." However, in Exodus 20:5 we are informed that God visits "the iniquity of the fathers on the children to the third and fourth generations." These seem flatly contradictory.

SOLUTION: Ezekiel is speaking of the *guilt* of the father's sin never being held against the sons, but Moses was referring to the *consequences* of the fathers' sins being passed on to their children. Unfortunately, if a father is a drunk, the children can suffer abuse and even poverty. Likewise, if a mother has contracted AIDS from drug use, then her baby may be born with AIDS. But, this does not mean that the innocent children are guilty of the sins of their parents.

Further, even if the Exodus passage implied that moral guilt was somehow also visited on the children, it would only be because they too, like their fathers, had sinned against God. Noteworthy is the fact that

God only visits the iniquities of "those who hate" Him (Ex. 20:5), not those who do not (see also comments on Rom. 5:12).

EZEKIEL 18:32 – Does God rejoice over the sinner's doom?

PROBLEM: According to this verse, God declares, "I have no pleasure in the death of one who dies [in his sins]." Yet in Proverbs 1:26, God declares to the sinner, "I also will laugh at your calamity; I will mock when your terror comes." But, these seem to be contrary attitudes toward the doom of the sinner.

SOLUTION: The answer lies in the fact that the passages are speaking about two different types of people. God does not rejoice in the death of an ultimately unrepentant sinner, since He knows "it is appointed for men to die once, but after this the judgment" (Heb. 9:27). However, God does "laugh" (is satisfied) when the unwise learn the consequence of their imprudence in this life (cf. Prov. 1:31). "Laugh" is a figure of His indignation at their spurning the path of wisdom for foolishness. God is rightly indignant over the foolhardy and the ways of those who do not fear Him (v. 29) and who bring disaster on themselves. But, in no way does He rejoice in those who go to their ultimate doom without Him, for He takes no pleasure in the death of the wicked.

EZEKIEL 20:25 – Are God's statutes evil?

PROBLEM: Ezekiel tells us that God "gave them up to statutes that were not good, and judgments by which they could not live." However, the Bible declares that God's laws are perfect and holy (Lev. 11:45; Ps. 19:7; Rom. 7:7).

SOLUTION: First of all, Ezekiel is probably not referring to the laws of God, but to pagan statutes to which God turned over His people when they disobeyed His holy law. Notice the text says, God also gave them up to statutes that were not good because "they rebelled against Me" (20:21).

Second, there is a sense in which God's holy law can be said to be not good, namely, disobedience to it brings evil results. The Apostle Paul put it this way: "Is the law sin? Certainly not! . . . But sin, taking opportunity by the commandment, produced in me all manner of evil desire. For apart from the law sin was dead" (Rom. 7:7-8). That is, the *purpose* of the law is good (namely, to reveal God's righteousness), but the *result* to the law is evil (since it is the occasion of man's sinfulness).

EZEKIEL 26:3-14 — How can Ezekiel's prophecies be included in Scripture if they are wrong about Nebuchadnezzar?

PROBLEM: According to the prophecies in Ezekiel 26, God would bring Nebuchadnezzar against the proud city of Tyre and would utterly destroy it. However, Ezekiel 29:18 indicates that Nebuchadnezzar failed to capture Tyre. How can these two statements be reconciled?

SOLUTION: Nebuchadnezzar did destroy the coastal cities. However, the people of the port of Tyre had obviously relocated to the island city, which they were able to successfully defend against the Babylonian invaders. Nebuchadnezzar had defeated and plundered the cities on the shore, as Ezekiel prophesied in 26:7-11, but he could not defeat the island city. This fact is reported in Ezekiel 29:18.

Further, verse 12 marks a shift from the prophecy concerning Nebuchadnezzar to prophetic declarations about other invaders. Verse 3 had already introduced the idea of many invaders in the statement, "I . . . will cause many nations to come up against you." As history records, many nations did come up against the island city of Tyre, but it was Alexander the Great, laying siege against the island city of Tyre in about 332 B.C., who finally conquered the city and left it in total ruins so that it was never rebuilt. When rightly understood, Ezekiel's prophecy perfectly fits the historical record.

EZEKIEL 28:1 — Who is the prince of Tyre?

PROBLEM: Many conservative scholars equate the prince of Tyre with Satan. However, such statements as "you are a man, and not a god" (28:2) indicate that this is a reference to a human prince, not to Satan. Who is the prince of Tyre?

SOLUTION: Evangelical scholars hold differing positions concerning the identity of the prince of Tyre. Some hold that the language in chapter 28 is highly poetic with figurative expressions that are designed to emphasize the arrogance of the prince of Tyre. These commentators understand this to be a human prince, although there is difference of opinion about exactly who this man would be. Some identify this prince as Ethbaal III who ruled from about 591 to about 572 B.C. Others identify him as Ithobal II, who may have been the same person under a different name. Some commentators propose that the language cannot be applied to any specific person, but is a personification of the city itself. The "king" serves as a symbol of the government and the people as a whole.

Other commentators propose that verses 1-11 refer to the human prince, but that verses 11-19 refer to Satan. Those who advocate this view point to the change of reference from "the prince (*nagid*) of Tyre" in verse 2, to "the king (*melek*) of Tyre" in verse 12. This change of reference from prince to king, coupled with such statements as "you were in Eden" (v. 13), "you were the anointed cherub" (v. 14), and "you were perfect in your ways from the day you were created" (v. 15) may indicate that this section is about Satan. To the contrary, others simply understand these phrases as hyperbolic (literary exaggeration) references to the human prince and king.

All conservative commentators agree, however, that chapter 28 is a prophecy against the city of Tyre and its ruler, whoever that might be. This ruler exalted himself above God and deserved the judgment that God would bring upon him. Although the specific identity of the prince and king of Tyre is a debated issue, the application of this passage extends to all those who exalt themselves in pride and arrogance against God, whether they be kings, demons, or common people. And, of course, Satan himself is the ultimate example of all such proud creatures (cf. 1 Tim. 3:6).

EZEKIEL 29:17-20 — Does Ezekiel prophesy about an invasion of Egypt by Nebuchadnezzar which never actually took place?

(For a discussion of the historical accuracy of the prophecies of Nebuchadnezzar's invasion of Egypt, see comments under Jer. 43:8-13.)

EZEKIEL 40–48 — How can these prophecies be understood literally when the NT declares that the sacrificial system has been abolished by Christ's death?

PROBLEM: Ezekiel seems to predict that, in the messianic period, the sacrificial system used by the Jews before the time of Jesus will be reinstituted (chaps. 40–48). However, the NT in general and the Book of Hebrews in particular is emphatic in declaring that Christ has by one sacrifice forever done away with the need for animal sacrifices (10:1-9).

SOLUTION: There are two basic interpretations of this passage of Scripture. Some take it spiritually and others view it literally.

First, some argue for a *spiritual* interpretation that these sacrifices are not to be understood literally, but only as symbols or foreshadows of what was fulfilled in Christ's all-sufficient sacrifice on the Cross (Heb. 1:1-2). They give the following reasons for their view.

1. The NT teaches that Christ fulfilled and abolished the OT sacrificial system and priesthood (Heb. 8:8-10).

2. The Book of Revelation describes the Heavenly City of the future with no temple or sacrifices, only Christ the Lamb (21:22-27).

3. Ezekiel portrays the Gentiles as excluded from Israel's temple, which is contrary to the NT teaching that Jew and Gentile are one in Christ (Gal. 3:28; Eph. 2:12-22).

4. The NT speaks of the church as a spiritual Israel in which OT predictions are fulfilled (Gal. 6:16; Heb. 8:8-10).

Those who object to this view point out, first, that this violates the normal, historical-grammatical way to interpret the text. Further, it illegitimately reads NT meaning back into the OT text, rather than understanding the OT text as it is written. They also argue that the sacrifices predicted by Ezekiel could be pointing back to the Cross, just as the OT ones pointed forward to it.

The *literal* interpretation looks to an actual restoration of the temple and sacrificial system, just as Ezekiel predicted it to be fulfilled during Christ's millennial reign on earth (Rev. 20). They support their position with the following points:

1. Ezekiel presents a highly detailed description, with numerous measurements, and historical scenes that do not fit with a spiritual interpretation.

2. If this passage is spiritualized, then on similar grounds most of the OT prophecies could be spiritualized away, including the obviously literal ones about Christ's first coming, which we know from their fulfillment was literal. The same, then, applies to His second coming.

3. The Bible distinguishes between Israel and the church (1 Cor. 10:32; Rom. 9:3-4). Promises unique to Abraham and his literal descendants, such as the Promised Land (Gen. 12:1-3), are not fulfilled in the church, but remain yet to be fulfilled in the future (Rom. 11; Rev. 20).

4. The picture in Revelation 21 is not that of the millennium (Rev. 20), but of the eternal state that follows it. Ezekiel's prediction (40–48) will be fulfilled in the millennium. Later, in the new heaven and the new earth, there will be no temple or sacrifices.

5. The sacrifices mentioned by Ezekiel have no atoning significance. They are merely *memorial* in nature, looking back to the accomplished work of Christ on the Cross, much as the Lord's Supper does for believers today.

6. The rest of Ezekiel's prophecy will be fulfilled in a literal 1,000-year reign of Christ (Rev. 20:1-7) as He sits on a literal throne with His 12 apostles sitting on 12 literal thrones in Jerusalem (Matt. 19:28). If so,

then there is no reason not to take the prophecy about the sacrifices as literal too.

7. The OT did not foresee *how* Jew and Gentile would be joined together (cf. Eph. 3:4-6), but it did envision *that* the Gentiles would be blessed (Isa. 11:10-16). Ezekiel's presentation does not exclude this later revelation (cf. Col. 1:26).

8. The Book of Hebrews speaks only of abolishing animal sacrifices as in an *atoning* sense, not in a *memorial* sense.

DANIEL

DANIEL 1:1a — Wasn't the Book of Daniel actually written after about 170 B.C.?

PROBLEM: Daniel contains an incredible amount of detail concerning the kingdoms of the Gentiles from the reign of Nebuchadnezzar, from about 605 B.C., down to the Roman empire which began to exercise dominance as early as 241 B.C. and, under the Roman general Pompey, took over the Promised Land in 63 B.C. However, conservative scholars have maintained that Daniel wrote in the 6th century B.C. How could Daniel have given such historically accurate details of events in the future?

SOLUTION: The Book of Daniel contains supernatural prophecies that, from Daniel's time, extended hundreds of years into the future (Dan. 2:7). Daniel 11 presents a sweeping display of detailed prophecy that stretches from the reign of Cyrus the Great to the reign of antichrist, to the millennial kingdom, to the end of the age and into eternity. The record of the movement of nations and events is so accurate, it reads as the historical account of an eyewitness. However, conservative scholarship places the date of the Book of Daniel at a time before any of these events took place. The book itself claims to be predictive prophecy (cf. 9:24ff). To avoid the conclusion that Daniel's prophecy was a supernatural act of God, modern scholars have proposed a number of explanations including a late date of writing. However, the historical accuracy of Daniel's record confirms a 6th century composition, and the best conclusion is that the Book of Daniel is a revelation from God about historical events that were future to Daniel, many of which are still future to us today.

DANIEL 1:1b — Is the date given here of Nebuchadnezzar's invasion in contradiction to the date given in Jeremiah 46:2?

PROBLEM: The Book of Daniel begins with the dating of the invasion of Nebuchadnezzar in the third year of the reign of Jehoiakim of Judah.

However, in Jeremiah 46:2, the date of Nebuchadnezzar's invasion is given as during the fourth year of the reign of Jehoiakim of Judah. Which is correct?

SOLUTION: Both statements are correct. The difference is a result of two different calendar systems used by the two prophets. Daniel employed the *Tishri* (around October) calendar system which was the first month of the new year on the Hebrew calendar. Jeremiah, whose prophecy concerned the coming invasion of the Assyrian armies, employed the calendar of the Assyrians that marked *Nisan* (around April) as the first month of the new year. Jehoiakim came to the throne in the month of *Tishri* in 609 B.C. The official reckoning of a king's first year starts on the first day of the new year, *Tishri* 1. Since Jehoiakim became king of Judah several days after the first day of the new year, his first official year as king did not begin until the first day of the following year. For Daniel, this meant that Jehoiakim's first official year began on the first day of *Tishri,* almost a whole year later. For Jeremiah, this meant that Jehoiakim's first official year began about six months later on the first day of *Nisan.*

609 B.C.

Jehoiakim becomes
king of Judah

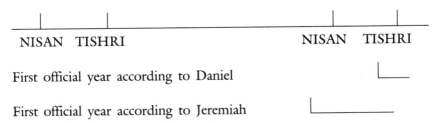

Nebuchadnezzar's invasion took place in the summer of 605 B.C., between the months of *Nisan* and *Tishri.* This means that according to Daniel's reckoning, it was only the third official year of Jehoiakim's reign, but according to Jeremiah's reckoning it was Jehoiakim's fourth official year as king of Judah.

DANIEL

■

605 B.C.

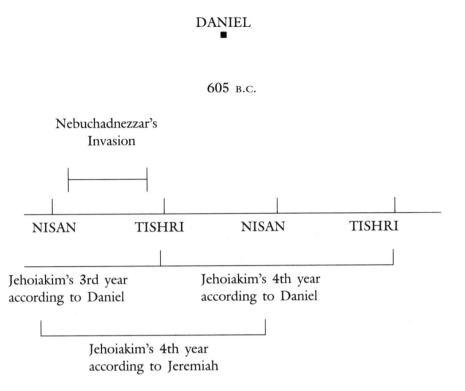

Nebuchadnezzar's
Invasion

NISAN   TISHRI   NISAN   TISHRI

Jehoiakim's 3rd year   Jehoiakim's 4th year
according to Daniel   according to Daniel

Jehoiakim's 4th year
according to Jeremiah

There is no contradiction here.

DANIEL 2:2 — Why does Daniel refer to the Chaldeans as a group of wise men here when he refers to them as an ethnic group in 5:30?

PROBLEM: When Daniel refers to those whom Nebuchadnezzar summoned to interpret his dream, he identifies these as magicians, astrologers, sorcerers, and Chaldeans. Each of these is a group of wise men who functioned as advisors to Nebuchadnezzar. However, in 5:30 Daniel refers to the Chaldeans as an ethnic group when he refers to Belshazzar as king of the Chaldeans.

SOLUTION: There is no contradiction here. Although these two verses use the same word, *kasdim,* this word has two distinct uses in the Hebrew language. The Hebrew word can refer to a class of astrologer-priests, as it is used in Daniel 2:2. It can also refer to the ethnic group of Chaldeans as it is used in 5:30. Due to its development through several languages and cultures, what originally started out as the Sumerian word *Gal-du,* which was applied to the astrologers meaning "master builder," has ultimately become confused with the Hebrew word for the ethnic group, Chaldeans *(kasdim).* Consequently, Daniel employs the same word in its two common uses.

DANIEL 3:12 — If Daniel was faithful to God, why did he not refuse to bow to this idol too?

PROBLEM: In the first chapter, Daniel and the three other young men refused to do anything that violated their conscience (cf. Dan. 1:8ff). However, here only the three young men refused to bow to the image. Why didn't Daniel refuse to perform this idolatrous act also?

SOLUTION: He undoubtedly would have refused, if he had been there. But, there is absolutely no indication that Daniel was present. Since he was a government official (cf. Dan. 1:19), he may have been out of the capital on business at this time. We do know that later (Dan. 6) he stood firm on his spiritual convictions, even under the threat of death. So, had he been present, we can be assured that he would not have engaged in this idolatry either.

DANIEL 5:1 — How can Daniel say the last king of Babylon was Belshazzar when history records that it was Nabonidus?

PROBLEM: Daniel 5 records the downfall of Babylon and identifies the king of Babylon as Belshazzar. However, neither Babylonian nor Greek historians record the existence of any such person. In fact, ancient historians report that Nabonidus was the last king of the Babylonian empire. Is Daniel's record in error?

SOLUTION: Daniel's historical record of Belshazzar has been confirmed by recent archaeological evidence. Nabonidus was the king of Babylon from 556 to 539 B.C. However, according to a cuneiform document known as the "Persian Verse Account of Nabonidus," in the third year of his reign, about 553 B.C., Nabonidus departed from Babylon on a long journey and entrusted the rule of Babylon into the hands of his first born son, Belshazzar. When Cyrus overthrew Babylon, Nabonidus was in Tema in North Arabia. Since Belshazzar was the subordinate of Nabonidus, his name was forgotten, because the ancient Babylonian and Greek historians were primarily interested in the reigns of the official kings. Daniel's record has proven to be amazingly accurate.

DANIEL 5:31 — How can the Book of Daniel be inspired if it makes reference to a man that modern scholarship says never existed?

PROBLEM: According to Daniel 5:31, the kingdom of Belshazzar fell to the invading armies, and Darius the Mede took over as king. However, modern scholars have rejected the historical accuracy of the Book of Daniel. They argue that there never was a Darius the Mede, since there is no mention of such a person in ancient documents. Is this an error in Daniel's historical account?

SOLUTION: Like the historical record of Belshazzar, which modern scholars questioned until archaeological evidence vindicated Daniel's accuracy, Daniel has again recorded the existence of a man that other ancient historical documents omit.

Some modern scholars claim that the author of Daniel mistakenly thought that the Medes conquered Babylon instead of the Persians. They claim that this author then confused Darius I, king of Persia (521-486 B.C.) with the conqueror of Babylon and identified this figure as Darius the Mede. However, there is no reason to assume that the Book of Daniel is in error. Darius the Mede is a different person from Darius I of Persia. Darius the Mede was a subordinate to Cyrus the Great. Cuneiform texts refer to Darius the Mede as Gubaru who was appointed by Cyrus to be governor over all of Babylonia. The tendency to deny the historical accuracy of Daniel simply because there is currently no corroborating historical information stems from the antisupernatural bias of modern scholarship. Daniel's historical record has proven to be a reliable source of information.

DANIEL 10:1 — Did Daniel continue until the first year of Cyrus or the third year of his reign?

PROBLEM: Daniel 1:21 asserts that Daniel "continued until the first year of King Cyrus." But Daniel 10:1 says that Daniel was still there until the "third year of Cyrus king of Persia."

SOLUTION: The first passage (Dan. 1:21) does not say Daniel did not continue to live longer. It simply notes that he lived until that glorious year when the Jewish exiles received permission to return to their homeland (cf. Ezra 1:3). The second passage (Dan. 10:1) notes that Daniel also lived even beyond that time.

Further, the word "continued" may imply that he retained his position or continued in Babylon. Although he lived on after Cyrus took over, Daniel would not necessarily have retained his government position with Babylon (cf. Dan. 1:19) after this time, since the Medo-Persians took over.

DANIEL 12:2 — Will the resurrection be partial or universal?

PROBLEM: Some Scriptures leave the impression that only some will be raised from the dead. Daniel says *"many* of those who sleep in the dust of the earth shall awake" (Dan. 12:2). The NT often refers to resurrection "out from among" (Gk., *ek*) the dead, implying that not all will be raised (e.g., Luke 20:35; Acts 4:2; Rom. 1:4; 1 Cor. 15:12).

SOLUTION: There will be both a partial resurrection and then later a complete resurrection. There are two resurrections — the resurrection of the "just" and then later the resurrection of the "unjust" (Acts 24:15). First, "those who have done good" will come forth and then "those who have done evil" (John 5:29). John informs us that these two resurrections are separated by "a thousand years." The "first resurrection" is before the thousand years (Rev. 20:6). This is the resurrection of the saved who "lived and reigned with Christ for a thousand years" (v. 4). But, "the rest of the dead [the unsaved] did not live again until the thousand years were finished" (v. 5). So, the first resurrection is partial, consisting only of the saved, and the second resurrection completes the picture, resurrecting all the rest, namely, the unsaved.

HOSEA

HOSEA 1:2 – How could a holy God who condemns harlotry command Hosea to marry a harlot?

PROBLEM: God commanded Hosea to "take yourself a wife of harlotry." However, according to Exodus 20:14, adultery is a sin; and according to 1 Corinthians 6:15-18, to have sexual relations with a harlot is immoral (cf. Lev. 19:29). How could a holy God command Hosea to take a harlot as his wife?

SOLUTION: Some scholars have attempted to avoid the difficulty by claiming this is an *allegory*. However, while God obviously intended this as a dramatic illustration to Israel of their unfaithfulness to Him (cf. 1:2), there is no indication in the text that it is anything but a literal event. How else could it have been such a forceful example to the way-ward people of Israel.

Taken *literally*, there is no real contradiction with any other Scripture for several reasons. First of all, when God commanded Hosea to take Gomer, the daughter of Diblaim, to be his wife, Gomer may not yet have actually committed adultery. However, God knew what was in her heart, and He knew that she would ultimately be unfaithful to Hosea. This is similar to the angel of the Lord calling Gideon a "mighty man of valor" before he had fought a single battle (Jud. 6:11-12). God knew that Gideon would become a great leader in Israel even though he was not yet. God commanded Hosea to take a woman whom He knew would become a harlot. God commanded this as a picture of how Israel had committed spiritual adultery against Him. When God brought Israel out of Egypt, she was a brand new nation. She had not yet broken the covenant which God would establish with her in the wilderness. Just like Israel had committed spiritual adultery by worshiping other gods, so Gomer would commit physical adultery by having relations with other men. The relationship between Hosea and Gomer was an object lesson for all Israel.

Second, the passage does not condone harlotry. In fact it is a strong condemnation of harlotry, of both the physical and spiritual (idolatry) kind (cf. 4:11-19). The fact that the grave sin of idolatry is depicted as spiritual harlotry reveals God's disapproval of harlotry.

Third, Hosea was commanded to *marry* a harlot, not to commit adultery with her. God said, "Go, take yourself a *wife*." God did not say go in and commit fornication with her. Rather, He said marry her and be faithful to her, even though she will be unfaithful to you. Not only does this not violate the commitment of marriage, it actually intensifies it. Hosea was to be faithful to his marriage vows even though his wife would become unfaithful to hers.

Fourth, the command in Leviticus 21:14 to not marry a harlot was given to the levitical priests, not to everyone. Salmon apparently married Rahab the harlot (Matt. 1:5) from whose legal genealogy Christ eventually came. At any rate, Hosea was a prophet, not a levitical priest, hence, the prohibition to not marry a harlot did not apply to him.

Finally, the command in 1 Corinthians 6:16 not to be joined to a harlot is not a command never to marry a woman who was a harlot. Rather, the command is directed against those who were having sexual relations outside of the marriage relationship. But, Hosea did not have sexual relations outside of marriage. God commanded Hosea to marry Gomer and always be faithful to her.

HOSEA 6:6 — Do the prophets disavow the sacrificial system of Moses?

PROBLEM: Moses commanded the use of sacrifices in the worship of the Lord, saying, "And you shall burn the whole ram on the altar. It is a burnt offering to the Lord; it is a sweet aroma, an offering made by fire to the Lord" (Ex. 29:18). However, the later prophets seemed to repeatedly repudiate the sacrificial system. Hosea quotes the Lord, saying, "I desire mercy and not sacrifice, and the knowledge of God more than burnt offerings" (Hos. 6:6). David confessed to God, "You do not desire sacrifice, or else I would give it; You do not delight in burnt offering" (Ps. 51:16). God declared through Jeremiah, "Your burnt offerings are not acceptable, nor your sacrifices sweet to Me" (Jer. 6:20).

SOLUTION: The later prophets did not repudiate the OT sacrificial system — they only stressed that God did not desire mere *outward* observance, but also *inward* obedience. This is clear from three lines of evidence. First, God expressed approval with the offering of sacrifices, even during the same period in which many of the above quoted verses were written, which are mistakenly taken to express His disapproval. For example, Solomon offered thousands of burnt offerings to the Lord, which God accepted by a supernatural manifestation of fire from heaven (2 Chron. 7:1-4). The godly King Josiah manifested his obedience to the Law of Moses by eating the passover lamb (cf. 2 Kings 23:21-23). Other good kings offered burnt sacrifices which were acceptable to God (cf. 2 Kings 16:15; 2 Chron. 29:18). Even after the captivity, at the end of the OT, sacrifices were offered during the time of Ezra (cf. Ezra 3:5; 8:35) and Nehemiah (cf. Neh. 10:33) which were accepted by God.

Second, even the later prophets themselves offered sacrifices and/or encouraged others to do so. Samuel offered a "burnt offering to the Lord" (1 Sam. 7:9). Elijah offered a "burnt sacrifice" on Mt. Carmel which God accepted (1 Kings 18:38). The prophet Joel lamented that "the grain offering and the drink offering have been cut off from the house of the Lord" (Joel 1:9, 13). Likewise, Zephaniah prophesied of a time when worshipers would return with an "offering" to the Lord (Zeph. 3:10). Ezekiel also predicted the continuance of offerings in the future kingdom (Ezek. 40:38). Even David, who stressed the need for inner purity of heart, nevertheless, in the same psalm, spoke of the need to offer a "burnt offering" (Ps. 51:19).

Finally, the verses that seem to speak against sacrifices and offerings do not condemn them *as such,* but only in the *vain way* in which they were being offered. It was *ritual* without *reality* that God condemned. They had a "form of godliness but denying its power" (2 Tim. 3:5). That this is what the verses mean is evident from several facts: (1) As just noted, during this same period God was accepting sacrifices offered with a right heart. (2) Also, as just observed, even the prophets themselves offered sacrifices to the Lord. (3) Samuel the prophet, who made one of the condemning statements (1 Sam. 15:22), offered a sacrifice to the Lord in the very next chapter (1 Sam. 16:2, 5). (4) The very wording of this condemnation implies that God was not against sacrifices as such. For example, the prophet Samuel said "to obey is *better than* sacrifice, And to heed than the fat of rams" (1 Sam. 15:22). It is clear that this is not a condemnation of sacrifices, but of sacrifices without an obedient heart.

HOSEA 8:13 – How can this verse say that Ephraim will return to Egypt when 11:5 says that Ephraim will not return there?

PROBLEM: According to the prophecy of 8:13, because Israel, or Ephraim, had sinned against God, Hosea prophesied that they would return to

Egypt (cf. 9:3). However, in 11:5 God specifically states that Israel "shall not return to the land of Egypt." Is this a contradiction?

SOLUTION: There is no contradiction because the statements refer to different aspects of Israel's experience. In Hosea 8:13, God is remembering the sin of Israel in worshiping other gods. In their hearts, the people of Israel were always "returning to Egypt." In Hosea 11:5, God is reiterating the promise of Deuteronomy 17:16 that Israel would not return to the captivity of Egypt. Although God would punish the sin of His people, He would not cause them to return to the captivity of Egypt. Rather, He would bring the Assyrian armies to enact His judgment, and Israel would be carried away as the captives of this foreign enemy. On several occasions Israel had sought help from Egypt against the Assyrians. The promise that they would not return to Egypt was not only a restatement of the promise of Deuteronomy 17:16, but it was also a warning that Egypt would not be able to help Israel any more against the invading Assyrians. Although their hearts were turning away from God, and returning to the pagan influence of Egypt, God would not drive them back there. Rather, He would break the bond with Egypt that Israel continued to rely upon instead of relying upon their God. He would do this by bringing about their captivity in Assyria. These two statements are in perfect harmony.

JOEL

JOEL 3:6 — How could Joel mention the Greeks if his book was written before the 4th century B.C.?

PROBLEM: According to many scholars, Joel was written in the 9th century B.C. However, the Greek reference in Joel 3:6 indicates that the earliest the book could have been written is the late 4th century B.C.

SOLUTION: It is not necessary to suppose that the mention of Greeks places the composition of the book in the late 4th century B.C. The context of chapter 3 is the judgment of the nations. God promises punishment specifically upon the Phoenicians and the Philistines because they had plundered His people and sold them into slavery to the Greeks. Verse 6 states that these nations had sold His people to the Greeks: "That you may remove them far from their borders." If Joel had been written after the expansion of the empire of Greece by Alexander the Great in the middle of the 4th century B.C., then God could not have accused the Phoenicians and the Philistines of selling the Jews to the Greeks who were "far from their borders." The Greeks are referred to in ancient Neo-Babylonian inscriptions as early as the 7th-century B.C., and the Cretan Linear B tablets indicate the beginning of the Greek civilization and language from about 1500 B.C. So, it is not possible to use this reference to date Joel's prophecy in the fourth century B.C.

JOEL 3:12 — Does God sit or stand to judge?

PROBLEM: Joel declares that God will "sit to judge all the surrounding nations." But, elsewhere the Bible says God "stands to judge the people" (Isa. 3:13). Which is true?

SOLUTION: Both are figures of speech which express literal and compatible truths. God "sits" to hear everyone impartially and *decide* their guilt or innocence. Then He "stands" to *execute* the judgment on the case. Each expression describes a different aspect of God's rule as judge.

AMOS

AMOS 8:11 — What does Amos mean when he says there will be a famine of hearing the words of the Lord?

PROBLEM: Because of the sin of Israel, God pronounced through His prophet Amos that He would bring judgment upon the people. One aspect of that judgment was that there would be a famine of hearing the words of the Lord. However, there is no indication from history that the Hebrew Scriptures were destroyed or removed from Israel at this time. To what does the "famine" in hearing the words of the Lord refer?

SOLUTION: This verse addresses the lack of messengers from God, such as His prophets. Israel had not only despised the messengers of God, but had put many of them to death for their words. In God's judgment upon Israel, there would come a time when Israel would seek for help and guidance, but God would be silent (compare Ezek. 7:26 and Micah 3:7). He would not send any messengers to them. Although they would still have the written Hebrew Scriptures, there would be a famine of the words of the Lord through His prophets.

AMOS 8:14 — Does this contradict the Bible's teaching on the resurrection?

(See comments on Job 7:9.)

OBADIAH

OBADIAH – If the Book of Obadiah is inspired Scripture, then why is it not quoted in the NT?

(For a discussion of this question, see Ecc. 1:1.)

OBADIAH – Is the prophecy of Obadiah simply an expression of Jewish nationalism?

PROBLEM: The prophecy of Obadiah is essentially a message of divine moral judgment upon the nations. Of the 21 verses that comprise this book, 16 are directed as pronouncements of coming judgment against Edom, and 5 verses are dedicated to the prophecies of the future triumph of Israel over Edom. But, isn't this simply an example of Jewish nationalism rather than a revelation of God?

SOLUTION: The Book of Obadiah is a revelation of the sovereignty of God presented in the midst of national disgrace and defeat. The impotence of God's people against their enemies was a reflection upon the power of the God of Israel. Wasn't Yahweh a defeated God? Wasn't He powerless to resist the enemies of His people? No is Obadiah's resounding reply! The God of Israel will keep His promises even though the future looks black. The nations have not understood that their temporary victory over God's people was the very work of God. The message of Obadiah is that the God of Israel is always in complete control, and He will accomplish His purpose. It is a message of faith and hope, and triumph against the enemies of God. But the triumph of Israel will be a blessing to all nations. Israel's apostasy brought judgment. But, "if their being cast away is the reconciling of the world, what will their acceptance be but life from the dead?" (Rom. 11:15) This book is not simply an expression of Jewish nationalism. It is a declaration of the faithfulness of God, and a testimony to His moral justice by which He will ultimately establish justice in the earth.

JONAH

JONAH 1:1 – Is the Book of Jonah fact or fiction?

PROBLEM: Traditional Bible scholarship has held that the Book of Jonah records events that actually took place in history. However, because of the literary style of the book and the amazing adventures that are said to have befallen the prophet Jonah, many modern scholars propose that it is not a book of actual historical events, but a fictional story designed to communicate a message. Did the events of Jonah actually happen or not?

SOLUTION: There is good evidence that the events recorded in the Book of Jonah are literal historical events that took place in the life of the prophet Jonah.

First, the tendency to deny the historicity of Jonah stems from an antisupernatural bias. If miracles are possible, there is no real reason to deny that Jonah is historical.

Second, Jonah and his prophetic ministry is mentioned in the historical book of 2 Kings (14:25). If his supernatural prediction is mentioned in a historical book, why should the historical nature of his prophetical book be rejected?

Third, the most devastating argument against the denial of the historical accuracy of Jonah is found in Matthew 12:40. In this passage Jesus predicts His own burial and resurrection, and provides the doubting scribes and Pharisees the sign that they demanded. The sign is the experience of Jonah. Jesus says, "For as Jonah was three days and three nights in the belly of the great fish, so will the Son of Man be three days and three nights in the heart of the earth." If the tale of Jonah's experience in the belly of the great fish was only fiction, then this provided no prophetic support for Jesus' claim. The point of making reference to Jonah is that if they did not believe the story of Jonah being in the belly of the fish, then they would not believe the death, burial, and resurrection of Jesus. As far as Jesus was concerned, the historical fact of His own death, burial, and resurrection was on the same historical ground as Jonah in the belly of the fish. To reject one was to cast doubt on the other (cf. John 3:12). Likewise, if they believed one, they should believe the other.

Fourth, Jesus went on to mention the significant historical detail. His own death, burial, and resurrection was the supreme sign that verified His claims. When Jonah preached to the unbelieving Gentiles, they repented. But, here was Jesus in the presence of His own people, the very people of God, and yet they refused to believe. Therefore, the men of Nineveh would stand up in judgment against them, "because they [the men of Nineveh] repented at the preaching of Jonah" (Matt. 12:41). If the events of the Book of Jonah were merely parable or fiction, and not literal history, then the men of Nineveh did not really repent, and any judgment upon the unrepentant Pharisees would be unjust and unfair. Because of the testimony of Jesus, we can be sure that Jonah records literal history.

Finally, there is archaeological confirmation of a prophet named Jonah whose grave is found in northern Israel. In addition, some ancient coins have been unearthed with an inscription of a man coming out of a fish's mouth.

JONAH 3:3 – Is Jonah's testimony to the size of Nineveh accurate?

PROBLEM: When Jonah arrived at the city of Nineveh, he observed that the city was so large, that it took a three-day journey to pass through it. However, such a statement must be an exaggeration, since it is argued that the average man could walk only from 50 to 70 miles in three days. A city of 50 to 70 miles in diameter is not recorded in all of history until modern times. Is this an error?

SOLUTION: There have been several proposals to explain this observation by Jonah. Some commentators propose that Jonah is commenting on the circumference of the city. A city 50 miles in circumference would be about 16 miles in diameter. This size more nearly fits the estimated population of about 600,000 people in this major ancient city.

Other commentators propose that Jonah is not claiming that it would take three days to walk straight through the city. Rather, Jonah observed that it would take three days to go through all the various areas in the entire city. Those who hold this position point out that Jonah went to Nineveh in order to proclaim the message of judgment to the people. This would require him to go to every part of the city, not simply to walk through the middle from one side to the other. This also fits the statement of verse 4 in which Jonah enters the city and, in the first day's walk, proclaimed the message as he went along.

JONAH

∎

JONAH 3:6 — Why does Jonah refer to the king of Assyria simply as the king of Nineveh?

PROBLEM: Conservative scholars maintain that the Book of Jonah was written by the prophet Jonah who actually experienced the events recorded in the book. However, if the Book of Jonah was written by a Hebrew prophet who lived in the time of the Assyrian empire, why would he refer to the king of the Assyrian empire simply as the king of Nineveh?

SOLUTION: All of the ancient records regarding the history of Assyria testify to the fact that it was common knowledge that Nineveh was the capital city of Assyria. Simply because Jonah identifies this king as the king of Nineveh does not mean that Jonah did not also realize that this man was the king of the Assyrian empire of which Nineveh was the capital. The king of Assyria would certainly be the king of its capital city. To identify the king of a nation as the king of its capital city was not uncommon. In 1 Kings 21:1 Ahab, king of Israel, is referred to as the king of Samaria. So, Jonah's use of this title is not anachronistic, and does not provide evidence for a late date.

MICAH

MICAH 3:4 – Does God ever withhold His blessing from those who cry out for it?

PROBLEM: This text and other passages of Scripture (cf. Isa. 1:15; James 4:3) speak of God withholding His blessing from those who cry unto Him. But, the Bible contends, on the other hand, that God "gives to all liberally" who ask (James 1:5), "for everyone who asks, receives" (Luke 11:10).

SOLUTION: These diverse texts are speaking about different kinds of people. God never withholds His promised blessing from those who call with a sincere and repentant heart. But, He does withhold it from those who do not call in "faith with no doubting" (James 1:6) or who "ask amiss" to spend it on their own pleasures (James 4:3). In brief, God always grants His promised blessings on the faithful, but He does not always promise the same blessings to the unfaithful.

Second, not all of God's promised blessings are unconditional, as was His unilateral land promise to Abraham and his descendants (Gen. 12; 14–15; 17). Many of His blessings are conditioned on His people's obedience, such as the bilateral covenant with Israel ("If you will indeed obey my voice," Ex. 19:5).

Likewise, God never promises that He will heal everyone in this life of all diseases. In fact, God refused to heal Paul though he pleaded three times with Him to be relieved of his burden (2 Cor. 12:8-9). Nor does God promise that He will make all believers rich in this life. Even Jesus became poor for us (2 Cor. 8:9), and He declared that there would always be poor (Matt. 26:11), spiritually blessed though they be (Matt. 5:3). In these cases, no matter how much faith one musters, God will not necessarily bestow the blessing in this life, since He never unconditionally promised to do so.

NAHUM

NAHUM 1:2 – Does God get angry?

PROBLEM: Nahum declares that God "avenges and is furious." Indeed, God is often represented as being angry in the Bible (cf. Isa. 26:20; Jer. 4:8). At the same time, the Bible urges believers not to be angry, since it is a sin (cf. Gal. 5:20). But if it is a sin, then how can God do it?

SOLUTION: Anger as such is not sinful. It depends on the purpose, nature, and/or object of anger. Even Jesus, our perfect moral example, was angry at sin (cf. Matt. 23:15-36). Paul exhorted us, "Be angry, and do not sin" (Eph. 4:26). In short, we should be angry at sin, but we should not sin in being angry. The problem with human anger, even in the good sense of anger at sin, is that it is easy to carry it too far so that we sin in our anger. Unlike God, who is "slow to anger" (Neh. 9:17), we are often quick to anger. In short, there is good and bad anger for humans.

GOOD ANGER	BAD ANGER
Over sin	Over being sinned against
Against sin	Against sinners
Expressed righteously	Expressed unrighteously
Being slow to anger	Being quick to anger
Done in justice	Done in retaliation

HABAKKUK

HABAKKUK 3:3 – If God is everywhere, then how could He "come from Teman"?

PROBLEM: This verse seems to contradict God's omnipresence. If God is everywhere (Ps. 139:7-10; Jer. 23:23), then how could He be localized in the city of Teman from which He was to come to judge His enemy?

SOLUTION: This is not a reference to God in His omnipresence, but to a special manifestation of God, such as a theophany. Just as God came down in a special display of His glory to Moses on Mt. Sinai (Deut. 33:2), or as the angel of the Lord to Manoah (Jud. 13), even so here He came from Teman.

HABAKKUK 3:3 – Is this a prediction of the Prophet Mohammed?

PROBLEM: Many Muslim scholars believe this refers to the prophet Mohammed coming from Paran (Arabia), and use it in connection with a similar text in Deuteronomy 33:2.

SOLUTION: As already noted (see comments on Deut. 33:2), Paran is not near Mecca where Mohammed came, but is hundreds of miles away. Furthermore, the verse is speaking of "God" coming, not Mohammed. Finally, the "praise" could not refer to Mohammed (whose name means "the praised one"), since the subject of both "praise" and "glory" is God ("His"), and Mohammed is not God.

ZEPHANIAH

ZEPHANIAH 1:1 – Hasn't it been demonstrated that Zephaniah is actually composed of two books with different messages?

PROBLEM: Conservative scholars maintain that the Book of Zephaniah is a single work composed by the prophet Zephaniah. However, modern scholarship claims that the book is actually two books with different messages put together as if it were one. The very beginning of this book is a message of dread and coming judgment. The overriding theme is the devastation and destruction that is about to fall in the swiftly approaching Day of the Lord (1:7, 8, 10, 14-15, etc.) However, verses 8-13 of chapter 3 present a message of hope that seems completely out of keeping with the theme of the book as a whole. How can this book be considered the sole work of one person, Zephaniah?

SOLUTION: There is no reason to suppose that the messages of judgment and hope are incompatible. In fact, it is the message of the Book of Zephaniah that the coming judgment of the Day of the Lord is the very means by which God would bring about the ultimate restoration of His people. The Day of the Lord is a day of purification from sin and salvation of the remnant. The hope of salvation in the midst of judgment, is found as early as 2:1-3 and 3:8-9, clearly pointing out that it is this purifying judgment that will prepare the way for the restoration of God's people. Zephaniah is a single unified work by the prophet Zephaniah.

HAGGAI

HAGGAI 1:2 – How could the indifference of the leaders have caused the work to cease when Ezra 4:23 blames foreign influence?

PROBLEM: Haggai 1:2 implies that the people were indifferent toward the building of the temple, while Ezra 4:7-23 claims that foreign enemies came up to force the people to stop the rebuilding project. Was the reason indifference or opposition?

SOLUTION: Both statements are true. The military force of the enemy caused the rebuilding *to stop,* but it was the indifference of the people that prevented the project from being *restarted.* (See comments on Ezra 4:23.)

HAGGAI 2:15 – Why does this verse imply that the building of the temple began in 520 B.C.?

PROBLEM: Haggai 2:15 implies that the building of the temple did not begin until 520 B.C. Ezra 3:8-13 claims that the rebuilding of the temple began in about 536 B.C., while Ezra 4:24 says the rebuilding of the temple took place during the reign of Darius, king of Persia. Which one of these is correct?

SOLUTION: All of them are correct. They are simply referring to different aspects of the work. For a discussion of these passages see under Ezra 3:10.

ZECHARIAH

ZECHARIAH 11:12-13 – How can these verses be part of Zechariah when Matthew 27:9 says they belong to the Book of Jeremiah?

PROBLEM: When Matthew presents the prophetic prediction that related to the death of Judas, he quoted from Jeremiah 32:6-9. However, he also quoted from Zechariah 11:12-13, but he asserts that these quotes are from the prophet Jeremiah. Does the Zephaniah passage actually belong in Jeremiah?

SOLUTION: It is not exactly accurate to say that Matthew quoted exclusively from Zechariah 11 or Jeremiah 32. There are other passages in Jeremiah that refer to the potter's field (Jer. 18:2; 19:2, 11), and Matthew's rendering is not an exact quote from any of the passages. Matthew is combining the various elements of these prophecies to make his point. Because Jeremiah is the more prominent prophetic book, Matthew simply mentions Jeremiah's name as the source of the prophetic message which he is bringing out. Matthew did this earlier (Matt. 5:2) where he cites from two passages (Micah 5:2 and 2 Sam. 5:2). It was a common practice of the day to cite the more popular prophet.

MALACHI 1:3 — If God is love, how could He hate any person?

PROBLEM: In the latter part of verse 2 and the first part of verse 3, God says, "Yet Jacob I have loved; But Esau I have hated." But, John says, "God is love" (1 John 4:16). How can a God of love hate any one person?

SOLUTION: First of all, God is not speaking about the *person* Esau, but of the *nation* that came from him, namely, Edom. So God is not expressing hate toward any person here.

Further, the nation Edom was deserving of God's indignation for their "violence against your brother Jacob [Israel]" (Obad. 10). They sided with Israel's enemies, blocked the way of their escape, and even delivered up those who remained (vv. 12-14).

Finally, like the Nicolaitans, God hates the *works* of the sinner, not the sinner himself. John commends the believers that "hate the *deeds* of the Nicolaitans, which I also hate" (Rev. 2:6; also see comments on Ps. 5:5).

MATTHEW

MATTHEW 1:8 – Is Joram the father of Uzziah or of Ahaziah?

PROBLEM: Matthew says "Joram begot Uzziah." However, 1 Chronicles 3:11 lists "Joram [and then] his son, Ahaziah." Which one is correct?

SOLUTION: Ahaziah was apparently the immediate son of Joram, and Uzziah was a distant "son" (descendant). Just as the word "son" in the Bible also means grandson, even so the term "begot" can be used of a father or grandfather. In other words, "begot" means "became the ancestor of," and the one "begotten" is the "descendant of."

Matthew, therefore, is not giving a *complete chronology,* but an *abbreviated genealogy* of Christ's ancestry. A comparison of Matthew 1:8 and 1 Chronicles 3:11-12 reveals the three generations between Joram and Uzziah (Azariah):

MATTHEW 1:8	1 CHRONICLES 3:11-12
Joram	Joram
. . . . .	Ahaziah
. . . . .	Joash
. . . . .	Amaziah
Uzziah	Uzziah (also called Azariah)

MATTHEW 1:9 – Did Matthew make a mistake concerning the father of Jotham?

PROBLEM: In 2 Kings 15:1-7, the Bible mentions the father of Jotham as Azariah, and in 2 Kings 15:32 and 34, Jotham's father is named Uzziah. Some have concluded that the Bible made a mistake by listing two different people as the father of Jotham.

SOLUTION: These are two different names for the same person. For different reasons, the Bible occasionally gives two different names for one individual. For example, Paul was also named Saul (Acts 13:9).

Also, in Judges, Gideon receives the second name, Jerubbaal (6:32; 7:1). Jehoiakim's son Jehoiachin is also known as Jeconiah (cf. 2 Kings 24:6 and 1 Chron. 3:16). Daniel, Hananiah, Mishael, and Azariah were all given new names. They are Belteshazzar, Shadrach, Meshach, and Abednego (Daniel 1:7). Also, some of Jesus' disciples had two names, for example, Simon (Peter) and Lebbaeus (Thaddaeus) (Matt. 10:2-3).

MATTHEW 1:17 — How many generations were listed between the captivity and Christ, 14 or 13?

PROBLEM: Matthew says the generations "from the captivity in Babylon until the Christ are fourteen generations" (1:17). However, he lists only 13 names after the captivity is counted. So, which is correct, 13 or 14 ?

SOLUTION: Both are correct. Jeconiah is counted in both lists, since he lived both before and after the captivity. So, there are literally 14 names listed "from the captivity in Babylon until the Christ," just as Matthew says. There are also literally 14 names listed between David and the captivity, just as Matthew claims (Matt. 1:6-12). There is no error in the text at all.

MATTHEW 2:2 — Why does the Bible commend the Magi for following the star, when it condemns astrology?

PROBLEM: The Bible condemns the use of astrology (see Lev. 19:26; Deut. 18:10; Isa. 8:19), yet God blessed the wise men (Magi) for using a star to indicate the birth of Christ.

SOLUTION: First, we need to ask what astrology is. Astrology is a belief that the study of the arrangement and movement of the stars can enable one to *foretell* events — whether they will be good or bad.

Second, the star used in the biblical account was to *announce* the birth of Christ, not to *foretell* this event. God gave the star to the Magi to proclaim to them that the child had already been born. We know the child was already born, because in Matthew 2:16, Herod gives a command to kill all the boys in Bethlehem and vicinity that are two years old or younger in accordance with "the time which he had ascertained from the Magi" (NASB).

Third, there are other cases in the Bible in which the stars and planets are used by God to reveal His desires. Psalm 19:1-6 affirms that the heavens declare God's glory, and Romans 1:18-20 teaches that creation reveals God's existence. Christ refers to what will happen to the sun, moon, and stars in connection with His second coming (Matt 24:29-30), as did the prophet Joel (2:31-32). The star guiding the Magi was not used to *predict,* but to *proclaim* the birth of Christ.

MATTHEW 2:6 — How can we explain Matthew's apparent misquotation of Micah 5:2?

PROBLEM: Matthew 2:6 quotes Micah 5:2. However, the words Matthew uses are different than those used by Micah.

SOLUTION: Although Matthew seems to have changed some of the words from the passage in Micah, there is no real deviation in the meaning of the text. Matthew, in some instances, seems to have paraphrased.

First, Matthew inserts the phrase "land of Judah" for the word "Ephrathah." This does not really change the meaning of the verse. There is no difference between the land of Judah and Ephrathah, except one is more specific than the other. In fact, Ephrathah refers to Bethlehem in the Micah passage, and Bethlehem is located in the land of Judah. However, this does not change the basic meaning of this verse. He is speaking of the same area of land. Interestingly, when Herod asked the chief priests and the scribes where the child was to be born, they said, "in Bethlehem of Judea" (Matt. 2:5, NASB).

Second, Matthew describes the land of Judah as "not the least" but Micah states that it is "little." Here, Matthew may be saying that since the Messiah is to come from this region, it is by no means least among the other areas of land in Judah. The phrase in Micah only says that Bethlehem is too little or small, as compared to the other areas of land in Judah. The verse does not say it is the least among them, only very little. Matthew is saying the same thing in different words, namely, that Bethlehem is little in *size,* but by no means the least in *significance,* since the Messiah was born there.

Finally, Matthew uses the phrase "who will shepherd My people Israel" and Micah does not. Micah 5:2 recognizes that there will be a ruler in Israel, and Matthew recognizes this as well. However, the phrase that is not mentioned in Micah is actually taken from 2 Samuel 5:2. The combining of verses does not take away what is being said, but it strengthens the point that the author is making. There are other instances where an author combines one Scripture with another. For example, Matthew 27:9-10 combines some of Zechariah 11:12-13 with Jeremiah 19:2, 11 and 32:6-9. Also, Mark 1:2-3 combines some of Isaiah 40:3 with Malachi 3:1. Only the first passage is mentioned, since it is the main passage being cited.

In brief, Matthew is not misrepresenting any information in his quotation of Micah 5:2 and 2 Samuel 5:2. Matthew's quote is still accurate even though he paraphrases part of it and combines another portion of Scripture with it.

MATTHEW 2:23 — Didn't Matthew make a mistake by claiming a prophecy that is not found in the OT?

PROBLEM: Matthew claims that Jesus moved to Nazareth to live, in order "that it might be fulfilled which was spoken by the prophets, He shall be called a Nazarene" (Matt. 2:23). However, no such prophecy is found in any OT prophet. Did Matthew make a mistake?

SOLUTION: Matthew did not say that any particular OT "prophet" (singular) stated this. He simply affirmed that the OT "prophets" (plural) predicted that Jesus would be called a Nazarene. So we should not expect to find any given verse, but simply a general truth found in many prophets to correspond to His Nazarene-like character. There are several suggestions as to how Jesus could have "fulfilled" (brought to completion) this truth.

Some point to the fact that Jesus fulfilled the righteous requirements of the OT Law (Matt. 5:17-18; Rom. 8:3-4), one part of which involved the holy commitment made in the vow of the "Nazarite." The Nazarite took this vow "to separate himself to the Lord" (Num. 6:2), and Jesus perfectly fulfilled this. However, the word is different both in Hebrew and Greek, and Jesus never took this particular vow.

Others point to the fact that Nazareth comes from the basic word *netzer* (branch). And many prophets spoke of the Messiah as the "Branch" (cf. Isa. 11:1; Jer. 23:5; 33:15; Zech. 3:8; 6:12).

Still others note that the city of Nazareth, where Jesus lived, was a despised place "on the other side of the tracks." This is evident in Nathaniel's response, "Can anything good come out of Nazareth?" (John 1:46) In this sense, "Nazarene" was a term of scorn appropriate to the Messiah whom the prophets predicted would be "despised and rejected of men" (Isa. 53:3; cf. Ps. 22:6; Dan. 9:26; Zech. 12:10).

MATTHEW 4:5-10 (cf. LUKE 4:5-12) — Is there a mistake in recording the wilderness temptation of Christ by Matthew or Luke?

PROBLEM: According to both Matthew and Luke, the first temptation was to turn stones into bread to satisfy Jesus' hunger. The second temptation listed by Matthew took place at the pinnacle of the temple. The third temptation listed by Matthew involved all the kingdoms of the world. However, although Luke mentions these same two events, he lists them in reverse order—the kingdoms of the world are mentioned second and the pinnacle of the temple is mentioned third. Which is the correct order?

SOLUTION: It may be that Matthew describes these temptations *chronologically* while Luke lists them *climactically,* that is, topically. This may be to express the climax he desired to emphasize. Matthew 4:5 begins with the word "then" while verse 8 begins with the word "again." In Greek, these words suggest a more sequential order of the events. In Luke's account, however, verses 5 and 9 each begins with a simple "and" (see NASB). The Greek in the case of Luke's account does not necessarily indicate a sequential order of events. Furthermore, there is no disagreement on the fact that these temptations actually happened.

MATTHEW 4:14-16 — Why does Matthew incorrectly quote Isaiah?

PROBLEM: Matthew does not seem to quote Isaiah 9:1-2 accurately. Rather, he seems to have changed it.

SOLUTION: It is not necessary to quote a passage *verbatim* to cite it *accurately.* Matthew does not distort the meaning of this passage. He simply condenses or summarizes it. To *paraphrase* accurately is not to *distort.* Otherwise, no news report or historical account was ever accurate, since summary is essential to history.

MATTHEW 5:14 — Are believers the light of the world, or is Jesus?

PROBLEM: In this passage, Jesus said to His disciples, "You are the light of the world." However, in John 9:5, Jesus declared, "I am the light of the world." Who is the light of the world, Jesus or His disciples?

SOLUTION: Both. Jesus is the *primary* light, and we are the *secondary* light. As the light of the sun is to the moon, so Jesus is the *source* of the light, and we are the *reflectors* of the light. Jesus said, "as long as I am in the world, I am the light of the world" (John 9:5). Now that He is no longer here, we are His reflected light in the world.

MATTHEW 5:17-18 — Did Jesus come to do away with the Law of Moses?

PROBLEM: Jesus said very explicitly, "Do not think that I came to destroy the Law or the Prophets. I did not come to destroy, but to fulfill."

However, on one occasion Jesus approved of His disciples when they broke the Jewish law about working on the Sabbath (Mark 2:24), and Jesus Himself apparently did away with the ceremonial law by declaring all meats clean (Mark 7:19). Jesus' disciples clearly rejected much of the OT law, including circumcision (Acts 15; Gal. 5:6; 6:15). Indeed, Paul declared that "You are not under law but under grace" (Rom. 6:14) and that the Ten Commandments engraved in stone have been "taken away in Christ" (2 Cor. 3:14).

SOLUTION: In the matter of whether the Law of Moses was done away with by Christ, confusion results from failing to distinguish several things.

First of all, there is a confusion of *time*. During His lifetime, Jesus always kept the Law of Moses Himself, including offering sacrifices to the Jewish priests (Matt. 8:4), attending Jewish festivals (John 7:10), and eating the passover lamb (Matt. 26:19). He did on occasion violate the pharisaical (and false) traditions that had grown up around the Law (cf. Matt. 5:43-44), chiding them, "You have made the commandment of God of no effect by your tradition" (Matt. 15:6). The verses that indicate the law has been fulfilled refer to *after* the Cross when there is "neither Jew nor Greek . . . for you are all one in Christ Jesus" (Gal. 3:28).

Second, there is a confusion of *aspect*. At least some of the references (if not all) to the Law being done away with in the NT are speaking of OT ceremonies and types. These ceremonial and typological *aspects* of the OT Law of Moses were clearly done away with when Jesus, our passover lamb (1 Cor. 5:7), fulfilled the Law's types and predictions about His first coming (cf. Heb. 7–10). In this sense, Jesus clearly did away with the ceremonial and typological aspects of the Law, not by destroying the Law, but by fulfilling it.

Finally, there is a confusion about *context*. Even when the moral dimensions of the law are discussed, there is a confusion. For example, not only did Jesus fulfill the moral demands of the Law for us (Rom. 8:2-3), but the *national* and *theocratic* context in which God's moral principles were expressed in the OT no longer apply to Christians today. For example, we are not under the commands as Moses expressed them for Israel, since, when expressed for them in the Ten Commandments, it had as its reward that the Jews would live "long upon the land [of Palestine] which the Lord your God is giving you [Israelites]" (e.g., Ex. 20:12). When the moral principle expressed in this OT commandment is stated in the NT, it is expressed in a *different context,* namely, one that is not national or theocratic, but is personal and universal. For all persons who honor their parents, Paul declares that they will "live long on the earth"

(Eph. 6:3). Likewise, Christians are no longer under the commandment of Moses to worship on Saturday (Ex. 20:8-11), for, since the Resurrection, appearances, and Ascension (all of which occurred on Sunday), Christians worship on Sunday instead (see Acts 20:7; 1 Cor. 16:2). Sabbath worship, declared Paul, was only an OT "shadow" of the real substance which was inaugurated by Christ (Col. 2:16-17). Since even the Ten Commandments *as such* were expressed in a national Jewish, theocratic framework, the NT can speak correctly about that which was "engraved on stones" being "taken away in Christ " (2 Cor. 3:7, 13-14).

However, this does not mean that the moral principles embodied in the Ten Commandments, that reflect the very nature of an unchanging God, are not still binding on believers today. Indeed, every one of these principles contained in the Ten Commandments is restated *in another context* in the NT, except of course the command to rest and worship on Saturday.

Christians today are no more under the Ten Commandments as given by Moses to Israel than we are under the Mosaic Law's requirement to be circumcised (see Acts 15; Gal. 3) or to bring a lamb to the temple in Jerusalem for sacrifice. The fact that we are bound by similar moral laws against adultery, lying, stealing, and murder no more proves we are still under the Ten Commandments than the fact that there are similar traffic laws in North Carolina and Texas proves that a Texan is under the laws of North Carolina. The truth is that when one violates the speed laws in Texas he has not thereby violated a similar law in North Carolina, nor is he thereby bound by the penalties of such laws in North Carolina. In like manner, although both the OT and NT speak against adultery, nevertheless, the penalty was different — capital punishment in the OT (Lev. 20:10) and only excommunication from the church in the NT (1 Cor. 5:1-13), with the hope of restoration upon repentance (cf. 2 Cor. 2:6-8).

MATTHEW 5:29 — Is hell the grave or a place of conscious torment?

PROBLEM: Jesus refers here to the "body" being "cast into hell," and the psalmist speaks of "bones" being "scattered at the mouth of hell [*sheol*]" (Ps. 141:7, KJV). Jacob talked about his "gray hairs" being brought down to hell (Gen. 42:38, KJV; cf. 44:29, 31). However, Jesus referred to hell as a place where the soul goes after one dies and is in conscious torment (Luke 16:22-23). Is "hell" just the grave, as the Jehovah's Witnesses and some other cults claim?

SOLUTION: The Hebrew word translated "hell" (*sheol*) is also translated "grave" or "pit." It simply means "unseen world," and can refer either to the grave, where the body is unseen after burial, or to the spirit world, which is invisible to mortal eyes. In the OT, *sheol* often means grave, as indicated by the fact that it is a place where "bones" (Ps. 141:7) and "gray hairs" (Gen. 42:38) go at death. Even the resurrection of Jesus' body is said to be from "hell" (i.e., the grave) where it did not see corruption (Acts 2:30-31).

While there may be some allusions to "hell" as a spirit world in the OT (cf. Prov. 9:18; Isa. 14:9), "hell" (Gk., *hades*) is clearly described as a place of departed spirits (souls) in the NT. Angels are there and they have no bodies (2 Peter 2:4). Unrepentant human beings are in conscious torment there after they die and their bodies are buried (Luke 16:22-25). In the end those in hell will be cast into the lake of fire with the devil where they will be "tormented day and night forever" (Rev. 20:10, 14-15). Jesus spoke many times of hell as a place of conscious and eternal suffering (cf. Matt. 10:28; 11:23; 18:9; 23:15; Mark 9:43, 45, 47; Luke 12:5; 16:23).

MATTHEW 5:33-37 — Did Jesus condemn all oath taking, even in court?

(See comments on James 5:12.)

MATTHEW 5:42 — Should believers literally give anything to anyone who asks?

PROBLEM: Here Jesus clearly said, "Give to him who asks you, and from him who wants to borrow from you do not turn away" (cf. Luke 6:30). But, if we took this literally we would have nothing to provide for our own families. Also, Paul says that those who do not provide for their own families are worse than infidels (1 Tim. 5:8).

SOLUTION: A text out of its context is a pretext. We must understand the context in which Jesus said "give to him who asks you." First of all, as we know from other things Jesus said and did, this does not mean to give to people what will harm them. As Jesus said, no good father would give a serpent to his child (Matt. 7:10). Furthermore, it does not mean give to those who can work, but refuse to. Paul said emphatically, "If anyone will not work, neither shall he eat" (2 Thes. 3:10). Finally, the whole context of Jesus' statements here are to reaffirm the spirit of the law which He came to fulfill (Matt. 5:17-18), as opposed to what they "heard" (cf. Matt. 5:21, 27, 33, 38, 43) — what had been said by oral tradition and misinterpretation (cf. Matt. 15:3-6).

Here Jesus is explicitly addressing the legalistic misinterpretation of the OT that says take revenge on your enemy with "an eye for an eye and a tooth for a tooth" (Matt. 5:38). By contrast Jesus says, don't retaliate against your enemy. Love him, and give to help him (cf. v. 44). But Jesus no more expected His listeners to take, without qualification, the command to "give to him who asks you" than He intended them to literally cut off their hands and pluck out their eyes if they offended them (vv. 29-30)!

MATTHEW 5:43 – Why did the OT prescribe that one could hate his enemies?

PROBLEM: Jesus said here of the OT, "You have heard that it was said, 'You shall love your neighbor and hate your enemy.' " How could a God of love (Ex. 20:2, 6; 1 John 4:16) command them to hate their enemies?

SOLUTION: God never commanded His people at any time to hate their enemies (see comments on Mal. 1:3). God is an unchanging God of love (cf. 1 John 4:16; Mal. 3:6), and He cannot hate any person, nor can He command anyone else to do so. Jesus said the greatest commands were to love God and to love our neighbor as ourself (Matt. 22:36-37, 39). In point of fact, this very command is taken by Jesus from the OT. Leviticus 19:18 declares: "you shall love your neighbor as yourself"!

Why then did Jesus say the OT taught that we should "hate our enemy" (Matt. 5:43)? He didn't, and for a very good reason. Nowhere in the OT can any such verse be found. In fact, Jesus is not quoting the OT here, but the pharisaical misinterpretation of the OT. Notice, Jesus does not say "it is *written*," as He often did when quoting the OT (cf. Matt. 4:4, 7, 10). Rather, He said, "you have *heard*," by which He meant the Jewish "tradition" that had grown up around the OT and by which they had made the commandment of God of no effect (cf. Matt. 15:3, 6). The truth is that the God of love commanded love both in the OT and NT and never at any time commanded that we hate other persons.

MATTHEW 6:6 – If Jesus said prayer should be in private, why does the Bible commend public prayer?

PROBLEM: In this text, Jesus urged His disciples to pray in private, saying, "When you pray, go into your room, and when you have shut your door, pray to your Father who is in the secret place." However, elsewhere the Bible commends praying in public. For example, Daniel prayed with his window open so he could be seen (Dan. 6:10). Solomon offered his great dedicatory prayer for the temple in public (1 Kings 8:22). And Paul urged public prayers "for men everywhere" (1 Tim. 2:8).

SOLUTION: It is not *public* prayers which Jesus condemned, but *ostentatious* prayers. He was not opposed to people praying in *appropriate* public places, but in *conspicuous* places. It was not the *place* of prayer so much as the *purpose* of their prayer that Jesus spoke against, namely, "that they may be seen by men" (Matt. 6:5).

MATTHEW 6:13 — Why should we pray that God would not lead us into temptation when God cannot tempt anyone?

PROBLEM: The Bible says emphatically, "God cannot be tempted by evil, nor does He Himself tempt anyone" (James 1:13). Why, then, does Jesus ask us here to pray, "and lead us not into temptation"?

SOLUTION: God can *test* us, but He cannot *tempt* us to sin. When we are tempted, we are drawn away by our own lusts (see comments on James 1:2). So, God should be invoked to order our lives in such a way that we are not led into situations in which we will be tempted. In other words, this is a plea for providential guidance through the mine field of sin in this fleshly sojourn. It is a request of God that He help us to "make no provision for the flesh" (Rom. 13:14).

MATTHEW 8:5-13 (cf. LUKE 7:2-10) — Is there a mistake in the accounts concerning Jesus and the centurion?

PROBLEM: Matthew seems to present the centurion as the one who seeks the help of Jesus (Matt. 8:5); but, Luke seeems to say that the centurion sent elders to see Jesus (Luke 7:3). Also, Matthew appears to say that the centurion himself comes to talk with Jesus. However, in Luke, the Bible says only the centurion's representatives saw Jesus.

SOLUTION: Both Matthew and Luke are correct. In the 1st century, it was understood that when a representative was sent to speak for his master, it was as if the master was speaking himself. Even in our day this is still the case. When the Secretary of State meets individuals from other countries, he goes out in the name of the president of the United States. In other words, what he says, the president says. Therefore, Matthew states that a centurion came entreating Jesus about his sick slave, when in fact the centurion sent others on his behalf. So, when Matthew declares that the centurion was speaking, this was true, even though he was (as Luke indicated) speaking through his official representative.

MATTHEW 8:12 — Is hell a place of darkness, or is there light there?

PROBLEM: Jesus described hell as a place of "outer darkness" (Matt. 8:12; cf. 22:13 and 25:30). By contrast, the Bible says hell is a place of "fire" (Rev. 20:14) and "unquenchable flames" (Mark 9:48). But, fire and flames give off light. How can hell be utterly dark when there is light there?

SOLUTION: Both "fire" and "darkness" are powerful figures of speech which appropriately describe the unthinkable reality of hell. It is like fire because it is a place of destruction and torment. Yet, it is like outer darkness because people are lost there forever. While hell is a literal place, not every description of it should be taken literally. Some powerful figures of speech are used to portray this literal place. Its horrible reality, wherein body and soul will suffer forever, goes far beyond any mere figure of speech that may be used to describe it. But, it is a serious mistake to take a figure of speech literally. By doing so, one can conclude that God has feathers, since He is described as having wings! (Ps. 91:4) There are other figures of speech used to describe the eternal destiny of the lost that, if taken literally, contradict each other. For example, hell is depicted as an eternal garbage dump (Mark 9:43-48), which has a bottom. But, it is also portrayed as a bottomless pit (Rev. 20:3). Each is a vivid depiction of a place of everlasting punishment.

MATTHEW 8:20 (cf. MATT. 20:18; 24:30; etc.) — If Jesus was the Son of God, why did He call Himself the Son of Man?

PROBLEM: Jesus referred to Himself most often as the Son of Man. This seems to point to His humanity more than His deity. If He was really the Messiah, the Son of God, why did He use the self-description, "Son of Man"?

SOLUTION: First of all, even if the phrase "Son of Man" is a reference to Jesus' humanity, it is not a denial of His deity. By becoming man, Jesus did not cease being God. The Incarnation of Christ did not involve the subtraction of deity, but the addition of humanity. Jesus clearly claimed to be God on many occasions (Matt. 16:16-17; John 8:58; 10:30). But, in addition to being divine, He was also human. He had two natures conjoined in one person.

Furthermore, Jesus was not denying His deity by referring to Himself as the Son of Man. The term "Son of Man" is used to describe Christ's deity as well. The Bible says that only God can forgive sins (Isa. 43:25; Mark 2:7). But, as the "Son of Man," Jesus had the power to forgive sins (Mark 2:10). Likewise, Christ will return to earth as the "Son of Man" in clouds of glory to reign on earth (Matt. 26:63-64). In this passage, Jesus is citing Daniel 7:13 where the Messiah is described as the "Ancient of Days," a phrase used to indicate His deity (cf. Dan. 7:9).

Further, when Jesus was asked by the high priest whether He was the "Son of God" (Matt. 26:63), He responded affirmatively, declaring that He was the "Son of Man" who would come in power and great glory (v. 64). This indicated that Jesus Himself used the phrase "Son of Man" to indicate His deity as the Son of God.

Finally, the phrase "Son of Man" emphasizes who Jesus is in relation to His Incarnation and His work of salvation. In the OT (see Lev. 25:25-26, 48-49; Ruth 2:20), the kinsman redeemer was a close relative of someone who was in need of redemption. So Jesus, as our Kinsman Redeemer, was identifying Himself with humankind as its Savior and Redeemer. Those who knew the OT truth about Messiah being the Son of Man understood Jesus' implicit claims to deity. Those who did not, would not so recognize this. Jesus often said things in this way so as to test His audience and separate believers from unbelievers (cf. Matt. 13:10-17).

MATTHEW 8:22 (cf. LUKE 9:60) — Wasn't it absurd for Jesus to tell the dead to bury their own dead?

PROBLEM: A man wanted to follow Jesus but first asked Jesus if he could go and bury his father. Jesus responded, "let the dead bury their own dead." But the dead can't bury anyone. This doesn't seem to make any sense.

SOLUTION: Jesus was not speaking of those who were *physically* dead, but of those who are *spiritually* dead (cf. Eph. 2:1). Jesus requested that the man follow Him (Luke 9:59). The man responded saying he wished to take care of his family first. So the issue is, who comes first—one's family or Jesus Christ. The answer Jesus gives indicates the spiritual state of this man's family. They were apparently not believers, and the Bible says that those who are not Christians are "dead in trespasses and sins" (Eph. 2:1, 5). Jesus was telling the man that his spiritually dead family should take care of the burial. Jesus wanted this man to follow Him. Christian discipleship calls for high commitment.

MATTHEW 8:28-34 (cf. MARK 5:1-20; LUKE 8:26-39) — Where were the demoniacs healed?

PROBLEM: The first three Gospels (Matthew, Mark, and Luke) each give an account of Jesus healing demoniacs. Matthew states that the place where the healing took place was the country of the Gadarenes. However, Mark and Luke say it was in the country of the Gerasenes.

SOLUTION: There is a textual problem here. The critical text of the Greek NT (Nestle-Aland/United Bible Societies) renders Mark and Luke the same as Matthew, namely, in the country of the "Gadarenes." However, some manuscripts give the name of the country as the Gerasenes. It is possible to account for the variant reading in these manuscripts as a scribal error. Gadara may have been the capital of the region, and Matthew therefore referred to the area as the "country of the Gadarenes" because the people of that region, whether they lived in Gadara or not, were identified as Gadarenes. Mark and Luke were perhaps giving a more general reference to the country of the Gerasenes, which was the wider area in which the incident occurred. However, a scribe, confusing the reference in Matthew as a reference to the town instead of the people of the region, may have attempted to correct the manuscripts and altered the references to make them uniform. It seems that the best textual evidence is in favor of Gadara, although there are varying opinions among commentators. There is no contradiction or error here, because the problem developed as a result of transcription, and there is no evidence to demonstrate that there was a conflict in the original manuscripts.

MATTHEW 8:28-34 (cf. MARK 5:1-20; LUKE 8:26-39) — How many demoniacs were healed?

PROBLEM: Matthew reports that two demoniacs came to Jesus, while Mark and Luke say that only one demoniac approached Him. This appears to be a contradiction.

SOLUTION: There is a very fundamental mathematical law that reconciles this apparent contradiction—wherever there are two, there is always one. There are no exceptions! There were actually two demoniacs that came to Jesus. Perhaps Mark and Luke mentioned the one because he was more noticeable or prominent for some reason. However, the fact that Mark and Luke only mention one does not negate the fact that there were two as Matthew said. For wherever there is two, there is always one. It never fails. If Mark or Luke had said there was *only* one, then that would be a contradiction. But, the word "only" is not in the text. The critic has to change the text to make it contradict, in which case the problem is not with the Bible, but with the critic.

MATTHEW 10:5-6 — Did Jesus come only for Jews or also for Gentiles?

PROBLEM: Jesus told His disciples to "make disciples of all the nations" (Matt. 28:19), because He had "other sheep . . . which are not of this fold" (John 10:16). Even the OT prophets declared that Jesus would be "a light to the Gentiles" (Isa. 49:6). However, Jesus Himself instructed His disciples, "Do not go into the way of the Gentiles, and do not enter a city of the Samaritans" (Matt. 10:5). Later, He affirmed, "I was not sent except to the lost sheep of the house of Israel" (Matt. 15:24).

SOLUTION: These apparently contradictory commands refer to two different periods. It is true that Jesus' original mission was to the Jews. But, the Scriptures testify that "He came to His own, and His own did not receive Him" (John 1:11). The official Jewish position was to reject Him as their Messiah and to crucify Him (Matt. 27; Mark 14; Luke 22; John 18).

Therefore, it was after His crucifixion and resurrection that the mission of the disciples was to go to the nations. This was in fulfillment of prophecies about the Gentiles. Thus, the Apostle Paul could tell the Roman Christians that the Gospel was "for the Jew first and also for the Greek" (Rom. 1:16). Because of their rejection of Jesus, the nation of Israel was cut off (Rom. 11:19), but, when the subsequent "fullness of the Gentiles" (11:25) has been completed, then Israel will be grafted in again (11:23, 26). Of course, even though Jesus' mission was officially to the Jews, He did not neglect Gentiles. He healed the Syro-Phoenician woman's daughter (Mark 7:24-30). He went out of His way to minister to the woman of Samaria (John 4). He told His disciples of His anticipated work (through them) among the Gentiles (John 10:16), and His Great Commission was to "make disciples of all the nations" (Matt. 28:18-20). But, both in order of priority and time, the message of Christ came first to the Jew and then to the Gentile. The difference, then, between the two sets of verses can be contrasted in this way:

JESUS CAME FOR THE JEWS	JESUS CAME FOR THE GENTILES ALSO
Officially	Actually
Initially	Subsequently
Primarily	Secondarily
Before His rejection	After His rejection

MATTHEW 10:10 (cf. MARK 6:8) — Did Jesus command that the disciples take a staff or not?

PROBLEM: In Matthew, Jesus seems to say that the disciples should not take a staff, but in Mark it appears that He allows them to have one.

SOLUTION: A closer examination reveals that the account in Mark (6:8) declares that the disciples are to take nothing except a staff, which a traveler would normally have. Whereas the account in Matthew states that they are not to acquire another staff. There is no discrepancy between these texts. Mark's account is saying that they may take the staff that they have, while Matthew is saying that they should not take an *extra* staff or tunic. The text reads "Provide neither . . . two tunics, nor sandals, nor staffs" (plural: vv. 9-10). It does not say that they should not take a staff (singular). So there is no contradiction.

MATTHEW 10:23 — Did Jesus promise to return to earth during the lifetime of the disciples?

PROBLEM: Jesus sent His disciples on a mission and promised them, "you will not have gone through the cities of Israel before the Son of Man comes." However, it is obvious that He never even went to heaven, to say nothing of returning again, before they had returned from their evangelistic tour.

SOLUTION: There are many interpretations of this passage. Some take it to be a reference to the destruction of Jerusalem (A.D. 70) and the end of the Jewish economy. But this hardly suits as a fulfillment of the phrase "before the Son of Man comes."

Others understand Jesus' statement to refer to an outpouring of the Holy Spirit or a great revival before the return of Christ to earth to set up His kingdom. They believe the preaching of the Gospel will usher in the kingdom (cf. Matt. 24:14). But, this too seems to go far beyond the literal meaning of the text here.

Still others see it as containing a projection from their immediate mission to their continuing mission to proclaim the Gospel "even to the end of the age" (Matt. 28:20). Note the fact that the disciples would probably have not gone through all "the cities of Israel" in the short mission on which Jesus sent them. One problem with this is that there is no direct indication in the text that Jesus was referring to the distant future.

Another alternative is to take the promise literally and immediately and to interpret the phrase "before the Son of Man comes" as a reference to the fact that Jesus rejoined the disciples after their mission. This view may be supported by several facts. First, the phrase "before the Son of Man comes" is never used by Matthew to describe the Second Coming. Second, it fits with a literal understanding of the first part of the verse. The disciples went literally and immediately into "the cities of Israel" to preach, and Jesus literally and immediately rejoined them after their itinerant ministry. Third, there is no indication here or anywhere else that the disciples believed that Jesus was going to go to heaven while they were gone on their preaching tour. This certainly would have startled them (cf. John 14:1-5). Furthermore, He had already told them that He had to die and rise from the dead (John 2:19-22) before He could go to heaven and return.

MATTHEW 10:34-36 – Did Jesus come to bring peace or war?

PROBLEM: Here Jesus affirms, "I did not come to bring peace but a sword." However, elsewhere He is called "the prince of peace" (Isa. 9:6) who said, "My peace I give to you" (John 14:27) and told His disciples to put away the sword, "for all who take the sword will perish by the sword" (Matt. 26:52). So, which are we to believe? Did Jesus come to bring peace or the sword?

SOLUTION: We must distinguish between the *purpose* of Christ's coming to earth and the *result* of it. His *design* was to bring peace—peace with God for unbelievers (Rom. 5:1) and eventually, the peace of God for believers (Phil. 4:7). However, the immediate consequence of Christ's coming was to divide those who were for Him and those who were against Him—the children of God from the children of this world. But, just as the *goal* of an amputation is to relieve pain, so the immediate *effect* is to inflict pain. Likewise, Christ's ultimate mission is to bring peace, both to the human heart and to earth. Nonetheless, the immediate effect of His message was to divide those in the kingdom of God from those in the kingdom of Satan.

MATTHEW 11:12 – How can God's sovereign and peaceful kingdom be entered by force?

PROBLEM: Paul declared that the kingdom (rule) of God is "peace and joy in the Holy Spirit" (Rom. 14:17). However, Matthew says "the kingdom of heaven suffers violence, and the violent take it by force." How can one enter God's kingdom by force?

SOLUTION: This is a difficult passage, and it has been interpreted several ways. Some take it to mean that the kingdom is violently taken by its enemies. That is, the forceful religious leaders of Jesus' day were resisting the kingdom introduced by John. They wanted a kingdom, but not the kind that was being offered by John and Jesus (cf. Rom. 10:3). However, some object that this is opposed to the context that is expressing the greatness of John the Baptist and the contrast between his day and Christ's.

Others see the "violence" as a figure of speech meaning, first, that the kingdom breaks through or intrudes itself with great power and abruptness. Then, the intense endeavors of people who on the preaching of John were taking the kingdom by storm. On this view, it is speaking of the response to John's preaching as a great popular uprising, a storming of the kingdom of God by people rushing with eagerness to get in it with a violent zeal. This explains the use of the term "violence" and fits the overall context.

MATTHEW 11:14 – Didn't Jesus say John the Baptist was Elijah reincarnated?

PROBLEM: Jesus refers here to John the Baptist as "Elijah who is to come" (cf. Matt. 17:12; Mark 9:11-13). But, since Elijah had died many centuries before, John must have been a reincarnation of Elijah.

SOLUTION: There are many reasons why this verse does not teach reincarnation. First, John and Elijah did not have the same *being* – they had the same *function*. Jesus was not teaching that John the Baptist was literally Elijah, but simply that he came "in the spirit and power of Elijah" (Luke 1:17), namely, to continue his prophetic ministry.

Second, Jesus' disciples understood that He was speaking about John the Baptist, since Elijah appeared on the Mount of Transfiguration (Matt. 17:10-13). Since John had already lived and died by then, and since Elijah still had the same name and self-consciousness, Elijah had obviously not been reincarnated as John the Baptist.

Third, Elijah does not fit the reincarnation model for another reason – he did not die. He was taken to heaven like Enoch, who did not "see death" (2 Kings 2:11; cf. Heb. 11:5). According to traditional reincarnation, one must first die before he can be reincarnated into another body.

Fourth, if there is any doubt about this passage, it should be understood in the light of the clear teaching of Scripture opposing reincarnation. Hebrews, for example declares, "it is appointed for men to die once, but after this the judgment" (Heb. 9:27; cf. John 9:2).

MATTHEW 11:28-30 — Is Jesus' yoke easy or hard?

PROBLEM: Jesus said here, "My yoke is easy and My burden is light." However, Hebrews declares that "whom the Lord loves He chastens, And scourges every son whom He receives" (Heb. 12:6). Which is it— easy or hard?

SOLUTION: These verses are referring to different aspects of the Christian life. The life of a believer is "easy" in that it brings "rest for your souls" (Matt. 11:29), but it is hard on the "flesh," which often needs the disciplining hand of God to keep it in line. Salvation brings "peace with God" (Rom. 5:1), but it also brings conflict with the world (1 John 2:15-17; Gal. 5:17). The Apostle Paul himself experienced God's grace in his life, but he also had a thorn in his flesh (2 Cor. 12:7-9).

MATTHEW 12:1-5 — Did Jesus' disciples break the Jewish Sabbath law?

PROBLEM: Jesus said, "Do not think that I came to destroy the Law or the Prophets. I did not come to destroy but to fulfill" (Matt. 5:17). Yet Jesus' disciples deliberately and knowingly picked grain on the Sabbath, thus arousing the ire of the Pharisees by doing "what is not lawful to do on the Sabbath" (Matt. 12:2).

SOLUTION: Jesus kept the OT law perfectly (see comments on Matt. 5:17-18). By eating grain on the Sabbath when hungry, Jesus' disciples did not break *God's law*. However, it did violate the *Pharisees' law*. Jesus often rebuked the Pharisees for adding their "traditions" (cf. Matt. 5:43 and 15:6) to God's laws. Deeds of mercy and necessity were permitted on the OT Sabbath. Jesus' disciples were not *harvesting* bushels full of grain on the Sabbath. They were merely *eating* handfuls of it as they passed through the field, which was permitted by OT law (see Deut. 23:25).

Further, as Jesus noted on this occasion, "The Sabbath was made for man, and not man for the Sabbath" (Mark 2:27). He also pointed out that "the Son of Man is Lord even of the Sabbath" (Matt. 12:8). In short, the Sabbath law was not the highest law, for there were "weightier matters" (cf. Matt. 23:23), such as justice and mercy. Jesus, as the Messiah and the Son of God, was not the servant of the Sabbath—He was Lord of it. He made it! And He could (and later did) change it, if He so desired (see comments on Matt. 5:17-18).

MATTHEW 12:40 (cf. JOHN 19:14) – If Jesus was crucified on Friday, how could He have been in the grave three days and nights?

PROBLEM: Christ rose on Sunday (Matt. 28:1), but He stated that He would be "three days and three nights in the heart of the earth." If Christ was crucified on Friday, how could He have been three days and three nights in the earth and rise on Sunday only two days later?"

SOLUTION 1: Some scholars believe Jesus was in the grave for three full days and nights (72 hours), being crucified on Wednesday. They offer the following in support of this contention.

First, they insist that this is the literal meaning of the phrase "three days and nights." Second, they point out that, on the view that Jesus was crucified on Friday, there is no explanation for what He did on Wednesday. All other days are accounted for. Third, they argue that the passover was not a fixed day (Friday), but floated.

SOLUTION 2: Most biblical scholars believe that Jesus was crucified on Friday. They take the phrase "three days and nights" to be a Hebrew figure of speech referring to any part of three days and nights. They offer the following in support of their position.

First, the phrase "day and night" does not necessarily mean a complete 24 hour period. The psalmist's reference to meditating "day and night" on God's Word does not mean one has to read the Bible all day and all night (Ps. 1:2).

Second, it is clear from the use of the phrase "three days and three nights" in the Book of Esther that it does not mean 72 hours. For, although they fasted three days and nights (4:16) between the time they started and the time she appeared before the king, the passage states that Esther appeared before the king "on the third day" (5:1). If they began on Friday, then the third day would be Sunday. Hence, "three days and nights" must mean any part of three days and nights.

Third, Jesus used the phrase "on the third day" to describe the time of His resurrection after His crucifixion (Matt 16:21; 17:23; 20:19; cf. 26:61). But, "*on* the third day" cannot mean "*after* three days" which 72 hours demands. On the other hand, the phrase "on the third day" or "three days and nights" can be understood to mean within three days and nights.

Fourth, this view fits best with the chronological order of events as given by Mark (cf. 14:1), as well as the fact that Jesus died on Passover day (Friday) to fulfill the conditions of being our Passover Lamb (1 Cor. 5:7; cf. Lev. 23:5-15).

The two views can be compared as follows:

THE LAST WEEK BEFORE THE CRUCIFIXION

	Fri.	Sat.	Sun.	Mon.	Tue.	Wed.	Thur.	Fri.	Sat.	Sun.
Wednesday Crucifixion "Re-construction View"	Arrived in Bethany	Day the Passover Lamb Was Caught EX. 12:3	Triumphal Entry JOHN 12:13	Cursing of Fig Tree	Contest with Jewish Leaders	Jesus Died EX. 12:6	A Sabbath JOHN 19:31	▲ JESUS' BODY IN TOMB ▲		
	Feast in Bethany JOHN 12:1				Mt. of Olives Sermon	Day of Preparation for Passover JOHN 19:14	Thurs.—Day and Night / Fri.—Day and Night / Sat.—Day and Night MATT. 12:40			
Jewish First Month (March/April)	9 Nisan	10 Nisan	11 Nisan	12 Nisan	13 Nisan	14 Nisan	15 Nisan	16 Nisan	17 Nisan	18 Nisan
Friday Crucifixion "Traditional View"		"6 Days before the Passover" / The Jews Plan Jesus' Death JOHN 12:8-11	"The Next Day" JOHN 12:12 / Triumphal Entry into Jerusalem He Wept over the City LUKE 19:41	"On the Morrow" MARK 11:12 / Curse of Fig Tree MARK 11:14 / Cleanse the Temple MARK 11:15-18 / Receive Praise from Children MATT. 21:14-16	"The Following Day" MARK 11:20 / Dead Fig Tree MARK 11:20 / Contest with Jewish Leaders / Olivet Sermon MARK 13:1		"After Two Days" MARK 14:1 / Sends Peter into City LUKE 22:7-13 / Last Supper MARK 14:12	"In the Morning" MARK 15:1 / Gethsemane MARK 14:32 / Arrest MARK 14:48-52 / Trial / Crucified / Buried JOHN 19:38-42		"The Sabbath Was Past" MARK 16:1 / Resurrection
							▼ JESUS' BODY IN TOMB ▼			

MATTHEW
∎

MATTHEW 13:12 — Is God unfair in giving to those who have?

PROBLEM: God is presented in the Bible as fair and evenhanded (Rom. 2:11; Gen. 18:25). Jesus, as God incarnate, is set up as the perfect moral example (Heb. 4:15). However, in this passage Jesus said we should take away from "whoever does not have" and give to "whoever has." What could be more unfair?

SOLUTION: "Give to him who has and take from him who has not" is a proverbial saying used by Jesus in this context to mean that when Jesus spoke in parables (Matt. 13:10), the result was that those who thought they had some insight into the kingdom had less because they were more confused. Their unbelief caused their confusion, so that "seeing they do not see, and hearing they do not hear" (v.13). On the other hand, those who received Jesus' words (namely, His disciples) had even a greater understanding than before.

MATTHEW 13:31-32 — Did Jesus make a mistake when referring to the mustard seed as the smallest of all seeds?

PROBLEM 1: Jesus said that the mustard seed was "the least of all the seeds." However, today we know that the mustard seed is not the smallest seed of all. Some think Jesus was speaking of the black mustard seed. But, even this is not the smallest of all seeds.

SOLUTION 1: Jesus was not referring to all the seeds in the world, but only those that a Palestinian farmer sowed in his field. This is made clear by the qualifying phrase "which a man took and sowed in his field" (v. 31). And it is a fact that the mustard seed was the smallest of all seeds which the 1st century Jewish farmer *sowed in his field*. So there is no contradiction here between science and Scripture. What Jesus said was literally true in the context in which He said it.

PROBLEM 2: Some claim that the mustard seed cannot grow big enough to house birds, let alone grow to tree size.

SOLUTION 2: But this is not so, because there is evidence that some mustard seeds grow into trees about ten feet tall. This would certainly provide enough branch space for a bird to build a nest (Matt. 13:32).

MATTHEW 13:34 — Did Jesus always speak in parables or not?

PROBLEM: This text states distinctly that "without a parable He [Jesus] did not speak to them." However, Jesus gave His whole Sermon on the Mount (Matt. 5–7) without a single parable in it.

SOLUTION: There are two qualifying factors that must be noted, one of which is stated and another implied. First, Matthew 13:34 states that Jesus spoke these things "to the multitude," whereas the Sermon on the Mount was given to His "disciples" (Matt. 5:1-2; cf. Luke 6:20), even though the multitudes apparently listened in (cf. Matt. 7:28). What is more, Jesus' statement may have only a reference to what He was doing at that time, not on every occasion. It does not say that He always and on every occasion spoke to a crowd only in parables. However, this interpretation is possible, since we have only a limited record of what Jesus spoke (cf. John 21:25).

MATTHEW 13:45 — Was Mary a perpetual virgin, or did she have other children after Jesus' virgin birth?

PROBLEM: Roman Catholicism teaches that Mary was a perpetual virgin, that is, that she never had sexual intercourse, even after Jesus was virgin born. Is it true that when the Bible refers to Jesus' "brothers and sisters" (Matt. 13:56) it means cousins or close relatives?

SOLUTION: It is true that the words for brother and sister can mean close relative. This must be determined by the context and from other Scriptures. And in the case of Jesus' brothers and sisters, the context indicates they were his real half brothers and sisters.

First, nowhere does the Bible affirm the doctrine of Mary's perpetual virginity. Like the Roman Catholic doctrine of Mary's sinlessness (see comments on Luke 1:46), there is no statement anywhere in the Bible that supports this teaching.

Second, when "brothers and sisters" are used in connection with father or mother, then it does not mean cousins, but actual blood brothers and sisters (cf. Luke 14:26). Such is the case with Jesus' brothers and sisters. Matthew 13:55 says, "Is not this the carpenter's son? Is not His mother called Mary? And His brothers James, Joses, Simon, and Judas?" (cf. Mark 6:3)

Third, there are other references in the Bible to Jesus' "brothers." John informs us that "even His brothers did not believe in Him" (John 7:5). And Paul speaks of "James, the Lord's brother" (Gal. 1:19). On another occasion Mark refers to "His [Jesus'] brothers and His mother" (Mark 3:31). John spoke of "His mother, His brothers, and His disciples" (John 2:12). Luke mentions "Mary the mother of Jesus, with His brothers" being in the Upper Room (Acts 1:14).

MATTHEW 16:16 — Why does Peter's confession here differ from that recorded in Mark and Luke?

PROBLEM: Peter's confession of Christ in Caesarea Philippi is stated differently in the three Gospels:
>Matthew: "You are the Christ, the Son of the living God."
>Mark: "You are the Christ" (8:29).
>Luke: "The Christ of God" (9:20).

If the Bible is the inspired Word of God, why are there three different reports of what Peter said? What did he really say?

SOLUTION: There are several reasons why the Gospel accounts of Peter's statements differ. First, Peter probably spoke Aramaic, while the Gospels are written in Greek. So, some changes come naturally as a result of translating the words differently. Second, the Gospel writers sometimes paraphrased the essence of what people said, much like the way journalists do today. Third, other writers selected and abbreviated what was said to fit the theme of their book or the emphasis they wished to make.

What is important to notice is that the Gospel writers never *created* these sayings, rather, they *reported* them. Further, their reports were in accordance with journalistic standards of the day (and even today for that matter). Also, whenever there are multiple reports, they all give the essence of what was said. For example, all three reports note that Peter confessed that Jesus is "the Christ of God." Sometimes, all the reports can be put together as a whole, giving what may have been the word-for-word original statement of Peter. For example, Peter may have said exactly what Matthew reported, and the others may have reported the important parts of Peter's confession, as illustrated in the following:
>Matthew: "You are the Christ, the Son of the living God."
>Mark: "You are the Christ [the Son of the living God]."
>Luke: "[You are] the Christ [the Son] of [the living] God."

MATTHEW 16:18 — Is Peter the rock on which the church is built?

PROBLEM: Roman Catholics use this passage to support their belief in the primacy of Peter, that is, that he is the rock on which the church is built. But Paul said the church is built on Christ, not Peter (1 Cor. 3:11). Is Peter the "rock" in this passage?

SOLUTION: There are different ways to understand this passage, but none of them support the Roman Catholic view that the church is built on St. Peter, who became the first Pope — infallible in all his official pronouncements on faith and doctrine. This is evident for many reasons.

First of all, Peter was married (Matt. 8:14), and Popes do not marry. If the first Pope could marry, why later pronounce that no priest (or Pope) can marry.

Second, Peter was not infallible in his views on the Christian life. Even Paul had to rebuke him for his hypocrisy, because he was not "straightforward about the truth of the Gospel" (Gal. 2:14).

Third, the Bible clearly declares that Christ is the foundation of the Christian church, insisting that "no other foundation can anyone lay than that which is laid, which is Jesus Christ" (1 Cor. 3:11).

Fourth, the only sense in which Peter had a foundational role in the church, all the other apostles shared in the same way. Peter was not unique in this respect. For Paul declared that in this sense the church is "built on the foundation of the apostles and prophets, Jesus Christ Himself being the chief cornerstone" (Eph. 2:20). Indeed, the early church continued steadfastly in the apostles' doctrine [not just Peter's]" (Acts 2:42). Even "keys of the kingdom" given to Peter (Matt. 16:19) were also given to all the apostles (cf. Matt. 18:18).

Fifth, there is no indication that Peter was the head of the early church. When the first council was held at Jerusalem, Peter played only an introductory role (Acts 15:6-11). James seems to have a more significant position, summing up the conference and making the final pronouncement (cf. Acts 15:13-21). In any event, Peter is never referred to as *the* "pillar" in the church. Rather, Paul speaks of "pillars" (plural), such as, "James, Cephas, and John" (Gal. 2:9). Peter (Cephas) is not even listed first among the pillars.

Sixth, many Protestant interpreters believe that Jesus' reference to "this rock" (Matt. 16:18) upon which His church would be built was to Peter's solid (rock-like) testimony that Jesus was "the Christ, the son of the living God" (Matt. 16:16). But even if this rock has reference to Peter (*Petros,* rock), which is certainly a possible interpretation, he was only *a* rock in the apostolic foundation of the church (Matt. 16:18), not *the* rock. Nor is he the *only* apostolic rock. Even Peter himself admitted that Christ is the chief rock ("cornerstone," 1 Peter 2:7). And Paul notes that the other apostles are all part of the "foundation" (Eph. 2:20).

MATTHEW 16:20 — Why did Jesus instruct His disciples to tell no one He was the Christ?

PROBLEM: Jesus commissioned His disciples, "Go therefore and make disciples of all nations" (Matt. 28:19). Yet over and over again throughout His ministry He insisted that His followers "tell no man" (cf. Matt. 8:4; 16:20; 17:9; Mark 7:36; 8:30; 9:9; Luke 5:14; 8:56; 9:21). Doesn't this contradict His Great Commission?

SOLUTION: The problem is easily resolved if several things are remembered. First, there was often a stated or implied condition on this command to "tell no man." Jesus said clearly to His disciples on one occasion, "tell no one . . . till the Son of Man ha[s] risen from the dead" (Matt. 17:9; cf. Mark 9:9). There is no contradiction between this and His pronouncement to tell everyone after He rose from the dead (in Matt. 28:19).

Second, sometimes Jesus was simply trying to keep down the crowds so that He could continue His ministry. Mark writes, "He commanded them that they should tell no one; but the more He commanded them, the more widely they proclaimed it" (Mark 7:36). Likewise, Luke reports that immediately after Jesus instructed the cleansed leper to "tell no one" (Luke 5:14), "then the report went around concerning Him all the more. . . . So He Himself often withdrew into the wilderness and prayed" (vv. 15-16).

Finally, Jesus did not wish to parade His messianic claims, especially among the Jews, since they had a false expectation of a political redeemer who would deliver them from the yoke of Rome (see comments on John 4:26). On one occasion, they even wanted to make Him king by force because of the signs which He did (see John 6:14-15). Since that was not His purpose, He withdrew from them, for His purpose was to die on the cross (see Mark 10:45 and John 10:10, 15).

MATTHEW 16:28 — Did Jesus make a mistake about His disciples seeing the kingdom come in their lifetimes?

PROBLEM: Jesus told His disciples that some of them would not see death until they saw Him coming in His kingdom. Yet during the life of the apostles, Jesus never returned to set up His kingdom.

SOLUTION: This is a question of *when* this was going to take place, not *whether* it would. There are three possible solutions.

First, some have suggested that this may be a reference to the Day of Pentecost where Christ's Helper, the Holy Spirit, came to descend upon the apostles. In John's Gospel (14:26), Jesus promised to send the Holy Spirit, and, in the beginning of Acts (1:4-8), He tells them not to leave Jerusalem until they have received the Holy Spirit. But this hardly seems to fit the description of seeing Christ coming in His kingdom (Matt. 16:28).

Second, others believe this might be a reference to the destruction of Jerusalem and the temple in A.D. 70. This would mean that He would return to bring judgment upon the city that rejected Him and crucified Him. While this is a possible explanation, it does not seem to account for the fact that Jesus appears to be coming for believers (those "standing there" with Him), not simply coming in judgment on unbelievers. Nor does the judgment on Jerusalem in A.D. 70 adequately express seeing the "Son of Man coming in His kingdom" (v. 28), a phrase reminiscent of His second coming (cf. 26:64). Nor does it explain why Jesus never appeared in A.D. 70.

A third and more plausible explanation is that this is a reference to the appearance of Christ in His glory on the Mount of Transfiguration which begins in the very next verse (17:1). Here Christ does literally appear in a glorified form, and some of His apostles are there to witness the occasion, namely Peter, James, and John. This transfiguration experience, of course, was only a foretaste of His Second Coming when all believers will see Him come in power and great glory (cf. Acts 1:11; Rev. 1:7).

MATTHEW 19:16-30 (cf. MARK 10:17-31; LUKE 18:18-30) — If Jesus was God, why did He seem to rebuke the rich young ruler for calling Him good?

PROBLEM: The rich young ruler called Jesus "Good Teacher," and Jesus rebuked him, saying, "Why do you call Me good? No one is good but One, that is, God." Yet on other occasions Jesus not only claimed to be God (Mark 2:8-10; John 8:58; 10:30), but He accepted the claim of others that He was God (John 20:28-29). Why did Jesus appear to deny that He was God to the young ruler?

SOLUTION: Jesus did not deny He was God to the young ruler. He simply asked him to examine the implications of what he was saying. In effect, Jesus was saying to him, "Do you realize what you are saying when you call Me Good? Are you saying I am God?"

The young man did not realize the implications of what he was saying. Thus Jesus was forcing him to a very uncomfortable dilemma. Either Jesus was good and God, or else He was bad and man. A good God or a bad man, but not merely a good man. Those are the real alternatives with regard to Christ. For no good man would claim to be God when he was not. The liberal Christ, who was only a good moral teacher but not God, is a figment of human imagination.

MATTHEW 19:21 – Should Christians sell all they have and give it away?

(See comments on 1 Tim. 6:17-18.)

MATTHEW 19:26 – Is anything impossible for God?

PROBLEM: According to this verse, "with God all things are possible." However, Hebrews 6:18 declares that "It is impossible for God to lie."

SOLUTION: The context in Matthew indicates that Jesus is speaking of what is *humanly* impossible, whereas, Hebrews informs us that some things (e.g., lying) are *actually* impossible for God. Note that in the former passage, Jesus said, *"with men* this is impossible," indicating that He was only speaking of what was humanly impossible, but not divinely impossible. However, there are some things that even God cannot do. For example, He cannot do anything that would contradict His nature, such as, cease being God, or be unholy, or do what is logically impossible (like making a square circle, or forcing people to freely love Him). God cannot make a stone so big that He cannot lift it, since the created cannot be greater than the Creator. However, God can do anything that is possible to do. He is all-powerful (omnipotent), the "Almighty" (cf. Job 5:17; 6:14; 42:2).

MATTHEW 20:1ff – Are rewards the same for all, or do they differ in degree?

PROBLEM: Jesus told a parable of His kingdom in which each servant got the same pay even though each had worked a different number of hours. Yet in other places, the Bible speaks of different degrees of reward for working in God's kingdom (cf. 1 Cor. 3:11-15; 2 Cor. 5:10; Rev. 22:12).

SOLUTION: There are different degrees of reward in heaven, depending on our faithfulness to Christ on earth. Jesus said, "I am coming quickly, and My reward is with Me, to give to every one *according to his work"* (Rev. 22:12). Paul said each believer's work will be tried by fire and "if anyone's work which he has built on it endures, he will receive a reward" (1 Cor. 3:14). In 2 Corinthians 5, he says we must all appear before the judgment seat of Christ "that each one may receive the things done in the body, *according to what he has done,* whether good or bad" (v. 10, emphasis added).

The point of the parable in Matthew 20 is not that all rewards will be the same, but that all rewards are *by grace*. It is to show that God rewards on the basis of *opportunity*, not simply on accomplishment. Not all the servants had the opportunity to work for the master the same amount of time, but all, nevertheless, were given the same pay. God looks at our *disposition* as well as our *actions* and judges accordingly.

MATTHEW 20:20 (cf. MARK 10:35) — Who came to talk with Jesus, the mother of James and John or James and John?

PROBLEM: In Matthew, the mother of James and John made a request of Jesus. However, Mark states that it was James and John who came to Jesus to make their request.

SOLUTION: It is clear that both the mother and her sons came to Jesus to make the request, since the text declares "the mother . . . came to Him with her sons" (v. 20). It is possible that the mother spoke first with the two sons closely following to reiterate the request. This is supported by Matthew's account because when Jesus responds "are you able to drink the cup that I am about to drink?" the Bible says "*they* said to Him, '*we* are able' " (v.22). So, there is no unsolvable conflict here. The two accounts are harmonious.

MATTHEW 20:29-34 (cf. MARK 10:46-52; LUKE 18:35-43) — Did Jesus heal two blind men or just one?

PROBLEM: Matthew says that Christ healed two men, but Mark refers to only one man being healed (10:46). This appears to be a clear contradiction.

SOLUTION: Although Mark records one individual getting healed, this does not mean that there were not two, as Matthew says there were. First of all, Mark does not declare that there was *only* one blind man healed. Matthew says there were two, and where there are two there is always one, every time! Matthew earlier mentions two demoniacs where Mark and Luke mention one (Matt. 8:28-34), so Matthew again mentions the two blind men where Mark mentions just one. Further, the fact that Mark mentions the name of one blind man, Bartimaeus, and his father (Timaeus, 10:46), indicates that Mark is centering on the one that was personally known to him. If two men were to receive a medal of honor from the president of the United States and one was your friend, it is understandable that when you relate the story you might only speak of the one whom you knew receiving the medal.

MATTHEW 20:29-34 (cf. MARK 10:46-52; LUKE 18:35-43) — Did Jesus heal the blind man coming into or going out of Jericho?

PROBLEM: According to Luke, a blind man was healed as Jesus entered the city of Jericho (18:35), but Matthew and Mark declare that the healing took place as Jesus left the city of Jericho. Again, the accounts do not seem to be harmonious.

SOLUTION: Some believe that the healing in Luke may have actually taken place as Jesus left Jericho, claiming that it was only the initial contact that took place as "He was coming near Jericho" (Luke 18:35) and the blind man may have followed Him through the city, since he was continually begging Jesus to heal him (vv. 38-39). But this seems unlikely, since even after the healing (v. 43) the very next verse (19:1) says, "then Jesus entered and passed through Jericho."

Others respond by noting there were two Jerichos, the old and the new, so that as He went out of one He came into the other.

Still others suggest that these are two different events. Matthew and Mark clearly affirm the healing occurred as Jesus left the city (Matt. 20:29; Mark 10:46). But Luke speaks of healing one blind man as He entered the city. This is supported by the fact that Luke refers only to a "multitude" of people being present as Jesus entered the city (18:36), but both Matthew (20:29) and Mark (10:46) make a point to say there was a "great multitude" of people there by the time Jesus left the city. If the word spread of the miraculous healing on the way into the city, this would account for the swelling of the crowd. It might also explain why two blind men were waiting on the other side of the city to plead for Jesus to heal them. Perhaps the first blind man who was healed went quickly to tell his blind friends what happened to him. Or maybe the other blind men were already stationed at the other end of the city in their customary begging position. At any rate, there is no irresolvable difficulty in the passage. The two accounts can be understood in a completely compatible way.

MATTHEW 21:2 (cf. MARK 11:2; LUKE 19:30) — Were there two donkeys involved in the triumphal entry or just one?

PROBLEM: Matthew's account records Jesus' request of two disciples to go into a village and get two donkeys. But in Mark and Luke, He requests that the two disciples get just the colt.

SOLUTION: Both animals were involved in Jesus' triumphal entry into Jerusalem. There is no mistake in the accounts because Mark and Luke mention just the colt (*pōlos*), and Matthew refers to the colt (*pōlos,* 21:5) and its mother. The passage in Matthew is pointing out the literal fulfillment of the prophecy of Zechariah 9:9 which states, "Behold your king is coming to you . . . humble, and mounted on a donkey, even on a colt, the foal of a donkey." The Greek version of the OT uses the same word for colt (*pōlos*) as the NT passages. Matthew literally states that once the disciples placed their garments on the donkeys, Jesus sat on them, that is, on their garments. Matthew does not say that Jesus rode on both the mother and the colt. It merely states that Jesus sat on the garments that the disciples had placed on the donkeys. Perhaps they placed some garments on the mother and others on the colt, and Jesus sat on those garments which were placed on the colt. The fact is the text of Matthew simply does not say on which donkey Jesus sat. Mark and Luke focus on the colt on which Jesus rode, while Matthew mentions the presence of the colt's mother. Her presence may have been necessary because the colt was so young. Mark 11:12 states that no one had ridden on the colt, and that the colt would be taking a passenger through a noisy crowd (Mark 11:9). Perhaps the mother was brought along in order to be a calming influence upon her young.

MATTHEW 21:12-19 (cf. MARK 11:12-14, 20-24) — When was the fig tree cursed by Jesus, before or after the temple was cleansed?

PROBLEM: Matthew places the cursing of the fig tree after the cleansing of the temple. But Mark places the cursing before the temple was cleansed. But, it cannot be both. Did one Gospel writer make a mistake?

SOLUTION: Jesus actually cursed the fig tree on His way to the temple as Mark said, but this does not mean that Matthew's account is mistaken. Christ made two trips to the temple, and He cursed the fig tree on His second trip.

Mark 11:11 says that Christ entered the temple the day of His triumphal entry. When Christ enters the temple, Mark does not mention Christ making any proclamations against any wrongdoing. Verse 12 says "Now the next day," referring to the trip to the fig tree on the way to the temple on the second day. On this day, Christ threw out those buying and selling in the temple. Matthew, however, addresses the two trips of Christ to the temple as though they were one event. This gives the impression that the first day Christ entered the temple He drove out the buyers and sellers as well. Mark's account, however, gives more detail to the events, revealing that there were actually two trips to the temple. In view of this, we have no reason to believe that there is a discrepancy in the accounts.

MATTHEW 22:30 – Will we be like angels (spirits) in heaven, beings without physical bodies?

PROBLEM: Jesus said that in the resurrection we will be "like the angels of God" (Matt. 22:30). But angels have no physical bodies – they are spirits (Heb. 1:14). Thus, it is argued that we will have no physical bodies in the resurrection. This, however, is contradictory to those verses that claim there will be a resurrection of the physical body from the grave (John 5:28-29; Luke 24:39).

SOLUTION: Jesus did not say that we would be like angels in that they are spirits, but like them in that they *do not marry*. Two observations are relevant here.

First of all, the context is not talking about the nature of the resurrection body, but whether or not there will be marriage in heaven. The question Jesus answered with this statement was, "In the resurrection, whose wife of the seven [husbands she had] will she be, for they all had her?" (22:28) Jesus' reply was that, like angels, there will be no marriage in heaven. So the woman will not be married to any of these seven husbands in heaven. But Jesus said nothing here about having immaterial bodies in heaven. Such a conclusion is totally unwarranted by the context.

Second, when Jesus said "in the resurrection . . . [they] are like angels of God," He obviously meant like angels in that they will "neither marry nor are given in marriage" (v. 30). He did not say they would be like angels in that they would have no physical bodies. Rather, they would be like angels in that they would be *without sexual propagation*.

MATTHEW 22:39 – Does Jesus want us to love ourself first or others?

PROBLEM: Jesus says in Matthew that we are to love our neighbor as ourselves. But, if we love ourselves first, before we love our neighbor, then this would be putting self before neighbor. Is Jesus teaching that we should be selfish?

SOLUTION: Loving others *as we love ourselves* can be understood in different ways, but in no way is Jesus implying that we should be selfish. The Bible condemns "lovers of themselves" (2 Tim. 3:2). It exhorts us not to consider only our own interests, but also the interest of others

(Phil. 2:4). There are three ways to understand the phrase, "love others as yourself."

First, some believe that Jesus is saying that we ought to love others as we ought to love ourselves, namely, *unselfishly*. This, however, seems far too subtle and dialectical for Jesus' normally straight-forward moral assertions. It would have been more forthright to simply say do not be selfish than the tangled command of loving oneself unselfishly.

Second, Jesus could have meant that we should love others as we ought to love ourselves, namely, *properly*. There is a legitimate self-respect or self-love. Ephesians tells us to care for our own bodies, "for no one ever hated his own flesh, but nourishes and cherishes it" (5:28-29). There is nothing wrong with a legitimate self-care and self-respect. The Bible condemns someone for "thinking of himself more highly than he ought," but urges him to think "soberly" (Rom. 12:3). In this sense, Jesus may be saying love others as you ought to love yourselves.

Third, Jesus could have meant that we should love others *as much as we do love ourselves*. That is, He might have been saying that we should measure how we *ought* to love others by how we actually *do* love ourselves without implying that the way we love ourselves is correct. Rather, God may be simply pointing to love for self as the standard by which we should judge how much to love others. In this way, there would be an automatic check on our selfish love, since we would have to love others this much too.

MATTHEW 23:9-10 — Is it wrong to call others our father?

PROBLEM: Here Jesus commanded: "Do not call anyone on earth your father." Yet elsewhere the Bible not only tells us "honor your father and mother" (Ex. 20:12), but even uses the term "father" of those who are spiritual mentors (2 Kings 2:12; cf. 1 Cor. 4:15).

SOLUTION: The context of Jesus' statement indicates that He is referring to taking human beings as *infallible* spiritual masters, not that He is opposed to having *fallible* spiritual mentors. In fact, Paul was a spiritual father to Timothy (1 Cor. 4:15) whom he called, "my beloved son" (2 Tim. 1:2). However, Paul was careful to instruct his spiritual children only to "Imitate me, just as I also imitate Christ" (1 Cor. 11:1). Showing *proper respect* to our spiritual leaders is one thing (cf. 1 Tim. 5:17), but giving them *unquestioned obedience* and reverence that is due only to God is another.

MATTHEW 23:17 — Why did Jesus call people fools and yet condemn others for doing the same thing?

PROBLEM: Jesus said, "whoever says [to his brother], 'You fool!' shall be in danger of hell fire" (Matt. 5:22). Yet He Himself said to the scribes and Pharisees, "Fools and blind!" (Matt. 23:17) The Apostle Paul, following suit, said, "O foolish Galatians" (Gal. 3:1; cf. 1 Cor. 15:36).

SOLUTION: There are good reasons why there is a strong difference between the two uses of the term "fool." First, this is another example of the principle that the same word can be used with different meanings in different contexts (see Introduction). For instance, the word "dog" can be used of a canine animal or a detested person.

Second, in Matthew 5, it is used in the context of someone who is "angry" with his brother, indicating a hatred. Neither Jesus nor Paul harbored hatred toward those to whom they applied the term. Thus, their use of the term "fool" does not violate Jesus' prohibition against calling others a fool.

Third, technically speaking, Jesus only commanded that a "brother" (Matt. 5:22) not be called a "fool," not an unbeliever. In fact the scriptural description of a fool is one who "has said in his heart, 'There is no God' " (Ps. 14:1). In view of this, one can see the seriousness of calling a brother a fool; it is tantamount to calling him an unbeliever. Hence, when He who "knew what was in man" (cf. John 2:25) called unbelievers "fools," it was a most appropriate description of what they really were.

MATTHEW 23:34-35 — Did Jesus make a mistake in referring to Zechariah the son of Berechiah rather than to Zechariah the son of Jehoiada?

PROBLEM: Jesus said to the scribes and Pharisees that the guilt of all the righteous blood from Abel to Zechariah will fall on them. Concerning Zechariah, Jesus said he was killed between the sanctuary and the altar. Some conclude that the Zechariah referred to by Christ is the son of Jehoiada (2 Chron. 24:20-22).

SOLUTION: The Zechariah referred to has to be the son of Berechiah. This Zechariah is one of the minor prophets, and his father is listed as Berechiah (Zech. 1:1). He would be the most likely candidate because the other Zechariah (son of Jehoiada) died about 800 B.C. If one thinks Christ referred to this Zechariah, then the time span from Abel to this Zechariah would not cover the OT period, which extended to 400 B.C.

Abel to Zechariah the son of Berechiah would make a much better sweep of the OT period than would the period from Abel to Zechariah the son of Jehoiada. Since many Zechariahs are mentioned in the OT, it would not be too difficult to imagine two Zechariahs dying from similar circumstances.

MATTHEW 24:29 – Did Christ come to earth immediately following the Tribulation or sometime later?

PROBLEM: In Matthew, Jesus represents His coming as "immediately after" (24:29) the Great Tribulation. But Luke seems to separate it by the "times of the Gentiles" (Luke 21:24, 27).

SOLUTION: The interval referred to by Luke is the time between the destruction of Jerusalem (A.D. 70), which began God's judgment on Jerusalem (cf. Matt. 24:2), and the return of Christ to earth "with power and great glory" (Matt. 24:30). So, when Matthew affirms that Christ's coming is "immediately after the tribulation of those days" (24:29), he is referring to the end of the "times of the Gentiles" mentioned by Luke (21:24). Hence, there is no irresolvable conflict between the two accounts.

MATTHEW 24:34 – Did Jesus err by affirming that the signs of the end time would be fulfilled in His era?

PROBLEM: Jesus spoke of signs and wonders regarding His second coming. But Jesus said "this generation" would not end before all these events took place. Did this mean that these events would occur in the lifetime of His hearers?

SOLUTION: These events (e.g., the Great Tribulation, the sign of Christ's return, and the end of the age) did not occur in the lifetime of Christ's hearers. Therefore, it is reasonable to understand their fulfillment as something yet to come. This calls for a closer examination of the meaning of "generation" for meanings other than that of Jesus' contemporaries.

First, "generation" in Greek (*genea*) can mean "race." In this particular instance, Jesus' statement could mean that the Jewish race would not pass away until all things are fulfilled. Since there were many promises to Israel, including the eternal inheritance of the land of Palestine (Gen. 12; 14–15; 17) and the Davidic kingdom (2 Sam. 7), then Jesus could be referring to God's preservation of the nation of Israel in order to fulfill His promises to them. Indeed, Paul speaks of a future of the nation of

Israel when they will be reinstated in God's covenantal promises (Rom. 11:11-26). And Jesus' response to His disciples' last question implied there would yet be a future kingdom for Israel, when they asked: "Lord, will You at this time restore the kingdom to Israel?" Rather than rebuking them for their misunderstanding, He replied that "It is not for you to know times or seasons which the Father has put in His own authority" (Acts 1:6-7). Indeed, Paul in Romans 11 speaks of the nation of Israel being restored to God's promised blessings (cf. vv. 25-26).

Second, "generation" could also refer to a generation in its commonly understood sense of the people alive at the time indicated. In this case, "generation" would refer to the group of people who are alive when these things come to pass in the future. In other words, the generation alive when these things (the abomination of desolation [v.15], the great tribulation such as has never been seen before [v. 21], the sign of the Son of Man in heaven [v. 30], etc.) begin to come to pass will still be alive when these judgments are completed. Since it is commonly believed that the tribulation is a period of some seven years (Dan. 9:27; cf. Rev. 11:2) at the end of the age, then Jesus would be saying that "this generation" alive at the beginning of the tribulation will still be alive at the end of it. In any event, there is no reason to assume that Jesus made the obviously false assertion that the world would come to an end within the lifetime of His contemporaries.

MATTHEW 26:11 — Was Jesus always present with His disciples?

PROBLEM: According to Jesus' statement here, He would not always be with the disciples, for He said: "but Me you do not have always" with you. On the other hand, in Matthew 28:20 Jesus said, "Lo, I am with you always, even to the end of the age."

SOLUTION: In the first passage, Jesus was speaking of His *physical* presence (which would not be with them between His ascension and second coming), and, in the later text, He is referring to His *spiritual* presence with them as they preached the Gospel in all the world. There is no contradiction here whatsoever.

MATTHEW 26:34 (cf. MARK 14:30) — When Peter denied Christ, did the rooster crow once or twice?

PROBLEM: Matthew and John (13:38) say before the rooster crows once, Peter will have denied the Lord three times. But Mark affirms that before the rooster crows *twice* Peter will deny Christ three times. Which account is right?

SOLUTION: There is no contradiction between the two accounts because, given the correctness of the text, Matthew and John do not expressly state how many times the rooster will crow. They simply say Peter will deny Christ three times "before the rooster crows," but they do not say how many times it will crow. Mark may simply be more specific, affirming exactly how many times the rooster would crow.

It is also possible that different accounts are due to an early copyist error in Mark, that resulted in the insertion of "two" in early manuscripts (at Mark 14:30 and 72). This would explain why some important manuscripts of Mark mention only one crowing, just like Matthew and John, and why "two" appears at different places in some manuscripts.

MATTHEW 26:52 — Is Jesus advocating pacifism and denouncing capital punishment in this passage?

PROBLEM: When the soldiers came to arrest Jesus, Peter took out his sword and cut off the ear of the high priest's servant. Jesus told Peter to put back the sword because those who take up the sword will die by the sword. Some use this verse to support pacifism and to oppose capital punishment, which the Bible affirms elsewhere (Gen. 9:6).

SOLUTION: Total pacifism is not taught in this Scripture. Indeed, Abraham was blessed by the Most High God (Gen 14:19) after engaging in a war against the unjust aggression of the kings who had captured his nephew Lot. In Luke 3:14, soldiers come to inquire of John the Baptist about what they should do. John never told them to leave the army. Likewise, Cornelius, in Acts 10, was a centurion. He was called a devout man (v. 2), and the Scriptures say that the Lord heard the prayers of Cornelius (v. 4). When Cornelius becomes a Christian, Peter does not tell him to leave the army. Also, in Luke 22:36-38, Christ says that the one who has no sword should sell his robe and buy one. The apostles responded saying that they had two swords. Jesus responded saying that "it was enough." In other words, they did not need to get rid of their swords. The Apostle Paul accepted the protection of the Roman army to save his life from unjust aggressors (Acts 23). Indeed, he reminded the Roman Christians that God had given the sword to the king who did not bear it in vain (Rom. 13:1-4). When Jesus returns to earth, He will come with the armies of heaven and will war against the kings of the earth (Rev. 19:11-19). So, from the beginning to the end, the Bible is filled with examples of the justification of war against evil aggressors.

What, then, did Jesus mean when He commanded Peter to put away his sword? Peter was making two mistakes in using his sword. First, while the Bible permits the sword by the government for *civil* purposes (Rom. 13:1-4), it does not endorse its use for *spiritual* ends. It is to be used by the *state*, not by the *church*. Second, Peter's use was *aggressive*, not purely *defensive*. His life was not being unjustly threatened. That is, it was not clearly an act of self-defense (Ex. 22:2). Jesus appears to have endorsed the use of the sword in civil self-defense (Luke 22:36), as did the Apostle Paul (Acts 23).

Likewise, capital punishment is not forbidden in Scripture, but rather was established by God. Genesis 9:6 affirms that whoever sheds man's blood, the blood of the killer will also be shed. Numbers 35:31 makes a similar statement. In the NT, Jesus recognized that Rome had capital authority and submitted to it (John 19:11). The Apostle Paul informed the Romans that governing authorities are ministers of God and that they still possessed the God-given sword of capital authority (13:1, 4). So Jesus in no way did away with the just use of the sword by civil authorities. He simply noted that those who live lives of aggression often die by the same means.

MATTHEW 27:5 (cf. ACTS 1:18) — Did Judas die by hanging or by falling on rocks?

PROBLEM: Matthew declares that Judas hanged himself. However, the Book of Acts says that he fell and his body burst open.

SOLUTION: These accounts are not contradictory, but mutually complementary. Judas hung himself exactly as Matthew affirms that he did. The account in Acts simply adds that Judas fell, and his body opened up at the middle and his intestines gushed out. This is the very thing one would expect of someone who hanged himself from a tree over a cliff and fell on sharp rocks below.

MATTHEW 27:37 (cf. MARK 15:26; LUKE 23:38; JOHN 19:19) — Why are all the Gospel accounts of the inscription on the cross different?

PROBLEM: The wording of the accusation above Christ's head on the cross is rendered differently in each Gospel account.

Matthew: "This is Jesus the king of the Jews" (27:37).

Mark: "The king of the Jews" (15:26).

Luke: "This is the king of the Jews" (23:38).

John: "Jesus of Nazareth, the king of the Jews" (19:19).

SOLUTION: While there is a difference in what is omitted, the important phrase, "the king of the Jews," is identical in all four Gospels. The differences can be accounted for in different ways.

First, John 19:20 says, "Then many of the Jews read this title, for the place where Jesus was crucified was near the city; and it was written in Hebrew, Greek, and Latin." So then, there are at least three different languages in which the sign above Christ's head was written. Some of the differences may come from it being rendered in different languages.

Further, it is possible that each Gospel only gives part of the complete statement as follows:

Matthew: "This is Jesus [of Nazareth] the king of the Jews."

Mark: "[This is Jesus of Nazareth] the king of the Jews."

Luke: "This is [Jesus of Nazareth] the king of the Jews."

John: "[This is] Jesus of Nazareth the king of the Jews."

Thus, the whole statement may have read "This is Jesus of Nazareth, the king of the Jews." In this case, each Gospel is giving the essential part ("the king of the Jews"), but no Gospel is giving the whole inscription. But neither is any Gospel contradicting what the other Gospels say. The accounts are divergent and mutually complementary, not contradictory.

MATTHEW 27:44 – Did both robbers revile Christ, or did only one do this?

PROBLEM: Matthew says here, "even the robbers who were crucified with Him reviled Him." However, according to Luke, only one reviled Him (Luke 23:39) while the other one believed in Him, asking, "Lord, remember me when You come into Your kingdom" (Luke 23:42).

SOLUTION: This difficulty is easily resolved on the supposition that at first both reviled the Lord, but that later one repented. Perhaps, he was so impressed hearing Jesus forgive those who crucified Him (Luke 23:34) that he was convinced that Jesus was the Savior and asked to be part of His coming kingdom (v. 42).

MATTHEW 27:48 – Did Jesus die on the cross or just swoon?

PROBLEM: Many skeptics, as well as Muslims, believe that Jesus did not die on the cross. Some say that He took a drug that put Him in a coma-like state and that He later revived in the tomb. Yet the Bible says repeatedly that Christ died on the cross (cf. Rom. 5:8; 1 Cor. 15:3; 1 Thes. 4:14).

SOLUTION: Jesus never fainted or swooned, nor was He drugged on the cross. In fact, He refused the drug customarily offered to the victim before crucifixion to help deaden pain (Matt. 27:34), and He accepted only "vinegar" later (v. 48) to quench His thirst. Jesus' actual physical death on the cross is supported by overwhelming evidence.

First of all, the OT predicted that Christ would die (Isa. 53:5-10; Ps. 22:16; Dan. 9:26; Zech. 12:10). And Jesus fulfilled the OT prophecies about the Messiah (cf. Matt. 4:14-16; 5:17-18; 8:17; John 4:25-26; 5:39).

Second, Jesus announced many times during His ministry that He was going to die (John 2:19-21; 10:10-11; Matt. 12:40; Mark 8:31). Typical is Matthew 17:22-23 that says, "The Son of Man is about to be betrayed into the hands of men and they will kill Him, and the third day He will be raised up."

Third, all the predictions of His resurrection, both in the OT (cf. Ps. 16:10; Isa. 26:19; Dan. 12:2) and in the NT (cf. John 2:19-21; Matt. 12:40; 17:22-23), are based on the fact that He would die. Only a dead body can be resurrected.

Fourth, the nature and extent of Jesus' injuries indicate that He must have died. He had no sleep the night before He was crucified. He was beaten several times and whipped. And He collapsed on the way to His crucifixion carrying His cross. This in itself, to say nothing of the crucifixion to follow, was totally exhausting and life-draining.

Fifth, the nature of the crucifixion assures death. Jesus was on the cross from 9 o'clock in the morning until just before sunset. He bled from wounded hands and feet plus from the thorns that pierced His head. There would be a tremendous loss of blood from doing this for more than six hours. Plus, crucifixion demands that one constantly pull himself up in order to breathe, thus sending excruciating pain from the nails. Doing this all day would kill nearly anyone even if they were previously in good health.

Sixth, the piercing of Jesus' side with the spear, from which came "blood and water" (John 19:34), is proof that He had physically died before the piercing. When this has happened, it is a medical proof that the person has already died (see point eleven below).

Seventh, Jesus said He was in the act of dying on the cross when He declared "Father, into Your hands I commend My spirit" (Luke 23:46). And "having said this, He breathed His last" (v. 46). John renders this,

"He gave up His spirit" (John 19:30). His death cry was heard by those who stood by (vv. 47-49).

Eighth, the Roman soldiers, accustomed to crucifixion and death, pronounced Jesus dead. Although it was a common practice to break the legs of the victim to speed death (so that the person can no longer lift himself and breathe), they did not even break Jesus' legs (John 19:33).

Ninth, Pilate double-checked to make sure Jesus was dead before he gave the corpse to Joseph to be buried. "Summoning the centurion, he asked him if He had been dead for some time. And when he found out from the centurion, he granted the body to Joseph" (Mark 15:44-45).

Tenth, Jesus was wrapped in about 75 pounds of cloth and spices and placed in a sealed tomb for three days (John 19:39-40; Matt. 27:60). If He was not dead by then, which He clearly was, He would have died from lack of food, water, and medical treatment.

Eleventh, medical authorities who have examined the circumstances and nature of Christ's death have concluded that He actually died on the cross. An article in the *Journal of the American Medical Society* (March 21, 1986) concluded:

> Clearly, the weight of historical and medical evidence indicates that Jesus was dead before the wound to his side was inflicted and supports the traditional view that the spear, thrust between his right rib, probably perforated not only the right lung but also the pericardium and heart and thereby ensured his death. Accordingly, interpretations based on the assumption that Jesus did not die on the cross appear to be at odds with modern medical knowledge (p. 1463).

MATTHEW 27:54 (cf. MARK 15:39; LUKE 23:47) — What did the centurion really say about Christ on the cross?

PROBLEM: Matthew records the centurion saying, "Truly this was the Son of God," while Mark says substantially the same thing, adding only the word "man," rendering it, "Truly this Man was the Son of God." Luke records the words of the centurion as follows: "Certainly this was a righteous Man!" What did he really say?

SOLUTION: He may have said both. The centurion's words need not be limited to one phrase or sentence. The centurion could have said both things. In accordance with his own emphasis on Christ as the perfect man, Luke may have chosen to use this phrase rather than the ones used by Matthew and Mark. There is no major difference between Matthew and

Mark, for in Greek the word "man" is implied by the masculine singular use of the word "This." It is also possible that Luke may have been paraphrasing or drawing an implication from what was actually said.

Christian scholars do not claim to have the exact words of the speakers in every case, but only an accurate rendering of what they really said. First of all, it is generally agreed that they spoke in Aramaic, but the Gospels were written in Greek. So the words we have in the Greek text on which the English is based are already a translation. Second, the Gospel writers, like writers today, sometimes summarized or paraphrased what was said. In this way, it is understandable that the renderings will be slightly different. But in this case, as in all other cases, the essence of what was originally said is faithfully produced in the original text. While we do not have the *exact words,* we do have the *same meaning.* Finally, when the sentences are totally different (but not contradictory), then we may reasonably assume that both things were said on that occasion and that one writer uses one and another writer the other. This is a common literary practice even today.

MATTHEW 28:5 – Why does Matthew say there was only one angel at the tomb when John says there were two?

PROBLEM: Matthew 28:5 refers to the "angel" at the tomb after Jesus' resurrection, and yet John says there were "two angels" there (John 20:12)?

SOLUTION: Matthew does not say there was *only* one angel. John says there were two, and wherever there are two there is always one; it never fails! The critic has to add the word "only" to Matthew's account in order to make it contradictory. But in this case, the problem is not with what the Bible actually says, but with what the critic adds to it.

Matthew probably focuses on the one who *spoke* and "said to the women, 'Do not be afraid' " (Matt. 28:5). John referred to how many angels they *saw;* "and she saw two angels" (John 20:12).

MATTHEW 28:9 – To whom did Christ appear first, the women or His disciples?

PROBLEM: Both Matthew and Mark list women as the first ones to see the resurrected Christ. Mark says, "He appeared first to Mary Magdalene" (16:9). But Paul lists Peter (Cephas) as the first one to see Christ after His resurrection (1 Cor. 15:5).

SOLUTION: Jesus appeared first to Mary Magdalene, then to the other women, and then to Peter. The order of the twelve appearances of Christ goes as follows:

THE ORDER OF THE TWELVE
APPEARANCES OF CHRIST

	PERSON(S)	SAW	HEARD	TOUCHED	OTHER EVIDENCE
1.	Mary (John 20:10-18)	X	X	X	Empty tomb
2.	Mary & Women (Matt. 28:1-10)	X	X	X	Empty tomb
3.	Peter (1 Cor. 15:5)	X	X*		Empty tomb, Clothes
4.	Two Disciples (Luke 24:13-35)	X	X		Ate with Him
5.	Ten Apostles (Luke 24:36-49; John 20:19-23)	X	X	X**	Saw wounds Ate food
6.	Eleven Apostles (John 20:24-31)	X	X	X**	Saw wounds
7.	Seven Apostles (John 21)	X	X		Ate food
8.	All Apostles (Matt. 28:16-20; Mark 16:14-18)	X	X		
9.	500 Brethren (1 Cor. 15:6)	X	X*		
10.	James (1 Cor. 15:7)	X	X*		
11.	All Apostles (Acts 1:4-8)	X	X		Ate with Him
12.	Paul (Acts 9:1-9; 1 Cor. 15:8)	X	X		

*Implied   **Offered Himself to be touched

Paul was not giving a complete list, but only the important one for his purpose. Since only men's testimony was considered legal or official in the 1st century, it is understandable that the apostle would not list the women in his defense of the resurrection here.

MATTHEW 28:18-20 — How can three persons be God when there is only one God?

PROBLEM: Matthew speaks of the "Father, Son, and Holy Spirit" all being part of one "name." But these are three distinct persons. How can there be three persons in the Godhead when there is only "one God" (Deut 6:4; 1 Cor. 8:6)?

SOLUTION: God is one in *essence,* but three in *Persons.* God has one *nature,* but three *centers of consciousness.* That is, there is only one *What* in God, but there are three *Whos.* There is one *It,* but three *I's.* This is a mystery, but not a contradiction. It would be contradictory to say God was only one person, but also was three persons. Or that God is only one nature, but that He also had three natures. But to declare, as orthodox Christians do, that God is one essence, eternally revealed in three distinct persons is not a contradiction.

MARK

MARK 1:1 — Why does Mark omit giving any genealogy of Jesus like Matthew and Luke do?

PROBLEM: Both Matthew (chap. 1) and Luke (chap. 3) give an ancestry of Jesus (see Matt. 1:1). However, Mark provides no genealogy whatsoever. Why the omission?

SOLUTION: Mark presents Christ as a servant, and servants need no genealogy. The Roman audience to whom Mark directed his Gospel was not interested in *where* a servant came from, but in *what* he could do. Unlike Mark's Roman audience, Matthew's Jewish audience looked for the Messiah, the King. Thus, Matthew traces Jesus back to His Jewish roots as the Son of David the king (Matt. 1:1). Likewise, Luke presents Christ as the perfect man. Hence, Christ's ancestry is traced back to the first man, Adam (Luke 3:38). John, on the other hand, presents Christ as the Son of God. Therefore, he traces Christ back to His eternal source with the Father.

Consider the following comparison of the four Gospels which explains why Mark needed no ancestry for Jesus.

	Matthew	**Mark**	**Luke**	**John**
Christ Presented	King	Servant	Man	God
Symbol	Lion	Ox	Man	Eagle
Key	Sovereignty	Ministry	Humanity	Deity
Audience	Jews	Romans	Greeks	World
Ancestry	To royalty	In anonymity	To humanity	To deity

MARK 1:2 — How can Mark's misquotation of this OT prophecy be justified?

PROBLEM: Mark misquotes Malachi, as indicated by the italicized words:

MALACHI 3:1	MARK 1:2
Behold, I send My messenger, And he will prepare the way before Me.	Behold, I send My messenger *before Your face,* Who will prepare *Your way* before *You.*

SOLUTION: First, it should be pointed out that, in spite of the change in words, the *original sense* is retained. In view of one of the fundamental principles of understanding difficult texts (see Introduction), "A NT citation need not be an exact quotation." As long as the meaning is retained, the words can differ. Second, in this case, Mark simply draws out the meaning by adding "before Your face." This is implied in the original passage, but made explicit by Mark. Third, the change from "Me" (first person) to "You" is necessitated because God is speaking in the Malachi passage, whereas Mark is speaking about God. Had he not changed the words he would have changed the meaning.

MARK 2:26 — Was Jesus wrong when He mentioned Abiathar as high priest instead of Ahimelech?

PROBLEM: Jesus says that at the time David ate the consecrated bread, Abiathar was high priest. Yet 1 Samuel 21:1-6 mentions that the high priest at that time was Ahimelech.

SOLUTION: First Samuel is correct in stating that the high priest was Ahimelech. On the other hand neither was Jesus wrong. When we take a closer look at Christ's words we notice that He used the phrase "in the *days* of Abiathar" (v. 26) which does not necessarily imply that Abiathar was high priest at the time David ate the bread. After David met Ahimelech and ate the bread, King Saul had Ahimelech killed (1 Sam. 22:17-19). Abiathar escaped and went to David (v. 20) and later took the place of the high priest. So even though Abiathar was made high priest after David ate the bread, it is still correct to speak in this manner. After all, Abiathar was alive when David did this, and soon following he became the high priest after his father's death. Thus, it was during the *time* of Abiathar, but not during his *tenure* in office.

MARK 5:1-20 — How many demoniacs were there? Where was the demoniac healed?

(See comments on Matt. 8:28-34.)

MARK 6:5 — If Jesus is God, why couldn't He do mighty works here?

PROBLEM: First of all, the Bible describes Jesus as God (John 1:1) who has, with the Father, "all authority in heaven and earth" (Matt. 28:18). However, on this occasion Jesus "could do no mighty work there" (v. 5). Why couldn't He, if He is all powerful?

SOLUTION: Jesus is almighty as God, but not almighty as man. As the God-man, Jesus has both a divine nature and a human nature. What He can do in one nature He cannot necessarily do in the other. For example, as God, Jesus never got tired (Ps. 121:4), but as man He did (cf. John 4:6).

Furthermore, just because Jesus *possessed* all power does not mean that He always chose to *exercise* it. The "could not" in Mark 6:5 is moral, not actual. That is, He chose not to perform miracles "because of their unbelief" (6:6). Jesus was not an entertainer, nor did He cast pearls before swine. So the necessity here is moral not metaphysical. He had the ability to do miracles there and in fact did some (v. 5), only He refused to do more because He deemed it a wasted effort.

MARK 6:8 — Did Jesus command the disciples to take a staff or not?

(See discussion on Matt. 10:10.)

MARK 8:11-12 — Did Jesus contradict Himself by saying there would be no sign given (cf. Matt. 12:38-39)?

PROBLEM: In Mark, the Pharisees ask for a sign from Jesus, but He says that no sign shall be given to that generation. But Matthew's account says that Christ responded that the sign of the Prophet Jonah would be given (namely, Jesus' resurrection).

SOLUTION: First, the main point here is that Christ was not willing to grant their *immediate* request for a sign. Jesus does not say in Matthew that the sign of the Prophet Jonah will be immediately given. This sign (of His death and resurrection) occurred *later*. So, even in Matthew He did not grant the requests of the Pharisees. Jesus refused to do miracles just to entertain (Luke 23:8). He did not "cast pearls before swine." However He did perform miracles to confirm His messiahship (John 20:31), and the Resurrection was the crowning miracle of that nature (cf. Acts 2:22-32).

Second, it is evident that on more than one occasion Jesus was asked to give a sign. Luke 11:16, 29-30 states that others sought for a sign. Here in Luke, Jesus responds very similar to the way He does in Matthew 12. Also, again in Matthew 16:1-4 the Pharisees ask for a sign from Jesus to which He responds that none will be given except the sign of Jonah, just as He had in chapter 12. So, it is clear that on other occasions Jesus was asked to give a sign and each time, Jesus refused to agree to their immediate demands. Miracles are performed according to God's will, not according to human want (cf. Heb. 2:4; 1 Cor. 12:11).

MARK 9:48 — Why did Jesus say worms would not die in hell?

PROBLEM: Jesus said that hell is a place "where 'their worm does not die and the fire is not quenched' " (Mark 9:48). But what do everlasting worms have to do with hell?

SOLUTION: Jesus is not speaking of earthworms, nor any other kind of animal here. He is speaking about the human body. Notice, He did not say "where the worm does not die" but, rather, "where *their* worm does not die." The antecedent of "their" is a human being who sins and dies without repentance (cf. 9:42-47). "Worm" is simply a way to refer to the human "worm," or shell known as the body. This fits with the context where He is speaking of the parts of the body, such as, "hands" and the "foot" (9:43-45). Jesus said here that we should not fear the one (man) who could destroy our body, but not our soul, but, rather, to fear the One (God) who could send soul and body into the everlasting flames (Luke 12:4-5; cf. Mark 9:43-48).

MARK 10:17-31 — Did Jesus deny He was God to the rich young ruler?

(See comments on Matt. 19:16-30.)

MARK 10:35 — Who came to talk with Jesus, the mother of James and John or James and John?

(See discussion on Matt. 20:20.)

MARK 10:46-52 — Did Jesus heal two blind men or just one?

(See comments on Matt. 20:29-34.)

MARK 11:2 — Were there two donkeys involved in the triumphal entry or just one?

(See discussion on Matt. 21:2.)

MARK 11:12-14, 20-24 — When was the fig tree cursed by Jesus?

(See comments on Matt. 21:12-19.)

MARK 11:23-24 — Did Jesus promise to give literally anything we ask in faith?

PROBLEM: On the face of it, this verse seems to be saying that God will grant any request we make of Him as long as we believe. On the other hand, Paul asked God three times to be relieved of his thorn in the flesh, and God refused (2 Cor. 12:8-9)

SOLUTION: There are limitations on what God will give, indicated both by the context and by other texts, as well as by the laws of God's own nature and the universe.

First of all, God cannot literally give us anything. Some things are actually impossible. For example, God cannot grant a request of a creature to be God. Neither can He answer a request to approve of our sin. God will not give us a stone if we ask for bread, nor will He give us a serpent if we ask for fish (cf. Matt. 7:9-10).

Second, the context of Jesus' promise in Mark 11 indicates that it was not unconditional, for the very next verse says "*If* you . . . forgive" your brother then God will forgive your trespasses. Thus, there is no reason to believe that Jesus intended us to take His promise to give us "whatever things" we ask without any conditions.

Third, all difficult passages should be interpreted in harmony with other clear statements of Scripture. And it is clear that God does not promise, for example, to heal everyone for whom we pray in faith. Paul wasn't healed, though he prayed earnestly and faithfully (2 Cor. 12:8-9). Jesus taught that it was not the blind man's lack of faith that hindered his being healed. Rather, he was born blind "that the works of God should be revealed in him" (John 9:3). In spite of the Apostle Paul's divine ability to heal others (Acts 28:9), later he apparently could not heal either Epaphroditus (Phil. 2:25ff) or Trophimus (2 Tim. 4:20). It clearly was not unbelief that brought Job's sickness on him (Job 1:1). What is more, if faith of the recipient were the condition for receiving a miracle, then none of the dead Jesus raised would have come back to life, since the dead cannot believe!

Finally, when the rest of Scripture is taken into consideration there are many conditions placed on God's promise to answer prayer in addition to faith. We must "abide in Him" and let His Word "abide in us" (John 15:7). We cannot "ask amiss" out of our own selfishness (James 4:3). Furthermore, we must ask "according to His will" (1 John 5:14). Even Jesus prayed, "Father, *if it is possible,* let this cup [His death] pass from Me" (Matt. 26:39). Indeed, on all except God's unconditional promises, this "if it be your will" must always be stated or implied. For prayer is not a means by which God serves us. Rather, it is a means by which we serve God. Prayer is not a means by which we get our will done in heaven, but a means by which God gets His will done on earth.

MARK 13:32 – Was Jesus ignorant of the time of His second coming?

PROBLEM: The Bible teaches that Jesus is God (John 1:1) and that He knows all things (John 2:24; Col. 2:3). On the other hand, He "increased in wisdom" (Luke 2:52) and sometimes did not seem to know certain things (cf. John 11:34). Indeed, He denied knowing the time of His own second coming here, saying, "but of that day and hour no one knows, neither the angels in heaven, nor the Son, but only the Father."

SOLUTION: We must distinguish between what Jesus knew *as God* (everything) and what He knew *as man.* As God, Jesus was omniscient (all-knowing), but as man He was limited in His knowledge. The situation can be schematized as follows:

JESUS AS GOD	JESUS AS MAN
Unlimited in knowledge	Limited in knowledge
No growth in knowledge	Growth in knowledge
Knew time of His coming	Did not know time of His coming

MARK 14:12ff – Did Jesus institute the Lord's Supper on the day of the Passover or the day before?

PROBLEM: If the first three Gospels (synoptics) are correct, then Jesus instituted the Lord's Supper "on the first day of Unleavened Bread, when they killed the Passover lamb" (cf. Matt. 26:17; Luke 22:1). But John places it "before the feast of the Passover" (13:1), the day before the crucifixion on which "they might eat the Passover" (18:28).

SOLUTION: There are two basic positions embraced by evangelical scholars on this point. Those who hold that Jesus ate the Passover lamb (and instituted the Lord's Supper at the end of it) on the same day it was observed by the Jews, support their view as follows: (1) It was the day required by OT Law, and Jesus said He did not come to destroy the Law, but to fulfill it (Matt. 5:17-18). (2) It seems to be the meaning of Mark 14:12 which says it was "on the first day of Unleavened Bread, when they killed the Passover lamb." (3) When John 19:14 speaks of it being "the Preparation Day of the Passover" they take this to mean simply the preparation for the Sabbath which occurred in that paschal week.

Other scholars contend that Jesus ate the Passover lamb on the day before the Jews did because: (1) He had to eat it a day early (Thursday) in order that He might offer Himself the next day (Good Friday) as the Passover Lamb (cf. John 1:29) to the Jews, in fulfillment of OT type on the very day they were eating the Passover lamb (1 Cor. 5:7). (2) The plain reading of John 19:14 is that it was "the Preparation Day of the *Passover*" [not the Sabbath], or in other words, the day before the Passover was eaten by the Jews. (3) Likewise, John 18:28 affirms that the Jews did not want to be defiled on the day Jesus was crucified "that they might eat the Passover."

Either view is possible without contradiction. However, the latter view seems to explain the texts more forthrightly. (See also comments on Matt. 12:40.)

MARK 14:30 – When Peter denied Christ, how many times did the rooster crow, once or twice?

(See comments on Matthew 26:34.)

MARK 15:25 (cf. JOHN 19:14) — Was Jesus crucified in the third hour or the sixth hour?

PROBLEM: Mark's Gospel account says that it was the third hour (9 a.m. Jewish time) when Christ was crucified (15:25). John's Gospel says that it was about the sixth hour (12 noon Jewish time) when Jesus was still on trial (19:14). This would make His crucifixion much later than specified by Mark. Which Gospel is correct?

SOLUTION: Both Gospel writers are correct in their assertions. The difficulty is answered when we realize that each Gospel writer used a different time system. John follows the *Roman* time system while Mark follows the *Jewish* time system.

According to Roman time, the day ran from midnight to midnight. The Jewish 24 hour period began in the evening at 6 p.m. and the morning of that day began at 6 a.m. Therefore, when Mark asserts that at the third hour Christ was crucified, this was about 9 a.m. John stated that Christ's trial was about the sixth hour. This would place the trial *before* the crucifixion and this would not negate any testimony of the Gospel writers. This fits with John's other references to time. For example, he speaks about Jesus being weary from His journey from His trip from Judea to Samaria at the "sixth hour" and asking for water from the woman at the well. Considering the length of His trip, His weariness, and the normal evening time when people come to the well to drink and to water their animals, this fits better with 6 p.m., which is "the sixth hour" of the night by Roman time reckoning. The same is true of John's reference to the tenth hour in John 1:39, which would be 10 a.m., a more likely time to be out preaching than 4 a.m.

MARK 15:26 — Why is the inscription on the cross different in all the Gospels?

(See comments on Matt. 27:37.)

MARK 15:39 — What did the centurion actually say about Jesus on the cross?

(See discussion on Matt. 27:54.)

MARK 16:2 – Was Mary at the tomb before sunrise or after?

PROBLEM: Mark states that Mary was there "very early in the morning . . . when the sun had risen" (v. 2). But John says it was "early, while it was still dark" (John 20:1).

SOLUTION: There are two general possibilities here. One possibility suggests that the phrase "when the sun had risen" (Mark 16:2) merely denotes early dawn (cf. Ps. 104:22), when it was "still dark" (John 20:1), relatively speaking.

Another view holds that Mary came alone at first when it was still dark before sunrise (John 20:1), and then again later after sunrise, she returned with the other women (Mark 16:1). In support of this is the fact that only Mary is mentioned in John, but Mary and the other women are named in Mark. Also, Luke (24:1) says it was "very early in the morning," implying after sunrise, when the "women" [not just Mary] had come. Likewise, Matthew (28:1) speaks of it being "after the Sabbath, as the first day of the week began to dawn" that "Mary Magdalene and the other Mary came to see the tomb." Only John mentions Mary being there alone "while it was still dark" (John 20:1).

MARK 16:8 – Did the women tell of their experience at the tomb or not?

PROBLEM: Mark says that the women returning from the empty tomb "said nothing to anyone, for they were afraid" (16:8). But Matthew asserts that they "ran to bring His disciples word" (Matt. 28:8; cf. v. 9).

SOLUTION: In response, it should be observed that Matthew does not actually say the women told the disciples, but they went back with the *intention* to tell them. Also, since Mark reveals that they did not speak because "they were afraid," it may be that *at first* they held their peace (as Mark indicated), and then *later* spoke up (as Matthew may imply). It is also possible that the women left the tomb in two groups at slightly different times, Mark referring to one and Matthew to the other.

MARK 16:9-20 – Why is this passage of Scripture omitted in some Bibles?

PROBLEM: Most modern Bibles contain this ending of the Gospel of Mark, including the KJV, ASV, NASB, and the NKJV. However, both the RSV and the NIV set it off from the rest of the text. A note in the NIV says, "Most reliable early manuscripts and other ancient witnesses do not have

Mark 16:9-20." Were these verses in the original Gospel of Mark?

SOLUTION: Scholars are divided over the authenticity of these verses. Those who follow the received text tradition point to the fact that this text is found in the majority of biblical manuscripts down through the centuries. Thus, they believe it was in the original manuscript of Mark.

On the other hand, those who follow the critical text tradition insist that we should not *add* evidence, but *weigh* it. Truth is not determined, they say, by majority vote, but by the most qualified witnesses. They point to the following arguments for rejecting these verses: (1) These verses are lacking in many of the oldest and most reliable Greek manuscripts, as well as in important Old Latin, Syriac, Armenian, and Ethiopic manuscripts. (2) Many of the ancient church fathers reveal no knowledge of these verses, including Clement, Origen, and Eusebius. Jerome admitted that almost all Greek copies do not have it. (3) Many manuscripts that do have this section place a mark by it indicating it is a spurious addition to the text. (4) There is another (shorter) ending to Mark that is found in some manuscripts. (5) Others point to the fact that the style and vocabulary are not the same as the rest of the Gospel of Mark.

Whether or not this piece of *text* belongs in the original, the *truth* it contains certainly accords with it. So, the bottom line is that it does not make any difference, since if it does belong here there is nothing in it contrary to the rest of Scripture. And if it does not belong, there is no truth missing in the Bible, since everything taught here is found elsewhere in Scripture. This includes tongues (see Acts 2:1ff), baptism (Acts 2:38), and God's 1st century supernatural protection of His messengers unwittingly bitten by poisonous snakes (cf. Acts 28:3-5). So, in the final analysis, it is simply a debate about whether this particular *text* belongs in the Bible, not over whether any *truth* is missing.

MARK 16:12 — Did Jesus appear in different bodies after His resurrection?

PROBLEM: According to Mark, Jesus appeared here in "another form." From this, some argue that after the resurrection Jesus assumed different bodies on different occasions, but did not have the same continuously physical body He had before the Resurrection. But this is contrary to the orthodox understanding of the Resurrection, as is indicated by many other verses (see comments on Luke 24:34).

SOLUTION: This conclusion is unnecessary for several reasons.

First, there are serious questions about the authenticity of the text involved. Mark 16:9-20 is not found in some of the oldest and best manuscripts (see comments on Mark 16:9-20 above). And in reconstructing the original texts from the existing manuscripts, many scholars believe that the older texts are more reliable, since they are closer to the original manuscripts.

Second, even granting its authenticity, the event of which it is a summary (cf. Luke 24:13-32) simply says "their eyes were prevented from recognizing Him" (Luke 24:16, NASB). This makes it clear that the miraculous element was not in Jesus' body, but in the eyes of the disciples (Luke 24:16, 31). Recognition of Jesus was kept from them until their eyes were opened.

Third, at best this is an obscure and isolated reference. And it is never wise to base any significant doctrinal pronouncement on such a text.

Fourth, whatever "another form" means, it certainly does not mean a form other than His real physical, material body. For, on this very occasion Jesus ate physical food (Luke 24:30), which later in this very chapter He gave as a proof that He was "flesh and bones" and not an immaterial "spirit" (vv. 38-43).

Finally, "another form" probably means other than that of a *gardener* for which Mary mistook Him earlier (John 20:15). Here Jesus appeared in the form of a *traveler* (Luke 24:13-14).

LUKE

LUKE 1:26ff—Was the announcement of the birth of Christ made to Mary or to Joseph?

PROBLEM: Matthew says the announcement of Jesus' birth was made to Joseph (Matt. 1:20), but Luke asserts that it was made to Mary (Luke 1:26ff). Who is correct?

SOLUTION: The announcement was made to Mary first and then to Joseph. Mary had to know first, since she would have been the first to know she was going to have the baby. Joseph needed to know next, since his wife was going to have a baby that was not his! This kind of pairing of visions on important matters is found elsewhere in Scripture. Compare Peter and Cornelius (Acts 10:3, 15) and Saul and Ananias (Acts 9:6, 10-16).

LUKE 1:27—How could Elizabeth be related to Mary when she was from the tribe of Aaron?

PROBLEM: According to Luke 1:5, Elizabeth was from the priestly tribe of Aaron. But here in Luke 1:36 she is described as a relative of Mary, who was from the tribe of Judah (1:39; 3:30).

SOLUTION: Being a relative of someone in the tribe of Judah does not mean she was from that tribe. She could have been related by marriage. Intermarriage between tribes was permitted, except in the case of an heiress. Aaron himself married someone from the tribe of Judah (Ex. 6:23; 1 Chron. 2:10).

LUKE 1:28ff—Should Christians worship Mary?

PROBLEM: The angel said Mary was the most blessed of all women, declaring to her, "Rejoice, highly favored one, the Lord is with you;

blessed are you among women!" (Luke 1:28) Although the highest form of worship is reserved for God alone (*latria*), Roman Catholics believe that Mary should be venerated in a lesser sense (*hyperdulia*) as the most highly favored above all other creatures since she is the "Mother of God" and "Queen of Heaven." Why do Protestants not give Mary her proper due?

SOLUTION: Protestants do honor Mary as the blessed "mother of . . . [our] Lord" (Luke 1:43). But for many reasons, we believe it is idolatry to worship Mary. First of all, Mary was a human being, not God. The Bible commands us, "You shall worship the Lord your God, and Him only you shall serve" (Matt. 4:10).

Second, Mary confessed that she was a sinner in need of a Savior just like any other human being. She said, "my soul magnifies the Lord, And my spirit has rejoiced in God my Savior" (see comments on Luke 1:46).

Third, the angel from God did not affirm that Mary was to be blessed *over* all women, but simply *among* all women. He declared only, "Blessed are you *among* women" (Luke 1:28, emphasis added). In practice many Roman Catholics have exalted Mary above all women, virtually to the place of God.

Fourth, the cult of Mariolatry grew in the Roman Catholic Church during the Middle Ages, adding to her such titles as "Coredemtrix," and "Queen of Heaven." However, this manifests a pagan influence on Christianity patterned after the old Babylonian goddess called by this very name "the queen of heaven" in Jeremiah (Jer. 7:18; 44:17-19, 25).

LUKE 1:46 – Was Mary born sinless as Roman Catholics claim?

PROBLEM: Roman Catholics claim that Mary the mother of Jesus was immaculately conceived (i.e., conceived without sin). However, with the exception of Christ, the Bible asserts that every human being is born in sin (Ps. 51:5; Rom. 5:12). Was Mary immaculately conceived?

SOLUTION: Mary the mother of Jesus was the most blessed among women (see comments on Luke 1:28ff). However, she was not sinless, and the Bible makes this clear in many ways. First, David declared for all human beings, "Behold, I was brought forth in iniquity, and in sin my mother conceived me" (Ps. 51:5).

Second, Paul affirmed that every human born of natural parents since Adam's time sinned in Adam, for "through one man sin entered the world, and death through sin, and thus death spread to all men, because all sinned [in Adam]" (Rom. 5:12).

Third, there is absolutely no trace anywhere in the Bible that Mary was an exception to the rule that "all have sinned and fall short of the glory of God" (Rom. 3:23). In Christ's case, however, it points out repeatedly that He was human, yet without sin (2 Cor. 5:21; Heb. 4:15; 1 Peter 3:18; 1 John 3:3).

Finally, Mary proclaimed her own sinfulness when she confessed, "my spirit has rejoiced in God my Savior" (Luke 1:46). Like everyone else, Mary too needed a Savior.

LUKE 2:1 — Did Luke make a mistake when he mentioned a worldwide census under Caesar Augustus?

PROBLEM: Luke refers to a worldwide census under Caesar Augustus when Quirinius was governor of Syria. However, according to the annals of ancient history, no such census took place.

SOLUTION: Until recently, it has been widely held by critics that Luke made an error in his assertion about a registration under Caesar Augustus, and that the census actually took place in A.D. 6 or 7, (that is mentioned by Luke in Gamaliel's speech recorded in Acts 5:37). The lack of any extra-biblical support has led some to claim this is an error. However, recent scholarship has reversed this trend, and it is now widely admitted that there was in fact an earlier registration as Luke records. This has been asserted on the basis of several factors.

First of all, since the people of a subjugated land were compelled to take an oath of allegiance to the emperor, it was not unusual for the emperor to require an imperial census as an expression of this allegiance and as a means of enlisting men for military service, or, as was probably true in this case, in preparation to levy taxes. Because of the strained relations between Herod and Augustus in the later years of Herod's reign, as the Jewish historian Josephus reports, it is understandable that Augustus would begin to treat Herod's domain as a subject land, and consequently would impose such a census to maintain control of Herod and the people.

Second, periodic registrations of this sort took place on a regular basis every 14 years. According to the very papers that recorded the censuses, (see W.M. Ramsay, *Was Christ Born in Bethlehem?* 1898), there was in fact a census taken in about 8 or 7 B.C. Because of this regular pattern of census taking, any such action would naturally be regarded as a result of the general policy of Augustus, even though a local census may have been instigated by a local governor. Therefore, Luke recognizes the census as stemming from the decree of Augustus.

Third, a census was a massive project which probably took several years to complete. Such a census for the purpose of taxation was begun in Gaul between 10–9 B.C. that took a period of 40 years to complete. It is quite likely that the decree to begin the census, in about 8 or 7 B.C., may not have actually begun in Palestine until some time later. Problems of organization and preparation may have delayed the actual census until 5 B.C. or even later.

Fourth, it was not an unusual requirement that people return to the place of their origin, or to the place where they owned property. A decree of C. Vibius Mazimus in A.D. 104 required all those who were away from their home towns to return there for the purpose of the census. For the Jews, such travel would not have been unusual at all since they were quite used to the annual pilgrimage to Jerusalem. There is simply no reason to suspect Luke's statement regarding the census at the time of Jesus' birth. Luke's account fits the regular pattern of census taking, and its date would not be an unreasonable one. Also, this may have been simply a local census that was taken as a result of the general policy of Augustus. Luke simply provides us with a reliable historical record of an event not otherwise recorded. Since Dr. Luke has proven himself to be a reliable historian in other matters (see Sir William Ramsey, *St. Paul the Traveler and Roman Citizen*, 1896), there is no reason to doubt him here (see also comments on Luke 2:2).

LUKE 2:2 — Why does Luke say the census was during Quirinius' governorship since Quirinius was not governor until A.D. 6?

PROBLEM: Luke states that the census decreed by Augustus was the first one taken while Quirinius was governor of Syria. However, Quirinius did not become governor of Syria until after the death of Herod in about A.D. 6. Is this an error in Luke's historical record?

SOLUTION: Luke has not made an error. There are reasonable solutions to this difficulty.

First, Quintilius Varus was governor of Syria from about 7 B.C. to about 4 B.C. Varus was not a trustworthy leader, a fact that was disastrously demonstrated in A.D. 9 when he lost three legions of soldiers in the Teutoburger forest in Germany. To the contrary, Quirinius was a notable military leader who was responsible for squelching the rebellion of the Homonadensians in Asia Minor. When it came time to begin the census, in about 8 or 7 B.C., Augustus entrusted Quirinius with the delicate problem in the volatile area of Palestine, effectively superseding the authority and governorship of Varus by appointing Quirinius to a place of special authority in this matter.

It has also been proposed that Quirinius was governor of Syria on two separate occasions, once while prosecuting the military action against the Homonadensians between 12 and 2 B.C., and later beginning about A.D. 6. A Latin inscription discovered in 1764 has been interpreted to refer to Quirinius as having served as governor of Syria on two occasions.

It is possible that Luke 2:2 reads, "This census took place *before* Quirinius was governing Syria." In this case, the Greek word translated "first" (*prōtos*) is translated as a comparative, "before." Because of the awkward construction of the sentence, this is not an unlikely reading.

Regardless of which solution is accepted, it is not necessary to conclude that Luke has made an error in recording the historical events surrounding the birth of Jesus. Luke has proven himself to be a reliable historian even in the details. Sir William Ramsey has shown that in making reference to 32 countries, 54 cities, and 9 islands he made no mistakes!

LUKE 3:23 – Why does Luke present a different ancestral tree for Jesus than the one in Matthew?

PROBLEM: Jesus has a different grandfather here in Luke 3:23 (Heli) than He does in Matthew 1:16 (Jacob). Which one is the right one?

SOLUTION: This should be expected, since they are two different lines of ancestors, one traced through His *legal* father, Joseph and the other through His *actual* mother, Mary. Matthew gives the *official* line, since he addresses Jesus' genealogy to Jewish concerns for the Jewish Messiah's credentials which required that Messiah come from the seed of Abraham and the line of David (cf. Matt. 1:1). Luke, with a broader *Greek* audience in view, addresses himself to their interest in Jesus as the *Perfect Man* (which was the quest of Greek thought). Thus, he traces Jesus back to the first man, Adam (Luke 3:38).

That Matthew gives Jesus' paternal genealogy and Luke his maternal genealogy is further supported by several facts. First of all, while both lines trace Christ to David, each is through a different son of David. Matthew traces Jesus through Joseph (his *legal father*) to David's son, *Solomon* the king, by whom Christ rightfully inherited the throne of David (cf. 2 Sam. 7:12ff). Luke's purpose, on the other hand, is to show Christ as an actual human. So he traces Christ to David's son, *Nathan,* through his *actual mother,* Mary, through whom He can rightfully claim to be fully human, the redeemer of humanity.

Further, Luke does not say that he is giving Jesus' genealogy through Joseph. Rather, he notes that Jesus was "as was supposed" (Luke 3:23) the son of Joseph, while He was actually the son of Mary. Also, that Luke would record Mary's genealogy fits with his interest as a doctor in mothers and birth and with his emphasis on women in his Gospel which has been called "the Gospel for Women."

Finally, the fact that the two genealogies have some names in common (such as Shealtiel and Zerubbabel, Matt. 1:12; cf. Luke 3:27) does not prove they are the same genealogy for two reasons. One, these are not uncommon names. Further, even the same genealogy (Luke's) has a repeat of the names Joseph and Judah (3: 26, 30).

The two genealogies can be summarized as follows:

MATTHEW	LUKE
David	David
Solomon	Nathan
Rehoboam	Mattathah
Abijah	Menan
Asa	Melea
Jehoshaphat	Eliakim
. . . . .	. . . . .
Jacob	Heli ———┐
Joseph — Mary — legal wife (legal father)	Joseph — Mary — actual mother (legal husband) ┘
Jesus	Jesus

LUKE 4:1-13 — Is there a mistake in the temptation of Jesus recorded by Matthew and Luke?

(See comments on Matt. 4:5-10.)

LUKE 4:19 — Why does Jesus not quote this passage accurately?

PROBLEM: When Jesus cited this prophecy, He lopped off the rest of the verse in Isaiah 61:2 which adds, "And the day of vengeance of our God." Why didn't He quote it accurately?

SOLUTION: First of all, Jesus did quote the passage *accurately,* but He didn't quote it *completely.* That is neither uncommon nor unacceptable. It is still done by authors today. Indeed, we have done it many times in this very book, usually indicated by ellipses (. . .). Furthermore, Jesus had a very good reason for not quoting the rest of the verse — it would have been wrong. Jesus told His audience that the quotation was limited to what "is fulfilled in your hearing" (Luke 4:21). But the only part of the verse that was fulfilled in His first coming was exactly the part He cited. Had He continued and read "And the day of vengeance of our God" (which refers to His second coming, Isa. 61:2), then what He said would not have been true.

LUKE 6:17 — Why does Luke say Jesus gave this sermon on a level place when Matthew declares it was given on the mountain?

PROBLEM: Luke affirms that Jesus "stood on a level place" when He gave this famous sermon, but Matthew says "He went up on a mountain" to deliver it (Matt. 5:1). How can this discrepancy be resolved?

SOLUTION: Granted that the two accounts are referring to the same event (see comments on Luke 6:20 below), they can be reconciled by noting that the mountain only refers to the *general area* where everyone was, while the level place denotes the *particular spot* from which Jesus spoke. It says "He *stood* on a level place." It does not say all the people were *seated* in a level place. A level place from which to preach to a multitude on a mountain side would make a natural amphitheater.

LUKE 6:17 – Why does Luke say Jesus stood to teach them when Matthew declares that He sat to teach them?

PROBLEM: Luke says that Jesus "stood on a level place" to preach. But Matthew recorded that "when He was seated . . . He opened His mouth and taught them" (Matt. 5:1-2).

SOLUTION: These references may be of slightly different times during the same event. One possibility is that Matthew's reference is to the beginning of the event when "His disciples came to Him . . . and [He] taught them" (Matt. 5:1-2). Then when the "great multitude [that] followed Him" gathered to listen in, Jesus would naturally want to stand to project His voice so that all could hear, as Luke records.

Another possibility is that Luke's reference to Jesus' standing is before He gave the sermon while He is still healing people (Luke 6:17-19). Then, since "the whole multitude sought to touch Him" Jesus may have found a place to sit where "He lifted up His eyes toward His disciples and said . . . [His message]" (6:20). This fits the order given in Luke and would also explain why Matthew declares that Jesus was sitting when He spoke to His disciples. In any event, there is no irreconcilable difference in the two accounts, even assuming they both refer to the same occasion.

LUKE 6:20 (cf. MATT. 5:3) – Why does Luke's version of the Beatitudes differ from those in Matthew?

PROBLEM: Luke's version of the first beatitude states "Blessed are you poor." While Matthew's account says "Blessed are the poor in spirit." Luke appears to be speaking about poverty in a financial sense and Matthew about poverty in a spiritual sense.

SOLUTION: Some believe that the difference in renditions could be because these are two different occasions. They point to the fact that Matthew says it was given to a multitude *including* His disciples (Matt. 5:1), while Luke's version was given to His disciples (Luke 6:20). Also, in Matthew, Jesus spoke on a hill (5:1) while in Luke He spoke on level ground (6:17). Then too, Luke's account is much more brief than Matthew's. (But see "Solution" to Luke 6:17.)

Others, however, note that both sermons were given at the same time, in the same geographical area, to the same group of people, with many of the exact same sayings. In both accounts His sermon was preceded by special healings, and followed by His going to Capernaum. Furthermore, although Luke introduces the sermon by saying Jesus "lifted up His eyes toward His disciples," like Matthew, he notes that Jesus gave "all His sayings in the hearing of the people" (Luke 7:1; cf. Matt. 5:1). All of this makes it unlikely that two different events are represented.

The difference in the accounts can be accounted for in several ways. First, Luke's account is much more brief than Matthew's. Second, Jesus may have said much more on this occasion than either writer recorded. So each writer is selecting from a larger body of material that which suited their theme. Third, Luke places a different emphasis on Jesus' words, stressing the significance for those who were poor. Matthew does not exclude financial poverty but speaks of that poverty of spirit which the poor often have as opposed to the rich (cf. Luke 16; 1 Tim. 6:17).

LUKE 6:26 – Is a good name a blessing or a curse?

PROBLEM: In this text, Jesus told His disciples that people would speak evil of them, as they had of the prophets before them. On the other hand, Solomon taught that "A good name is better than precious ointment" (Ecc. 7:1). But if a good name is to be chosen over riches (Prov. 22:1), then why did Jesus tell His disciples to rejoice when people spoke evil of them?

SOLUTION: A good name does not necessarily mean all people will speak well of those who possess it. Many persons with good names have evil enemies. Who has a more blessed name than Jesus Himself, and yet who is cursed more. Jesus warned His disciples in the Luke passage to be wary when those who are willing to sacrifice principle for popularity speak well of you. The acclaim of crowd pleasers is disastrous, but the recognition of the righteous is blessed.

LUKE 7:2-10 – Is there a mistake in the accounts concerning Jesus and the centurion?

(See comments on Matt. 8:5-13.)

LUKE 8:26-39 – How many demoniacs were there? Where was the demoniac healed?

(See discussion on Matt. 8:28-34.)

LUKE 9:50 — Did Jesus contradict Himself when He referred to those who are for Him (cf. Luke 11:23)?

PROBLEM: In Luke 9:50, Jesus says that "he who is not against us is for us." Yet in Luke 11:23 Jesus says that "He who is not with Me is against Me." Which position is correct?

SOLUTION: First, Luke 9:50 is better translated "he who is not against *you* is for *you*." The KJV translates the word "you" for "us," but it is better translated the other way around. The original Greek is clear on which pronouns should be used. Most all Greek manuscripts older than the 8th century A.D. do not contain the "against us . . . for us" rendition. If this is so, then the problem dissolves.

Second, the contexts of each particular account are different. In both passages, the casting out of demons are in view. In Luke 9, an individual who is not one of Christ's 12 disciples is casting out demons in Christ's name and John tried to stop him (9:49). Jesus instructed His disciples not to hinder him "for he who is not against us is for us." In Luke 11 the situation is different. Here, Jesus has cast out a demon from someone and some people were saying that Jesus casts out demons by Beelzebub, the ruler of demons (vv.14-15). The people here were *against* the work of the Lord while the man in Luke 9 was *doing* the work in the name of the Lord. One was *for* the Lord while others were *against* Him. Thus there is no real contradiction.

LUKE 9:52-53 — Did the Samaritans receive Christ or reject Him?

PROBLEM: Luke says clearly that "they did not receive Him." Yet, when Jesus spoke to the Samaritan woman at the well, a great multitude flocked to meet Him (John 4:39-40).

SOLUTION: These passages refer to different times and different places. First of all, Luke is speaking of a specific village, not all Samaritans. Further, Luke gives the reason for the rejection at this time, "because His [Jesus'] face was set for the journey to Jerusalem" (v. 53). Finally, the positive response of the Samaritans in John was because of the testimony of the woman who told her friends that she had found a prophet, one "who told me all things that I ever did" (John 4:29).

LUKE 9:60 — How can the dead bury their own dead?

(See comments on Matt. 8:22.)

LUKE 10:23 – Are those who see blessed, or those who do not see?

PROBLEM: Here Jesus tells His disciples: "Blessed are the eyes which see the things you see." However, later He said to them, "Blessed are those who have not seen and yet have believed" (John 20:29). Which one is right?

SOLUTION: First of all, there is a different meaning to the word "blessed" in each passage. In the first case, it seems to mean that they were *highly favored* because they were seeing these miracles occur (cf. 10:17-19). In the John passage, "blessed" means worthy of praise, which is a reference to those who believe in Christ without having the opportunity to place their finger into the crucifixion wounds in His resurrection body.

Further, even if "blessed" is taken in the same sense, there is still an important difference in the object of Jesus' commendation for what they saw or didn't see. There is a difference between requiring sight as *the ground* of faith, as Thomas apparently did, and using sight in *process* of exercising their faith, as the disciples did. There is nothing wrong with evidence used to *support* one's faith, but it should not be used as the very *basis* of it. God alone and His self-revelation is the basis for believing, not the miraculous evidence for it. So we should believe in God because of Himself, not merely because of the evidence for Him. Evidence, at best, merely give us grounds for belief *that* God exists. Only God Himself, through our free choice, can persuade us to believe in Him. Therefore, to demand that we "see" more evidence before believing in Him diminishes the merit of faith (i.e., our blessedness).

LUKE 13:24 – Do all seekers find God?

PROBLEM: Jesus says, "Seek and you will find." Other passages of Scripture reaffirm the same truth (1 Chron. 28:9; Isa. 55:6; Acts 10:35). Yet, according to Jesus, "many . . . will seek to enter and will not be able" (Luke 13:24). Likewise, Jesus said in John, "You will seek Me and not find Me" (John 7:34).

SOLUTION: All who earnestly seek God, find Him, for "He is a rewarder of those who diligently seek Him" (Heb. 11:6). In fact, God is "longsuffering toward us, not willing that any should perish" (2 Peter 3:9).

Of course, there are those who seek God *on their own terms* (by human works) who will not be saved, since it is "not by works of righteousness which we have done, but according to His mercy He saved us" (Titus

3:5). The Bible says, "there is a way which seems right to a man, But its end is the way of death" (Prov. 14:12). Further, there are those who *seek too late,* namely, after they die for "it is appointed for men to die once, but after this the judgment" (Heb. 9:27). But there is no one who comes to God in this life in penitence, falling upon His mercy, that does not receive His gracious gift of salvation.

SEEKERS WHO DO FIND GOD	SEEKERS WHO DO NOT FIND GOD
Those coming God's way	Those coming their own way
Those who come in time	Those who wait too late
Those coming in repentance	Those coming in remorse

Judas regretted his sin (Matt. 27:4), but Peter repented of his. Hence, Judas is lost (John 17:12), and Peter is saved.

LUKE 16:31 – Do miracles prove Jesus' divine mission?

PROBLEM: Beginning with Moses, miracles were given as a proof of the divine mission of His servants (cf. Ex. 4:1-17). Nicodemus knew Jesus was sent from God because, he said to Jesus, "No one can do these signs that You do unless God is with him" (John 3:2). Luke tells us that Jesus was "attested by God to you by miracles, wonders, and signs which God did through Him" (Acts 2:22). The writer of Hebrews declared that God bore "witness both with signs and wonders, with various miracles, and gifts of the Holy Spirit" (Heb. 2:4).

On the other hand, it is evident that miracles do not work to confirm the divine message to those who do not believe. Jesus Himself admitted this fact in this passage when He said, "Neither will they be persuaded though one rise from the dead" (Luke 16:31). And in a pivotal verse in John, after Jesus performed His many miraculous signs, John conceded, "But although He had done so many signs before them, they did not believe in Him" (12:37). So, it would seem from these verses that miracles do not really work to confirm a divine mission.

SOLUTION: The reason for this discrepancy is not difficult to find. There is a difference between *proof* and *persuasion.* Given the theistic context, Jesus' miracles were a *confirmation* of His claims, but that does not mean everyone who saw them would be *convinced* by them. They were an *objective* demonstration of His claims, but not everyone was *subjectively* convinced by them. Even the best evidence is effective only on the willing, not the unwilling. Those who are closed to God will hear only "thunder," while those who are open hear the very voice of God (cf. John 12:27-29).

LUKE 18:1ff — Should prayer be continuous or brief?

PROBLEM: Jesus condemned the long and repetitious prayers of the Pharisees who thought they would "be heard for their many words" (Matt. 6:7). Yet in this parable Jesus encouraged incessant prayer of those "who cry out day and night" to God (Luke 18:7). But these passages seem to be in conflict.

SOLUTION: What Jesus spoke against was not *long* prayers but *repetitious* prayers. He was more concerned with the *strength* of the prayer than the *length* of the prayer. Petitioners before God are not heard for their "many words," but they are heard for their sincere "cry."

LUKE 18:18-30 — If Jesus is God, why did He rebuke the young ruler for calling Him good?

(See discussion on Matt. 19:16-30.)

LUKE 18:35-43 — Did Jesus heal two blind men or just one?

(See comments on Matt. 20:29-34.)

LUKE 19:30 — Were there two donkeys involved in the triumphal entry or just one?

(See discussion on Matt. 21:2.)

LUKE 22:19 — What did Jesus mean when He said "This is My body"? Should it be taken literally?

PROBLEM: Orthodox Protestants believe in interpreting the Bible literally. But if Jesus' statement here is taken literally, it seems to support the Roman Catholic view of transubstantiation, namely, that, when consecrated, the communion bread becomes the actual body of Christ.

SOLUTION: Jesus no more meant that the statement "This is My body" should be taken literally than the statement "I am the true vine" (John 15:1). The Roman Catholic doctrine of transubstantiation (that the bread becomes the actual body of Christ) is without biblical or rational support for many reasons.

First, the *context* is opposed to taking this literally. All agree that when Jesus made this statement, He was referring to the bread. Luke says "He took the bread, gave thanks, and broke it . . . saying, 'This is My body' " (Luke 22:19). But it was obvious to all that Jesus' actual body was holding the bread in His hands. So none of His disciples present could possibly have understood Him to mean the bread was His actual body.

Second, *common sense* is opposed to taking this literally. God created the senses, and all of life depends on our trusting the information they give us about our world. But those who believe in transubstantiation admit that the consecrated bread (host) looks, smells, and tastes like real bread. Why then would God call on us to distrust the very senses that He created and asks us to trust continually for our very life.

Third, *parallel statements by Jesus* are opposed to taking this literally. Jesus often spoke in figurative language. He said, "I am the Door" (John 10:9) and we should "eat the flesh of the Son of Man." But neither Catholics nor Protestants take these literally (see comments on John 6:53-54). Why then should we take His statement ("This is My body") about the communion bread literally?

LUKE 23:38 — What did the sign on the cross really say?

(See comments on Matt. 27:37.)

LUKE 23:43 — Did Christ err when He told the thief on the cross that he would be in paradise the day Christ died?

PROBLEM: If Christ did not go to heaven until at least three days after His death, how can the thief be in paradise the day Christ died?

SOLUTION: Christ's *soul* went immediately to paradise, which is the third heaven (2 Cor. 12:2-4), but His *body* went to the grave for 3 days. Jesus said on the cross, "Father, into Your hands I commit My Spirit" (Luke 23:46, NIV), which indicates His soul went to be with the Father in heaven the very instant He died. When Jesus said to Mary after His resurrection, "I have not yet ascended to My Father," He was referring to His *body* ascending into heaven 40 days after His resurrection (Acts 1), not to his *soul* going to heaven between death and resurrection. The phrase "descended into hell" is not in the earliest Apostles' Creed but was added much later. (See comments on Eph. 4:8.)

LUKE 23:47 — Is the remark of the centurion about Jesus accurately recorded?

(See comments on Matt. 27:54.)

LUKE 24:23 — Were Jesus' resurrection appearances physical or mere visions?

PROBLEM: Jesus spoke of His resurrection body having "flesh and bones" (Luke 24:39). He ate physical food (v. 42) and was touched by human hands (Matt. 28:9). But Luke calls it a "vision" in this passage, which implies that it was not a real physical appearance. In addition, some point to the fact that those who were with Paul during his Damascus road experience did not see Christ (see Acts 9:7).

SOLUTION: The Resurrection appearances were literal, physical appearances. This is evident for several reasons. First of all, the passage cited above from Luke (24:23) does not refer to seeing Christ. It refers only to the women seeing angels at the tomb, not to any appearance of Christ. The Gospels never speak of a resurrection appearance of Christ as a vision, nor does Paul in his list in 1 Corinthians 15.

Second, the post-resurrection encounters with Christ are described by Paul as literal "appearances" (1 Cor. 15:5-8), not as visions. The difference between a mere vision and a physical appearance is significant. Visions are of invisible, spiritual realities, such as God and angels. Appearances, on the other hand, are of physical objects that can be seen with the naked eye. Visions have no physical manifestations associated with them, but appearances do.

People sometimes "see" or "hear" things in their visions (Luke 1:11ff; Acts 10:9ff), but not with their naked physical senses. When someone saw angels with the naked eye, or had some physical contact with them (Gen. 18:8; 32:24; Dan. 8:18), it was not a vision but an actual appearance of an angel in the physical world. During these appearances the angels temporarily assumed a visible form after which they returned to their normal invisible state. However, the Resurrection appearances of Christ were experiences of seeing Christ with the naked eye in His continued visible, physical form. In any event, there is a significant difference between a mere vision and a physical appearance.

VISION	APPEARANCE
Of a Spiritual Reality	Of a Physical Object
No Physical Manifestations	Physical Manifestations
Daniel 2; 7	1 Corinthians 15
2 Corinthians 12	Acts 9

Third, certainly the most common way to describe an encounter with the resurrected Christ is as an "appearance." These appearances were accompanied by physical manifestations, such as, the audible voice of Jesus, His physical body and crucifixion scars, physical sensations (as touch), and eating on three occasions. These phenomena are not purely subjective or internal—they involve a physical, external reality.

Finally, the contention that Paul's experience must have been a vision because those with him did not see Christ is unfounded, since they both heard the physical sound and saw the physical light, just as Paul did. Only Paul looked into the light, and so only he saw Jesus.

LUKE 24:31a — Did Jesus dematerialize when He suddenly disappeared from the disciples after an appearance?

PROBLEM: Jesus could not only suddenly appear after His resurrection (cf. John 20:19), but He could also instantly disappear. Is this evidence, as some critics claim, that Jesus dematerialized on these occasions?

SOLUTION: Jesus rose in the same physical, albeit glorified, body in which He died. Such a body is an important dimension of His continuing humanity both before (cf. John 1:18) and after (Luke 24:39; 1 John 4:2) His resurrection.

First of all, the fact that He could appear or disappear quickly does not diminish His humanity but enhances it. It reveals that, while the post-resurrection body has *more* powers than a pre-resurrection body, it was not *less* than physical. That is, it did not cease to be a material body even though by resurrection it gained powers beyond mere physical bodies.

Second, it is the very nature of a miracle that it is immediate, as opposed to the natural gradual process. When Jesus touched the man's hand, *"immediately* his leprosy was cleansed"* (Matt. 8:3). Likewise, at Jesus' command the paralytic *"immediately* . . . arose, took up the bed, and went out in the presence of them all"* (Mark 2:10-12). When Peter proclaimed that the man born crippled be cured, *"immediately* his feet and ankle bones received strength . . . leaping up, [he] stood and walked"* (Acts 3:7-8).

Third, Philip was immediately transported from the presence of the

Ethiopian eunuch in his physical pre-resurrection body. The text says, after baptizing the eunuch "the Spirit of the Lord caught Philip away, so that the eunuch saw him no more" (Acts 8:39). One moment Philip is with the eunuch; the next he suddenly and miraculously disappeared and later appeared in another city (Acts 8:40). Such a phenomenon does not necessitate an immaterial body. Hence, sudden appearances and disappearances are not proofs of the immaterial, but of the supernatural.

LUKE 24:31b — If Jesus had the same physical body after His resurrection, why did His disciples not recognize Him?

PROBLEM: These two disciples walked with Jesus, talked with Him, and ate with Him and still did not recognize Him. Other disciples had the same experience (see verses below). If He rose in the same physical body (cf. Luke 24:39; John 20:27), then why didn't they recognize Him.

SOLUTION: Jesus did rise in the numerically same body of flesh and bones in which He died (see comments on 1 Cor. 15:37). There were many reasons why He was not immediately recognized by His disciples:

1. Dullness — Luke 24:25-26
2. Disbelief — John 20:24-25
3. Disappointment — John 20:11-15
4. Dread — Luke 24:36-37
5. Dimness — John 20:1, 14-15
6. Distance — John 21:4
7. Different Clothes — John 19:23-24; cf. 20:6-8

Notice, however, two important things: the problem was only *temporary,* and before the appearance was over they were absolutely convinced that it was the same Jesus in the same physical body of flesh, bones, and scars that He had before the resurrection! And they went out of His presence to turn the world upside down, fearlessly facing death, because they had not the slightest doubt that He had conquered death in the same physical body in which He had experienced it.

LUKE 24:34 — Was Jesus invisible to mortal eyes before and after He appeared?

PROBLEM: The phrase "He appeared" means "He made Himself visible" to them (cf. 1 Cor. 15:5-8). Jesus also disappeared (Luke 24:31). Some take this to mean that Jesus was not essentially material, but simply materialized when He appeared to His disciples and dematerialized when He disappeared. However, other passages declare that Jesus had the same continuously material body of flesh and bones in which He died (Luke 24:39; John 20:27).

SOLUTION: That Jesus' resurrection body was essentially material is clear from the following facts. First of all, Christ's resurrection body could be seen with the naked eye during His appearances. They are described by the word *horaō* ("to see"). Although this word is sometimes used of seeing invisible realities (cf. Lk. 1:22; 24:23), it often means to see by the naked eye. For example, John uses the same word (*horaō*) of seeing Jesus in His earthly body before the Resurrection (6:36; 14:9; 19:35) and also of seeing Him in His resurrection body (20:18, 25, 29). Since the same word for body (*sōma*) is used of Jesus before and after the Resurrection (cf. 1 Cor. 15:44; Phil. 3:21), and since the same word for seeing it (*horaō*) is used of both, there is no reason for believing the resurrection body is not the same literal, physical body.

Furthermore, even in the phrase "he let Himself be seen" (aorist passive, *ophthē*), it simply means that Jesus took the initiative to show Himself to the disciples, not that He was essentially invisible. The same form ("He [they] appeared") is used in the Greek OT (2 Chron. 25:21), in the Apocrypha (1 Mac. 4:6), and in the NT (Acts 7:26) of purely human beings appearing in normal physical bodies. In this passive form the word means to initiate an appearance for public view, to move from a place where one is not seen to a place where one is seen. It does not necessarily mean that what is by nature invisible becomes visible. Rather, it means more generally "to come into view." There is no reason to understand it as referring to something invisible by nature becoming visible, as some do. For in this case it would mean that these human beings in normal pre-resurrection bodies were essentially invisible before they were seen by others.

Furthermore, the same event that is described by "He appeared" or "let Himself be seen" (aorist passive), such as the appearance to Paul (1 Cor. 15:8), is also described in the active voice. Paul wrote of this same experience in the same book, "Have I not seen Jesus Christ our Lord?" (1 Cor. 9:1). But if the resurrection body can be seen by the naked eye, then it is not invisible until it makes itself visible by some alleged "materialization."

Jesus also disappeared from the disciples on other occasions (see Luke 24:51; Acts 1:9). But if Jesus could disappear suddenly, as well as appear, then His ability to appear cannot be taken as evidence that His resurrection body was essentially invisible. For by the same reasoning His ability to disappear suddenly could be used as evidence that it was essentially material and could suddenly become immaterial.

Finally, there are much more reasonable explanations for the stress on Christ's self-initiated "appearances." First of all, they were the proof that He had conquered death (Acts 13:30-31; 17:31; Rom. 1:4). Jesus said, "I am He who lives, and was dead, and behold I am alive forever more. Amen. And I have the keys of Hades and of Death" (Rev. 1:18; cf. John 10:18). The translation ("He let Himself be seen," 1 Cor. 15:5ff) is a perfectly fitting way to express this self-initiated triumphalism. He was sovereign over death as well as His resurrection appearances.

Furthermore, no human being saw the actual moment of the Resurrection. But the fact that Jesus appeared repeatedly in the same body for some 40 days (Acts 1:3) to over 500 different people (1 Cor. 15:6) on 12 different occasions is indisputable evidence that He really rose bodily from the dead. In brief, the reason for the stress on the many appearances of Christ is not because the resurrection body was essentially invisible and immaterial, but rather to show that it was actually material and immortal. Without an empty tomb and repeated appearances of the same body that was once buried in it, there would be no proof of the Resurrection. So it is not surprising at all that the Bible strongly stresses the many appearances of Christ. They are the real proof of the physical Resurrection.

LUKE 24:44 — Was the OT divided by the Jews of Jesus' day into two or three parts?

PROBLEM: The Jewish Bible is divided into three sections — the Law, the Prophets, and the Writings. Many believe that Jesus is alluding to this threefold division in the phrase "the Law of Moses and the Prophets and the Psalms." However, the standard NT way of referring to the entire OT by Jesus and the NT writers was by the phrase "the Law and the Prophets" (cf. Matt. 5:17; Luke 24:27). Which is correct?

SOLUTION: The earliest reference to divisions or sections in the OT is twofold — Law and Prophets. This is true during the period of the Jewish exile (6th century B.C.), as indicated by Daniel (9:2, 11, 13), and also after the exile (Zech. 1:4; 7:7, 12; cf. Mal. 4:4, 5). References to the OT continued between the OT and NT in the Apocrypha (1 Mac. 4:45; 9:27; 2 Mac. 15:9), as well as in the Qumran community (*Manual of Discipline* 9.11). Also, as indicated, this is the standard way to refer to the divisions of the OT in the NT (cf. Matt. 5:17; Luke 24:27).

Furthermore, this phrase "Law and Prophets" included the whole OT (all 39 books), since Jesus said it referred to "all the Scriptures" (Luke 24:27). It also includes everything God revealed through prophets up to John the Baptist (Matt. 11:13). Indeed, the emphatic manner in which Jesus referred to not a "jot or tittle" of the OT passing away from the "Law or the Prophets" (Matt. 5:17-18) indicates He is referring to the entire OT.

However, there apparently was an early alternate way of dividing "the Prophets" into two sections which came to be known as Prophets and Writings. The "Prologue of Ecclesiasticus" (ca. 132 B.C.) uses a threefold division, as did the Jewish philosopher Philo (ca. A.D. 40). So did the Jewish historian Josephus (A.D. 37–100) just after Jesus' time (*Against Apion,* 1.8), even though he did not place the exact same books in this division as later Jewish groups did. The modern threefold classification into Law, Prophets, and Writings found in today's Jewish Bibles is derived from the *Babylonia Talmud* (ca. A.D. 4th cent.). So Jesus' reference in Luke 24:44 may or may not refer to this threefold division. It is interesting that He did not call the third group "Writings," but referred only to the Book of "Psalms." Some believe that He may have singled it out only because of its messianic significance. At any rate, Jesus had just referred to the standard twofold division of Law and Prophets calling it "all the Scriptures" (in Luke 24:27).

LUKE 24:49 – Why did the disciples go to Galilee when Jesus commanded them to stay in Jerusalem?

PROBLEM: According to Luke, the apostles were told to "tarry in the city of Jerusalem" until Pentecost. But Matthew tells us that they went into Galilee (Matt. 28:10, 16).

SOLUTION: First, it is possible that the command was not given until after they had been in Galilee. In this event there would be no conflict whatsoever. Furthermore, the command to "tarry" simply meant to make Jerusalem their headquarters. It did not preclude taking short trips elsewhere. Jerusalem was the place they were to receive the Holy Spirit (Luke 24:49) and to begin their work.

LUKE 24:50-51 — Did Jesus ascend from Bethany or from the Mountain of Olives near Jerusalem?

PROBLEM: Luke says Jesus ascended from Bethany (Luke 24:50), but Acts 1:9-11 affirms that He ascended from the Mt. of Olives near Jerusalem.

SOLUTION: Bethany was on the eastern slope of the Mt. of Olives, which is just east of Jerusalem. Luke, who wrote both passages (cf. Acts 1:1), saw no contradiction in referring to both places as the general location of Christ's ascension. Jesus may have begun His ascension from the mount, passing to the east over Bethany as He disappeared from their sight.

JOHN

JOHN 1:1 – Is Jesus God or just a god?

PROBLEM: Orthodox Christians believe Jesus is God and often appeal to this passage to prove it. However, Jehovah's Witnesses translate this verse "and the Word (Christ) was a god" because there is no definite article ("the") in the Greek of this verse.

SOLUTION: In Greek, when the definite article is used, it often stresses the *individual,* and, when it is not present, it refers to the *nature* of the one denoted. Thus, the verse can be rendered, "and the Word was of the nature of God." The full deity of Christ is supported not only by general usage of the same construction, but by other references in John to Jesus being God (cf. 8:58; 10:30; 20:28) and the rest of the NT (cf. Col. 1:15-16; 2:9; Titus 2:13).

Furthermore, some NT texts use the definite article and speak of Christ as "the God." So it does not matter whether John did or did not use the definite article here – the Bible clearly teaches that Jesus is God, not just a god (cf. Heb. 1:8).

That Jesus is Jehovah (Yahweh) is clear from the fact that the NT attributes to Jesus characteristics which in the OT apply only to God (cf. John 19:37 and Zech. 12:10).

JOHN 1:18 – Why does John say no one has seen God when other verses declare we will see God?

PROBLEM: On the one hand the Bible claims no one can see God, but on the other hand it says "Blessed are the pure in heart for they shall see God" (Matt. 5:8) and His servants "shall see His face" (Rev. 22:4) and "we shall see Him as He is" (1 John 3:2).

SOLUTION: The verses which teach that no man can see God are referring to no mortal man in this life. Even Moses was refused this honor (Ex. 33:23). Mortal man is not suited for that exposure. However, what mortal man cannot see in this life, immortal man will see in the next life (1 Cor. 13:12; Rev. 22:4). This is known as the beatific (blessed) vision and will be the spiritual climax of the believer to see God face-to-face, to know Him directly in His essence and not merely indirectly as reflected through created things (Rom. 1:18-20).

JOHN 1:18 – Was Jesus alone the Son of God?

PROBLEM: Jesus is called "the only begotten Son" in this verse. Yet only a few verses earlier John informs us that we can by faith "become children of God" (1:12). If then we are sons of God, how can Jesus be the only Son of God?

SOLUTION: There is a gigantic difference between the senses in which Jesus is the "Son of God" and we are "sons of God." First, He is the unique Son of God; I am only a son of God. He is the Son of God with a capital "S"; human beings can become sons of God only with a small "s." Jesus was the Son of God by eternal right of inheritance (Col. 1:15); we are only the sons of God by adoption (Rom. 8:15). He is the Son of God because He is God by His very nature (John 1:1), whereas we are only made in the image of God (Gen. 1:27) and remade in "the image of Him" by redemption (Col. 3:10). Jesus is *of* God by His very nature; we are only *from* God. He *is* divine in nature, but we only participate in it by salvation (2 Peter 1:4). And we can participate only in God's moral attributes (like holiness and love), not in His non-moral attributes (like infinity and eternality). To summarize the differences:

JESUS AS THE SON OF GOD	HUMANS AS SONS OF GOD
Natural Son	Adopted sons
No beginning	Beginning
Creator	Creature
God by nature	Not God by nature

JOHN 1:33 – Did John the Baptist know Jesus before His baptism or not?

PROBLEM: Before His baptism John said categorically, "I did not know Him." Yet in Matthew 3:13-14 John recognized Jesus before he baptized Him and said, "I have need to be baptized by You."

SOLUTION: John may have known Jesus before His baptism only by *reputation,* not by *recognition.* Or, he may have known Jesus only by *personal acquaintance,* but not by *divine manifestation.* After all, Jesus and John were relatives (Luke 1:36), even though they were reared in different places (Luke 1:80; 2:51). However, even though John may have had some previous family contact with Jesus, He had never known Jesus as He was revealed at His baptism when the Spirit descended on Him and the Father spoke from heaven (Matt. 3:16-17). The context indicates that, up to His baptism, no one really knew Jesus as He would then "be revealed to Israel" (John 1:31).

JOHN 1:37-49 – Were the apostles called at this time or later?

PROBLEM: John records that Jesus called Andrew, Peter, Philip, Nathanael, and another disciple at this time. However, the other Gospels record their call as taking place much later (cf. Matt. 4:18-22; Mark 1:16-20; Luke 5:1-11). When were they called?

SOLUTION: The first passages indicate Jesus' *initial interview* of the disciples, not their *permanent call.* As a result of this first contact they only stayed with Jesus "that day" (John 1:39), after which they returned to their homes and regular employment. The later passages indicate the time they left their former jobs and took up their full-time ministry as disciples of Christ.

JOHN 3:3 – Does being "born again" indicate that Jesus taught reincarnation?

PROBLEM: Traditionally, Christians have believed that the Bible does not teach the doctrine of reincarnation (cf. Heb. 9:27). However, many groups use this verse to claim that Jesus taught that it was necessary to be reincarnated.

SOLUTION: What Jesus is teaching in this passage is not reincarnation, but regeneration. This is clear from several facts. First, the doctrine of reincarnation teaches that, after a person dies, he enters another mortal body to live on this earth again. This process repeats itself over and over in a virtually endless cycle of birth, death, and rebirth into yet another mortal body. If Jesus were advocating reincarnation, He should have said, "unless someone is born again and again and again and again. . . ."

Second, the doctrine of reincarnation teaches that people die over and over until they reach perfection (Nirvana). However, the Bible clearly teaches that "it is appointed for men to die *once,* but after this the judgment" (Heb. 9:27).

Third, in the verses that follow, Jesus explains what He means by being born again. Jesus says, "unless one is born of water and the Spirit, he cannot enter the kingdom of God" (John 3:5). Although there are commentators who differ on exactly what this "water" means (see comments on John 3:5), they are all agreed that it cannot possibly refer to reincarnation. Being born again, then, is being cleansed from our sins, and being given the life of God by the Spirit of God (Rom. 3:21-26; Eph. 2:5; Col. 2:13).

JOHN 3:5 – Does this verse teach baptismal regeneration?

PROBLEM: Jesus told Nicodemus that "unless one is born of water and the Spirit, he cannot enter the kingdom of God." Does this mean a person has to be baptized to be saved?

SOLUTION: Baptism is not necessary for salvation (see comments on Acts 2:38). Salvation is by grace through faith and not by works of righteousness (Eph. 2:8-9; Titus 3:5-6). But baptism is a work of righteousness (cf. Matt. 3:15). What then did Jesus mean when He referred to being "born of water"? There are three basic ways to understand this, none of which involve baptismal regeneration.

Some believe Jesus is speaking of the *water of the womb,* since He had just mentioned one's "mother's womb" in the preceding verse. If so, then He was saying "unless you are born once by water (at your physical birth) and then again by the "Spirit" at your spiritual birth, you cannot be saved."

Others take "born of water" to refer to the "washing of *water by the word*" (Eph. 5:26). They note that Peter refers to being "born again . . . through the word of God" (1 Peter 1:23), the very thing John is speaking about in these verses (cf. John 3:3, 7).

Still others think that "born of water" refers to the *baptism of John* mentioned (John 1:26). John said he baptized by water, but Jesus would baptize by the Spirit (Matt. 3:11), saying, "repent for the kingdom of heaven is at hand (Matt. 3:2). If this is what is meant, then when Jesus said they must be "born of water and the Spirit" (John 3:5) He meant that the Jews of His day had to undergo the baptism of repentance by John and also later the baptism of the Holy Spirit before they could "enter the kingdom of God."

JOHN 3:13 — How could Christ say no one has ascended to heaven when Elijah had?

PROBLEM: Jesus declared in this text that "No one has ascended to heaven. . . ." However, the OT records Elijah's ascension into heaven in a chariot (2 Kings 2:11).

SOLUTION: In this context, Jesus is setting forth His superior knowledge of heavenly things. In essence He is saying, "No other human being can speak from firsthand knowledge about these things, as I can, since I came down from heaven." He is claiming that no one has ascended to heaven to bring down the message that He brought. In no way is He denying that anyone else is *in* heaven, such as Elijah and Enoch (Gen. 5:24). Rather, Jesus is simply claiming that no one on earth has gone *to* heaven and *returned* with a message such as He offered to them.

JOHN 3:17 — Did Jesus come to judge the world or not?

PROBLEM: According to this verse, God did not "send His Son into the world to condemn the world, but that the world through Him might be saved." He added later, "I judge no one" (John 8:15; cf. 12:47). However, in other places Jesus claimed "authority to execute judgment also, because He is the Son of Man" (John 5:27). Indeed, He even claimed, "For judgment I have come into this world" (John 9:39) and the Father "has committed all judgment to the Son" (John 5:22).

SOLUTION: These verses were spoken in different contexts and with different references. In general, the references to Jesus sitting in judgment on the human race are references to His second coming (see Rev. 19–20), while verses about His not coming to judge but to save have His first coming in mind. Sometimes Jesus is simply speaking about not acting as an earthly judge during His life on earth. A case in point is His answer to the man who wanted him to arbitrate the family inheritance: "Man, who made Me a judge or an arbitrator over you?" (Luke 12:14).

Another distinction that clears up some difficulties is found between the real *purpose* of Christ's coming (to save those who believe) and the net *effect* of it (to judge those who don't believe). His statement that "for judgment I have come into this world" (John 9:39) seems to fit this latter category (cf. v. 40).

JOHN 4:26 – Why did Jesus confess He was the Messiah here, but avoid doing it elsewhere?

PROBLEM: In the synoptic Gospels (Matthew, Mark, and Luke) Jesus seemed to go out of His way to avoid claiming He was the Jewish Messiah. He would ask His disciples in private (Matt 16:13) and would sometimes exhort people who discovered it "to tell no man" (see comments on Matt. 16:20). Yet here in John the woman of Samaria said, "I know that Messiah is coming who is called Christ" (John 4:25). Jesus forthrightly volunteered, "I who speak to you am He" (v. 26).

SOLUTION: Here Jesus was in Samaria, not Judea. The Jews of Jesus' day had a distorted concept of the Messiah, namely, as one who would deliver them from the political oppression of Rome. In this context, Jesus was more careful to make His claims more covert, so as to elicit from His disciples a more spiritual concept of the one who came to redeem His people (cf. Luke 19:10; John 10:10).

Indeed, this is why Jesus so often spoke in parables, so that those who were truly seeking would understand, but those who had a false concept would be confused (see Matt. 13:13). This is why when Jesus performed miracles He would sometimes exhort the person to tell no one, since He did not want to be thronged by the curious. Indeed, Jesus rebuked those who, having seen Him multiply the loaves, wanted to make Him king (John 6:15), declaring that they followed Him "because you ate of the loaves and were filled" (v. 26). However, in Samaria, where this false Jewish concept of a political deliverer from Rome who could feed the masses did not prevail, Jesus did not hesitate to claim that He indeed was the true Messiah. Furthermore, Jesus said this to only one Samaritan woman in private, not to the masses of Jews in Judea.

Nonetheless, Jesus did claim to be the Messiah in public, in Judea and to the Jews. Usually, however, His claim was more covert, trying to get them to discover for themselves who He was. However, when the chips were down and it became necessary to declare Himself before the high priest, Jesus explicitly answered the question "Are You the Christ, the Son of the Blessed" by declaring, "I am [the Christ]" (Mark 14:61-62; cf. Matt. 26:64; cf. Luke 22:70).

JOHN 5:28-29 – Is Jesus advocating salvation by works?

PROBLEM: Jesus says in John's Gospel that the time is coming when people in the graves will hear His voice "and come forth – those who have done good, to the resurrection of life, and those who have done evil, to the resurrection of condemnation" (v. 29). This seems to be a clear contradiction to salvation by grace (cf. Eph. 2:8-9).

SOLUTION: First, Jesus does not believe in salvation by works. In the beginning of John's Gospel, John writes, "But as many as received Him, to them He gave the right to become children of God, even to those who believe in His name: who were born, not of blood, nor of the will of the flesh, nor of the will of man, but of God" (John 1:12-13). Jesus says in John 3:16-18:

> For God so loved the world that He gave His only begotten Son, that whoever *believes* in Him should not perish but have everlasting life.
>
> For God did not send His Son into the world to condemn the world, but that the world through Him might be saved. He who *believes* in Him is not condemned; but he who does not believe is condemned already, because he has not *believed* in the name of the only begotten Son of God.

Furthermore, in John 5:24, Jesus says, "Truly, truly, I say to you, he who hears My word, and *believes* Him who sent Me, has eternal life" (NASB). From these passages it is clear that Jesus did not believe in works salvation.

Second, Jesus' reference to good works in John 5:28-29 is to that which occurs after saving faith. To be saved, one needs the grace of God (Eph. 2:8-9), but authentic faith expresses itself in good works (v. 10). The Apostle Paul in the Book of Romans, says something very similar to what Jesus says in John 5:28-29. In Romans Paul says that God "will render to every man according to his deeds: to those who by perseverance in doing good seek for glory and honor and immortality, eternal life; but to those who are selfishly ambitious and do not obey the truth, but obey unrighteousness, wrath and indignation" (Rom. 2:6-8, NASB). But Paul also wrote, "For by grace you have been saved through faith, and that *not of yourselves;* it is the gift of God" (Eph. 2:8). In the passage in Romans, Paul is not talking about the one who obtains eternal life by faith, but the individual who shows this life in his good works. In Ephesians, Paul is saying that none can save himself by works *prior* to salvation. (See also comments on James 2:21.)

So, Jesus does not contradict Himself nor the rest of Scripture concerning the matter of salvation. Those who receive the resurrection of life have shown their saving faith by their works.

JOHN 5:31 — Was Jesus' self-testimony true or false?

PROBLEM: In John 8:14 Jesus said, "If I bear witness of Myself, My witness is true." But here in John 5:31 He seems to say just the opposite, namely, "If I bear witness of Myself, My witness is not true."

SOLUTION: There are two ways to understand this verse — hypothetically or actually. On the first interpretation, Jesus is saying in essence, "Even *if* you don't accept my testimony about Myself, you should accept that of John the Baptist in whose ministry you rejoiced" (cf. 5:32).

Others take the verse as declarative, not hypothetical, claiming both texts are true, but in different senses. That is, everything Jesus said was actually true, but officially it was only considered true if it was verified by "two or three witnesses" (Deut. 19:15). Since Jesus was "truth" incarnate (John 14:6), everything He said was true. However, since He is trying to establish His claims to the Jews, He notes that they need not accept His words alone, but also the witness of the Scriptures and the Father. The difference between these two passages can be outlined as follows:

JESUS' SELF-WITNESS WAS TRUE	JESUS' SELF-WITNESS WASN'T TRUE
Actually	Officially
Personally	Legally
In itself	To the Jews

JOHN 5:34 — Did Jesus accept human testimony about who He was?

PROBLEM: In this verse Jesus rejected human testimony about Himself, insisting, "I do not receive testimony from man." But elsewhere He accepted Peter's testimony that He was the Christ, the Son of the Living God (Matt. 16:16-18). In fact, even in this same book (John 15:27) Jesus said to His disciples, "And you also will bear witness, because you have been with Me from the beginning."

SOLUTION: The difference in these statements is due to the circumstances of the testimony. He did not accept mere human testimony to *establish* who He was, but He did accept it to *propagate* who He was. God, by miraculous acts, established who Jesus was (cf. Acts 2:22; Heb. 2:3-4), not human beings. On the other hand, once humans *discovered* what God had *disclosed,* their testimony was valid. Even after Peter's great confession, Jesus reminded him that "flesh and blood has not revealed this to you" (Matt. 16:17). The matter can be summarized in this way:

HUMAN TESTIMONY COULD NOT	HUMAN TESTIMONY COULD
Disclose who Jesus was Establish who He was Prove who He was	Discover who Jesus was Disseminate who He was Propagate who He was

JOHN 5:37 – Can God's voice be heard?

PROBLEM: Jesus declared to the Jews, "You have neither heard His [God's] voice at any time, nor seen His form." Yet the voice of God was heard many times in the OT (cf. 1 Sam. 3:4-14), and the Father spoke from heaven three times during Jesus' earthly ministry (Matt. 3:17; 17:5; John 12:28).

SOLUTION: There are a number of interpretations of this passage. First, some claim that Jesus is simply referring to the crowd to whom He is ministering here, thus, not excluding the fact that God's voice had been heard by others. However, this seems unlikely in view of the sweeping phrase "at any time," as well as the fact that Jesus seems to be addressing the Jewish nation in general which rejected Him (cf. John 1:10-11; 5:39; 12:37).

Second, still others believe Jesus is contrasting their state of knowledge with that of the OT prophets who heard God's voice and saw His form (manifested in theophanies). If so, their inability to understand it was due to the fact that they were "not willing" to respond to God speaking in and through it (John 5:40).

Third, many scholars hold that this refers to their not heeding God's *unique* or inner voice speaking to their hearts, since they were not receptive to His Word (cf. 1 Cor. 2:14). This fits with the fact that they could search the Scripture (John 5:39) and still miss its main message, Christ. In addition, the reference to the Father's testimony of Him (v. 37) may be a reference to the voice from heaven at Jesus' baptism, which, like the later voice from heaven (John 12:28), they dismissed as "thunder" (John 12:29).

JOHN 6:35 – Why are the "I AM" statements of Jesus only mentioned in John?

PROBLEM: John mentions numerous times that Jesus said "I Am" (e.g., John 6:35; 8:58; 10:9; 14:6). Yet not one of these statements is mentioned in any other Gospel. Did John make these up, or did Jesus actually say them?

SOLUTION: John reported accurately what he heard and saw. First of all, he was an eyewitness of the events (John 21:24; cf. 1 John 1:1). His Gospel is filled with details of geography (3:23), topography (6:10), and private conversations that betray a first-hand, first-century knowledge of the events (cf. John 3; 4; 13–17).

Further, when John records events and/or conversation found in the other Gospels, he does so in substantially the same way they do. This includes the preaching of John the Baptist (1:19-28), the feeding of the 5,000 (6:1-14), Jesus' walking on the water (6:15-21), eating the Passover with His disciples (13:1-2), Peter's denial (13:36-38; 18:15-27), Judas' betrayal (18:1-11), His trials (18-19), His crucifixion (19), and His resurrection (20-21).

In addition, the other Gospels record some of the same types of conversation recorded in John. Matthew 11:25-30 sounds like something right out of the Gospel of John. Even Jesus' characteristic use of "verily" (KJV), ("truly," NASB; "assuredly," NKJV) in John (cf. 1:51; 3:3, 11; 5:19, 24, etc.) is found in other Gospels (cf. Matt. 5:18, 26; Mark 3:28; 9:1; Luke 4:24; 18:17), though John alone doubles it perhaps for emphasis.

Finally, John's differences from the synoptics can be accounted for in several ways. First of all, John writes primarily about Jesus' Judean ministry, whereas the other Gospels speak largely about His Galilean ministry. Second, John records many of Jesus' private conversations (cf. chaps. 3–4; 13–17), whereas the other Gospels speak mostly about His public ministry. Third, clear "I Am" statements come usually after Jesus has been challenged and He declares His point simply and emphatically. Even so, they are not without parallel in the other Gospels, where Jesus says "I am" [the Christ] (Mark 14:62).

JOHN 6:53-54 — What did Jesus mean when He said we should eat His flesh?

PROBLEM: Evangelical Christians believe in taking the Bible literally. But Jesus said, "unless you eat the flesh of the Son of Man and drink His blood, you have no life in you" (John 6:53). Should this be taken literally too?

SOLUTION: The literal (i.e., actual) meaning of a text is the correct one, but the literal meaning does not mean that everything should be taken literally. For example, the literal meaning of Jesus' statement, "I am the true vine" (John 15:1) is that He is the real source of our spiritual life.

But it does not mean that Jesus is a literal vine with leaves growing out of His arms and ears! Literal meaning can be communicated by means of figures of speech. Christ is the actual foundation of the church (1 Cor. 3:11; Eph. 2:20), but He is not literally a granite cornerstone with engraving on it.

There are many indications in John 6 that Jesus literally meant that the command to "eat His flesh" should be taken in a figurative way. First, Jesus indicated that His statement should not be taken in a materialistic sense when He said, "The words that I speak to you are spirit, and they are life" (John 6:63). Second, it is absurd and cannibalistic to take it in a physical way. Third, He was not speaking of physical life, but "eternal life" (John 6:54). Fourth, He called Himself the "bread of life" (John 6:48) and contrasted this with the physical bread the Jews ate in the wilderness (John 6:58). Fifth, He used the figure of "eating" His flesh in parallel with the idea of "abiding" in Him (cf. John 15:4-5), which is another figure of speech. Neither figure is to be taken literally. Sixth, if eating His flesh and drinking His blood be taken in a literalistic way, this would contradict other commands of Scripture not to eat human flesh and blood (cf. Acts 15:20). Finally, in view of the figurative meaning here, this verse cannot be used to support the Roman Catholic concept of transubstantiation, that is, eating Jesus' actual body in the communion (see comments on Luke 22:19).

JOHN 7:1 — Why did Jesus fear death and yet tell His disciples not to do so?

PROBLEM: John informs us here that "Jesus walked in Galilee; for He did not want to walk in Judea, because the Jews sought to kill Him." Yet Jesus said to His disciples, "My friends, do not be afraid of those who kill the body" (Luke 12:4).

SOLUTION: Jesus did not fear death; He merely avoided dying *prematurely*. Before the appropriate time Jesus would say, "My hour has not yet come" (John 2:4; 8:20). But when "His hour came" (cf. John 12:23), Jesus faced death bravely and courageously. Though humanly speaking Jesus shrunk from the horror of the Cross (see comments on Heb. 5:7b); nevertheless, He prayed, "what shall I say? 'Father, save Me from this hour'?" to which He answered with an emphatic *no*: "But for this purpose I came to this hour" (John 12:27). Jesus knew from the very beginning that He had come to die (cf. John 2:19-20; 10:10-11), and He never hesitated in His resolute purpose "to give His life a ransom

for many" (Mark 10:45). However, to accomplish this as God had ordained and the prophets predicted, Jesus had to watch out for attempts
on His life before the appointed time and way. For example, He was to
be crucified (cf. Ps. 22:16; Zech. 12:10), not to be stoned, as the Jews
sought to do on one occasion (see John 10:32-33).

JOHN 7:8 – Did Jesus lie to His brothers?

PROBLEM: Jesus' unbelieving brothers challenged Him to go up to Jerusalem and show Himself openly if He was the Messiah (7:3-4). Jesus
refused, saying, "I am not yet going up to this feast, for My time has not
yet fully come" (v. 8). However, only a few verses later Jesus "went up to
the feast" (v. 10).

SOLUTION: Jesus did not go up to Jerusalem in the way in which His
brothers suggested. They suggested He go and be "known openly"
(7:4). But the Scripture explicitly declares that "He also went up to the
feast, *not openly,* but as it were in secret" (7:10).

**JOHN 7:53-8:11 – Why do some scholars question whether this story
should be in the Bible?**

PROBLEM: This story of the woman taken in adultery is found in the
KJV, the ASV, the NASB, and the NIV. However, the NEB places it at the
end of the Gospel under the caption "An incident in the temple." And
since 1971 the RSV places it in special print set off from the rest of the
text, as does the NRSV. The standard Greek NT (Nestle-Aland Text,
United Bible Societies) places brackets around it, indicating that it is not
part of the text of John. Why do many scholars believe this story is not
part of the original manuscript of the Gospel of John?

SOLUTION: There are several reasons why many scholars question
whether this passage belongs here in John's Gospel. (1) The passage does
not appear in the oldest and most reliable Greek manuscripts. (2) It is
not found in the best manuscripts of the earliest translations of the Bible
into Old Syriac, Coptic, Gothic, and Old Latin. (3) No Greek writer
commented on this passage for the first 11 centuries of Christianity.
(4) It is not cited by most of the great early church fathers, including
Clement, Tertullian, Origen, Cyprian, Cyril, and others. (5) Its style does
not fit that of the rest of the Gospel of John. (6) It interrupts the flow of
thought in John. John reads better if one goes right from John 7:52 to
8:12. (7) The story has been found in several different places in Bible

manuscripts—after John 7:36; after John 21:24; after John 7:44; and after Luke 21:38. (8) Many manuscripts that include it in John 7:53–8:11 have marked it with an obelus, indicating they believe it is doubtful.

In spite of this, many Bible scholars believe this story is authentic. It certainly contains no doctrinal error and fits with the character of Jesus and His teaching, but there is no certainty that it was in the original text of John.

JOHN 8:3-11 (cf. ROM. 13:4) — Did Jesus repudiate capital punishment in this text?

PROBLEM: Passages like Romans 13:4 present a good case for capital punishment, for the passage says, "for it [the government] does not bear a sword for nothing; for it is a minister of God, an avenger who brings wrath upon the one who practices evil" (NASB). In John 8 a woman is caught in an adulterous situation, which was cause for stoning according to the Mosaic Law. Yet Jesus did not seek her death, but rather forgave her sin. Did Jesus thereby reject capital punishment?

SOLUTION: First, the authority in Romans 13 is the Roman government and the authorities in John 8 are Jewish ones. The point is that the Jews had to act under Roman law. For instance, if they were really going to stone a woman, why did they seek the help of Pilate in the crucifixion of Jesus? For in John 18:31 the Jews respond to Pilate saying, "It is not lawful for us to put anyone to death." But in the case of the adulterous woman, they were ready to stone her.

Second, they did not act in accordance with the Law itself. The Law stated that *both* the parties, male and female, had to be brought before the people (Deut. 22:22-24). Since this woman was caught in the very act (v.4), why wasn't the man brought out with the woman to be stoned? The scribes and Pharisees who were supposed to be law abiding citizens failed in a key aspect of their own law.

Third, the motives of these scribes and Pharisees were wrong. They used this opportunity to try to trap Jesus so that they might have a reason for accusing Him (v.6). The crime of adultery did not seem important to them. Rather, it seemed more important to find cause for accusation against Jesus.

This passage, then, is not a good text for anyone who wants to propose that Jesus opposed capital punishment. In fact, other places of Scripture seem to support the very idea (see Gen. 9:6 and Matt. 26:52).

JOHN 9:31 — Does God hear the prayers of sinners?

PROBLEM: John said here, "Now we know that God does not hear sinners." Yet Jesus said God heard the publican who prayed, "God be merciful to me a sinner" (Luke 18:13). Does He hear sinners when they pray?

SOLUTION: God hears sinners when they confess they are sinners and accept His forgiveness. For "whoever calls upon the name of the Lord shall be saved" (Rom. 10:13). Jesus promised, "the one who comes to Me I will by no means cast out" (John 6:37).

However, God does not promise to answer the prayers of sinners who are not serving the true God. Jesus said, "if anyone is a worshiper of God and does His will, He [God] hears him" (John 9:31). Even so, God's grace exceeds His promise, and He apparently does on occasion respond to the prayer of an unsaved person as part of His overall providential plan to bring them to Himself (cf. Jonah 1:14-15). In this sense, God's response to the prayer of the unsaved is part of the "goodness of God [that] leads you to repentance" (Rom. 2:4).

JOHN 10:11 — Is Jesus the shepherd or a sheep?

PROBLEM: John presents Christ here as the "Good Shepherd." Yet elsewhere He is a sheep (lamb) that dies for our sins (John 1:29, 36). Which is He?

SOLUTION: Christ is appropriately presented by both figures of speech. He died as our Passover Lamb (1 Cor. 5:7), and He leads and guides His people as a Good Shepherd. In one context, believers are like the people of Israel who need the passover lamb to die for them. In the other, we are like wandering sheep who need a shepherd to lead us. Both are true.

JOHN 10:11 — Did Jesus die just for His friends or for His enemies too?

PROBLEM: John quotes Jesus as claiming that He laid down His "life for the sheep" (cf. 15:13). But Paul claims "Christ died for the ungodly" while they were still "enemies" (Rom. 5:6, 10). How can both be true?

SOLUTION: Jesus died for both His friends (disciples) and His enemies. In fact, His "friends" were enemies when He died for them. There is no contradiction here, since the text does not say that Christ died *only* for His friends. He did die for those who would become His friends, but He also died for those who would remain His enemies. Peter refers to the apostates who were "denying the Lord who bought them" (2 Peter 2:1).

JOHN 10:30 – Was Christ one with the Father?

PROBLEM: Jesus said here, "I and My Father are one." But on other occasions He distinguished Himself from the Father, saying "I came forth from the Father and . . . I leave the world and go to the Father" (John 16:28). Further, He prayed to the Father as one person to another (John 17), and even said, "the Father is greater than I."

SOLUTION: Jesus was one with the Father in *nature,* but distinct from Him in *person.* The triune Godhead has one *essence,* but three distinct *persons* (see comments on John 14:28). So, Jesus was both the same in substance and yet was a different individual from the Father.

JOHN 10:34 – Did Jesus advocate that man could become God?

PROBLEM: Jesus answered a group of Jews and said, "Is it not written in your law, 'I said, you are gods'?" Does this mean that humans can become God as pantheistic religions and New Age advocates claim?

SOLUTION: The context of this passage reveals that Christ had just pronounced Himself one with the Father saying, "I and My Father are one" (10:30). The Jews wanted to stone Him because they thought Christ was blaspheming since He was making Himself out to be equal with God (vv. 31-33).

Jesus responded by quoting Psalm 82:6 which says, "I said, you are gods." This psalm addresses judges who are judging unjustly. The title of "gods" is not addressed to everyone, but only to these judges about whom Jesus said are those to "whom the word of God came" (v. 35). Jesus was showing that if the OT Scriptures could give some divine status to divinely appointed judges, why should they find it incredible that He should call Himself the Son of God? Thus, Jesus was giving a defense for His own deity, not for the deification of man.

JOHN 11:4 – Did Jesus make a mistake when He said Lazarus' sickness was not unto death?

PROBLEM: Jesus at first said, "This sickness is not unto death" (John 11:4). However, later even Jesus admitted that "Lazarus is dead" (v. 14). Was Jesus mistaken when He thought Lazarus would not die?

SOLUTION: Jesus knew all along that Lazarus would die and that He would raise him from the dead so that God would receive the glory (v. 4). He used different figures of speech to teach the disciples that Lazarus' death was not final. He called it "sleep" (v. 11) and said it was "not unto death" (v. 4), meaning that it would not *eventuate* in Lazarus' being dead, but in his being alive by Jesus' resurrection power. That is, although Lazarus' sickness would *temporarily* bring death, Jesus' power would restore him to life.

JOHN 11:26 – How could Jesus say we will never die when the Bible declares all will eventually die?

PROBLEM: God Himself said to Adam, "In the day that you eat of it you shall surely die" (Gen. 2:17). Paul reaffirmed this, declaring that "through one man sin entered the world, and death through sin, and thus death spread to all men, because all sinned" (Rom. 5:12). But Jesus seems to contradict this when He affirmed, "whoever lives and believes in Me shall never die" (John 11:26).

SOLUTION: First of all, even taken literally, Jesus was not denying that believers would die. In fact, He affirmed it in the previous verse, saying, "though he may die, he shall live." In other words, Jesus claimed that because He was "the resurrection and the life" (v. 25), He would resurrect those who believe in Him unto eternal life (cf. John 5:28-29).

Further, Jesus may have been speaking about spiritual life and spiritual death. In this sense, those who believe in Him will have spiritual life (John 3:16, 36), even though they will experience physical death. For those who are born only once will die twice, once physically and once again at the "second death" (Rev. 20:14) or final separation from God. But those who are born twice (John 3:3, 7) will only die once (physically), but will live with God forever.

JOHN 11:44 – How could Lazarus come forth from the tomb if he was bound hand and foot?

PROBLEM: This verse states what seems impossible, namely, when Jesus raised Lazarus "he who had died came out bound hand and foot."

SOLUTION: It is not impossible. The Jewish corpses were not wound so tight (like an Egyptian mummy) that it precluded all motion. When life came back into Lazarus body he was no doubt jolted into action. He could have slid from his slab, stood upright on the floor, and if necessary, even jumped to the cave opening. Nothing more than this is implied in the term "came forth." Having done what only He could do (namely, raise Lazarus from the dead), Jesus expected Lazarus and others to do what they could do. So Jesus asked them to unloose Lazarus' cords.

JOHN 14:2-3 — Was heaven prepared from eternity or is Jesus still preparing it?

PROBLEM: Matthew affirms that heaven was "prepared for you from the foundation of the world" (25:34). But here in John 14:2 Jesus said, "I go to prepare a place for you," implying that it was not yet prepared at that time.

SOLUTION: The first text speaks about the *creation* of heaven and the second about its *preparation*. The former passage speaks in *general* about the preexistence of heaven; the latter *specifically* about its preadaptation to each particular soul. There is a dual preparation of heaven for each person and each person for heaven. Since individual believers will have different rewards (1 Cor. 3:11-15; 2 Cor. 5:10), then their reward in heaven, which already exists, will have to be suited to their particular service.

JOHN 14:16 — Are Muslims right in referring this promise of the coming "helper" to Mohammed?

PROBLEM: Muslim scholars see in this reference of the promised "Helper" (Gk., *paraklētos*) a prediction of Mohammed, because the Quran (Surah 61:6) refers to Mohammed as "Ahmad" (*periclytos*) which they take to be the correct rendering of *"paraklētos."*

SOLUTION: There are absolutely no grounds for concluding the "Helper" (*paraklētos*) Jesus mentioned here is Mohammed. First of all, of the 5,366 Greek manuscripts of the NT, not a single manuscript contains the word *periclytos* ("praised one"), as the Muslims claim it should read. Second, Jesus clearly identifies the "Helper" as the Holy Spirit, not Mohammed. Jesus referred to "the Helper, the Holy Spirit, whom the Father will send" (John 14:26). Third, the "Helper" was given to His disciples ("you," v. 16), but Mohammed was not. Fourth, the "Helper" was to abide with them "forever" (v. 16), but Mohammed has been dead for 13 centuries! Fifth, Jesus said to the disciples, "You know Him [the Helper]" (v. 17), but they did not know Mohammed. He wasn't even born for 6 more centuries. Sixth, Jesus told His apostles, the Helper will be "in you" (v.17). In no sense was Mohammed "in" Jesus' apostles. Seventh, our Lord affirmed the Helper would be sent "In My [Jesus'] name" (John 14:26). But no Muslim believes Mohammed was sent by Jesus in His name. Eighth, the Helper Jesus would send would not "speak on His own authority" (John 16:13), whereas Mohammed constantly testifies to himself in the Quran (cf. Surah 33:40). Ninth, the

Helper would "glorify" Jesus (John 16:14), but Mohammed claims to supersede Jesus, being a later prophet. Finally, Jesus asserted that the Helper would come in "not many days" (Acts 1:5), whereas Mohammed did not come for 600 years.

JOHN 14:28 – Did Jesus think of Himself as less than God?

PROBLEM: Orthodox Christianity confesses Jesus is both fully man and fully God. Yet Jesus said in John 14:28, "My Father is greater than I." How can the Father be greater if Jesus is equal to God?

SOLUTION: The Father is greater than the Son by *office,* but not by *nature,* since both are God (see John 1:1; 8:58; 10:30). Just as an earthly father is equally human with, but holds a higher office than, his son, even so the Father and the Son in the Trinity are equal in *essence,* but different in *function.* In like manner, we speak of the president of our country as being a greater man, not by virtue of his *character,* but by virtue of his *position.* Therefore, Jesus cannot ever be said to say that He considered Himself anything less than God by nature. The following summary helps to crystalize the differences:

JESUS IS EQUAL TO THE FATHER	THE FATHER IS GREATER THAN JESUS
In essence	In function
In nature	In office
In character	In position

JOHN 15:1 – Was Jesus the vine or the root?

PROBLEM: John portrays Jesus as the vine of which believers are the branches. But elsewhere the Bible calls Him a "root out of dry ground" (Isa. 53:2).

SOLUTION: Both of these are appropriate figures of Christ, each describing a different aspect of His ministry. Jesus was a root (source of life) in relation to the vine (Israel) in the OT. But He is the vine in which believers abide for spiritual life in the NT (John 15:1, 3).

JOHN 16:12 – Did Jesus reveal everything to His disciples or hold back some things?

PROBLEM: Only a short time earlier Jesus left His disciples with the impression that He had told them everything He wanted to communicate to them, saying, "all things that I heard from My Father I have made known to you" (John 15:15). However, here in John 16:12 He reveals, "I still have many things to say to you, but you cannot bear them now." It appears that these statements are in conflict.

SOLUTION: Some scholars believe that the first statement is proleptical, envisioning in the present everything He was about to tell them in the future as well. In this case, the "many things" (of 16:12) would refer to what the Holy Spirit was yet to teach them (cf. 16:13).

However, in light of the fact that these are in the same discourse, the latter seems to be a qualification of the former. Thus, the earlier statement means "All that the Father has designed for you *at present,* I have revealed to you." In other words, Jesus faithfully communicated what the Father wanted them to know and *when* the Father wanted them to know it.

JOHN 17:9 – Did Jesus ever pray for unbelievers?

PROBLEM: Jesus said here, "I pray for them [the disciples]. I do not pray for the world." But elsewhere Jesus prayed for unbelievers, even those who crucified Him, saying, "Father, forgive them, for they do not know what they do" (Luke 23:34).

SOLUTION: In His high priestly prayer, Jesus was *focusing* on His disciples, not on the world. This does not mean that we should never pray for the world. Indeed, Jesus died for the sins of the world (John 3:16; 1 John 2:1-2; Rom. 5:6-8). He prayed that the Father would forgive those who crucified Him (Luke 23:34). He also asked His disciples to "pray the Lord of the harvest to send out laborers into His harvest" (Luke 10:2). Jesus' followers urged "prayers . . . for all men" (1 Tim. 2:1). And, the Apostle Paul prayed passionately for his unsaved kinsmen (Rom. 10:1).

JOHN 18:31 – Was it lawful for the Jews to exercise capital punishment?

PROBLEM: In this verse, the Jews of Jesus' day claimed that "It is not lawful for us to put anyone to death." However, in the very next chapter, they insisted that "We have a law, and according to our law He ought to die" (John 19:7). Which was correct?

SOLUTION: Both statements are correct. According to the *Jewish Law* of Moses, anyone who blasphemes God was to be given capital punishment (see Lev. 24:16). However, when speaking to Pilate, the Roman governor, the Jews correctly noted that the Romans did not allow their subjects to exercise capital punishment, but retained that right for themselves. Thus, the Jews correctly said to Pilate, "it is not lawful [according to *Roman law*] for us to put anyone to death" (John 18:31).

JOHN 19:14 – Was Jesus crucified on Friday?

(See discussion on Matt. 12:40.)

JOHN 19:14 – What time was Jesus placed on the cross?

(See comments on Mark 15:25.)

JOHN 19:19 – What did the sign on the cross really say?

(See discussion on Matt. 27:37.)

JOHN 20:17 – If Jesus had not yet ascended to the Father, how could He have committed His Spirit to the Father?

PROBLEM: Jesus said here "I have not yet ascended to My Father." But earlier on the cross He said, "Father, into Your hands I commend My spirit" (Luke 23:46). If He was already with the Father, then why did He say that He had not yet ascended to Him?

SOLUTION: The day He died, Jesus' spirit went to be with the Father (as Luke 23:43, 46 records). So His *spirit* had been with the Father, but His *body* had not yet ascended into heaven when He spoke to Mary. The bodily ascension took place some 40 days later (cf. Acts 1:3, 9-10).

JOHN 20:19 – How could Jesus walk through a closed door with a physical body?

PROBLEM: It is inferred by some critics that, since the resurrected Christ could appear in a room with closed doors (John 20:19), this proves that

His body must have dematerialized to do so, showing that His resurrection body was not essentially or continuously material. However, many other Scriptures indicate that Jesus' resurrection body was literal "flesh and bones" (Luke 24:39) that could eat physical food and even had the crucifixion scars in it (Luke 24:40-43).

SOLUTION: Jesus' resurrection body was essentially and continuously material (see comments on Luke 24:34). The fact that Jesus could get into a room with a closed door in no way proves that He had to dematerialize in order to do it. This is clear for several reasons.

First, the text does not actually say Jesus passed through a closed door. It simply says that "when the doors were shut where the disciples were assembled, for fear of the Jews, Jesus came and stood in the midst" (John 20:19). The Bible does not say *how* He got into the room.

Second, if He chose to do so, Jesus could have performed this same miracle before His death in His pre-resurrection material body. As the Son of God, His miraculous powers were just as great before the Resurrection.

Third, even before His resurrection Jesus performed miracles with His physical body that transcended natural laws, such as walking on water (John 6:16-20). But walking on water did not prove that His pre-resurrection body was immaterial. Otherwise, Peter's pre-resurrection walk on water (Matt. 14:29) would mean his body dematerialized for a moment and then quickly rematerialized!

Fourth, although physical, the resurrection body is by its very nature a supernatural body (see comments on 1 Cor. 15:44). Hence, it should be expected that it can do supernatural things, such as appearing in a room with closed doors.

Fifth, according to modern physics, it is not an impossibility for a material object to pass through a door. It is only statistically improbable. Physical objects are mostly empty space. All that is necessary for one physical object to pass through another is for the right alignment of the particles in the two physical objects. This is no problem for the One who created the body in the first place.

JOHN 20:22 — Was the Holy Spirit given to the disciples before Pentecost?

PROBLEM: In Acts, the apostles are told to wait until Pentecost before they receive the Holy Spirit (Acts 1:4-8; cf. 2:1-2). Yet even before His crucifixion Jesus breathed on His disciples and said, "Receive the Holy

Spirit" (John 20:22). Didn't they receive the Holy Spirit at this point and not later at Pentecost?

SOLUTION: First of all, the John passage is a difficult one, with no direct parallels, and it is hard to know exactly what it means. And like all obscure passages, one should not base any major teaching on it.

Second, some scholars believe that the imperative "receive" is intended to denote the future "you will receive." If so, then there is no conflict.

Third, even if Jesus meant them to receive the Holy Spirit at that moment (in John 20:22), it was apparently in a *different sense*. Here the Spirit is given *"to forgive the sins"* (v. 23). But in Acts 1:8 the Spirit was to be given to provide *"power ... [to] be witnesses"* for Him to the "end of the earth."

Fourth, the promise of the Spirit in John was for His *indwelling* the believer (cf. John 14:16), not for His being baptized by the Holy Spirit (Acts 1:5; cf. 1 Cor. 12:13), which is a different act of the Holy Spirit. In this sense, then, there is no conflict between the two passages, since they speak of different activities of the Spirit which came at different times.

JOHN 20:22-23 – Does this passage support the Roman Catholic view that priests have the power to forgive sins?

PROBLEM: Roman Catholics claim that Jesus gave His disciples the power to forgive sins and that this power has been passed on to Roman Catholic priests down through the centuries. Does this text support their position?

SOLUTION: Jesus did give His disciples the power to forgive sins, and this power still exists today. However, it is not unique to Roman Catholic priests. Any believer in Christ possesses the same power to pronounce someone's sins forgiven, based on their trust in the finished work of Christ. Notice the context of the passage.

First of all, many see this as an extension of the power promised in Matthew 18:18 to bind and loose sins with the "keys of the kingdom" (Matt. 16:19). It is given to all the apostles, not just Peter (see comments on Matt. 16:18). And inasmuch as the mission of the church extends "to the ends of the age" (Matt. 28:20), Christ is "present" to forgive sins with all who preach the Gospel at any time or place.

Further, this is John's parallel to the Great Commission. Jesus introduces it by the words, "as the Father has sent Me, I also send you" (John 20:21). But the clergy (priesthood) is not the only group commissioned to serve Christ; every believer is to be a witness (cf. Matt. 28:18-20; 2 Cor. 4:1ff).

Finally, this power is present only through the Holy Spirit. Jesus said, "Receive the Holy Spirit" (John 20:22). This is parallel to what Jesus said later, "You shall receive power when the Holy Spirit has come upon you; and you shall be witnesses to Me in Jerusalem, and in all Judea and Samaria, and to the end of the earth" (Acts 1:8). But all believers have this same power to pronounce forgiveness of sins as the witness to the good news of Christ throughout the world. There is absolutely no mention here about any unique priestly power resident in a select clergy. It is simply John's equivalent of the Great Commission to all believers to proclaim the message of Christ's forgiveness to all the world (cf. Luke 24:47).

ACTS

ACTS 1:18 – In what way did Judas die?

(See comments on Matt. 27:5.)

ACTS 2:16-21 – Did Peter make a mistake in quoting Joel?

PROBLEM: In Acts 2, Pentecost arrives, and the disciples are filled with the Holy Spirit. In response to criticism, Peter says that what they hear and see was "spoken by the prophet Joel" (cf. Joel 2:28-32). Yet, in the passage that Peter quotes, there are events in it that did not happen at Pentecost, like the moon turning to blood. Does Peter err on this occasion?

SOLUTION: First, Peter was simply showing that Pentecost involved a partial or initial fulfillment of Joel 2:28-32. This partial fulfillment was in regard to the indwelling Holy Spirit for believers. And this is exactly what happened on the day of Pentecost. Joel says that God "will pour out My spirit on all flesh . . . I will pour out My Spirit in those days" (Joel 2:28-29). And God did pour forth His Spirit on the day of Pentecost.

Second, Peter's reference was to indicate that the last days had been inaugurated (cf. Heb. 1:1-2; 2:4). The wonders of the sky above and the signs on the earth beneath (Acts 19–21) are to take place later on in earth's history at the time of Christ's second coming. Notice that these things will happen "before the . . . great and notable day of the Lord" (v. 20) which is yet future (cf. Matt. 24:1ff).

ACTS 2:34 – Is David in heaven or not?

PROBLEM: Peter seems to imply here that David was not in heaven. He wrote, "David did not ascend into the heavens." Yet the Bible indicates that David was one of God's choice servants (Acts 13:22) who obviously went to be with his Lord when he died (cf. Matt. 22:42-46).

SOLUTION: Peter is not speaking of David's *soul* here, but of his *body*. David's soul is in heaven along with all other believers, but his body is still in the grave (Acts 2:29). Since David's body has not yet been raised, it is clear that he has not yet "ascended" bodily into heaven either. It is for this same reason that Jesus said to Mary, "I have not yet ascended to My Father" (John 20:17). The day He died, Jesus' spirit went to be with the Father (see Luke 23:43, 46). So, His spirit had been with the Father, but His body had not yet ascended into heaven when he spoke to Mary. The bodily ascension took place several weeks later (cf. Acts 1:3, 9-10). (See also comments on Eph. 4:9.)

ACTS 2:38 – Did Peter declare that baptism was necessary for salvation?

PROBLEM: Peter seems to be saying that those who responded had to repent and be baptized before they could receive the Holy Spirit. But this is contrary to the teaching of Paul that baptism is not part of the Gospel (1 Cor. 1:17) and that we are saved by faith alone (Rom. 4:4; Eph. 2:8-9).

SOLUTION: This is resolved when we consider the possible meaning of being baptized "for" the remission of sins in the light of its usage, the whole context, and the rest of Scripture. Consider the following:

First, the word "for" (*eis*) can mean "with a view to" or even "because of." In this case, water baptism would be *because* they had been saved, not *in order to* be saved.

Second, people are saved by receiving God's word, and Peter's audience "gladly received his word" before they were baptized (Acts 2:41).

Third, verse 44 speaks of "all who believed" as constituting the early church, not all who were baptized.

Fourth, later, those who believed Peter's message clearly received the Holy Spirit *before* they were baptized. Peter said, "Can anyone forbid water, that these should not be baptized who have received the Holy Spirit just as we have?" (Acts 10:47)

Fifth, Paul separates baptism from the Gospel, saying, "Christ did not send me to baptize, but to preach the Gospel" (1 Cor. 1:17). But it is the Gospel which saves us (Rom. 1:16). Therefore, baptism is not part of what saves us.

Sixth, Jesus referred to baptism as a work of righteousness (Matt. 3:15). But the Bible declares clearly it is "not by works of righteousness which we have done, but according to His mercy He saved us" (Titus 3:5).

Seventh, not once in the entire Gospel of John, written explicitly so that people could believe and be saved (John 20:31), does it give baptism as part of the condition of salvation. It simply says over and over that people should "believe" and be saved (cf. John 3:16, 18, 36).

In view of all these factors it seems best to understand Peter's statement like this: "Repent and be baptized with a view to the forgiveness of sins." That this view looked backward (to their sins being forgiven after they were saved) is made clear by the context and the rest of Scripture. Believing (or repenting) and being baptized are placed together, since baptism should follow belief. But nowhere does it say, "He who is not *baptized* will be condemned" (cf. Mark 16:16). Yet Jesus said emphatically that "he who does not *believe* is condemned already" (John 3:18). So neither Peter nor the rest of Scripture makes baptism a condition of salvation.

ACTS 2:44-45 – Did early Christians practice communism?

PROBLEM: Some have inferred from the fact that these early Christians "sold their possessions" and had "all things in common" that they were practicing a form of communism. However, even the Ten Commandments imply the right to private property, forbidding one to "steal" or even "covet" what belongs to another (Ex. 20:15, 17).

SOLUTION: There are several reasons to believe that this passage does not teach an abiding form of Christian communism or socialism. First, these passages are not *prescriptive,* but are simply *descriptive.* Nowhere does it lay this down as normative. It simply describes what the believers were doing.

Second, so far as the text indicates, the system was only *temporary,* not a permanent arrangement. They apparently stayed together in Jerusalem, since that is where the Holy Spirit had descended and the first great turning to Christ had occurred. The necessities of living together away from home occasioned this sort of common arrangement.

Third, the communal arrangement was *voluntary.* There is no indication in the text that this was a compulsory arrangement. It was apparently simply a temporary and voluntary convenience for the furtherance of the Gospel in those early and crucial days of the Christian church.

Fourth, the selling of property and giving of money was only *partial.* The text implies that they sold only extra land and other possessions, not that they sold their only place of residence. After all, they all eventually left Jerusalem, to which they had come for the Feast of Pentecost (Acts 2:1), and went back to their homes which were scattered all over the world (cf. Acts 2:5-13).

ACTS 3:21 — Will all things be restored to God or just some things?

PROBLEM: On the one hand, this verse speaks of the "restoration of all things," which seems to imply that all will eventually be saved. On the other hand, the Scriptures declare that many will be lost (Matt. 25:41; Rev. 19:20–20:15). Will everyone eventually be saved?

SOLUTION: God desires that all people be saved (1 Tim. 2:4; 2 Peter 3:9). However, some are simply "not willing" to accept His grace (cf. Matt. 23:37). Since God is love (1 John 4:16) and humans are free, God cannot force them to freely love Him. Forced freedom is a contradiction in terms. Hence, God will allow the unrepentant to have it their way. Those who do not say to God, "Your will be done," will eventually hear God declare to them, "your will be done." Such is the nature of hell. Nowhere in the Bible does it hold out hope for those who refuse to accept God's love. A loving God cannot force anyone to love Him. Forced love is a contradiction in terms. Love always works persuasively, but never coercively (see also comments on Col. 1:20).

What then does "the restoration of all things" mean? Peter is speaking here to the Jews and makes reference to the "restoration of all things, which God has spoken by the mouth of all His holy prophets since the world began" (Acts 3:21). Peter said it is referring to the "covenant which God made with our [Jewish] fathers, saying to Abraham, 'And in your seed all the families of the earth shall be blessed' " (Acts 3:25). This Abrahamic covenant was unconditional and included the promises of possessing the land of Palestine "forever" (Gen. 13:15). It is to the future fulfillment of this Abrahamic covenant that Peter refers. It is the restoration of all *things* to Israel, not to the salvation of all people (see also comments on Rom. 11:26-27).

ACTS 4:12 — Is Christ the only way of salvation?

PROBLEM: Peter declares that "there is no other name under heaven given among men by which we must be saved." But isn't this a narrow exclusivism? What about the sincere pagan or Buddhist? Is God going to send them to hell?

SOLUTION: Several observations are relevant to this question. First of all, sincerity is not a good test of truth. Many people can and have been sincerely wrong about many things (Prov. 14:12).

Second, all *truth* is exclusive. The truth that "two plus three equals five" is very exclusive too. It does not allow for any other conclusion. The same is true of value statements, such as "Racism is wrong" and "People should not be cruel." These views do not tolerate any alternatives.

Third, all truth *claims* are exclusive. For example, if humanism is true, then all non-humanisms are false. If atheism is true, then all who believe in God are wrong. Every truth claim excludes its opposite. Hence, if Jesus is the only way to God, then there are no other ways. This is no more exclusive than any other truth claim. The question is whether the claim is true.

Fourth, Jesus and the NT clearly and repeatedly emphasize that Jesus is the only way of salvation. (1) Jesus said, "I am the way, the truth, and the life. No one comes to the Father except through me" (John 14:6). (2) Jesus also claimed He was the door (John 10:9), insisting that "he who does not enter the sheepfold by the Door . . . the same is a thief and a robber" (v. 1). (3) The Apostle Peter added, "Nor is there salvation in any other, for there is no other name under heaven given among men by which we must be saved" (Acts 4:12). (4) And Paul contended that "there is one God and one Mediator between God and men, the Man Christ Jesus" (1 Tim. 2:5).

ACTS 4:34-35 — Did early Christians practice communism?

(See comments on Acts 2:44-45.)

ACTS 5:31 — Is repentance a gift of God or an act of man?

(See discussion on 2 Tim. 2:25.)

ACTS 5:36-37 — Does Luke make a mistake concerning Theudas and Judas?

PROBLEM: In Acts, a Pharisee named Gamaliel makes mention of a Theudas and Judas of Galilee. Yet, the 1st century Jewish historian Josephus also refers to a Theudas and Judas. Some think that there is a discrepancy between the individuals to whom Gamaliel and the ones to whom Josephus refers.

SOLUTION: First, concerning Theudas, Luke's account and that of Jose-phus are talking about two different individuals. The Theudas in the Josephus account revolted in A.D. 44 while the Theudas in Acts revolted before the census which took place around A.D. 7 (cf. Acts 5:37). In other words, there were two different men named Theudas. We know this because Theudas preceded Judas of Galilee who arose during the days of the census. Therefore, the Theudas Gamaliel refers to is different than the one mentioned by Josephus.

Secondly, concerning Judas of Galilee, there is no discrepancy between Gamaliel and Josephus. Once the question of Theudas is clear, so is the problem of Judas. The Theudas Gamaliel speaks of is different than the one to whom Josephus refers. Yet Josephus refered to the same Judas that Gamaliel does, because the words attributed to Gamaliel are said to have been spoken around A.D. 33. This period of time is much sooner than the Judas of A.D. 44 mentioned by Josephus. There is no contradic-tion concerning Judas because Gamaliel and Josephus refer to the same individual.

ACTS 7:14 — Why does this text say "seventy-five people" when Exodus 1:5 says there were "seventy persons"?

PROBLEM: According to Exodus 1:5 there were only 70 descendants who went down into Egypt with Jacob. But, when Stephen relates this same incident in Acts 7:14, he gives the number as 75. This appears to be a flat contradiction.

SOLUTIONS: There are several possible ways to explain the difference between these accounts. First, some scholars suggest that Acts 7:14 is correct in stating 75. They note that both the Greek translation of the OT (Septuagint) and a Hebrew manuscript found in the Dead Sea area use the number 75 just as Stephen said.

Others suggest that while Luke accurately records Stephen's sermon, that Stephen nevertheless made a mistake. Thus Acts is an inerrant record of the speech in which Stephen made this error. The parallel account in Genesis 46:27 also gives the number as 70. The main objection to this view is the fact that Luke's inclusion of this speech carries with it the implication that what he said is correct. Further, the text states that Stephen was "full of the Holy Spirit" when he gave the addresses (7:55).

Another explanation points out that the discrepancies can be explained by the fact that Stephen was probably quoting from the Septuagint (the

Greek version of the OT) which states, "And all the souls from Jacob were seventy-five" (Ex. 1:5), rather than the Hebrew, which states "And all the persons who came from the loins of Jacob were seventy in number, but Joseph was already in Egypt" (Ex. 1:5, NASB). The difference arises from the difference in the way the totals are calculated.

Jacob has twelve sons. Adding Jacob's grandsons and great-grandsons, the total was 66. Adding Ephraim and Manasseh who were born to Joseph in Egypt, the total is 68. When you add Jacob and his wife the total is 70, as the Hebrew records. The Septuagint, however, starting with Jacob's 12 sons, added Jacob's grandsons and great-grandsons for a total of 66. Then, it added the seven additional descendants of Joseph who were probably sons of Ephraim and Manasseh who were born to Joseph's sons some time after the migration of Jacob to Egypt, but before Jacob died. The Septuagint also omitted Jacob and his wife. This makes a total of 75 as Stephen mentions in the Acts passage.

	HEBREW TEXT	GREEK TEXT
Jacob and his wife	2	not counted
Jacob's sons	12	12
Jacob's grandsons and great grandsons	54	54
Joseph's sons Ephraim and Manasseh	2	2
Joseph's additional descendants in Egypt	not counted	7
TOTAL	70	75

ACTS 15:20 — Does this passage indicate that it is a sin to receive a blood transfusion?

PROBLEM: The ability of modern medicine to sustain life by blood transfusion is a common practice that has no doubt been used by Christians. However, this verse is used by some religious groups, such as the Jehovah's Witnesses, to claim that blood transfusions are against God's will.

SOLUTION: This passage is talking about the OT restriction against eating or drinking blood (Gen. 9:3-4; cf. Acts 15:28-29). However, a blood transfusion is not "eating" or "drinking" blood. This is clear from several facts. First, even though a doctor might give food to a patient intravenously and call this "feeding," it is simply not the case that giving blood intravenously is also "feeding." This is clear from the fact that blood is not received into the body as "food."

Second, to refer to the giving of food directly into the blood stream as "eating" is only a figurative expression. Although the food is absorbed into the blood in a way similar to the way it is absorbed through the normal digestive functions, eating is the literal taking in of food in the normal manner through the mouth and into the digestive system. The reason intravenous injections are referred to as "feeding" is because the ultimate result is that, through intravenous injection, the body receives the nutrients that it would normally receive by eating. This is similar to calling food "healthy." Food is not really healthy, because health is a characteristic of living things, not of food. But, we call food "healthy" because it produces health in the body.

Third, the only possible way to understand the word "eating" in both the OT and NT is the literal process of taking something into the body as food through the mouth and into the digestive system. This is evident since the technology to enable intravenous injections had not been invented at the time these passages were written.

Fourth, it is clear that this OT passage is not primarily concerned with the eating of blood. Rather, it is primarily concerned with the fact that the life is in the blood. Leviticus 17:10-12 makes this plain:

> And whatever man of the house of Israel, or of the strangers who sojourn among you, who eats any blood, I will set My face against that person who eats blood, and will cut him off from among his people. For the *life of the flesh is in the blood,* and I have given it to you upon the altar to make atonement for your souls; for it is the blood that makes atonement for the soul. Therefore I said to the children of Israel, "No one among you shall eat blood, nor shall any stranger who sojourns among you eat blood."

The prohibitions in Genesis 9:3-4 and Leviticus 17:10-12 were primarily directed at eating flesh that was still pulsating with life because the lifeblood was still in it. But, the transfusion of blood is not eating flesh with the lifeblood still in it.

Finally, the prohibition in Acts was not necessarily given as a law by which Christians were to live, for the NT clearly teaches that we are not under law (Rom. 6:14; Gal. 4:8-31). Rather, the Jerusalem counsel may have been advising Gentile Christians to respect their Jewish brethren by observing these practices, thereby not giving offense "either to the Jews or to the Greeks or to the church of God" (1 Cor. 10:32). In any event, the restriction can in no way be construed as a prohibition against blood transfusions.

ACTS 16:1-3 — Why did Paul have Timothy circumcised when he himself spoke so strongly against it?

PROBLEM: Paul's main point in Galatians can be summarized in his words, "If you become circumcised, Christ will profit you nothing" (Gal. 5:2). Yet Paul admits that he had Timothy circumcised "because of the Jews who were in that region" (Acts 16:3). Wasn't this a contradiction to his own teaching.

SOLUTION: Even if Paul were wrong here in his action, it would not prove that the Bible erred in its teaching, but simply that Paul erred. Paul, like any other human being, was capable of error. Since the Bible is the Word of God (see Introduction), it is not capable of erring in anything it teaches.

Furthermore, Paul's action in having Timothy circumcised is not necessarily inconsistent with what he taught in Galatians, since the two cases are different. Paul was violently opposed to any who made circumcision *necessary for salvation*. But he never opposed it as *helpful for evangelism*. Indeed, Paul said elsewhere, "to the Jews I became as a Jew, that I might win Jews" (1 Cor. 9:20). However, when Judaizers insisted that "unless you are circumcised according to the custom of Moses, you cannot be saved" (Acts 15:1), then Paul took an intractable stand against circumcision.

ACTS 16:6 — Why did the Holy Spirit forbid Paul to preach in Asia when Jesus said to go into all the world?

PROBLEM: Jesus commanded His followers to "make disciples of all the nations" (Matt. 28:19) and to be witnesses to "the end of the earth" (Acts 1:8). But in Acts 16 Paul and Timothy "were forbidden by the Holy Spirit to preach the word in Asia" (v. 6).

SOLUTION: Paul was only forbidden *immediately*. God had a more strategic route for the Gospel through Europe first (Acts 16:9). *Eventually*, however, the Gospel got to Asia and to every place through Paul's converts in Europe (cf. 1 Thes. 1:7) and by Paul himself (Acts 19:10, 22, 26; 20:4, 16, 18; 1 Cor. 16:19). So, the prohibition was only *temporary*, not *permanent*.

ACTS 17:28 – Why did Paul quote an uninspired pagan poet?

(See comments on Titus 1:12.)

ACTS 20:9-10 – How could Eutycus be dead if he had life in him?

PROBLEM: Verse nine says he was "taken up dead." But in the very next verse Paul said, "his life is in him."

SOLUTION: His life was in him only *after* Paul had performed the miracle (v. 10), not before (v. 9).

ACTS 23:5 – Did Paul lie when he said he didn't know the high priest?

PROBLEM: The high priest Ananias commanded that Paul be struck on the mouth. Paul rebuked him for doing so, and those who stood by condemned Paul for reviling the high priest. Paul responded by claiming, "I did not know . . . that he was the high priest" (Acts 23:5). But this is highly unlikely, since Paul himself was a member of the Jewish Sanhedrin and worked closely with him before his conversion (Acts 9:1-3).

SOLUTION: There are several views taken on this passage. Some suggest that Paul may have not known the high priest personally, even though he was previously a member of the Jewish Council. Others claim that Paul may have had poor vision (perhaps his "thorn in the flesh") and not been able to see him clearly. Still others believe that Paul could have been lying to get himself out of a bad situation. Apostles sinned too (cf. Gal. 2:11-13). In this case, Acts is simply giving us a true record of Paul's sin.

It seems more plausible, however, to take Paul's statement as sarcastic but not false. In this case, his statement, "I did not know . . . he was the high priest," could be translated something like this: "This is the high priest of God's Law? I would never have known it by his unlawful command to strike me!"

ROMANS

ROMANS 1:19-20 – Are the heathen lost?

PROBLEM: Jesus said, "I am the way, the truth, and the life. No one comes to the Father, except through Me" (John 14:6). Also, Acts 4:12 says of Christ, "And there is salvation in no one else; for there is no other name under heaven that has been given among men, by which we must be saved" (NASB). But what if someone has never heard the Gospel of Christ, will he be eternally lost? Paul seems to answer this in the affirmative. But is it fair to condemn people who have never even heard about Christ?

SOLUTION: Paul's answer is clear. He said that the heathen are "without excuse" (1:20) because "what may be known of God *is manifest in them,* for *God has shown it to them.* For since the creation of the world His invisible attributes *are clearly seen, being understood* by the things that are made" (1:19-20). So, the heathen are justly condemned for several reasons. First, Romans 2:12 states, "For as many as have sinned without Law will also perish without Law, and as many as have sinned in the Law will be judged by the Law." This passage teaches that the Jew is judged by the Law, the Hebrew Scriptures, but the Gentile is condemned by "the Law written in their hearts."

"For when Gentiles who do not have the Law do instinctively the things of the Law, these, not having the Law, are a law to themselves, in that they show the work of the Law written in their hearts, their conscience bearing witness, and their thoughts alternately accusing or else defending them" (Rom. 2:14-15, NASB).

Second, the question assumes innocence on the part of the saved man who hasn't heard the Gospel. But the Bible tells us that "all have sinned and fall short of the glory of God" (Rom. 3:23). In addition, Romans 1:18-20 says that God clearly reveals Himself through natural revelation "so that they are without excuse." Human beings are not innocent regarding God's natural revelation.

Third, if a person who has not heard the Gospel lives his life to the best of his ability he simply is doing works for salvation. But salvation is by grace, "For by grace you have been saved through faith, and that not of yourselves; it is the gift of God" (Eph. 2:8). Not in any way, shape, or form can anybody do anything to gain access into heaven. If there was such a way, then the work of Christ on the Cross was a futile act.

Finally, the Bible says in essence, "seek and you will find." That is, those who seek the light they have through nature, which is not sufficient for salvation, will get the light they need for salvation. Hebrews 11:6 says, "But without faith it is impossible to please Him, for he who comes to God must believe that He is, and that He is a rewarder of those who diligently seek Him." Acts 10:35 adds, "But in every nation whoever fears Him and works righteousness is accepted by Him." God has many ways to get the truth about salvation through Christ to those who seek Him. He can send a missionary (Acts 10), or a Bible (Ps. 119:130), give them a vision (Dan. 2; 7), or send an angel (Rev. 14). But those who turn their back on the light they have (through nature) and find themselves lost in darkness, have no one to blame but themselves. For "men loved darkness rather than light, because their deeds were evil" (John 3:19).

ROMANS 1:26 — Does this verse mean that homosexuals should not be heterosexual because it is unnatural to them?

PROBLEM: According to some homosexuals, when Paul spoke against what is "unnatural" in Romans 1:26, he was not declaring that homosexuality was morally wrong, but simply that it was unnatural for homosexuals. "Unnatural" is used in a sociological, not a biological way. So rather than condemning homosexual practices, it is argued that this passage actually approves of them for homosexuals.

SOLUTION: When the Bible declares that homosexual practices are "against nature" (Rom. 1:26), it is referring to biological nature, not sociological nature. First, sex is defined biologically in Scripture from the very beginning. In Genesis 1, God created "male and female" and then told them to "be fruitful and increase in number" (Gen. 1:27-28, NIV). This reproduction was only possible if He was referring to a biological male and female.

Second, sexual orientation is understood biologically, not sociologically, when God said "for this reason a man will leave his father and mother and be united to his wife, and they will become one flesh" (Gen. 2:24,

NIV). For only a biological father and mother can produce children, and the reference to "one flesh" speaks of a physical marriage.

Thirdly, the Romans passage says that "men committed indecent acts with other men." This clearly indicates that this sinful act was homosexual in nature (Rom. 1:27, NIV).

Fourth, what they did was not natural to them. They "exchanged" the "natural relations" for the unnatural ones (Rom. 1:26, NIV). So the homosexual acts were pronounced unnatural for homosexuals too.

Fifth, homosexual desires are also called "shameful lusts" (v. 26, NIV). So it is evident that God is condemning sexual sins between those of the same biological sex. Homosexual acts are contrary to human nature as such, not just to a homsexual's sexual orientation.

ROMANS 2:7 — Is immortality acquired or possessed?

PROBLEM: Paul speaks here of "seeking" immortality. He also refers to acquiring it at the resurrection (1 Cor. 15:53). However, Jesus taught that the soul is immortal, that is, it cannot be destroyed by death (Luke 12:5). Paul also insists that the soul survives death (2 Cor. 5:8; Phil. 1:23; cf. Rev. 6:9). But which is it — do we already possess immortality or do we only acquire it at the resurrection?

SOLUTION: The Bible reserves the *term* "immortality" for humans in their resurrected state. It is something acquired, not possessed before the Resurrection, since Christ, who was the first one to attain an immortal resurrection body (1 Cor. 15:20), "brought life and immortality to light" (2 Tim. 1:10) for the rest of the race.

Nevertheless, the *fact* of immortality includes the human soul as well. For the soul is not destroyed by physical death, just as Jesus said (Luke 12:5). It survives death and goes into either God's presence (2 Cor. 5:8; Phil. 1:23), if it is saved, or into conscious hell (Luke 16:22-26; Rev. 19:20–20:15), if it is lost. Since the soul (and/or spirit) is not mortal, as the body is, in this sense it is proper to say the soul *is* immortal. However, the whole person — soul and body — is resurrected to immortality. So in this sense, the soul *gains* immortality at the resurrection of the body.

However, in the biblical sense of living forever in an immortal body, human beings do not possess immortality before the resurrection. Even so, only God is intrinsically immortal (see comments on 1 Tim. 6:16); whatever immortality humans have, they derive from God. The matter can be summarized as follows:

SINCE THE SOUL IS IMMORTAL	SINCE THE SOUL IS NOT IMMORTAL
Indestructible by man	Indestructible by God
Survives physical death	Can avoid second death
Has beginning but no end	Has no beginning or end
Derived from God	Inherent like God's

ROMANS 2:14-15 — How can those who are by nature sinners keep God's laws of nature?

PROBLEM: Ephesians 2:3 asserts that all humans are "by nature children of wrath." But Paul speaks here of unbelieving Gentiles who "by nature do the things contained in the law" (Rom. 2:14). These two things seem mutually opposed.

SOLUTION: Ephesians is speaking of the *cause* of sinful actions, whereas Romans refers to the *rule* for our actions. The former relates to our *propensity* to sin and the latter to the *norm* for what is sin. There is a difference between what humans are *inclined* to do by nature and what they *ought* to do according to the natural law "written in their hearts" (Rom. 2:15).

ROMANS 5:12 — Does this statement imply that we were only potential humans before we were born, not actual human beings?

PROBLEM: According to this text, "all [human beings] sinned [in Adam]." But, we were not yet even conceived, let alone born, when Adam sinned. Therefore, we could not possibly have been actual human beings. Hence, we must have been merely potential human beings.

SOLUTION: For several reasons it is evident that this text does not prove that unborn human beings are not fully human. First, the passage is not speaking about an embryo in the womb, but about the way all humans were in Adam, the head of the human race.

Second, the fact that we were all genetically, representatively, or potentially in Adam, and therefore responsible in his sin, reveals that there is a corporateness about human nature. That is, there is a unity in humanity, so that we cannot separate off one member from another (cf. Rom. 14:7), no matter where we are located.

Third, the very fact that we are all declared sinners from conception (see comments on Ps. 51:5), by virtue of being in Adam, reveals that even from the point of conception one is considered to be part of the actual human race, not merely a potential human being.

ROMANS 5:14 — Is it fair to judge all people because of Adam's sin?

PROBLEM: Death came to all people because of the sin of Adam (Rom. 5:12), but Romans 5:14 says, "Nevertheless death reigned from Adam to Moses, *even over those who had not sinned according to the likeness of the transgression of Adam*." But, if they did not sin like Adam, why are they held accountable?

SOLUTION: There are two types of people who may fall into this category: (1) infants, and (2) those who do not deliberately disobey God's dictate.

First, many Bible scholars believe that infants and small children who die before the age of moral accountability will go to heaven. This is based on the following verses. (1) In 2 Samuel 12:23, when David's baby died, he said "I shall go to him, but he shall not return to me." This implies that the baby was with the Lord. (2) In Psalm 139, David speaks of even an unborn baby as written in God's book in heaven (v. 16). (3) Further, Isaiah distinguishes between those who are not yet old enough to "know to refuse the evil and choose the good" (7:15), which implies they are not yet morally accountable. (4) Jesus added, "if you were blind, you would have no sin" (John 9:41). (5) And Paul speaks of Christ's sacrifice making all righteous (Rom. 5:19), which would cover even little children who are born in sin (Ps. 51:5). (See also comments on 2 Sam. 12:23.)

Second, we "all sinned [in Adam]" as our representative, and as a consequence the guilt of Adam's sin was imputed to all of us. But Christ's death cancelled this and released the human race from this judicial guilt (Rom. 5:18-19). Even so, those who attain the age of accountability are responsible for their personal sin and therefore are justly condemned.

So those who did not sin in the likeness of Adam, nevertheless still sinned in Adam (Rom. 5:12). That is why death still reigned from the time of Adam and Moses. Romans 2:14-15 affirms that the Gentiles, even if they have not the Mosaic Law, still were a law to themselves. They have the Law written in their hearts and their conscience bears witness to their actions. Humans after Adam are still sinful and responsible for their actions.

Just because people do not sin in the likeness of Adam does not mean that they are not sinful. In other words, it doesn't mean that humans are not held accountable by God for their actions. Man dies because man sins (Rom 6:23). God is just in condemning sin, and He is merciful in providing salvation for those who will receive it.

ROMANS 5:19 — If all are made righteous by Christ why aren't all saved?

PROBLEM: It is agreed by scholars that in Paul's contrast between the "one" and the "many" here, that "many" means all. For the "many" were "made sinners" by the "one" (Adam's) sin, and Paul had already concluded that "all have sinned [in Adam]" a few verses earlier (Rom. 5:12). But if all were "made sinners" means all actually became sinners, then why doesn't all "will be made righteous" in the same verse mean that all will be saved? (Rom. 5:19)

SOLUTION: There are two broad answers to this question—universalism and particularism. That is, those who claim this verse as proof that all people will eventually be saved and those who believe only some will be saved. Since the Bible clearly rejects universalism (see comments on Col. 1:20), we will focus here on the two general responses of particularists.

The Potential View: Some scholars believe Paul is simply referring to being "made righteous" by Christ's death in a *potential* sense. That is to say, by the Cross all people are made *savable,* but not all people will be saved. Those who hold this position point to the fact that the parallel is not perfect, for we were "made sinners" in Adam without our personal free choice. Nevertheless, we cannot be "made righteous" in Christ without freely receiving the "gift" (5:16-17).

The Judicial View: According to this position, all persons were "made sinners" and "made righteous" in the same sense—*judicially.* That is, both Christ and Adam were our *legal* representatives. And while in Adam all his race were before God made sinners *officially,* nonetheless, in Christ all are officially made righteous, though not actually and personally. And just as every person, when they come to the age of accountability (see comments on 2 Sam. 12:23 and Rom. 5:14), must personally sin to be personally guilty, even so everyone must personally accept Christ to be personally saved. Christ removed the official and judicial guilt that was imputed to the race because of Adam's sin. This does not mean that everyone is *actually* saved, but only that they are no longer *legally* condemned.

ROMANS 8:3 — Was Jesus actually in human flesh or only in its likeness?

PROBLEM: Paul asserts that Jesus was made "in the *likeness* of sinful flesh," but he does not assert that Jesus *is* human flesh. Yet the Bible speaks repeatedly of Jesus being incarnated *in* human flesh, that is, of being truly human, not just like a human.

SOLUTION: Jesus was not just similar to humans—He was human. He did not come simply in something *like* of human flesh. He came in real human flesh. On this the Scriptures are clear. John declared, "The Word [Christ] became flesh and dwelt among us" (John 1:14). Later, he warned that anyone who "does not confess that Jesus Christ has come in the flesh is not of God" (1 John 4:3; cf. 2 John 7). Likewise, Paul insisted that "God was manifested in the flesh" (1 Tim. 3:16).

Elsewhere in the same book Paul uses the phrase "likeness" to mean being actually like, not just similar (Rom. 1:23; 5:14; 6:5). So, it may be that Paul intended no difference between "likeness" and "the same as." Or, perhaps when Paul affirmed (in Rom. 8:3) that Jesus was only in the "likeness" of it, he was not speaking of human flesh as such, but of "*sinful* human flesh." Jesus was exactly like human flesh but only similar to sinful human flesh, since He had no sin (Heb. 4:15; 1 Peter 3:18; 1 John 3:3).

In any event, in Philippians 2 Paul speaks of Christ being "in the likeness of men" as meaning the same as being human (v. 7). So even without the qualifier "sinful," Paul speaks of Jesus' "likeness" to humans as meaning the same as "being human."

ROMANS 8:26 — Is the Holy Spirit our mediator or is Christ?

PROBLEM: First Timothy 2:5 asserts that "there is one . . . Mediator between God and men, the Man Christ Jesus." But Romans 8:26 informs us that the Holy Spirit intercedes for us to God "with groanings which cannot be uttered." How can Christ be the only mediator when the Holy Spirit also mediates?

SOLUTION: Christ is the only *mediator;* the Holy Spirit is only an *intercessor.* Christ alone died for our sins (Heb. 1:1-2), making reconciliation with God possible (2 Cor. 5:19). The Holy Spirit did not die for our sins; He prays to the Father on our behalf, based on the redeeming work of Christ. Further, the intercession of the Holy Spirit is not *in heaven,* as Christ's work is (1 John 2:1-2). Rather, it is *in us.* The indwelling Spirit pleads in us to the Father on the grounds of the mediating work of the Son.

ROMANS 8:30 — Are all the called ones saved or only some?

PROBLEM: Paul indicates here that all who are "called" by God are eventually "justified" and "glorified" (Rom. 8:30). But Jesus said that "many are called, but few chosen" (Matt. 20:16).

SOLUTION: The word "called" is being used in different senses. This is not uncommon in languages. Take, for example, the following sentence: "The dog would *bark* by the tree but did not scratch the *bark* from the tree." Clearly the word "bark" is used in two different senses. Likewise, Paul and Jesus are using different senses of the word "called" which can be contrasted as follows:

GENERAL CALL	SPECIFIC CALL
Call for salvation	Call of salvation
For all men	Only for believers
Not effectual	Effectual for salvation

In brief, when Jesus referred to a "call" He was speaking of a general invitation for all to believe. Paul, however, has reference to the specific "call" of God by which God brings believers to salvation. The first is the call for salvation to all; the last is the call of salvation to some.

ROMANS 9:13 – How can God hate Esau when He is a God of love?

(See comments on Mal. 1:3.)

ROMANS 9:17 – How can Pharaoh be free if God hardened his heart?

PROBLEM: God said to Pharaoh, "For this very purpose I raised you up, to demonstrate my power in you, and that my name might be proclaimed throughout the whole earth" (Rom. 9:17, NASB). In fulfillment of this, it says that God hardened Pharaoh's heart (Ex. 4:21; cf. Ex. 7:3). But if God raised up Pharaoh and even hardened his heart to accomplish His divine purposes, then isn't Pharaoh exempt from responsibility for his actions?

SOLUTION: First, God in His omniscience foreknew exactly how Pharaoh would respond, and He used it to accomplish His purposes. God ordained the means of Pharaoh's free but stubborn action as well as the end of Israel's deliverance. In Exodus 3:19, God told Moses, "But I am sure that the king of Egypt will not let you go, no, not even by a mighty hand." Pharaoh rejected the request of Moses and only after ten plagues did Pharaoh finally let the people go.

Second, it is important to note that Pharaoh first hardened his own heart. When Moses initially approached Pharaoh concerning the release of the Israelites (Ex. 5:1), Pharaoh responded, "Who is the LORD that I should obey His voice to let Israel go? I do not know the LORD, nor will I let Israel go" (Ex. 5:2). The passage Paul quotes (in Rom. 9:17) is Exodus 9:16 which, in context, is the plague of the boils, the sixth plague. But Pharaoh hardened his own heart before God made this statement. Just because God raised up Pharaoh does not mean that Pharaoh is not responsible for his actions.

Third, God uses the unrighteousness of humans to show His glory. God still holds Pharaoh accountable, but in the process of his hardened heart God used Pharaoh to display His greatness and glory. God sometimes uses evil acts to bring about good results. The story of Joseph is a good example of this point. Joseph is sold by his brothers and later becomes a ruler in Egypt. In Egypt, Joseph saves many lives during a famine. When he later reveals himself to his brothers and forgives them, he says, "But as for you, you meant evil against me; but God meant it for good, in order to bring it about as it is this day, to save many people alive" (Gen. 50:20). God can use bad actions to bring about His glory (see also discussion on Ex. 4:21).

ROMANS 10:5 — Does keeping the law bring life?

PROBLEM: Paul seems to imply that law-keeping brings life when he cites Leviticus (18:5) that "the man who does those things [written in the law] shall live by them" (Rom. 10:5). But elsewhere Paul himself calls it "the law of sin and death" (Rom. 8:2). He affirms flatly, "the commandment, which was to bring life, I found to bring death" (Rom. 7:10).

SOLUTION: Keeping the law does not bring saving life to anyone. On this the Bible is crystal clear. Paul told the Galatians, "if there had been a law given which could have given life, truly righteousness would have been by the law" (Gal. 3:21). He added, "by the deeds of the law no flesh will be justified in His sight (Rom. 3:20). For "no one is justified by the law in the sight of God," for "the just shall live by faith" (Gal. 3:11).

What then do the passages mean that seem to imply that the law will bring life? These are to be understood hypothetically, not actually. Theoretically, if one were to keep the law perfectly he would be perfect, but in actual fact no one can do that. For "all have sinned and fall short of the glory of God" (Rom. 3:23). And "whoever shall keep the whole law, and yet stumble in one point, he is guilty of all" (James 2:10). To summarize: can keeping the law bring life?

YES	NO
Hypothetically	Actually
Theoretically	Practically
If it is kept	But no one keeps it

ROMANS 11:26-27 — How can there be a future for the nation of Israel since they rejected the Messiah?

PROBLEM: The nation of Israel clearly rejected Christ as their Messiah (Romans 9–10; cf. John 1:10-11). And the Bible says that the promises of Abraham go to his spiritual seed, not his descendants according to the flesh (Rom. 4; Gal. 3). Why then does Romans 11 speak of a future for the nation of Israel?

SOLUTION: Abraham has both a spiritual seed (descendants) and literal descendants. Anyone who believes in Christ can become a *spiritual* heir of the promise for justification (Rom. 4; cf. Gen. 15), because Christ came of the seed of Abraham (Gal. 3:16).

However, there are also promises to Abraham's *literal* descendants, the Jews, that have never yet been completely fulfilled. For example, God unconditionally promised that Abraham's literal descendants would inherit the land of Palestine forever (Gen. 12:1-3; 13:15-17; 15:7-21; 17:8). Only one short time in Israel's history did they inherit this land (Josh. 11:23), but God gave it to them by an unconditional oath (cf. Gen. 15:7-21) "forever" (Gen. 13:15), as an "everlasting possession" (17:8). Since God cannot break an unconditional promise (Heb. 6:17-18; 2 Tim 2:13), this promise is yet to be fulfilled for the nation of Israel.

Paul is speaking of the literal descendants of Abraham, the children of Israel in Romans 9–11. He calls them "my kinsmen according to the flesh, who are Israelites" (Rom. 9:3-4) and "Israel" (Rom. 10:1). This same national group (Israel) that was temporarily cut off will be grafted in again into the tree, and "all Israel will be saved" (Rom. 11:26). Jesus spoke of this time in Acts 1 when asked by His disciples, "Will You at this time restore the kingdom to Israel?" (Acts 1:6) His answer was not a stern rebuke for misunderstanding the Scriptures, but an assurance that only the Father knows the "times or seasons" in which this will occur (v. 7). Earlier Jesus spoke of "the regeneration, when the Son of Man sits on the throne of His glory, [and] you who have followed Me will also sit on twelve thrones, judging the twelve tribes of Israel" (Matt. 19:28). Indeed, in the final book of the Bible, the Apostle John spoke of God redeeming out of the tribulation "one hundred and forty-four thousand of all the tribes of the children of Israel" (Rev. 7:4). So there is every reason to believe that God will honor His unconditional covenant to Israel to give them the land of Palestine forever.

1 Corinthians

1 CORINTHIANS 1:17 — Did Paul oppose water baptism?

PROBLEM: Paul declares that Christ did not send him to baptize. Yet Christ commissioned His disciples to "make disciples of all the nations, baptizing them in the name of the Father, and of the Son, and of the Holy Spirit" (Matt. 28:19). Does Paul contradict Christ?

SOLUTION: Paul was not opposed to baptism, but neither did he believe it was a condition of salvation (see comments on Acts 2:38). Paul himself was baptized by water (Acts 9:18; 22:16), and he taught water baptism in his epistles (cf. Rom. 6:3-4; Col. 2:12). Indeed, in this very passage (1 Cor. 1), Paul admits that he baptized several people (vv. 14, 16) as he did the Philippian jailor after he was saved (Acts 16:31-33). While Paul believed water baptism was a symbol of salvation, he did not believe it was part of the Gospel or essential to salvation.

1 CORINTHIANS 2:8 — How could Paul say the rulers of this world did not know Christ, when Christ came before them at His trial?

PROBLEM: The apostle affirms that "none of the rulers of this age knew [Christ]; for had they known, they would not have crucified the Lord of glory." Yet Jesus came before both Jewish and Gentile rulers, including Pilate, Herod, and Caiaphas (cf. Matt. 26–27; Mark 14–15; Luke 22–23; John 18–19).

SOLUTION: First of all, Paul does not say they did not know Christ; he said they did not know the "mystery" about Christ's redemption that was hidden for ages (1 Cor. 2:7-8; cf. Eph. 3:3-4). Second, they knew that they had allowed Christ to be crucified (cf. Matt. 21:38), but they "did it in ignorance" (cf. Acts 3:17), not realizing the implications of their decision. They were morally blinded (cf. John 16:3), even though they were physically and socially aware of the fact that Jesus of Nazareth was crucified.

1 CORINTHIANS 3:11 — Who is the foundation of the church, Christ or the apostles?

PROBLEM: In this text, Paul insists that "no other foundation can anyone lay than that which is laid, which is Jesus Christ." On the other hand, Paul told the Ephesians that the church is "built on the foundation of the apostles" (Eph. 2:20). Which is it?

SOLUTION: The answer is in the very next phrase in the last quote: "Jesus Christ Himself being the chief cornerstone" (Eph. 2:20). Christ is the foundation in a *primary sense,* and His chosen apostles are the foundation in a *secondary sense.* Christ is, as it were, the substructure, and the apostles are the foundation built on that (see Matt. 16:16-18). Christ is the kingpin that holds the apostolic foundation of the church together. It was His *deeds* (death and resurrection) and their *doctrine* (cf. Acts 2:42) about Him that formed the foundation of the Christian church.

1 CORINTHIANS 3:13-15 — Does this passage support the Roman Catholic view of purgatory?

PROBLEM: Roman Catholics appeal to this passage in support of the doctrine of temporary punishment for those not good enough to go directly to heaven. They point to the fact that it speaks of people who "suffer loss" when their works are "burned" by fire and yet they are eventually "saved" (1 Cor. 3:15). Does the Bible teach that there is a temporary hell (purgatory) where people suffer for their sins before they are let into heaven?

SOLUTION: Nowhere does the Bible teach the doctrine of purgatory. This doctrine is contrary to many facts of Scripture. First, hell is a permanent place of "everlasting fire" (Matt. 25:41). It entails "everlasting destruction from the presence of the Lord" (2 Thes. 1:9; see comments on that passage). Jesus declared it is a place where the fire "shall never be quenched" and where the body "does not die" (Mark 9:45, 48).

Second, once one goes to hell, he can never get out. Jesus said there is "a great gulf fixed, so that those who want to pass" from one side to the other cannot do so (Luke 16:26). This is true even if they regret being there (Luke 16:23, 28).

Third, the doctrine of purgatory is an insult to the all-sufficiency of the death of Christ on the cross. When Jesus died for our sins (1 Cor. 15:3) He announced, "It is finished" (John 19:30). Looking forward to the cross, He prayed to the Father, "I have finished the work which you have given Me to do" (John 17:4). Hebrews informs us that "after He [Jesus] had offered one sacrifice for sins forever, [He] sat down at the right hand of God" (Heb. 10:12). "For by one offering He has perfected forever those who are being sanctified" (Heb. 10:14).

Fourth, the only purgatory ever to be experienced was experienced by Christ on the cross when He purged our sins. Hebrews declares that "when He had by Himself purged our sins, [He] sat down at the right hand of the Majesty on high" (Heb. 1:3).

Fifth, the doctrine of purgatory is based on the apocryphal book of 2 Maccabees (12:46, Douay) which says it is a holy and wholesome thought to pray for the dead that they may be loosed from their sins. But this second century B.C. book never claimed to be inspired, nor did any of the apocryphal books. First Maccabees even disclaims inspiration (1 Mac. 9:27). These apocryphal books were never accepted by Judaism as inspired. Neither Jesus nor the NT writers ever cite them as inspired. Even Jerome, the Roman Catholic translator of the great Latin Vulgate Bible, rejected 2 Maccabees along with the other apocryphal books. Furthermore, 2 Maccabees was not officially added to the Bible by the Roman Catholic Church until A.D. 1546, some 29 years after Luther started his reformation during which he spoke out against purgatory and prayers for the dead. Finally, even when 2 Maccabees was added by Rome to the Bible (along with other apocryphal books), it rejected another apocryphal book which spoke against prayers for the dead. Second Esdras (called 4 Esdras by Roman Catholics), speaking of the day of death, declares, "no one shall ever pray for another on that day" (2 Esdras 7:105). Rejecting this book and accepting Maccabees manifests the arbitrariness of the decision to choose books to support doctrines they had added to the Bible.

Finally, in 1 Corinthians, Paul is not speaking of purgatory, but of the "judgment seat of Christ," before which all believers must come to receive their rewards "for the things done in the body" (2 Cor. 5:10). All our "work" will be "revealed by fire." And "if anyone's work . . . endures, he will receive a reward" (1 Cor. 3:13-14). And "if anyone's work is burned, he will suffer loss [of reward]; but he himself will be saved, yet so as through the fire" (1 Cor. 3:14-15). Since salvation from hell is by grace, not by works (Rom. 4:5; Eph. 2:8-9; Titus 3:5-7), it is clear that this passage is speaking about the "work" and "reward" of the believer for serving Christ, not about any alleged purgatory where they (instead of Christ) suffer for their sins.

1 CORINTHIANS 3:19 — How could Paul consider the words of Eliphaz inspired when God rebuked Eliphaz for saying them to Job?

PROBLEM: In 1 Corinthians 3:19 the Apostle Paul quotes from the Book of Job a statement made by one of Job's friends Eliphaz which says, "For it is written, 'He catches the wise in their own craftiness' " (cf. Job 5:13). Yet later in Job, God says to Eliphaz, "My wrath is aroused against you and your two friends, for you have not spoken of Me what is right, as My servant Job has" (Job 42:7). If what Eliphaz spoke was not right, then can his words be considered inspired?

SOLUTION: First, God did not say that everything uttered by Eliphaz was false, but only his accusations that God was punishing Job because of his sin. On this point Eliphaz and his friends did not speak what was right of God. For God considered Job perfect, a man who did good and turned away from evil (Job 2:3). Satan thought that, given the right circumstances, Job would curse God (2:4-5). Therefore, the things that happened to Job were allowed by God to show that Job would not curse Him. They did not happen because he had sinned. In light of this, Job's friends were wrong. But this does not mean that they never said anything that was true in their speeches. For example, Eliphaz is certainly correct in asserting that "He [God] gives rain on the earth, and sends waters on the fields" (Job 5:10). Likewise, he is right in affirming that God "catches the wise in their own craftiness" (Job 5:13).

Second, Paul uses the phrase "It is written" to introduce the quoted material. This is a standard practice in the NT to show that a particular passage is authoritative (cf. Matt. 4:4, 7, 10). Thus the inspired NT places its approval on this statement as true. Indeed, the fact that God takes up this same basic truth in His declaration to Job (37:24) gives divine approval to it and makes it appropriate for Paul to quote it as inspired.

1 CORINTHIANS 5:9 — If Paul wrote an inspired epistle, how could God allow it to be lost?

PROBLEM: Paul refers to a previous epistle he "wrote" to the Corinthians which is not in existence. But since it was written by an apostle to a church and contained spiritual and authoritative instruction, it must be considered inspired. This raises the question as to how an epistle inspired of God could be allowed by Him to be lost.

SOLUTION: There are three possibilities here. First, it may be that not all apostolic letters were intended to be in the canon of Scripture. Luke refers to "many" other gospels (1:1). John implies that there was much more Jesus did that was not recorded (20:30; 21:25). Perhaps this so-called "lost" letter to the Corinthians was not intended by God to be collected in the canon and preserved for the faith and practice of future generations, as were the 27 books of the NT (and 39 of the OT).

Second, others believe that the letter referred to (in 1 Cor. 5:9) may not be lost at all, but is part of an existing book in the Bible. For example, it could be part of what we know as 2 Corinthians (chaps. 10–13), which some believe was later put together with chapters 1–9. In support of this is offered the fact that chapters 1–9 have a decidedly different tone from the rest of the Book of 2 Corinthians (chapters 10–13). This may indicate that it was written on a different occasion. In addition, they point to the use of the word "now" (in 5:11) in contrast to an implied "then" when the former book was written. They also note that Paul refers to "letters" (plural) he had written in 2 Corinthians 10:10.

Third, others believe that Paul is referring to the present Book of 1 Corinthians in 1 Corinthians 5:9, that is, to the very book which he was writing at the time. In support of this they note the following:

1) Even though the Greek aorist tense used here ("I wrote") may refer to a past letter, it could also refer to the book at hand. This is called an "epistolary aorist," because it refers to the very book in which it is being used.

2) In Greek, the aorist tense is not a past tense as such. It has reference to the *kind* of action, rather than to the *time* of action. It identifies a completed action that may have even taken a long time to be accomplished (cf. John 2:20).

3) The aorist tense often implies a decisive action, in which case Paul would be saying something like this: "I am now decisively writing to you." This certainly fits the context of this passage in which he is urging the church to take immediate action to excommunicate a wayward member.

4) An "epistolary aorist" is used by Paul elsewhere in this very letter when he said, "I am not writing these things that it may be done so in my case" (1 Cor. 9:15, NASB).

5) There is absolutely no indication in early church history that any such letter of Paul, other than the existing 1 and 2 Corinthians, ever existed. The reference in 2 Corinthians 10:10 saying, "his letters are weighty" may mean no more than "what he writes is weighty." And the "now" of 1 Corinthians 5:11 need not indicate a later letter. It can be translated "rather" (RSV) or "actually" (NASB).

1 CORINTHIANS 6:2-3 — How will the saints judge the world and angels?

PROBLEM: The Bible asserts that God is the judge of the world (Ps. 96:13; Acts 17:31; Rev. 20:11-15), including evil angels (2 Peter 2:4; Rev. 12:9). Why, then, does Paul affirm that Christians will be the judges of the world and angels?

SOLUTION: Obviously, God is the judge of wicked humans and angels in a different sense in which Christians will be. Whatever judgment we have will be as God's *delegates* or *representatives,* not by any right we have inherent in ourselves. We are simply the *instruments* through which God executes His judgment. We do not make the ultimate decisions.

It is not clear exactly what Paul envisioned in this passage, but we do know from other Scriptures that there are some legitimate senses in which it can be said that Christians will judge the world. First, during Christ's reign, the apostles "will also sit on twelve thrones, judging the twelve tribes of Israel" (Matt. 19:28).

Second, those who were faithful to Christ during the tribulation "reigned with Christ for a thousand years" (Rev. 20:4). John said, "I saw thrones, and they sat on them, and judgment was committed to them" (Rev. 20:4).

Third, some believe that God will judge the godless by the godly conduct of believers. Jesus said even of the men of Nineveh that they "will rise in the judgment with this generation and condemn it, because they repented at the preaching of Jonah" (Matt. 12:41). Apparently, God will hold up repentant sinners as examples to those who did not repent, and those who did not repent will, therefore, be justly condemned by their own contemporaries. Likewise, the angels who sinned in the perfect environment of heaven will be judged on the basis of the conduct of humans who were saved in the imperfect environment of earth (cf. 2 Peter 2:4).

1 CORINTHIANS 6:9 — Was Paul's condemnation of homosexuality merely his private opinion?

PROBLEM: Paul told the Corinthians that "neither fornicators . . . nor homosexuals . . . will inherit the kingdom of God" (6:9-10). But in the same book he admitted that he was only giving his private "opinion" (1 Cor. 7:25, NASB). In fact, Paul admitted, "I have no commandment from the Lord" (v. 25), and "I [say this], not the Lord" (v. 10). Was not this, by his own confession, merely Paul's own nonbinding opinion on this issue?

SOLUTION: Paul's condemnation against homosexuality is divinely authoritative and not merely his private opinion. This is made plain once the evidence is fully examined. First of all, Paul's clearest condemnation of homosexuality is in Romans 1:26-27, the divine authority of which is not challenged by anyone who accepts the inspiration of Scripture.

Second, Paul's apostolic credentials are firmly established in Scripture. He delcared in Galatians that his revelations were not something that man made up, but were "received . . . by revelation from Jesus Christ" (Gal. 1:12).

Third, Paul declared to the Corinthians that, "The things that mark an apostle — signs, wonders, and miracles — were done among you" (2 Cor. 12:12, NIV). In short, he had exercised apostolic authority in his ministry to the Corinthian Christians.

Fourth, even here in the Book of 1 Corinthians where Paul's authority is severely challenged by his critics, his divine authority is made evident in three ways. (1) He begins the book by claiming that he has "words taught by the Spirit" (1 Cor. 2:13, NIV). (2) He concludes the books claiming, "what I am writing to you is the Lord's command" (14:37, NIV). (3) Even in the disputed chapter 7 where Paul is alleged to be giving his own uninspired opinion, he declares "I too have the Spirit of God" (v. 40, NIV). Indeed, when he said "I, not the Lord" he does not mean his words are not from the Lord; this would contradict everything he says elsewhere. Rather, it means that Jesus did not speak directly to this matter while on earth. But Jesus promised His apostles that He would send the Holy Spirit to "guide you into all truth" (John 16:13). And Paul's teaching in 1 Corinthians was a fulfillment of that promise.

1 CORINTHIANS 6:9 — Was Paul against all homosexual acts or only offensive ones?

PROBLEM: According to the NIV, 1 Corinthians 6:9 speaks only against "homosexual offenders," not against homosexuality as such. That is, the passage only condemns *offensive* homosexual acts, but it is not against homosexual activity per se. Was Paul against homosexual behavior or only offensive homosexual behavior?

SOLUTION: When Paul speaks of "homosexual offenders" (NIV) it means the offense of homosexuality, not an offensive homosexual act as opposed to a non-offensive one. This is made plain by several factors. First, "homosexual" qualifies "offenders," not the reverse. That is, it speaks against a homosexual kind of offense, not an offensive kind of homosexual.

Second, if only offensive kinds of homosexual acts were evil, then what about adulterers and idolaters spoken against in the same passage. Are we to conclude that only offensive kinds of adultery and idolatry are evil.

Third, no such qualification — that only offensive kinds of homosexuality are wrong — is made anywhere else in Scripture in the numerous times it is condemned (see Lev. 18:22-24; Rom. 1:26; cf. also 1 Tim. 1:10; Jude 7).

1 CORINTHIANS 6:13 – If God is going to destroy the body, then how can it be resurrected?

PROBLEM: Paul said, "Foods for the stomach and the stomach for foods; but God will destroy both it and them" (1 Cor. 6:13). On this basis, some argue that the resurrection body will not have the anatomy or physiology of the pre-resurrection body. On the other hand, Paul inferred that we would recognize our loved ones in heaven (1 Thes. 4:13-18).

SOLUTION: The body that goes into the grave is the same body, made immortal, that comes out of it. This is proven by the fact that Jesus' tomb was empty, He had the crucifixion scars in His body (John 20:27), that His body was "flesh and bones" (Luke 24:39), that people could and did touch it (Matt. 28:9), and that He could and did eat physical food (Luke 24:40-42).

As for 1 Corinthians 6:13, a careful study of the context here reveals that, when Paul says God will destroy both food and the stomach, he is referring to the *process* of death, not to the *nature* of the resurrection body. For he refers to the process of death by which "God will destroy both it and them" (v. 13). Further, while the resurrection body may not have the need to eat, it does, however, have the ability to eat. Eating in heaven will be a joy without being a need. So, the body that death "destroys" (decays), is the same one that resurrection restores. To argue that there will be no resurrection body because the stomach will be "destroyed" is tantamount to claiming that the rest of the body — head, arms, legs, and torso — will not be resurrected because death will also turn them into dust.

1 CORINTHIANS 7:10-16 – Does Paul contradict what Jesus said about divorce?

PROBLEM: This passage from 1 Corinthians talks about a Christian who has an unbelieving mate. At one point, Paul says, "But if the unbeliever departs, let him depart; a brother or a sister is not under bondage in such cases" (v. 15). Jesus said in Matthew 5:32 and 19:8-9 that one can divorce a spouse only in the case of marital unfaithfulness. Does Paul advocate divorce or abandonment?

SOLUTION: There is no discrepancy between what Paul says and the words of the Lord Jesus. First, Paul says that if one spouse is a Christian and the other isn't, and if that unbelieving spouse does not want to leave, the Christian should not insist they do (vv. 12-13). Second, Paul says that if the wife leaves her husband, she should remain unmarried (v. 11). This would also hold true for a husband who leaves his wife.

Also, Paul does not tell the spouse to divorce or remarry if the unbelieving spouse leaves. Rather, he suggests that they remain unmarried (v. 11), undoubtedly in hope for reconciliation. God's ideal for marriage is one man and one woman united till death (1 Cor. 7:2; cf. Rom 7:1-2). Hence, as long as there is hope for reunion, both partners are obligated to work to that end. This accords completely with what Jesus said about permanence of marriage (in Matt. 5:33 and 19:7-9).

1 CORINTHIANS 7:12 (cf. 7:40) — How can Paul's words be inspired if he says he is merely giving his own opinion?

PROBLEM: In two places in 1 Corinthians (7:12, 40), the Apostle Paul seems to imply that he is writing on his own authority, not the Lord's. First, in 7:12 Paul says, "But to the rest I, not the Lord." And in 7:40 he says "and I think I also have the Spirit of God" which seems to imply that Paul is not sure if he has the Holy Spirit. How can these verses be harmonized with the divine authority claimed by Paul in his epistles (cf. Gal 1:11-17; 2 Tim. 3:16-17)?

SOLUTION: First, concerning 1 Corinthians 7:12, Paul is referring to the fact that the Lord did not directly address this issue when He spoke about divorce and marriage (Matthew 5:31-32; 19:4-12). So Paul does speak to it here, giving his authoritative view on whether a believing wife should stay with an unbelieving husband.

Second, Paul was not uncertain of his possession of the Holy Spirit on this matter, since he said clearly "I also have the Spirit of God" (1 Cor. 7:40). So this passage cannot be used to show that Paul disclaimed divine authority.

Finally, Paul clearly affirmed his divine authority in this very book, declaring what he wrote as "words . . . the Holy Spirit teaches" (1 Cor. 2:13). Indeed, he concludes the book by saying, "the things which I write to you are the commandments of the Lord" (14:37). So his words in chapter 7 should be taken in harmony with these emphatic claims.

1 CORINTHIANS 8:4 — If idols are nothing, why does God condemn idolatry?

PROBLEM: Paul affirms here that "an idol is nothing in the world." Yet the Bible repeatedly condemns idolatry (cf. Ex. 20:4), and even Paul said there are demons behind idols (1 Cor. 10:19). Is he then claiming that demons are nothing?

SOLUTION: Paul does not deny the *existence* of idols, but simply their *ability* to affect mature believers who eat meat that has been offered to them (cf. 8:1). It is not the *reality* of idols, but their *divinity* which Paul denies. The devil does deceive idolaters (1 Cor. 10:19), but he cannot destroy the meat which God has created and pronounced good (Gen. 1:31; 1 Tim. 4:4), even if someone else has offered it to an idol.

1 CORINTHIANS 9:24 — Does Paul encourage or discourage running to obtain a spiritual goal?

PROBLEM: In this text, the apostle encourages the believer to "run in such a way that you may obtain it." However, in Romans, Paul informs us that "it is not of him who wills, nor of him who runs, but of God who shows mercy" (9:16).

SOLUTION: The first passage is speaking about *rewards* which do depend on our works (cf. 1 Cor. 3:11ff and 2 Cor. 5:10), while the last passage is speaking about *salvation* which is by grace and not by works (Rom. 4:5; Eph. 2:8-9; Titus 3:5-7).

1 CORINTHIANS 10:8 — Does Paul make a mistake in quoting how many people died?

PROBLEM: Paul says in this verse that 23,000 people died. In Exodus 32:28, the number of people listed as having died is 3,000. This would seem to be an error.

SOLUTION: First, the people killed in Exodus 32:28 were killed by the sword, and those Paul mentions are those killed by the sword and a plague. Exodus 32:35 says, "So the LORD plagued the people because of what they did with the calf which Aaron made." Paul gives a complete total from the plague as well as the sword. But Exodus 32:28 gives only the number of those killed by the sword.

Second, some feel that the number of people killed that Paul gives relates to an account of judgment in Numbers 25:9 which says that 24,000 were killed. This may be answered in two ways. First of all, the passage in Numbers does not give a specific time period in which how many people died. Yet, the Apostle Paul says that 23,000 died in one day. Here Paul is giving an account of those killed in one day as opposed to the passage in Numbers which does not specify how many were killed in one day, but gives the total. Further, some say that Paul does not refer to this passage in Numbers because 1 Corinthians 10:7 quotes from Exodus 32:6 which would fit the context of 1 Corinthians and Exodus 32:28.

1 CORINTHIANS 11:5 – Should women wear veils when they pray?

PROBLEM: Paul insisted here that "every woman who prays or prophesies with her head uncovered dishonors her head" (v. 5). Does this mean that women should wear veils in church today, or is this purely cultural? And if it is cultural, then how do we know what is cultural and what is not?

SOLUTION: Several considerations will cast light on this difficult problem. First, a distinction should be made between the *meaning* of the text and its *significance*. The meaning is *what* it says to people in that culture, and the significance is *how* it applies to our cultural situation today. There is little doubt about its meaning. It means exactly what it says. When the women of Corinth threw back their veils and prayed in church, they dishonored their head (husband, 11:3, 7, 9, 11). In that day, the veil was a symbol of a woman's respect for her husband. In such a cultural context, it was imperative that a woman wear a veil in church while praying or prophesying.

Second, there is a difference between *command* and *culture*. The commands of Scripture are absolute – culture is relative. For example, few believe that Jesus' command to His disciples not to have an extra pair of sandals with them while on an evangelistic tour applies today. And most Christians do not literally "Greet all the brethren with a holy kiss" anymore (1 Thes. 5:26). Nor do they believe that "lifting up holy hands in prayer" is essential to public prayer (1 Tim. 2:8). There is a *principle* behind all these commands that is absolute, but the *practice* is not. *What* Christians must do is absolute, but *how* they do it is culturally relative. For example, Christians must greet one another (the *what*), but *how* they greet each other will be relative to their respective cultures. In some cultures, as in the NT, it will be with a kiss, in others with a hug, and in still others with a handshake. Many Bible scholars believe that this principle is also true of the practice of wearing a veil. That is, women in all cultures at all times must show respect for their husbands (the *what*), but *how* this respect is manifest may not always be with a veil. For example, it might be with a wedding ring or some other cultural symbol.

1 CORINTHIANS 11:14 — How can nature teach that long hair is wrong for a man when length of hair is culturally relative?

PROBLEM: Paul asked, "Does not even nature itself teach you that if a man has long hair, it is a dishonor to him?" But, the length of a man's hair is relative to the culture and time in which he lives. It is not something that is known by nature.

SOLUTION: This is a difficult passage, and commentators are not in agreement on it. But, there are two general kinds of answers.

Nature Understood Subjectively. In this sense, "nature" denotes the instinctive feelings or intuitive sense of what is proper. This, of course, may be affected by habits and practices unique to the culture. If this is the sense of the passage, then Paul's statement means something like this: "Do not your own customs teach you that long hair is a shame for a man to have?" This interpretation is difficult to justify in terms of the normal meaning of the word "nature" (*phusis*) which has a much stronger sense than "custom" in the NT (cf. Rom. 1:26; 2:14).

Nature Understood Objectively. In this sense, "nature" means the order of natural laws. Paul speaks of homosexuality as being "against nature" (Rom. 1:26) and of Gentiles knowing "by nature" — that is, by the "law written in their hearts" (Rom. 2:15) — what is right and what is wrong. In this sense, Paul is saying something like this: "Even heathen, who have no special revelation, still have a natural inclination to distinguish the sexes by the length of their hair, women generally having fuller and longer hair." Human beings instinctively distinguish between the sexes in different ways, one of which is the length of hair. There were exceptions arising out of necessity (health, safety), perversity (homosexuality), or special sanctity (the vow of the Nazarite). But, these only serve to prove the general rule based on the natural tendency to differentiate the sexes based on length of hair.

Of course, no absolute standard of what is "long" was in mind. This would vary with the culture. The main point was to aid in distinguishing the sexes. It was for this reason that the OT also forbade a man to dress like a woman (Deut. 22:5), a practice that would have given rise to all sorts of improprieties, both social and moral.

1 CORINTHIANS 12:31 — If coveting is wrong, why does Paul encourage coveting the best gifts?

PROBLEM: One of the Ten Commandments says, "You shall not covet" (Ex. 20:17). Yet Paul encourages the Christian church at Corinth to "covet earnestly the best gifts" (1 Cor. 12:31, KJV).

SOLUTION: "Covet" is used here in the good sense of *"earnestly desire"* (NKJV), rather than in the bad sense of an *unlawful craving* of what does not belong to us.

1 CORINTHIANS 15:5-8 — Did Jesus only appear to believers?

PROBLEM: Some critics have attempted to cast doubt on the validity of Christ's resurrection by insisting that He appeared only to believers, but never to unbelievers. Is this so?

SOLUTION: It is incorrect to claim that Jesus did not appear to unbelievers. This is clear for several reasons. First, He appeared to the most hostile unbeliever of all, Saul of Tarsus (Acts 9:1ff). The Bible devotes much of several chapters to relate this story (Acts 9; 22; 26).

Second, even Jesus' disciples were unbelievers in the resurrection when He first appeared to them. When Mary Magdalene and others reported that Jesus was resurrected "their words seemed to them like idle tales, and they did not believe them" (Luke 24:11). Later, Jesus had to chide the two disciples on the road to Emmaus about disbelief in His resurrection, "O foolish ones, and slow of heart to believe in all that the prophets have spoken!" (Luke 24:25) Even after Jesus had appeared to the women, to Peter, to the two disciples, and to the ten apostles, still Thomas said, "Unless I see the nail marks in His hands and put my finger where the nails were, and put my hand into His side, I will not believe it" (John 20:25, NIV). He was hardly a believer in the resurrection.

Finally, in addition to appearing to His unbelieving disciples, Jesus also appeared to some who were not His disciples at all. He appeared to His brother James (1 Cor. 15:7), who, with his other brothers, was not a believer before the Resurrection (John 7:5). So, it is simply false to claim that Jesus did not appear to unbelievers.

1 CORINTHIANS 15:5-8 – Why did Jesus appear to only a select few?

PROBLEM: Some critics have suggested that the fact that only a few saw Jesus after His resurrection indicates that He was essentially invisible to the human eye, and only materialized to a few people on select occasions. But this is contrary to the orthodox contention that Jesus' resurrection was literal and physical.

SOLUTION: First of all, Jesus did not appear to only a few people. He appeared to over 500 people (1 Cor. 15:6), including many women, His own apostles, His brother James, and to Saul of Tarsus (the chief anti-Christian of the day).

Second, Jesus did not simply appear on a few occasions. He appeared on at least 12 different occasions. These were spread over a 40-day period of time (Acts 1:3) and in many different geographical locations. (See chart on Matt. 28:9.)

Third, Jesus did not allow just anyone to lay hands on Him even before His resurrection. On one occasion, an unbelieving crowd tried to take Jesus and "throw Him down over the cliff. Then passing through the midst of them, He went on his way" (Luke 4:29-30; cf. John 8:59; 10:39).

Fourth, even before His resurrection, Jesus was selective about those for whom He performed miracles. He refused to perform miracles in His own home area "because of their unbelief" (Matt. 13:58). Jesus even disappointed Herod who had hoped to see Him perform a miracle (Luke 23:8). The truth is that Jesus refused to cast pearls before swine (Matt. 7:6). In submission to the Father's will (John 5:30), He was sovereign over His activity both before and after His resurrection. But this in no way proves that He was essentially invisible and immaterial either before or after His resurrection.

1 CORINTHIANS 15:10 – Was Paul's boasting contrary to Scripture?

PROBLEM: Paul boasted here when he declared, "I labored more abundantly than they all." In 2 Corinthians 11:16, Paul even admitted that he was bragging, claiming that none of the other apostles had anything on him (cf. 2 Cor. 12:11). But Paul himself admitted that boasting was wrong and "that no flesh should glory in His presence" (1 Cor. 1:29). And Proverbs exhorts, "Let another man praise you, and not your own mouth" (Prov. 27:2).

SOLUTION: It is important to note, first of all, that when Paul boasted he admitted, "I speak not according to the Lord, but as it were, foolishly" (2 Cor. 11:17). Furthermore, Paul qualified his boasts by phrases like "though I am nothing" (2 Cor. 12:11) and "not I, but the grace of God" (1 Cor. 15:10). His "boasts" must be understood in the light of his confession that "by the grace of God I am what I am" (1 Cor. 15:10). In addition, Paul's motive was not one of self-applause or self-vindication, but the defense and spread of the Gospel. Finally, Paul did not glory in the *flesh*. He gloried rather in the Lord and in the privilege to be humiliated and persecuted for Him (2 Cor. 11:22ff). This kind of "boasting" is in perfect harmony with true humility.

1 CORINTHIANS 15:20 — Was Jesus the first one ever to be resurrected from the dead?

PROBLEM: The Bible seems to claim here that Christ was the first one ever to rise from the dead, calling Him "the firstfruits of those who have fallen asleep." However, there are many other resurrections recorded in the Bible before Jesus' resurrection, both in the OT (cf. 1 Kings 17:22; 2 Kings 13:21) and in the NT (cf. John 11:43-44; Acts 20:9). How then could Jesus' resurrection be the first one.

SOLUTION: When Jesus returned from the dead, it was the first real *resurrection*. Every other raising from the dead was merely a *resuscitation* or *revivification* of a dead body. There are some crucial differences between a true resurrection and a mere resuscitation.

First of all, a resurrection is to an immortal body, whereas a resuscitation is merely back to a mortal body (cf. 1 Cor. 15:53). That is to say, Lazarus and everyone else who was raised from the dead before Christ eventually died again. Christ's resurrection was the first to declare anyone "alive forevermore" (Rev. 1:18).

Further, resurrection bodies manifest some supernatural qualities, not inherent in mortal bodies, such as, the ability to appear and disappear from sight immediately (Luke 24:31) or to get inside a closed room (John 20:19).

Finally, while a resurrection is more than a resuscitation, it was not less than one. Resuscitated corpses die again, but Jesus' resurrection body was immortal. He conquered death (Heb. 2:14; 1 Cor. 15:54-55), whereas merely resuscitated bodies will eventually be conquered by death. However, that Jesus was the first to be raised in an immortal body does not mean it was an immaterial body. It was more than a reanimation of a material corpse, but it was not less than that. It was His same body of "flesh and bones" (Luke 24:39).

1 CORINTHIANS 15:29 – Doesn't advocating baptism for the dead contradict Paul's teaching that each person must believe individually?

PROBLEM: Paul said, "what will they do who are baptized for the dead?" This seems to imply that if a person gets baptized on the account of a dead person, then the deceased will be saved. But, this is in conflict with the clear teaching of Scripture that anyone old enough must believe for himself or herself (John 3:16; Rom. 10:9-13; cf. Ezek. 18:20) to be saved.

SOLUTION: This is an obscure and isolated passage. It is unwise to base any doctrine on such a passage. Rather, one should always use the clear passages of Scripture to interpret the unclear ones. The Bible is emphatic that baptism does not save (see comments on Acts 2:38). We are saved by grace through faith, not by works (Eph. 2:8-9; Titus 3:5-7; Rom. 4:5). Further, we cannot do anything that would obtain salvation for another person. Each person must personally believe (John 1:12). Everyone must make his own free choice (Matt. 23:37; 2 Peter 3:9).

Scholars differ as to what Paul means in this passage. The following interpretations are possibilities.

Some believe Paul is referring to a cultic practice among the Corinthians who had many other false beliefs (cf. 1 Cor. 5; 12). In effect, Paul would be saying, "If you don't believe in the Resurrection, then why engage in the practice of baptizing people for the dead. You are inconsistent with your own (false) beliefs." They think that the practice was so obviously wrong that Paul does not need to condemn it explicitly. They point to the fact that Paul says "they" (others) not "we" baptize the dead (v. 29).

Others suggest that Paul is simply referring to the fact that baptism of new converts is replenishing the depleted ranks of believers who have died and gone on to be with the Lord. If so, then his sense here would be, "Why do you continue to fill the church with baptized converts, who replace those who have died, if you do not really believe there is any hope for them beyond the grave?"

Some suggest that Paul is referring to the fact that baptism symbolizes the believer's death with Christ (Rom. 6:3-5). The Greek word "for" (*eis*) can mean "with a view to." In this sense, he would be saying, "Why are you baptized with a view to your death and resurrection with Christ, if you do not believe in the Resurrection?"

Still others, point out that the preposition "for" in Greek (*huper*) can mean "for the sake of." In this case, baptism would be for the sake of those who are dead. They point to the fact that Paul says "If the dead do not rise at all; Why then are they baptized for the dead?" (v. 29) Since it was common in the NT period to be baptized as one accepted the Gospel, this was a sign of one's faith in Christ. Thus Paul would be saying, "Why be baptized if there is no resurrection?" For Paul later says that if there is no resurrection, then "let us eat and drink, for tomorrow we die" (v. 32). Whatever the correct interpretation, there is no reason to believe Paul is here contradicting his clear teaching elsewhere or the rest of Scripture which insists that every person must freely choose or reject God's gift of salvation.

1 CORINTHIANS 15:33 — By quoting a pagan poet as part of Scripture, doesn't Paul thereby pronounce this pagan writing a part of Scripture?

(See comments on Titus 1:12.)

1 CORINTHIANS 15:37 — Is Paul teaching that the resurrection body is a different one from the one that is sown — a kind of reincarnation?

PROBLEM: According to this verse, we "do not sow that body that shall be." Some take this to mean the resurrection body is a different one, a "spiritual" (v. 44) body that is not essentially material (see comments on 1 Cor. 15:44). Does this prove that we are not raised in the same physical body of flesh and bones in which we die?

SOLUTION: There are real changes in the resurrection body, but it is not changed into a nonphysical body — one substantially different from the one we possess now. The seed that goes into the ground brings forth more seeds that are the same kind, not immaterial seeds. It is in this sense that Paul can say "you do not sow [cause to die] the body that shall be," since it is immortal and cannot die. The body that is raised is different in that it is immortal (1 Cor. 15:53), not in that it is immaterial. Of His resurrection body Jesus said, "It is I Myself. Handle Me and see, for a spirit does not have *flesh and bones* as you see I have" (Luke 24:39).

There are many reasons for holding that the resurrection body, though transformed and glorified, is the *numerically same body* of flesh and bones Jesus possessed before His resurrection. And since our resurrection bodies will be like His (Phil. 3:21), the same is true of the believer's resurrection body. Notice these characteristics of Jesus' resurrection body: (1) It was the same body with the crucifixion scars it had from before the resurrection (Luke 24:39; John 20:27). (2) It was the same body that left the empty tomb behind (Matt. 28:6; John 20:5-7; cf. John 5:28-29).

(3) The physical body of Jesus did not corrupt in the tomb (Acts 2:31). (4) Jesus said the same body that is destroyed will be built up again (John 2:21-22). (5) The immortal body is "put on" over, but does not replace, the mortal body (1 Cor. 15:53). (6) The plant that springs forth from the seed is both genetically and physically connected with the seed. What is sown is what is reaped (1 Cor. 15:37-38). (7) It is the same body of "flesh and bones" (Luke 24:39) that could be touched (Matt. 28:9; John 20:27) and could eat physical food (Luke 24:41-42).

The "change" (1 Cor. 15:51) Paul referred to at the resurrection is a change *in* the body, not a change *of* the body. The changes in the resurrection are *accidental,* not *substantial.* They are changes in *secondary* qualities, not changes in *primary* qualities. It is changed from a corruptible physical body to an incorruptible physical body. It is not changed from a physical body into a nonphysical body. It is changed from a mortal to an immortal physical body. But it is not changed from a material to an immaterial body.

1 CORINTHIANS 15:44 — Is the resurrection body material or immaterial?

PROBLEM: Paul declares that the resurrection body is a "spiritual body" (1 Cor. 15:44), but a spiritual body is an immaterial body. However, elsewhere the Bible says Jesus' resurrection body was made of "flesh and bones" (Luke 24:39).

SOLUTION: A "spiritual" body denotes an immortal body, not an immaterial body. A "spiritual" body is one dominated by the spirit, not one devoid of matter. The Greek word *pneumatikos* (translated "spiritual" here) means a body directed by the spirit, as opposed to one under the dominion of the flesh. It is not ruled by flesh that perishes, but by the spirit that endures (1 Cor. 15:50-58). So "spiritual body" does not mean immaterial and invisible, but immortal and imperishable. This is clear from several facts:

First, notice the parallelism mentioned by Paul:

PRE-RESURRECTION BODY	POST-RESURRECTION BODY
Earthly (v. 40)	Heavenly
Perishable (v. 42)	Imperishable
Weak (v. 43)	Powerful
Mortal (v. 53)	Immortal
Natural (v. 44)	[Supernatural]

The complete context indicates that "spiritual" (*pneumatikos*) could be translated "supernatural" in contrast to "natural." This is made clear by the parallels of perishable and imperishable and corruptible and incorruptible. In fact, this same Greek word (*pneumatikos*) is translated "supernatural" in 1 Corinthians 10:4 when it speaks of the "supernatural rock that followed them in the wilderness" (RSV).

Second, the word "spiritual" (*pneumatikos*) in 1 Corinthians refers to material objects. Paul spoke of the "spiritual rock" that followed Israel in the wilderness from which they got "spiritual drink" (1 Cor. 10:4). But the OT story (Ex. 17; Num. 20) reveals that it was a physical rock from which they got literal water to drink. But the actual water they drank from that material rock was produced supernaturally. When Jesus supernaturally made bread for the five thousand (John 6), He made literal bread. However, this literal, material bread could have been called "spiritual" bread (because of its supernatural source) in the same way that the literal manna given to Israel is called "spiritual food" (1 Cor. 10:3).

Further, when Paul spoke about a "spiritual man" (1 Cor. 2:15) he obviously did not mean an invisible, immaterial man with no corporeal body. He was, as a matter of fact, speaking of a flesh and blood human being whose life was lived by the supernatural power of God. He was referring to a literal person whose life was Spirit directed. A spiritual man is one who is taught by the Spirit and who receives the things that come from the Spirit of God (1 Cor. 2:13-14). The resurrection body can be called a "spiritual body" in much the same way we speak of the Bible as a "spiritual book." Regardless of their spiritual source and power, both the resurrection body and the Bible are material objects.

1 CORINTHIANS 15:45 — Was Christ a life-giving spirit after His resurrection, or did He have a physical body?

PROBLEM: Paul asserts here that Christ was made a "life-giving spirit" after His resurrection. Some have also used this passage to prove that Jesus had no physical resurrection body.

SOLUTION: This does not follow for many reasons.

First, "life-giving spirit" does not speak of the *nature* of the resurrection body, but of the divine *origin* of the resurrection. Jesus' physical body came back to life only by the power of God (cf. Rom. 1:4). So Paul is speaking about its spiritual *source,* not its physical *substance* as a material body (see also comments on 1 Cor. 15:44).

Second, if "spirit" describes the nature of Christ's resurrection body, then Adam (with whom He is contrasted) must not have had a soul, since he is described as "of the earth, made of dust" (v. 47). But the Bible clearly says that Adam was "a living being [soul]" (Gen. 2:7).

Third, Christ's resurrection body is called "spiritual body" (v. 44) which, as discussed under 1 Corinthians 15:44, is the same word used by Paul to describe material food and a literal rock (1 Cor. 10:4).

Fourth, it is called a "body" (sōma) which always means a physical body when referring to an individual human being.

In summation, the resurrection body is called "spiritual" and "life-giving spirit" because its source is the spiritual realm, not because its substance is immaterial. Christ's supernatural resurrection body is "from heaven," as Adam's natural body was "of the earth" (v. 47). But just as the one from "earth" also has an immaterial soul, even so the One from "heaven" also has a material body.

1 CORINTHIANS 15:50 — If flesh and blood cannot enter heaven, then how can there be a physical resurrection?

PROBLEM: The Bible speaks of the resurrection of the physical body from the grave (John 5:28-29), which is composed of "flesh and bones" (Luke 24:39) and which leaves an empty tomb behind (Matt. 28:6). However, according to this verse, "flesh and blood cannot inherit the kingdom of God."

SOLUTION: To conclude from this phrase that the resurrection body will not be a body of physical flesh is without biblical justification. First of all, the very next phrase omitted from the above quotation clearly indicates that Paul is speaking not of flesh as such, but of *corruptible* flesh. For he adds, "nor does corruption inherit incorruption" (v. 50). So, Paul is not affirming that the resurrection body will not have flesh, but that it will not have *perishable* flesh.

Second, to convince the frightened disciples that He was not an immaterial spirit (Luke 24:37), Jesus emphatically told them, "Look at My hands and My feet. It is I Myself! Touch Me and see; a ghost does not have *flesh and bones,* as you see I have" (Luke 24:39, NIV). Peter declared that the resurrection body would be the same body of *flesh* that went into the tomb and never saw corruption (Acts 2:31). Paul also reaffirmed this truth in a parallel passage (Acts 13:35). And John implies that it is against Christ to deny that He remains "in the *flesh*" even after His resurrection (1 John 4:2; 2 John 7).

Third, this conclusion cannot be avoided by claiming that Jesus' resurrection body had flesh and bones, but not flesh and blood. For if it had flesh and bones, then it was a literal, material body, whether or not it had blood. "Flesh and bones" stresses the solidity of Jesus' physical post-resurrection body. They are more obvious signs of tangibility than blood, which cannot be as easily seen or touched.

Fourth, the phrase "flesh and blood" in this context apparently means *mortal* flesh and blood, that is, a mere human being. This is supported by parallel uses in the NT. When Jesus said to Peter, "Flesh and blood has not revealed this to you" (Matt. 16:17), He could not have been referring to the mere substance of the body as such, which obviously could not reveal that He was the Son of God. Rather, the most natural interpretation of 1 Corinthians 15:50 seems to be that *humans, as they now are, earth-bound and perishable creatures,* cannot have a place in God's glorious, heavenly kingdom.

2 CORINTHIANS

2 CORINTHIANS 3:7, 13 — Did Moses wear a veil when speaking to the people or not?

PROBLEM: Exodus 34:33 (KJV) asserts that, "Till Moses had done speaking with them, he put a vail [*sic*] on his face" (cf. v. 35). This implies he had the veil on while speaking with them. But this seems to contradict the statement here in 2 Corinthians 3 that they could not look "steadily" on it, which implies that they were looking at it when Moses spoke (vv. 7, 13).

SOLUTION: Recent translations have corrected this problem, rendering Exodus 34:33 as follows: "when Moses had finished speaking with them [the people], he put a veil on his face." This fits the context better as well, since this verse is followed by the assertion that "whenever the children of Israel saw the face of Moses, that the skin of Moses' face shone, then Moses would put the veil on his face again, until he went in to speak with Him [God]" (v. 35). Then Moses would come out, take the veil off and speak to the people until they could not bear the glory, and he would cover it up until he again went in before the Lord (v. 34).

2 CORINTHIANS 5:21 — How could Jesus be made sin when He was sinless?

PROBLEM: Paul asserts here that Jesus was "made to be sin." However, many other Scriptures insist that Jesus was "without sin" (Heb. 4:15; cf. 1 Peter 3:18). But how could Jesus be without sin if He was made sin for us?

SOLUTION: Jesus was always without sin *actually*, but He was made to be sin for us *judicially*. That is, by His death on the Cross, He paid the penalty for our sins and thereby cancelled the debt of sin against us. So, while Jesus never committed a sin *personally*, He was made to be sin for us *substitutionally*. The issue can be summarized as follows:

CHRIST WAS NOT SINFUL	CHRIST WAS MADE TO BE SIN
In Himself	For us
Personally	Substitutionally
Actually	Judicially

2 CORINTHIANS 11:5 — Was Paul the greatest or the least of apostles?

PROBLEM: Here Paul claimed, "I am not at all inferior to the most eminent apostles" (2 Cor. 11:5). And elsewhere he would have us believe that he is "the least of the apostles" (1 Cor. 15:9). But it would seem that both cannot be true.

SOLUTION: Paul is speaking in different contexts. In one passage, he is speaking with respect to his *ability, training, and zeal.* However, unlike the other apostles, Paul had persecuted the church of Christ before his conversion and, therefore, considered himself unworthy even to be an apostle (cf. Gal. 1:13; Acts 9:1). So with respect to his *preconversion antagonism to Christ* he rightly considered himself "the least of the apostles."

GALATIANS

GALATIANS 1:15-16 – Is Paul teaching reincarnation in this passage?

(See comments on Jer. 1:5.)

GALATIANS 3:13 – Is Christ blessed or cursed?

PROBLEM: Paul declares that Christ was cursed of God, "having become a curse for us." However, the Bible declares repeatedly that Christ was blessed of God (cf. Ps. 72:17), the one worthy to receive "glory and blessing" forever (Rev. 5:12).

SOLUTION: These passages view Christ under different aspects. He is blessed in heaven, but He became a curse for us on earth. He is blessed in Himself, but was cursed for us on the Cross. Actually, as the perfect Son of God, He is the most blessed of all persons. Yet, judicially, as He became our substitute – He was the most cursed of all. The difference is manifest in this contrast:

CHRIST WAS BLESSED OF GOD	CHRIST WAS CURSED OF GOD
Actually	Judicially
For who He is	For what He did for us
In heaven	On the cross
For the kind of person He is	For the kind of death he died

GALATIANS 3:17 – Does Paul err in the amount of time between Abraham and the time the Law was given?

PROBLEM: In Galatians 3:17, the apostle states that a period of 430 years elapsed between the time of God's promises to Abraham (Gen.

12:1-3), which was about 2000 B.C., and the giving of the law to Moses, which was around 1450 B.C. This would be a mistake of over 100 years.

SOLUTION: The time that Paul refers to is not the initial *giving* of the Abrahamic covenant (Gen. 12–15), but the later *confirmation* of the covenant to Jacob (Gen. 46), which was about 1877 B.C. Since the Exodus occurred around 1447 B.C. (cf. 1 Kings 6:1), this would be exactly 430. There is good indication that Paul is referring to the confirmation to Jacob, not to the initiation of the covenant to Abraham. The text clearly dates the 430 years from "the covenant that was *confirmed*" (Gal. 3:17). Thus, the time period is the final reaffirmation of the Abrahamic promises to the descendants (seed) of Abraham which takes place in Genesis 46:2-4 to Jacob, a descendent of Abraham, which was 430 years before the children of Israel came out of Egypt.

GALATIANS 6:5 — Are we to bear other's burdens or our own?

PROBLEM: In Galatians 6:2, Paul exhorts us to "bear one another's burdens, and so fulfill the law of Christ." But only a few verses later he says "every man shall bear his own burden" (v. 5, KJV).

SOLUTION: The word for "burden" is different in each case. In the first passage, Paul urges *sympathy for others*. In the other, he is speaking of taking *responsibility for ourselves*. There is no conflict between being *accountable for our own lives* and being *helpful to others*.

EPHESIANS

EPHESIANS 1:10 — Does this verse teach that all will be saved (universalism)?

(See comments on Col. 1:20.)

EPHESIANS 2:1 — How can a person believe if he or she is dead in sins?

PROBLEM: The Bible repeatedly calls on the unbeliever to "believe on the Lord Jesus Christ and . . . be saved" (Acts 16:31). However, this passage declares that unbelievers are dead in their sins, and dead people cannot do anything, including believe.

SOLUTION: "Death" in the Bible is not to be understood as annihilation, but as separation. Isaiah said, "Your iniquities have separated you from your God" (Isa. 59:2). If death were annihilation, then the second death would be eternal annihilation, but the Bible declares that the lost will be consciously separated from God, as was the rich man in hell (Luke 16), as will be the beast and false prophet who will be "tormented day and night forever and ever" (Rev. 20:10). Indeed, they were cast "alive" into the lake of fire at the beginning of the 1,000-year reign of Christ (Rev. 19:20), and they were still alive at the end of the 1,000 years (20:10). So, the second "death" is eternal conscious separation from Christ.

Furthermore, believers die physically, but their souls survive death and are consciously in the presence of God. Paul said, "absent from the body and . . . present with the Lord" (2 Cor. 5:8). And he went on to say, "having a desire to depart and be with Christ, which is far better" (Phil. 1:23).

Likewise, spiritual death is also separation from God, not annihilation. Adam and Eve, for example, died spiritually the moment they ate the forbidden fruit (Gen. 3:6; cf. Rom. 5:12), yet they were still alive and could hear God's voice speaking to them (Gen. 3:10). So, whereas the image of God in fallen man is effaced, it is not erased. It is marred, but not destroyed. Thus, unsaved persons can hear, understand the Gospel, and believe it to be regenerated or made alive in a spiritual sense (Eph. 2:8-9; Titus 3:5-7).

EPHESIANS 3:5 — How could the mystery of Christ be hidden in previous ages and yet known by the OT Prophets?

PROBLEM: According to this passage, the mystery of the church, the body of Christ, was not known in other ages. Yet the apostle goes on to say that it was revealed to the "apostles and prophets." But the prophets lived prior to the time of Paul. How could the prophets have known if people in the OT did not know the mystery?

SOLUTION: There are several reasons for believing that Paul is referring to NT prophets, not OT ones. First, the order in which he mentions them is not prophets and then apostles, but "apostles and prophets."

Second, this same phrase is used to describe the foundation of the NT church which is built on the "foundation of the apostles and prophets" (Eph. 2:20). But the NT church did not begin in the OT, but only after Christ announced it in Matthew 16:18.

Third, the text says clearly that the mystery of the spiritual body of Christ "was not made known" to the sons of men "in other ages" but only now to "the apostles and prophets" (Eph. 3:5).

Finally, the parallel passage in Colossians says emphatically, "the mystery . . . has been hidden from ages and from generations, but now has been revealed to His saints" (1:26). Thus, the "prophets" to whom it was made known were NT prophets (cf. 1 Cor. 12:28; Eph. 4:11).

EPHESIANS 4:8 — Does Paul inaccurately quote Psalm 68:18?

PROBLEM: Paul quotes Psalm 68:18 saying, "When He ascended on high, He led captivity captive, and *gave* gifts to men" (Eph. 4:8). Yet the OT Psalm reads, "You have ascended on high, you have led captivity captive; you have *received* gifts among men." Is there a discrepancy here between these two texts?

SOLUTION: Some say that Paul did not quote from the Septuagint, but from the Aramaic Targum which is used by orthodox Jews to interpret the text. The Septuagint translates the Hebrew as "You have taken," while the Targum translates the Hebrew "You have given."

In any event, the idea given by these two translations of the Hebrew is that God received or took gifts so that they could then be distributed to men. Since both ideas are in the text, both renderings are correct. Thus, Paul says, "He Himself gave some to be apostles, some prophets, some evangelists, and some pastors and teachers" (Eph. 4:11). In other words, Paul quotes this OT passage to show that Christ was victorious over our spiritual enemies, taking from them the spoils of battle and passing on the gifts to believers who in the exercise of these gifts can be victorious over the enemy. Therefore, there are no discrepancies to be found in Paul's use of this Psalm, since this is precisely what David did when he robbed his enemy of their gifts and gave them to his men.

EPHESIANS 4:9 – Did Jesus descend into hell?

PROBLEM: Paul claims here that Jesus "descended into the lower parts of the earth." And the Apostles' Creed declares that after Jesus died, He "descended into hell." However, when Jesus was dying, He committed His spirit into His Father's hand (Luke 23:46) and told the thief that He would be with Him in "paradise" (Luke 23:43) which is in the "third heaven" (2 Cor. 12:2, 4). Where did Jesus go—to heaven or to hell?

SOLUTION: There are two views as to where Jesus went the three days His body was in the grave before His resurrection.

The Hades View. One position claims that Christ's spirit went to the spirit world, while His body was in the grave. Here, they believe, He spoke to the "spirits in prison" (1 Peter 3:19) who were in a temporary holding place until He would come and "lead captivity captive," that is, take them to heaven. According to this view, there were two compartments in Hades (or *sheol*), one for the saved and another for the unsaved. They were separated by a "great gulf" (Luke 16:26) which no person could pass. The section for the saved was called "Abraham's bosom" (Luke 16:23). When Christ, as the "firstfruits" of the resurrection (1 Cor. 15:20), ascended, He led these OT saints into heaven with Him for the first time.

The Heaven View. This teaching holds that the souls of OT believers went directly to heaven the moment they died. It offers the following arguments in support of its teaching. First, Jesus affirmed that His spirit was going directly to heaven, declaring, "Father, into Your Hands I commend My spirit" (Luke 23:46).

Second, Jesus promised the thief on the cross, "Today, you will be with me in Paradise" (Luke 23:43). But "Paradise" is defined as "the third heaven" in 2 Corinthians 12:2, 4.

Third, when OT saints departed this life, they went directly to heaven. God took Enoch to be with Himself (Gen. 5:24; cf. Heb. 11:5), and Elijah was caught up into "heaven" when he departed (2 Kings 2:1).

Fourth, "Abraham's bosom" (Luke 16:23) is a description of heaven. At no time is it ever described as hell. It is the place that Abraham went, which is the "kingdom of heaven" (Matt. 8:11).

Fifth, when OT saints appear before the cross, they appear from heaven, as Moses and Elijah did on the Mount of Transfiguration (Matt. 17:3).

Sixth, OT saints had to await Christ's resurrection before their *bodies* could be resurrected (1 Cor. 15:20; cf. Matt. 27:53), but their *souls* went directly to heaven. Christ was the Lamb slain "from the foundation of the world" (Rev. 13:8), and they were there on the merits of what God knew Christ would accomplish.

Seventh, "descending into the lower parts of the earth" is not a reference to hell, but to the grave. Even a woman's womb is described as "lowest parts of the earth" (Ps. 139:15). The phrase simply means caves, graves, or enclosures on the earth, as opposed to higher parts, like mountains. Besides this, hell is not in the lower parts of the earth — it is "under the earth" (Phil. 2:10).

Eighth, the phrase, "descended into hell," was not in the earliest Apostles' Creed. It was not added until the 4th century. Further, as a creed, it is not inspired — it is only a human confession of faith.

Ninth, the "spirits in prison" were not saved, but unsaved beings. Indeed, they may refer to angels, not to human beings (see comments on 1 Peter 3:19).

Finally, when Christ "led captivity captive," He was not leading friends into heaven, but bringing foes into bondage. It is a reference to His conquering the forces of evil. Christians are not "captives" in heaven. We are not forced to go there against our own free choice (see Matt. 23:37; 2 Peter 3:9).

EPHESIANS 4:26 — Is anger a sin or not?

PROBLEM: On the one hand, the Bible seems to approve of anger, saying, "be angry" (Eph. 4:26). On the other hand, the Bible seems to disapprove of it, listing it as one of the "works of the flesh" (Gal. 5:19-20).

SOLUTION: Anger *as such* is not necessarily wrong. In fact, anger *at sin* is definitely right. Jesus was angry at unbelief and hypocrisy (cf. Matt. 23; John 2:13-17), and God is angry at unrighteousness and apostasy (cf. Ex. 4:14; Num. 11:1). What is wrong is not anger *at sin,* but sinning *in anger*. Briefly, there is both a good sense and a bad sense of anger:

GOOD ANGER	BAD ANGER
Righteous indignation	Unrighteous eruptions
Under self-control	In loss of self-control
Anger at sin	Anger in sin
As a spiritual expression	As a natural passion

EPHESIANS 6:5 – Doesn't this command perpetuate the institution of slavery?

(See comments on Phile. 16.)

PHILIPPIANS

PHILIPPIANS 2:5-7 — If Christ emptied Himself of deity while on earth, then how could He be God?

PROBLEM: Paul seems to say that Jesus "emptied Himself" of His deity or "equality with God" (vv. 6-7), becoming "a man" (v. 8). But elsewhere Jesus claimed to be God on earth (John 8:58; 20:28). But how could Jesus be God while on earth if He left His deity aside to become man?

SOLUTION: Jesus did not cease being God while on earth. Rather, in addition to being God, He also became man. His incarnation was not the subtraction of deity, but the addition of humanity. Several things in this text support this position. First, it does not say Christ gave up or emptied Himself of His deity, but merely of His *rights* as deity, assuming the "form of a servant" (v. 7) so as to be an example for us (v. 5). Second, the text declares that He was in the "form of God" or "in very nature God" (v. 6, NIV). Just as the "form of a servant" (v. 7) is a servant by nature, so the "form of God" (v. 6) is God by nature. Third, this very passage declares that every knee will one day confess Jesus is "Lord," a citation from Isaiah 45:23 that refers to *Yahweh,* a name used exclusively of God.

PHILIPPIANS 2:25 — If Paul had the gift of healing, why couldn't he heal his coworker, Epaphroditus?

PROBLEM: In the Book of Acts, Paul healed the sick and even raised the dead (Acts 20:9-10). On one occasion he even healed everyone in an entire city (Acts 28:9). But here, he apparently could not even heal a needed coworker.

SOLUTION: There are two possible responses to this.

Some believe that possessing the gift of healing did not guarantee that one could always heal everyone. On one occasion the disciples could not heal a demon-possessed young man (Matt. 17:16). They insist that the gift of healing did not make a person 100 percent successful, any more than the gift of teaching made one infallible.

Others insist that the gift of healing was always successful, noting that Jesus healed the young man (in Matt. 17) and rebuked the disciples for not exercising their God-given power to do it (vv. 17-18). They claim that the gift of healing was 100 percent successful, just as no one with the gift of prophecy ever uttered a false prophecy with it. For a false prophecy was a proof that someone was not exercising the gift of prophecy (cf. Deut. 18:22).

The reason Epaphroditus was not healed is not stated in the text. But neither does it say Paul attempted to heal him and failed. Since no exercise of the gift of healing is recorded past about A.D. 61 (Acts 28:8), it may be that the special apostolic gift of healing (cf. 2 Cor. 12:12; Heb. 2:4) had passed away by this time. It is not listed in the much briefer list of gifts in Ephesians 4 (ca. A.D. 60), as it was earlier in 1 Cor. 12:30.

PHILIPPIANS 3:15 – Are Christians perfect, or still on the way?

PROBLEM: In this verse, Paul calls on those who "are perfect" (KJV) to act as he did, but only three verses earlier he claimed that he was not "already perfect" (v. 12), but that he was still pressing on to attain perfection. Which one should we believe?

SOLUTION: Here is a good example of how the same word can be used in different senses. This is not uncommon in languages, as the English word "board" illustrates. Take this sentence for example: "The *board* members took a stroll on the *board*walk and then stopped at the desk to inquire about room and *board*." It is obvious that the same word "board" is being used here in three different senses. Likewise, Paul uses the word "perfect" in different senses. Some believers are "perfect" in the sense of being *mature* or *complete*. But no believer this side of death is perfect in the sense of having *fully arrived* or having *reached the ultimate goal*. This only comes, as Paul indicated, at "the resurrection from the dead" (Phil. 3:11).

PHILIPPIANS 4:4 – How can we rejoice always when Jesus said "blessed are those who mourn"?

PROBLEM: Paul commands us here to "Rejoice in the Lord always," but Jesus insisted that "Blessed are those who mourn" (Matt. 5:4).

SOLUTION: Properly understood, these are not mutually exclusive. Mourning is the *condition* and rejoicing is the *result* of a proper relation to God. It is those who humble themselves whom God lifts up (cf. James 4:10). So it is those who mourn in their spirit who will be able to rejoice in their Lord. True sorrow for sin is the *antecedent* of the *consequent* joy of salvation.

PHILIPPIANS 4:5 – Is the Lord's coming at hand or far off?

PROBLEM: According to this passage, "The Lord is at hand" (cf. 1 Peter 4:7). However, other passages portray Christ's coming as not being immediate, but as having intervening events. "For that Day will not come," writes Paul, "unless the falling away comes first" (2 Thes. 2:3).

SOLUTION: Bible scholars respond to this problem in two different ways, depending on their view of future things (eschatology).

Non-imminent View. Those who believe Christ's coming is not imminent take the verses that speak of it as "at hand" as only general descriptions, but not specific time frames. They note that the "last days" includes the whole period of time between Christ's first and second comings (cf. Heb. 1:1; 1 John 2:18). Thus, they see no difficulty with passages (like 2 Thes. 2:3) that speak of some events that must occur first before Christ can return. That is, they believe that it is true *in a general sense* that "the Lord is at hand," but deny that this means that He could literally come at any moment. Some specific events, like the "falling away," must come first before Christ will actually return.

Imminent View. Other Bible scholars, including the authors, take the verses declaring that Christ's coming is "at hand" (Phil. 4:5; cf. 1 Peter 4:7) literally. They claim that otherwise it could not be "the blessed hope" spoken of by Paul (Titus 2:13), nor the purifying hope by John (1 John 3:2-3). Further, why should the believer be exhorted to "watch" for it and not to be taken by surprise (cf. 1 Thes. 5:1-2). In addition, they believe that if there were discernable signs and events that must occur before Christ returns for believers, then we could know "the day and hour" (Matt. 24:36) or "times or seasons" (Acts 1:7) which Christ said we cannot know.

According to this view, then, when the Bible speaks of Christ's return as a sign-less, imminent event that could happen at any moment, it is speaking about Christ's coming in the air *for* His saints before the tribulation (i.e., the rapture of 1 Thes. 4:13-18). And when the Scriptures talk about signs and events that must occur before the coming of Christ, it is referring to His coming *with* His saints to earth after the tribulation (Matt. 24:29-30).

The two aspects of Christ's return can be diagramed in this manner:

COMING FOR HIS SAINTS	COMING WITH HIS SAINTS
Before the tribulation	After the tribulation
In the air	On earth
No signs	Many signs
Imminent	Not imminent
At hand	Yet to come
A "now" coming	A near coming

COLOSSIANS

COLOSSIANS 1:18 – If Christ is only the firstborn in creation, then how can He be God?

PROBLEM: John declared Christ to be eternal and equal with God (John 1:1; 8:58; 20:28). But here Paul seems to say that Christ was only a creature, the first one born (created) in the universe.

SOLUTION: Paul clearly declares Christ to be God in this very letter by saying He "created all things" (1:16) and has "the fullness of the God-head" (2:9). The reference to "firstborn" does not mean He is the first-born *in* creation, but the firstborn *over* creation (v. 15), since "He is before all things" (v. 17). "Firstborn" in this context does not mean the first one to be born, but the heir of all, the Creator and owner of all things. As Creator of "all things," He could not have been a created thing.

COLOSSIANS 1:20 – Does this verse teach that all will be saved (universalism)?

PROBLEM: The Apostle Paul wrote to the Colossians, "For it was the Father's good pleasure . . . *through Him [Christ] to reconcile all things to Himself,* having made peace through the blood of His cross; through Him, I say, whether things on earth or things in heaven" (Col. 1:19-20, NASB). If Paul says that all things are reconciled to Christ by His death and resurrection, this seems to imply that all people are saved. But other Scriptures declare that many will be lost (e.g., Matt. 7:13-14; 25:41; Rev. 20:11-15).

SOLUTION: First of all, Paul is not speaking about universal *salvation* here, but simply universal *sovereignty* of Jesus Christ. In other words, all authority has been given to Jesus Christ in heaven and on earth (Matt. 28:18). By virtue of His death and resurrection, Christ as the Last Adam is Lord over all that was lost by the First Adam (cf. 1 Cor. 15:45-49).

Note the contrast between two crucial passages by Paul:

EPHESIANS/COLOSSIANS	PHILIPPIANS
All *in* Christ	All bow *before* Christ
All in:	All in:
heaven	heaven
earth	earth
. . . . .	under the earth
All in Salvation	All in Subjection

When Paul speaks of being "in Christ" (i.e., being saved), he does not include "those under the earth" (i.e., the lost). However, all persons, saved and unsaved, will one day bow before Christ and acknowledge His universal lordship. But nowhere do the Scriptures teach that all people will be saved. Jesus will say to many, "Depart from Me, you cursed, into the everlasting fire prepared for the devil and his angels" (Matt. 25:41). John spoke of the devil, the beast and the false prophet, and all whose names are not written in the Book of Life being cast into the lake of fire forever (Rev. 20:10-15). Luke speaks of a great impassible gulf between heaven and hell in which those who have rejected God are living in torment (Luke 16:19-31). Paul speaks of punishment on the wicked as "everlasting destruction from the presence of the Lord" (2 Thes. 1:7-9). Jesus declared Judas was lost and called him "the son of perdition" (John 17:12). It is evident from all these passages that not everyone will be saved.

COLOSSIANS 1:24 — How can Christ's death on the Cross be sufficient for salvation when Paul speaks of what is lacking in the sufferings of Christ?

PROBLEM: The Bible declares that Jesus' death on the cross was both sufficient and final for our salvation (John 19:30; Heb. 1:3). Yet Paul states that we are to fill up what is "lacking in the afflictions of Christ." But if the Cross is all-sufficient, then how can anything be lacking in Christ's suffering for us?

SOLUTION: Christ's death on the Cross is sufficient for our salvation. The Bible makes this emphatically clear. Anticipating the Cross, Jesus said to His Father, "I have finished the work which You have given Me to do" (John 17:4). On the cross He cried out, "It is finished!" (John 19:30). The Book of Hebrews declares unequivocally that "by one offering [on the cross] He has perfected forever those who are being sanctified" (Heb. 10:14). And this He did "by Himself" (Heb. 1:3), with no help from anyone else.

Nevertheless, there is a sense in which Christ still suffers after His death. Jesus said to Paul, "Why are you persecuting Me?" In this sense, we too can suffer for Him, since "it has been granted on behalf of Christ, not only to believe on Him, but also to suffer for His sake" (Phil. 1:29). But in no sense is our suffering for Christ a means of atoning for sin. Only Jesus suffered *for* sin. We suffer *because* of sin (ours and others), but never for sin. Each person must bear the guilt of his own sin (Ezek. 18:20) and accept the fact that Christ suffered for his sin (1 Peter 2:21; 3:18; 2 Cor. 5:21). When we suffer for Christ, we are undergoing pain as part of His spiritual body, the church, but only what Christ suffered in His physical body on the Cross is efficacious for our sins. Our suffering, then, is in *service,* not for *salvation.*

COLOSSIANS 2:8 – Does this verse mean Christians should not study philosophy?

PROBLEM: Paul warned here, "Beware lest anyone cheat you through philosophy and empty deceit." Does this mean that Christians should not study philosophy? If so, then why did God give us a mind and command us to think (Matt. 22:37) and reason (1 Peter 3:15)?

SOLUTION: First of all, the Bible is no more against philosophy than it is against religion. It is not against philosophy, but against *vain* philosophy, which Paul calls "empty deceit" (v. 8). Likewise, the Bible is not opposed to religion, but only against *vain* religion (cf. James 1:26-27).

Further, Paul is not speaking about philosophy *in general,* but about a *particular* philosophy, usually understood as an early form of Gnosticism. This is indicated by his use of the definite article (in Greek), which should be translated "*the* philosophy" or "*this* philosophy." So Paul was referring to this particular gnostic-like philosophy that had invaded the church in Colosse and involved legalism, mysticism, and asceticism (cf. Col. 2) and not to all philosophy.

What is more, Paul himself was well trained in the philosophies of his day, even quoting them from time to time (cf. Acts 17:28; Titus 1:12). Paul successfully "reasoned" with the philosophers on Mars Hill, even winning some to Christ (Acts 17:17, 34). Elsewhere he said a bishop should be able "to exhort and convict those who contradict" (Titus 1:9) and that he was "appointed for defense of the Gospel" (Phil. 1:17). Peter exhorted believers to "always be ready to give a defense to everyone who asks you a reason for the hope that is in you" (1 Peter 3:15). Indeed, Jesus said the great command is to love the Lord "with all your *mind*" (Matt. 22:37).

Finally, God places no premium on ignorance. In fact, He knows we cannot "beware of philosophy" unless we are aware of it. No one would go to a doctor who did not study sickness. But, herein lies the danger. The Christian should approach the false philosophies of the world the way a medical researcher approaches the AIDS virus. The scientist should study them objectively and carefully to find out what is wrong with them, but not subjectively and personally so that he or she catches the "disease."

COLOSSIANS 2:16 — Are Christians obligated to keep the Sabbath?

(See comments on Ex. 20:8-11 and Matt. 5:17-18.)

COLOSSIANS 3:20 — Does Paul contradict Jesus when he exhorts children, "obey your parents in all things"?

PROBLEM: While Paul told children to obey their parents in everything, Jesus said, "He who loves father or mother more than Me is not worthy of Me" (Matt. 10:37). Surely children should not obey a parent who commands them to curse God, or hate Jesus, or kill their brother.

SOLUTION: A text must be understood in its context. The "all things" in Colossians 3:20 does not include things that displease the Lord, since the very next phrase says, "for this is well pleasing to the Lord." Furthermore, in the parallel passage in Ephesians, written at the same time, Paul explicitly qualifies this command, saying, "children, obey your parents *in the Lord*" (Eph. 6:1). This makes it clear that a child is not to obey his or her parents if they command the child to do something against the Lord.

COLOSSIANS 3:22 — Doesn't this command perpetuate the institution of slavery?

(See discussion on Phile. 16.)

COLOSSIANS 4:16 — What happened to the lost epistle of the Laodiceans?

PROBLEM: Paul refers to the "epistle from Laodicea" as a book he wrote that should be read by the church at Colosse, just as the inspired Book of Colossians was to be read by the Laodiceans. However, no such 1st century epistle to the Laodiceans exists (though there is a 4th century fraud). But, it is very strange that an inspired book would perish. Why would God inspire it for the faith and practice of the church (2 Tim. 3:16-17) and then allow it to be destroyed?

SOLUTION: There are two possibilities. First, it is possible that not all divinely authoritative or inspired books were intended by God to be in the Bible. Luke refers to other gospels (Luke 1:1), and John affirmed that there were many other things Jesus did that are not recorded in his Gospel (John 20:30; 21:25). So, it is possible that only those inspired books that God preserved by His providence were intended to be in the canon of Scripture.

Second, there are some good reasons to believe that "the epistle from Laodicea" is not really lost, but is really the Book of Ephesians. First of all, the text does not call it the epistle *of* the Laodiceans, but the "epistle [coming] *from* Laodicea" (Col. 4:16), whatever name it may have had. Second, it is known that Paul wrote Ephesians at the same time he wrote Colossians and sent it to another church in the same general area. Third, there is evidence that the Book of Ephesians did not originally bear that title, but was a kind of cyclical letter sent to the churches of Asia Minor. As a matter of fact, some early manuscripts do not have the phrase "in Ephesus" in Ephesians 1:1. It is certainly strange that Paul, who spent three years ministering to the Ephesians (Acts 20:31), sent no personal greetings to them, if the book known as "Ephesians" was intended for them alone. By contrast, Paul had never visited Rome, but he greeted numerous people in his letter to them (Rom. 16:1-16). Fourth, no epistle of the Laodiceans is cited by any early church father, though they make over 36,000 NT citations including every book and almost every verse of the NT. A fraudulent epistle of the Laodiceans appeared in the 4th century, but scholars do not believe it is the one referred to by Paul. Indeed, it is largely a collection of quotations from Ephesians and Colossians which the Church Council of Nicea (A.D. 787) called a "forged epistle."

1 THESSALONIANS

1 THESSALONIANS 4:13 — Did Paul teach the doctrine of soul-sleep?

PROBLEM: Several times the Bible refers to the dead as being asleep. Does this mean that the soul is not conscious between death and resurrection?

SOLUTION: The souls of both believers and unbelievers are conscious between death and the resurrection. Unbelievers are in conscious woe (see Luke 16:23; Mark 9:48; Matt. 25:41) and believers are in conscious bliss. "Sleep" is a reference to the body, not the soul. Sleep is an appropriate figure of speech for death of the body, since death is temporary until the resurrection when the body will "awake" from it.

The evidence that the soul (spirit) is conscious between death and resurrection is very strong:

1. Enoch was taken to be with God (Gen. 5:24; Heb. 11:5).

2. David spoke of bliss in God's presence after death (Ps. 16:10-11).

3. Elijah was taken up into heaven (2 Kings 2:1).

4. Moses and Elijah were conscious on the Mount of Transfiguration (Matt. 17:3) long after their time on earth.

5. Jesus said He went to the Father the day He died (Luke 23:46).

6. Jesus promised the repentant thief that he would be with Him in paradise the very day he died (Luke 23:43).

7. Paul said it was far better to die and be with Christ (Phil. 1:23).

8. Paul affirmed that when we are "absent from the body" then "we are present with the Lord" (2 Cor. 5:8).

9. The writer of Hebrews refers to heaven as a place where "the spirits of just men [are] made perfect" (Heb. 12:23).

10. The "souls" of those martyred during the tribulation were conscious in heaven, singing and praying to God (Rev. 6:9).

1 THESSALONIANS 4:15 — Did Paul teach that he would be alive when Christ returned?

PROBLEM: Paul spoke here to the Thessalonian Christians of *"we* who are alive and remain until the coming of the Lord." This seems to imply that he was affirming that Christ would come before he died. But Christ did not come before the death of Paul (2 Tim. 4:6-7). Did Paul make a mistake here?

SOLUTION: There are two ways to understand this verse without alleging that Paul made a mistake. First of all, it could be an *editorial "we."* That is, it may be a literary expression that is the equivalent of "those" who are alive. This is a perfectly acceptable way of speaking, which authors often use. For example, in view of a friend's death, I might say "we never know when such an eventuality may overtake us," without expressing either the belief or hope that it will occur to me.

Second, Paul may simply be *expressing his own hope* here, without affirming that he would in actual fact be alive when Christ returns. After all, Christ's return is the blessed hope (cf. Titus 2:13) of all believers. Had Paul wanted to affirm that he would be alive when Christ came back, he could have said very clearly, "I will be alive and remain until the coming of the Lord." But he did not say this. The "we" could have implied a *hope* he had without making any *affirmation* about whether he would or would not remain alive until the rapture.

2 THESSALONIANS

2 THESSALONIANS 1:9 — Will the wicked be annihilated or suffer conscious punishment forever?

PROBLEM: In some passages of Scripture, like this one, it speaks of the wicked being "destroyed" by God, suffering "the second death" (Rev. 20:14), or going to "perdition" (2 Peter 3:7). Yet in other places, it speaks of them suffering conscious torment (e.g., Luke 16:22-28). Will unsaved persons be annihilated, or will they consciously suffer forever?

SOLUTION: "Destruction" does not mean annihilation here, otherwise it would not be "everlasting" destruction. Annihilation only takes an instant, and it is over. If someone undergoes everlasting destruction, then they have to have everlasting existence.

Furthermore, "death" does not mean annihilation, but separation. Adam and Eve died spiritually the moment they sinned, yet they still existed and could hear God's voice (Gen. 2:17; cf. 3:10). Likewise, before one is saved, he is "dead in trespasses and sins" (Eph. 2:1), and yet he is still in God's image (Gen. 1:27; cf. 9:6; James 3:9) and is called on to believe (Acts 16:31) and to repent (Acts 17:30) and be saved.

Likewise, when the wicked are said to go into "perdition" (2 Peter 3:7), and Judas is called the "son of perdition" (John 17:12), it does not mean they will be annihilated. The word "perdition" (*apōleia*) simply means to perish or to come to ruin. But junk cars have perished in the sense of having been ruined. But they are still cars, ruined as they may be, and they are still in the junk yard. In this connection, Jesus spoke of hell as a junk yard or dump where the fire would not cease and where a person's resurrected body would not be consumed (see comments on Mark 9:48).

Finally, there are several lines of evidence that support the everlasting consciousness of the lost. First, the rich man who died and went to hell was in conscious torment (Luke 16:22-28), and there is absolutely no indication in the text that it was ever going to cease.

Second, Jesus spoke repeatedly of the people in hell as "weeping and gnashing of teeth" (Matt. 8:12; 22:13; 24:51; 25:30), which indicates they were conscious.

Third, hell is said to be of the same duration as heaven, namely, "everlasting" (Matt. 25:41).

Fourth, the fact that their punishment is everlasting indicates that they too must be everlasting. One cannot suffer punishment, unless a person exists to be punished (2 Thes. 1:9).

Fifth, the beast and the false prophet were thrown "alive" into the lake of fire at the beginning of the 1,000 years (Rev. 19:20), and they were still there, conscious and alive, after the 1,000 years (Rev. 20:10).

Sixth, the Scriptures affirm that the devil, the beast, and the false prophet "will be tormented day and night forever and ever" (Rev. 20:10). But there is no way to experience torment forever and ever without being conscious for ever and ever.

Seventh, Jesus repeatedly referred to hell as a place where "the fire is not quenched" (Mark 9:48), where the very bodies of the wicked will never die (cf. Luke 12:4-5). But it would make no sense to have everlasting flames and bodies without any souls in them to experience the torment.

Eighth, the same word used to describe the wicked perishing in the OT (*abad*) is used to describe the righteous perishing (see Isa. 57:1; Micah 7:2). The same word is used to describe things that are merely lost, but then later found (Deut. 22:3), which proves that "lost" does not here mean go out of existence. So, if perish means to annihilate, then the saved would have to be annihilated too. But we know they are not.

Ninth, it would be contrary to the created nature of human beings to annihilate them, since they are made in God's image and likeness, which is everlasting (Gen. 1:27). For God to annihilate His image in man would be to attack the reflection of Himself.

Tenth, annihilation would be demeaning both to the love of God and to the nature of human beings as free moral creatures. It would be as if God said to them, *"I will allow you to be free only if you do what I say! If you don't, then I will snuff out your very freedom and existence!"* This would be like a father telling his son he wanted him to be a doctor, and, when he chose instead to be a park ranger, the father shot him! Eternal suffering is an eternal testimony to the freedom and dignity of humans, even unrepentant humans.

■

2 THESSALONIANS 2:11 – How can God send a lie for people to believe and yet not allow liars in heaven?

PROBLEM: Paul wrote, "And for this reason God will send them strong delusion, that they should believe the lie" (2 Thes. 2:11). But Revelation 21:8 says, "the cowardly, unbelieving, abominable, murderers, sexually immoral, sorcerers, idolaters, *and all liars,* shall have their part in the lake which burns with fire and brimstone, which is the second death." But it seems inconsistent for God to condemn liars and yet send such a strong delusion that people should believe a lie.

SOLUTION: God does not send a lie but simply confirms those who do not wish to believe the truth. God is not responsible (i.e., culpable) for those who go to hell. For it is because of their rejection of the Gospel that they eventually end up there, not because of God's negligence. The context of this passage reveals that man has already rejected the Gospel of Christ. Paul says that when the Antichrist comes, he will come with signs and false wonders with all deception of wickedness (2 Thes. 2:8-10). These things happen for "those who perish, *because they did not receive the love of the truth, that they might be saved*" (v. 10). When God sends the deluding influence, Paul says He does so in order "that they all may be condemned who *did not believe the truth,* but had pleasure in unrighteousness" (v. 12). They have chosen to *reject* God rather than to *accept* His provision of salvation. God is not sending the lie to trick people, but He sends delusions to reveal human depravity in which they choose evil over good.

1 TIMOTHY 2:12-14 – Does the Bible limit the ministry of women?

PROBLEM: Paul said here that he did not "permit a woman to teach or to have authority over a man, but to be in silence." Likewise, in 1 Corinthians 14:34 he added, "Let your women keep silent in the churches, for they are not permitted to speak" (cf. 1 Peter 3:5-6). Doesn't this deny women a ministry and degrade their personality?

SOLUTION: Not at all. When properly understood in context, these and many other passages in the Bible exalt the role of women and give them a tremendous ministry in the body of Christ. Several things should be kept in mind on the topic of the role of women in the church.

First, the Bible declares that women, like men, are in the image of God (Gen. 1:27). That is, they are equal with men by nature. There is no essential difference – both male and female are *equally human by creation*.

Second, both women and men are *equal by redemption*. They both have the same Lord and both share equally in exactly the same salvation. For in Christ "there is neither male nor female; for you are all one in Christ Jesus" (Gal. 3:28).

Third, there are no sex symbols on the ministry gifts listed in the Bible. It does not say, "gift of teaching – male; gift of helps – female." In other words, women have the same gifts for ministry to the body of Christ that men do.

Fourth, throughout the Bible, God gifted, blessed, and greatly used women in the ministry. This includes Miriam, the first minister of music (Ex. 15:20), Deborah (Jud. 4:4), Huldah the prophetess (2 Chron. 34:22), Anna the prophetess (Luke 2:36), Priscilla the Bible teacher (Acts 18:26), and Phoebe the deaconess (Rom. 16:1).

Fifth, Jesus had many women who assisted Him in the ministry (cf. Luke 23:49; John 11). Indeed, it is very significant that in a patriarchal culture that Jesus chose women for His first *two* resurrection appearances

(Matt. 28:1-10; John 20:10-18). St. Peter did not make it until the third round (1 Cor. 15:5)!

Sixth, whatever Paul may have meant by the "women be silent" passages, he certainly did *not* mean that they should have no ministry in the church. This is clear for several reasons. For one thing, in the same book (of 1 Corinthians), Paul instructed women on *how they should pray and prophesy* in the church, namely, in a decent and orderly way (cf. 11:5). Further, there were also times when all the men were to be "silent" as well, namely, when someone else was giving an utterance from God (cf. 14:28). Finally, Paul did not hesitate to use women to assist him in the ministry, as is indicated by the crucial role he gave to Phoebe in delivering to its destination the great epistle to the Romans (Rom. 16:1).

Seventh, when understood in context, the "silence" passages are not negating the *ministry* of women, but are limiting the *authority* of women. Paul asserts that women were not permitted "to have authority over a man" (1 Tim. 2:12). Likewise, he follows his exhortation to "keep silent" by reminding them to be "submissive" (1 Cor. 14:34). Of course, men too were under authority and needed to submit to the headship of Christ over them (1 Cor. 11:3). Indeed, the ultimate proof that there is nothing degrading about being submissive is that Christ, who was God in human flesh, is always submissive to the Father, both on earth (Phil. 2:5-8) and even in heaven (1 Cor. 15:28). That male headship and leadership is not simply a cultural matter is evident by the fact that it is based on the very order of creation (1 Cor. 11:9; 1 Tim. 2:13). Thus, elders are to be men, "the husband of one wife" (1 Tim. 3:2). This, however, in no way demeans or diminishes the role of women, either in the family or in the church. The fact that men cannot have babies is not demeaning to their humanity or their role in the family. It is simply that God has not granted them this function, but a different one.

Eighth, God has given women an exalted role both by order of creation and redemption. First of all, Eve was not created from Adam's feet to be walked on by him, nor from his head to rule over him, but from his side to be equal to him and companion of him (cf. Gen. 2:19-25). Furthermore, every man ever born was carried in a woman's womb (1 Cor. 11:12) and then, the vast majority were nurtured by her through infancy, childhood, and youth until they grew up. In addition, when God chose the vessel by which He Himself would become manifest in human flesh (John 1:14), it was not by direct creation of a body (as Adam), or in assuming a visible form (as the angel of the Lord), nor was it by cloning a male human being. Rather, it was by being miraculously conceived and carried to full term in a woman's womb, the blessed virgin

Mary (Matt. 1:20-21; Gal. 4:4). What is more, God has, through the birth and nurturing process, endowed woman with the most marvelous role in forming all human beings, including every man, at the most tender and impressionable time in their lives, both prenatal (cf. Ps. 139:13-18) and postnatal. Finally, in the church, God has made women "one in Christ Jesus" (Gal. 3:28) and bestowed upon them the gifts of the spirit (1 Cor. 12; 14; Rom. 12) whereby they can edify the body of Christ, including prophecy (cf. Acts 2:17-18; 21:9) and teaching (Acts 18:26; Titus 2:4).

1 TIMOTHY 5:8 – Does this contradict Jesus' instruction about not storing treasures on earth?

PROBLEM: Jesus exhorted His disciples, "Do not lay up for yourselves treasures on earth" (Matt. 6:19). Luke added, "Give to everyone who asks of you" (Luke 6:30). By contrast, Paul affirmed that "If anyone does not provide for his own . . . he has denied the faith and is worse than an unbeliever" (1 Tim. 5:8). And Proverbs 13:22 claims that "a good man leaves an inheritance to his children's children." But how can we give all our treasure to God and others and still have an inheritance left for our family.

SOLUTION: The Bible does not command us to give away *all* our money to God and others. The OT laid down the tithe as the minimum all should give (cf. Mal. 3:8), and proportionally blessed those who brought more offerings (cf. 1 Cor. 16:2; 2 Cor. 8:14-15). In addition to this, we should help those in need, especially our own family and other believers (1 Tim. 5:8).

Jesus in no way intended that we should give away all that we possess. His advice to the rich young ruler to do so was a special case, since money had become an idol to this man (see Luke 18:22). Jesus encouraged prudence and economy and forbade making "treasures" our chief good. He encouraged us not to be unduly "anxious" about our earthly provisions (Matt. 6:25) nor to selfishly hoard treasures for ourselves on earth (Matt. 6:19-20). But in no way did He say we should not invest our money or plan for the future. Indeed, He gave parables about investing our treasures (Matt. 25:14ff) and about counting the cost before building a tower (Luke 14:28).

Neither is there any indication that the early believers ever took Jesus' statement (to give to those who ask) to the extreme of giving away everything they possessed. In spite of some misunderstood verses to the contrary (see comments on Acts 2:44-45), the early church did not practice any abiding form of communism or socialism. Most of them apparently owned their own homes and/or other property. Otherwise, how could they have fulfilled the command to provide for their own and to leave an inheritance to their families. The prudent believer gives of his or her possessions first to God (see Matt. 6:19, 33), then for family and other believers (1 Tim. 5:8), and then, as much as is possible, to help the poor (Gal. 2:10).

1 TIMOTHY 5:23 — Was Paul recommending wine-drinking for Christians?

PROBLEM: The Bible repeatedly warns against abuse of strong drink and drunkenness (Prov. 20:1; 31:4-5; Isa. 24:9; 1 Cor. 6:9-10; Eph. 5:18). However, here Paul tells Timothy to "no longer drink only water, but use a little wine for your stomach's sake and your frequent infirmities." Doesn't this commend wine drinking?

SOLUTION: Once the entire context is understood, there is no basis here for Christians to engage in the social drinking of wine (or other alcoholic beverages). First, Paul says "a little," not a lot. Paul elsewhere urges Christian leaders to be temperate (1 Tim. 3:3, 8).

Second, it was "for his frequent infirmities" not for pleasure. In other words, it was recommended for medicinal purposes, not for social purposes.

Third, the Bible speaks often of the evil of wine drinking. It pronounces woes on those who drink in excess (Isa. 5:11; Amos 6:6; Micah 2:11). All are warned that too much alcohol will lead to disgrace and judgment (Amos 6:6-7).

Finally, the wine that was used in the biblical times was mixed with three parts water to one part wine, thus diluting it to a relatively harmless amount of alcohol. When this was taken in this minimal amount in conjunction with a meal, there was little chance in a non-alcoholic society for it to be personally or socially harmful. The same is not true today, since the wine, beer, and whiskey being imbibed is by biblical standards "strong drink." And this is even more problematic in an alcoholic culture where one out of ten persons who begins to drink becomes a problem drinker. In this context it is better to follow the advice of Paul elsewhere when he said, "it is good neither to eat meat nor drink wine nor do anything by which your brother stumbles or is offended or is made weak" (Rom. 14:21).

1 TIMOTHY 6:16 — Does only God have immortality or do humans also have it?

PROBLEM: According to Paul in this passage, God "alone has immortality, dwelling in unapproachable light." However, in other places, Paul speaks of Christians being raised in "immortal" physical bodies (1 Cor. 15:53) and partaking of "immortality" through the Gospel (2 Tim. 1:10). But if God alone has immortality, then how can anyone else have it?

SOLUTION: God is the only one who has immortality *intrinsically,* by virtue of His very nature. All believers get it as a gift from God, but it is not inherent to their very nature as creatures. Or, to put it another way, only God *is* immortal — human beings simply *have* immortality. Likewise, God alone *is* existence (cf. Ex. 3:14) — creatures only *have* existence (cf. Acts 17:28). Further, God's immortality is *without beginning or end.* Our immortality has *a beginning with no end.* In summary:

GOD'S IMMORTALITY	HUMAN IMMORTALITY
Intrinsic to His nature	Not intrinsic to our nature
Something God *is*	Something humans *have*
Possesses by His essence	Possess by participation
Inherent	Derived
No beginning or end	A beginning but no end

1 TIMOTHY 6:16 — Does God dwell in darkness or in light?

PROBLEM: According to Paul, God "dwells in unapproachable light." However, the Bible repeatedly says things like "the Lord said He would dwell in the dark cloud" (1 Kings 8:12) because "He made darkness His secret place (Ps. 18:11; cf. 97:2). Which is it — darkness or light?

SOLUTION: In considering this discrepancy, we must remember, first of all, that "light" and "darkness" may be figures of speech and need not be taken literally. Both describe God's unsearchableness (cf. Rom. 11:33).

Furthermore, even if taken literally, they are not necessarily contradictory, for what is light to God can be darkness to us. For example, the dawn brings light to the robin, but darkness to the bat. Indeed, the blinding light of His transcendent deity can create darkness for our finite attempt to comprehend God. So there is no necessary conflict, even if light and darkness are understood literally.

1 TIMOTHY 6:17-18 — Should wealth be avoided or retained?

PROBLEM: Jesus urged the rich young ruler to "sell what you have and give to the poor" (Matt. 19:21). The early disciples sold their possessions and laid the money at the apostles' feet (Acts 4:34-35). And Paul warned that "the love of money is a root of all kinds of evil" (1 Tim. 6:10). However, God blessed Abraham and Job with riches, and Paul does not instruct the rich to give away all they have, but to use and "richly enjoy" (1 Tim. 6:17-18).

SOLUTION: It should be observed, first of all, that Jesus' instruction to "sell what you have and give to the poor" (Matt. 19:21) was to a rich young man who had made money his god, not to those who have not. There is nothing wrong with *possessing riches* — there is something wrong with *being possessed by riches*.

Further, there is no indication that the early disciples in Acts were either urged to sell all, or that they actually did. The land sold (Acts 4:34-35) may have been extra property. It is noteworthy that it does not say they sold their homes (see discussion on Acts 2:44-45). Finally, Paul does not say that money is evil, but only that the *love* of money is the root of all kinds of evil. Seeking riches for their own sake is wrong, but seeking to have something to share with others in need is not. Thus, while God "gives us richly all things to enjoy" (1 Tim. 6:17), in the same breath He warns, "not . . . to trust in uncertain riches."

2 TIMOTHY

2 TIMOTHY 1:10 – If Jesus abolished death, why do we still die?

PROBLEM: Paul affirms in this text that Christ "has abolished death and brought life and immortality to light through the Gospel." But death is not abolished, since "death spread to all men" (Rom. 5:12), and "it is appointed for men to die once" (Heb. 9:27).

SOLUTION: First of all, Christ did not abolish physical death *immediately,* but by His death and resurrection it will be abolished *eventually.* Christ is the first one to experience resurrection in an immortal body (1 Cor. 15:20) – the rest of the human race will experience this later, at His second coming (1 Cor. 15:50-56). Second, Christ abolished death *officially* when He personally defeated it by His resurrection. However, physical death will not be completely destroyed *actually* until He returns again and "death is swallowed up in victory" (1 Cor. 15:54). For Paul tells us that "the last enemy that will be destroyed is death" (1 Cor. 15:26).

2 TIMOTHY 2:14 – Is it wrong for Christians to argue about theological matters?

PROBLEM: Paul seemed to forbid theological arguments when he instructed Timothy "not to strive about words to no profit" (2 Tim. 2:14) and to "avoid foolish and ignorant disputes" (v. 23). On the other hand, Paul himself argued with the Jews in their synagogues (Acts 17:2, 17) and disputed with the philosophers on Mars Hill (Acts 17:18ff). Indeed, Jude exhorted us "to contend earnestly for the faith which was once for all delivered to the saints" (Jude 3).

SOLUTION: A distinction must be made between the two senses of what it means to argue or to contend. *Arguing* is not necessarily wrong, but being *argumentative* is. We should *contend* for the faith, but we should not be *contentious* in so doing. Making an *earnest effort* to defend the faith is good (cf. Phil. 1:17; 1 Peter 3:15). But engaging in *fruitless quarrels* is not. Likewise, Paul did not oppose disputing about *what words really mean* in a given context—he simply opposed *mere semantical wrangling.*

2 TIMOTHY 2:25 – Is repentance a gift of God or an act of man?

PROBLEM: Paul speaks here of God "granting them repentance, so that they may know the truth" (cf. Acts 5:31). Yet in other places, repentance is considered a person's own act. Jesus, for example, calls on people to "Repent, and believe in the Gospel" (Mark 1:15). Paul tells us that God "commands all men everywhere to repent" (Acts 17:30). But doesn't it have to be either an act of God or else an act of the individual believer?

SOLUTION: There are two possible answers here, neither of which negates a person's God-given responsibility to exercise free choice. First, repentance could be an actual gift of God, but like other gifts, it must be received to be enjoyed. On this view, God offers all who are willing the gift of repentance unto eternal life. Those who are not willing do not get repentance. In this way, God is impartial in His offer, but man is still responsible to accept or reject the gift of repentance necessary for salvation.

A second view simply notes the two different senses in which repentance is used in these seemingly opposed verses. One set of verses is speaking of repentance as an *opportunity* and the other as an *act.* The former is simply a *disposition* given by God, leaving the actual *action* of repenting to human beings. The former is a God-given *provision,* while the latter is a man-made *decision.* This view can be summarized as follows:

TWO DIFFERENT SENSES OF REPENTANCE

As a God-given opportunity	As a free human act
As a disposition from God	As an action of man
As a provision of God	As a decision of man

So understood, there is no contradiction in the diverse texts on repentance. Whichever interpretation is taken, one thing is certain, there is no verse saying God repents for us. Each free moral creature is responsible to repent for himself. The same can be said about whether faith is a gift of God or not.

2 TIMOTHY 3:12 — Are all who live godly lives persecuted, or only some?

PROBLEM: Here the apostle makes the sweeping statement that "all who desire to live godly in Christ Jesus will suffer persecution." This appears to be in flat contradiction to Solomon's claim that "When a man's ways please the Lord, He makes even his enemies to be at peace with him" (Prov. 16:7). How can both be true?

SOLUTION: Neither of these passages should be taken universally. Proverbs were only general statements, not universal truths. Likewise, Paul's statement seems hardly appropriate for persons who die shortly after becoming believers or who live in a Christian environment all their life.

Even if taken with strict literalness, being at "peace" with one's enemies does not mean they are not persecuting us. It simply means that the believer, like Christ commanded, is not retaliating against his enemy or fighting back (cf. Matt. 5:39-40).

2 TIMOTHY 3:16 — Does this passage prove the inspiration of all Scripture or just some?

PROBLEM: Paul says in this passage that "All Scripture is given by inspiration of God." Some think that the word "all" should be replaced by the word "every." Plus, some believe that the copula "is" should be placed after the remark concerning the inspiration of the Scriptures, not before. In doing so this can lead to the conclusion that some Scripture is not inspired.

SOLUTION: First, most versions translate this verse "All Scripture is God-breathed," except those that translate this verse with the copula "is" after the word "God." This makes it sound like there are some Scriptures that are not inspired of God (e.g., RSV, ASV), although the marginal notes in these translations give a more accurate rendering. But, most Bibles see the verse as reading "All Scripture is inspired of God."

Second, concerning whether the word "all" should be translated "every," some argue that it should on the grounds of, if the definite article is missing in reference to this word, the verse should be translated "every." However, whenever the word "Scripture" (*graphē*) is used in the NT, it always refers to authoritative and inspired writings — never the opposite — with or without the definite article in Greek. This word is used of the Hebrew Scriptures (as in our present verse) or NT writings (2 Peter 3:16).

Third, the word for "inspired of God" suggests that God so guided the

NT authors as to write the very word of God. As we notice in 2 Peter 1:20-21, no prophecy of Scripture came about by the will of man but by the Holy Spirit moving (carrying along) the writers of Scripture to speak from God. The word for "moved" (*pherō*) in 2 Peter is the same word used in Acts 27:15 where the ship which carried Paul was so caught up in a storm that they could not face the wind. They gave way to it, and they let themselves be "driven along" by the storm. This is true of the Holy Spirit inspiring the authors of Holy Scripture to write the Word of God. But if all the authors of Scripture were moved by God, then the words of Scripture were breathed out by God and without error, since God cannot err (Heb. 6:18; Titus 1:2; John 17:17).

Finally, even if it could be argued from the NT that not every use of "the Scriptures" refers to an inspired writing, nonetheless, it would not undermine Paul's teaching here that the entire OT is inspired of God. For the context makes it clear that the "Scripture" to which he refers is "the Holy Scriptures" (1:15) which Timothy's Jewish mother and grandmother had taught him (cf. 2 Tim. 1:5), and this could be none other than the whole Jewish OT.

TITUS

TITUS 1:12 – Doesn't Paul involve himself in a paradox or contradiction here?

PROBLEM: Paul quoted a Cretan who said that "Cretans are always liars" (1:12). But if this was said by a Cretan and Cretans always lie, then he too was lying. But if this Cretan was lying when he said Cretans always lie, then Cretans do not always lie and there is a lie in the Scripture. If, on the other hand, this Cretan was telling the truth about Cretans, then Cretans do not always lie, at least not the one who said this. In either event, by incorporating this statement in Scripture, the apostle seems to have included a falsehood.

SOLUTION: Paul seemed to be aware of this dilemma and quickly added, "This testimony is true" (v. 13). In other words, the Cretans generally lie, but at least on this one occasion a Cretan uttered the truth when he characterized the Cretans as liars. In this way the paradox is broken, and no falsehood is thereby included in Scripture.

TITUS 1:12 – Doesn't Paul pronounce this pagan poet inspired by making him part of Scripture?

PROBLEM: Christians believe that only the Bible is the Word of God (2 Tim. 3:16). Yet the Apostle Paul quotes pagan poets on at least three occasions. But in so doing he seems to give assent to the sources he quotes as inspired, just as when he quotes OT Scripture as the Word of God (cf. Matt. 4:4, 7, 10).

SOLUTION: Paul is not quoting this non-Christian source *as inspired,* but simply *as true.* All truth is God's truth, no matter who said it. Caiaphas the Jewish high priest uttered a truth about Christ (John 11:49). The Bible often uses non-inspired sources (cf. Num. 21:14; Josh. 10:13; 1 Kings 15:31). Three times Paul cites non-Christian thinkers (Acts 17:28; 1 Cor. 15:33; Titus 1:12). Jude alludes to truths found in two non-canonical books (Jude 9, 14). But never does the Bible cite them as divinely authoritative, but simply as containing the truth quoted. The usual phrases, such as, "thus saith the Lord" (cf. Isa. 7:7; Jer. 2:5, KJV) or "it is written" (cf. Matt. 4:4, 7, 10) are never found when these non-inspired sources are cited. Nonetheless, truth is truth wherever it is found. And there is no reason, therefore, that a biblical author, by direction of the Holy Spirit, cannot utilize truth from whatever source he may find it.

TITUS 3:10 — Should the wayward be instructed or expelled from the church?

PROBLEM: This verse says we should "reject" them, and in 1 Corinthians 5 the adulterous member was excommunicated (v. 5). But in 2 Timothy 2:25 leaders are exhorted, "in humility correcting those who are in opposition, if God perhaps will grant them repentance."

SOLUTION: The severity of the action of the church will depend on the *seriousness of the sin* of the member being disciplined. Those who are living in immorality should, after being exhorted to change, be excommunicated, since their sin has a leavenous or contagious effect on others (1 Cor. 5:5-7). Even so, if they repent, they should be reinstated in the church (cf. 2 Cor. 2:6-7), since the primary purpose of discipline is not to reject, but to reform.

The main difference in the severity of the discipline was in the *penitence of the person* being disciplined. If the person repented, he was to be reinstated (2 Cor. 2:6-7). If not, then "after the first and second admonition" (Titus 3:10) he was to be rejected.

PHILEMON

PHILEMON 16 – Doesn't Paul approve of the institution of slavery?

PROBLEM: The Apostle Paul seems to favor the institution of human slavery by sending a runaway slave, Onesimus, back to his owner. But slavery is unethical. It is a violation of the principles of human freedom and dignity.

SOLUTION: Slavery is unethical and unbiblical and neither Paul's actions nor his writings approve of this debasing form of treatment. In fact, it was the application of biblical principles that ultimately led to the overthrow of slavery. Several important facts should be noted in this connection.

First, from the very beginning, God declared that all humans participate in the image of God (Gen. 1:27). The apostle reaffirmed this, declaring, "we are the offspring of God" (Acts 17:29), and He "has made from one blood every nation of men to dwell on all the face of the earth" (Acts 17:26).

Second, in spite of the fact that slavery was countenanced in the semitic cultures of the day, the law demanded that slaves eventually be set free (Ex. 21:2; Lev. 25:40). Likewise, servants had to be treated with respect (Ex. 21:20, 26).

Third, Israel, itself in slavery in Egypt, was constantly reminded by God of this (Deut. 5:15), and their emancipation became the model for the liberation of all slaves (cf. Lev. 25:40).

Fourth, in the NT, Paul declared that in Christianity "there is neither Jew nor Greek, there is neither slave nor free, there is neither male nor female; for you are all one in Christ Jesus" (Gal. 3:28). All social classes are broken down in Christ; we are all equal before God.

Fifth, the NT explicitly forbids the evil system of this world that traded the "bodies and souls of men" (Rev. 18:13). Slave trade is so repugnant to God that He pronounces His final judgment on the evil system that perpetrated it (Rev. 17–18).

Sixth, when Paul urges, "Servants, be obedient to those who are your masters" (Eph. 6:5; cf. Col. 3:22), he is not thereby approving of the institution of slavery, but simply alluding to the de facto situation in his day. Rather, he is instructing them to be good employees, just as believers should be today, but he was not thereby commending slavery.

Seventh, a closer look at Philemon reveals that Paul did not perpetuate slavery, but actually undermined it, for he urged Philemon, Onesimus' owner, to treat him as "a beloved brother" (v. 16). So, by emphasizing the inherent equality of all human beings, both by creation and redemption, the Bible laid down the very moral principles that were used to overthrow slavery and help restore the dignity and freedom of all persons of whatever color or ethnic group.

HEBREWS

HEBREWS 2:10 — If Jesus was already perfect, how could He be made perfect through suffering?

PROBLEM: The Bible declares that Jesus was absolutely perfect and without sin, even in His human nature (2 Cor. 5:21; Heb. 4:15; 1 Peter 2:22; 3:18; 1 John 3:3). But according to this verse, Jesus was made "perfect through sufferings." But to be made perfect implies that He was not perfect to begin with, which is a contradiction.

SOLUTION: Jesus was absolutely and unchangeably perfect in His divine nature. God is perfect (Matt. 5:48), and He cannot change (Mal. 3:6; Heb. 6:18). But Jesus was also human, and as such was subject to change, though without sin. For example, "Jesus increased in wisdom and stature" (Luke 2:52). If his knowledge as a man increased, then his experience also did. Thus, He "learned obedience by the things which He suffered" (Heb. 5:8). In this sense He was "made perfect" in that He experienced the perfecting work of suffering in His own sinless life (cf. Job 23:10; Heb. 12:11; James 1:2-4). That is, He gained all the experiential benefits of suffering without sinning (Heb. 4:15). In this way He can be of real comfort and encouragement to those who suffer.

HEBREWS 2:14 — Does the devil have the power of death or does God?

PROBLEM: The writer of Hebrews speaks here about Christ's coming so "that through death He might destroy him who had the power of death, that is, the devil." But in other places the Bible asserts that only God has the power over life and death: "I kill and I make alive" (Deut. 32:39; cf. Job 1:21).

SOLUTION: God is sovereign over all life. Only He can create it, and only He has determined the number of our days (Ps. 90:10-12) and has "appointed" the day of our death (Heb. 9:27). But by tempting Adam and Eve, the devil succeeded in bringing on the human race God's pronounced judgment of death for disobedience (Gen. 2:17; Rom. 5:12). So, in this sense, the devil may be said to have had the power of death (Heb. 2:14). However, by tasting death for every man (Heb. 2:9) and rising triumphantly from the grave (Rom. 4:25), Christ now holds "the keys of Hades and of Death" (Rev. 1:18), having "abolished death and brought life and immortality to light through the Gospel" (2 Tim. 1:10).

HEBREWS 2:17-18 — Was it possible for Christ to have sinned?

PROBLEM: The writer of Hebrews says that Christ "had to be made like His brethren in all things. . . . For since He Himself was tempted in that which He has suffered, He is able to come to the aid of those who are tempted" (2:17-18, NASB). Does this mean that Christ could have sinned?

SOLUTION: Some argue that Christ *could not* have sinned. They believe that our Lord was tempted like we are and that He can sympathize with our weaknesses, but that He was incapable of sinning. In support of this view they argue, first, that since Christ was God, and since God cannot sin (Heb. 6:17; James 1:13), it follows that Christ could not sin either. Second, since Christ had no fallen human nature, as we do, He had no propensity to sin. Finally, they observe that His temptation was only from without, not from within. Hence, He could be tempted without having the real possibility of sinning.

Other orthodox scholars believe that Christ had the ability to sin (since He had the power of free choice), but did not sin. In short, sin was possible, but not actual in Jesus' life. To deny this possibility, they believe, would deny His full humanity, His ability to "sympathize with our weaknesses" (Heb. 4:15), and would make His temptation into a charade. They note that while Jesus could not sin *as God*, nonetheless, He could have sinned (but didn't) *as man*. Since Jesus had two natures, one divine and one human, a distinction must be made in what He could do in each nature. For example, He could not get tired, hungry, or sleepy as God. But He did all of these as man. His divine nature could not die. Yet He died as man. Likewise, they argue, Christ could not have sinned as God but could have sinned as man.

HEBREWS 5:7a — Did Christ have flesh only before His resurrection?

PROBLEM: Speaking of the "days of His [Jesus'] flesh" as past seems to imply that Jesus did not rise in the flesh and ascend into heaven in the same physical body in which He died. Yet Jesus Himself said that His resurrection body was one of "flesh and bones" (Luke 24:31) and the *Apostles' Creed* confesses the "resurrection of the flesh."

SOLUTION: The phrase "days of His flesh" simply refers to Jesus' *earthly sojourn*. It affirms nothing about the nature of the resurrection body. It is clear from many passages that Jesus rose in literal, physical, human flesh (see comments on Luke 24:39; 1 John 4:2-3).

HEBREWS 5:7b – Did Christ shrink from death or face it courageously?

PROBLEM: On the one hand, it would seem that Christ shrunk from death, since He prayed "with vehement cries and tears to Him who was able to save Him from death" (Heb. 5:7). He said, "O My Father, if it is possible, let this cup pass from Me" (Matt. 26:39). On the other hand, we are led to believe that He faced death obediently and boldly, for He "steadfastly set His face to go to Jerusalem" (Luke 9:51), calmly facing His arrest, trial, and crucifixion, and repeatedly assuring His disciples He would rise again (Matt. 12:40-42; John 10:18).

SOLUTION: Christ faced dath *boldly* but not *eagerly*. He met it *willingly* but not *apathetically*. Christ was "obedient to the point of death" (Phil. 2:8). He approached it boldly and bravely, declaring, "I have power to lay it down, and I have power to take it again" (John 10:18). He willingly submitted to the Father, saying, "not as I will, but as You will" (Matt. 26:39).

Christ's willingness and boldness notwithstanding, He nevertheless felt the full emotional and existential impact of His impending death. He did pray with "vehement cries and tears," but the writer adds, He "was heard because of His godly fear" (Heb. 5:7). Jesus *wished* as a man that His cup (death) could pass from Him (Matt. 26:39), but He *willed,* as the Father willed, that it would take place for the salvation of the world. While His soul was "troubled" about death, He never prayed, "Father, save me from this hour." He only asked, "shall I say" this? His answer was no, "for this purpose I came to this hour. 'Father glorify Your name' " (John 12:27-28). He never feared death as such, but banishment from the Father (Matt. 27:46). In fact, by His death Jesus overcame the power and fear of death, defeating the devil (Heb. 2:14).

HEBREWS 6:4-6 (cf. 10:26-31) — Does this passage teach that it is possible for Christians to lose their salvation?

PROBLEM: Hebrews 6:4-6 seems to be written for Christians because it contains certain characteristics that would be true only of them, such as "partakers of the Holy Spirit" (v. 4). But it declares that if they fall away, it is impossible "to renew them again to repentance, since they crucify again for themselves the Son of God, and put Him to an open shame" (v. 6). Does this mean that Christians can lose their salvation?

SOLUTION: There are two basic interpretations of this passage. Some take it to refer to believers and others to nonbelievers.

Those who say this refers to unbelievers argue that all of these characteristics could belong to those who merely *profess* Christianity, but who do not really *possess* the Holy Spirit. They note that they are not depicted in the normal ways of describing a true Christian, such as, being "born again" (John 3:3), being "in Christ" (Eph. 1:3), or being "sealed by the Holy Spirit" (Eph. 4:30). They point to Judas Iscariot as a classic example. He walked with the Lord, was sent out and commissioned by Jesus on missions having "power over unclean spirits, to cast them out, and to heal all kinds of sickness and all kinds of disease" (Matt. 10:1). However, Jesus, in His prayer in John's Gospel, spoke of Judas as "the son of perdition" (John 17:12).

There are several problems with taking this to refer to nonbelievers, even for those who hold that a believer can lose his salvation (i.e., Arminians). First, the passage declares emphatically that "it is impossible . . . to renew them again to repentance" (Heb. 6:4, 6). But few Arminians believe that once a person has backslidden it is impossible for him to be saved again. Further, while the description of their spiritual status differs from other ways of expressing it in the NT, some of the phrases are very difficult to take any other way than that the person was saved. For example, (1) those spoken of had experienced "repentance" (Heb. 6:6), which is the condition of salvation (Acts 17:30); (2) they were "enlightened and have tasted the heavenly gift" (Heb. 6:4); (3) they were "partakers of the Holy Spirit" (v. 4); (4) In addition, they had "tasted the good word of God" (v. 5); and (5) have tasted the "powers of the age to come" (v. 5).

Of course, if they were believers, then the question arises as to their status after they had "fallen away" (v. 6). Here interpretations differ along theological lines. Arminians often argue that these people actually lost their salvation. However, the text seems to indicate that they cannot be saved again, something even most Arminians reject.

On the other hand, those who hold a Calvinistic point of view (such as the authors) point to several facts. First, the word for "fall away" (*parapesontas*) does not indicate a one-way action. Rather, it is the word for "drift," indicating that the status of the individuals is not hopeless. Second, the fact is that it is "impossible" for them to repent again indicates the once-for-all nature of repentance. In other words, they don't need to repent again since they did it once and that is all that is necessary for "eternal redemption" (Heb. 9:12). Third, the text seems to indicate that there is no more need for "drifters" (backsliders) to repent again and get saved all over any more than there is for Christ to die again on the cross (Heb. 6:6). Finally, the writer of Hebrews calls those he is warning "beloved," a term hardly appropriate for unbelievers.

In any event, there is no problem here with the *inspiration* of Scripture. It is simply an intramural question of *interpretation* of Scripture among Christians who share in common the belief that the Bible is the inspired Word of God in whatever it affirms.

HEBREWS 7:3 — Does this verse support reincarnation?

PROBLEM: Hebrews tells us that Melchizedek, "having neither beginning of days nor end of life, but made like the Son of God, remains a priest continually." Since Jesus assumed this priesthood (7:21), some reincarnationalists use this verse to prove that Jesus is a reincarnation of Melchizedek. Are they correct?

SOLUTION: No, this is a misuse of this passage. This is clear for several reasons. First of all, it says Melchizedek was only *"made like"* Jesus, not that Jesus *was* Melchizedek (Heb. 7:3). Second, Christ was only a priest *"according to the order of"* (Heb. 7:21) Melchizedek. It does not affirm that He *was* Melchizedek. Finally, the fact that Melchizedek had a mysterious and unrecorded birth and death (Heb. 7:3) does not prove reincarnation — it was merely used as an analogy for the eternal Messiah, Jesus Christ.

HEBREWS 7:9-10 — Do these verses indicate that an embryo is merely a potential human being, not an actual human person?

PROBLEM: The writer of Hebrews declares that Levi paid tithes to Melchizedek through Abraham. However, Levi was not even born until hundreds of years after this time. So Levi could not possibly have actually paid tithes to Melchizedek — he could only have done it potentially.

SOLUTION: This text is not speaking of an embryo, to say nothing of calling it a potential human being. First, it does not say that Levi was potentially in Abraham. He was probably only there representatively or figuratively.

Second, even if Levi was potentially in Abraham, it certainly does not follow that he was an embryo in Abraham.

Third, if Levi, who was not even conceived when he was said to be "in Abraham," was a potential human being, then we are potential humans before we are even conceived.

Fourth, if this is so, then even human sperm (before they fertilize an ovum) are potential human beings just like embryos. But this is genetically incorrect. Sperm have only 23 chromosomes while embryos have 46 (see comments on Ps. 139:13-16).

HEBREWS 7:19 — Was the Law of Moses perfect or imperfect?

PROBLEM: The psalmist declared that the "law of the Lord is perfect" (Ps. 19:7). It reflects the very character of God (cf. Lev. 11:45). Yet the writer of Hebrews insists that "the law made nothing perfect" (7:19), and thus God brought in a "better covenant" (v. 22). This, he contends, would not have been necessary "if that first covenant had been faultless" (Heb. 8:7). So, who is right? Is the law perfect or imperfect?

SOLUTION: The law was perfect in its *nature,* but imperfect in its results. It was a perfect expression of God's righteousness, but an imperfect means of making man righteous. Of course, that is not the fault of the law itself or the purpose for which God gave it. For the law was never given to redeem sinners (Titus 3:5-6; Rom. 4:5), but to *reveal sin.* As a standard and means of revealing sin, the law was an impeccable norm and teacher. But it was only "our tutor to bring us to Christ, that we might be justified by faith" (Gal. 3:24). Like a mirror, the law was intended to reveal our imperfections as we look into it; but it, no more than the mirror, was intended to correct our imperfections. So the law is perfect in itself, as a rule and revealer of sin, but it is imperfect as a means of empowering us to overcome sin.

HEBREWS 8:1 — Is Jesus our priest or our sacrifice?

PROBLEM: Christ is presented here as the "High Priest" of believers (cf. 7:21). However, later Jesus is depicted as the "sacrifice" for our sins (Heb. 9:26, 28; 10:10). Which is He?

SOLUTION: Jesus is represented correctly by both figures. He is our

Priest in that He speaks to God on behalf of man. Yet He is our Sacrifice, since He offered Himself on the Cross for our sins. He is the Offerer and the Offered; both Sacrificer and Sacrificed. "He offered up Himself" (Heb. 7:27).

HEBREWS 9:3-4 — Was the altar of incense in the Holy Place or in the Most Holy Place behind the veil?

PROBLEM: According to Exodus 30:6 (cf. 26:33; 40:3), the altar of incense was in the Holy Place in front of the veil, not in the Most Holy Place behind the veil. However, Hebrews 9:3-4 states that it was "behind the . . . veil, [in] the part of the tabernacle which is called the Holiest of all."

SOLUTION: Several possible solutions have been suggested to this difficulty. Any one of them would resolve the problem.

1. The text has been corrupted by a copyist mistake. Some scholars note that there is a possible textual dislocation here, that the phrase about the "golden altar" (v. 4) really belongs in verse 2 along with the other furniture in the Holy Place. This they note is the way it is in some early manuscripts, such as, Vaticanus (A.D. 4th century), the Coptic, and the Ethiopic versions.

Others object that the overwhelming textual evidence and virtually all modern translations oppose these isolated exceptions. They further note that the few texts which disagree leave the impression that they result from an attempt to "correct" the text which they found difficult to understand.

2. The altar was inside the veil. Following Hebrews 9:3-4, it has been argued that the Altar of Incense was always inside the Most Holy Place. This view is supported with the following arguments. First, it is in accord with the clear statement in Hebrews 9:3-4. Second, it is implied in other passages which speak of this altar as "before the ark of the testimony" (Ex. 40:5), which was in the Most Holy Place. Third, 1 Kings 6:20 speaks of the altar of incense as "belonging to the inner sanctuary" (Phillip E. Hughes translation).

Opponents of this view have noted several objections. First, it is contrary to clear statements in the OT (e.g., Ex. 30:10) that place the altar of incense in the Holy Place, along with the bread and the candles. The priest, who was forbidden to enter the Most Holy Place (except on the Day of Atonement), served at the altar of incense daily (Ex. 30:6-11). Second, Philo, Josephus, and other Jewish authorities all placed it outside the veil in the Holy Place. Finally, the NT locates it outside the veil where ordinary priests like Zechariah ministered (Luke 1:5ff).

3. *The Veil was moved on the Day of Atonement.* According to this position, the altar of incense was *usually* stationed outside the veil in the Holy Place. However, they believe the veil was moved back on the Day of Atonement so the priest could have ready access to the altar of incense in order to use it in the Most Holy Place. Support for this view is derived from the following: First, the Bible usually speaks of the altar of incense as being separated from the Most Holy Place by a veil (cf. Ex. 30:6; Lev. 16:12, 15, 17). The only time it speaks of this altar being accessible to the priest in the Most Holy Place is on the Day of Atonement (cf. Lev. 16:2; Heb. 9:7). Finally, this fits with the typology of the OT high priest who did once a year what Christ did once for all time (cf. Heb. 10:10-11), namely pull back the veil that separates us from God. In this connection it is noted that Christ has rent the veil (Matt. 27:5) and there is no longer a separation between the Holy Place and the Most Holy Place.

The main problems with this view are these: First of all, there is no passage that actually states the veil was moved back on the Day of Atonement. Second, it may be pushing a type too far. After all, not everything the OT priest did prefigured Christ. For example, they continued to offer sacrifices after their Day of Atonement (Heb. 10:11); Christ did not after His. Third, there are passages which clearly imply the veil was still in place on the Day of Atonement, speaking of the priest going "inside the veil" to do his work (Lev. 16:12; cf. 15, 17, 23, 27).

4. *There were two altars of incense.* Some scholars posit two altars to resolve the difficulty, one stationed inside and one outside the veil. This view has the merit of explaining all the data and of avoiding the difficulties of the two previous views.

However, there are major problems with this position. First, there is no reference to two altars of incense in either the OT or NT. Second, Jewish authorities (such as Philo and Josephus) make no reference to any such second altar. Third, if there were two altars, then the author of Hebrews must be charged with a gross omission, since he makes no reference to the altar of incense in the Holy Place, which was a regular daily part of the priestly ministry (Heb. 9:3-4). Finally, this suggested solution seems harmonistic, that is, suggested as a solution without any substantial evidence for it.

5. *The golden censer differs from the golden altar.* This position contends that the Greek word *thumiaterion* often translated "golden altar" (Heb. 9:4) should be rendered "golden censer." This would resolve the difficul-

ty, since the altar of incense would be outside the veil and the golden censer would be inside the veil where the priest could use it on the Day of Atonement. In support of this position the following can be offered: First, "censer" is an acceptable translation of the Greek word *thumiatērion,* which can mean either the place or the instrument of incense. Second, the same Greek word is used of a censer elsewhere in the Greek translation of the OT (cf. Ezek. 8:11; 2 Chron. 26:19). Third, this view is supported by the Jewish Mishnah which gives a detailed description of this golden censer. Fourth, it avoids a flat contradiction which involves having one altar in two places. Fifth, it fits with the fact that the altar of incense is usually mentioned with the bread and candles (which are always in the Holy Place), whereas the golden censer is used only once a year in the Most Holy Place (Lev. 16:2, 12, 29). Sixth, Aaron the high priest was expressly commanded to burn incense in a censer before the mercy seat on the Day of Atonement (Lev. 16:12-13). Seventh, as a Jewish teacher familiar with the law, the author of Hebrews would have been familiar with the temple furniture and ritual. Eighth, his message would have had no credibility with his Hebrew readers had he made a gross mistake in the positioning of the altar of incense. Ninth, since this instrument for incense was used only once a year in the Most Holy Place, it is only reasonable that it would be kept in the most sacred place.

As much as there is to commend it, this view is not without objections. First of all, the Greek word in question is usually translated "golden altar" (e.g., ASV, NASB, RSV, NIV, NKJV), not a "golden censer." Second, if it is translated "golden censer," then the author of Hebrews must be charged with a gross omission of the altar of incense, which seems unlikely given its importance in the tabernacle furniture and daily ministry. Third, if "censer" was meant it would not have been made of gold but of brass to house the hot coals for the incense. Finally, the same term is used by contemporary Jewish authorities (Philo and Josephus) to refer to the altar of incense.

6. *The altar of incense was moved on the Day of Atonement.* Other scholars affirm that Hebrews 9:3-4 is a reference to the "golden altar" of incense which was moved from its *regular* location outside the veil on the *special* occasion of the Day of Atonement. There are several arguments in favor of this view. First, it resolves the apparent conflict by holding that there was only one ark which is located in two different places at the appropriate times. Second, it explains all the data consistently. Third, it avoids the speculative nature of the two altar theory. Fourth, it seems inconceivable that the author of Hebrews, writing to Hebrew

Christians familiar with the facts, would place such an important item of tabernacle furniture in the wrong place. This view avoids such an unlikely situation. Fifth, it explains how the high priest could have used this altar so readily in cleansing the Most Holy Place on the Day of Atonement, since it was moved there on that occasion. Sixth, it fits with the other references of Scripture which speak of incense being offered in the very presence of a holy God (Rev. 8:3; 9:13). Seventh, it is congruent with 1 Kings 6:22 which can be rendered, "the entire altar [of incense] . . . was in the inner sanctuary." Eighth, Exodus 30:6 (cf. 40:5) may be instructions to move the altar of incense to the Most Holy Place on the Day of Atonement. Likewise, Hebrews 9:6 may encompass this move when it says, "now when these things had been thus prepared." Ninth, the Jewish *Apocalypse of Baruch* (6.7), which belongs to this same period, describes the Most Holy Place as containing the altar of incense.

It has been suggested that the lack of explicit reference to moving the altar of incense for the Day of atonement makes this view problematic. Likewise, some have queried how the high priest could have moved this heavy altar by himself. But neither of these is telling arguments, since not everything is explicitly noted in Scripture and the other priests were available to make any arrangements necessary for the Day of Atonement.

7. The altar was "inside" by doctrinal association. Some Bible students have suggested that the altar of incense was actually located outside the veil but that it was listed as "inside" in Hebrews 9:3-4 because of its close association with the ark of the covenant and the atoning sacrifice offered there. In brief, Hebrews is speaking of it being "inside" by *doctrinal association* but not in its *spatial location*. In support of this conclusion they cite the fact that the author of Hebrews uses the participle "having" (*echousa*) instead of the expression "in which" (*en hē*) which would clearly mean spatial location.

This view, of course, would solve many of the problems associated with other views, but it creates problems of its own. First of all, the same word (*echousa*) translated "having" is used spatially in this very passage (cf. v. 4). Furthermore, the two phrases are used interchangeably in this text, indicating that it is more a matter of variation in style than a desire to give a non-spatial relational impression.

In summary, while any one of these views is *possible* and would remove the difficulty, some seem unlikely (1 and 7). Others seem more probable (5 and 6). Whichever is correct, there is certainly no demonstrated error here in the Bible. On the contrary, several plausible solutions are available.

HEBREWS 9:4 – Were there three things in the ark or only the tables of stone?

PROBLEM: This passage claims that the ark of the covenant had the golden bowl of manna, Aaron's rod that budded, and the two tables of stone. But elsewhere it affirms that only the tables of stone were there (Ex. 40:20; Deut. 10:5; 1 Kings 8:9). Which is correct?

SOLUTION: The two "tables of stone" (i.e., the Ten Commandments) are not the same as the "book of the law." The latter was not put in the ark, but was placed along side of it (Deut. 31:26). *Originally,* all three items (tables of stone, pot of manna, and Aaron's rod) were in the ark (as Heb. 9:4 says). *Subsequently,* the last two were removed (Ex. 40:20).

HEBREWS 10:6-7 – How can we explain the distorted quotation of Psalm 40?

PROBLEM: Psalm 40:6 cites the Messiah as saying "My ears You have opened," but the writer of Hebrews quotes it as "a body You have prepared for Me" (10:5). There is no similarity whatsoever in these quotations. The NT seems to totally distort this OT passage.

SOLUTION: The difficulty arises here from the fact that the writer of Hebrews cites a version of the Greek translation of the OT (the Septuagint), whereas Psalm 40 was originally written in Hebrew. However, this does not solve the difficulty for anyone who believes in the inspiration of the Bible, since once the NT cites a passage this guarantees its truthfulness. How, then, can this apparent misquotation be resolved?

The solution may lie in the fact that Hebrews is a loose rendition, and Psalms is a more literal translation of the same idea, namely "You have fitted me for obedient service." The Psalm phrase, "My ears you have opened," may be a figure of speech referring to the boring of a slave's ear to signify his willing submission to his master. In which case, Hebrews actually clarifies the meaning of this now obscure figure of speech by its more "loose" rendition.

Others claim this is a synecdoche, in which one part stands for the whole. That is to say, if God is to "dig out the ears" (so that the Messiah can obey God and become a sacrifice for sin), then He must "prepare a body" for Him in which He can enter the world and accomplish His divine mission (cf. Heb. 10:5). Either way would satisfactorily resolve the difficulty and satisfy the principle that the NT citations need not be exact quotations as long as they are faithful to the truth contained in the OT text.

HEBREWS 10:11 – Did OT sacrifices make atonement for sins?

PROBLEM: Leviticus 17:11 affirmed that God gave blood sacrifices "to make atonement" for our souls. But Hebrews seems to contradict that, insisting that the Aaronic priest "stands ministering daily and offering repeatedly the same sacrifices, which can never take away sins" (10:11).

SOLUTION: The sacrifices in the OT were not intended to *take away* sin, but only to *cover over* sin until Christ came who could do away with it. Each blood sacrifice before Christ looked forward to Christ. The passover lamb was a type that anticipated fulfillment in "Christ, our Passover, [who] was sacrificed for us" (1 Cor. 5:7). They provided only a *temporary* covering for sins until Christ could bring in the *permanent* solution to the sin question. Old Testament offerings had, as it were, an IOU attached to them, awaiting the price to be paid by the "Lamb of God who takes away the sin of the world" (John 1:29).

HEBREWS 11:8 – Did Abraham know where he was going when he left his homeland to follow God?

PROBLEM: The writer of Hebrews informs us here that Abraham "went out, not knowing where he was going." Yet Genesis 12:5 asserts that Abraham "departed to go to the land of Canaan."

SOLUTION: Abraham did not know at the time he was called by God where he would eventually go. He was simply told by God to go to "a land that I will show you" (Gen. 12:1). Or, as Hebrews renders it, "to the place which he would afterward receive as an inheritance" (Heb. 11:8). The statement (in Gen. 12:5) that he "departed to go to the land of Canaan" is a comment by the author looking back, not the condition of Abraham's mind at the time.

HEBREWS 11:21 (cf. GEN. 47:31) – Is there a discrepancy regarding the death of Jacob?

PROBLEM: Hebrews mentions that Jacob died worshiping, "leaning on the top of his staff" (11:21). Yet Genesis 47:31 mentions Jacob "bowed himself on the head of the bed." How do we reconcile this apparent contradiction?

SOLUTION: The Hebrew words for "staff" and "bed" are spelled the same in their consonants. Since the vowels were not written in the original text, but were added around A.D. 700, words like the two above would look identical, since they had the same consonants. The Septuagint renders the passage in Genesis "staff" while later Jewish Masoretes translated the word "bed" instead of "staff." In light of this, "top of his staff" would be the likely rendition of the verses (Heb. 11:21) and the rendering "bed" (in Gen. 47:31) would be a vowel-pointing mistake.

HEBREWS 11:32 — Should some of the men listed in this "hall of faith" really be included?

PROBLEM: Why should Barak, Samson, and Jephthah be listed among the great men of faith such as Abraham, Moses, and Joseph? After all, they failed in many ways.

SOLUTION: It is true that Barak did not want to go to war without Deborah and showed lack of leadership. Samson had a flare for women, and Jephthah negotiated with the Ammonites which he should not have done. Yet none of these acts should necessarily exclude these men from being listed. For, as the NT says, "all have sinned and fall short of the glory of God" (Rom. 3:23). This is true even of others mentioned in the list of great men of faith. Abraham lied concerning Sarah his wife, and Moses killed a man. David will always be remembered for his adulterous act with Bathsheba, yet God called him a man "who followed Me with all his heart" (1 Kings 14:8). What separates these men from other individuals is their *faith,* not their sinfulness. Their heroic faith warranted their inclusion in the "Faith Hall of Fame." For example, even after Samson's decline, he performed mighty acts of faith and accomplished great things for God, destroying more of God's enemies in his death than he did in his life (Jud. 16:30).

HEBREWS 12:17 — Why couldn't Esau repent if he sought it with tears?

PROBLEM: The Bible informs us here that Esau "was rejected, for he found no place for repentance, though he sought it diligently with tears." But why wouldn't God accept his sincere repentance, when He commands all men everywhere to repent (Acts 17:30) and is patiently waiting for people to repent (2 Peter 3:9).

SOLUTION: There are two important things to observe about this passage. First, the statement "no place for repentance" may refer to his father's inability to change his mind about giving the inheritance to Jacob, and not to Esau's change of mind. At any rate, the circumstances did not afford Esau the opportunity to reverse the situation and get the blessing.

Second, tears are not a sure sign that a person has genuinely repented. One can also have tears of regret and remorse that fall short of true repentance or change of mind (cf. Judas, Matt. 27:3).

Finally, this text is not talking about *spiritual blessing* (salvation), but *earthly blessing* (inheritance). God always honors the sincere repentance of sinners and grants them salvation (Acts 10:35; Heb. 11:6).

JAMES

JAMES 1:2 – Is it desirable to avoid trials and temptation?

PROBLEM: Jesus instructed His disciples to pray, "do not lead us into temptation" (Matt. 6:13). But James says here, "count it all joy when you fall into various trials."

SOLUTION: The two situations are different, as indicated by several factors. First, James is speaking of trials we *"fall into,"* and Jesus is referring to things we should not want to be *"led into."* Second, James is speaking of *trials,* and Jesus is speaking about *temptations.* It is not a sin to fall into trials, but sin does result from being led into temptations. Finally, while the believer should not masochistically *seek* trials, neither should he try to *avoid* them at all cost. God can work in and through them to perfect our lives (cf. Job 23:10; Heb. 12:11; James 1:3-4). (See comments on Matt. 6:13.)

JAMES 1:15 – If God doesn't tempt anyone, then why did He tempt Abraham?

PROBLEM: The Bible says "God tempted Abraham" (Gen. 22:1, KJV), and Jesus taught His disciples to pray to God, "do not lead us into temptation" (Matt. 6:13). How then can James say of God, "nor does He Himself tempt anyone" (James 1:13).

SOLUTION: God did not *tempt* Abraham (nor anyone) to sin. Rather, He *tested* Abraham to see if he would sin or be faithful to Him. God allows Satan to tempt us (cf. Matt 4:1-10; James 4:7; 1 Peter 5:8-9), but James is correct in saying, never does God "Himself tempt anyone." God cannot be tempted by sin, since He is absolutely and unchangeably perfect (Matt 5:48; Heb. 6:18), nor can He tempt anyone else to sin (James 1:13). When we sinful human beings are tempted, it is because we allow ourselves to be drawn away by our own lustful desires (James 1:14-15). The source of temptation comes from within, not from without. It comes from sinful man, not from a sinless God.

While God does not and cannot actually tempt anyone to sin, He can and does allow us to be tempted by Satan and our own lustful desires. Of course, His purpose in permitting (but not producing or promoting) evil is to make us more perfect. God allowed Satan to tempt Job so that Job could say "When He has tested me, I shall come forth as gold" (Job 23:10). God allowed evil to befall Joseph at the hands of his brothers. But in the end Joseph was able to say to them, "you meant evil against me; but God meant it for good" (Gen. 50:20).

JAMES 2:12 – Does the law bring liberty or bondage?

PROBLEM: By James' account, the law of God brings liberty into the Christian's life, since he describes it here as the "law of liberty." This appears to be in direct conflict with the Apostle Paul's contention that the Law of Moses "gives birth to bondage" (Gal. 4:24).

SOLUTION: James and Paul are speaking of two different laws. Paul is speaking of the OT Law of Moses, "the one from Mount Sinai" (Gal. 4:24). And James is speaking of the NT "law of liberty," which Paul calls the "law of Christ" (Gal. 6:2) that has set us free from the law of bondage. As Paul put it, "what the Law [of Moses] could not do in that it was weak through the flesh," nevertheless "the law of the Spirit of life in Christ Jesus has made me free from the law of sin and death" (Rom. 8:2-3). The Law of Moses was written in stone, but the law of Christ is inscribed by the Spirit in our hearts (Jer. 31:31; 2 Cor. 3:3-7). The two laws can be summarized as follows:

THE LAW OF MOSES	THE LAW OF CHRIST
Brings bondage	Brings liberty
Weak through the flesh	Powerful by the Spirit
Written on stone	Written on the heart

JAMES 2:19 – If the demons believe in God, then why are they not saved?

PROBLEM: According to the Bible, all that is necessary to be saved is to "believe on the Lord Jesus Christ" (Acts 16:31), for "whoever believes in Him should not perish but have everlasting life" (John 3:16). Paul said salvation comes "to him who does not work but believes on Him" (Rom. 4:5). If this is so, then why are not the demons saved, since the Bible admits that "even the demons believe" (v. 19).

SOLUTION: The demons are not saved because they do not exercise a saving kind of faith. This is James' very point, namely, not any kind of faith can save a person. Only the kind of faith that produces good works can save (James 2:17). While we are saved by faith alone, nevertheless, the faith that saves is not alone. It is always accompanied by good works. We are not saved *by* works (Eph. 2:8-9), but we are saved *for* works (Eph. 2:10).

The difference between saving faith and non-saving faith is that the former is only belief *that* God exists. The latter is faith *in* God. No one can be saved by believing *that* God exists and *that* Christ died for their sins and rose again. They must believe in Him (i.e., trust Him). In like manner, no one can get to the top floor by an elevator if she simply believes *that* elevators can get her there. She must believe *in* the elevator (i.e., trust it) enough to step in it and allow it to get her there. The demons do not believe *in* (trust God) for their salvation—they simply believe *that* God exists, but they continue in their rebellion against Him (Jude 6; Rev. 12:4).

JAMES 2:21 — If Abraham was saved by works, why does the Bible say he was justified by faith?

PROBLEM: Paul clearly teaches that we are justified by faith and not by works (Rom. 1:17). He declared, "But to him who does not work but believes on Him who justifies the ungodly, his faith is accounted for righteousness" (Rom. 4:5). It is "not by works of righteousness which we have done, but according to His mercy He saved us" (Titus 3:5). For "by grace you have been saved through faith, and that not of yourselves; it is the gift of God, not of works, lest anyone should boast" (Eph. 2:8-9).

But James seems to flatly contradict this by declaring, "a man is justified by works, and not by faith only" (2:24), for "faith without works is dead" (2:26). Indeed, while Paul said Abraham was justified by faith (Rom. 4:1-4), James declares, "Was not Abraham our father justified by works" (2:21). Are these not flatly contradictory?

SOLUTION: James and Paul would be contradictory if they were speaking about the same thing, but there are many indications in the text that they are not. Paul is speaking about justification *before God,* while James is talking about justification *before humans.* This is indicated by the fact that James stressed that we should "show" (2:18) our faith. It must be something that can be seen by others in "works" (2:18-20). Further, James acknowledged that Abraham was justified before God by faith, not works, when he said, "Abraham believed God, and it was accounted to him for righteousness" (2:23). When he adds that Abraham was "justified by works" (v. 21), he is speaking of what Abraham *did that could be seen by people*, namely, offer his son Isaac on the altar (2:21-22).

Further, while Paul is stressing the *root* of justification (faith), James is stressing the *fruit* of justification (works). But each man acknowledges both. Immediately after affirming that we are "saved by grace through faith" (Eph. 2:8-9), Paul quickly adds, "we are His workmanship, created in Christ Jesus for good works, which God prepared beforehand that we should walk in them" (Eph. 2:10). Likewise, right after declaring that it is "not by works of righteousness which we have done, but according to His mercy He saved us" (Titus 3:5-7), Paul urges that "those who have believed in God should be careful to maintain good works" (Eph. 2:8). The relation between Paul and James can be summarized this way:

PAUL	JAMES
Justification *before God*	Justification *before humans*
The *root* of justification	The *fruit* of justification
Justification *by* faith	Justification *for* works
Faith as *producer of works*	Works as the *proof of faith*

JAMES 3:6 — Does the "course of nature" refer to reincarnation?

PROBLEM: James makes reference to the "course of nature," which has been translated "wheel of beginning." Some take this to be a reference to reincarnation, since they believe life goes around in cycles of birth, death, and rebirth (into another body). Is this a correct interpretation of the passage?

SOLUTION: James is not writing about reincarnation. This is evident for several reasons. First, the context is speaking about the power and persuasiveness of the human "tongue," with its far reaching effects. Second, the "course of nature" refers to the ongoing of life in general, not the recycling of individual souls. Third, James affirmed forgiveness of sins (cf. 5:20) and petitionary prayer (5:15-17), both of which are contrary to the doctrine of Karma behind reincarnation, which affirms that whatever is sown in this life, must be reaped in the next life (no exceptions). Finally, even if there were some question as to how this verse should be interpreted, an unclear passage should always be understood in the light of a clear one. And the Bible clearly opposes reincarnation (see Heb. 9:27; John 9:2).

JAMES 5:1-6 — Are riches a blessing or a curse?

PROBLEM: Solomon lauded riches as a blessing from God, saying, "In the house of the righteous there is much treasure" (Prov. 15:6; cf. Ps. 112:3). However, James warned the rich to "weep and howl for your miseries that are coming upon you!" (5:1). Which is it?

SOLUTION: The texts that speak about God blessing the righteous with riches refer to the general promise of God to supply the needs of those who live righteous lives. Exceptions to this establish the general rule, not diminish it. The passages that warn of the woes of wealth are written to those who idolize it, setting affection on it rather than on God (cf. also Luke 12:21). Both are true and complementary.

JAMES 5:12 — Is oath-taking forbidden or blessed?

PROBLEM: This and many other verses (cf. Hosea 4:2; Matt. 5:33-37) condemn oath-taking. In James' words, "Above all, my brethren, do not swear, either by heaven or by earth or with any other oath." Jesus had said the same thing, namely, "Do not swear at all: neither by heaven . . . nor by the earth" (Matt. 5:34-35). On the other hand, there are many places in the Bible where oaths were taken and blessed by God (cf. Gen. 21:24; Deut. 6:13). Indeed, angels took oaths (Rev. 10:5-6), as did God Himself (Heb. 6:13).

SOLUTION: Obviously there is a good sense of oath-taking and a bad sense that can be contrasted in the following manner:

GOOD OATHS	BAD OATHS
True ones	False ones
To do good	To do evil
Sacred ones	Profane ones
Meaningful ones	Vain ones
Serious ones	Frivolous ones
Judicial ones	Secret ones

Nothing in the Bible condemns taking a courtroom oath "to tell the truth, the whole truth, and nothing but the truth, so help me God." On the other hand, secret oaths taken in fraternal organizations which are contrary to God's Word are forbidden by the Scriptures cited above. Even Jesus submitted to being put under oath by the high priest at His trial (Matt. 26:63).

JAMES 5:17 — Was the drought three years or three-and-a-half years?

PROBLEM: Both here and in Luke 4:25 it speaks of a three and one-half year drought in the days of Elijah. But in 1 Kings 17:1 (and 18:1) it refers to the drought being three years.

SOLUTION: There are three possible solutions here. First, the three years may be a round number. Second, the third year in Kings may be reckoned from the time of Elijah's stay with the widow of Zarephthah, not the full time of the drought. Third, it is possible that the *drought* began six months before the *famine* did, making both passages precise but referring to different things.

1 PETER

1 PETER 1:2 – Are we sanctified by God's truth or by God's Spirit?

PROBLEM: Peter speaks in this text about "sanctification of the Spirit," but Jesus prayed, "Sanctify them by Your truth" (John 17:17). Which way are we set apart to God – by His Spirit or by His truth?

SOLUTION: We are sanctified *through* God's truth which is *from* God's Spirit. The Spirit of God is the *efficient* cause (that by which God works in our hearts), and the truth of God is the *instrumental* cause (that through which God works in our hearts). In short, God is the *source,* and God's truth is the *means* of our sanctification.

1 PETER 3:15 – Why does Peter command believers to reason about their faith when the Bible says elsewhere to simply believe?

PROBLEM: Over and over again the Scriptures insist that one should simply believe in God (cf. John 3:16; Acts 16:31). Hebrews declares that "without faith it is impossible to please God" (Heb. 11:6). Paul contended that, "the world through wisdom did not know God" (1 Cor. 1:21). Yet Peter here instructs believers to "defend" and give a "reason" for their faith. Aren't faith and reason opposed?

SOLUTION: Faith and reason are not mutually exclusive. A person should not believe in something without first inquiring whether it is a worthy object of belief. For example, few people would undergo a serious medical operation by a totally unknown person whom they had no reason to believe was anything but a quack. Likewise, God does not call on us to exercise blind faith.

Since God is a God of reason (Isa. 1:18), and since He has made us rational creatures in His image (Gen. 1:27; Col. 3:10), He wants us to look before we leap. No rational person should step into an elevator without first looking to see if there is a floor. Likewise, God wants us to take a step of faith in the light of the evidence, but not a leap of faith into the dark.

The Bible is filled with exhortations to use our reason. Jesus commanded, "You shall love the Lord . . . with all your *mind*" (Matt. 22:37, emphasis added in all quotes here). Paul added, "whatsoever things are true . . . *think* on these things" (Phil. 4:8, KJV). Paul also "reasoned" with the Jews (Acts 17:17) and with the philosophers on Mars Hill (v. 22ff) winning many to Christ (v. 34). Bishops were instructed to be able "to *refute* those who contradict" (Titus 1:9, NASB). Paul declares that he was "appointed for the *defense* of the gospel" (Phil. 1:17). Jude urged us to "*contend* earnestly for the faith which was once for all delivered to the saints" (Jude 3). And Peter commanded, "be ready to give a *defense* to everyone who asks you a *reason* for the hope that is in you" (1 Peter 3:15).

There are two kinds of belief. Understanding the relation between them is a key to discerning the relation between faith and reason.

FAITH

THAT	IN
Prior	Subsequent
Evidence	No evidence
Mind	Will
Proof	Persuasion
Human reason	Holy Spirit

The devil believes *that* God exists, but He does not believe *in* God. Belief *that* is a matter of the mind knowing something based on the evidence human reason can see. Belief *in* God (or Christ), however, is a choice of the human will under the persuasion of the Holy Spirit. So belief *that* will never save anyone (cf. James 2:14-20) — only belief *in* Christ can do that. However, no rational person should ever believe *in* something, unless he first has evidence to believe *that* it is true. No sensible traveler gets into an airplane with a broken off wing. So, reason is valid as a basis for belief *that,* but is wrong to demand as a basis for belief *in* (cf. John 20:27-29).

1 PETER 3:18 — Was Jesus raised in the Spirit or in a physical body?

PROBLEM: Peter declares that Christ was "put to death in the flesh but made alive in the spirit" (NASB). This seems to imply that Jesus did not rise in the flesh, but only in His spirit, which conflicts with Jesus' statement that His resurrection body was "flesh and bones" (Luke 24:39).

SOLUTION: To interpret this as proof of a spiritual, rather than a physical resurrection, is neither necessary nor consistent with the context of this passage and the rest of Scripture. Several reasons support this conclusion.

First of all, the passage can be translated, "He was put to death in the body but made alive by the [Holy] Spirit" (NIV). The passage is translated with this same understanding by the NKJV and others.

Second, the parallel between death and being made alive normally refer to the resurrection of the body in the NT. For example, Paul declared that "Christ died and rose and lived again" (Rom. 14:9), and "He was crucified in weakness, yet he lives by the power of God" (2 Cor. 13:4).

Third, the context refers to the event as "the resurrection of Jesus Christ" (3:21). But this is everywhere understood as a bodily resurrection in the NT (cf. Acts 4:33; Rom 1:4; 1 Cor. 15:21; 1 Peter 1:3; Rev. 20:5).

Fourth, even if "spirit" refers to Jesus' human spirit (not to the Holy Spirit), it cannot mean He had no resurrection body. Otherwise, the reference to His "body" (flesh) before the resurrection would mean He had no human spirit then. It seems better to take "flesh" in this context as a reference to His whole condition of humiliation before the resurrection and "spirit" to refer to His unlimited power and imperishable life after the resurrection.

1 PETER 3:19 — Does Peter support the view that a person can be saved after he dies?

PROBLEM: First Peter 3:19 says that, after His death, Christ "went and preached to the spirits in prison." But the Bible also says that "it is appointed for men to die once, but after this the judgment" (Heb. 9:27). These two verses appear to teach mutually opposing positions.

SOLUTION: The Bible is clear that there is no second chance after death (cf. Heb. 9:27). The Book of Revelation records the Great White Throne Judgment in which those who are not found in the book of life are sent to the lake of fire (Rev. 20:11-15). Luke informs us that, once a person dies, he goes either to heaven (Abraham's bosom) or to hell and that there is a great gulf fixed "so that those who want to pass" from one to the other cannot (Luke 16:26). The whole urgency of responding to God in this life before we die gives further support to the fact that there is no hope beyond the grave (cf. John 3:36; 5:24).

There are other ways to understand this passage, without involving a second-chance at salvation after death. Some claim that it is not clear that the phrase "spirits in prison" even refers to human beings, arguing that nowhere else is such a phrase used of human beings in hell. They claim these spirits are fallen angels, since the "Sons of God" (fallen angels, see Job 1:6; 2:1; 38:7) were "disobedient . . . in the days of Noah" (1 Peter 3:20; cf. Gen. 6:1-4). Peter may be referring to this in 2 Peter 2:4, where he mentions the angels sinning immediately before he refers to the Flood (v. 5). In response, it is argued that angels cannot marry (Matt. 22:30), and they certainly could not intermarry with human beings, since angels, being spirits, have no reproductive organs.

Another interpretation is that this refers to Christ's announcement to departed spirits of the triumph of His resurrection, declaring to them the victory He had achieved by His death and resurrection, as pointed out in the previous verse (see 1 Peter 3:18). Some suggest that Jesus offered no hope of salvation to these "spirits in prison." They point to the fact that the text does not say Christ *evangelized* them, but simply that He *pro-claimed* the victory of His resurrection to them. They insist that there is nothing stated in this passage about preaching the Gospel to people in hell. In response to this view, others note that in the very next chapter Peter, apparently extending this subject, does say "the Gospel was preached also to those who are dead" (see comments on 1 Peter 4:6). This view fits the context here, is in accord with the teaching of other verses (cf. Eph. 4:8; Col. 2:15), and avoids the major problems of the other view.

1 PETER 4:6 — Is the Gospel preached to people after they die?

PROBLEM: Peter says that "the Gospel was preached also to those who are dead." This appears to claim that people have a chance to be saved after they die. But this runs into conflict with Hebrews 9:27, which insists that "it is appointed for men to die once, but after this the judgment."

SOLUTION: In response it should be noted, first, that there is no hope held out anywhere in Scripture for salvation after death. Death is final, and there are only two destinies — heaven and hell, between which there is a great gulf that no one can pass over (see comments on 1 Peter 3:19). So, whatever preaching to the "dead" may mean, it does not imply that one can be saved after he dies.

Second, this is an unclear passage, subject to many interpretations, and no doctrine should be based on an ambiguous passage like this. The difficult texts should be interpreted in the light of the clear ones and not the reverse.

Third, there are other possible interpretations of this passage that do not conflict with the teaching of the rest of Scripture. (1) For example, it is possible that it refers to those who are now dead who heard the Gospel while they were alive. In favor of this is cited the fact that the Gospel "was preached" (in the past) to those who "are dead" (now, in the present). (2) Or, some believe this might not be a reference to human beings, but to the "spirits in prison" (angels) of 1 Peter 3:19 (cf. 2 Peter 2:4 and Gen. 6:2). (3) Still others claim that, although the dead suffer the destruction of their flesh (1 Peter 4:6), yet they still live with God by virtue of what Christ did through the Gospel (namely, His death and resurrection). This victorious message was announced by Christ Himself to the spirit world after His resurrection (cf. 1 Peter 3:18).

2 PETER

2 PETER 1:1 — Did the Apostle Peter really write this book?

PROBLEM: The style of writing in 1 Peter is different than 2 Peter. Also the tone used in the first epistle is different than that of the second epistle. How can evangelicals claim that Peter wrote this epistle?

SOLUTION: First, in his earlier epistle, Peter had Silas as a secretary (5:12, NIV), but in the second epistle Peter seems to have written it himself. This could account for the lack of smoothness and style between the two epistles.

Second, different styles and tones should be expected in two different letters written for two different purposes which were written at different times. First Peter is written to encourage believers who are suffering, while 2 Peter contains warnings against false teachers. So, some of the difference in style and tone can be accounted for in the light of the different circumstances. After all, one would not write to his girlfriend the same way he would write to his congressman.

Third, there is good internal evidence that the letter is from Peter. Verse 1 claims it is from the Apostle Peter. Peter remembers the words of Jesus concerning His death, as recorded in John 21:18-19 (cf. 2 Peter 1:14). The author of this letter was an eyewitness to the Mount of Transfiguration, which is recorded in Matthew 17:1-8 (cf. 1:16-18). Peter even calls this his "second letter" (3:1, NIV) which presupposes a first. And he is aware of the writings of the Apostle Paul and calls him "our beloved brother Paul" (3:15-16).

Fourth, there are not only some differences between epistles, but also some likenesses. Both place emphasis on Christ, 1 Peter on His suffering and 2 Peter on His glory. And in both epistles Peter refers to Noah and the flood (1 Peter 3:20; 2 Peter 2:5; 3:5-6).

Fifth, there is good external evidence that it was written in the 1st century by someone like Peter who was a contemporary of the events. The noted archaeologist William F. Albright dated 2 Peter before A.D. 80. The discovery of the Bodmer papyri (P72, ca. A.D. 250) reveals that it was highly respected in Egypt at an early date. The book was cited as authentic by numerous early church fathers, including Origen, Eusebius, Jerome, and Augustine.

Finally, if it was not written by Peter, then it is a biblical forgery, because the letter is said to be written by him. If it has not been written by Peter, then it is deceiving us and cannot be trusted in what it purports to tell us (i.e., his testimony to be a witness of the Transfiguration). Consideration of all the above factors provides strong evidence that the Apostle Peter is the writer of this epistle and not someone else. So we have no reason to distrust its content.

2 PETER 2:4 — Are fallen angels bound or are they free to tempt human beings?

PROBLEM: Peter affirms in this passage that God cast the fallen angels "down to hell and delivered them into chains of darkness, to be reserved for judgment" (cf. Jude 6). However, it is evident from the NT that demons roam freely over the earth, oppressing and even possessing people (cf. Matt. 12:22; 17:14-17; Acts 16:16-18; Rev. 16:14).

SOLUTION: There are two basic explanations of this apparent contradiction. First, it is possible that Peter is speaking of the *official* and *ultimate* destiny of fallen angels (demons), not their *actual* and *immediate* status. That is, while they are already sentenced by God to eternal damnation, they have not yet actually started serving their term. Nonetheless, they know their time is coming (Matt. 8:29; Rev. 12:12).

Second, these passages may be speaking of two different classes of fallen angels, some already in chains (2 Peter 2:4) and the rest yet loose. Some believe Peter is referring to the "sons of God" (angels) of Genesis 6 who instigated intermarriage with women just before the Flood, since the very next verse refers to Noah (v. 5). If so, then this may account for why these particular angels are already in chains (so they cannot repeat their feat), as opposed to other demons who are loose.

2 PETER 3: 7 — Does perdition mean the unsaved will be annihilated?

(See comments on 2 Thes. 1:9.)

1 JOHN

1 JOHN 3:9 — Doesn't John contradict himself when he asserts that Christians are without sin?

PROBLEM: John affirms here that "Whoever has been born of God does not sin." But in the first chapter he insisted that "If we say that we have no sin, we deceive ourselves, and the truth is not in us" (1:8).

SOLUTION: John nowhere claims that believers are without sin or never commit a sin. First John 3:9 is in the present continuous tense and should be translated "Whoever is born of God does not continually practice sin." Conversely, if a person habitually practices sin, he is not born of God. As James argued, true faith will produce good works (James 2:14ff). If a pig and a lamb fall into the mud, the pig wants to stay there, but the lamb wants to get out. Both a believer and an unbeliever can *fall* into the same sin, but a believer cannot *stay* in it and feel comfortable.

1 JOHN 4:2-3 — Does this refer to Jesus being in the flesh before or after His resurrection?

PROBLEM: John declares that those who deny "Jesus Christ has come in the flesh" are of Antichrist. While all orthodox Christians take this to mean Jesus was fully human, including having a physical body of flesh before His resurrection, some contend that Jesus was not raised from the dead in the same body of flesh and bones in which He died, but in a body that was not essentially material. What does this verse mean?

SOLUTION: John uses the perfect tense here in Greek, meaning past action with continuing results in the present. Thus, he affirms that Jesus came in the flesh in the past and continues in the flesh in the present (i.e., when he is writing, which was after the Resurrection).

This is further clarified by John's use of the same phrase, only in the present tense. He declared that many deceivers do not "confess Jesus

Christ as coming [present tense] in the flesh" (2 John 7). From this it is clear that, even after the Resurrection when John wrote, he insisted that Jesus was still continuing in the flesh.

Finally, in addition to these two passages in John's epistles, there are two other NT texts which explicitly declare Christ's resurrection body to be one of flesh. Referring to the resurrection of Christ, Peter declared that "nor did His *flesh* see corruption" (Acts 2:30-31). Jesus Himself said to His disciples in one of His post-resurrection appearances, "Handle Me and see, for a spirit does not have *flesh* and bones as you see I have" (Luke 24:39).

1 JOHN 4:18 — If love casts out all fear, why are we told to fear God?

PROBLEM: John affirms here that "perfect love casts out all fear." Yet we are told that the "fear of the Lord is the beginning of knowledge" (Prov. 1:7) and that we should "serve the Lord with fear" (Ps. 2:11). Indeed, Paul said, "knowing . . . the terror [fear] of the Lord, we persuade men" (2 Cor. 5:11).

SOLUTION: Fear is being used in different senses. Fear in the good sense is a *reverential trust* in God. In the bad sense it is a sense of *recoiling torment* in the face of God. While proper fear brings a healthy respect for God, unwholesome fear engenders an unhealthy sense that He is out to get us. Perfect love casts out this kind of "torment." When one properly understands that "God is love" (1 John 4:16), he can no longer fear Him in this unhealthy sense. For "he who fears has not been made perfect in love" (1 John 4:18). Nonetheless, at no time does proper love for God ever show disrespect for Him. Rather, it is perfectly compatible with a reverential awe for Him, which is what the Bible means by "fearing God" in the good sense (cf. 2 Cor. 7:1; 1 Peter 2:17).

1 JOHN 5:7 — Why is this verse on the Trinity missing in many modern translations?

PROBLEM: John declares that "there are three who bear witness in heaven: the Father, the Word, and the Holy Spirit; and these three are one" (KJV). This is the clearest statement on the Trinity in the Bible. However, most modern translations omit this verse. Why?

SOLUTION: The reason is very simple. This verse has virtually no support among the early Greek manuscripts, though it is found in Latin manuscripts. Its appearance in late Greek manuscripts is based on the fact that Erasmus was placed under ecclesiastical pressure to include it in his Greek NT of 1522, having omitted it in his two earlier editions of 1516 and 1519 because he could not find any Greek manuscripts which contained it.

Its inclusion in the Latin Bible probably results from a scribe incorporating a marginal comment (gloss) into the text as he copied the manuscript of 1 John. But including it in the text violates almost every rule of textual criticism. Even the NKJV, which generally retains the longer readings and disputed passages (see Mark 16:9ff and John 7:53-8:11), comments in the margin that this is "a passage found in only four or five very late *Greek* mss."

1 JOHN 5:16 — What is a sin unto death? Is it forgivable?

PROBLEM: On the one hand, the Scriptures speak of God's free and unconditional forgiveness to all who want it (cf. Acts 13:38-39; Rom. 5:20; 1 John 2:1). On the other hand, Jesus spoke of an unpardonable sin that can never be forgiven. And John declares here that there is a "sin leading to death."

SOLUTION: Bible commentators differ on just what John had in mind here. Some say he was referring to *repeated* sin (see comments on 1 John 3:9). Others believe he was speaking of a *grave* sin. Still others believe he had *apostasy* in mind (cf. 2 Peter 2).

Whatever John envisioned, there is no reason that it could not refer to a sin so serious that it would eventuate in physical death. Paul mentioned that the Corinthians had so participated in the Lord's Supper in an unworthy manner that some were sick and others were dead as a result (1 Cor. 11:29-30). In fact, the priests Nadab and Abihu were smitten dead for their disobedience to the Lord (Num. 3:4), as were Ananias and Saphira for their sin (Acts 5:1-9). So, it is entirely possible that John has some such serious sin in mind here whereby the believer is turned over to Satan for "the destruction of the flesh, that his spirit may be saved in the day of the Lord Jesus" (1 Cor. 5:5).

1 JOHN 5:18 — Can Satan injure God's children or not?

PROBLEM: Even Jesus admitted to Peter, "Satan has asked for you, that he may sift you as wheat" (Luke 22:31). However, John insists here that "he who has been born of God keeps himself, and the wicked one does not touch him." These passages appear to conflict with each other.

SOLUTION: There is an apparent conflict here, but no contradiction for several reasons. First of all, it does not really say that Satan actually injured Peter. Jesus simply states that Satan "asked" for permission to do so.

Second, just as was the case with Job, Satan cannot do anything to a believer that God does not permit him to do, because God has "made a hedge around him" (Job. 1:10).

Third, technically speaking, there is a difference between "sifting" wheat (believers) and destroying them. God may allow the former, but He will never permit Satan to do the latter to one of His children (cf. Rom. 8:38-39).

2 JOHN

2 JOHN 1 – Who was the "elect lady"?

PROBLEM: John addresses his second letter to "the elect lady." Some have argued that because this was strictly a personal letter addressed to a particular lady, that it does not belong in the canon of Scripture. Was the "elect lady" a person or not?

SOLUTION: First of all, if the "elect lady" were a particular person, this would not exclude it from the canon of Scripture. Several of the epistles of Paul were personal letters to particular individuals (e.g., Timothy, Titus, Philemon).

Second, it is possible that the elect lady was not a particular person. The proposals of commentators basically fall into two categories, the literal and the figurative. Those who understand this address to be *literal* hold that this was indeed a certain individual whom John knew. The following points are offered in favor of this view. First, it seems to be more natural to take the words as an address to an actual lady and her children. Further, this view fits with the references to the children of the elect lady, her sister (v. 13), and her sister's children (v. 13). Also, the basic structure of the greeting in verse 1 fits with the basic structure of the greeting of 3 John 1 ("To the . . . whom I love in truth") which itself was an address to a certain individual. Finally, if the term "lady" refers to the church, then to whom does the word "children" refer. Are the "children" not included in the church? Are they somehow different from the church?

Third, those who hold the view that this is a *figure of speech* maintain that this is a reference to the church as a whole, or to a particular local church. The following points are made in support of this view. First, John states that the lady is loved not only by him, but by "all those who have known the truth" (v. 1). This would mean that she was known by everyone. However, this kind of observation would fit better with reference to a local church than an individual. Second, although John uses the singular pronoun "you," he does switch to the plural in verse 8 where he seems to be warning the lady "Look to yourselves." But, if this was a literal woman, why would he use a plural at all? Third, the appeal to "love one another" (v. 5) makes more sense when directed to a community of believers than to a woman and her children. Fourth, the personification of the church in feminine terms is a common use in the Bible (e.g., Eph. 5:29ff where Paul develops the idea that the church is the bride of Christ; 1 Peter 5:13 where Peter uses the feminine expression of the church).

Although we may not be able to decide the issue definitively on the basis of our current information, it is clear that, if this was a personal letter to a literal woman, this fact would not exclude it from the canon of Scripture. And, it is not at all clear that it is a reference to an individual lady.

2 JOHN 10 — Why does this verse tell us not to receive certain people when Jesus told us to love our enemies?

PROBLEM: According to Jesus, we are supposed to love our enemies, bless those who curse us, and do good to those who hate us (Matt. 5:44). However, according to John, we are not to receive into our house or even greet anyone who comes to us and does not believe that Christ is come in the flesh. Which are we supposed to do?

SOLUTION: We are supposed to follow both instructions. The apparent discrepancy between these directives arises from the fact that they are talking about two totally different situations.

In the passage in Matthew, Jesus is contrasting His own teaching to that of the Pharisees. The divine principle of love should be the guiding principle of one's life. Even though some people are the enemies of God, He still allows the rain to fall upon their crops and causes the sun to shine on them. God treats the wicked with loving kindness. However, He never condones their wickedness. As Paul points out in Romans, the goodness of God is not a sign of His approval of their actions. Rather, the goodness of God is designed to lead to repentance (Rom. 2:4).

The passage in 2 John is not talking about someone who simply comes to visit. Rather, John is talking about false teachers who are deceivers (v. 7) and who come to present their doctrines.

First, John is instructing the local church, and the individuals of the local church, not to extend hospitality to these persons, because that would imply that the church accepted or approved of their teaching. The people of the local church were directed not even to give a Christian greeting to them, lest this be misconstrued as an attitude of tolerance of their false doctrines. This was by no means a command not to love one's enemy. In fact, following John's directives would be the supreme act of love for one's enemy. By clearly demonstrating an intolerance for false doctrine, it would be possible to communicate to false teachers that they needed to repent. On the contrary, if the church or individual were to extend hospitality to a false teacher, he would be encouraged in his position and take this action as an acceptance of his doctrine, or as a covering of his unrighteousness.

Second, it must be remembered that, in the early church, the evangelistic and pastoral ministry of the church was conducted primarily by individuals who traveled from location to location. These itinerant pastors depended on the hospitality of the people of a local congregation. John is directing the church not to extend this kind of hospitality to teachers of false doctrine. This is not contradictory to Jesus' teaching. We are to love our enemies, but not encourage them in their evil deeds. We are to do good to them that hate us, but not to condone their wickedness. As Jesus said, we are to show ourselves to be children of our Father. In the very same Sermon on the Mount, Jesus went on to warn His disciples to beware of false prophets "who *come* . . . in sheep's clothing" (Matt. 7:15). John gave practical application to this warning, and thereby encouraged the local church to maintain its purity and devotion to Christ.

3 JOHN

3 JOHN 7 — Should money be taken from unbelievers to do God's work?

PROBLEM: John claims here that the brethren took no support for their ministry from unbelievers. Yet when Solomon built the temple he accepted gifts from Gentiles (1 Kings 5:10; 2 Chron. 2:13-16). Is it always wrong to take money from unbelievers for God's work?

SOLUTION: As a rule, God's work should be supported by God's people. For those who benefit spiritually should share materially with their teachers (1 Cor. 9:1-14). On the other hand, it may offend an unbeliever to turn down his gift and place an obstacle in the way of his becoming a believer. Moses did not reject gifts from Egypt (Ex. 12:25-36). Nor did Solomon reject the gifts and help of the Gentile King Hiram (2 Chron. 2:13-16) or from the Queen of Sheba (1 Kings 10:10). So, while money should not be sought from unbelievers, neither should it be rejected, unless of course there are strings attached. Under no conditions should spiritual or other favors be bought by anyone.

Furthermore, it should be noted that this passage in 3 John is not prescriptive, but descriptive. It does not say "Never take money from unbelievers." It simply notes that these believers on this journey did not accept help from the heathen. No doubt they wanted to refrain from any appearance of selling the truth (cf. 2 Cor. 11:7; 1 Thes. 2:9). Rather, as it should have been, they depended on other believers to "send them forward on their journey in a manner worthy of God" (v. 6). We should not expect unbelievers to support the cause of faith.

JUDE

JUDE 9 – Isn't the dispute between Michael the Archangel and the devil based on an apocryphal story?

PROBLEM: Jude records an account in which Michael the archangel and the devil have a dispute over the body of Moses, saying, "Yet Michael the archangel, in contending with the devil, when he disputed about the body of Moses, dared not bring against him a reviling accusation, but said, 'The Lord rebuke you!' " (v. 9) This account is not found in the OT and is also considered to be found in a pseudepigraphal book (false writing) titled *The Assumption of Moses*.

SOLUTION: Just because the account is not found in any OT passages of Scripture doesn't mean that the event did not occur. The Bible often cites truths from books that are not inspired, but which contain, nevertheless, some true statements. A biblical author is not limited to citing only Scripture. All truth is God's truth, wherever it is found.

JUDE 14 – Doesn't Jude cite the uninspired Book of Enoch as divinely authoritative?

PROBLEM: Jude quotes *The Book of Enoch,* saying, "Now Enoch, the seventh from Adam, prophesied about these men also, saying, 'Behold, the Lord comes with ten thousands of His saints' " (v. 14). However, *Enoch* is not an inspired book but is considered pseudepigraphal (a false writing) by the Christian church.

SOLUTION: First, it is not certain that Jude is actually citing the *Book of Enoch.* He may simply be mentioning an event which is *also* found in this uninspired book. It is noteworthy that Jude does not affirm that Enoch wrote this statement. He simply records that "Enoch *said*" (v. 14). Jude may have been using a valid oral tradition and not the *Book of Enoch.*

Furthermore, even if Jude took this statement from the *Book of Enoch,* it is still true. Many true statements can be found outside of Scripture.

Just because Jude quoted from a non-canonical (extra-biblical) source does not mean that what he says is necessarily wrong. Not everything in the *Book of Enoch* is correct, but this does not warrant the conclusion that everything in it is wrong.

Further, the Apostle Paul cites truths from pagan poets (Acts 17:28; 1 Cor. 15:33; Titus 1:12) without implying that these books are inspired. Indeed, even Balaam's donkey uttered a truth (Num. 22:28). The inspiration of the Book of Jude does not guarantee whatever else is said in an uninspired source it cites—it only guarantees the truth it cites.

Finally, the external evidence for Jude is extensive from the time of Irenaeus (ca. A.D. 170) onward. It is in the Bodmer papyri (P72) of A.D. 250, and traces of it are found even earlier in the *Dicache* (2:7) which probably dates from the second century. So there is evidence for the authenticity of the Book of Jude which is not diminished by this allusion to what Enoch said. The existence of Enoch and his communication with God is a fact established elsewhere, both in the OT (Gen. 5:24) and NT (Heb. 11:5).

REVELATION 1:4 — How can the Holy Spirit be seven spirits if He is one person?

PROBLEM: According to the orthodox doctrine of the Trinity, the Holy Spirit is one person, the third person of the triune Godhead. Jesus referred to the Holy Spirit as "He" (singular). But John referred to "the seven Spirits who are before His [God's] throne" (Rev. 1:4), which many commentators see as a reference to the Holy Spirit. But how can the Holy Spirit be seven spirits?

SOLUTION: The Book of Revelation contains a good bit of symbolism, and this is only one example. There is similar symbolism in other portions of this book. For instance, most agree that Revelation 12:3 speaks about Satan, but he is called a "great red dragon" with "seven heads and ten horns." Here, the seven heads and ten horns are attributed to one individual, Satan. Also, speaking of the beast from the sea, Revelation 13:1 says that he has "seven heads and ten horns." The number seven symbolizes completeness, as there are seven days in a complete week.

Other symbols are used of the Holy Spirit in Scripture. For instance, He is spoken of as a dove in Mark 1:10 and is likened to the "wind" in John 3:8 and water in John 4:14. He is also portrayed as "tongues as of fire" in Acts 2:3. And Ephesians 1:13 says we are "sealed" by the Holy Spirit, signifying God's ownership of us and the security of our salvation.

Many Bible students believe the sevenfold nature of the Holy Spirit may derive from the reference in Isaiah 11:2 where He is called the Spirit of the *Lord*, the Spirit of *wisdom*, of *understanding*, of *counsel*, of *might*, of *knowledge*, and of the *fear of the Lord* — seven different characteristics of one and the same Spirit.

REVELATION 5:5 — Will Jesus come again as a lion or a lamb?

PROBLEM: In this prophecy, Jesus is depicted as a Lion, the king of beasts. This fits with the fact that He will come as King to reign over all the earth (Rev. 19–20). However, the main symbol of Christ in the Book of Revelation is the Lamb, mentioned some 27 times.

SOLUTION: It is clear that both figures of speech are appropriate to Christ's second coming. John even speaks of the "wrath of the Lamb" (Rev. 6:16). While at His first coming Jesus was "the Lamb of God who takes away the sin of the world" (John 1:29), nonetheless, He will return as a wrathful Lamb. Why? Because He who died for the sins of the world has the right to execute judgment on those who reject His death for their sins. The only safe place to flee in the judgment is where God's judgment already fell — on the Cross. Those who do not take refuge in the Lamb who took the wrath of God for them (cf. 2 Cor. 5:21) will experience the wrath of the Lamb on them. The figure of a lamb, then, is an appropriate symbol of the love of a just God who is executing His judgment on those who reject Him.

REVELATION 6:16 — Is Christ merciful or wrathful?

PROBLEM: Throughout the Gospels Christ is presented as merciful, healing the sick, blessing the poor, comforting the sorrowing, and forgiving sinners (cf. Luke 9:56; 19:10). But the Book of Revelation speaks of "the wrath of the Lamb" (6:16) and the judgment of Christ on the whole world (Rev. 19:11-15).

SOLUTION: Often the differences in these passages is due to their reference to *different times* in Jesus' work on earth, namely, His first coming versus His second coming. His first coming was primarily a mission of mercy. His second coming, however, will be initially one of wrath. He who died as a Lamb (John 1:29) will also return as a Lion (Rev. 5:5). During His first coming, Jesus was a bruised reed (Isa. 42:3), but at His second coming He will rule with an iron rod (Ps. 2:9).

At other times, Jesus' *different attitudes and actions* were simply due to the fact that they were directed at different people or conditions. For example, even during His first coming Jesus was angry with hypocrites (Matt. 23) and indignant with those who had commercialized the house of God (John 2). He cursed the fig tree, which symbolized the fruitless nation of Israel that rejected their Messiah (Matt. 21:19). At all times, Jesus is merciful to the penitent and wrathful to the impenitent.

REVELATION 7:1 – Does the Bible teach that the world is square?

PROBLEM: John speaks here of the "four corners of the earth," which implies that the earth is square. But modern science teaches that it is round. Isn't this a mistake in the Bible?

SOLUTION: The Bible does not teach that the world is square. First of all, this is a figure of speech meaning "from every section of the globe" or as Jeremiah put it, "from the four quarters of heaven" (Jer. 49:36). It is a succinct way of referring to the four directions, "north, south, east, and west." In this sense it is akin to the phrase, "the four winds . . . of heaven" (Jer. 49:36).

The only references to the shape of the earth in the Bible speak of it as round. Isaiah spoke of God "who sits on the circle of the earth . . . (Isaiah 40:22, MKJV). And Job refers to the world as hanging in space, asserted that God "stretches out the north over the empty place, [and] He hung the earth on nothing" (Job 26:7, MKJV). There is certainly nothing unscientific about these statements.

REVELATION 7:4-8 – Who are the 144,000 of whom John writes here?

PROBLEM: In this passage, John mentions a specific group of 144,000 believers. Is this an exact number, and does it mean only this many will be saved? If not who are they?

SOLUTION: *Spiritual Interpretation.* Some take the "144,000 of all the tribes of Israel" to be a spiritual reference to Christians. However, this view is not supported by the facts. First, the word "tribes" is never used of anything but a literal ethnic group in Scripture.

Furthermore, if the number is taken seriously, surely it grossly under represents the number of believers there will be in heaven. True, the Bible nowhere reveals the exact number of believers there will be in heaven, but since there are billions of humans alive, and since there are easily multiplied millions of these who are saved, this is obviously not a reference to the total number of redeemed of all time.

In addition, even the physical dimensions of the New Jerusalem (Rev. 21:16-17), to say nothing of the rest of God's vast universe, could contain a much larger number than 144,000 people.

Revelation 7:9 declares that there were, in addition to the 144,000, "a great multitude . . . of all nations" who were also redeemed, which not only indicates that the saved are not limited to them but that the passage makes more sense if taken literally.

Literal Interpretation. Others take this passage literally as a reference to 144,000 Jews who will be saved during the tribulation period, 12,000 from each tribe of the 12 tribes of Israel. They note, first of all, that Dan is not listed while Levi is listed among the 12 tribes, since Dan went into idolatry and was largely obliterated. Levi, however, who, because of its priestly function, was not given a separate land inheritance in the OT is numbered with the 12 tribes here, since the Levitical priesthood was fulfilled by Christ (Heb. 7–10). Likewise, Ephraim may be in the place of "Joseph" in this passage, since he was Joseph's son.

In further support of the literal interpretation is the fact that Jesus spoke of the 12 apostles (whom we know were literal persons) sitting on "twelve thrones, judging the twelve tribes of Israel" in the last day (Matt. 19:28). There is no reason not to take this as a reference to 12 literal tribes of Israelites.

In addition, the last question Jesus answered before His ascension directly implied that He would return and "restore the kingdom to Israel" (Acts 1:6-8).

Indeed, the Apostle Paul spoke of the restoration of the nation of Israel to its former privileged position in Romans 11 (cf. vv. 11-26).

Many Bible scholars believe in a literal restoration of the nation of Israel, because God's land 'promises to Abraham's literal descendants (Gen. 12; 14; 15; 17; 26) have never been fulfilled "forever," as they were promised (cf. Gen. 13:15), but at best only for a short period during the time of Joshua (Josh. 11:23).

REVELATION 14:13 — Is heaven a place of rest and quiet or of incessant praise and singing?

PROBLEM: According to this verse, heaven is a place in which the saints "rest from their labors." However, earlier in the Book of Revelation heaven is described as a place of constant praise and singing (Rev. 4–5). Which is it?

SOLUTION: Heaven is both. There is no contradiction between resting from labor and singing praises to God. It is exactly what God's people do today on their day of rest and worship. Heaven is just an extension of what we do on the Lord's Day now. "Labor" implies what is wearisome and painful. Resting from this and praising God forever are not mutually exclusive. In fact, they go hand in hand.

REVELATION 16:14 – Can demons perform miracles?

PROBLEM: The Bible sometimes uses the same words (sign, wonders, power) to describe the power of demons as those used to describe miracles of God (Rev. 16:14; 2 Thes. 2:9). However, a miracle is a supernatural act of God, and only God can perform such acts. The devil is a created being and has only limited power.

SOLUTION: Although Satan has great spiritual powers, there is a gigantic difference between the power of the devil and the power of God. First, God is infinite in power (omnipotent); the devil (and demons) is only finite and limited. Second, only God can create life (Gen. 1:1, 21; Deut. 32:39); the devil cannot (cf. Ex. 8:19). Only God can raise the dead (John 10:18; Rev. 1:18); the devil cannot, though he gave "breath" (animation) to the idolatrous *image* of the Antichrist (Rev. 13:15).

The devil has great power to deceive people (Rev. 12:9), to oppress those who yield to him and even to possess them (Acts 16:16). He is a master magician and a super scientist. And with his vast knowledge of God, man, and the universe, he is able to perform "lying wonders" (2 Thes. 2:9; cf. Rev. 13:13-14). But true miracles can be performed only by God. The devil can do the supernormal but not the supernatural. Only God can control the natural laws He has established, though on one occasion He granted Satan the power to bring a whirlwind on Job's family (Job. 1:19). Further, all the power the devil has is given him by God and is carefully limited and monitored (cf. Job 1:10-12). Christ had defeated the devil and triumphed over him and all his host (Heb. 2:14-15; Col. 2:15), thus giving power to His people to be victorious over demonic forces (Eph. 4:4-11). Thus, John informed believers: "He who is in you is greater than he who is in the world" (1 John 4:4).

APPENDIX 1

System of Transliteration
The following system of transliteration will be used through this book for all Hebrew and Greek words.

HEBREW	ENGLISH	GREEK	ENGLISH
א	none	α	a
ב	b	β	b
ג	g	γ	g
ד	d	δ	d
ה	h	ε	e
ו	v	ζ	z
ז	z	η	ē
ח	ch	θ	th
ט	t	ι	i
י	y	κ	k
כ/ך	k	λ	l
ל	l	μ	m
מ/ם	m	ν	n
נ/ן	n	ξ	x
ס	s	ο	o
ע	none	π	p
פ/ף	p/ph	ρ	r
צ/ץ	ts	σ/ς	s
ק	q	τ	t
ר	r	υ	u
שׂ	s	φ	ph
שׁ	sh	χ	ch
ת	t/th	ψ	ps
(ַ)(ָ)(ֲ)	a	ω	ō
(ֵ)(ֶ)(ְ)(ֱ)	e	(ʽ)	h
(ִ)(ֵ)	i		
(וֹ)(ֹ)(ָ)(ֳ)	o		
(וּ)(ֻ)	u		
(ְ)	e or none		

Appendix 2

The Hebrew Language

The Hebrew language consists of 22 different signs that represent the 23 letters of the Hebrew alphabet. All of the letters of the Hebrew alphabet are consonants. In the earliest manuscripts of the Scriptures, the vowels are not written in the text. It was not until a group of scribes known as the Masoretes codified the Hebrew text between A.D. 500 and 950 that the vowel pointing and punctuation marks were added into the written text. The vowel points which the Masoretes systematized consists of a series of dots and dashes that mostly appear beneath the Hebrew letters. The following list will illustrate these instances.

CONSONANT	VOWEL POINT	CONSONANT AND VOWEL POINT
א	◌ָ	אָ
ב	◌ַ	בַ
ג	◌ִ	גִ
ד	◌ֶ	דֶ
ו	◌ֹ	וֹ

Historical Discrepancies

When critics claim that the Bible has historical errors, they like to draw attention to discrepancies in the spellings of personal names, or the discrepancies in numerical notations. Many of these differences can be explained as the result of scribal errors in the copying of manuscripts. It is easy to understand how these scribes made errors in copying manuscripts once we have seen the similarity in appearance of many Hebrew characters.

Personal Names

In 2 Samuel 23:27 we find the name "Mebunnai." Using the Hebrew characters, this name appears like this: מבני. In 1 Chronicles 11:29 we find a mention of the same person, but his name is spelled "Sibbecai." In Hebrew characters this name would appear, סבכי. Putting the two names side-by-side we can see a similarity between the letters: סבכי מבני. It must also be pointed out that ancient manuscripts were hand written and not mechanically reproduced. Under these circumstances, it is easy to see how the letters may have been confused by a copyist. Likewise, a comparison of the names of the sons of Dishon in Genesis 36:26 and 1 Chronicles 1:41 yields a different spelling of the name of one of his descendants—Hemdan (חמדן) in Genesis, and Hamran (חמרן) in 1 Chronicles. The similarity between the letters "r" and "d" in these names is obvious (r = ר; d = ד). Even in the ancient Hebrew script we find the same types of similarities between letters. The following chart represents Hebrew scripts from the 9th to the 5th centuries B.C., from the 1st to the 4th centuries A.D., alongside modern Hebrew script, and the name of each letter. In some instances the similarities are even more striking in the ancient scripts than in the modern script.

9TH–5TH CENTURY A.D.	1ST–4TH CENTURY A.D.	MODERN SCRIPT	NAME
⟨	⟨ Y N N	א	Aleph
9	געב	ב	Beth
1	ג	ג	Gimel
⊲	דד	ד	Daleth
⟍	⊓	ה	He
Y	וו	ו	Waw
I	וו	ז	Zayin
H	⊦⊓⊓	ח	Heth
⊗	⊍	ט	Teth

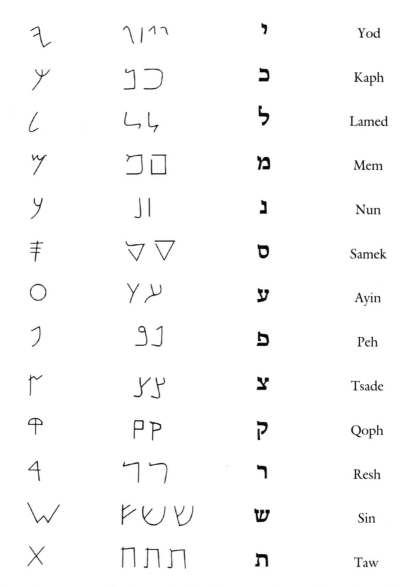

٦	٦١٦	י	Yod
Y	ו٦	כ	Kaph
८	५५	ל	Lamed
৵	ロロ	מ	Mem
y	ال	נ	Nun
‡	▽ ▽	ס	Samek
○	Y ﻻ	ע	Ayin
٦	٦٦	פ	Peh
୮	YY	צ	Tsade
ዋ	PP	ק	Qoph
4	77	ר	Resh
W	۴ ᄂ ᄂ	ש	Sin
X	ΠΠΠ	ת	Taw

A very important point is revealed by the comparison of the various kinds of Hebrew script from the different points of history. Not only is there a similarity between letters of the same period, but different letters from different periods are written similarly. For example, the *Nun* from the 9th to 5th century B.C. script is quite similar to the *Ayin* of the 1st to 4th century A.D. script, and the *Gimel* from the 9th to 5th century B.C. script is similar to the *Yod* from the 1st to 4th century A.D. script. Consequently, a scribe not only had to deal with similarities between the letters of the language of his own time, but he may have also had to deal with letters of an ancient script that were similar to different letters of his own script.

Numeric Figures

We have already dealt with some numeric discrepencies in the body of this book. However, it would be wise to restate some of the dynamics which have given rise to these types of discrepencies. The same principle is at work in copying numbers as in copying names. Unlike English, the ancient Hebrew language did not have a set of numerals. Rather, ancient Hebrews employed words and letters of their alphabet to stand for numbers. Just like English uses the word "one" as the name for the numeral "1," so, Hebrew used names for numbers.

ENGLISH	HEBREW
One	אֶחָד
Two	שְׁנַיִם / שְׁתַּיִם
Three	שָׁלֹשׁ
Four	אַרְבַּע
etc.	etc.

Large numbers employ additional words, just like in English.

| Five hundred | חָמֵשׁ מֵאוֹת |
| Five thousand | חֲמֵשֶׁת אֲלָפִם |

Very large numbers were also written out. Although there was no hard and fast rule, usually the larger number would be first, then the next largest number and so on. For example, the number 503 would be written just like the English order

חָמֵשׁ מֵאוֹת וּשְׁלֹשָׁה (five hundred and three).

Sometimes, however, the numbers would be written in reverse order, "77 years and 700 years."

Ancient Hebrew also employed the Hebrew letters to stand for numbers:

ENGLISH	ANCIENT HEBREW	BIBLICAL HEBREW
One	⟨	אֶחָד
Two	9	שְׁנַיִם
Three	1	שָׁלֹשׁ
etc.	etc.	

It is easy to see how transcribing numbers from one document to another could become confusing and lead to copying errors. Some of the words are very similar in spelling, and even some of the lettes are quite similar. This is compounded by the fact that later generations were not as familiar with the ancient alphabets as the original authors. Indeed, it is a testimony to the providential care of God that He has preserved His written revelation throughout history in spite of the frailty of His human instruments.

INDEX OF UNORTHODOX RELIGIOUS DOCTRINES

TOPICAL INDEX OF BIBLE DIFFICULTIES

APPARENT CONTRADICTIONS

APPARENT ERRORS

CHRISTIAN APOLOGETICS

CHRISTIAN LIFE

DISCREPANCIES

■

■

SCRIPTURE INDEX

SELECT BOOKS
ON BIBLE DIFFICULTIES

Archer, Gleason L. *An Encyclopedia of Biblical Difficulties*. Grand Rapids: Zondervan, 1982.

Arndt, William. *Bible Difficulties*. St. Louis: Concordia, 1971.

——————. *Does the Bible Contradict Itself*. St. Louis: Concordia, 1955.

Clark, Gordon. *Can I Trust My Bible?* Chicago: Moody, 1963.

DeHoff, George. *Alleged Biblical Contradictions Explained*. Dehoff Publications, 1950.

Ellis, Edward. *Paul's Use of the Old Testament*. Grand Rapids: Eerdmans, 1957.

Guilleband, H.E. *Some Moral Difficulties of the Bible*. InterVarsity Christian Fellowship, 1941.

Haley, John. *An Examination of Alleged Discrepancies of the Bible*. 1874. Reprint. Grand Rapids: Baker, 1963.

Kaiser, Walter. *Classical Evangelical Essays in Old Testament Interpretations*. Grand Rapids: Baker, 1972.

Orr, James. *The Problem of the Old Testament Considered with Reference to Recent Criticism*. New York: C. Scribner's Sons, 1931.

Pettingill, William. *Bible Questions Answered*. Wheaton, Ill.: Van Kampen Press, n.d.

Sproul, R.C. *Objections Answered*. Ventura, Calif.: Regal, 1978.

Thiele, Edwin. *Mysterious Numbers of the Kings of Israel*. Grand Rapids: Eerdmans, 1965.

Torrey, R.A. *Difficulties in the Bible*. Chicago: Moody, 1907.

Tuck, Robert, ed. *A Handbook of Biblical Difficulties*. E. Stock, n.d.